Rev. J. G. Atterbury —
From his friend
A. Sheley
Detroit Mich

THE SABBATH.

THE SABBATH

VIEWED IN THE LIGHT

OF

REASON, REVELATION, AND HISTORY,

WITH

SKETCHES OF ITS LITERATURE.

BY THE REV. JAMES GILFILLAN,
STIRLING, SCOTLAND.

WE ARE TO ACCOUNT THE SANCTIFICATION OF ONE DAY IN SEVEN A DUTY WHICH GOD'S IMMUTABLE LAW DOTH EXACT FOR EVER.—HOOKER.

PUBLISHED BY THE
AMERICAN TRACT SOCIETY,
150 NASSAU-STREET, NEW YORK:
AND THE
NEW YORK SABBATH COMMITTEE,
5 BIBLE HOUSE, ASTOR PLACE.

THE stereotype plates of this volume were generously presented to the New York Sabbath Committee, by JOHN HENDERSON, Esq., of Glasgow, Scotland. In issuing it without revision, neither that Committee nor the Publishing Committee assume the responsibility of any sentiment that may have the aspect of denominational controversy.

"The first creature of God in the works of the days was the light of the sense, the last was the light of reason, and his Sabbath work ever since is the illumination of his Spirit." LORD BACON.

PREFACE.

THE author of the following work accounts it his happiness to have been connected from his earliest days with a class, of whom the sacred observance of the Lord's Day has been a prominent distinction. That there have been among them no insincere characters, presenting a distorted image of their creed, it would be too much to affirm; but sure he is, that both ministers and private individuals, with whom, from his circumstances, he has been brought into intercourse, have been, for the most part, upright, holy, kind-hearted, cheerful Christians, with whom, he had reason to believe, it would be good for him to live and die. Of persons in sacred office, there rise to his view, his relative, Mr. Barlas, Crieff; Dr. Pringle and Mr. Black, Perth; Mr. Jameson, Methven; Mr. Beath, Pitcairn Green; Dr. Mitchell, Anderston, afterwards of Glasgow; Dr. Ferrier, Paisley; Dr. Jamieson and Professor Paxton, Edinburgh; Mr. Culbertson, Leith. Others, who occupied a less public station, he must not name; but he sees them attending to the claims of their fellow-creatures equally as to their own affairs—visiting the poor and suffering—sitting by their bed-sides with the impression that a dying immortal is near, and with the tear and the tone of sympathy—tending the steps of the aged and the neglected—showing in their countenances the serenity and benevolence which they have catched from the face of the Saviour—their very steps indicating that they

> "Walk thoughtful on the silent, solemn shore
> Of that vast ocean we must sail so soon."

His education among such persons, with the circumstance that his father had published an "Essay" on the subject, gave him an early interest in the Sabbath. The work, which is the result, has for years employed those moments which he could spare from the duties of a laborious profession. His own collection of books that treated of the institution, though ultimately of some extent, being insufficient for his purpose, he has had to draw upon various public libraries. For securing him access to their treasures, or for otherwise aiding his researches, he is under great obligations to Professors Pillans, Edinburgh, and Fleming, Glasgow; Messrs. George Offor, and William H. Black, London; Mr. Haig, Dublin; and the Rev. Alex. B. Grosart, Kinross: and to the librarians, the Rev. A. L. Simpson, Messrs. Small, Laing, Halkett (Edinburgh), Jones (Glasgow), and Christie (Innerpeffray), he is indebted for manifold acts of attention and kindness.[1] He may be allowed to express special gratitude for the encouraging interest shown, and the various assistance rendered, in connexion with

[1] Of public libraries, the writer found those of the British Museum and the Edinburgh University to be the richest in Sabbatic literature. In the Advocates' Library, and that of the University of Glasgow, he met with works on the subject which he had not discovered anywhere else in Scotland. The library of the United Presbyterian Church is peculiarly valuable in the department of Theology, which it owes in no small measure to the portion of it that belonged to the learned Robertson of Kilmarnock, and has a select number of volumes on the Sabbath. The most extensive and valuable collection of books and pamphlets relative to the institution that he has had the opportunity of seeing was that of Mr. W. H. Black, minister of a Sabbatarian Church, London, and an accomplished scholar. He regretted that with the most liberal permission to make use of it on the spot, the rule of the Library, which precluded the removal of any book from the premises, and his limited time, put it out of his power to derive much benefit from its stores.

his undertaking, by the late Professor More, the Rev. Dr. Somerville, John Henderson, Esq. of Park, and his friends, the Rev. James Young, and Mr. John Taylor, Edinburgh. He would also cordially acknowledge the approbation which his labours have met with in not a few public journals.

The alterations which the work has undergone in this second edition have, it is believed, improved, without substantially changing its character. This he can affirm with some confidence as far as respects the General Index, prepared by the practised pen of the Rev. James Anderson, author of the "Ladies of the Covenant," and of other kindred and approved publications. With these remarks, he again commits his volume, such as it is, to the candid consideration of his readers, and to Him, who, he trusts, will mercifully accept and bless the offering.

STIRLING, *April* 17, 1862.

CONTENTS.

SKETCHES OF SABBATIC CONTROVERSIES AND LITERATURE.

PROOFS, FROM REASON AND EXPERIENCE, OF THE EXCELLENCE AND DIVINE ORIGIN OF THE SABBATH.

CHAPTER IV.

CHAPTER V.

CHAPTER VI.

CHAPTER VII.

TESTIMONY OF REVELATION TO A SACRED AND PERPETUAL SABBATH.

CHAPTER I.

CHAPTER II.

CHAPTER III.

CHAPTER IV.

CHAPTER V.

CHAPTER VI.

CHAPTER VII.

EVIDENCE FROM HISTORY FOR A WEEKLY DAY OF REST AND WORSHIP.

THE SABBATH DEFENDED AGAINST OPPOSING ARGUMENTS, THEORIES, AND SCHEMES.

CHAPTER I.

CHAPTER II.

CHAPTER III.

CHAPTER IV.

CHAPTER V.

CHAPTER VI.

CHAPTER VII.

THE CLAIMS OF THE SABBATH PRACTICALLY ENFORCED.

INDICES.

SKETCHES OF SABBATIC CONTROVERSIES AND LITERATURE.

THE Sabbath dates, as we believe, from the creation of the world. Traces of it have been found among pagan nations, ancient and modern. It has run parallel in Judea with the greater part of Jewish history. It has been identified for eighteen centuries with the ecclesiastical and civil affairs of Christendom. The object of ardent regard, and of intense dislike, it has been the occasion of earnest controversy and of multiplied writings. Although it has not received the attention, still less the full elucidation, which its character, antiquity, and value might prepare us to expect, it could not fail long ere this time to furnish materials for a chapter in the polemics, and another in the literature of religion. And yet these chapters, so far as we know, remain unwritten. A comprehensive view, however, of the manner in which so important a department of knowledge has been cultivated, and some account of the labourers, while fitted as matters of general intelligence to gratify and instruct, seem to be necessary for guiding further research, and for shedding a direct light on the subject of inquiry.[1] As there is little hope that we shall be favoured in this, as in various other branches of study, with a reproduction of the abler treatises of former days, might not the authors of the new works, which new times and circumstances demand, supply in some degree the want, and enhance the value,

[1] After these sketches were written, and several sheets printed, the author was happy to meet with the excellent *De Histoire* of Koelman, and, after the whole had passed from the press, with the annotated *Aphorisms* of C. Vitringa, and the *Sunday* of Dr. Hessey. These works supply *in part* what he here desiderates.

of their own volumes, by presenting a *résumé* at least of previous theories and arguments ?

If the following sketches should prove that it is easier to point out than to supply a *desideratum*, it will be to the writer a satisfying result of considerable labour expended on an attempt made in a somewhat untrodden walk and with limited space, if by any impulse imparted to more successful exertion, or by the information brought together, a service shall be rendered to the cause which it is the object of this volume to illustrate and recommend —the cause, he believes, of Divine law, and of human happiness.

During the period comprehended in the sacred records of the Old Testament, though Sabbatic privileges were in repeated instances despised, no professed friend of the true religion is found to dispute the Divine appointment or sacred character of the seventh-day's services and rest. A similar unanimity prevailed for many centuries among Christians with regard to the claims of the Lord's day. But there wanted not differences between the Jews and the heathen; and between the Christians and both. And it is necessary to pass these differences under a brief review, before we proceed to describe the strifes by which the Church itself came to be agitated.

PAGANS AGAINST JEWS—BOTH AGAINST CHRISTIANS.

While kindred observances are discovered in pagan countries from the remotest times, it appears from a few scattered notices in history, that the true Sabbath, as observed by the patriarchs and the Jews, was the object of bitter and even violent hostility to those heathen men who were brought into intercourse with its friends. In Cain and Pharaoh, we see types—the one, of a class who deliberately abandon scenes and seasons of worship uncongenial to their hearts, and so leave to their descendants a legacy of atheism and moral death ; the other, of persons in power who refuse to their subjects or servants the periodical respite from labour demanded by the necessities of body and soul. The anti-Sabbatic spirit comes out subsequently in the conduct of the Babylonian "adversaries of Jerusalem," who not only "mocked at her

Sabbaths," but compelled her people to labour without any rest;[1] and in the cruel edict of Antiochus Epiphanes, who proclaimed the keeping of their Sabbath, and every observance of their law by the Jews, to be a capital offence.[2] A similar feeling is betrayed in another form by the Greek and Roman writers at various times —Democritus, Cicero, Strabo, and Ovid, Seneca, Juvenal, Persius, Tacitus, Plutarch, and Appian, who ridicule or denounce the Jewish religion—some of them singling out for special derision or reprehension its weekly and other holy days. Ovid brands these as foreign Sabbaths, unsuited for business, and fit to be ranked with seasons of noted calamity and gloom:—

> "Quâque die redeunt rebus minus apta gerendis
> Culta Palæstino septima festa Syro."[3]

> "Nec pluvias vites: nec te peregrina morentur
> Sabbata: nec damnis Allia nota suis."[4]

According to Augustine, Seneca, in censuring the rites of Judaism, charges its Sabbaths in particular with causing the neglect and obstruction of urgent affairs, and dooming to idleness and waste the seventh part of life.[5] Juvenal repeats the latter charge, when, lampooning Roman perverts to Judaism, he says,—

> "By them no cooling spring was ever shown,
> Save to the thirsty circumcised alone!
> Why? but each seventh day their bigot sires
> Rescind from all that social life requires."[6]

He is followed by Tacitus, who affirms that the Jews so enjoyed the repose from labour which every seventh day afforded, as to be led by the blandishments of idleness to give up every seventh year also to sluggish inaction.[7] Persius sneers at the voiceless prayers, and the Sabbaths of the circumcised:—

> "Thou mutterest prayers—nor dost refuse
> The fasts and Sabbaths of the curtailed Jews."[8]

1 Lam. i. 7; v. 5.
2 Jahn's *Jewish Antiq.*, p. 108.
3 *Art. Am.* i. 415, 416.
4 *Remed. Am.* 219, 220.
5 *De Civit. Dei*, lib. vi. c. 11.
6 "Quæsitum ad fontem," etc.—Juv. *Sat.* xiv. 105.
7 "Septimo quoque die otium placuisse," etc.—*Hist.*, lib. v. sec. 5.
8 "Labra moves tacitus recutitaque Sabbata palles."—Pers. *Sat.* v. 184.

Whence, it may be asked, this antipathy to Jewish sacred days? These writers were familiar with seasons of rest and worship as observed by their own countrymen in a manner not unlike the practice of the Jews. Plato, in a remarkable passage, extols festivals as the gift of the gods for the relief of toil-doomed man.[1] Cicero, though he stigmatizes the religion of the Jews as abhorrent from the ancestral ordinances of Rome, commends festival days.[2] And Seneca, while he sees nothing but damage and loss of time in the Sabbaths of Moses, applauds the holidays of heathendom as the wise appointments of legislators, for the necessary attempering of human labour.[3] The reason, therefore, of dislike to the former must be sought for in prejudice, not in calm consideration and rational conviction. The sanctity and unworldliness which are repulsive to human depravity now, were equally obnoxious then. It is true that some of the heathen, surmounting this obstacle, embraced Judaism,[4] and that many of the Jews had spread themselves over the Empire, and had been admitted to the privileges of citizenship. To this latter fact the words of Horace apply :—

"'This is the Jews' grand feast; and, I suspect,
You 'd hardly like to spurn that holy sect.'
'Nay, for such scrupulous whims I feel not any.'
'Well, but I do; and, like the vulgar many,
Am rather tender in such points as these.'"[5]

But the prevalence of the system and its friends only served to exasperate the aversion of others into a bitterness of feeling not at all favourable to the discoveries or utterances of truth. Under this feeling Seneca represents the hateful Jews as able by their numbers and power to rule their masters; and Juvenal complains:

"There be, who, bred in Sabbath-fearing lore,
The vague divinity of clouds adore;
Who, like their sires, their skin to priests resign,
And hate like human flesh the flesh of swine.

[1] Θεοὶ δὲ οἰκτείραντες—*De Leg.* lib. ii. [2] *De Leg.* lib. ii. sec. 19. Orat. pro. Flac.

[3] *De Tranq. Anim.* c. 15.

[4] Josephus not only mentions Fulvia, a woman of rank in Rome, as having been converted to the Jewish religion, but informs us that in the reign of Nero all the married women in Damascus were addicted to that religion.

[5] "Hodie tricesima Sabbata," etc.—*Sat.* 9 of B. 1.

The laws of Rome those blinded bigots slight,
In superstitious dread of Jewish rite;
To Moses and his mystic volume true,
They set no traveller right, except a Jew." [1]

The translator, Badham, remarking on the ignorance betrayed by Juvenal in these lines, adds :—"Had Providence permitted to him the use of that volume of their (the Jews') great lawgiver, how much would he have been astonished at the benevolence and mercy which it inculcates! and how little would he have felt disposed to boast of the light which the world had received from 'Athens or from Rome.'" But that volume in Greek was accessible to Juvenal, and both he and Tacitus had abundant means of avoiding their ignorant misrepresentations of the Jewish religion. The latter has in one instance done it justice, and let his beautiful words be a reply to the poet's fancy of "cloud-worship," though, as the translator observes, if he gave them no credit for a more pure abstract notion of the Deity, a cloud was as good as a stone: "The Jews acknowledge one God only, and him they see in the mind's eye, and him they adore in contemplation, condemning as impious idolaters all who with perishable materials wrought into the human form, attempt to give a representation of the Deity. The God of the Jews is the great governing mind that directs and guides the whole frame of nature, eternal, infinite, and neither capable of change, nor subject to decay." [2]

In defending their religion and its institutions, the Jews had recourse to various means according to circumstances. Sometimes, as under Ahasuerus, and in the Maccabæan wars, they successfully stood for their lives and for their faith. It frequently happened, that in consequence of their oppressed condition, they could vindicate their cause only by heroic suffering on its account. Of this means of defence we have some noble instances in the Babylonian captivity.—(Dan. ii. vi.) We cannot accord the same unmixed feeling of admiration to the conduct of those Jews[3] in later times, who, to the number of a thousand, allowed themselves to be massacred rather than resist their assailants on the day of holy rest, or those twelve thousand who perished, and their priests

[1] "Quidam sortiti metuentem Sabbata patrem," etc.—Juv. *Sat.* xiv. 97.
[2] *Hist.* Book v. sec. 5.
[3] Joseph. *Antiq.* xii. vi. 2; *Wars*, i. vii. 5.

whose blood was mingled with their sacrifices, because, though they had come to believe it right to withstand their enemies, they still held it unlawful to adopt offensive measures on that day. At other times we find them resorting to the arts of diplomacy, and the aid of foreign power. They pleaded effectually, for example, with Agrippa and Augustus. The latter, in answer to their appeal, issued, and inscribed on a pillar in the temple of Cæsar, an order in their favour, commanding, with other things, that they should not be obliged to go before any judge on the Sabbath-day, or on the day of preparation for it, after the ninth hour.[1]

Nor was the pen wanting. After the cessation of the prophetic spirit with Malachi, the books called the Apocrypha were written, it is supposed, by individuals of the Jewish people belonging mostly to Alexandria. These books, though nowhere pretending, and, in some instances, as they well might, even disavowing any claim to inspiration, contain, amidst flagrant errors and imperfections, many wise maxims, with our most authentic information respecting the history, doctrines, and practice of the divinely selected nation, and of the Church of God, during the period of above four hundred years.[2] Re-echoing Scripture facts relative to the Sabbath, they describe the care, amounting to austerity, with which in the days of the Maccabees that holy institution was observed. To two other writers, who amongst various services to Judaism, stood forward in the character of its apologists, we owe answers to anti-Sabbatic calumnies, as well as warm eulogiums on the septenary rest. One of them was the learned and eloquent Philo-Judæus [3] The other was the well-known Josephus,[4] whose works, prized alike by the intelligent many, and the learned few, have shed much light, including a few rays on our subject, over

1 Joseph. *Antiq.* xvi. ii. 3; xvi. vi. 1, etc.

2 Dr. Pye Smith's *First Lines of Christ. Theol.* p. 472.

3 Philo represents himself as advanced in life in A.D. 40. His language on certain subjects is so strikingly coincident with the phraseology of the Apostles John and Paul, as to be regarded by an able writer (Dr. J. Jones) as a proof of his conversion to Christianity.

4 He was born about A.D. 37, but belongs in the character of historian to the close of the first century. Sad it is, that living when the Gospel had begun to pour its effulgence on the world, he refused its illumination. For, that Josephus was a Christian, as the writer already referred to has laboured to show, is disproved by stubborn facts.

the Sacred Scriptures, and the history and character of his nation. Any defence of Judaism, however, at the time when these able men wrote, was encumbered with serious disadvantages. The friends of the system were far from being happy illustrations of its moral tendency, and the system itself had fallen under the description : "In that he saith, A new covenant, he hath made the first old. Now that which decayeth and waxeth old is ready to vanish away."—(Heb. viii. 13.)

The Sabbatic controversy now passes into two—one between Jews and Christians; the other between Christians and the adherents of Paganism. In each of these new conflicts, as in the old, one of the parties is subjected for a time to persecution for its opinions. A new power, it is felt, has come into the field. Its wider and more rapid ascendency produces a more determined resistance than had been offered to the less aggressive and energetic system which it has succeeded. Christianity is assailed with a proportionate severity by the heathen. The Jews also turn persecutors, and, like Herod and Pilate, they and the Pagans, who before were at enmity between themselves, are made friends together. From the days of the apostles downwards for many years, the followers of Christ had no enemies more fierce and unrelenting than that people, who cursed them in the synagogue, sent out emissaries into all countries to calumniate their Master and them, and were abettors, wherever they could, of the martyrdom of men, such as Polycarp, of whom the world was not worthy. Among the reasons of this deadly enmity was the change of the Sabbatic day. The Romans, though they had no objection on this score, punished the Christians for the faithful observance of their day of rest, one of the testing questions put to the martyrs being, *Dominicum servasti?*—Have you kept the Lord's day?[1] Such, however, was the success of truth, and of the example of these good men, that the Lord's day soon passed from being an object of opprobrium into a law of a great empire. And Julian himself was so impressed with the power of its arrangement of rest and instruction as to contemplate the adoption of a similar provision for reviving and propagating heathen error.

[1] Baron. *An. Eccles.* A.D. 303. Num. 35, etc.

But the opposition of the Jews and Pagans to Christianity was conducted in the form also of assault against its principles and institutions by argument and ridicule. Celsus and Porphyry proved, if not abler, yet more zealous and subtle combatants against Jesus, than Seneca and Tacitus had been against Moses. Trypho may be considered as expressing the grounds of Jewish antagonism to the Christian faith. Its friends had, therefore, in addition to the work of propagating truth, to defend it against this twofold opposition. The defence was undertaken by the eminent men who are so well known under the name of the Fathers, and occupies not the least valuable portion of their works.

The Sabbatic views of the Fathers will fall to be presented in another part of this volume. Let it be sufficient in this place to say, that by one or more of them, uncontradicted by the others, has each of the doctrines been held, which in our days have, though improperly, been termed Sabbatarian—the primæval appointment and patriarchal observance of a weekly day of rest and worship—the substitution by Divine authority of the first day of the week as the Christian Sabbath for the Jewish seventh day—and the consecration by the same authority of the former, or Lord's day, entirely to rest from secular labour, and to the immediate service of God, as required and directed in the Fourth Commandment, cases of necessity and mercy being, as they were, also, under the former economy, excepted.

The Fathers had on the subject of the Sabbath, as on others, to engage in dialectic conflicts with the Jews. Besides frequent passages which touch on Judaism, we find some of them devoting entire treatises—others, large portions of works, to the subject.[1] The Sabbatic institution in particular is treated of by Novatian, and in a work ascribed to Athanasius, and is referred to in various patristic writings, with special respect to Jewish opinions. In Justin Martyr's Dialogue with Trypho, a Jew—whether a real or fictitious person, is not certain—the Christian and Jewish arguments on, besides other points, the continued observance of the seventh day as a holy day, are presented. Trypho charges Justin and other Christians, as affecting superior excellence, and

[1] As Justin Martyr, Clement of Alexandria, Tertullian, Hippolytus, Cyprian, Eusebius, Basil, Chrysostom, and Augustine.

yet not at all differing from the Gentiles, inasmuch as they observed neither the feasts nor the Sabbaths. To this Justin replies, that as circumcision was not necessary before Abraham, nor the celebration of the Sabbath and festivals and oblations before Moses, neither now is there any need of these observances after Christ has come.[1] Irenæus and Tertullian reason in the same way. "Abraham," says the former, "believed God without circumcision and the Sabbath."[2] "Let them show me," says the latter, "that Adam sabbatized, or that Abel in presenting his holy offering to God pleased him by sabbatic observance, or that Enoch who was translated, was an observer of the Sabbath, or that Noah, the builder of the Ark on account of the great deluge, kept the Sabbath, or that Abraham amidst Sabbath-keeping offered his son Isaac, or that Melchisedec in his priesthood received the law of the Sabbath."[3]

The word *Sabbath*, as will afterwards more fully appear, must be understood in these passages to signify the Jewish Sabbath. The connexion of the word with "festivals and oblations" in the argument of Justin Martyr, shows that this was the sense in which he used the term. That Tertullian employed it in the same acceptation follows from the drift of his reasoning, and from his usual mode of writing; as for example, "We celebrate the day after Saturday in distinction from those who call this day their Sabbath, and who devote it to ease and eating, departing from the old custom, of which they are now very ignorant;"[4] and "All anxiety is to be abstained from, and business postponed on the Lord's Day."[5] Neither Justin nor Tertullian can intend to question the need or the obligation of a weekly holy day under Christianity, for they have both not only detailed the manner in which "Sunday" was observed by the Christians in their times, but positively affirmed the Divine authority of the day. Irenæus, too, mentions the Sabbath along with circumcision, thus making it manifest that he refers to Mosaic ordinances, and has plainly stated his conviction that the Decalogue is of perpetual obligation, as well as that the Lord's Day is supreme among the days of the week, being the only season on which it was right to celebrate

[1] C. 12. [2] *Adv. Hæres*, lib. iv. c. 30. [3] *Adv. Judæos*, sec. 4.
[4] *Apol.* c. 16. [5] *De Orat.* c. 23.

the resurrection of Christ.[1] "The Fathers," observes Bishop Patrick on Gen. ii. 3, "in saying that there was no Sabbath among the patriarchs, meant Jewish Sabbaths." How would Justin Martyr and Tertullian have indignantly spurned the interpretation put on their words by a recent writer, when, to accomplish the ungodly and unphilanthropic purpose of overthrowing a Divine institution, he neglects to ascertain the meaning of words employed by ancient writers, or of their views elsewhere expressed, and charges them with saying what warranted the inference that, "except during the time of divine service, the Christians of that period lawfully might, and actually did, follow their worldly pursuits on the Sunday!"[2]

There is a phase of the controversy which has led to the mistaken notion that the Christian Church itself was for a considerable time divided on the subject of a weekly holy day. There were even in the days of the apostles persons who wished to impose upon converts from heathenism the obligation of observing the times of the Jewish calendar, along with the other parts of the ancient ritual, an obligation from which the Apostle of the uncircumcision declared them to be free (Col. ii. 16, 17), and which was not to be required on the one hand (Acts xv. 19), or to be yielded to on the other (xxi. 25). Yet a party, the Ebionites, who professed to be Christians, though they denied the Divinity of the Saviour, not only held and acted on the necessity of keeping the whole law of Moses, but insisted that all others should do the same. This party continued to exist for four or five centuries. But although, as Eusebius informs us, they celebrated the Sundays in remembrance of the resurrection of our Saviour, yet, as they observed the Jewish Sabbath, and other ceremonies like the Jews,[3] as they made this observance an indispensable part of religion, and as they disbelieved the doctrine of Christ's Deity, they had no claim to be considered Christians. They were accordingly ranked among heretics, and some of the Fathers wrote against them as such. Epiphanius devotes a part of his *Panarium* to the Ebionites, in which, while he holds that the first

1 *Adv. Hæres*, iv. 31. Euseb. *Hist. Eccles.* lib. v. c. 24.
2 *Examin. of the Six Texts*, by a Layman, p. 274.
3 *Hist.* lib. iii. c. 27.

Sabbath has revolved in its septenary cycle from the beginning of the world, he also contends that the Jewish day had been discharged.

Besides the Ebionites, there was a class, who were sometimes confounded with them, but who, for a long period at least, remained distinct, the Nazarenes. These believed in the Divinity of our Lord, but clung to the Jewish ritual, which, however, they sought not to impose upon others. Although to some extent sympathized with by the Church, they were not considered as belonging to it. Justin Martyr remarks, that it was a question in his time whether a Christian who observed the Sabbath, that is Saturday, should be admitted or not to the holy mysteries.[1] Against such Sabbatarianism, not only he, but Clement and Dionysius of Alexandria, Tertullian, Victorine, Novatian, and others, testified. Notwithstanding these efforts, respect for Saturday gained ground. This feeling was especially cherished in the Eastern Churches, in which, from deference to the Jews, who were numerous in the East, they distinguished the day by two of the supposed prerogatives of the Lord's Day, the standing posture in prayer, and the exclusion of fasts. Tertullian informs us that a very few persons in his time began to introduce the former practice in the West. The historians, Socrates and Sozomen, attest the general observance of the Lord's Supper on both the seventh and first days of the week, the former excepting the Churches of Alexandria and Rome—a very large exception—who followed an old tradition.[2] And Bingham states, that towards the close of the fourth century, the observance of Saturday, like Sunday, prevailed generally throughout the East, and the greater part of the Christian world.[3] But the former day was in no period of the Church's history placed on a level with the latter. In earlier times, a religious regard to the seventh day was paid by few, and disapproved by Christians in general. It was by many never recognised as an appropriate season for the celebration of the communion, and, as Bingham says, "there were no ecclesiastical laws obliging men to pray

[1] *Dial. cum Trypho*, p. 266.
[2] Socr. *Hist.* lib. v. c. 22, and lib. v. c. 8. Soz. *Hist.* lib. vii. c. 19.
[3] *Antiq.* Book xx. c. 3, sec. 1.

standing on the Sabbath; nor, secondly, are there any imperial laws forbidding lawsuits and pleadings on this day; nor, thirdly, any laws prohibiting the public shows and games, as on the Lord's Day; nor, fourthly, any laws obliging men to abstain wholly from bodily labour."[1] The views and practice of Christians, as respected the Saturday, therefore, did not amount to a want of unanimity in reference to the exclusive claim of the Lord's Day to Divine authority, and peculiar sacredness. The facts bear out the statement of Archbishop Ussher, that "where Saturday was kept holy day, it was not as a Sabbath, but as a preparation-day for the Christian Sabbath."

The literary conflicts of the Christians and Pagans, in reference to the Lord's Day, afford few materials of remark. In the first instance the persecutions of the Church, and then her ascendency in the Roman Empire, went to preclude, in a great measure, the strife of words. It appears that so late as the beginning of the fifth century, Pagan poetry shot some envenomed shafts at the Christians on account of their weekly holy day, though under the pretence of aiming them at the so-called and less-dreaded Jews.[2] At an earlier period, the heathen assailed the Christian ritual as contemptibly mean, and the Christian Sabbath as a season devoted to concealed impurity and crime. The charges of immorality, as practised on the Lord's Day by its friends, were triumphantly disproved. Justin Martyr and Tertullian present unvarnished accounts of the harmless and holy manner in which the Christians passed the day. The latter, and Minucius Felix, turn the weapons of their enemies against themselves, for which the flagrant and shameless profligacy of paganism furnished ample occasion. The groundless allegation of Celsus, that the religion of Jesus was without a proper worship, because it had no altars, images, or temples, was met and disposed of by overpowering arguments in one of the ablest works of Origen, but for whose

[1] *Antiq.* Book xx. c. 3. sec. 3.

[2] Thus wrote Rutilius Numitianus,—

> Radix stultitiæ cui frigida Sabbata cordi:
> Sed cor frigidius religione sua est.
> Septima quæque dies turpi damnata veterno
> Tanquam lassati mollis imago Dei.

immortal pages the allegation itself must have been long ago forgotten.

Although no important discussion between Christians and unbelievers on the subject appears to have arisen in the period from the seventh century down to the time of the Reformation, and Sabbatic memorials were transferred for the most part to the canons of councils and the edicts of princes, to the abridgment of the literature of the question, yet the institution still employed the pens of the learned, and their testimony was of no little consequence to its preservation, as well as to the permanent evidence on its behalf. Many councils and synods directed their attention to the institution, and issued injunctions for its observance. It was the subject of frequent and uniformly favourable legislation by the civil powers. The dignitaries of the Church, particularly in England, exerted their commanding authority in their respective dioceses on its behalf. Even among the Popes, a few, awed by its sanctity, took its part. Such means, mixed up though they were in many instances with superstitious, and other impure ingredients, were the tributes of human reason and conscience to the sacred claims of the weekly rest, and helped to secure its preservation, with some measure of its hallowing and humanizing influence, during fifteen centuries. But a peculiar honour and interest attach to the men of those times, whether in higher or lower station, who breathed and shed around them the benignant spirit of the Divine institute, and to whom it owed, as to persons of the same character it will ever owe, its most congenial testimony, and best defence.

But, though the harmony of Christians on points directly affecting the authority and sacredness of the Lord's Day continued unbroken for upwards of fifteen centuries, and the Reformation itself, which stirred so many questions, led to no immediate contest on this, yet on a practice allied to the weekly day of rest, and tending to its wrong and injury, Rome and the Reformers were speedily at issue.

HOLIDAYS.

From an early time piety and zeal, by adding to the institutions of Heaven, began, unwittingly, to prepare the way for further errors and future strife. In these feelings originated the appointment of stated days for the commemoration of particular events in the history of the Saviour. The same feelings produced another class of sacred seasons. The day of martyrdom was regarded as "the day of birth to a happy life for ever," and, therefore, worthy of grateful celebration. Such days were called *Natalitia.* To ceremonies without Divine rule there was no limit. The saints entitled to the honour of commemoration amounted, in the course of some centuries, to a multitude for each day of the year,[1] and the annual holidays of man became more numerous than the Sabbath-days of God. Self-righteousness soon converted the invention and observance of new ceremonies into the price of salvation. Ambition saw in these things the means of promoting its objects; and the more surely to compass them, gradually withdrew the light of knowledge, while it ministered fresh fuel to the flame of superstition and fanaticism. Rome, holding in words the supremacy of the Lord's Day, indirectly impaired its authority and influence by ranking it with her own holidays, and by imposing on her votaries both classes of institutions under the same temporal penalties, and as alike necessary to salvation. The authority of the Church was sufficient to turn the scale in favour of those Sabbath-days on which the anniversaries of her own appointment fell, and in process of time human holidays were practically preferred to the day which Christ had consecrated for His worship. So multitudinous had sacred days and their assigned engagements become, that not only was a large amount of productive labour lost to society, but intellectual power was uselessly expended in framing and interpreting the rules of a prodigious system of fooleries, and conscience was perplexed as well as the spirit borne down by the endless "commandments of men." "All Christianity," says the Confession of Augsburg, "was placed in the observation of certain festivals, rites, fasts, and forms of apparel." "Daily, new ceremonies, new orders, new holidays, new fasts, were appointed;

[1] "Except the first day of January, when the Gentiles had been so intent upon their own riots as to have no leisure for martyring the Christians."—Durand. *Ration. Off.* lib. vii. fol. 242. Durandus, alleging Eusebius as his authority, gives the number of martyrs at 5000 a day. The Editor of Cosin's Works (v. 23, notes) alleges another authority than Eusebius, and reduces the number to 500!

and the teachers in the churches did exact these works at the people's hands as a service necessary to deserve justification, and they did greatly terrify their consciences if aught were omitted." "The doctrine of the gospel," it is further observed, "is hereby obscured, which teacheth that sins are forgiven freely by Christ—this benefit of Christ is transferred unto the work of man."[1] And thus, also, was the law of morality made void as well as the law of faith. Oppression tends to madness and anarchy; the over-tasked will seek relief in licentious liberty; holidays were turned into seasons for vice and riot; and, unprofitable for religious ends, they became auxiliaries of impiety and demoralization.

The growing evil met, for many centuries, with little resistance. The later Fathers were strangely betrayed into the encouragement of the system, notwithstanding its attendant mischiefs which they observed and deplored. Not only were particular feast-days made by them the subjects of homilies and extravagant encomiums, but Basil[2] and Chrysostom[3] congratulated their hearers on having the martyrs as the safeguards of their country and cities against all enemies. Yet there were individuals who were not entirely carried away by the prevailing delusion. Ærius, presbyter of Sabacte in Armenia, of the fourth century, may be regarded as one of these, in so far as he contended strenuously against stated days for fasting, and the perpetuation under Christianity of Jewish feast-days. Of this individual, who also advocated the equality of bishops and presbyters, an interesting account is given by Neander.[4] While Augustine was engaged in seeking support for the existing holidays in the authority of the apostles and councils, and Chrysostom, in lauding the pre-eminent virtues of Easter, the historian Socrates was preparing to strike a heavy blow at their doctrine in the avowal that neither the Saviour nor the apostles enjoined by any law the observance of that leading feast, which had crept in and was kept not from canon but from custom; and in censuring those who contended for holidays as for life itself, while they regarded licentiousness as a matter of indifference, thus despising the commands of God, and making canons of their own.[5] About

[1] Hall's *Harmony of Confessions* (1842), 391, 397.
[2] Orat. on the *Forty Martyrs*.
[3] *Hom.* 70, to the people of Antioch.
[4] *Gen. Hist.* iii. 461, 462.
[5] *Hist. Eccl.* lib. v. c. 21, 22.

the same time Vigilantius, a presbyter of Barcelona, denounced, along with other corruptions, the abuses connected with vigils and festivals. His treatise on the subject was assailed with much asperity by Jerome.[1] After an interval of four centuries, Claudius, bishop of Turin (fl. 817), appears on the arena as a combatant of dominant evils. "In the abolition of all saints' days, as in other things"—opposition to the worship of images, and the veneration of relics and crosses—"he preceded the Calvinists."[2] He was followed by the Waldenses, of whom Reinerus Sacco, an apostate from themselves, and a Jacobin inquisitor, thus wrote about A.D. 1254—"They hold that all customs of the Church, except those which are to be found in the gospel, are to be contemned; for example, the feast of light, and of palms, and the feast of Pasch, of Christ, and of the saints. They work on feast-days: they disregard the fasts of the Church, dedications, and the benedictions."[3] Another writer informs us, that they rejected not only holidays in memory of saints, but all others whatsoever, as having been introduced without proper warrant, and kept no day holy except the Lord's Day.[4] It appears that in his views on this, as on other subjects, Wycliffe anticipated the reformers, and that there were many in his time who held the same opinions. He says, that "*many* were inclined to be of opinion, that all saints' days ought to be abolished in order to celebrate none but the festival of Jesus Christ, because then the memory of Jesus Christ would always be recent, and the devotion of the people would not be parcelled out between Jesus Christ and his members."[5] So intolerable was the evil of multiplied holidays felt to be by thoughtful men in the following century as to produce a loud call for redress. The cardinal of Cambray brought the matter before the Council of Constance (A.D. 1414).[6] He also pleaded for the rectification of this and of some other disorders, in his Treatise on Reformation, holding, "that excepting Sundays and the great festivals instituted by the Church, people ought to be allowed to work on holidays after Divine service, as well on account of the

[1] Bruce, *Annus Secularis*, p. 199. Neander's *Gen. Hist.*, iii. 456.
[2] Gretserus, in *Altare Damascenum*, p. 490.
[3] Blair's *Hist. of the Wald.* i. 408.
[4] Leger, *Hist. Gén. des Eglis. Vaudois*, i. 123.
[5] Bruce's *An. Sec.* p. 20.
[6] Heylyn's *Hist. of the Sab.* part 2, p. 168.

debaucheries and enormities in which the generality of people indulge themselves on these days, as out of regard to labouring men who have need of all the time they breathe in to get their livelihood."[1] The subject called forth the eloquent and impassioned expostulations of Nicholas de Clemangis, who describes holidays as seasons distinguished alike by the abominable obscenities of Bacchus and Venus, and by the bloody rites of Mars and Bellona, —inquires what noble or great man would not revolt at the celebration of his birthday with such villanies,—and whether any handiwork on the solemnities of the saints would not be infinitely preferable to so horrible practices,—and observes, "If a man oppressed with penury, be found to have laboured in his field or vineyard, he is cited and severely punished, but he who is guilty of these worse things shall want both punishment and an accuser."[2] The council did adopt some measures of reformation. The Popes, however, disregarded all complaints, and not only retained the days already established, but added others daily as they saw occasion.[3]

If the reformers had been able to accomplish it, the evil would have been swept away. Luther repeatedly declared his disapproval of holidays, and his desire that they were abolished.[4] "I would to God," says Bucer, "that every holy day whatsoever, beside the Lord's Day, were abolished. That zeal, which brought them first in, was without all warrant or example of the Scripture, and only followed natural reason, driving out the holy days of the Pagans, as one nail is driven out with another. These holy days have been defiled with so gross superstition, that I marvel if there be any Christian who does not shake at their very names."[5] Farel and Viret achieved their removal from Geneva. On coming to reside there, Calvin acquiesced in the received custom. His refusal, and that of his colleagues, Farel and Couralt, to approve of the restoration of the former practice at the dictation of the

[1] Bruce's *An. Sec.* p. 162. Gerson, in a sermon before the Council on the Nativity of tho Virgin, expressed similar sentiments, but in the same breath proposed that a new festival should be instituted in honour of Joseph's virginity.

[2] Tractat. de Nov. Celebrit. non instit.

[3] Heylyn's *Hist. of the Sab.* part 2, p. 168.

[4] Consultum esse ut omnia festa aboleantur, solo Dominico Die retento.—*Lib. ad Nobil. German.* Utinam apud Christianos nullum esset festum, nisi dies Dominicus.—*De Bon. Oper.*

[5] Bucer on Matt. x. 11

Bernese, were among the reasons of their banishment from that city. On their departure, the holidays, as observed in Berne, with certain accompanying rites, were re-established, which, however, were again, after years of controversy, abolished by the people. Calvin declared that he had no hand in this, though he was not much displeased that it had so happened; and that had he been consulted, he would not have given his opinion in favour of such a measure.[1] "Nor is this," he elsewhere states, "the only church which retained no solemnities but those of the seventh day; the same custom had already been introduced into Strasburg." In no case was the dismissal of such observances more thorough and permanent than in Scotland. The First Book of Discipline declares, that "the holidays invented by men, such as Christmas, Circumcision, Epiphany, Purification, and other fond feasts of our Lady, with the feasts of the apostles, martyrs, and virgins, with others, we judge utterly to be abolished forth of this realm, because they have no assurance in God's Word." When, in 1566, the Helvetic Confession, a copy of which was sent to this country, was approved by a number of the superintendents, with some of the most learned ministers, and afterwards by the General Assembly, the part that sanctioned holy days, of which the Church of Scotland rejected all but the Sabbath-day, was in both cases excepted from the favourable verdict. In the General Assembly, held August 6, 1575, it was enacted, "That all days which heretofore have been kept holy, besides the Sabbath-days, such as Yule day, saints' days, and such others, may be abolished, and a civil penalty (be appointed) against the keepers thereof by ceremonies, banquetting, fasting, and such other vanities."[2] Hence the boast of King James VI., so much in contrast with his subsequent proceedings towards his native land—when, in addressing the Assembly of 1590, he praised God that he was born in such a time as in the time of the light of the Gospel, and in such a place as to be King in such a Kirk, the sincerest kirk in the world: "The Kirk of Geneva," he proceeded, "keepeth Pasch and Yule.[3] What have they for them? They have no institution. As for our

[1] For these facts, see Calv. *Epist. ad Haller et ad Min. Bur.* and Bonnet's *Letters of Calvin*, i. 40, 46, notes.

[2] *Book of the Univ. Kirk of Scotland* (1839), p. 151.

[3] Easter and Christmas.

neighbour Kirk in England, their service is an evil-said mass in English: they want nothing of the mass but the liftings."[1]

In other instances the success of the Reformers in this matter did not come up to their wishes. We learn from a letter of Bullinger to Calvin, written in 1551, that the Church of Zurich had recovered her tranquillity after no small discord produced by her having discarded twelve feast-days of Rome. It appears from the Acts of Synod held at Dort in 1574, that the Belgic Churches had agreed to be content with the observance of the Sabbath.[2] But the magistrates interfered to maintain some of the old holidays, so that the Synod held at the same place in 1578 adopted a modified resolution, to the effect—that it were to be wished that the liberty allowed by God of working six days in the week were retained in the churches, and the Lord's Day alone devoted to rest; but since by the authority of the magistrates some other holidays are observed—Christmas, etc., the ministers of the Word shall labour by their preaching to turn the useless and hurtful practice of holiday-keeping, or idleness, into the occasion of holy and profitable employment, aud shall do the same in cities where more festivals are kept by the authority of the magistrates; and that the churches shall endeavour, as far as possible, to have the stated observance of every feast, except Christmas, Easter, Ascension-day, and Whitsunday, abolished with all due speed.[3] The French Protestants entertained the same views,[4] only being compelled by the Edict of Nantes to abstain from working on the holidays of the Roman Catholic Church, they agreed to congregate on these days either for hearing the word preached, or for prayer, as the consistories might find convenient, that the time might not be spent in idleness or vice.[5] In England, for upwards of a century after holiday abuses had been canvassed in the Council of Constance, nothing was done by the authorities in the shape of remedy beyond a few attempts to secure the better observance of the existing days. In 1523, six years after Luther had begun his career of reform, Cuthbert, bishop of London, reduced the many anniversaries of church dedications in his diocese to one annual

1 Calderwood's *Hist.* (1678), p. 286.
2 *Kerkelyk Hantboekje* (1738), Art. 53.
3 *Kerkelyk Hantboekje* (1738), Art. 75, *Voet. Disput. Select.* iii. 1309.
4 *Voet.* ibid.
5 *Order of Synod at Vitre,* Bruce's *An. Sec.* p. 206.

celebration, "in order," as he said, "to diminish the number of holidays which encouraged the people to indulge in riotous excesses."[1] But the most effectual assault on the evil was that of Henry VIII., who, having broken with the Pope, and set himself to dissolve the monasteries, authorized Cromwell, his vicar-general, to declare in the famous convocation of June 1536, "that it was his Majesty's pleasure that the rites and ceremonies of the Church should be reformed by the rules of Scripture, and that nothing should be maintained which did not rest on that authority;" following up the intimation of this noble principle with an order for the abolition, as demanded by the moral and social interests of the community, of "the feast of the patron of every Church, and all those feasts which fall either in harvest-time—July 1 to Sept. 29—or in term-time at Westminster, except the feasts of the Apostles, of our blessed Lady, and of St. George, and those holidays on which the judges were not wont to sit in judgment." This order distinguishes "the Sabbath-day" from holidays "instituted by man." The fickle monarch, by an ordinance in 1541, restored the feasts of St. Luke, St. Mark, and St. Mary Magdalene, "their names being often and many times mentioned in plain and manifest Scripture," but the feasts of the Invention, Exaltation of Holy Cross, and St. Lawrence, were abolished. "Divers superstitions and childish observances" were also placed under ban. And thus was fixed—except that the feast of St. Mary Magdalene was excluded in 1552—the precise number of holidays which is still to be found in the Prayer-book.

The conflict of the Reformers with the Church of Rome on the subject before us was soon ended. That Church was true to her motto, "Always the same." After the Reformers had laboured for years to correct abuses of every kind, these were all stereotyped by the Council of Trent. Rome even asserted more daringly an authority over times and seasons; and so late as 1549, consigned to the flames a poor man who ventured to maintain his right to work on one of her festival days that he might not starve.[2] On the other hand, the Reformed Churches generally settled down in the observances which they were able to secure. Although most of their leaders failed to attain in this respect all that they desired.

[1] *Wilk. Concil.* iii. 701. Fox's *Acts and Mon.*, *Table of French Martyrs*, K. Hen. VIII.

much nevertheless was gained. Happy had it been, as events have shown, for the peace and prosperity of all the Churches, if they had adopted the principle, that the Lord's Day is the only stated holy day appointed by Christ, who has, however, given to his followers the right of appropriating occasional seasons for public worship as circumstances may require. But the popular prejudice operated so strongly in various parts of Europe, as to prevent so desirable a consummation. There were many, however, in England who were not satisfied with this state of things, and hence a contest, earnest and prolonged, on the subject of rites and ceremonies among the Protestants of that country, which resulted in the expatriation of many of her best people, and in the disruption of the Church.

In this contest, as in others already noticed, there was on the one side power, the power of the oppressor. In the reign of Elizabeth, valuable though the services rendered to the Reformation were, acts were passed and measures employed, in not a few instances through the active influence of the Queen, which grieved the hearts of good men, and excluded from their churches, reduced to poverty, consigned to prison, or forced into banishment, thousands of ministers—a third, says Hume,[1] of all the ecclesiastics in the kingdom, many of them learned and excellent men—because they could not conscientiously submit to unnecessary compliances, which no earthly power had the right to exact. The consequent results to the nation were, that great numbers of churches were without ministers, and that three thousand others were supplied with mere readers who could not preach at all, to the promotion everywhere of Popery, ungodliness, and immorality.[2]

It was expected that on the accession of James to the throne of England, a prince who had avowed his attachment to "the sincerest kirk in the world," and his abhorrence of every vestige of Popery, would do justice to the persecuted and their cause. A deputation of the Puritans, accordingly, presented to his Majesty during his progress to London, the celebrated Millenary address, entitled "The humble Petition of the Ministers of the Church of England, desiring reformation of certain ceremonies and abuses of the Church," in which they say, "that being more than a thou-

[1] *Hist.* (1805), vol. v. p. 463. [2] Brook's *Puritans*, i. 60.

sand ministers groaning under the burden of human rites and ceremonies, they with one consent threw themselves at his royal feet, for a reformation in the Church-service, ministry, livings, and discipline," praying "that the Lord's Day be not profaned, and the rest upon holidays not so strictly urged." The petitioners had their fears as well as hopes, but they were not kept in suspense. The king soon after declared at the Hampton Conference, that "he would compel them to conform, or 'harrie' them out of the land, or else do worse;" and in his first Parliament avowed, that while he was content to meet "our Mother-Church," the Church of Rome, half way, the Puritans were insufferable in any well-regulated state. Accordingly, four hundred of his petitioners were in the course of a few years cast into prison, or driven from their country. These doings were followed by the introduction into Scotland of Prelacy, and four holidays against "the sense of the Kirk and nation," and with consequences the most disastrous to both. Measures more atrocious were employed against the Nonconformists in England and the Presbyterians in Scotland, by Charles I., till both parts of the kingdom were roused to arms, and Laud, the chief instigator of persecution, and the King himself, perished on the scaffold. Under the remarkable rule which succeeded, and which, absolute though it was, granted full toleration to all professing Christians, the Parliament passed an ordinance, setting aside all festivals, commonly called holidays, and appointing the second Tuesday in each month to be a day of recreation "for all scholars, apprentices, and other servants, the leave and approbation of their masters being first had and obtained." The restored monarchy and ecclesiastical system brought with them the increased oppression of the Puritans, of which the crowning instance in the time of Charles II. was the passing in 1662, of the "Act of Uniformity," requiring every one to conform to the Prayer-book, rites and ceremonies of the Church, and causing the deprivation of nearly two thousand five hundred ministers, the death of three thousand nonconformists, and the ruin of sixty thousand families. The undiminished severity of the following reign is clearly indicated, when to the mention of the name of Jeffreys, it is added, that no dissenting minister could appear in public, or travel, except in disguise, and that fourteen hundred and sixty Quakers were in prison, not for crime, but for nonconformity.

There is no satisfaction in recalling these depraved exhibitions of our common nature, except with the view of serving the ends of utility and truth. And it is pleasant to turn from them to the succession of noble-minded men who sympathized with the victims of wrong,[1] and to the salutary effects of measures which, though they set at nought the claims of justice and humanity, expatriated some thirty thousand citizens, and drained the country of so much of its wealth and moral worth, were, under Providence, the occasion of establishing our rights at the Revolution, of training a race of men who have made America and England what they are, and of sounding in the ears of oppressors notes of warning which can never die away.

From the circumstances of the Puritans, it might be presumed that there could be little intellectual controversy on questions which were summarily disposed of by authority. When, as in the days of Elizabeth, a person for saying, "that to keep the Queen's birthday as a holy day was to make her an idol," might be committed to the Fleet, and another for vindicating him, might be sent to the Marshalsea,—when, as at the Hampton Court Conference, and on many other occasions, the Puritans were subjected to browbeating and abuse,—and when, as afterwards, a physician, for denying the Divine right of bishops above presbyters, a barrister for writing against plays, and two ministers for publishing pamphlets against recent innovations and prelacy respectively, were degraded, imprisoned, fined, and, in two of the cases, barbarously maimed in their persons, it may be conceived, that the prosecutors had no need, and the sufferers small encouragement, to enter the arena of disputation. Yet the former did sometimes descend from their vantage ground, and the latter,

[1] The Earls of Bedford and Warwick, Lord Rich, Sir Francis Knollys, Sir William Cecil, Beza, the General Assembly, the Parliament at various times, Mr. Attorney Morrice, Archbishops Grindal and Abbot (repeatedly), Bishops Rudd and Williams, etc. Grindal for his favour to the Puritans was under censure for some years, and Williams for saying that "they were the King's best subjects, and he was sure they would carry all at last," was fined £11,000, and committed to the Tower, his library and goods being sold to pay the fine, to which was added a fine of £8000 on the discovery among his papers of two letters addressed to him, and containing certain dark expressions.

under all their disabilities, ventured to encounter them, or even to be the assailants. Howe has condensed the history of the conflict before his time in his letter to Bishop Barlow : "Few metaphysical questions are disputed with nicer subtlety than the matter of the ceremonies has been by Archbishop Whitgift, Cartwright, Hooker, Parker,[1] Dr. Burgess, Dr. Ames, Gillespy, Jeanes,[2] Calderwood, Dr. Owen, Baxter, etc." [3]

The subject had, indeed, been canvassed in the days of Edward VI., when Hooper and others, supported by a majority of the reforming clergy, contended against the vestments and other relics of Popery, and again during the earlier years of Elizabeth's reign, particularly in the Convocation of 1562, at which the petition for the removal of the rites and ceremonies was rejected by a single proxy vote. But Howe has accurately commenced his list with the names of Whitgift and Cartwright, since it was not till these learned men—professors of Divinity in the University of Cambridge—wrote, that the points of difference received a full and formal discussion. They published each two works, in the course of the years 1572-77, which nearly exhausted the question. How Cartwright acquitted himself on the occasion may be conceived from Beza's recommendation of him to Queen Elizabeth, as a person far better qualified to refute "the Rhemish New Testament" than he himself was; and from the words upon another occasion of the same reformer when writing to a friend in England he said, "Here is now with us your countryman, Thomas Cartwright, than whom, I think, the sun doth not see a more learned man." [4] Whitgift's part in the controversy has been pronounced learned, and, in some instances, eloquent. But it lay open to this cutting remark of Ballard, a Popish priest, "I would desire no better books to prove my doctrine of Popery than Whitgift's against Cartwright, and his injunctions set forth in her Majesty's name." [5] Within a few years there followed a discussion between

[1] Robert Parker, a rector of the Church, author of *De Politica Ecclesiastica*, an able treatise.

[2] Henry Jeanes, also a rector, and according to Wood, "a noted and ready disputant, a noted metaphysician." He is the author of controversial publications against Goodwin, Milton, Drs. Hammond and Jeremy Taylor, of a subtlety quite according to Sir W. Hamilton's own heart; and, also, of several excellent sermons.

[3] *Works* (1836), p. 23. [4] Clark's *Lives*, pp. 18, 19. [5] Strype's *Whitgift*, p. 285.

Hooker and Travers, when both were lecturers at the Temple. Travers was silenced by authority. Declining an invitation to a professorship in the University of St. Andrews, he accepted the provostship of Trinity College, Dublin, where he had Ussher as a pupil. He had a principal share in the composition of the *Book of Discipline,* afterwards the ecclesiastical directory of the Commonwealth. The dispute brought out the remarkable sentence from Hooker,—"Schisms and disturbances will arise in the Church, if all men may be tolerated to think as they please, and publicly speak what they think." But its chief result was, that by means of it he was induced to prepare his great work, for which purpose he withdrew to a more retired situation. The *Ecclesiastical Polity* has received even from those most unfriendly to its views the praise of extraordinary erudition, research, eloquence, and moderation; and of having superseded all other defences of the Church of England. But it has been too truly said, that, if written in support of the Popish hierarchy and ritual, the greater part of it would have required little alteration.

The name of Dr. Ames, or Amesius, has given importance and fame to a contest between him and Bishop Morton, with Dr. Burgess, on whom the bishop devolved the task of defending his work on *The Innocence of the Three Ceremonies.* Dr. Ames had suffered for his nonconformity, having been obliged to retire to Holland, whither he was pursued by the hostile influence even of Archbishop Abbot, who procured his removal from the English Church at the Hague, of which he had been chosen minister, and prevented his appointment to a chair in the University of Leyden. He was for twelve years the admired professor of divinity at Franeker. His third work in the controversy, *A Fresh Suit against Human Ceremonies in God's Worship,* which was published in 1633, after the death of its author, and was the means of converting Baxter to nonconformity on several points, is, says Orme, "one of the most able works of the period, on the subject on which it treats. Its author was a man of profound learning, great acuteness, and eminent piety. . . . Though not professedly an answer to Hooker's *Ecclesiastical Polity,* it embraces everything of importance in that noted work."[1]

[1] *Life and Times of Richard Baxter,* p. 19.

The imposition of Prelacy, and the Five Articles of Perth, on the people of Scotland, extended the controversy to that country, where men of no ordinary endowments were found prepared to defend their religious polity. Henderson stood forward in the Assembly of 1618, to oppose the innovations, and was, along with Calderwood and others, author of a book (1619) proving the nullity of that Assembly. *The Course of Conformitie* (1622) seems to have been the production of William Scot, minister of Cupar-Fife.[1] Mr. John Murray, minister of Leith, and afterwards of Dunfermline, was the author of *A Dialogue, etc.* (1620), on the recent innovations. In a memoir of this individual, Dr. M'Crie remarks, "As Christian experience and practical godliness have been so often pressed to the disparagement of all contendings about the external form and discipline of the Church, it may be observed, that in this eminent person they were closely united, as they have been in 'a great cloud of witnesses with which we are compassed about.'"[2] It may be added, that even were the latter class of subjects admitted to be on some accounts less important than the other, it is "the least in the kingdom of heaven who breaks or teaches men to break one of these least commandments," and "the great" in that kingdom who "do and teach these commandments." The Nonconformists both in England and in Scotland were religiously and morally, as well as intellectually, the *élite* of the community. It was not among them that the profane, the dishonest, the dissolute, and the ignorant were to be found. Circumstances sometimes required of them, as in the case of Calderwood, to devote their energies to the defence of points connected with ecclesiastical government and discipline. But it will generally be found that their writers were still more prolific on subjects of doctrine and personal piety, and that they were the contributors of our best works in both these departments. Jeanes, Ames, Owen, and Baxter, are a few out of many instances. The spirit of Adam Gib has been common among such men: "I have used," he says, "my best endeavours all along," for forty-five years, "through 'evil report and good report,' to maintain the cause of the Secession testimony which I profess, on behalf of the Reformation-principles of the Church of Scotland, against the manifold errors and corrup-

[1] Scot's *Narr.*, Pref. p. vi. note (Wod. Soc. Works). [2] *Miscell. Writings* (1841), p. 152.

tions of the present age. But I have very seldom entertained my hearers from the pulpit with any peculiarities of that cause. It has been always my principal, and almost only business there, to explain and enforce those doctrines and duties which are accounted of among Christians of all denominations, so far as they take the substance of their Christianity from the Bible. And I have a particular satisfaction in this providential ordering, that my former appearances before the world, in favour of the special testimony which I have espoused, are succeeded by the present appearance on behalf of the common interests of Christianity."[1] A work of Gillespie, under the title, *The English Popish Ceremonies obtruded upon the Church of Scotland* (1637), though the production of a mere youth, was deemed worthy of being "discharged by a proclamation." Baillie extols it as a marvellous composition, and "far above such an age."[2] But the most voluminous writer on the subject was Calderwood, author of the *True History of the Church of Scotland* (1678), who, besides replies to Dr. Morton maintaining his "innocent" to be "nocent" ceremonies (1623), a *Re-examination of the Five Articles enacted at Perth*, etc. (1636), with other books and tracts, published in 1623 the *Altare Damascenum*, "beyond comparison the most learned and elaborate work ever written on the subject, embracing the whole controversy between the English and Scottish Churches as to government, discipline, and worship. It was never answered, nor is it easy to see how it could be answered. It was held in high estimation by foreign divines, having been printed more than once on the Continent."[3]

It would be unnecessary to dwell on the writings of the decided

[1] *Sacred Contemplations*, Preface—a work which discovers a profound acquaintance with Divine truth, and powers of vigorous thinking and writing, even when its author was in his seventy-third year.

[2] Stevenson's *History*, ii. p. 217. Baillie's *Letters*, i. pp. 67, 68.

[3] M'Crie's *Miscell. Writings* (1841), words of the editor, p. 78. In an advertisement to the reader, prefixed to the Leyden edition (1708) of the *Altare Damascenum*, we have the now well-known remark of James I., the implacable enemy of Calderwood, that the work was unanswerable, as there was nothing in it but Scripture, reason, and the Fathers. In his Appendix to his History, Spotswood, another enemy, is constrained to acknowledge its consummate erudition. It is mentioned by Orme as one of the means by which Baxter was brought to "the full conviction that the English Episcopacy is a totally different thing from the primitive, that it had corrupted the churches and the ministry, and destroyed all Christian discipline."—*Life of Baxter*, pp. 22, 33.

Owen, or of the more moderate Baxter, in this controversy, or to recall the lucubrations of Bancroft and Durell, with those of their respective opponents, Bradshaw and Hickman. And it is sufficient to do little more than name the remaining principal writers on our subject, Nicholls and Pierce, who present the substance of the controversy between the Church and the Nonconformists; Calamy and Bishop Hoadly, whose writings have been said to give the fullest view of the points of difference between these parties to be found in our language; and, in reference to holidays in particular, Wheatly, who has done justice to the arguments for such seasons,[1] with Professor Bruce of Whitburn, who applied his remarkable powers and acquirements to a work in which he endeavours to prove that holidays are contrary to Scripture, and fraught with injury to the best interests of society.[2]

We may add, that it fitly devolved on the intimate friend of Bruce, Dr. M'Crie, to appear in defence of the principles of the Scottish Reformation, when, in 1817, the Court papers announced that the churches throughout the country were to be opened for divine service on the day appointed for the funeral of the Princess Charlotte. The late Dr. Andrew Thomson positively refused to comply with the order. A discussion ensued, which, after several pamphlets had appeared on both sides, was terminated by a publication from the pen of Dr. M'Crie[3] under the name of *Scoto-Britannus*, a brochure not discreditable to the philosophy and genius of the distinguished author.

As to the question of the propriety of those measures which were employed to compel compliance with the rites and ceremonies of the dominant Church, we believe that the progress of knowledge has left, in the minds of all enlightened Protestants, no doubt that such measures were inexpedient, incompetent, and unjust. On the question, however, of the appointment of stated days for the commemoration of good men, or of some remarkable particulars in the life of Christ, there is still a difference of opinion. Wheatly thus defends the practice as regards "the remembrance

[1] In *Rational Illustration, etc.*, ch. v. *Of the Sundays and Holydays.*

[2] *Annus Secularis, or the British Jubilee, etc.* (1788.)

[3] *Free Thoughts on the late Religious Celebration of the Funeral of her Royal Highness the Princess Charlotte of Wales; and on the Discussion to which it has given rise in Edinburgh.*—See Dr. M'Crie's *Miscell. Writings*, pp. 356, 357.

of some special acts and passages of our Lord in the redemption of mankind." "That the observation of such days is requisite, is evident from the practice both of Jews and Gentiles. Nature taught the one, and God the other, that the celebration of solemn festivals was a part of the public exercise of religion. Besides the feasts of the Passover, of Weeks, and of Tabernacles, which were all of Divine appointment, the Jews celebrated some of their own institution, viz., the feast of Purim, and the Dedication of the Temple, the latter of which even our blessed Saviour himself honoured with his presence. As to the celebration of Christian festivals, the first Christians thought themselves as much obliged to observe them as the Jews were to observe theirs. They had received greater benefits, and therefore it would have been the highest degree of ingratitude to have been less zealous in commemorating them. And, accordingly, we find that in the very infancy of Christianity, some certain days were yearly set apart to commemorate the Resurrection and Ascension of Christ, the coming of the Holy Ghost, etc., and to glorify God by a humble and grateful acknowledgment of these mercies granted to them at those times. Which laudable and religious custom so soon prevailed over the universal Church, that in five hundred years after our Saviour, we meet with them distinguished by the same names we now call them by; such as Epiphany, Ascension-day, Whitsunday, etc., and appointed to be observed on those days on which the Church of England now observes them."[1] In the absence of a summary by any eminent writer of the argument on the other side, we present two or three brief extracts from the writings of Amesius and Owen. The former, in the preface to his *Fresh Suit*, says :—"The state of this war is this; we, as it becometh Christians, stand upon the sufficiency of Christ's institutions for all kind of worship. *The Word*, say we, and nothing but the Word, in matters of religious worship. The prelates rise up on the other side, and will needs have us allow and use certain human ceremonies in our Christian worship. We desire to be excused as holding them unlawful. Christ we know, and all that cometh from Him we are ready to embrace; but these human ceremonies we know not, nor can have anything to do with them. Upon

[1] *Rational Illustration, etc. Of the Sundays and Holydays*, ch. v. Introd.

this they make fierce war upon us; and yet lay all the fault of this war, and the mischiefs of it, on our backs." In his *Truth and Innocence Vindicated*, Dr. Owen shows that all worship under the Mosaic dispensation was to be exclusively of Divine appointment (Exod. xx. 4, 5; xl.; Deut. iv. 2; xii. 32; 1 Kings xii. 33; Prov. xxx. 6; Mal. iv. 4); that every human addition to it was rejected in that word of the blessed Holy One, "In vain do they worship me, teaching for doctrines the commandments of men;" that the churches of the New Testament had their foundation laid in the command of our Saviour, "Go ye, and disciple all nations, teaching them to observe all things whatsoever I have commanded you;" that his presence was promised, "Lo, I am with you always," to accompany the teaching and observance of His own ordinances, not of any human super-additions; and that in no one instance did the apostles impose anything on the practice of the churches in the worship of God, to be necessarily or for a continuance observed among them, but what had the express warrant and authority of our Lord Christ.[1] "I shall take leave to say," are his words in his treatise on Communion with God, "what is on my heart, and what (the Lord assisting) I shall willingly make good against all the world, namely, that that principle, that the Church hath power to institute and appoint any thing or ceremony belonging to the worship of God, either as to matter or to manner, beyond the orderly observance of such circumstances as necessarily attend such ordinances as Christ himself hath instituted, lies at the bottom of all the horrible superstition and idolatry, of all the confusion, blood, persecution, and wars, that have for so long a season spread themselves over the Christian world; and that it is the design of a great part of the revelation to make a discovery of this truth."[2]

It is more than probable, that, when men of the greatest learning, wisdom, and piety, engage earnestly in a controversy, persevere in it, and "suffer the loss of all things," rather than abandon the principles which they conceive it to involve, the matter in dispute is no trifle. What must raise this probability as to the case before us into certainty, are the two considerations; first, that such questions had to be settled as, Whether Christ be the

[1] *Works* (1826), xxi. 336, 337.

[2] *Ibid.* x. 184, 185.

sole lawgiver in his Church? and Whether the Scriptures be a sufficient rule of worship? and, second, that history has proved the opinions on one side to have been productive of great good, and, on the other, of incalculable evil. And if we bear in mind the superior intelligence and morals of the Puritans as a body to those of their neighbours—the impossibility of vindicating the ceremonies without striking at the above-mentioned scriptural principles, and at Protestantism generally—with the results of the systems, written, respectively, in the blessings of knowledge, religion, and prosperity, and in the reverse, we seem to have the means of determining, along with the value of the contest, the side on which the truth lay; in other words, that the one class of opinions were importantly right, and the other gravely wrong. How happy for the Church of England were she warned by her own history, and the recent mutinies in her camp, yet to fulfil the desires of her early reformers by purging away her remaining Popery! And how sad for the churches in Scotland, should they, instead of holding fast and making real progress, come to weary of their simple religious forms, and yield to the insidious attempts of recreant sons to secularize a system of polity and worship which has been the glory and blessing of their country! On this subject let us employ the weighty words of a distinguished Scottish writer: "This thorough reform"—the "abolishing at the Reformation of holidays, and a multitude of other ceremonies"—says M'Crie, "constitutes the high distinction of Scotland among the Protestant Churches. Its beneficial influence has extended to all departments of society; it has improved our temporal as well as our spiritual welfare; it has freed us from many galling impositions which diminish the comforts and fret the spirits of other nations. It may be seen in the superior information of our people, in their freedom from childish fears and vulgar prejudices, in the purity of their morals, and in that practical regard which, unconstrained by forms, and unattracted by show, they voluntarily pay to the ordinances of religion. One of the worst symptoms of our state, and which may justly occasion foreboding apprehensions, is, that we are not duly sensible of our privileges, nor aware of the cause to which, under Providence, we are principally to ascribe them; and that there are many among us whose conduct gives too much ground to suspect that they would be ready to part at a very cheap rate with those privileges which their fathers so dearly won.

'O fortunatos nimium sua si bona norint.'

. . . . If ever the time come when the attachment of the people of Scotland to Presbytery shall be loosened and give way, its effects will not be confined to religion. To this attachment—to the soul-inspiring recollections by which it has been cherished—to the unfettered genius of our worship—to our exemption from the benumbing bondage of recurring holidays, political or religious, and from forms of prayer dictated on particular occasions by the Court, and to the freedom of discussion yet retained in our ecclesiastical assemblies, we hesitate not to ascribe, more than to any other cause, the preservation of public spirit and independence, which many things in our political situation and local circumstances have a powerful tendency to weaken and to crush. Those who view every expression of these feelings with jealousy, will, of course, encourage or connive at whatever is calculated to blunt them. But all who wish well to the public spirit of Scotland, as well as to her religious purity, are called upon to deprecate and resist such acts of conformity. And this resistance cannot be opposed to the evil at too early a stage.

'Principiis obsta; sero medicina paratur,
Cum mala per longas invaluere moras.'"[1]

ENGLAND.

No country has owed more to the Lord's Day than Scotland, and in none was the institution more indebted to the Reformation. There it rose at once, from a position almost on a level with Rome's crowd of fasts and feasts, to its proper honours as the one permanent holy day of the Christian Church. In other Protestant lands its claims were neither so definitely settled nor so fully recognised. Among the evils remaining unredressed, not the least important were certain days of man's consecration—those plants, which, as not of divine planting, the Reformers would have "rooted up," but which, left to cluster round the sacred tree of

[1] *Miscell. Writings*, pp 574, 585.

liberty, drew to themselves the nourishment necessary to its vigour and luxuriance. It is a matter rather of regret than marvel, that these great and good men, in exposing the prevalent error that the observance, however perfunctory, of rites and holy days, atoned for sin and exhausted moral obligation, should have let fall expressions in reference to the Lord's Day, hardly reconcilable with their decided testimonies on other occasions to its authority and excellence, or with their practical regard to its claims. Nor is it surprising, though also to be regretted, that amidst their manifold engagements they should have failed to present in their writings a full exposition of sabbatic doctrine and law, instead of those unsatisfactory notices of the subject which an able writer has thus described: "There is no regular and systematic treatise on the Sabbath in the works of the more eminent divines of that period; it is only incidentally alluded to in connexion with other points, such as the power of the Church in decreeing ceremonies, or briefly discussed in their commentaries on Scripture; or, finally, made the subject of a few paragraphs under the Fourth Commandment, in their elements of Christian doctrine. A few minutes might suffice to read what each one of the Reformers has left on record concerning the permanent obligation of the Sabbath; indeed, that part of the question is rather summarily decided on than calmly and satisfactorily examined." [1]

It is a peculiar responsibility of such men that they exert a powerful and far-reaching influence. Scotland's Reformers did early justice to the Lord's Day, and so, notwithstanding some unrighteous and violent attempts from without to wrest it from her, she still retains, bedimmed though it is, her sabbatic crown. The countries of the Reformation abroad felt for a time the impulse of the doctrines taught, and of the example set, by Zuinglius, Luther, and Calvin; but as Christianity and its weekly holy day, which are mutually conservative and stimulating, were not fully adjusted to each other, nor consequently brought to act with concentrated power on the people, the decay of both ensued; and though a war on the Sabbath question (from which Scotland was happily free) kindled by a spark from this country, prevailed for a century in Holland, and extended to parts of Germany, yet as

[1] Fairbairn's *Typology*, vol. ii. p. 462.

it ended in what Hengstenberg calls "the gradual advance of more liberal views," that is, such views as have left these countries well-nigh without a religion at all, another must yet be waged over the entire continent of Europe. The Reformation in England was not so thorough as in some countries, but the spirit of its people was too ardent to let a great question be compromised and slumber, as occurred in so many Protestant States. Hence to that country accrued the glory, as respected one party—the discredit as regarded another, of being the scene of the earliest conflict within the Christian Church on subjects affecting the Divine authority, the sacred character, and thus the very existence of one of the noblest, most indispensable, and most beneficent institutions of Heaven.

When the claims of the Lord's Day are advocated on the ground that the doctrine of its Divine authority was held by the Church down to the time of the Reformation, it is not necessary to prove that the institution was never misrepresented or misapplied. It is enough to the argument that the doctrine was received by the universal Church, although she chose to add holidays, superstitious rites, and one of six ecclesiastical precepts to the simple ordinance of Heaven. Nor is this argument, founded as it is on the harmony of many centuries, destroyed by the fact that sabbatic unanimity was disturbed at the Reformation, unless it can be shown that the ordinance was the cause of the disturbance. That peaceful ordinance, however, was guiltless. The Reformers were not aggrieved at the celebration of the weekly holy day. This formed no reason of their protest against Rome, or of their secession from her pale. It was her own interminable contrivances that at last rent the Church; and it was this, her will-worship, imitated naturally enough by one class, but rejected by another, which largely contributed to alienate from each other the friends of the Reformation. Rome, ever boasting of her concord, has least exemplified it in her own community, and has been the chief cause of the divisions and distractions in civil and ecclesiastical society around her;—and thus new evidence has been added to the old, in proof of the Divine power of an institute which has continued to exist among Protestant sects and controversies, not less than it was, and still is, preserved amidst all the corruptions of the Papacy.

Although nothing entitled to the name of a general or prolonged contest on our subject, except in so far as it was indirectly concerned with that on holidays, was the immediate result of the Reformation, yet there wanted not indications, then and afterwards, that diversified, and in some instances confused notions of the institution were entertained, arising from the system with which it had been mixed up, and showing that an open collision was, in the case of England at least, at hand. Luther, in his zeal against the profane and mischievous perversions of Divine commandments and ordinances in the Church of Rome, laid himself open, by strong expressions respecting the Mosaic Law and the Sabbath, to the charge preferred against him by John Agricola, of affirming the abrogation of the Decalogue—a charge which he vehemently denied, and obliged his accuser to retract, though only to be renewed.[1] Cardinal Tolet maintained, "that the observance of the Lord's Day is not a law of God, but an ecclesiastical precept, and a custom of the faithful."[2] The position was substantially asserted by Sir Thomas More in his *Dialogues*, where he avowed that the first day came in place of the seventh by virtue of tradition, and that the observance of the Sunday rested on the commandment of the Church,—"The Sundays hear thou mass." It is not for us to attempt harmonizing the views of such men with the doctrine taught in their Church throughout her history even to the present day—that the apostles changed the Jewish Sabbath into the Lord's Day, and that the duties of the latter are prescribed in the Decalogue. In his *Answer to Sir Thomas More* (1530), William Tyndale wrote slightingly of those circumstances of time to which the Church attached so superstitious and fatal an importance; and, as extremes meet, seemed to claim for the Christian people a right to alter the stated day of worship, no less unwarranted than that assumed by his opponent for the hierarchy in its appointment. "We be lords," he says, "over the Sabbath, and may yet change it into the Monday, or any other day, as we see need; or may make every tenth day holy day only, if we see a cause why; we may make two every week if it were expedient, and one not enough to teach the people. Neither

[1] Rutherford's *Survey of the Spiritual Antichrist*, pp. 68-80.
[2] Toleti *Insti. Sacerdot.* lib. iv. c. 13.

was there any cause to change it from the Saturday, but to put difference between us and the Jews, and lest we should become servants unto the day after their superstition. Neither needed we any holy day at all, if the people might be taught without it."[1] Tyndale, having finished his education at Oxford and Cambridge, conceived the purpose of translating the Scriptures into the English language, but finding it impossible to accomplish this in his native country, proceeded to the Continent, where he had completed a version of the New Testament with portions of the old, and had had the satisfaction of seeing many editions of the former printed and circulated, when he fell a victim to assassination in 1536, offering up with his last breath, the prayer, "Lord, open the eyes of the king of England!" Although it does not appear that he had personal intercourse with Luther, his residence on the Continent had led him to adopt, in reference to the Sabbath, the same strange phraseology, which appears, however, in both cases, to have been compatible with substantially sound views, and reverent observance of the institution. "When the Sunday came," says John Fox, "then went he to some one merchant's chamber or other (in Antwerp), whither came many other merchants, and unto them would he read some one parcel of Scripture; the which proceeded so fruitfully, sweetly, and gently from him, much like to the writing of John the Evangelist, that it was a heavenly comfort and joy to the audience to hear him read the Scriptures; likewise after dinner he spent an hour in the same manner."[2] Frith, his convert and friend, who suffered martyrdom for the Protestant faith in 1533, had in the year of his death written his *Treatise on Baptism*—in which, touching on the Sabbath, he follows Tyndale's train of thought, and asserts the same liberty for Christians to choose a day of worship, but with this difference, that the right was in the hands of "the forefathers," or apostles, and that "though they might have kept Saturday with the Jews as a thing indifferent, yet they did much better."

Without dwelling on the statement of the Convocation in 1536—"That sith the Sabbath-day was ordained for man's use, and therefore ought to give way to the necessity and be-

1 *Works* (1831) vol. ii. p. 101.
2 Anderson's *Annals of the English Bible*, vol. i. p. 521.

hoof of the same," "*much rather any other holiday instituted by man*,"[1]—we come to a declaration of sabbatic opinion, which, like that of the Convocation, has the advantage of coming from the collective wisdom of the English Church at the time. It is contained in *The Godly and Pious Institution of a Christian*, which appeared in 1537, with the signatures of Archbishop Cranmer and Bishop Latimer, Protestants ; and of Bishops Stokesley, Tonstall, Gardiner, Archdeacons Bonner and Heath—all, except in the matter of the Pope's supremacy, Romanists ; and, substantially repeated in the editions of 1540 and of 1543, the latter bearing the new title—*A Necessary Doctrine and Erudition for any Christian Man*, states that "the fourth commandment is distinguished from the other nine—the latter being merely moral, the former ceremonial as regards 'rest from bodily labour the seventh day,' which belonged only to the Jews, but moral as respects the spiritual rest from sin, which binds Christians at all times—the command, however, binding also to rest from all bodily labour, and to the exclusive service of God at certain times—not as formerly on the Saturday, instead of which succeedeth the Sunday, and many other holy and feastful days, ordained from time to time by the Church and called holy days, not because one day is more acceptable to God than another, but because the Church hath ordained that on these days we give ourselves wholly to holy works without impediment." Directions follow to the bishops and clergy to teach the people not to be over-scrupulous in time of necessity in abstaining from labour on the holy day, and that idleness, gluttony, or other vain and idle pastimes on that day, do not please God, but offend Him.

There appeared in 1545, *The Primer ; or Book of Prayers*, containing the Lord's Prayer, the Creed, the Ten Commandments, etc.,—"where," to borrow the remarkable statement of another, "the general confession, enumerating the violation of each of the commandments, on the fourth says, 'I have not sanctified *the holy days* with works which be acceptable unto thee, nor instructing my neighbour in virtue accordingly ;' when we turn to the Decalogue, we find, in strict conformity with this notion, nothing more of the fourth commandment than these words only—'Re-

[1] *Wilk. Concil.* iii. 827.

member that thou keep holy the Sabbath day.' This lopping off all mention of the six days' creation, and of the hallowed rest on the seventh, in order to make the commandment square with the Romish doctrine, might have been a hint to Cranmer, that his opinions on this head were not yet those we are taught in the Ten Commandments of Almighty God." [1]

Cranmer's Catechism (1548) states, that Christians are freed from the Mosaic law as regards differences of times and meats—that they have the liberty of using other sacred days than the Jewish—that to maintain this liberty they observe not Saturday but Sunday, and certain other days, as the magistrates, whom in this thing they ought to obey, judge it convenient—that they must employ and bestow the Sabbath-day upon godly works and business—and that to spend the holy days in the neglect of such works, or "in idleness, banqueting, dancing," etc., is "a great sin," "for which God punisheth us with divers kinds of plagues, but specially with need and poverty." [2]

It appears from the preceding extracts, that, while the Romanists were disposed to support their practical abuse of the Lord's Day by corrupting its doctrine, the Reformers, as religious earnest men, would have the institution applied to pious and practical use, but knew not how to carry out, or did not clearly apprehend, the only theory by which their object could be fully gained—the theory, we mean, of a Sabbath, moral, perpetual, and admitting of no competitor. It was reserved for Bishop Hooper to make the nearest approach to this theory that had been made since the time of Wycliffe. In his *Exposition of the Ten Commandments*, published in 1550, he not only advocates, with Cranmer, abstinence from ordinary labour, and from pastimes, on the Lord's Day, but, though admitting the Jewish Sabbath, as regarded its specific day of the week, to have been ceremonial, "during for the time," holds that the fourth commandment is no more ceremonial than the second, "all the commandments being of one virtue and strength."

[1] James' *Four Sermons on the Christian Sacraments and Sabbath*, p. 228.

[2] The original work, written in German "for the use of the younger sort" in Nuremberg, was, in 1539, translated by Justus Jonas, junior, into Latin, from which it was rendered into English by the archbishop, Jonas being at the time his guest.

These views, which were not new but very old, cannot reasonably be conceived to have been then peculiar to Hooper. But it is not unlikely that the writings of so learned and good a man would, with his preaching, exercise a powerful influence on sabbatic opinion in his lifetime, and that this would receive fresh energy from his heroic death in the cause of the doctrines and institutions of Christ. Whatever truth there may be in this supposition, certain it is, that so early after the appearance of his treatise as 1551, when the *Book of Common Prayer* was confirmed by Parliament, though the Preamble of the Act rang the old changes on holidays, the commandments were for the first time added to the *Liturgy*, the fourth, "Remember that thou keep holy the Sabbath-day," etc., being, as well as the others, succeeded by the prayer, "Lord, have mercy upon us, and incline our hearts to keep this law;" and that in Cranmer's *Forty-two Articles*, agreed to at a convocation of bishops and learned men in 1552, are to be found the following positions of vital importance to our subject, and expressed in singularly clear and decided terms:—First, the exclusive competency of the Scriptures of the Old and New Testaments to the establishment of any doctrine; and, Second, the threefold distinction in the law given from God by Moses, which as touching ceremonies does not bind Christian men, as respects civil precepts ought not of necessity to be received in any commonwealth, and as moral consists of commandments from the obligation of which no Christian man whatsoever is free.

A blank in sabbatic discussion and literature of fully five years (1553-58) is accounted for by the reign of Mary and Popery, under which Coverdale, Jewell, Becon, Fox, with many more, were obliged to quit their country, and Rogers, Hooper, Bradford, Ridley, Latimer, Cranmer, and others, were committed to the flames. But good resulted. The blood of the martyrs was the life of their creed, and the exiles returned, after the death of Queen Mary, only the more qualified to take part in the recovery and advancement of the Reformation. To the impression of those martyrdoms, and to the efforts of the men whose characters had been matured by their residence abroad, England in no small measure owed her free Bible, her improved Articles and Homilies, her Augustan age of learning, and her Puritans, with the liberty, virtue, enterprise, and prosperity, which were the fruits of the principles, labours, and sufferings of these oppressed but noble men. To the same means was she indebted for not the least of her privileges—a Sabbath doctrinally recognised as an institution of perpetual obligation, having its changed day divinely appointed, as well as its Christian observance ruled by the fourth commandment; and which, but for her own princes and prelates, would, through the removal of useless and pernicious devices from Divine worship, have reached a closer conformity to the Word of God. Queen Elizabeth had not been above four years seated on the throne when, at her desire, the Convocation of 1562 was assembled for the settlement of doctrine in the Church. The publication of thirty-eight Articles, and of the Second Book of Homilies, now appended to the First, as all agreed to by that body, was one of the chief results. These documents, supplemented with a thirty-ninth Article, and otherwise slightly changed, were approved by the Convocation of 1571, and in the same year confirmed by the Queen and Parliament, as constituting, with the Book of Common Prayer, the formularies of Doctrine and Worship in the Church of England. As such, with one important and several minor alterations subsequently made, they have been recognised by her members down to the present day.[1]

When we examine these documents, we find the following to be their doctrine respecting the Sabbath:—That while we ought always and everywhere gratefully to remember our beneficent Creator, it appears to be His good-will and pleasure that there should be special times and places for His worship and glory—that the appointed solemn time is ascertained from the Fourth Commandment, and is a standing day in the week—that this commandment does not require of us, as of the Jews, abstinence

[1] The important alteration referred to was the introduction into the Twentieth Article of the words,—"The Church hath power to decree rites or ceremonies, and authority in controversies of faith." As this, or any similar clause, had no place in the Forty-two Articles of Edward VI., none in the subscribed MS. Articles of 1562 and 1571, and none in any such book—"an imprinted *English* book"—as was alone confirmed by this Act of Parliament, it follows that the Church did not in her Articles of either of those years claim the power which the clause arrogates for her.

from ordinary labour in time of great necessity, or the observance of the seventh day—that Christians keep the first day of the week, and make that their Sabbath, or day of rest, in honour of Christ, who upon that day rose from, and conquered, death—that God hath given express charge by this commandment as a thing belonging to the law of nature, and therefore as most godly, just, and good, to be retained and kept of all good Christian people, that all men shall, upon the Sabbath-day, which is now our Sunday, cease from all weekly and work-day labour in which they ought to be employed during the six days, and give themselves wholly to heavenly exercises of God's true religion and service, even as God wrought six days and rested the seventh, and blessed and sanctified it, and consecrated it to quietness and rest from labour—that this example and commandment of God the godly Christian people began to follow immediately after the ascension of our Lord, and to choose for their standing day of worship in the week, the Lord's Day, the day after the seventh, of which mention is made in 1 Cor. xvi. and Apoc. i.—that since that time the day has been observed without gainsaying in the Church—that notwithstanding the warning against the breach of it given in the stoning to death of the man who gathered sticks on the Sabbath-day, there are still those that would be counted God's people who devote the Sunday to travelling and business without extreme need, or to what is worse, gluttony, drunkenness, quarrelling and fighting, excess and superfluity, toyish talking, and fleshly filthiness, so that God is more dishonoured, and the Devil better served on that day than upon all the days of the week besides; and that if men will be negligent, and not forbear to labour and travel on the Sabbath-day, or Sunday, and do not resort together to magnify His name in quiet holiness and godly reverence, they have reason to fear the displeasure and just plagues of Almighty God.[1] To this analysis of what is contained in the Homilies on the subject, let us add an extract from the *Book of Common Prayer*: "*Minister.*—Remember that thou keep holy the Sabbath-day. Six days shalt thou labour, and do all that thou hast to do, but the seventh day is the Sabbath of the Lord thy God. In it thou shalt do no manner of work, etc. *People.*

[1] *Homily of the Place and Time of Prayer. Homilies*, edit. London, 1687.

—Lord, have mercy upon us, and incline our hearts to keep this law."[1]

Such was in 1562 and 1571, and such is at this day the sabbatic creed of the English Church. As prior to 1562, no secession from her pale beyond that of an individual or two had taken place, the Church may be said to have then comprised nearly the entire population of the country; and as her creed was to exert no slight influence on the existing as well as many future generations, it was certainly of great moment that it should be accordant with Scripture. Of the one adopted different opinions have been entertained. Many, including persons of her own communion, have shown by their writings or practice that they have regarded it as rigid and unscriptural. Others, deploring its alliance with a hierarchy and ritual viewed by them as foreign from the letter and spirit of the gospel, may also take exception to some of its statements as incorrect or defective. The holidays of human appointment, for example, with which it is bound up, and which of course it does not condemn, are justly held to be a grievous wrong and bane to the Christian Sabbath. But surely it is a matter of well-founded congratulation that the Church of England has since 1562 distinctly recognised the Decalogue as a law of permanent authority, and as giving in its fourth precept a Divine and express charge to all men, that upon the Sabbath-day, which is now the first day of the week, and observed in honour of Christ and His conquest of death, they should, excepting in cases of necessity, rest from the common labour required of them on the other days of the week, and apply themselves wholly to heavenly exercises, as they would avoid the displeasure and just plagues of the Almighty, and "declare themselves to be his loving children in following the example of our gracious Lord and Father." And it is as gratifying as it is surprising, that a Convocation, almost equally divided on the proposal made to it of rejecting most of the old ceremonies, and actually debating the question, Whether they should conform in outward appearances as closely as possible

[1] *Order of the Administration of the Lord's Supper.* Partly as it was a minor authority, and partly as it expresses itself only less fully than the *Homilies*, on the Fourth Commandment, we have not cited Noell's *Catechism*, which was approved by the Convocation, as was also Jewell's *Apology*.

to Popish practice, should harmonize in a verdict respecting the weekly day of worship and rest containing so much precious truth. Jewell is supposed to have been engaged with Parker in completing the *Second Book of Homilies.* At all events, that learned man, so desirous, some years before, that every vestige of Popery, "the relics of the Amorites," were removed, but soon to be a strict enforcer of subscription; and the hardly less learned Sampson, who would submit to no human impositions; appear to have concurred with the Archbishop and his courtly friends, in approving the homily on "The place and time of prayer." The Queen, "the Governor of the Church," who was said, Argus-like, to have an eye on everything, *centum luminibus cinctum caput,* and who conceived that the reading of the Homilies might supersede every other means of public religious instruction, may be presumed to have read what she sanctioned. And neither those Nonconformists who separated from the Church in 1566, nor the Roman Catholics who followed their example in 1569, seem to have offered any protest against her sabbatical doctrine, or to have withdrawn on its account.

The decision thus harmoniously passed was not without an influence for good. It proved somewhat of a shield to the friends of the Lord's Day in their efforts on its behalf, and doubtless contributed materially to the fact, that the Church of England has from that time ever numbered amongst its members many enlightened defenders and conscientious observers of an entire weekly day of sacred rest. But its beneficial operation was lamentably counteracted by the intolerant principles and proceedings of many of those who were concerned in its adoption. This they accomplished not chiefly by direct attacks on the institution, although Whitgift, writing under the direction of Parker, claimed for the Church a power by virtue of which she had appointed the first day of the week to be the Christian Sabbath,[1] and the Queen

[1] "The Scripture hath not appointed what day in the week should be most meet for the Sabbath-day, whether Saturday, which is the Jews' Sabbath, or the day now observed, which was appointed by the Church." Cartwright, in replying to Whitgift's work, waives the point, "as not wishing to raise up other questions than those in hand," only saying, "There was no great judgment to make the Lord's Day as arbitrary and changeable as the hour and place of prayer."—Whitgift's *Works*, vol. i. pp. 200, 201.

asserted an arbitrary right sometimes to stifle bills brought by the bishops into Parliament in favour of Sabbath observance, and anon to banish profane players, and raze theatres and gambling-houses to the ground. It was mainly by other means that the injury was inflicted.

There is nothing by which the sabbatic institution, in regard to both its theory and its practice, is more favourably or unfavourably affected than the manner in which its relative ordinances are treated. In the commencement of Elizabeth's reign, persons of the greatest learning and piety were precluded by the compliances requisite to the exercise of the ministry, from accepting charges, which were in consequence supplied by mechanics, and other equally uneducated and unscrupulous men. Thousands of the former class, who had either got over their difficulties to some extent, or been tolerated by such prelates as Grindal, were afterwards suspended, and punished as felons. In 1559, the Bishop of Bangor wrote, that "he had only two preachers in all his diocese."[1] There were in 1583 only 2000 preachers to serve 10,000 parishes.[2] At this latter period the inferior clergy of England were very generally not only ignorant and unable to preach, but men of profane and profligate characters. In a petition to Parliament from the inhabitants of the county of Cornwall in 1579, it is said, "We have about one hundred and sixty churches, the greatest part of which are supplied by men who are guilty of the grossest sins ; some fornicators, some adulterers, some felons, bearing the marks in their hands for the said offence, some drunkards, gamesters on the Sabbath-day, etc. We have many non-residents who preach but once a quarter."[3] "The conformable clergy," it has been affirmed, "obtained all the benefices in their power, and resided upon none, utterly neglecting their cures ; many of them alienated the Church lands, made unreasonable leases, wasted the wood upon the lands, and granted reversions and advowsons for their own advantage. The churches fell greatly into decay, and became unfit for Divine service. Among the laity there was little devotion ; and the Lord's Day was generally profaned. Many were mere heathens, epicures, or atheists, espe-

[1] Brook's *Puritans*, vol. i. p. 21. [2] *Ibid.* p. 49. [3] *Ibid.* p. 41.

cially those about the Court; and good men feared that some sore judgment hung over the nation."[1]

That the general profanation of the Lord's Day should be one of many evils attendant on such a scarcity and abuse of the other Christian institutions, was a necessary result. For as an author of that time observes: "Wheresoever the preaching of the Word is not, or where men have it, and come not to it, there can they not sanctify the day in that manner that they should; because they want the principal part of God's service, and that which should direct them in all the rest, and make these most profitable unto them. . . . And if this be the state of the poor people, ... what can be said or thought sufficiently and answerably unto the sin of them who, being called the ministers of God, as they that should be chief in his service, and go before others in it, by preaching unto them, are able and willing to do nothing less in the world than that? For partly they are ignorant and cannot do it; partly, they are given to ease, and will not do it; and partly, they have so many charges to look unto, that they know not where to begin to do it. And so do not only unhallow every Sabbath-day that they live, and do bestow no day in the week so ill as that which they should bestow best of all, because they neglect that which God requireth most of all at their hands; but also are the only chief causes everywhere of unhallowing the Sabbath, and do compel the people to break it whether they will or no."[2] Accordingly, in city and country, this species of profaneness abounded. In a petition from the city of London to Parliament in 1579, it is said: "There are in this city a great number of churches, but the one-half of them at the least are utterly unfurnished of preaching ministers; . . . . (as to) the other half, partly by means of non-residents, which are very many, and partly through the poverty of many meanly qualified, there is scarcely the *tenth* man that makes conscience to wait upon his charge, whereby the Lord's Sabbath is often wholly neglected or miserably mangled, ignorance increaseth, and wickedness comes upon us like an armed man. Therefore, we humbly on our knees beseech this honourable assembly, in the bowels and blood of Jesus

[1] Brook's *Puritans*, vol. i. p. 34; Strype's *Parker*, p. 395.

[2] Bownd's *Sab. Vet. et Nov. Test.* (1606), pp. 328, 329.

Christ, to become humble suitors to her Majesty, that we may have guides, that the bread of life may be brought home to us, that the pipes of water may be brought into our assemblies, that there may be food and refreshing for us, our poor wives, and forlorn children."[1] We have discovered no proof that this heart-rending appeal met with any success or even attention. The Queen could not, indeed, grant the petition consistently with her procedure only two years before, and with her cherished principles on that occasion expressed. When in 1577 she sent for Archbishop Grindal, and commanded him to put down the exercises or prophesyings, which he had been careful so to regulate as to preclude the possibility of any reasonable objection to them, she told him that "it was good for the Church to have but few preachers, three or four in a county being sufficient." Curates, though incapable of preaching, might, in her view, adequately discharge their duty by simply reading the Homilies. In vain did the archbishop remonstrate with her in "a long and earnest letter," in which he declared that the Homilies, originally intended only to supply the lack of preachers, were, by the statute of Edward VI., to give place to sermons whensoever they might be had—that by the Canons every bishop had authority to appoint exercises for the improvement of inferior ministers, and that whereas, before the exercises were commenced there were not three able preachers, thirty were now fit to preach at St. Paul's Cross, and forty or fifty besides were qualified to instruct their own cures. The only result was, that by an order from the Star-Chamber, and without consulting with the bishops or any of the clergy, she confined him to his house, and suspended him from his archiepiscopal functions for six months.[2] Neal says, "Towards the close of this letter, his Grace declares himself willing to resign his bishopric, if it should be her Majesty's pleasure, and then makes these two requests: 1. That your Majesty would refer ecclesiastical matters to the bishops and divines of the realm, according to the practice of the first Christian emperors; and 2. That when your Majesty deals in matters of faith and religion, you would not pronounce so peremptorily as you may do in civil matters; but remember

1 Bownd's *Sab. Vet. et Nov. Test.* (1606), p. 41.

2 Neal's *History of the Puritans* (1732), vol. i. pp. 352-58.

that in God's cause, his will, and not the will of any earthly creature, is to take place. 'Tis the antichristian voice of the Pope, '*Sic volo sic jubeo, stet pro ratione voluntas.*' He then puts her in mind, that though she was a great and mighty princess, she was nevertheless a mortal creature, and accountable to God; and concludes with saying, that he could not without offence of the majesty of God send out injunctions for suppressing the exercises." The truth is, Elizabeth could not have favoured a free and general gospel without consciously endangering that arbitrary power which would "suffer no one to decline either to the left or to the right hand from the drawn line limited by authority and her own laws and injunctions," and which punished with ruinous fines, suspension, and even death, worthy and learned men for declining to observe foolish and unscriptural practices, required in some instances by laws that were unconstitutional, and in others by no law at all. But had she with enlarged and true wisdom desired to reign on principles of justice alike to herself and to her subjects, she might have rejoiced in the most extended supply of the preached word, the best of all means for securing stability to the throne, and prosperity to the people. Of this mind were the citizens of London who thus continue their address to the Parliament: "So shall the Lord have his due honour, you shall discharge good duty to her Majesty, many languishing souls shall be comforted, atheism and heresy banished, her Majesty have more faithful subjects, and you have more hearty prayers for your prosperity in this life, and full happiness in the life to come." Could any petition have been more respectful and courteous? And yet the petitioners belonged to a class, who because a few of their number were driven by oppression to the use of strong and even unbecoming language—was it wonderful? —have as a body been maligned as rude and troublesome men. They were so regarded even by the Queen, and most of the prelates, who, bound, the one to be a nursing-mother to the Church, a terror not to good works but to the evil, and the others, to feed the flock of God, not as being lords over His heritage, but ensamples to the flock, were, in reality, more active and zealous in putting down the instrumentalities of good, than in enlightening ignorance, or rooting out profaneness and vice.

Contemporary writers bear melancholy testimony to the prevalent violation of the Fourth Commandment in those times. The chief transgessor was the leading personage in the country, who had nearly as little veneration for the day as she had for the name of God.[1] Instances are indeed given of the Queen's presence at public worship. Wood says, that Noell, Dean of St. Paul's, "for thirty years together preached before her the first and last sermons in the time of Lent, wherein he dealt plainly and faithfully with her, without dislike."[2] This was good, and it would be well if, instead of thanking one chaplain for his "pains and piety" in defending "the real presence," or ordering another—Noell himself, if we mistake not—to desist from "his ungodly digression" against "the sign of the Cross," she had sunk the Papist in the Christian, and merged the monarch in the subject of a higher Sovereign. It was well, too, that sometimes in her numerous "progresses" she rested on the Lord's Day, and attended the nearest parish church; but it would have been better not to subject the servile functionaries at Cambridge to the repetition of any part of the worship by her caprice and lateness, or to conclude the day by countenancing the representation of a play of Plautus in "the King's College Church." "Unfortunately," as Miss Strickland observes, "her respect for the Sabbath was confined to the act of joining in public worship, for the rest of the day was devoted to sports not meet for any Christian lady to witness, much less to provide for the amusement of herself and Court; but Elizabeth shared in the boisterous glee with which they were greeted by the ruder portion of the spectators. Bear and bull baitings, tilts, tourneys, and wrestling, were among the noon-day divertissements of the maiden Majesty of England; dancing, music, cards, and pageants brought up the rear of her Sabbath amusements. These follies were justly censured by the more rigid reformers."[3]

1 We are informed that the practice of profane swearing, so much a national sin and disgrace, had in the preceding century grown to be so conspicuous, as to secure on the Continent for an Englishman a name taken from one of his own imprecations—that, by which he desired for himself the most fearful of all calamities—and that the masculine daughter of the bluff Harry was particularly distinguished in her time by the terrible vigour and roundness of her oaths.—Eccleston's *Antiquities*, pp. 222, 223, 319.

2 *Athen. Oxon.* vol. i. p. 271.

3 *Lives of the Queens of England* (1843), vol. vi. p. 422.

The sabbatic practice of the ministers of religion was, for the most part, little better than that of their Sovereign. Men of their order had been for centuries the writers and actors of the mysteries, miracle-plays, and moralities, or scenic representations, which, after the model of the Roman stage, had been introduced into the service of the Church. The original design of these representations was to impress on the minds of the people the facts of Scripture, the deeds of martyrs, and the lessons of virtue, but the performers in course of time applied their pens and histrionic powers to such exhibitions as the Feast of the Ass, and the Feast of Fools, till places of worship were turned into theatres, and the clergy became common players. "To what base uses we may return, Horatio!" Cardinal Wolsey attempted to put an end to this plurality of functions, and Bishop Bonner endeavoured to exclude common plays from the churches, but in both cases in vain. And when it is considered that of thousands of Popish ecclesiastics, only two hundred and forty-three were honest enough to quit their livings in 1558, at the accession of Elizabeth,[1] and that in 1579, many of the incumbents of churches were "disguised Papists, more fit to sport with the timbrel and pipe than to take into their hands the book of God,"[2] it does not surprise us to learn that in 1572 such things were enacted as an author of that year, when describing clerical neglect of duty, thus portrays: "He posteth it (the service) over as fast as he can gallop; for either he hath two places to serve, or else there are some games to be played in the afternoon, as lying for the whetstone, heathenish dauncing for the ring, a beare or a bull to be bayted, or else jackanapes to ride on horseback, or an enterlude to be played; and if no place else can be gotten, it must be doone in the church."[3]

The progress of society, however, brings a division of labour; and these performers, satisfied with the pleasures of remembered exploits, and with the prospect of their posthumous fame as the founders of the English drama, must soon bid farewell to the sock and buskin, in some such words as Shakspere would shortly put

[1] Neal's *History of the Puritans* (1732), vol. i. pp. 156, 157.
[2] Strype's *Aylmer*, p. 32.
[3] Whitgift's *Admonition* (*Works*—Parker), vol. i. p. 384.

into the mouth of Othello, "Our favourite occupation's gone." Already have rivals made their *début*, who, though excluded from the consecrated boards, find ampler scope for their versatile talents in "large inns," and are not prevented from imitating their spiritual guides in the selection of the sacred day as the most convenient time for their exhibitions. In 1574, when a plague was decimating the population of London, these persons so outraged all religion, decorum, and humanity, in pandering by their "unshamefaced speeches and doings," to seduction and robbery—for which these inns afforded every facility—as to compel the Common Council to subject the plays to a rigid censorship, a measure which the Queen and her Council, appealed to against it by the players, followed up with an order restricting the performances to certain hours before sunset.[1] These weak and partial remedies having failed, and the proposal made in 1579 of the only effectual one—increased religious instruction—being opposed to the royal creed and will, it was deemed necessary to resort to violence, and in the following year we find her Majesty yielding to the suit of the magistrates for authority to "interdict plays and interludes on the Sabbath-day," and to that, moreover, of "many citizens and gentlemen," for leave to "expel the players out of the city, and to pull down all the play-houses and dice-houses within the liberties."[2] A writer of that year, lamenting the "corruption of youth, the profanation of the Sabbath," and other evils, which "the infamous players" had inflicted on society, says, "The Lord is never so ill-served as on the holidays, for *then hell breaks loose*."[3] The Queen's passionate partiality for the more barbarous and equally profane and demoralizing sports, which had for many years drawn crowds to the Paris garden in Southwark on Lord's Days, may have discouraged any petition, as certainly it would prevent on her part any spontaneous effort for their suppression. They received in 1583 a temporary check, though not from "governors, who are sent by Him for the punishment of evil-doers, as well as for the praise of them that do well." On January 13, of that year, being the Sabbath-day, a thousand persons

[1] *London, etc.*, by Brayley, vol. i pp. 284, 285.
[2] Morer *On the Lord's Day*, pp. 300, 301.
[3] *Blast of Retreat from Plays*, in Bruce's *An. Sco.* p. 174.

having assembled to enjoy a bear-baiting, "one of the scaffolds" broke down, when eight men and women were killed and many were "hurt and bruised to the shortening of their days." The "foul abuse," however, "shamelessly lifted up its head again," till it was finally removed by king James.[1] It was in the same year that Elizabeth first allowed a public company of players to act under her name and authority. "When a regular theatre was at length established, plays were acted at first *only on Sundays*, but the actors soon contrived to make four or five Sundays a week. The hour at which the play usually commenced was one o'clock in the day, when a flag was hoisted on the top of the building, where it remained till the close of the entertainment, which lasted generally about two hours."[2]

There were other flagrant abuses of the Sabbath. Throughout that holy day provisions were everywhere bought and sold, and pedlars disposed of their wares in the porches of the churches—offences, which it appears to have been accounted no small feat of legislation to restrain during canonical hours.[3] In the rural districts, that day was the chosen time for shooting, hunting, hawking, tennis, fencing, and similar exercises, and for the performances of strolling players and buffoons. These votaries of gain and pleasure would visit the churches, some, possibly, to quiet their consciences, and some to express their contempt. Falconers were to be seen there with their bows and arrows, with their dogs at their heels, and their hawks upon their fists.[4] And morrice-dancers, with suchlike characters, would play unseemly parts, with scoffs, jests, wanton gestures, and ribald talk, in the place, and during the progress, of Divine worship.[5]

To this manner of spending sacred time there were happily many exceptions. But the facts presented give evidence of a wide-spread disregard for the sanctities of the Sabbath, while they not

[1] Bownd's *Sabbatum*, etc., p. 257; Neal, vol. i. p. 390.

[2] Eccleston's *Antiquities*, p. 309.

[3] This was all that was attempted in Cranmer's *Visitation Articles*, the Canons of 1571, and Grindal's *Injunctions*. The restrictions upon publicans and pedlars, in following their vocations, were limited to the time of common prayer, preaching, reading of the homilies or Scriptures, or (as it is in one case provided with all the simplicity of the Elizabethan style of religious education), "to the time of sermon, if there be any sermon."—Wilk. *Concil.* iv. pp. 24, 266, 269; Neale's *Feasts and Fasts*, pp. 184, 185.

[4] Bownd's *Sabbatum* (1606), pp. 263, 264.

[5] Brook's *Puritans*, vol. i. p. 256.

obscurely indicate a corresponding measure of immorality in the country and period under review. When it is added, that the criminal calendar, much lighter than that of modern Spain, was yet three times heavier than that of Ireland in the most disturbed of its recent years—the annual number of executions in a population of scarcely five millions being four hundred—we see reason to concur in a remark which has been made, that "merry England under Elizabeth was rather a terrible country to live in."[1]

For this state of things the responsibility appears to have attached chiefly to the highest authorities in the Church. They refused to comply with the demands of many for further reformation. They set themselves against measures for instructing an ignorant clergy. They exercised hardly any discipline on wrong-doers, however scandalous, whether ecclesiastics or people. Their main religious business, indeed, for the greater part of Elizabeth's reign, seems to have consisted in persecuting, when they ought to have been employed in encouraging, their most learned and useful ministers, against whom no occasion could be found except as concerned the law of their God. And thus they reaped as they had sown. The sanctioned remains of the old oppression, superstition, and ignorance, yielded, according to their amount, the natural and wonted produce of profaneness, profligacy, and crime. Nor was their example without its blighting influence on the religion and morals of the land. We have already adverted to some of the lessons practically inculcated by the Sovereign, whose sex, early sufferings, acquirements, energy, self-identification with her people, dignified bearing, and successful government, made her the object of the nation's honour and love, and thus the more powerful for good or evil. Of Archbishop Parker it has been said, "His Grace had too little regard for public virtue ; his entertainments and feastings being chiefly on the Lord's Day : nor do we read among his episcopal qualities of his diligent preaching, or pious example."[2] After his death, Aylmer, bishop of London, and Archbishop Whitgift, may be said to have been the leading men of the Church for many years. The former, the honoured tutor of Lady Jane Grey, then an exile for his Protestantism,

[1] Wade's *Middle and Working Classes* (1842), p. 23.
[2] Neal's *Puritans* vol. i. p. 341.

afterwards on the accession of Elizabeth an ardent reformer, justly though coarsely assailing, in his *Harbour for Faithful Subjects*, the extravagant emoluments, dignities, and authority of the bishops, became in due time a conformist, alleging, on being twitted with his former opinions, that "when he was a child he spake as a child, and thought as a child." The latter, though he shrank from being a confessor in the days of Mary, felt a transient glow of indignation at the treatment by Parker of the Puritans, but he also, on reaching the years of discretion, devoted himself to the support of things as they were. Both were persons of talent and learning, but they alike fell into an error fatal to their character as ministers of religion, when they surrendered their consciences to the will of an earthly sovereign. "The eye was not single," and hence the dark procedure of severity to faithful "fellow-servants," of indulgence to the unfaithful, of forbidding some, and not providing others, to speak to the ignorant that they might be saved. While we recognise with pleasure the sympathy of Aylmer with the sufferers in the plague of 1578, and the interest taken by Whitgift in public charities, with his ultimate relenting towards Cartwright, when this great antagonist, in appearing before him, "behaved with so much modesty and respect," we are bound to say that their standard of Christian principle and conduct was far from being high. Love to the Sabbath, reverence for the name of God, regard to truth, mercy, humility, and justice, are among the plainest marks of moral excellence. The bishop "usually played at bowls on the Sundays in the afternoons, and used such language at his game as justly exposed his character to reproach;"[1] the archbishop "called in" a book which was producing a "more solemn and strict observation of the Lord's Day" in the country,[2] and was in the "constant custom" of making promises to the great, of kindness towards the nonconformists, which he never fulfilled.[3] The spirit of the one was as high as that of the greatest lord in the land;[4] the spirit of the other

[1] Neal's *Puritans*, vol. i. p. 576.

[2] Fuller's *Church History* (1655), Book ix. p. 227. Fuller cites Rogers, as in Preface to the Articles, alleging that Bownd's *Sabbatum*, the book referred to, was called in by Whitgift. The same allegation is made by Heylyn, though, as we shall see, discredited by Twisse.

[3] Neal's *Puritans*, vol. i. p. 218.

[4] Strype's *Aylmer*, p. 84.

showed itself in affecting a pomp, which in his retinue, of some times a thousand horsemen including a hundred servants, many of them with gold chains, resembled that of Wolsey, and in his cathedral worship emulated the gorgeous ceremonial of the Pope's chapel.[1] His lordship of London, instead of carrying out his early proposal that the bishops should apply the superfluities of their large revenues to the maintenance of the wars which they had procured, and to the extension of schools and preaching, became an accumulator of money,[2] while his Grace of Canterbury "seldom failed to offer" "the perpetual incense of profuse adulation at the shrine of secular power,"[3] of which a mournful instance was afforded when he ascribed the King's medley of learning and folly uttered at the Hampton Court Conference to the special assistance of the Spirit of God. Both were choleric men, who poured out the language of the most undignified abuse on the Puritan ministers, and indulged in a treatment of them, which, on the part of the bishop, amounted sometimes to brutality and outrage on common justice,[4] and, on that of the primate, "savoured," according to Lord Burghley, "of the Romish Inquisition;" and, in the complication of toils spread for entrapping victims, exceeded the Inquisition of Spain—the whole being a device to *seek* for rather than to *reform* offenders, and tending to encourage Papists as well as endanger the Queen's safety.[5] Let not ignorance of the principles of true liberty be assigned as an apology for any doings of the kind, still less for their grosser forms, or for the conduct of Puritans, whether in submitting to them then, or in imitating them in any measure afterwards. These principles lay clearly before them in the Bible. They were not altogether unknown to Zuinglius, Luther, or Queen Elizabeth's council. And persecution is the error, not of mere times and circumstances, but of human nature—of the heart rather than of the head.

That under such an ecclesiastical rule the nation did not revert to Popery, as more than once it was apprehended it would, or that it did not sink to a lower depth, was owing to the measure of reformation which it retained, and to the agencies and means

1 Paule's *Life of Whitgift* (Lond. 4to, 1612), pp. 78, 79.
2 Neal, vol. i. pp. 441-443.
3 Toplady's *Works* (1837), p. 212.
4 Neal, vol. i. pp. 365, 374, 383, 432, etc.
5 Fuller's *Church History*, B. ix. p. 155.

of good, which, though crippled and borne down, were not extinguished. It was good for England that its civil affairs were under the direction of wise counsellors who knew how to influence the regal will, particularly Lord Burghley, one of the greatest of statesmen[1]—that the Queen, who dreaded the liberty of the press, of the pulpit, and of Parliament, made her subjects nevertheless welcome to the Homilies, to the Prayer-book, to the Catechism, to Jewell's *Apology* and *Reply*, to Fox's *Acts and Monuments*—all containing much precious truth ; and, above all, to an open Bible, of which one hundred and thirty distinct publications were issued in the course of her reign,[2]—and that neither she nor others could altogether prevent such men as Grindal, whom Bacon called "the greatest and gravest prelate of the land," Pilkington, Parkhurst, and Noell, from sowing beside all waters the seed of truth, or the Puritans from doing much good under the sheltering wings of these good men, and, when deprived of their protection, from being received into the houses of the nobility, gentry, and wealthy citizens, where they discharged the duties of chaplains and tutors with a beneficial effect which was experienced in the next generation. It was, under Providence, to such means as these, in other words, to the degree in which the principles of the Reformation exerted their enlightening and elevating power, that England was indebted for her superiority in commerce, wealth, literature, and military fame, to the other nations of Europe.

Of these means not the least salutary remains to be noticed. If any one thing more than another turned the people adrift on the sea of ungodliness and vice, and defeated the ends of religion and government, it was an unsanctified Sabbath. In proportion, therefore, as any applied the institution to its purposes of sacred rest and service, they kept themselves and those under their care from moral ruin, came with their families under the power of sanctifying objects and exercises, leavened instead of further corrupting the human mass around them, and brought down on their

1 "The High Church policy which may be traced in the councils of Elizabeth, from the death of Lord Burghley, certainly went far to weaken her popularity during the last years of her reign."—*British Quarterly Review* for February 1848, p. 74.

2 Anderson's *Annals of the English Bible*, vol. ii. p. 353.

country, in its arms, trade, and literary studies, the enriching blessing of Heaven. The men, too, who urged sabbatic claims on their brethren from the press or pulpit, were signal benefactors to the religion and every interest of the community. Wherever there is sound and practical Christianity, there must be friends and advocates of the Lord's Day. Tyndale in the twilight of a transition from the darkness of Popery to the light of Reformation, though he may utter crudities in the heat of his zeal against arrogant assumption, must, as the appropriated time in the weekly cycle comes round, obey at once the Divine command, and the instinct and necessities of his new nature, by retreating into an inner and holier sanctuary. Over England, there doubtless were many both before and after the Reformation, who, feeding on such portions of the word of God as they possessed, spent His day in sacred thoughts and acts, and wept in secret places over the abuse and waste of its golden hours. Various instances of reverence and zeal for that day have already appeared in the course of this sketch. And we must now hastily notice some other illustrations of this spirit, as it appears struggling against the opposite error and evil in the few years that must yet elapse ere the sabbatic institution be for the first time the occasion of convulsing the Church.

For twenty years after the settlement of the doctrines of the Church in 1562, the friends of the Sabbath seemed to have occasion for exerting themselves against practical rather than theoretical errors on the subject. Instances of their zeal in this respect have already been noticed. Let others be now added. There appeared about the year 1577, a treatise by John Northbrooke, minister and preacher of the word of God, reprinted, singularly enough, by "the Shakespeare Society" in 1843, which was designed to "reprove," by the authority of Scripture and ancient writers, a variety of idle pastimes, "commonly used on the Sabboth-day." It is the fourth instance in which the institution, so far as we have seen, has been mentioned in the title-page of any book; but on examining the work, we find that its sole object is to prove, that "dicing, dauncing, vaine plays, or enterludes," etc., are at all times improper and hurtful, from which we are left to draw the inference, that they are especially so on the

Lord's Day. Northbrooke was followed by Humphrey Robartes, in *A Complaint for Reformation* of similar abuses, published in 1580. We have not seen this publication, nor one of the year 1583, which considered the calamity in the Paris garden as a Divine judgment, and called for reform in reference to Sabbath observance. After mentioning the execution this year of two ministers, Messrs. Thacker and Copping, who, though "sound in the doctrinal articles of the Church of England, and of unblemished lives," were condemned to die for circulating a work against the Book of Common Prayer, the author himself, Robert Brown, being at the same time pardoned and set at liberty, Neal observes, "While the bishops were thus harassing honest and conscientious ministers for scrupling the ceremonies of the Church, practical religion was at a very low ebb; the fashionable vices of the time were profane swearing, drunkenness, revelling, gaming, and profanation of the Lord's Day; but there was no discipline for these offenders, nor do I find any such cited into the spiritual courts, or shut up in prisons. If men came to their parish churches, and approved of the habits and ceremonies, other offences were overlooked, and the court was easy."[1] The Lord Mayor of London evinced a concern for the Sabbath-day, which honourably distinguished not a few who held the office both before and after his time. Writing that year to the Lord Treasurer, soon after the tragic scene in the Paris garden, he says, that "it gives great occasion to acknowledge the hand of God for such abuse of his Sabbath-day, and moveth me in conscience to give order for redress of such contempt of God's service;" adding, that for this purpose he had treated with some Justices

[1] Neal, vol. i. p. 390. Bishop Aylmer displaced a minister, because he had informed him that "within the compass of sixteen miles there were twenty-two non-residents, thirty insufficient and scandalous ministers, and nineteen silenced for refusing subscription," and because it was alleged, that he was chosen by the people, had defaced the Book of Common Prayer, denied that Christ descended into the regions of the damned, and kept persons from the Communion, when there was more need to allure them to it; but refused compliance with the petition of the parishioners to remove that minister's successor, saying, "that he would not, for all the livings he had, put a poor man out of his living for the fact of adultery." And yet this rigid disciplinarian in rituals though not in morals—in transgressions of human, not of Divine injunctions, made his own porter minister of Paddington! Strype's *Aylmer*, pp 120, 121, 212, 213; Brook, vol. ii. pp 166, 168, *note*.

of Peace in Surrey, who expressed a very good zeal, but alleged want of commission, which he referred to the consideration of his Lordship.[1] Neal states that the Court paid no regard to such remonstrances. Neither the Queen nor the Bishop of London could consistently with their own practice interfere. But what has become of Burghley, who had made sacrifices for his religion, who had such power in the council, and who uttered the noble words, "I will trust no man if he be not of sound religion, for he that is false to God can never be true to man"? The person who had such views, and who "never retired to rest out of charity with any man," was not likely to forget his duty on this occasion; but how he acted we are not aware.

To the year 1583 belongs the first appearance of Gervase Babington (born 1551, died 1610) as an author on our subject. In his work of that year, *An Exposition of the Ten Commandments*, of which another edition appeared in 1586, and in his Commentary on Genesis, which is to be found in his collected works of 1596 and 1615, he maintained the primæval institution of the Sabbath,—the Divine authority of its transference from the seventh to the first day of the week,—and the obligation of devoting the Lord's Day, except in cases of absolute necessity, to holy rest and service, according to the prescription of the Fourth Commandment. Having been educated at Trinity College, Cambridge, of which he became Fellow, and having taken his degrees of A.M. and D.D., he was made domestic chaplain to the Earl of Pembroke, whose Countess he assisted in her version of the Psalms into English metre. After a course of diligent study, and showing himself a most impressive preacher, he was appointed prebendary of Wellington in 1588, and in 1591 advanced to the bishopric of Llandaff, "thence translated to Exeter, thence to Worcester, thence to Heaven," says Fuller, who adds, "He was an excellent pulpit man, happy in raising the affections of his auditory, which having got up, he would keep up, till the close of his sermon." It has been further said of him, that he was remarkably devoid of the failings which attach to some even of the best of men, and that his life was spent in the cultivation of his mind, and in the exercise of every virtue.

[1] Neal, vol. i. p. 390.

While a few were thus coping with a wide-spread, and, by the chief authorities, practically sanctioned evil, a greater number were applying the remedies of a preached gospel, and private religious instruction, in various parts of the kingdom. Greenham at Drayton, Bownd at Norton, and Perkins at Cambridge, had, for a longer or briefer space, proclaimed those weighty and impressive truths relative to the Sabbath, as to many other subjects, which were afterwards given to the world in their valuable works. Thomas Rogers at Horningsheath would, before his suspension for nonconformity, render good service to the institution, though he saw reason erelong to change his opinions, and turn informer against the culprit, who was, to his taste, unduly zealous for the just, holy, and good commandment, "Remember that thou keep holy the Sabbath-day." Others there were, in considerable numbers, who, if not so celebrated, were like-minded men. When Dr. Bownd was suspended, between two and three hundred ministers shared his fate. We wonder that the race of Puritans was not extirpated. But as hundred after hundred of them were suspended, others were seen to spring up as from the ground, like the fabled crop of armed warriors of old, or rather like the veritable people, of whom it is testified that, "the more they afflicted them, they more they multiplied and grew;" so that after thirty and forty years of oppression, there were in 1592, according to Sir Walter Raleigh's statement in Parliament, twenty thousand nonconformists *without*, and in 1603, according to the words of the Millenary Petition, upwards of a thousand ministers who were aggrieved at ceremonial strictness and sabbatic laxity, *within*, the pale of the Church. It was remarkable, moreover, that the pulpit and the press were left so free to the advocates of the Lord's Day. The Queen appeared to be content with the neglecting of petitions, and the quashing of Parliamentary bills, having for their object its better observance. The leading prelates, what with looking after unsurpliced incumbents, what with enjoying their entertainments or games, seemed to have their hands full. At all events, though Greenham, Perkins, and Dod suffered on account of the ceremonies, they, with Bishop Babington, and others, were all, excepting Smith and Bownd, permitted to plead the claims of the weekly holy day without harassment or hindrance.

It might be conceived, from the state of matters in 1584, that the efforts employed on behalf of the institution had been unsuccessful. A writer of that year informs us not only that few spent the Lord's Day in the public and private exercises of religion, "the greatest multitude of men and women of all degrees and callings, letting loose the reins and giving out the bridle unto all kinds of vanities and licentiousness," but, what has not previously appeared, that there were "manifold disputations among the learned," and "a great diversity of opinion among the vulgar people and simple sort, concerning the Sabboth-day, and the right use of the same"—some maintaining the unchanged and unchangeable obligation of the seventh-day Sabbath ; others utterly denying that there ought to be a dedication of any day to the Divine service ; and a third class, while they granted that the first day of the week should be appropriated to the use of the ministry and church meetings, holding that every man might lawfully follow his usual calling on that as on any other day. And yet, without questioning that bad practice in some had led to the adoption and avowal of bad principles, we have no doubt that the alleged disputes and diversities gave evidence that the general mind was awakened to thought and inquiry, which further information would guide to a good result. One effect would be that religious men would avail themselves of the spirit abroad in the community by imparting sound instruction. It was so in fact. The writer referred to was an instance. He translated and published that part of the works of Ursinus which treated of the Fourth Commandment, observing, in "The Epistle Dedicatory," from which the preceding information has been derived : "I have thought with myself that I could not do better than to seek out a remedy for the staying of the consciences of the weaker number in this great variety and doubtfulness of assertions, tending to the overthrow of religion and impeachment of God's service ;" and "finding the argument [of Ursinus] fit for the circumstance of the time, I have turned the same into our mother tongue, for the further benefit of the godly and christianly disposed, that they may have in this point wherewith to satisfy both themselves and others."[1]

[1] Of this worthy man we have ascertained nothing more than is stated on the title-page of his translation, where he designates himself "John Stockwood, Schoolmaster

Archbishop Whitgift, on his elevation to the primacy in September 1583, received from the Queen "a strait charge," as he afterwards termed it, to restore the discipline and uniformity of the Church, which, through some conniving prelates, the obstinate Puritans, and a few powerful noblemen, had "run out of square." And when we consider that within the year he had published his three Articles, procuring for their enforcement an ecclesiastical commission, with powers beyond those of any preceding one, and that, not satisfied with the domestic misery and spiritual desolation spread by these engines of cruelty and terror over many parts of the land, he has sought and obtained in 1585 a decree for a further restraint on the press, we are not surprised that under such a *régime* the sacred enclosure of the weekly rest should in that year be threatened with invasion, and a worthy man called to account for urging obedience to the sabbatic law of his country.[1] Nothing, indeed, came of the interference, but it showed how matters, under a growing intolerance, were tending. The case is thus stated by Neal:—"The Rev. Mr. Smith, M.A., in his sermon

of Tunbridge," beyond the fact, that he published a variety of other pieces, chiefly translations of portions of the writings of Bullinger, Beza, etc., under the character, in some instances, of "minister" as well as schoolmaster, and dating the preface to the first-mentioned, "Zurich, 1556," from which it might be supposed that he was then an exile. The work before us is dedicated to "Lady Pelham," a daughter-in-law of Sir N. Pelham, "a learned man and a favourer of the Reformation." We might conjecture that Stockwood was one of the men who, in those times of "sore travail," was driven from the profession of a minister to that of a teacher.

[1] This decree—the third instance in which the liberty of the press was abridged in this reign, each successive one worse than the preceding—restricted printing-presses to London and the two Universities, and ordered that no book should be printed against any of the laws in being, or any of the Queen's injunctions—that no new presses should be set up but by licence from the Archbishop, or Bishop of London for the time being, and that no person should print any book unless first allowed according to the foresaid injunctions, and seen and perused by one of these prelates or their chaplains.—Strype's *Whitgift*, p. 223. The press was thus "in the hands of the Archbishop, who took all possible care to stifle the writings of the Puritans, while he gave license to Ascanio, an Italian merchant and bookseller in London, to import what Popish books he thought fit, upon this very odd pretence, that the adversaries' arguments being better known by learned men might be more easily confuted." The Puritans, however, found ways and means from abroad to propagate their writings and expose the severity of their adversaries. Some of them purchased a private press in 1589, and carried it from one county to another to prevent discovery. Satirical pamphlets, answered with equal buffoonery, issued from it, and were dispersed over the kingdom, till the press being discovered and seized, some of its supporters were "deeply fined," and others were put to death.—Neal, vol. i. pp. 463, 482, 503, 507.

before the University of Cambridge, the first Sunday in Lent, maintained the unlawfulness of these plays"—plays on the evenings, and sometimes in the afternoons of Lord's Days—"for which he was summoned before the Vice-Chancellor, and upon examination offered to prove, that the Christian Sabbath ought to be observed by an abstinence from all worldly business, and spent in works of piety and charity; though he did not apprehend we were bound to the strictness of the Jewish precepts. The Parliament had taken this matter into consideration, and passed a bill for the better and more reverent observation of the Sabbath, which the Speaker recommended to the Queen in an elegant speech; but her Majesty refused to pass it, under the pretence of not suffering the Parliament to meddle with matters of religion, which was her prerogative. However, the thing appeared so reasonable, that, without the assistance of a law, the religious observation of the Sabbath grew into esteem with all sober persons, and after a few years became the distinguishing mark of a Puritan." [1]

If such a case as that of Smith was rare in this reign, not less so the necessity of defending the institution against an attack made on it through the press. This necessity arose in 1582, when the *Rhemes New Testament* appeared. The individuals who wrote and printed this book at Rheims, and the Old Testament at Douay in 1609, were four exiled Englishmen and Romanists, William Allyn, afterwards Cardinal, Gregory Martin, Richard Bristow, authors of the translation, and Thomas Worthington, writer of the notes. The whole was designed for the Roman Catholics in England, from whom it was seen that the Bible could no longer be withheld, and yet whom, as was also seen, it would be fatal to a bolstered-up system to trust with the Bible in a true and unglossed version. A work in which, by false renderings of the text, and a mass of sophistical notes, a portion of the Word of God was wrested in support of Popery, was conceived to demand a reply. Many, including Dr. Fulke, concurred with Beza in pointing to Cartwright as the fittest man to write it, and petitioned him to undertake the task. He had yielded to their importunities; but Whitgift, holding him to be too much of a Puritan, "forbade him to proceed," and recommended for the service Dr. Fulke, who published a con-

[1] Neal, vol. i. pp. 464, 465.—For a life of Smith (Smyth), see Brook's *Puritans*.

futation in 1589. "A View of the Marginal Notes in the Popish Testament," by Dr. George Withers, appeared in 1588. Cartwright proceeded with his work, which was published in 1618, fifteen years after his death, and though closing with Rev. xvii., was, according to Fuller, "so complete a refutation, that the Rhemists durst never answer it." Among the errors of the *Rhemes New Testament* were its sabbatic opinions. In the remarks on Rev. i. 10, the annotator declares, that the apostles and the faithful abrogated the Sabbath of the seventh day, and made the eighth day in count from the creation holy day in its place, and this without all Scriptures or commandment of Christ; and that if the Church had authority and inspiration to make Sunday (being a week-day before) an everlasting holy day, and the Saturday, that was before a holy day, now a common work-day, *the same Church* may prescribe and appoint the other holy feasts of Easter, Whitsuntide, Christmas, and the rest. No proofs are given of these statements and assumptions, and it is, therefore, sufficient to meet them with the following counter-assertions of Dr. Fulke :—"That the Lord's Day was sanctified instead of the Jewish Saboth, for the assemblies of the faithful to the public exercises of religion, we learn by this place. But that there were any other holy days beside this, we find not in the Scriptures. The apostles did not abrogate the Jewish Saboth, but Christ himself by His death, as He did all other ceremonies of the law that were figures and shadows of things to come, whereof He was the body, and they were fulfilled and accomplished in Him and by Him. And this the apostles knew, both by the Scriptures, and by the word of Christ, and by his Holy Spirit. By the Scripture also they knew, that one day of seven was appointed to be observed for ever, during the world, as consecrated and hallowed to the public exercises of the religion of God, although the ceremonial rest and prescript-day, according to the law, were abrogated by the death of Christ. Now for the prescription of this day before any other of the seven, they had without doubt, either the express commandment of Christ before His ascension, when He gave the precepts concerning the kingdom of God, and the ordering and government of the Church (Acts i. 2), or else the certain direction of His Spirit, that it was His will and pleasure it should be so, and that, also, according to the Scriptures. . . . To change the Lord's Day, and keep it on Monday, Tuesday, or any other day, the Church hath no authority. For it is not a matter of indifferency, but a necessary prescription of Christ himself delivered to us by His apostles." [1]

It has been observed respecting the learned and voluminous writings of this author, that they are "monuments of his industry and love of study, and furnish satisfactory evidence, that among contemporary scholars none surpassed him in erudition, in a grammatical and deep acquaintance with the learned tongues, in acuteness and closeness of reasoning, and vigorous and untiring energy in supporting the bulwarks," and it ought to be added, in labouring for the reformation "of the Church of England."[2] Dr. William Fulke (died 1589) was born in London, educated in St. John's College, Cambridge, of which he was chosen Fellow in 1564, expelled for his intimacy with Cartwright and suspected puritanism, presented successively to the rectories of Wesley and Dennington, and after accompanying the Earl of Lincoln on his embassy to the Court of France, appointed to the mastership of Pembroke Hall, where he found leisure for his literary labours.

The excellent and laborious Perkins had repeatedly appeared as an author before the year 1591, but in that year he published—*A Golden Chain; or the Description of Theology*, where, in a chapter on the Fourth Commandment, he for the first time treated of the sabbatic institution. The views there expressed, and afterwards repeated with more or less amplification in his *Cases of Conscience*, and in his Commentaries on the Epistle to the Galatians, and the first three chapters of the Revelation, though affirmed with diffidence, are substantially the same as those of Hooper, of the Homilies, of Babington, and Fulke. It appears, that previously to their publication in print, they had been propagated by written, as they had been by his oral, words. Zealous hearers took them down from his lips, and their notes were widely circulated. It is not unlikely that the shackled state of the press would promote, if it did not suggest, the practice. In

[1] *The Text of the New Testament, etc.* (1601), on Rev. i. 10.

[2] Biographical Account in *Defence of English Translations of the Scriptures.* Park. Soc edition.

this way the preacher had his sentiments conveyed from Cambridge to Dublin, and contributed to form the character of one of the most remarkable men in the following century. About 1590, when Ussher was only ten years of age, "his meeting with some notes taken from famous Mr. Perkins (his works being not then printed), concerning the sanctification of the Lord's Day, proved, through God's blessing, so effectual with him that ever after he was the more strict in the observing of it."[1] The discourses of Greenham seem to have been turned to account after the same fashion. For the editor of his collected works (1599) informs us in the preface, "that then"—the time of the author's death, which took place in 1591—"his works were dispersed far and near;" and states, at p. 228 of the volume, that his *Treatise of the Sabboth* "hath been in many hands for many years, and hath given light to some." Richard Greenham (1531-1591), M.A., minister for twenty-two years at Dry Drayton, and for two years at Christ Church, London, where he died of the plague, and William Perkins (1558-1602), for the most part of his brief life minister of St. Andrew's Church, Cambridge, had much in common. Alumni and fellows of colleges in the University of Cambridge, they became distinguished as fervent preachers, laborious ministers, excellent casuists, earnest friends and advocates from pulpit and press of the Lord's Day, Puritans who suffered at the hands of Whitgift—the former suspension, the latter deprivation—for their opinions, wise, blameless, and pious men, and instruments of largely promoting the interests of evangelical truth and practical religion. Among the circumstances which peculiarly marked the course of Perkins were his extraordinary conversion,[2] his successful zeal for the good of the prisoners in Cambridge jail, the European fame of his writings, written in elegant Latin, or translated into five of the continental languages, and the credit, not only of a style pronounced the best of his own and the following age, but of being the first, according to Mosheim, to give form, accuracy, and precision to the master-science which has virtue, life, and manners,

[1] Clark's *Collection of Lives* (1662), p. 191.

[2] While leading a profane and dissolute life at college, he heard a woman say to a troublesome child, 'Hold your peace, or I will give you to drunken Perkins, yonder.' The thought that his name was a bye-word for an intemperate man went to his heart, and was the means of rousing him to break the fetters of vice.

for its object.[1] The end of Perkins, as of Greenham, was peace. The death of the latter was "most comfortable and happy." The former expired crying for mercy and forgiveness, and thus again blessed that great and good archbishop, who, having often wished that he might die the death of holy Mr. Perkins, poured out his latest breath in the words, "Lord, especially forgive my sins of omission."

We have now come to the commencement of the earliest sabbatic contest, entitled to the name, in the Christian Church. The occasion of this intestine war was the publication, in 1595, of *The Doctrine of the Sabbath, plainely layde forth and soundly proved*, etc.: by Nicholas Bownd, D.D., a treatise in which the institution, for the first time probably, received a full and satisfactory consideration. Of the author little has been recorded. Educated at Cambridge, where he took his degrees, he became minister of Norton in Suffolk, and was one of sixty, who, in 1583, were suspended from the exercise of sacred functions for refusing to subscribe Whitgift's three Articles, which declared: 1. That the Queen was supreme head of the Church; 2. That the Ordinal and the Book of Common Prayer contained nothing contrary to the Word of God; and, 3. That the Thirty-nine Articles of the Church of England were to be admitted as agreeable to the Holy Scriptures.[2] Besides *The Doctrine of the Sabbath*, which, after being "perused" and enlarged, was reprinted in 1606, he published three works, according to Wood, who adds, "with other things which I have not seen."[3] His literary labours appear to have been all carried on at Norton, and to warrant the

[1] *History* (1825), vol. iv. pp. 412, 413.—Orton, who was descended from an elder brother of Perkins, says, in 1772 (*Practical Works*, vol. ii. p. 434): "His works are little known in England, but they are still in estimation in Germany." The three volumes folio might be seen in the libraries of some Scottish ministers half a century ago, and the writer once found them in the hands of a plain though somewhat *bein* Scotsman, who read and relished them not the less that they presented the truths of the Bible in a manner somewhat different from that of the more familiar works of Owen and Boston.

[2] By the 13th Elizabeth, the subscription of the clergy was limited to those Articles of the Church which related to the doctrines of faith and the administration of the sacraments, whereas Whitgift's Articles enjoined subscription to the whole thirty-nine, and were otherwise illegal and oppressive.

[3] The three works are—*The Holy Exercise of Fasting, etc., in certain Homilies or Sermons* (1604). *A Storehouse of Comfort for the afflicted in Spirit, set open in Twenty-one Sermons* (1604); and, *The Unbelief of Thomas the Apostle, laid open for Believers*, etc. (1608).

presumption that he had been permitted to resume the exercise of his ministry there.

Dr. Bownd's treatise on the Sabbath was regarded with so much favour and dislike by different classes, and produced so great a change in the sabbatic practice of Englishmen in his time, as to entitle its doctrines and history to more notice than they have of late received.

The positions which the writer copiously and learnedly maintains from Scripture, the Fathers, and Reformers, are the following :—The observation of the Sabbath is not a bare ordinance of man, or a merely civil or ecclesiastical constitution, appointed only for polity, but an immortal commandment of Almighty God, and therefore bindeth men's consciences. The Sabbath was given to our first parents, and so after carefully observed both by them and by their posterity.

It was revived on Mount Sinai by God's own voice to the Israelites, with a special note of remembrance, fortified with more reasons than the other precepts, and particularly applied to all sorts of men by name, showing how careful the Lord was, that every one should straitly keep it.

While the ceremonies of the law, which made a difference between Jew and Gentile, are taken away by the gospel, this commandment of the Sabbath abideth still in full force as moral and perpetual, and bindeth for ever all nations and sorts of men as before.

The apostles, by the direction of God's Spirit, changed the day from the seventh to the eighth, which we now keep in honour of Redemption, and which ought still to be kept of all nations to the world's end, because we can never have the like cause or direction to change it.

On this day we are bound straitly to rest from all the ordinary works of our calling, because six days in the week are appointed for them, and the seventh is sanctified and separated by God himself from the others to another end—the public service of God.

Much more ought we on that day to avoid every kind of lawful recreations and pastimes, which are less necessary than the works of our callings, and whatever withdraws the heart from God's service, because this law is spiritual, and binds the whole man as well as any other ; most of all ought we to renounce all such things as are not lawful at any time.[1]

Works of necessity and mercy, however, are excepted from this prohibition, and the governors of the church and commonwealth have a liberty above others to perform such works for the good of both, in which, as in other things, their reasons are not to be busily scanned.[2]

The day of rest ought to be spent altogether in God's service, partly in frequenting the public assemblies, where the Word of God is plainly read and purely preached, the sacraments rightly administered, and prayer made in a known tongue to the edifying of the people, and in attending upon these things from the beginning to the ending ; and partly in those private exercises which prepare for or promote the benefit of public worship, as private prayer, reading the Scriptures, singing of psalms, meditating or conferring about the word and works of God, and this either personally in the family or with neighbours, either in houses or abroad in the fields.

Masters, magistrates, and princes, ought especially to provide in their respective spheres for the observation of this commandment, and to compel those under their charge to at least an outward rest and its sanctification, as well as to the keeping of any other commandment, such as those against murder, adultery, theft, and such like.

We must aim at perfection here, not measuring our duty by our inability, but by the perfect reed of the temple, and, repenting of our failures, crave pardon for Christ's sake.

1 "In determining that we must give over then our ordinary recreations, we do not conclude that they should altogether be left, but advise men rather to take them at some other time; and we do exhort them that be in government, to give some time to their children and servants for their honest recreation on other days, that they be not driven to take it upon this, seeing they can no more want it altogether than their ordinary food. And as we have seen that they are bound to give them some time to work for themselves, unless they will by their overmuch straitness compel them to it upon the day of rest; so must they spare also some few hours for their refreshing now and then, seeing they can no more want the one than the other."—Pp. 271, 272.

2 "Necessitas non habet ferias."—This "is to be considered of us the rather, lest any through a gross superstition should fall into the extremity of the Jews of whom it is written, and namely, of certain heretics called Essaei, that they are over precise in this rest, so that they dress all their meat the day before, and kindle no fire," etc.—P. 223.

The treatise on its first appearance, produced an extraordinary sensation, which Fuller thus describes :—" About this time (1595), throughout England began the more solemn and strict observation of the Lord's Day (hereafter, both in writing and preaching, commonly called the Sabbath), occasioned by a book this year set forth by one P. (*sic*) Bound, Doctor of Divinity, (and enlarged with additions, anno 1606)."[1] After giving an abstract of its doctrines, the historian proceeds to say :—" It is almost incredible how taking this doctrine was, partly because of its own purity, and partly for the eminent piety of such persons as maintained it, so that the Lord's Day, especially in corporations, began to be precisely kept, people becoming a law to themselves, forbearing such sports as yet by statute permitted ; yea, many rejoicing at their own restraint herein. On this day the stoutest fencer laid down the buckler, the most skilful archer unbent his bow, counting all shooting besides the mark ; May-games, and Morish-dances grew out of request, and good reason that bells should be silenced from gingling about men's legs, if their very ringing in steeples were adjudged unlawful ;[2] some of them were ashamed of their former pleasures, like children which, grown bigger, blushing themselves out of their rattles and whistles. Others forbear them for fear of their superiors, and many left them off out of a politic compliance, lest otherwise they should be accounted licentious.

" Yet learned men were much divided in their judgments about these sabbatarian doctrines. Some embraced them as ancient truths consonant to Scripture, long disused and neglected, now seasonably revived for the increase of piety. Others conceived them grounded on a wrong bottom, but because they tended to the manifest advance of religion, it was pity to oppose them, seeing none have just reason to complain being deceived into their own good. But a third sort flatly fell out with these positions, as galling men's necks with a Jewish yoke, against the

1 " *Sabathum Veteris et Novi Testamenti, or the True Doctrine of the Sabbath before and under the Law, and in the time of the Gospel,* &c."

2 Fuller exaggerates the claims of Bownd to originality. The word " Sabbath " had been used by the Fathers, in the Homilies, by Becon, Babington, Perkins, and others. Among the injunctions of Edward VI. was the following :—" All ringing of bells, save one, shall be utterly forborn."

liberty of Christians : that Christ, as Lord of the Sabbath, had removed the rigour thereof, and allowed men lawful recreations : that the doctrine put an unequal lustre on the Sunday, on set purpose to eclipse all other holy days to the derogation of the Church : that the strict observance was set up out of faction to be a character of difference, to brand all for libertines who did not entertain it."

For a time no attempt was made to put down this stirring publication, whether by argument or by authority. "For some years together," continues Fuller, "Dr. Bound alone carried the garland away, none offering openly to oppose, and not so much as a feather of a quill in print did wag against him. Yet, as he in his second edition observeth, many, both in their preachings, writings, and disputations, did concur with him in that argument." Among the "many" were Babington, Perkins, and Dod. An edition of the works of Babington appeared in 1596. Perkins reprinted his *Golden Chain* in 1597. Both writers continued to maintain the sabbatic views which, before the publication of Bownd's treatise, they had given to the world, and which were in substance the same as his. *An Exposition of the Ten Commandments* by John Dod, minister at Hanwell, Oxfordshire, aided, as he was in other works, by Robert Cleaver, minister at Drayton in the same county, belonged to the year 1604, and treated copiously and practically of the Sabbath. The exposition is simple, lively, pithy, and worthy of both, Cleaver having been "a most pious, excellent, and useful preacher," and Dod, not only "a distinguished scholar," but "a most worthy man," of whom Ussher said, "Whatever some say of Mr. Dod's strictness, and scrupling some ceremonies, I desire, that when I die, my soul may rest with his." In the second edition of his work, Bownd refers to a writer who had published a digest of the first edition. This, or *An Abstract of the Doctrine of the Sabbath*, by William Burton, had preceded the volume in which it is referred to, only by some months, as they both came out in 1606. It appears that "disputations" had taken place, in which the doctrine of Bownd was successfully advocated. One of these is repeatedly mentioned by writers of the time. Heylyn evidently felt sore when he thus recorded it :—"In the year 1603, at the commencement held in Cambridge, this thesis or proposition, *Dies Dominicus nititur Verbo Dei*, was publicly maintained by a doctor there, and by the then Vice-Chancellor so determined ; neither the following doctors there, or any in the other University, that I can hear of, did ever put up any *antithesis* in opposition thereunto."[1]

Three supporters of Dr. Bownd's doctrine are particularly alluded to by him in the preface to the second edition of his work. After informing us that many concurred with him in his argument, he says, "And three several profitable treatises were within a few years successively written by three godly learned ministers." One of these treatises, according to Fuller, was "made by Greenham." Another was probably the plain and practical *Doctrine of the Sabbath, handled in Four Severall Bookes or Treatises*, by George Widley, A.M., Minister of the Word of God in Portsmouth," which maintains the perpetuity of the Sabbath, as well as the sanctity of the entire day, and was published in 1604. We find no third publication that fully answers Bownd's description.

The treatise of Greenham was extensively read, and productive of much good. It had, as already stated, been in many hands for many years before it appeared among his collected works, and these passed through five editions in the course of 1599-1612, two of them in the first of those years. "No book," says Fuller, "made a greater impression upon the minds of the people than his *Treatise on the Sabbath*, which greatly promoted the observance of it through the nation." Partaking of the qualities that distinguish all the writings of its author, the comprehensive brevity with which each topic is treated, great simplicity of language clothing not unfrequently original and striking thoughts, and a spirit of unaffected piety and benevolence, it presents, within some ninety small pages, the very pith of the subject as regards its doctrine, polemics, and duties. It has almost nothing of the patristic learning which appears in the volume of Dr. Bownd, as, except in one or two instances, it derives the support of its positions exclusively from the Scriptures. Nor does it exhibit the same power of reasoning as that writer has wielded. But it surpasses the volume now mentioned, as appears to us, in its more faultless exposition of the sabbatic institution.

[1] *History of the Sabbath*, part ii. p. 261.

There is scope for persons of all varieties of attainment to put forth their efforts in defence or recommendation of that institution. But if any class be more entitled and qualified than another to handle the subject, it must be the men who, to superior mental talents and acquirements, add a spirit imbued with the heavenly tastes and desires of the Christian. Such a man was Greenham. "He was," says Fuller, "a strict observer of the Lord's Day." It is also recorded of him, that "he loved the habitation of God's house," repairing to it however inferior might be the abilities of the preacher, and happy, like Chalmers, to hear those "intrinsically glorious and imperishable truths of the Christian system, which," as has been beautifully said, "language cannot embellish, nor the little arts of composition improve." It is such men alone who can fully perceive the excellence and value of the Sabbath. And the words of such come with power. In some measure, like their Master, they might say, "We speak that we do know, and testify that we have seen." Their united experience is an argument for the institution which admits of no answer. Their manifest character—an epistle which may be seen and read of all men—is another. Let the life of Greenham show that a strictly observed Lord's Day, though repulsive to the selfish and the self-indulgent, tends to encourage, not sourness, gloom, or unhappiness, but decision with meekness, labour with its dignity, beneficence with its pure pleasures, and faith in Christ with its safety and hope—the whole making a man good, useful, and blessed. Bearing in mind the particulars of that life already mentioned, let us consider some others. Every morning found that ardent man in his study at four o'clock. The preaching of six sermons, with two catechetical exercises, formed his ministerial labour in public each week, the services of the work-days being, for the convenience of his people, in the mornings. Much of his time and strength was expended in giving religious instruction and counsel in private to the multitudes who resorted to him with their difficulties and doubts, and in unwearied applications for stipends and exhibitions for the assistance of poor scholars at the University.[1] Rejecting every lucrative preferment offered to him, he yet abounded in acts of liberality to the needy and distressed, showing a pity for the

[1] Russell's *Memorials of Thomas Fuller, D.D.*, p. 14.

suffering, which, bringing by its resistless impulses himself and his family into frequent straits, it is far easier to condemn for imprudent excess, than to admire for its rare intensity. Nothing could make him subscribe to the rites and ceremonies which the prelates in his day so unjustly enforced, as they were in his view unsanctioned by Scripture, productive of much superstition, and hindrances to the success of the gospel; but while he "loved the truth," he loved also "the peace," and combined the *suaviter* with the *fortiter*—the meekness of wisdom with inflexibility of principle and purpose. When called before the bishop, Dr. Cox, upon a complaint of his nonconformity, and asked, Whether the blame of the schism in the Church was attachable to the conformists or nonconformists? he replied, "that it might be attached to *either* or to *neither*. For if both parties loved each other as they ought, and did acts of kindness for each other, thereby maintaining love and concord, the blame would be on *neither* side; but which party soever made the rent, the charge of schism belonged to them." The bishop is said to have been so well satisfied with this answer, that he dismissed him in peace.[1] Greenham was much esteemed and reverenced in his lifetime by the wise and good of various ranks. He died lamented. Bishops Hall and Wilkins, and others, have expressed high estimates of his works. From a number of tributes to his worth as a man and a writer, which appear in his collected works, we may be permitted, if not for their poetical merit, yet on account of their subject and their author, to present the following lines :—

Whiles Greenham writeth of the Sabboth's rest,
His soul enjoys that which his pen exprest:
His work enjoys not what itself doth say,
For it shall never find one resting day;
A thousand hands shall toss each page and line,
Which shall be scanned by a thousand eyne.
That Sabboth's rest, or this Sabboth's unrest,
Hard is to say whether is the happiest.—I. HALL.[2]

[1] Brook's *Puritans*, vol. i. pp. 416, 417. To this work, with Fuller's *Ch. Hist.*, and Greenham's *Works* (1599), we are indebted for most of the particulars relative to Greenham, in this and preceding pages.

[2] Fuller, in citing the lines, says, "as one (then a great wit in the University, now a grave wisdom in our Church) hath ingeniously expressed." The I. Hall must have

Thus far, and even down to the year 1605, the argument is all on one side, and not till 1599 was any opposition publicly made to the views of Dr. Bownd. In that year, however, his treatise, according to Thomas Rogers of Horninger, or Horningsheath, was called in. Rogers himself, not long before a cashiered Puritan, confesses, and glories in the fact, that he turned Queen's evidence against his former friend. "It is a comfort unto my soul," he says, in addressing Archbishop Bancroft, "and will be till my dying hour, that I have been the man and the means that the sabbatarian errors and impieties are brought into light and knowledge of the State, whereby whatsoever else, sure I am, this good hath ensued, namely, that the said books of the Sabbath . . . . hath been both called in, and forbidden any more to be printed and made common. Your Grace's predecessor, Archbishop Whitegift, by his letters, and officers at synods, and visitations, *Ann.* 99, did the one; and Sir John Popham, Lord Chief-Justice of England, at Burie S. Edmonds, in Suffolk, *Ann.* 1600, did the other."[1] Dr. Twisse questions these allegations, as there was no evidence of their truth but the word of Rogers, and as, in the year after they were published, Willet's Commentary on Genesis appeared, dedicated to King James and to Bancroft, under whose auspices it was undertaken, and highly commending as well as fully adopting the sentiments of Bownd.[2] There is, indeed, nothing in the second edition of the book to imply the alleged treatment of the first, and the manner in which the author writes of the Chief-Justice appears to be inconsistent with the representation of Rogers. He mentions "the very rare and honourable example" of that individual, in "resting for the most part on the Sabbath in his circuit journeys," which he does not utter in flattery, "seeing that it is like that these shall never come into his hands and eyes;" and adds, that he "travaileth so much the more early and late, and taketh up part of the night, that by extraordinary labouring upon other daies, hee might redeem the time to rest upon the Sabbath."[3] And yet both Heylyn and Fuller credit the

been Joseph Hall, afterwards the celebrated Bishop of Norwich, and author of the "Contemplations."—*Ch. Hist.* vol. ix. p. 220.

[1] Preface, sect. 23 (written "the 11 of March 1607"), tc *Catholic Doctrine of the Church of England*, 1625.

[2] *Morality of the Fourth Commandment*, pp. 164-166.

[3] Bownd's *Sabbatum* (2d edit. 1606), p. 231.

statement of Rogers, the former acknowledging that the measures of Whitgift and Popham were "good remedies, had they been soone inough applied," but lamenting "that they were not so good as those which formerly were applied to Thacker and his fellow, in the aforesaid towne of Burie, for publishing the bookes of Browne against the service of the Church."[1] Nor do we find that Neal, or any other writer, vindicates, or even notices, the doubts of Twisse. Certain it is, that in confessing to his having called the attention of the authorities to what he designates "Sabbath speculations," Rogers asserted for himself the unenviable distinction of being both the first of professed Christians to employ measures of violence against the friends of the Lord's Day, and the originator, Bownd being only the occasion, of the earliest sabbatic controversy within the pale of the Christian Church.

We have referred the commencement of the dialectic controversy to A.D. 1605, because, though it was not till 1607 that a blow of this kind was struck with any effect against the institution, the former year was the date of the first anti-sabbatical publication. This was a treatise,[2] dedicated to King James, which maintained that the Sabbath is partly ceremonial and partly moral—that it was not of primæval origin—that the Church was led by certain causes and reasons to substitute the first day of the week in place of the seventh as a Sabbath—that all days in Christian times are not Sabbath days, and that the Sabbath should be sacredly observed in rest of body and mind, and in doing good, the whole suffused with joy and the pleasures of music and sports. Although he turns his weapons against the Puritans under the general designation of Reformers, the author condescends to mention the name of no previous writer of his time, and he himself has been very seldom referred to by his successors. Rivet bestows two or three remarks on his views, and Heylyn, commending "one M. Loe of the Church of Exeter," as alone "declaring himself to be of different judgment from" the Sabbatarians, and as "laying downe, indeed, the truest and most justifiable doctrine of the Sab-

[1] *History of the Sabbath*, part ii. p. 254.
[2] *Effigiatio Veri Sabbathismi.* Authore Roberto Loeo, Exoniensis Ecclesiæ Thesaurario, 4to, Lond. 1605.

bath of any writer in that time,' complains that the treatise, "being written in the Latine tongue, came not to the people's hands, many of those which understood it never meaning to let the people know the contents thereof." [1] A failure as to popular effect, the work was not lost upon the learned King and Laud, and was a fitting precursor of the *Book of Sports.*

Fuller, "ignoring" Mr. Loe, observes, "The first that gave a check to the full speed of this" (Bownd's) "doctrine, was Thomas Rogers of Horninger, in Suffolk, in his preface to the Book of Articles." Rogers had published several editions of his Exposition of the Thirty-nine Articles, from 1579 downwards. In 1607, as we have seen, he wrote the Preface to which Fuller refers, and it appears in additions of the Exposition printed subsequently to that year. In this Preface he made his first attempt, as a disputant, to controvert the doctrine which, in the capacity of informer, he had already fruitlessly sought to extirpate. In the *Effigiatio* there is argument, in "the Preface" there is none. We wonder what there was in the latter to "check the speed" of the opposite doctrine, till we recollect that strong assertion stands frequently with certain minds for proof. A few words may suffice to tell the amount of what Rogers has to advance against the Puritans, or brethren, as he terms them, on the subject of their "Sabbatarian errors and impieties." Discomfited in the matter of the ceremonies, they adopted the stratagem of holding up the Sabbath at the expense of the holidays, whence sprang irreligion and every evil. They set up a new idol, their St. Sabbath (erst in the days of Popish blindness, St. Sunday) in the midst and minds of God's people, thereby introducing a worse than either Jewish or Popish superstition into the land. Their insisting on a rigid observance of the Lord's Day by all classes, if they would not incur the penalties of damnation, led to such heretical and horrible statements, as that to throw a bowl on the Sabbath-day is as great a sin as to kill a man, or commit adultery; and that to make a feast or wedding-dinner on the Lord's Day is as great a sin as for a father to take a knife and cut his child's throat; and that in the *Sabbatum* "are very many things to this effect." The reply of Dr. Twisse to these accusations, advanced by Rogers, and

[1] *Hist. of the Sabbath*, part ii. p 261.

endorsed by Heylyn, was the following : First, the sabbatic doctrine of Dr. Bownd was that of Perkins, Bishop Babington, Bishop Andrewes, Bishop Lake, Dr. Willet, as is shown by their own words. Dr. Willet is quoted as taking up the sentiments of Bownd, establishing them one by one from Scripture, and adding, "But these allegations are here superfluous, seeing there is a learned treatise of the Sabbath already published of this argument, which containeth a most sound doctrine of the Sabbath, as it is said in the former positions, which shall be able to abide the triall of the Word of God, and stand warranted thereby, when other humane fantasies shall vanish ; howsoever, some in their heat and intemperance are not afraid to call them *sabbatariorum errores*, yea, hereticall assertions, a new Jubilee, St. Sabbath, more than either Jewish or Popish institution ; God grant it be not layd to their charge that so speake or write, and God give them a better minde."[1] "Now I have made it manifest," says Twisse, "that the doctrines which he picks out of Dr. Bownd, and stiles sabbatarian doctrines, are the doctrines of Dr. Andrewes, afterwards bishop of Winchester ; I could show them to be the doctrines of many other worthy prelates that have been of this kingdome ; and it may be, that if the votes of the bishops of this kingdom were taken, the major part would concurre with us, as touching the doctrine of the Sabbath, rather than against us."[2] This answer was important, not because names can prove a doctrine to be true, but because in the present instance they set aside the silly though plausible argument, founded on the puritanic character of the men who had stood up for the Sabbath, and on the alleged singularity of their opinions. Second, the allegation as to the "heretical and horrible" assertions uttered by the supporters of Bownd's doctrine, referring as it does only to a few cases, could prove nothing even if true, and was itself without proof. Dr. Twisse says, generally, of such charges, which it became the fashion of anti-sabbatists to take up without inquiry, and to trumpet on all occasions, "As long as the world lasts, we shall be exercised with wild wits, and so no doubt we shall with tale-tellers too ;" and, examining those charges more particularly, he shows that the alleged

[1] Comment. on Gen. ii. 3, in Twisse's *Morality of the Fourth Commandment*, p. 166.
[2] Twisse, p. 164.

expressions are, in two instances, accompanied by no particulars of person or place, the imputations having no better authority than the accuser's own word; and that in cases where the particulars were specified, either the evidence was wanting, or the falsehood of the accusation was exposed. While it is possible, without at all affecting the doctrine of the Puritans, that an individual or two might use improper expressions in its illustration, it is certain that no such impropriety was proved, and it is more than probable that all the charges were, like the following one preferred against the Doctor himself, wretched fabrications in a kindred cause: "Lately, it hath beene brought unto mee, that one hath beene heard to lay to my charge behind my backe, that I should say, David sinned more in dancing about the Arke, than either in deflowring Bathshebath, or killing Uriah; though it is such a comparison that never entered into my thoughts, how much lesse to passe so prodigious a judgment upon the comparison."[1] Third, the averment, that "many things to this effect he had read before in the Sabbath doctrine, printed at London for I. Porter, and T. Man (An. 95)," was, like the other charges, unsubstantiated. Twisse says, "What this booke was I could not devise, but lately have gotten Dr. Bownde's book of the Sabbath. I finde by comparing it well, that this is the booke he girds at. Now I finde nothing in him to this effect, though I have gone over most of the first booke, and in the Index doe not finde anything that can give me probability in the second booke, tending to any such effect: and I wonder he spared to quote the place where such doctrines are to be found, nothing being more convenient to justifie his criminations (than to quote for it something that is to be seene in print) and thereby to cleare himself from the suspicion of a malignant."[2] The truth is, that "the many things to this effect, which he (Rogers) had read" in the *Sabbatum* were not there.[3]

Dr. Twisse having extracted the sting of the only effective part of the Preface, its tale-telling, conceived it superfluous, we presume, to answer any more charges against the friends of the Sab-

[1] *Morality of the Fourth Commandment*, pp. 162-164. [2] *Ibid.* p. 163.

[3] If they had, we should have heard of it from Heylyn, who repeats from Rogers "the horrible" expressions *con amore*, but neither affirms nor denies the occurrence of "many things to this effect" in Bownd. We have read the *Sabbatum*, 2d edit., more than once, without observing in it any such expressions.

bath, founded as these charges were on mere authority, and on such an authority. So slight, indeed, appears to have been the impression produced by the assertions of Rogers, that it was not till thirty-four years after they were published, and when Bishop White and Dr. Heylyn had, by their writings, given them currency and importance, that Twisse took notice of them. Let Fuller illustrate "the check to the full speed of Bound's doctrine" which he ascribes to the Preface, and show that the author in evoking the magistrate's sword from its sheath, as well as "wagging the feather of a quill," had increased the momentum. "But though minister and magistrate jointly endeavoured to suppress Bound's book, with the doctrine therein contained, yet all their care did but for the present make the Sunday set in a cloud, to arise soon after in more brightness. As for the archbishop, his known opposition to the proceedings of the brethren rendered his actions more odious, as if out of envy he had caused such a pearl to be concealed. As for Judge Popham, though some conceived it most proper for his place to punish felonious doctrines (which robbed the Queen's subjects of their lawful liberty), and to behold them branded with a mark of infamy, yet others accounted him no competent judge in this controversy; and though he had a dead hand against offenders, yet these sabbatarian doctrines, though condemned by him, took the privilege to pardon themselves, and were published more generally than before. The price of the doctor's book began to be doubled, as commonly books are then most called on, when called in, and many who hear not of them when printed, inquire after them when prohibited; and though the book's wings were clipped from flying abroad in print, it ran the faster from friend to friend in transcribed copies; and the Lord's day, in most places, was most strictly observed. The more liberty people were offered the less they used it, refusing to take the freedom authority tendered them; for the vulgar sort have the actions of their superiors in constant jealousy, suspecting each gate of their opening to be a trap, every hole of their digging to be a mine, wherein some secret train is covertly conveyed, to the blowing up of the subject's liberty, which made them almost afraid of the recreations of the Lord's day allowed them; and seeing it is the greatest pleasure to the mind of man to do what he pleaseth, it was sport for them to refrain from sports, whilst the forbearance was in themselves voluntary, arbitrary, and elective—not imposed upon them. Yea, six years after, Bound's book came forth with enlargements, publicly sold; and scarce any comment, catechism, or controversy was set forth by the stricter divines, wherein this doctrine (the diamond in this ring) was not largely pressed and proved; so that, as one saith, 'the Sabbath itself had no rest;' for now all strange and unknown writers, without further examination, passed for friends and favourites of the Presbyterian party, who could give the word, and had anything in their treatise tending to the strict observation of the Lord's day."[1]

Thus, "minister and magistrate" became the patrons of Dr. Bownd, and the best publishers of his volume, persecuting both into a notice and influence which they might never otherwise have obtained. And the remarkable success of that volume, which received not merely in several instances the *laudari a laudato*—the plaudits of the celebrated, but the approbation of many wise and good men unknown to fame, which stimulated and enlightened the zeal of writers and preachers on its great subject, and which effected an extensive improvement in the religious character of the nation, was a gratifying recompense to its author for the reproach and opposition of a few, and for the labour and time expended on its composition.[2]

Nor has the injury done to his posthumous reputation by such authors as Heylyn, and Collier, who attempted with too much effect to identify his name with all that is stern and repulsive in sabbatic doctrine and practice, been without reparation. That the only consistent, practical, and scriptural theory of the institution still prevails among the most moral and enterprising classes of England, owing in a great measure to the impulse originally communicated by his writings, is a noble tribute to his memory. And other tributes have been paid in occasional vindications of his treatise against unfounded objections, and more frequently in the advocacy of similar views, by able men. We

[1] Fuller's *Church History* (1845), vol. v. pp. 217-219.

[2] The respect which, according to Livingstone (*Missionary Travels*, Preface), the toil of authorship ought to inspire, was peculiarly merited by Bownd, as, in consequence of the unaccountable disappearance of his completed manuscript, the preparation for the second edition had to be repeated.

have seen that Dr. Twisse—"the very learned Twisse"—"this veteran leader, so well trained to the scholastic field," as Owen describes him, did his part. "Some say," observes the erudite Leigh, "that Dr. Bound was the first who set on foot the sabbatarian doctrines in the Church of England—if so, it was a great honour to him to be the first in so good a work."[1] Thomas Fuller, a conformist, though not of the Heylyn school, or "fierce for moderation," has rendered good and honest service, by recording the triumphs of the treatise, and testifying to the eminent piety of the men who held its doctrines. Another conformist has lately corrected one or two injurious misinterpretations of Bownd in Fuller's *History*, and affirmed that the charges of Rogers, which that history recorded, without either confirmation or censure, have no just application to the *Sabbatum*, which he commends as "written in a truly Christian spirit."[2] Its author has been followed in his opinions by Twisse, Owen, and a host of others. And we may trust that as the subject is more studied and understood, a larger measure of respect and gratitude will be accorded to one of the boldest and most successful advocates of the sabbatic institution.

A work by Mr. John Sprint, A.M., which appeared in 1607, calls for a brief notice. It consists of two parts—Propositions tending to prove the necessary use and Divine authority of the Lord's day, and the Practice of the sacred day framed after the rules of Scripture. The views of the author are coincident with those of Bownd, clear, decided, and learnedly maintained. The practical part supplies a defect found in some treatises on the subject, though it perhaps exceeds, like others, in the minuteness of its details. The son of Dr. John Sprint, dean of Bristol, Mr.

1 *System of Divinity*, p. 1100.

2 Fuller's *Ch. Hist.* (1845), edited by Brewer, vol. v. pp. 211-214, 217, notes. Fuller, for example, had represented Bownd as holding, that "no solemn feasts nor wedding-dinners were to be made on the Lord's day, with permission, notwithstanding, of the same to lords, knights, and gentlemen of quality;" whereas he only says that "the ordinary diet of these classes, which, in comparison, may be called feasts," is not to be condemned, but exhorts them so to divide the duties of servants as to admit of their attending churches. The nobility of those times kept open table, and required for their large households corresponding provisions. Bownd would have agreed with Dr. Paul Micklethwaite thus far, "that persons of quality, who rest from hard labour all the week long, are concerned in conscience to observe the Lord's day with the greater abstinence from recreations."—Fuller, *Ch. Hist.*, vol. vi. pp. 93, 94.

Sprint was educated in Christ's Church, Oxford, became minister at Thornbury in Gloucestershire, and was subsequently a popular preacher in London. While in creed a Puritan, regarding imposed ceremonies as "inconveniencies, and the Church's burdens," he was of opinion that a minister ought to conform to them under protest, rather than suffer deprivation. Wood says, he was a grave and pious divine, and cut off in the prime of his years when great things were expected from him.[1]

We have referred to the hopes entertained by the Puritans from the accession of King James VI. to the throne of England. Among these hopes was that of a more generally and strictly observed Sabbath. It was reasonable to suppose that a native and the Sovereign of a country where so much zeal had been evinced in favour of the institution, the man who had spoken out so strongly against the Popish days of Geneva and the English mass, and the author of the Βασιλικον Δῶρον, which allowed unsuperstitious and lawful amusements, and cheer, "alwaies provided that the Sabbaths be kept holy, and no unlawfull pastimes then be used" (p. 52), would be right glad to comply with such a request as that presented in the Millenary petition, which craved, "That the Lord's day be not profaned, and the rest upon holidays not so strictly urged." And though it was not long before his Majesty disclosed enough to confirm the fears that were blended with the expectations of his best subjects, yet the very earliest measures of his reign held out prospects of permanent favour to the sabbatic cause. We refer to his proclamation at Theobald's, May 7, 1603, the day of his entry into London, against bear and bull baitings, with other disorderly pastimes, being "frequented, kept, or used any time hereafter upon any Sabbath-day;" to the procedure of the Hampton Court Conference, January 1604, where Dr. Rainolds, the most learned man of his time, the originator of the present authorized version of the Scriptures, and afterwards one of the translators, having said "Great is the profanation of the Sabbath-day, and contempt of your Majesty's proclamation, which I earnestly desire may be reformed," the "motion found an unanimous consent;"[2] and to the enactment passed by the

[1] Brook's *Puritans*, vol. ii. pp. 305, 306; Calamy's *Account*, vol. ii. p. 343; Fuller's *Worthies*, vol. i. p. 564; Wood's *Athen. Oxon.* vol. i. p. 406. [2] Fuller, vol. v. p. 284.

first English Parliament after the Union of the Crowns, held in March of the same year, prohibiting shoemakers from selling the articles of their craft upon Sunday. But the Millenary petition was destined to receive a negative on the subject of the Sabbath as decided, if not so prompt, as on that of rites and ceremonies; and when, in the seventh year of this reign a second attempt to legislate for the stricter observance of the Lord's day proved unsuccessful, the petitioners might, notwithstanding the royal ratification of the Irish Church Articles in 1615,[1] have been prepared for the next act of the drama.

This was the publication in 1618 of *The Declaration for Sports on the Lord's day.* As Morton, bishop of Durham, had a considerable share in the preparation of this celebrated document, it is of importance to hear his almost entirely neglected account of its origin. It is given by Dr. Barwick, his biographer, who says he had often heard it from the bishop's own mouth, and is to the following effect: In Lancashire, where "the Popish recusants" abounded (then, as since) more than in any other county of England, it was the policy of their leaders to "keep the people from church by dancing, and other recreations, even in the time of Divine service, especially on holy days, and the Lord's day in the afternoon." This gross abuse the bishop endeavoured to redress in his primary visitation. "But it was represented to King James as a very great grievance, at his return out of Scotland through Lancashire in 1617, by some in Court who were too favourable to that party. And his readiness to hear any complaint against a thing that carried but the name of a public grievance, encouraged some to so much boldness the next Lord's day after, as even to disturb the public worship and service of God by their piping and dancing within the hearing of all those that were at church, whereof the King being fully informed by this bishop, utterly disavowed any thoughts or intention of encouraging such profaneness; and therefore left them that were guilty of it to the bishop's censure, which he inflicted only upon one that was the head and causer

[1] One of these Articles was as follows: "The first day of the week, which is the Lord's day, is wholly to be dedicated to the service of God; and, therefore, we are bound therein to rest from our common and daily business, and to bestow that leisure upon holy exercises, both private and public."

of it. There wanted not some still to complain to the King of the bishop's proceedings herein as rigorous and tyrannical, considering that the chief thing they desired was only some innocent recreation for servants and other inferior people on the Lord's day, and holy days, whose laborious callings deprived them of it at all other times; and thereupon to solicit his Majesty for some power therein, and the rather because it was the general desire of most of that country. Which the King finding to be true upon inquiry, and willing to give them satisfaction therein, consulted with this reverend person, being the bishop of that diocese, how he might satisfy their desires without endangering this liberty to be turned into licentiousness. The bishop hereupon, retiring from the court at Haughton Tower to his own lodging at Preston, considered of six limitations or restrictions, by way of conditions, to be imposed upon every man that should enjoy the benefit of that liberty, which he presented to the King in writing the next day, and which the King did very well approve of, and added a seventh; saying only, he would alter them from the words of a bishop to the words of a King."[1] Dr. Barwick adds, though he cannot positively affirm it, as he does the preceding details, that Bishop Andrewes, who then attended the King, "was therefore in all probability consulted in the same business." If consulted, of which, however, no evidence appears, it does not follow, but is, on the other hand, most improbable, that he approved of a measure so contrary to his principles, for he held that, "to indulge in dancing, *vacare choreis*, on the Lord's day is the Sabbath of the golden calf."[2] Barwick would have hazarded a happier conjecture by supposing that, instead of Andrewes, Laud was consulted, as this individual, who was also then in attendance upon the King, was, according to his own confession on his trial, favourable to the re-issue of the *Book of Sports* in the following reign.

On May 24, 1618, the Court being then at Greenwich, the King published the *Declaration*, of which it may suffice to present an abstract.

1. The document professes to be an explanation, rendered necessary by the calumnious misrepresentations of Papists and Puritans in Lancashire, of his Majesty's directions given there in the

[1] *Life of Bishop Morton*, p. 80. [2] *Patterne of Catech. on the Fourth Commandment.*

preceding year concerning Sunday sports, and to be also a publication of these directions to all his subjects, with a few additional words specially applicable to the people of that county.

2. It states that the report of a recently growing amendment amongst the inhabitants of Lancashire, a part of the country abounding more than any other in Popish recusants, made him the more sorry when with his own ears he heard the general complaint of his people, that they were barred from all lawful recreation and exercise upon the Sunday afternoon after the ending of all Divine service, which prohibition could not but produce two evils; first, preventing the conversion of many whom their priests would take occasion hereby to vex, persuading them that no honest mirth or recreation was lawful on those days; second, precluding the common people, occupied wholly in winning their bread on other days, from the exercises necessary to "make their bodies more able for war," and, in place thereof, setting up filthy tipplings and drunkenness, and breeding "idle discontented speeches in their ale-houses."

3. It directs that the clergy shall employ instruction and persuasion for the conversion of Papists, and shall "present them that will not conform themselves but obstinately stand out," to the civil authorities, who are required to put the laws in execution against them; and that the bishop of the diocese shall constrain "the Puritans and Precisians" to conform, or quit the country.

4. It provides that the people "be not disturbed, letted, or discouraged from any lawful recreation, such as dancing, either men or women, archery for men, leaping, vaulting, or any other such harmless recreation, nor from having of May-games, Whitsun-ales, and Morris-dances, and the setting up of May-poles, and other sports therewith used, so as the same be had in due and convenient time, without impediment or let of Divine service; and that women shall have leave to carry rushes to church for the decoring of it, according to their old custom." This order is accompanied with the following explanations and restrictions: First, "We do here account still as prohibited, all unlawful games to be used on Sundays only, as bear and bull baitings, interludes, and. at all times in the meaner sort of people by law prohibited,

bowling." Second, That all known recusants abstaining from coming to Church and Divine service, and any that, though "conform in religion," are not present in the church at the service of God before their going to the said recreations, are barred from this benefit and liberty. Third, That the authorities shall sharply punish all who abuse this liberty before the end of all Divine services for the day. Fourth, That no offensive weapon be carried or used in the said times of recreations.

5. It "straightly commands, that every person shall resort to his own parish church to hear Divine service, and each parish by itself to use the said recreations after Divine service."

6. It concludes with the words, "And our pleasure is, That this our *Declaration* shall be published by order from the bishop of the diocese, through all the parish churches, and that both our Judges of our Circuits, and our Justices of our Peace, be informed thereof."

It would not affect the principle involved in this extraordinary proclamation, even were it true, as Fuller and others relying on his authority have affirmed, that it was merely "local for Lancashire;" but the assertion is not true, for the document calls itself a publication to all his subjects of his Majesty's directions given in that county; and Charles I., when renewing the edict, states that his dear father of blessed memory did, in his princely wisdom, publish a declaration to all his loving subjects concerning lawful sports, from the want of which his people in all other parts of the kingdom suffered in the same kind, though perhaps not in the same degree, as the men and women of Lancashire. Nor is it a justification of the proceeding to say, that the Declaration contained no command to any to practise sports on the Lord's day, being simply a prohibition of interference with persons who chose so to recreate themselves. To concede the absence of positive injunction in the matter would still leave enough to constitute the measure an atrocity against the Sabbatic institution unparalleled at the time in history. Bidding defiance to the practice of good men in every age—to all that had been done by fathers, councils, and princes, for securing the weekly rest from the pollution of worldly pleasure, as for the most part also from the intrusion of secular work—to the doctrine of the Homilies and other formularies of the English Church,—above all, to the Law and Declaration of the King of kings, which respectively said, "Remember the Sabbath-day to keep it holy;" "If thou shalt honour me" by the abnegation of thine own ways, pleasure, and words, "I will make thee to ride on the high places of the earth;"—and disregarding the claims of his people to a stated time for rest, for reading, for reflection, for domestic worship and instruction, and for expressing sympathy in the sorrows of fellow-creatures around,—the King of England proclaims it to be right, patriotic, and beneficial for his subjects to abandon themselves to thought-dispelling, exhausting, and dissipating sports in the afternoon of the Lord's day, and wrong for any man to do his duty to his God, his conscience, his Church, and his country, by attempting to hinder this wholesale desecration of sacred time.

It was not surprising that the *Book of Sports* should produce the greatest alarm and sorrow among the best of the clergy and people.[1] Several of the bishops declared their opinion against it.[2] Archbishop Abbot being at Croydon, forbade it to be read in the church there on the day appointed.[3] Dr. Twisse not only refused to read, but condemned, the *Declaration* from his pulpit.[4] His Majesty was prudent enough to wink at these offences "against his spiritual supremacy."[5] And, though when the Lord Mayor of London commanded the royal carriages to be stopped as they were driving through the city on a Sunday during Divine service, James vowed that "he thought there had been no more kings in England but himself," and directed a warrant to his lordship, ordering him to let the carriages pass, yet when the civic officer yielded, with the answer, "While it was in my power I did my duty, but that being taken away by a higher power, it is my duty to obey;" the King, it is said, was pleased, and returned him his thanks.[6] It is generally agreed by writers that the *Declaration* proved a failure—that the matter, as Collier says, was dropt. Fuller states, that the King of his goodness removed the cause of

[1] Fuller (1845), vol. v. pp. 452, 453; Collier's *Eccl. Hist. of Britain* (1714), vol. ii. p. 712.

[2] Bishop Kennet's *Complete History of England*, vol. ii. p. 709; Neale's *Feasts and Fasts*, p. 223.

[3] *Life of Abbot*, p. 27.

[4] Brook's *Puritans*, vol. iii. p. 14.

[5] *Ibid.*; Neale's *Feasts and Fasts*, p. 228.

[6] Kennet's *Complete History of England*, vol. ii. p. 709.

alarm, and that no minister was obliged to read the document from the pulpit. But according to another account, the book came forth with a command, enjoining all ministers to read it to their parishioners; and those that did not were brought into the High Commission, imprisoned, and suspended.[1] Whatever might induce royalty to "drop" *The Dancing Book*, it certainly was not loving-kindness or tender mercy.

Before passing from England, and its Sabbath of 1618, we ought to mention another phase of the controversy which appeared there, in that unprecedented year of trespass against Sabbatic rights and sanctities. The opinion, that the seventh-day Sabbath is of unchanged and unchangeable obligation, was mooted, as we have seen, p. 60, so early as 1584, but it attracted little attention till 1618, when John Traske, a schoolmaster in his native county of Somerset, having obtained "orders," which had been at first refused him on the alleged ground of his unfitness, forthwith avowed himself a Sabbatarian, and began to "preach up the Levitical rites."[2] For these errors, or, according to another account, for "making of conventicles and factions, by that means which may tend to sedition and commotion, and for scandalizing the king, the bishops, and the clergy,"[3] "he was censured in the Star-Chamber to be set upon the pillory at Westminster, and from thence to be whipt to the Fleet, there to remain prisoner."[4] Mrs. Traske was, for maintaining the same opinions, also sent to prison, where she spent the remaining fifteen years of her life, resolutely holding by her creed to the last. Traske's views were opposed by Bishop Andrewes in a Star-Chamber speech which has frequently been referred to in the controversy. Lord Bacon, writing to Buckingham on December 1, 1619, says, "This day also, Traske in open Court made a retractation of his wicked opinions in writing. The form was as good as may be. I declared to him that this Court was the judgment-seat; the mercy-seat was his Majesty: but the Court would commend him to his Majesty; and humbly pray his Majesty to signify his pleasure speedily, because of the misery of the man; and it is a rare thing for a sectary that hath once

1 Kennet's *Complete Hist. of England*, vol. ii. p. 709; Rapin, vol. ix. p. 386.
2 Collenge's (Dr. Collinges) *Modest Plea for the Lord's Day*, p. 74.
3 Hobart's *Reports* quoted in Bishop Andrewes' Minor Works (1854), p. 83.
4 Pagitt's *Heresiog.* (1662), p. 161.

suffered smart and shame, to turn so unfeignedly as he seemed to do."[1] In 1621, Mr. Traske published his recantation, under the title, *Liberty from Judaism*, of which it has been said, "It is certainly not the production of a weak or an ignorant person, but is on the contrary remarkable for the excellence of its style and spirit."[2] According to the editor of Pagitt, he afterwards fell to Antinomian opinions. Fuller says, "he relapsed not into the same but other opinions, rather humourous than hurtful, and died obscurely at Lambeth."

The people of Scotland were treated to what was no less abhorrent to their views than a Book of Sports, in the famous Five Articles which the Court and bishops contrived to force upon them, through a Convention held at Perth, August 25, 1618. These articles prescribed (along with kneeling at the Lord's Supper, the administration of the same ordinance to the sick in their houses, private baptism, and confirmation), the observance henceforth in the Kirk of Scotland of the following festivals—Christmas, Easter, Whitsunday, and the Ascension of the Saviour. The King ordered these articles to be published at the Market Cross in each borough, and to be read by the ministers in their pulpits, the greater number of whom disobeyed the order. They were ratified by the Parliament in 1621.

An incident of the latter year exhibits the practice of the monarch as consistent with his principles, if not with either religion or decorum. *Technogamia* or the *Marriage of Arts*, a Comedy, was, after some alterations by the author, Barton Holyday, acted before the King at Woodstock, on a Sunday night, August 26, 1621. But it being too grave for the King, and too scholastic for the auditory (or as some have said, the actors having taken too much wine before they began), his Majesty, after two acts, offered several times to withdraw, but was induced to remain, which gave occasion to these lines by a certain scholar :—

"At Christ Church Marriage done before the King,
Lest that those mates should want an offering,
The King himself did offer, What? I pray ?
He offered twice or thrice to go away."[3]

[1] *Works* (1830), vol. xii. p. 379.
[2] Fuller's *Church History* (1845), vol. v. pp. 460, 461. Note by the editor.
[3] Wood's *Athen. Oxon.* vol. ii. p. 170.

The suspension of hostilities consequent on the proceedings of 1618, although of brief duration, affords an opportunity of turning for a little to the controversy which had already commenced in Holland.

THE NETHERLANDS.

No Sabbatic strife appeared in the Belgic Churches for a century after the doctrines of the Reformation had been embraced by a majority of the inhabitants of the Low Countries. The Churches, though engaged at an early period of their history in a fruitless struggle with the magistrates for the exclusion of Popish holidays, and in occasional conflicts with certain fanatics who abjured all distinction of days, were agreed among themselves on the subject of the weekly rest, their views on that point being substantially the views which have been held by the great body of Christians in all countries and times. John Robinson (1575-1625), so well known as the pastor of the Pilgrim Fathers, said in the year 1619, that in regard to the sanctification of the Lord's day, in which he and his friends then resident in Holland seemed "even superstitiously rigid," the Belgic Churches did not "differ from them in judgment, but in practice," and referred, in proof of his remark, to the lately published *Harmony of the Belgic Synods*."[1]

The unfailing result, however, of the addition of human to Divine ordinances soon discovered itself in a diminished practical regard for the Lord's day. "It seemeth not without all leaven of superstition," as the same writer remarks, "that the Dutch Reformed Churches do observe certain days consecrated as holy to the nativity, resurrection, and ascension of Christ, and the same also (as it commonly comes to pass where human devices are reared up by the side of Divine institutions), much more holy [holily] than the Lord's day by him himself appointed."[2] Robinson and his flock, "neither allowed to remain peacefully in England, nor suffered quietly to depart," had, in 1608, escaped to Holland, and, after a year's residence in Amsterdam, had settled

[1] *Works* (1851), vol. iii. p. 46. [2] *Works* (1851), vol. iii. p. 43.

in Leyden. Of various reasons for the resolution to quit their adopted country for America, one was, "that they could not bring the Dutch to observe the Lord's day as a Sabbath, or to reform anything amiss amongst them."[1]

A correspondingly low state of religion and morals was the fruit of a like neglect of the institution in Zealand. Happily, however, the remedial means employed were in this instance more successful. An ardent Zealander, thoroughly acquainted with the feelings and language of the people, was the instrument of reviving a respect for the Sabbath, and of advancing the cause of religion, not only in his own province, but throughout the Netherlands. "Where the Sabbath is at an undervalue in any country," said Hugh Peters, when under sentence of death, "say it be in France, Holland, Germany, etc., there you shall find religion wasting itself into disputes. I was a witness that Middleburgh, in Zealand, or Walcheren, grew famous for religion by Teeling, their preacher, fetching the keeping of the Sabbath from England."[2] Amesius, writing in 1630, the year after Teellinck's death, and referring to the distinguished piety of pastors and people in Zealand, as noted in all places around, singles out for special encomium "that remarkable servant of God, William Teellinck, who exerted himself so ardently in public and private, by his voice and by his writings, in promoting the cause of religion, as that the zeal of God's house may be said to have eaten him up, and who, having overcome the envy attendant on such excellence, has gained the crown which God has prepared for those that have turned many to righteousness."[3]

This "most popular preacher, and voluminous writer among the Dutch divines of his day," was born at Zierikzee, and having studied for some time at the University of St. Andrews,[4] took his degree at Poictiers in 1603, with a view to the legal profession. But in the course of a visit to England and Scotland, he was so deeply impressed at a prayer-meeting held in London by John Dod, Arthur Hildersham, and other pious ministers of the

[1] Morton's *N. England's Memorial* (1826), p. 19.

[2] *Dying Father's Legacy*, as quoted in Hanbury's *Memorials*, vol. iii. p. 581.

[3] *De Conscientiâ* (1670), Dedication, p. 2.

[4] "Gulielmus Teelingius" occurs in the list of foreign students at St. Andrews, A.D. 1600, when Andrew Melville was Principal. M'Crie's *Melville*, vol. ii. p. 49.

gospel, as to form the resolution of devoting himself to the ministry, a purpose which the unanimous concurrence of his English friends, after a day set apart by them and himself for invoking the Divine direction, contributed to strengthen. He became one of the ministers of the Dutch Reformed Church in Middleburg. Dr. Steven, to whom we are indebted for some of these particulars, mentions that Teellinck was a zealous friend of the British settlers in Walcheren, having been principally instrumental in the erection of their place of worship, and frequently employed in officiating to the congregation.[1] It is stated by Foppens, that he wrote or edited no fewer than 127 publications in the Dutch language.[2]

In regard to the Sabbath, as to other things, practical evil prepares the way for the adoption of such opinions as serve the offender for a justification of his conduct. If new views of the institution had previously to 1618 been partially entertained in the Belgic Churches, it was not till that year, according to a laborious and able writer, that they led to open strife.[3] A controversy, or "twist," as it is called in the language of the country, then commenced, which, extending beyond the scene of its origin, continued with occasional pauses for upwards of a century. It took its rise among the ministers of Zealand, though not as represented by Dr. Hengstenberg in these words: "From England the doctrine of the obligation of the Mosaic law of the Sabbath spread to Holland. Some English Puritans, who sought an asylum in Zealand, introduced it. It was first published in two works on Ethics, by Udemann in 1612, and Teelling in 1617. Several ministers embraced the new opinions; others retained the old."[4] The Puritans referred to by the writer must have been Thomas Cartwright, Robert Browne, Henry Jacob, and Hugh Broughton (or some of their number), who, with John Forbes, a Scotsman, had resided in Middleburg before the year 1617. But if the testimony of Robinson already adduced be true—and its truth admits of full confirmation—there was no call for the interference of foreigners in attempting to change the opinions of the Zealanders in reference to the institution, since both foreigners

[1] *Hist. of Scot. Church*, Rotterdam, p. 317. [2] *Bibliothec. Belgic* (1739), vol. i. p. 424.
[3] Koelman, *De Historie van den Sab.* p. 250. [4] *Lord's Day*, p. 69.

and Zealanders were substantially of the same mind on the subject, nor, though such men as Cartwright and his friends would, as occasion offered, declare their Sabbatic views, have we evidence that they felt it necessary to combat opinions opposite to their own. It was improved practice that was needed; and what English Puritans failed to effect in Holland, was by a native, profiting, indeed, by what he had witnessed of a well-observed Sabbath in England and Scotland, achieved in Zealand. And when Godfrey Udemann, minister at Zierikzee, and not the least able or energetic member of the Synod of Dort, maintained in his *Practice of the Christian Virtues*, as in other writings, the doctrines of a primitive—perpetual—moral, not "Mosaic" Sabbath transferred under Christianity to a new day, he and Teellinck, who also held these doctrines, instead of introducing novelties, or requiring to borrow their opinions from abroad, found their tenets already in the creed of their Church, and enunciated by Junius, Trelcatius, Acronius, and other expounders of her formularies—not to plead here that their views were as old, some of them as Christianity, others as the completed creation.

The earliest agitation of the Sabbath question in the Netherlands, though keen, was not lasting. The combatants agreed to submit the points at issue to the judgment of the celebrated Synod of Dort, which assembled November 13, 1618, for composing the more serious differences between the Calvinists and Arminians. Apart indeed from the case to be referred to it for decision, the Synod in reality declared its Sabbatic views at its fourteenth session, when it re-inforced the exposition of the Catechism by ministers in the afternoon of the Lord's day, and agreed to call on the magistrates for the prohibition by severer enactments of all servile or customary work, and especially games, compotations, and other profane practices so common, particularly in villages, on that part of the day, that the people might be induced to attend on religious instruction, and thus *learn to sanctify the entire Sabbath.*[1] The foreign deputies having taken their departure, May 9, 1619, the deputies of the Low Countries proceeded to deliberate on matters of local concern. According to the statement of Walæus, who was well qualified to speak on the subject, the remanent

[1] *Acta. Synod.* (Lug. Bat. 1620), p. 28.

members judged it to be beyond their province—*sui fori non esse*—to decide on questions of so general importance as had been raised respecting the Sabbath, and only recommended to the contending parties, laying aside other points of debate, to adhere to certain rules, in which, before arbiters, they had agreed to acquiesce.[1] The arbiters were Professors Gomarus, Walæus, Thysius, and Festus Hommius, who had also prepared the rules or articles of peace, as follows :—

First, In the fourth precept of the Divine law, there is something ceremonial and something moral.

Second, The ceremonial consists in the rest of the seventh day from the creation, and in the rigid observance of that rest enjoined specially on the Jews.

Third, The moral is the assignation of a certain and stated day to Divine worship, and so much rest as is requisite for Divine worship and holy meditation on that day.

Fourth, The Sabbath of the Jews having been abrogated, the Lord's day ought to be solemnly sanctified by Christians.

Fifth, This day was ever from the times of the Apostles observed by the ancient Catholic Church.

Sixth, This day ought to be so consecrated to Divine worship as that there may be a cessation thereon from all servile works, excepting works of charity and urgent necessity, and from such recreations as hinder the worship of God.[2]

These rules were, according to Walæus, commended by the Synod to the Churches of the Netherlands, and followed up by a petition to the States-General, adopted session 177, which, with other requests, craved that the strictest measures might be employed to suppress certain specified forms of prevailing Sabbath profanation.

For some years the spirit of controversy slumbered, or rather smouldered, under an agreement which it seems strange should have been assented to by either of the contending parties. Teellinck, intent on practical objects, published in 1621, *The Rest-time, or a Treatise on the Observance of the Christian Sabbath*, which

[1] Walæi *Opera* (1647), tom. i. p. 276.

[2] "In quarto legis divinæ præcepto," etc. Walæi *Op.* tom i. p. 276. We have translated the copy of the rules, which Walæus says he had transcribed from the authentic Acts of the Synod.

was approved by a Synod held at Rotterdam, and elicited from Gomar a friendly epistle, lauding the pious endeavours of that "eminently practical man," its author.[1]

The States-General, warned by recent events, resolved to select for the chairs of the University of Leyden, men not only of learning and worth, but also of sound doctrinal views. Walæus and Thysius in 1619, and Rivetus in 1620, were accordingly appointed colleagues to Polyander in the teaching of Theology. Desirous of bearing testimony to the great principles which had lately been in peril, but had triumphed, and of showing their agreement in religious sentiment—*fidei ac sententiæ nostræ πανάρμονιαν*, the four Professors published in 1625 the *Synopsis Purioris Theologiæ.* The chapter containing a *Disputation on the Sabbath and the Lord's Day*, was contributed by Thysius, who expresses opinions in harmony with the *Dortrechtan Articles*, only adding to them two important statements—the one affirming that "the certain and stated day" demanded by the morality of the Fourth Commandment, is a perpetual seventh portion of time ; the other explicitly declaring that the Lord's day is of "Apostolic ordination, and consequently of Divine authority," its very name, moreover, intimating that it was "consecrated *by* the Lord, and wholly *to* the Lord." Antonius Thysius (1565-1640) was born at Antwerp. Having studied under Bonaventura Vulcanius, whom he followed to Leyden,—under Isaac Casaubon, Beza, and Faius, at Geneva, —under Whitaker at Cambridge and Rainolds at Oxford, he became minister of a church at Haarlem, then pastor at Amsterdam, and Professor of Theology successively at Harderwick and Leyden.

The first book published in the Netherlands against the Sabbath, according to a Dutch authority, was *Een Weeklag der Kerke, etc.*, —*A Lamentation of the Church over the Doctrine of the Sabbath.*[2] It made its appearance in 1626 under the name of James Burs, minister at a village near Middleburg, and son of Mr. Giles Burs, colleague in the ministry to Teellinck and Walæus, though the author was understood to have been aided in the work by Gomar, his father's friend. "About this time," says the biographer of

[1] Koelman, *De Histoire*, etc. p. 255. Voet. *Select. Disput. Theol.* (1659), P. iii. p. 1242.
[2] Koelman, *De Histoire*, etc., p. 257.

Walæus, "the Churches of Zealand were agitated by the contentions of Teellinck and Burs. The former, studious to promote the interests of piety, while aiming at the correction of evil, went to the extreme of rigour in the opposite direction, as they are wont to do who try to straighten crooked timber. In this manner, he sought, in a published treatise, to remedy the profanation of the Sabbath. The son of Burs seized the occasion, and gave to the world the Threnody of the Weeping Church over the fancied violation of her liberty, attempting to refute Teellinck with regard to the observance of a seventh day, and the institution of the Lord's day, for which Gomar, sufficiently devoted to the Bursii, had supplied arguments. The friends of Teellinck were aggrieved, and there was a danger that they might break out into rejoinders, and that the Church might be split into parties. Voet had opposed the juvenile production, by which he appeared more to provoke the crocodile tears of the adversaries, less to edify the Church."[1]

The blame imputed by this writer to Teellinck amounted to his holding views which obtained for him, as they have for many others, the name of Sabbatarian, and which a great part of the Christian world have regarded as forming the only consistent and tenable theory of the weekly rest. The work of Voetius was published in 1627. The title, *Lachrymæ Crocodili abstersæ*—*The Tears of the Crocodile wiped away*, however happily terse and "telling," according to the modern demand, in such cases, or however much provoked by the enormity of the occasion, does seem unbecoming the subject and the author, as well as somewhat misapplied, since there was no reason to doubt the sincerity of the tears which were shed by the chief mourner, and which he would naturally conceive would be shed by others, over the threatened calamity of a generally-observed Sabbath.[2] How far the performance itself was liable to exception for provoking the complaints of his opponents rather than edifying the Church, we have not the means of judging, not having seen the *Lachrymæ*. But we can speak with some confidence of a chapter from the

[1] Walæi *Opera, Vita*, p. 40.

[2] If in this instance of the *seria mixta jocis*, which the discussions of the times occasionally elicited, there was more of the serious than was pleasant to the one party

same pen, *De Sabbato et Festis*,[1] which, if betraying "the deficiency in philosophical precision" ascribed to Voet by Mosheim, assuredly affords abundant indications of what the same authority accords to him, "uncommon application and immense learning." Gisbertus Voetius (1589-1676) was born at Heusden in Holland—was a pupil of Arminius and Gomarus at Leyden—became minister of a church in his native town—was a member of the Synod of Dort, the longest-lived of that distinguished assembly—and, latterly, Professor of the Oriental Languages, and for a time of Theology also, at Utrecht. It is interesting to mark how this ardent combatant of the Cartesian, Cocceian, and other errors of his time, evinced no less ardour in his ministerial duties, preaching at one period eight sermons every week, and resigning one of his professorships, that he might resume his earliest and favourite work. Of his various writings, that by which he is now best known is his *Select Theological Disputations*, where the curious in Sabbatic and other religious opinions may find ample stores.

Amesius (1576-1633), Professor of Theology at Franeker, published the first part of his *Medulla Theologica*, or *Marrow of Theology*, in 1623. The second part, which appeared along with the other in 1627, contained a chapter on "The Time of Worship," in which the whole doctrine of the Sabbath was briefly and lucidly presented, and the primæval appointment of the institution, the Divine authority of its transference from the seventh to the first day of the week, and the entire morality of the Fourth Commandment, were ably maintained. The contents of this work, and of that on Conscience, which latter supplied a practical supplement to the chapter on the "Time of Worship" in the *Medulla*, perfectly harmonize with their avowed object of recalling the attention of the Churches, too much engrossed with

or proper for the other, the remark applies still more to a pasquinade directed by an ill-natured wit against Voet himself during a controversy between him and Maresius—

"Voetius odit alit fallit defendit adoptat
Pacem, dissidium, Patres, absurda, malignos."

To which Paul, son of the lampooned divine, happily retorted thus—

"Voetius odit alit defendit prodit adoptat
Dissidium, pacem, Patres, malefacta, benignos."

—Foppen's *Bibliothec. Belgic, sub voce* Voet.

[1] *Select. Disput.* P. iii. pp. 1227-1353.

doctrinal disputes, to the moral influence and practice of the truth, for which, along with Perkins and Teellinck, his alleged models in the attempt, he has received the praise of Mosheim.[1] This good and learned man, the circumstances of whose retirement to Holland have been mentioned (p. 25), was a native of Norfolk, and educated at Cambridge under Perkins, to whom he appeared to have owed, by the Divine blessing, his earliest thorough impressions of religion. After being excluded through prelatic influence from his ministry at the Hague, he distinguished himself by a controversy with Grevinchovius, one of the leading remonstrants. We find him attending as a hearer the Synod of Dort, and regularly communicating intelligence of its proceedings to King James's Ambassador at the Hague. Apprehensive that the climate of Franeker would prove fatal to his constitution, and having a strong desire to preach the gospel to his countrymen, he accepted, in 1632, an invitation to the charge of the English Church at Rotterdam, where he died after a year's ministry. His works in Latin, of which a complete edition was published at Amsterdam in 1658, are said to have been "famous over Europe."

Previously to the appearance of the *Weeklag* and the *Lachrymæ*, Teellinck had been engaged in preparing his *Nootwendig Vertoogh, etc.—A Necessary Demonstration concerning the Present Afflicted State of God's People.* The author, on sending a copy of it to Walæus, says, "I only wish that it may be read with such a heart as is seemly, and then I trust it will produce an effect towards edification You have doubtless seen the *Complaint* of J. Bursius. I suppose you will not forbear any longer to publish your *Treatise on the Sabbath* at the first possible opportunity, though such writings, being published rather inconsiderately, would make a bad impression upon the people, and increase the power of sinning. I hope that you, by-the-bye, will declare me to be free from the suspicion which that man insinuates against me, in order to make my service fruitless. You know how D. D. G. has dealt with me. I do not know what the use of cordial friendship and zeal for the innocent is, if it keeps entirely quiet in such cases. But I leave this to your discretion, and will not

[1] In *Eccles. Hist.* vol. iv. pp. 412-414.

by this, my writing, press you to do anything which you yourself may not deem advisable."[1] In this spirited, and yet not intemperate style does Teellinck refer to writers who were combined against him in a work which we leave it to Udemann, in a letter shortly to be cited, to describe, and of one of whom, his eulogist but six short years before, he might have said, "And thou, too, Brutus!" After alluding to a circumstance bearing on the interests of the Church, he concludes with the characteristic prayer, "May the good God grant that we may act purely in these holy matters!" The *Nootwendig Vertoogh*, after being twice written, and submitted to the examination of the Faculties of Leyden and Franeker, came out in 1627, recommended by the theological professors of both these Universities, those of Leyden intimating that they differed from the author on certain points; and was dedicated to all holding office in the Churches, Universities, Guilds, and schools, and to all heads of families in the United Provinces. This, which has been called "a noble" work, has a relation to our subject, which must not be estimated by the number of pages devoted to its consideration. The chief part, including two brief chapters on "The observance of the Christian Sabbath, and its Rule in the Decalogue," must have been printed, though not issued, before the production of Bursius appeared. Teellinck felt that some counteractive to the mischievous tendency of such a book was necessary. He accordingly replied to it, not by argument, for which he referred to the *Rust-tijdt*, or by abuse, but by a *Declaration*, enunciating in distinct propositions his own Sabbatic creed. This was the fitting answer of a Christian to the scurrility of the *Weeklag;* and being published when the writer had only two more years to live, may be regarded as his dying testimony to opinions, by the advocacy of which he had eminently promoted the religion and morals of his country.

Many eyes were now turned to Walæus as the individual who ought to enter the lists with Bursius, or rather with the redoubtable Gomarus. The deep interest felt on the occasion appears from the language of Teellinck, already quoted, and from that of Udemann, both of them distinguished by their zeal in the Sabbatic cause. "G. V. Z.," that is, we have no doubt, "Godfrey Udemann, Zierik-

[1] Ick wenschste maer alleene, etc.; Wal. *Oper.* tom. ii. p. 446.

zee," in a letter to the Professor, having expressed his conviction that he must have seen the truly mournful dirge of Mr. James Burs, which was blazoned in all the book-shops, having obtested him by many sacred considerations to publish his anxiously looked for *Treatise*, and having assured him that the ministers could not interfere without injury, proceeds thus—" The remedy, under God, is expected from your Theological Faculty, which can, with greater authority and better success, confute so impudent calumnies, and still the rising tempest. This man boasts that his doctrine is the doctrine of the Church, and that others, who teach that one of seven days is to be sanctified, that the Sabbath is from the beginning, that the Lord's day took its origin from the Apostles themselves, that this day is unchangeable, etc., deliver opinions, new, erroneous, dangerous, Brownistic, and unheard-of by the ancient Church and first Reformers—and what not. You should say that some Nestor spoke, or rather that Apollo from his tripod poured forth his oracles, so haughtily does he assert his own views, and reject the views of other men. I pass over his sarcasms and numberless calumnies, which, as many opine, merit for his production the title of a Menippean Satire rather than the name of a Lament."[1]

The parents of Antonius Walæus (1573-1639) were, at the capitulation in 1584 of his native city Ghent, to the Spaniards, compelled to quit it for Middleburg. At the age of fifteen, when attending his father, who had collected a small force to resist the descent of the Spanish fleet on Walcheren, and lying beside him in his tent at night on a bed of straw, he "perceived, by some sacred instinct, that he was called to be a minister of the Church of God"—a scene which nothing in his future life had power to exclude from his thoughts. After a course of training under the ablest masters and professors of the time,[2] and visiting the most celebrated places on the Continent, he settled, in 1602, as minister of a village church in Zealand, whence he was translated to a

[1] Epist. Sept. 1627, Wal. *Oper.* tom. ii. p. 446.

[2] At Middleburg, Gruterus, and Murdisonius, a Scotsman, who shortly after this was promoted to a professorship in Leyden; at Leyden, Junius, Scaliger, and Gomarus; at Geneva, the octogenarian Beza and Faius; and at Basle, Grynæus, Polanus, and Buxtorf.

similar charge in the neighbouring city of Middleburg. There, having for his colleagues Giles Bursius, Faukelius, Teellinck, and others of less note, he laboured for fifteen years, distinguished as a popular preacher, as a laborious minister, as a zealous promoter of education and learning, and, latterly, as a leading man in the councils of the Calvinists, and at the Synod of Dort, where he was employed in all matters requiring superior acuteness, judgment, address, and powers of debate, and to take part in drawing up its acts and canons. An individual so educated and experienced—who had been selected to defend Calvinism when it was in peril, and to fill a theological chair at a critical juncture—whom Grotius, his intimate friend, admired, and Uitenbogart declined to encounter in discussion, and who was the publicly-appointed counsellor of Barneveldt in prison, the president of a missionary seminary, and one of the translators of the Scriptures from the original languages into the Belgic—could be no common man; and it was not surprising, particularly as he was known to have directed his attention to the question, that his interference should be sought in the present emergency, and that he should be desired and expected to apply his gifted mind to the settlement of Sabbatic differences.

"Yielding," says his biographer, "to the importunities of his admirers, Walæus reviewed what he had previously presented in his lectures, and extending it into a treatise, gave it to the world, to the great joy of the Churches, who, as they prized the learning of Walæus, so also in the present instance admired his wisdom."[1] Udemann himself was almost satisfied. "I rejoice," are his words in a letter of March 29, 1628, "that your *Treatise on the Sabbath* has at last been wrung from you, so as to see the light among your other learned lucubrations. The brethren in Zealand, in general, as far as I have been able to hear, applaud and thank you from the heart—at least, I have as yet met with none who has ventured to censure. Your preface appears to some sufficiently mild, and too guarded; but I have defended you as I could, because, doubtless, you acted not without a reason, although, to confess the truth, I should have wished a little more boldness against those sciolists who set up their own dreams for articles of

[1] Wal. *Oper.* tom. i.; *Vita*, p. 40.

faith. But it was impossible for you, in a matter so delicate, to please all in everything. You have laid the foundations soundly and solidly; let others take heed how they build thereon. A translation into the vernacular language is necessary."[1]

The *Treatise*[2] made its first appearance early in 1628, in Latin, "whence it was translated into Dutch by Silvius, pastor at Amsterdam." The accomplished writer maintains the positions, that the Sabbath was of primæval appointment—that the Fourth Commandment is partly moral and partly ceremonial—that the ceremonial part, which passed away with the Mosaic ritual, is the obligation to the observance of the seventh day of the week, and to a more rigid rest—that the moral part is that which has ever demanded, and still demands, the consecration of a seventh portion of our time to sacred rest and service—and that the Lord's day is partly of Divine authority, in so far as the Fourth Commandment is moral, and partly of ecclesiastical, yet apostolic institution, inasmuch as the Apostles, by virtue of the extraordinary commission given to them for settling the doctrine and laws of the Church, and by their example, altered the season of rest and worship from the last to the first day of the week. He would, it appears to us, have consulted a nobler and scriptural simplicity of doctrine, if he had regarded "the ceremonial as merely an appendage or circumstance which does not enter into the substance of the law," and if he had affirmed that the Lord's day is of Divine authority, inasmuch as the Lord of the Sabbath has by his own example, and by the inspired testimony of the Apostles, appointed it as the specific season in which, under the Christian dispensation, we are to appropriate sacred time for the purposes and in the proportion required in the Fourth Commandment. But there is no question, that he has rendered very important service to the institution by his unanswerable arguments for its antiquity, and for the enduring Divine claim on the seventh part of man's time to be consecrated and employed as prescribed in the Decalogue.

The writer of the author's life, after mentioning the pleasure with which the *Dissertation* was hailed, says, "Thus those billows

[1] Wal. *Oper.* tom. ii. p. 472.

[2] *Dissertatio de Sabbato seu vero sensu atque usu IV. Præcepti.*

of the Church were assuaged, and as it were broken in pieces on the objected rock, and would have entirely subsided, if Gomar had not believed that his interest was concerned in not allowing the things, which were known to have come from him, to be soon disregarded; wherefore he put forth a small book on the *Investigation of the Sabbath.* To which Rivet replied. Gomar defended himself; and although he found very few or no followers, Walæus, lest some ensnaring things should fasten, treated in public lectures whatever novelty might seem to have been advanced, and noted some things in aid of his memory, with the view of printing an enlarged edition of his *Treatise*—a purpose, however, the execution of which was hindered by the labour of the New Testament version, and then for ever arrested by the hand of death. These have been added in a second edition of his *Dissertation concerning the Sabbath,* posthumously published. Thus the differences in obscurer things are never better settled than by the prudence and authority of a great man."[1]

In September of the same year, Franciscus Gomarus (1563-1641), formerly Professor of Theology at Leyden, along with Arminius, whose views he then, and afterwards in the Synod of Dort, so ably opposed, and now Professor of Hebrew and Divinity at Groningen, gave to the world his *Investigation,* intended, he said, to bring men back to the middle course, which had been pointed out by pious and learned men, and which avoided equally the Charybdis of superstition and the Scylla of profaneness. The task, he further said, was not unwillingly undertaken, out of deference at once to the just expectation of his hearers, and to the honourable desire of many brethren in the ministry. The *Investigation* is an attempt to show that the Fourth Commandment prescribed a Sabbath only for the Jews, the statute applying to other men only as in a general manner it required, at certain and sufficient times, a holy vacation from mundane business and cares, in subserviency to the ministry of the Divine word, the public profession and exercises of religion, and the recruiting of man's strength; that the general command of a Sabbath, recurring not less seldom than that of the Jews, is obligatory on mankind, before and after Christ, by the eternal law of love; that

[1] Wal. *Oper.* tom. i.; *Vita,* p. 40.

the institution, taking its origin in the wilderness of Sin, and renewed at Sinai, was abrogated by the crucifixion of Christ, though, in tenderness to the Jews, its use, with some ceremonies, was retained for a time by the Apostles; and that, while it is not clearly evident that the Lord's day, or first day of the week, was appointed by the Apostles for the worship of God, it yet appears, from the general meaning of the Fourth Commandment, that it ought to be observed in the public worship of God, nor can be violated without the injury and unworthy scandal of religion. One cannot easily reconcile the author with himself in some of his proceedings on this question, or the opinions in the *Investigation* and *Defence* with the creed of his Church, and with the common sense views of Scripture, which, there is reason to rejoice, will ever overpower the crotchets of a few good men, and the perplexing distinctions of the learned, who occasionally darken counsel by words without knowledge. It has been remarked of Gomar, that, in the great doctrinal controversy of the time, he directed his mind mainly to the study, and brought extraordinary ability to the defence, of the one article of Justification by Faith—that criterion of a standing or falling Church. But certainly his Sabbatic efforts, though exhibiting not a few indications of the learning in which he excelled, have not added much to his reputation, either by their wisdom or by their power. It is but justice to him, however, to recollect that, unlike many opponents of the institution, who have claimed the patronage of his name and the use of his arguments, he pleaded for more, not less, than the sacred time of a seventh day, and that as in general morals, so in Sabbatic practice, to employ the words of an admiring though on the question before us dissenting pupil, he "bolted the door against all profaneness, and was as remote as possible from worldly indulgence."[1]

The celebrated Rivet (Andreas Rivetus, 1572-1661) replied to Gomar in "four or five pages of his prælections on Exodus xx.," which were published in March 1632, and which touched only on the question respecting the origin of the Sabbath. Of this point he had treated in a previous work on Genesis, but as Walæus and Gomarus had taken opposite sides on the question, he em-

[1] Voet in *Select Disput.* P iii. p. 1242.

braced the opportunity of his forthcoming commentary again to show his opinion, in which the *Dissertation* of his colleague had confirmed him. He vindicates the plain narrative of Genesis from the gratuitous gloss which makes it a proleptical account, or intimated destination, of an institution which was to be actually appointed 2500 years after the creation, and to be thenceforward during the Levitical economy sanctified and blessed ; and shows from Hebrews iv. that men had entered into the Sabbatic rest when the world was made. To his astonishment, these remarks called forth from Gomar an answer, under the formidable title of a *Defence of the Investigation*, which challenged the modest writer of a few pages to single combat, and having the name of the culprit inscribed on the title-page *majusculis literis*, was industriously disseminated in Amsterdam, Leyden, and in Zealand itself. In the *Defence* the author specifies two questions, on the right solution of which depend correct views of the Sabbath : First, Whether the institution was of primæval origin ; and, Second, Whether one day in seven is to be observed, by authority of the Fourth Commandment, in the worship of God. "Between us," he says, "there is on the second question a manifest agreement, but on the first, the bond of confidence and friendship remaining nevertheless unimpaired, there is some difference." Such Christian courtesy, which in the Sabbatic strife is not rare, it is pleasant to notice. Rivet resolved to be silent, "to sabbatize, as it were, on the question," and no further to contend with a man whose age he reverenced, and whose learning he admired ; or if he did publish any thing, to annex it at his leisure by way of appendix to his exercises on Genesis on which he was then employed. He was confirmed in this resolution by the affliction in which the loss of a son, and of a step-son, had plunged him and his family, and by the opinion of prudent friends, who conceived that the matter had been more than sufficiently canvassed. On paying a visit to Leyden, however, he was urged by so many and by such arguments to take the field again, as to be induced to abandon his purpose, and to prepare a rejoinder, which appeared in the same year, 1633,[1] as the *Defence*, and was afterwards inserted in the second edition of his work on the Decalogue published in 1637. The rejoinder is

[1] *Dissert. de Orig. Sab. Cont.*, Fr. Gomarum, 8vo.

chiefly devoted to a learned and able vindication of the Sabbath as a primæval institution—a doctrine, all opposition to which ought, after the triumphant refutations of Walæus and Rivet, to have expired with Gomar. On the Fourth Commandment, and the celebration of the Lord's day, our author takes low ground, holding that the commandment requires under the present economy only the consecration of some day—a sufficient time to sacred rest and service, and that the observance of the first day of the week is an arrangement not necessarily binding on Christians, but entitled to respect, as having been agreed to by the early Church —an arrangement that may be changed provided some necessity should call for it; which necessity, however, he considers as precluded by the already exercised moral right of the Church to choose her day of worship, and by the public authorization of the Lord's day. Here, as we saw in Gomar, and shall see in Dr. John Prideaux, is a case in which some peculiar bias leads a man of the greatest learning and of acknowledged piety, into views which respect for these qualities restrains us from characterizing. On these points he tries to defend himself against the objections, and to combat the opinions of John Robinson, who had in his *Just and Necessary Apology* maintained the cause of the Sabbath on the ground of a strictly Divine and immutable right. Rivet, conscious that his doctrine needed it, cautions his readers against using for a cloak of licentiousness the liberty which he has asserted for them, and recommends that the Lord's day be spent in holiness, rest, joyfulness, and beneficence. Dr. Twisse, who has occupied some sections of his volume on *The Morality of the Fourth Commandment*, with a review of Rivet's Sabbatic doctrine, refers to his practical application of it in these pungent terms: "As for Dr. Rivet's honest and pious instructions as concerning the duties and our demeanours to bee performed on this day, we may easily perceive how little worth they are, and how easily they vanish into smoake, after that he hath in the doctrinall part of the Sabbath layd so unhappy a foundation, and that by so poore reasons and meane carriage of himselfe, that as I verily thinke, throughout all his writings there is not to be found the like."[1]

The controversy, so far as it had proceeded before the appear-

[1] Page 144.

ance of the last-mentioned work, was ably reviewed in the *Inquisitio de Sabbato et Die Dominico*, which was published in 1633 at Franeker, where the author, Nathanael Eaton, a native of England, was at that time a student in the University. Referring in the Preface to the Sabbatic treatises of Walæus, Gomar, and Rivet, he says, "Pondering each of these works of learned theologians with an impartial and humble mind, as in all I perceived erudite and instructive writing, in some I acknowledged and embraced truth; so when I thought that the other was wanting in some things, I could not but indicate the defect to his eager admirer with a gentle and modest pen; lest carried away by the emptiest shadows, and by names in the very search of truth, he should fall into error, and embrace a cloud instead of Juno." The *Inquisitio*, or, as it was afterwards named, *Gulielmi Amesi Sententiæ de Origine Sabbati, et Die Dominico*, comprehends, like the *Medulla* of that writer, the whole existing controversy in small space, and passed in course of time through several editions. The second, published in 1653, is introduced with some remarks by Christian Schotanus (1603-1671), one of the ministers of Franeker, and Professor of Greek and Church History in its University, who says, "Again appears the judgment of our preceptor, Dr. Ames, concerning our controversies on the Sabbath and Lord's day, which an excellent young man set down in writing from the mind of that individual, and exhibited for public discussion many years since." Disclaiming the part of a Palaemon in the strife, he adds, "I am unwilling that this little book should a second time be seen by you, without a friendly word from me. The observance of the Lord's day ought to be commended to all, and held in such honour as is due to a law of the first table." In his remaining remarks, the learned and excellent professor sets the institution on its true foundation of Divine authority, and, distinguishing between the extremes of superstition and profaneness in the treatment of it, deplores especially the prevalence of the latter amongst those who, "called the reformed, were yet in truth the most deformed."

Before we turn our attention again to England, the chief arena of the strife, it may be well to trace, however rapidly, the remaining controversies in the Netherlands. What has been numbered the third of these, began in 1656, and was conducted by four Professors of Theology—Hoornbeek of Leyden, and Essen of Utrecht, on the one hand, who held that the Fourth Commandment is moral, and that the Lord's day is of Divine authority; Heidan and Cocceius of Leyden, on the other, who maintained that the Fourth Commandment was, like circumcision, merely ceremonial and Jewish; that it never required worship, public or private, or anything but rest, and has been repealed; and that the Lord's day is nothing more than an old custom and institution of the Church. The following is in substance the account of the origin and circumstances of the discussion, as given by Koelman, who was a person of great worth, thoroughly versant in Sabbatic history, and at the time a student at Leyden. The University and Church of Utrecht were in a very flourishing state about the middle of the seventeenth century. The sanctification of the Sabbath, strongly enforced by the ministers, was more exact and conscientious than was aimed at in other parts of the Netherlands. The students of theology, imbued with sound Sabbatic principles, were zealous in their efforts to make them known, being at the same time well indoctrinated in the Catechism, and accustomed to the repetition of sermons on the Lord's day. But those who had studied at Leyden were, for the most part, not so well-informed [in regard to the doctrine of the Sabbath], and their practice was not so uniform. The Utrecht graduates and students, before admission to the University of Leyden, were subjected, as Koelman himself witnessed and experienced, to vexatious examinations on the subject of the institution. Hoornbeek, who had in 1653 been appointed to a chair in Leyden, sympathized with the young men in their views and wrongs. In 1656, he published a work in which he sought at once to allay existing differences, and to promote the substantial doctrine and sacred observance of the Lord's day. This, however, had not the desired effect. Heidan wrote his *Disputatio de Sabbato et Die Dominico*, which, after being canvassed in public discussions, was translated and printed in 1658. It produced no small disturbance in the Church. "The scandal thereby given and taken was unspeakably great." As an antidote to the poison of a book which was in every one's hands, Essen published his *Dissertation on the*

Perpetual Morality of the Decalogue, first in Latin, and then in Dutch. There followed a variety of works by Heidan, Cocceius, Hoornbeek, with one by John Paschasius, under the *nom-de-guerre* of Nathanael Johnston, and republications of treatises by Prideaux, Broad, and Primerose, the last having been translated into Dutch. The States interfered in 1659 to suppress the discussion, but a second and enlarged edition of the Dissertation, including replies to Cocceius and his colleagues, made its appearance nevertheless in 1660.[1]

Abraham Heidanus (1597-1678) forms the subject of a eulogistic article in Bayle's *Dictionary*. He wrote, besides other works, a book on *The Origin of Error*, and a *Body of Divinity*, the latter published after his death. He was dismissed from the Theological Chair for disobeying and publicly animadverting on a decree of the curators of the University forbidding the professors to treat in any way of certain disputed propositions in theology and philosophy, and of Descartes's Metaphysics. John Coch, or Cocceius, by his uncommon acquirements in oriental and rabbinical lore, was enabled to throw light on the sacred page. But it may be questioned whether he did not contribute still more to darken it by his views of the Bible, which he regarded as throughout a book of types and of words that ought to be understood in every possible sense.[2] Agreeably to the former theory, though inconsistently with the latter, he held that the Ten Commandments were promulgated from Sinai, not as a law which was to be obeyed, but as one form of the covenant of grace. John Hoornbeek (1617-1666) was born at Haarlem. Having studied at Leyden, and for five years discharged the duties of the ministry at Mulheim, near Cologne, he became a professor of theology, and afterwards preacher also, at Utrecht. Much against his own inclination, and the wishes of the magistrates and people there, he removed in 1653 to fill the same offices at Leyden. To eloquence, consummate ability in theological controversy, and high integrity, he added extensive acquaintance with languages and science, which, with his numerous publications, attested the re-

[1] *De Histoire*, pp. 284-295.

[2] This canon—*verba valent, quod valere possunt*—was, in presence of Cocceius, applied by a Jesuit to prove transubstantiation from the words, "This is my body."—Melch. Leydeck, *Synop. Theol.* (1689), p. 37.

markable energy of one, who, though of singularly noble form—*præter dicta, insigni corporis formâ conspicuus*—laboured under frequent attacks of disease, and died when he had not completed the age of forty-nine.[1] His ally in the controversy, Andrew Essen (1618-1677), a native of Bommel, in Guelderland, after receiving part of his education there, and completing it at the Gymnasium and University of Utrecht, presided for ten years over the Church in Nederlangbroek. He was transferred in 1651 to the Church of Utrecht, and in 1653 appointed also one of the Professors of Theology in the University. He published some systematic works in Theology, and treatises on particular doctrines and controversies. One of his latest efforts was an eloquent and affectionate tribute to the memory of his preceptor, Voetius.[2] Witsius, in his *Dissertations on the Creed*, says, "Whoever wishes to see the whole doctrine of Episcopius completely overthrown may consult the accurate and solid *Dissertation on the Subjection of Christ*, by Andrew Essenius, a man whom I venerate as my preceptor and father in the Lord."[3]

That a contest in which such men were engaged should call forth displays of erudition and talent was to be expected. The least meritorious of the publications which it elicited were perhaps those of Heidan. He appears to have performed his part with as much regard to his own ease as possible, the *Disputation* that made so much noise, containing in its fifty small pages nearly ten in succession of borrowed matter, without a single expression of acknowledgment, much less of thanks to the author, soon, indeed, to be, if not already, removed beyond the reach of this world's censure or praise.[4] The share of Cocceius was considerable, but its worth was not a little lessened by his fanciful views of Scripture. Hoornbeek and Essen, on the other hand, treated the Bible as a book of definite meanings, and as forming in its

[1] *Traj. Erudit.* p. 150, etc. Hoffman's *Dict.*, where, on the authority of *The Life of Hoornbeek*, it is mentioned that he knew ten languages, and a little of two others.—Fraser's *Witsius on the Creed*, vol. ii. p. 612.

[2] *Traj. Erudit.* p. 95, &c.

[3] *Dissert.* vii. sect. 23, in Fraser.

[4] The work so unceremoniously pillaged was the *Disput. de Die Dominico* of Louis Chapelle. See Brown's *Causa Dei, etc.*, vol. ii. p. 896; Koelman's *De Histoire*, pp. 289-293.

two great divisions of the Old and New Testaments a Divine revelation to mankind. Of the works produced on the occasion that have come under our notice, the most comprehensive and complete appears to be the *Dissertation* of Essen, which without prolixity exhausts the subject as then agitated; and by its rational scriptural views of the Fourth Commandment, as well as of the Decalogue at large, reminds us of the best Sabbatic writers of our own country. Nor were Hoornbeek and Essen less distinguished by the spirit than by the ability which they showed in the discussion. They deported themselves entirely as became ministers of the gospel and professors of theology. Heidan was bitter; his "sharpest" passages, indeed, were said to be those which he had plagiarized; but this fault he made, and there was little else in the property that he could make, really his own. Cocceius is querulous, and, in his reply to Paschasius, who charged him with following and favouring the Socinians in his Sabbatic views, wrathful. Although he was the decided opponent of Socinian, as he was of Arminian and Popish errors, yet the undue heat of the *Indignatio*, and the feeling of uneasiness betrayed by him in other parts of the discussion, bespeak misgivings as to the goodness of his arguments and cause. We wonder, indeed, that such a cause and its obvious fruits in the increasing profaneness of the people did not induce a person, who, according to Mosheim, was possessed of "piety in an eminent degree," to pause, and thenceforth eschew the folly of conceiving that men can have religion on other days, who do not devote one day in seven to its exclusive study, and that there is any guarantee for a weekly holy day but in the fact and belief that it is an express ordination of Heaven.[1]

Four years had hardly elapsed when there arose a fourth controversy, attributable to Francis Burmann, Professor of Theology and Pastor at Utrecht. For a time after his appointment to

[1] The spirit of partisanship descended from Cocceius to his son, who, in the preface to the collected works of the former, imputes the blame of the controversy to Hoornbeek and Essen, proving it by arguments amounting to this—"My father and his col league very innocently introduced the subject for discussion among the students, and, when found fault with by their opponents, who recklessly disregarded the peace of the Church in so doing, must reply to them, because 'neither was truth to be abandoned, nor reputation to be thrown away.'"

these offices in 1662 and 1664 respectively, he acted warily in regard to the Sabbath question, particularly in the pulpit. It was not long, however, till he proceeded openly to proclaim his views, which he did in June 1665, when, in course of lecturing on the second part of the Catechism, he spent a great part of his hour in attempting to prove that in the matter of sanctifying the Lord's day, we are bound not by the force of the Fourth Commandment, but by a custom and ordinance of the Church. Many were astonished and offended at his doctrine. To others it was acceptable as it "promised them liberty." The professors and ministers of Utrecht were aggrieved at so flagrant a departure from the principles which they had so cordially held. Essen was not slack to encounter the challenger. They engaged in a series of public disputations. Thus far we have followed Koelman.[1] From the publications issued on both sides, we find that the war was carried to the press, and learn the following particulars respecting it. Burmann published his *Disquisitio*. Essen answered in his Διαλυσις. In the *Vindiciæ Disquisitionis*, which next appeared, Burmann apprehending, as he said, that the debate would rival the fabled river of the Jews which flowed with untiring rapidity on all days but the Sabbath, declared that he laid down his pen, not to take it up again *nisi digniores vindice nodi occurrant*, as he envied no one, neither coveted the fancied victory of having the last word. Essen issued the *Vindiciæ Quarti Præcepti*, so thorough and elaborate a discussion of the whole question as fully to warrant him in declining any further *ex professo* reply. He did so, and kept his promise. The other, rather readily overcoming his dislike to the last word, came out again in *Apologia pro Vindiciis Disquisitionis*. When we consider that the whole controversy was comprised in the period of about a year, and prosecuted amidst many professorial and ministerial engagements, we are constrained to admire the activity and vigour of the two disputants, especially of Essen, now past his prime, one of whose replies forms a considerable volume, and who was contemporaneously employed in settling the arrears of his debate with Heidan. In addition to energy, the praise of superior acquirements must be conceded to both writers. But here the

[1] *De Histoire*, p. 300.

resemblance ends. While Essen brings independent thinking and sound judgment in aid of his cause, Burmann does little more than present in attractive form and maintain with dialectic skill the dogmas of the more original and learned though crotchety Cocceius. He, in other words, supports with elaborate buttresses, and graces with ornaments, a building which has no proper foundation, thus deceiving some on-lookers, and devolving on men like Essen and Owen, the labour of pulling down useless and dangerous fabrics, and of clearing away the rubbish, when they are about to erect what is solid and profitable. The celebrated English writer just named, referring to the discussion five years after it had taken place, says, that though the objections made to the doctrine of a moral sacred rest had been "solidly answered and removed," yet as "they had lately been renewed and pressed by a person of good learning and reputation," he would "give them a new examination and remove them out of his way." Many will agree with Owen that Essen effectually disposes of the arguments of Burmann, particularly in the *Vindiciæ Quarti Præcepti*, the value of which is enhanced by the evidence adduced in the latter half of the volume to establish the substantial harmony of the reformers and reformed churches, on the great question of a weekly holy day. In nothing has he the advantage over his opponent more than the meekness and calmness, of which, it has been said, he was a rare example. That his manifestly reverent regard to the eye of the Great Taskmaster should once and again express itself in the language of prayer was in perfect keeping with the other parts of his consistent character, and this, as well as other considerations, ought to have repressed the sneer uttered towards the close of the *Apologia*, "A prolix writing is concluded with prolix prayers." Of the sentences which follow that remark, and which insinuate, without positively making an application to Essen of the case in Ezek. xiv. 4, we will only say, that all readers of right feeling must be ashamed and indignant, that such language should be employed in reference to a minister of religion and a professor of theology, whose general character was irreproachable, and whose only apparent offence in the present instance was that he held too firmly and defended too ably the doctrine of a Christian Sabbath.

Essen's lack of service in taking no notice of the *Apology* of Burmann was supplied with remarkable ability. Matthew Crawford, who afterwards took an able and earnest part in the affairs of his native Scotland, having finished his course of the liberal arts at a Scottish university, applied his mind to theological studies, and having been captivated with the writings of the Belgic divines, on account of their signal erudition, and complete agreement in doctrine with his own Church and the Westminster Assembly, had a strong desire to place himself under the tuition of some of those distinguished men. He accordingly repaired to Belgium.[1] "When," he says, after visiting its cities, "I observed the Lord's day profaned by labour, markets, merchandize, and in other forms, I was struck with astonishment, for never had I seen the like in Britain. Nay, when I understood that some learned men in published writings very strenuously contended that the Lord's day was only of human and ecclesiastical obligation, and condemned its stricter and pious sanctification, opinions which I conceived to be the profane and licentious doctrine of Socinians, Anabaptists, and Enthusiasts, and altogether unknown to the doctors of the Reformed Church, I thought it nothing wonderful that the people profaned the Sabbath, and that the magistrates did not punish them, such things being instilled by pastors and teachers." Under the influence of these feelings, and differing from those who regarded the controversy as of small moment, Crawford wrote several "disputations" in defence of chap. 21, sect. 7, of the Westminster Confession, which he resolved to maintain under the presidency of Voet or Essen. In June 1669 he submitted to examination, in a discussion presided over by the latter, the proleptical theory of Genesis ii. 2, 3, which Professor Burmann not long before had publicly advocated. That individual, however, whose views were assailed, though without any mention of his name, employed his powerful influence successfully, to quash the discussion.[2] If Crawford spoke as he afterwards wrote, it was certainly not for the credit of the professor, or of his opinions, that it should proceed. That the interests of truth might not suffer, the silenced student wrote out his thoughts on the subject more fully, and published them. The

[1] Preface to his *Exercitatio*.

[2] *Ibid.*

volume[1] was dedicated, with much respect and affection, to Voetius, then in his eighty-first year, and to Essenius, Nethenus, and Leusden. Koelman said in 1685, that it had never, whether by Burmann, or any other, been answered.[2]

Another Scotsman, who had been resident in Holland since the spring of 1663, might already be engaged in preparing his voluminous work on the Sabbatic institution, which appeared four years after the *Exercitatio*. We refer to the celebrated Mr. John Brown of Wamphray. Having for his opposition to the restoration of Charles II. been ejected from his parish and imprisoned, he was, in consequence of his own representation, that his life was in danger from confinement in a damp cell, liberated on condition that he "obliged himself to remove and depart off the King's dominions, and not to return without license from his Majesty and Council under pain of death." This good and learned man passed his remaining days in Holland,—residing partly at Utrecht and partly at Rotterdam, enjoying the intimate friendship of Leydecker, Spanheim, Borstius, and à Brakel, by all of whom he was highly esteemed for his theological attainments,—and engaged in occasional preaching, corresponding with his friends in Scotland, and in writing and publishing useful works, which the above-mentioned and other friends did everything in their power to circulate. The resentment of Charles followed him, and obliged him in 1677 to leave Rotterdam, where, however, after a brief sojourn in Utrecht or its neighbourhood, he again resided till his death in 1679.[3] His principal, though least popular work, and, we should suppose, the largest ever published on the subject, is the *De Causâ Dei contra Anti-Sabbatarios Tractatus*, or, *Treatise on the Cause of God against the Anti Sabbatarians*, which appeared at Rotterdam in two volumes, the first in 1674, the second in 1676. Prefixed

1 *Exercitatio Apologetica*, etc., Sumptibus Autoris 1670.

2 *De Histoire*, p. 315. Crawford was the editor of a reprint of Welch's Reply to Gilbert Brown, under the title *Popery Anatomized*, and author of *A Discovery of the bloody, rebellious, and treasonable principles and practices of Papists*, both of which, with an interesting life of Welch, also by Crawford, appeared in 1672. Wodrow refers to him as preaching at a Communion administered at Kippen in 1676 in the night season, and as in 1679 taken on trials for ordination as minister of the parish of Eastwood (*Hist.* vol. ii. p. 318; iii. p. 24. Ed. by Burns), where he laboured for a considerable time, and was succeeded by Woodrow himself.

3 Steven's *Scot. Church, Rotterdam*, pp. 38, 69.

are approving notices by Professors Arnold of Franeker, Voet and Essen of Utrecht, and Spanheim of Leyden. In an epistle dedicatory to the Rotterdam authorities, Brown expresses similar views and feelings to those of Crawford, in reference to the prevalent profanation of the Sabbath in Holland, and the encouragement given to it by the inculcation in writings, catechisings, and sermons, of opinions such as he had never before heard "even from the mouths of the most profligate." He sets forth, in their own words, the sentiments of the ablest writers for and against the Sabbath as a moral, catholic, perennial, Divine institution. Hence the formidable extent of the treatise, and yet its inestimable value to those particularly who have not the means of consulting the original authors. Nor is it a mere compilation. Not the least important portions are the clear, able, and conclusive statements of Brown himself. Koelman says, that no part of it was answered by Burmann. Neither he, indeed, nor any other, could be expected to attempt a full reply to a work of such dimensions. But why has it been so little noticed by the supporters of adverse views! Have not some of them felt that it would injure their cause to remit inquirers to the convincing arguments of such a man, of whom in his lifetime it was said by one well acquainted with him, and well able to estimate his character: "I know no minister alive (though the residue of the Spirit be with Him) that would fill his room if he were removed;" and further, "If our captivity were this day returned, Mr. Brown, now removed from the Scottish congregation of Rotterdam, would by a General Assembly be pitched upon to fill the most famous place in the Church of Scotland."[1]

Among the Dutch friends of Brown was the Rev. James Koelman, who, as Dr. Steven informs us, had been ejected from his charge at Sluis in Flanders for refusing to observe the festival days and formularies of the Church, and subsequently devoted himself to the publication of religious books, most of which he dedicated to his former flock.[2] What entitles him to notice here is the important contribution which he made to the Sabbath controversy in three works or parts of works, one of them printed in 1683, the other two in 1685, and the whole collected in a volume

[1] *Ibid.* Letter of M'Ward, pp. 54, 55. [2] *Ibid.* pp. 72, 73, note.

under the common title, *The Argument, History, and Practice of the Sabbath and the Lord's Day.*[1] The work is second in magnitude only to that of Brown, and, like it, is a complete *thesaurus* on its subject. The arrangement of topics, which is indicated by the title, is happy, and each of them receives its distinct and proportionate attention. It has a novel feature of peculiar interest in the historical account which it supplies of opinions on the Sabbath, and of Sabbatic controversies in England and the Netherlands. Mr. Koelman died at Utrecht in 1695. Dr. Steven says, that he appears to have been a very conscientious, worthy man, and that, besides being the author of many original and useful publications, including one that had for its subject the festival days of the Reformed Church in the Netherlands, he is advantageously known as the able translator of Rutherford's *Letters*, and many other works, all of which have gone through several editions. By his means some of Brown's more popular writings were translated into Dutch, and circulated in Holland, previously to being printed in the English language.[2]

"The controversy," says Hengstenberg, "was kept up in Holland till the eighteenth century, but with greater calmness. However, the more liberal views gradually advanced, and became more and more prevalent throughout the reformed churches, with the exception of Great Britain."[3] But has not this advancing liberalism on the Continent been moral and political retrogression, while British conservatism in respect of the weekly rest has been national progress? Were not Holland's two centuries of greatest temporal glory "the most glorious centuries of her Protestantism," and of her Sabbath? And is not Holland, where there is more respect for Divine institutions than in neighbouring countries, the dwelling-place of a more virtuous and happy community than Belgium, France, or Germany?

1 *Het Dispuit, en de Historie*, etc.

2 *Scot. Ch., Rotterdam*, pp. 72, 73. It is remarkable that in this instructive work, Dr Steven makes no mention of the Sabbatic writings and efforts of Brown and Koelman.

3 *Lord's Day*, p. 70.

ENGLAND.

We now approach a new era in the Sabbatic literature of England. The doctrine of the Church, which was declared in 1562, and conclusively settled in 1571, recognised the Lord's day as the divinely appointed Sabbath of Christianity, and as having for its rule the fourth precept of the abiding Decalogue. This doctrine continued to be held in good faith, and publicly maintained, by a succession of learned, excellent ministers for upwards of half a century, only a few professedly religious men, and these of little comparative weight, daring formally to assail it. Such views were not peculiar to the Puritans, but were entertained by Babington, Hooker, Andrewes, Lord Bacon, Hall, and Bayly, as they were by Fulke, Cartwright, Travers, Greenham, Perkins, Bownd, and Willet.[1] Hooker, in 1597, enunciated the noble and oft-cited sentence, "We are to account the sanctification of one day in seven a duty which God's immutable law doth exact for ever."[2] About the same time, in his lectures at Cambridge, Andrewes was employed in bearing that testimony to the primæval origin, the morality, the permanence, and the entire sacredness of the weekly day of rest, which is to be found in his posthumous writings.[3] "God demands and segregates for himself," says Bacon, "a tenth of our substance, but a seventh of our time."[4] Hall, who in 1599 eulogized the *Treatise* of Greenham, was heard preaching in 1611 the doctrine of which these memorable words may be regarded as the sum :—"The Sun of righteousness arose upon the first day of the week, and drew the strength of God's moral precept into it."[5] And Lewis Bayly, Bishop of Bangor, taught, when minister at Evesham, and subsequently published in his *Practice of Piety*, views of the Sabbath as Puritanic as those of

[1] An interpretation of the articles and homilies, in which all those writers concurred, is much more likely to be true than that of Dr. Heylyn and Bishop White, who wrote after the *Second Declaration of Sports* had appeared, and by the command of its author.

[2] *Works* (1662), p. 280.

[3] Particularly his *Pattern of Catechistical Doctrine*. See Oxford edit. (1846), pp. 154 etc.

[4] *Adv. of Learning*, lib. 8, c. 2, *ad fin.*

[5] Letter to Lord Denny—*Works* (1837), vol. vi. p. 270.

Bownd.[1] But in a Church so trammelled by civil and hierarchical authority, there was little security for the purity of religious ordinances. We have seen how the Sabbatic institution had sometimes fared under Elizabeth and her ecclesiastical minions. A worse fate, however, awaited it under her successors, James I. and Charles I. Their reigns, indeed, began with strong enactments against certain profanations of the institution ; but, besides that these measures were favourable, virtually in the one instance, and avowedly in the other, to the desecration of holy time, by so-called lawful amusements, each reign was signalized by a *Book of Sports*, by growing severity against the friends of a sacredly observed Sabbath, and by the complacent regard with which the Court smiled on men of more flexible consciences, and of more congenial opinions. But the spirit of Puritanism was not extinct. It lived even under a crushing tyranny, which it soon acquired strength to shake off. And nothing perhaps contributed more to overturn "the throne of iniquity" than its framing of mischief against the holy Sabbath by a law.

In his Church History of Britain, Fuller assigns to 1632 the begun revival of "the Sabbatarian controversy," and represents Theophilus Bradborn [Brabourne], a minister of Suffolk [Norfolk], as having in 1628 "sounded the first trumpet to the fight." Brabourne, indeed, uttered in 1628 a few unheeded notes ; but various trumpets had previously sounded.

The first attempt to excite the overborne yet peace-loving Sabbatists to further controversy was made by Thomas Broad, rector of Retcomb, who in 1621 published his *Three Questions on the Fourth Commandment ;* but his instrument gave so tremulous and uncertain a sound as to evoke from Heylyn the taunt : "One Thom. Broad, of Gloucestershire, had published something in this kind ; wherein to speak my minde thereof, he rather shewed that he disliked those Sabbath doctrines than durst disprove them."[2]

1 This popular work had reached its eleventh edition by 1619, and its sixty-second in 1757. The dedication to the Prince of Wales, afterwards Charles I., is followed by the faithful and almost prophetic distich :—

Ad Carolum Principem.
Tolle Malos, extolle Pios, cognosce Teipsum :
Sacra tene ; Paci consule ; disce pati.

2 *Hist. of the Sab.* pt. ii. 263.

Mr. Broad was followed by Dr. John Prideaux, rector and theological professor of Exeter College, Oxford, and afterwards Bishop of Worcester. By a Latin oration delivered in 1622, given to the world along with other discourses in 1625, and published by Dr. Heylyn in an English translation, with a preface, in 1634, he contributed to hasten, and subsequently to exasperate the renewed strife. His "Italian trills" tickled the ears of the young men who were attracted from all quarters to the prelections of the very learned and fascinating professor, in whom they found the rare union of the zealous Protestant and Calvinist with the anti-Sabbatic Conformist; but the trumpet had a comparatively limited range, till the translator awoke it to intelligible English strains. The discourse itself is unworthy of its author. It is employed in setting aside, by dogmatic assertion rather than on assigned grounds, "the things most surely believed among" Christians generally respecting the Sabbatic institution, and in affirming, without a word as to where he got them, the propositions, that all recreations which serve to refresh our spirits and nourish mutual neighbourhood, are permitted on the Lord's day, and that to such recreations it is the exclusive right of the religious magistrate to prescribe bounds and limits.[1] Sad it was for an eminent teacher of theology to authorize liberties with the Lord's day, which the monarch himself declined to take,[2] and to publish *his* license for sports at a time when the Government, alarmed at "the quarrels, bloodsheds, and other great inconveniences," which such amusements had spread over the land, ordained that "no man should use unlawful pastimes in his own parish, or go out of it for any pastime whatsoever, on the day, "the holy keeping of which," as was well said, "is a principal part of the true service of God."[3] It was not in consequence of its own merit, but that he might compromise with the Puritans, and attach to the measures of the court, a man of note, as well as, it has been said, to indulge a personal grudge, that Heylyn was at the pains

[1] *Orat. Inaug.* (1648), p. 68.

[2] "His Majesty (Charles I.) is much delighted in hunting; it is a recreation mixt with manly exercise well becoming a king; but I heare he never useth to hunt on the Lord's day."—Twisse on the *Morality of the Fourth Commandment*, Preface, p. 4.

[3] Neale's *Feasts and Fasts*, pp. 230, 231.

to translate and epitomize the performance; and it was to neutralize the influence of such a name that Twisse, after construing some parts of the work favourably, as far as possible, to the Sabbath, overpowered with calm argumentation the remainder.[1]

A posthumous treatise, by Robert Cleaver, already mentioned as associated with John Dod in various publications, appeared in 1625, and again in 1630, under the title, "A Declaration of the Christian Sabbath: wherein the Sanctifying of the Lord's Day is proved to be agreeable to the Commandment of God, and to the Gospell of Jesus Christ. Whereunto is added a briefe Appendix touching the limits of the C. S., the Lord's Day: that it beginneth and endeth after Midnight, not after the Sunne Setting in the Evening."[2]

The example of the Rector of Exeter College was not without its re-inspiring influence on the Rector of Retcomb, who, after a lapse of six years, had acquired sufficient breath and nerve to emit, though in outlandish tones which he had not practised for years,[3] a bold defiance to the whole race of Sabbatarians. In a Latin treatise on the Sabbath, which appeared in 1627, Broad attempted, in opposition to clear Scripture, the creed of his Church, and the facts of history, to establish the propositions, that it is one thing for God to sanctify a day, and another to command its sanctification by men,—that weeks, a division of time bounded and constituted by the Sabbath, are not mentioned prior to the Exodus,—that as the Fourth Commandment, which was ceremonial, has been abrogated, it cannot bind us to the sanctification of the Lord's day, and could not so bind us even if it were in force; and though all pious and learned men, as far as he knew, were of the mind that the first day of the week should be sanctified, there is no command of Christ or of his apostles to that effect, no fault is found by them with those who neglect it, and no religion must be placed in the observance of times. It was a fitting result of the writings of Broad and Prideaux, that Dr. Robinson, afterwards Archdeacon of Gloucester, publicly main-

1 See *Morality of the Fourth Commandment*, p. 187, etc.

2 We have not read this volume, which, we suppose, is now rare. The title is given from the second edition, which we have seen in the Marsh Library, Dublin. Both editions are marked in the Catalogue of the Bodleian.

3 Ignoscat Lector stilo minus eleganti: annus enim jam agitur vicesimus quartus ex quo lingua Latina vel decem tantum lineas exaravi. *Tract de Sab. Præfatiunc.*

tained at Oxford in 1628 the thesis, that recreations on the Lord's day are not at all prohibited by the Word of God.[1]

Nor, as extremes meet, was it an unconnected sequence of writings, which explained away the Fourth Commandment, that Brabourne was excited to such zeal on its behalf as, in *A Discourse upon the Sabbath-day*, published in 1628, to urge the claims of the last day of the week to be accounted the Sabbath of Christians. This work seems to have come into any notice only in consequence of the celebrity which circumstances gave to a subsequent production of the same author. Brabourne, who followed Traske in his Sabbatarianism as he did in his retractations, if his equal in ability was his inferior in the qualities of the heart.

An attempt by Edward Brerewood, the first-appointed Professor of Astronomy in Gresham College, and a learned writer,[2] to engage the no less learned Nicholas Byfield, minister of St. Peter's Church, Chester, in a conflict on the subject, has not yet been mentioned, because, though the challenge and the assault belonged to the year 1611, they had not, as Fuller might say, become trumpet-tongued till 1630, when the parties had for some time been silent in the dust. In the latter year, an officious publisher issued *A Learned Treatise of the Sabaoth*, consisting of an angry epistle from Mr. Brerewood to Mr. Byfield, with a brief reply by the latter and a rejoinder by the former. The circumstances of this correspondence were singular. The Professor, deceived by a worthless nephew, who pretended that having been converted by Mr. Byfield to strict views of Sabbath-keeping, he could not conscientiously remain in a situation where he was required to perform certain unnecessary works on the Lord's day, wrote to the minister of St. Peter's a formidable letter extending in print to fifty quarto pages, in which he poured out bitter reproaches, maintained extraordinary opinions, and insisted that the man who had wronged him should give him the satisfaction of a rencounter, not certainly with rapiers, but, according to Fuller's expression, by "brandishing pens." Byfield, in his brief reply, repudiated the charges, disclaimed the obligation to "answere every stranger's

[1] Heylyn's *Hist. of the Sab.* Pt. ii. p. 263.

[2] He wrote *Enquiries touching the Diversity of Languages and Religions*, 1622; *De Ponderibus et Pretiis vet Nummorum*, 1614, with other works.

vaine challenge," and having declared his Sabbatic creed, declined the controversy. It appears, however, that the reiterated accusations, demands, and strange doctrines of the Professor, in his Rejoinder, had compelled the aggrieved minister to forego his purpose of silence, and that, according to the belief of his brother, an answer was in the hands of the publisher, who suppressed it.[1] When in these writings of Mr. Brerewood we find him indulging "proud wrath," and stoutly asserting, that the moral part of the Sabbath *became on Sinai* one of the perpetual words, not before; that it is incompatible with the goodness of God to give to a man a command which, through the wickedness of other men, he cannot keep without being punished for his obedience; and that as the Fourth Commandment is given to the master, not to the servant, the performance of secular work by the latter on the Lord's day in obedience to the order of the former is the sin not of the servant but of the master,—we may say, that however versant in astral matters, or in the old coins, languages, and even religions, of this lower world, he was not much at home on the subject of moral obligation, or eminently fitted by his studies or temper for religious controversy. It is but justice, however, to note that he felt relentings towards the good man, whom he had unworthily treated, and under whose ministry, with the excellent John Bruen as his fellow-worshipper, he occasionally sat; and that his second *Treatise on the Sabbath*, which appeared in 1632, though not improved in its sentiments, is free from the faults of heat and abuse which disfigured the first. As for Nicholas Byfield, he has the honour to belong to "a cloud of witnesses," who by their character have attested the truth of their Sabbatic opinions, which, like other opinions, are "known by their fruits." As a minister in Chester, and afterwards as vicar of Isleworth in Middlesex, where he died, "he was a constant, powerful, and useful preacher, a thorough Calvinist, a nonconformist to the ceremonies, and a strict observer of the Sabbath. By his zeal for the sanctification of the Lord's day, his labours in the ministry, and his exemplary life, religion flourished, many were converted, and Puritanism gained ground."[2] He was the author of Expository Sermons on

[1] R. Byfield's *Doctrine of the Sabbath Vindicated*, p. 191.
[2] Brook's *Puritans*, vol. ii. p. 297.

the Epistle to the Colossians and other parts of Scripture, which obtained for him a place in the *Ecclesiastes* of Bishop Wilkins, among the most eminent of our English commentators and writers on "Practical Divinity."[1]

An ample and able reply to Brerewood made its appearance in 1631, under the title of "*The Doctrine of the Sabbath Vindicated*, by Richard Byfield, pastor in Long Ditton in Surrey." The author was half-brother of Nicholas, and one of the 2000 ministers who were ejected in 1662. Referring to "The Learned Treatise," he says, "When I first received this booke, a little before November last, though I was utterly ignorant of any such controversie to have passed between my brother and Master Edward Breerwood, and had not yet cast mine eye on the base language of the reply in the end of the Treatise, yet the very noveltie, and dangerous vilnesse of the doctrine, without any reference to things personall, strucke me. My spirit was stirred in me, when I saw the whole right of the Law for the time of God's worship alleviated, the consequence whereof must needs be this, the whole kingdome wholy given to Atheisme and profanenesse." He proceeds to show, that the Fourth Commandment is given to the servant and not to the master only; that the commandment is moral; that our own light works, as well as gainful and toilsome, are forbidden on the Sabbath; that the Lord's day is of Divine institution; and that the Sabbath was instituted from the beginning; doctrines to be found in the Homilies, and in the almost universal creed of Christendom.

The intrepid, if not always discreet Henry Burton, rector of St. Matthew's, Friday Street, London, had published several works against Popery, for which he was subjected in every instance to trouble by the ruling prelates, and in one of the cases, to suspension from his benefice. But the man who, referring to his various citations before Laud, could say, "I was not at any time before him, but methought I stood over him as a schoolmaster over his schoolboy, so great was the goodness of God upon me,"[2] was not to be deterred by any danger from contending for the sanctity and Divine authority of the Sabbath, which he did in *The Law and*

[1] *Eccles.* [1693], pp. 97, 101, 108.
[2] *A Narration of the Life of Mr. Henry Burton*, p. 7.

the Gospel Reconciled (1631), and in *Sermons for God and the King* (1636). Among the charges brought against him in the High Commission were these: that he had spoken against the putting down of afternoon sermons on the Lord's day, and against the setting up of crucifixes. It was on account of such acts as these, by which he sought to stem the tide of corruption in the Church and State, and not on account of disaffection to the Government, for he loved his King and the Constitution, that he was condemned to a series of grievous wrongs, and, along with Prynne and Bastwick, to savage indignities, which it is impossible even to read of without horror.

It was not in 1628, as Fuller states, but in 1632, that Theophilus Brabourne "set forth a book, dedicated to his Majesty, entitled, *A Defence of that most Ancient and Sacred Ordinance of God's, the Sabbath-day.*" This was a larger work than his *Discourse* of 1628 on the same subject; and if the author on neither occasion "sounded the first trumpet to the fight," he yet, by his second publication, blew a blast in the ear of royalty itself, which compelled attention, and provoked immediate as well as lasting hostilities. In the *Defence*, after laying down the position, that the Fourth Commandment is simply and entirely moral, containing nothing legally ceremonial in whole or in part, and ought therefore, in its full force and virtue, to be obeyed to the world's end, he proceeds to affirm that the Saturday, or seventh day of the week, ought to be an everlasting holy day in the Christian Church, the religious observation of which day obligeth Christians under the Gospel, as it did the Jews before the coming of Christ, and that the Sunday, or Lord's day, is an ordinary working day, which it is superstition and will-worship to make the Sabbath of the Fourth Commandment. "I am tied in conscience," were his words, "rather to depart with my life than with this truth; so captivated is my conscience and enthralled to the law of my God."[1] The "pride," however, which was thus confident, "went before a fall." He was called before the Court of High Commission, where, according to Bishop White, "there was yeelded unto him a deliberate, patient, and full hearing, together with a satisfactory answer to all his maine objections."[2] The result of this, and of

[1] *Defence*, Dedication, p. 1. [2] *Treatise of the Sabbath Day*, Dedication, p. 24.

a private conference, was a confession made in "a publike and honourable audience," that "his position touching the Saturday Sabbath was a rash and presumptuous error," and "the Sunday, or Lord's day, is an holy day of the Church, yea, and a most ancient holy day, and very honourable," with a humble submission unto his holy Mother, the Church of England, and the promise, "I will ever hereafter carry myselfe as an obedient sonne, in all peaceable and dutifull behaviour to my Mother the Church, and to the godly fathers and governors thereof."[1] It was a confirmation of the proverbial ardour of new converts, that the penitent had scarcely left the Commission, when he handed to one of its members a breviate, charging the Puritans with having led him astray, a charge which the bishop was not slack to re-echo, both he and Brabourne himself being willing that the latter, though a man of no mean parts, should pass for a simpleton, in order to excite against a harmless but hated class the already overheated zeal of the authorities.[2] There was something suspicious in such a conversion. A partial writer says all that could be said in its justification, and it is little: "For some reason, it is not possible to ascertain distinctly what, though probably he was overawed by the character of the assembly, he signed a recantation, and went back to the bosom of the Church. Nevertheless, he continued to assert, that if the Sabbatic institution be indeed moral and perpetually binding, the seventh day ought to be sacredly kept."[3] We are informed by Dr. Collinges of what appear to have been the latest opinions of Brabourne, who, he says, "came to assert three Gods, and grew to keep no Sabbath, making bargains, etc., on his Sabbath."[4]

We may here adopt the words of Fuller: "Pass we now from the pen to the practical part of the Sabbatarian difference. Somersetshire was the stage whereon the first and fiercest scene thereof was acted. Here wakes (much different, I daresay, from the watching prescribed by our Saviour) were kept on the Lord's day, with church-ales, bid-ales, and clerk's-ales." The wakes had their origin in the festivals instituted in memory of the dedication of churches, and were kept on the Lord's day before or after the

[1] *Treatise of the Sabbath Day*, pp. 305-7.
[2] *Ibid*, pp. 307, 308.
[3] Davy's *Hist. of the Sabbatar. Churches*, p. 127.
[4] *Modest Plea*, p. 74.

memorial-day of the saint to whom the churches were dedicated, because the people had not leisure to observe them on the week-days. The object of church-ales was to raise money for repairing churches, and for the poor by means of benevolences collected after divine service at pastimes in the churchyard, or at drinkings and merry-makings in the public-house. Clerk-ales were for behoof of the parish-clerk, to whose house the parishioners sent provisions, and then came on Sundays to feast with him, "whereby he sold more ale." A bid-ale was a Sunday's feast, at which contributions were made by his friends for the setting-up again of some decayed brother.[1]

In 1631, while going the Western Spring Circuit, the Lord Chief-Justice (Sir Thomas Richardson) and Baron Denham, were importuned by the gentry in Somersetshire "to make a severe order for the suppressing of all ales and revels on the Lord's day." They accordingly issued such an order, requiring the minister of each parish to publish it on three several Sundays every year. On "the return of the circuit," Judge Richardson punished certain persons who had violated the order, and gave a second strict charge against the revels. Laud complained to the King of the judge's proceedings as an invasion of the episcopal jurisdiction, whereupon Richardson was summoned before the Council. Although he pleaded that the order was issued at the request of the justices of the peace, with the consent of the whole Bench, and adduced precedents in the reigns of Elizabeth, James, and Charles himself, in vindication of his conduct, he received a reprimand, and was peremptorily enjoined to revoke his order at the next assizes, which he complied with, he said, "as much as in him lay." In a letter to Pierce, Bishop of Bath and Wells, requiring further information respecting the manner in which the church-feasts were "ordered," Laud observed, "While his majesty conceives, and that very rightly, that all outrages or disorders at those feasts may and ought to be prevented by the care of the justices of the peace, the feasts themselves ought to be kept for the neighbourly meeting and recreation of the people, of which he would not have them debarred under any frivolous pretences." The bishop, in his reply, stated, that the suppression of the feasts was very unacceptable,

[1] Bishop Pierce, in Neal's *Puritans* (1837), vol. i. pp 559, 560.

and that the restitution of them would be very grateful to the gentry, clergy, and common people; mentioned that he had "procured the hands of seventy-two of his clergy" in their favour, and might have had a hundred more, but was satisfied with the number, being that of the translators of the Old Testament into Greek, and recommended the Sunday recreations; because, besides other reasons, they brought the people more willingly to church, tended to civilize them, and compose differences, and served to increase love and beneficence. On the other hand, the justices of the peace addressed a petition to the King for the suppression of the revels, which, they said, had introduced not only a great profanation of the Lord's day, but riotous tippling, contempt of authority, quarrels, murders, with other evils, and were very prejudicial to the peace, plenty, and good government of the country.[1] "Here," according to Neal, "we observe the laity petitioning for the religious observation of the Lord's day, and the bishop, with his clergy, pleading for the profanation of it."[2] Laud was raised to the primacy, August 16, 1633. His letter to Bishop Pierce was dated October 4th of the same year. And a fortnight had not elapsed ere the *Second Declaration of Sports* appeared.

This document, after narrating the grounds and proceedings of James in issuing his Declaration of 1618, and repeating the Declaration itself word for word, says, "Now out of a like pious care for the service of God, and for suppressing of any humors that oppose truth, and for the ease, comfort, and recreation of our well-deserving people, we do ratify and publish this our blessed father's Declaration; the rather because of late in some counties of our kingdom, we find that under pretence of taking away abuses, there hath been a general forbidding, not only of ordinary meetings, but of the feasts of the dedication of the churches, commonly called wakes. Now, our express will and pleasure is, that these feasts, with others, shall be observed, and that our justices of the peace, in their several divisions, shall look to it, both that all disorders there may be prevented or punished, and that all neighbourhood and freedom, with manlike and lawful exercises, be used. And we farther command our justices of assize in their several circuits, to see that no man dare trouble or molest any of our loyal and

[1] Fuller and Neal, under A.D. 1633. [2] Neal (1837), vol. i. p. 560.

dutiful people, in or for their lawful recreations, having first done their duty to God, and continuing in obedience to us and our laws. And of this we command all our judges, justices of the peace, as well within liberties as without, mayors, bailiffs, constables, and other officers, to take notice of and to see observed, as they tender our displeasure. And we farther will, that publication of this our command be made, by order from the bishops, through all the parish churches of their general dioceses respectively. Given at our Palace of Westminster the eighteenth day of October, in the ninth year of our reign. God save the King."[1]

The Declaration "struck the sober part of the nation with a kind of horror; and the severe pressing of it made sad havoc among the Puritans for seven years." While some of the clergy devolved the publishing of the document on their curates, and others, after reading it, pronounced the words of the Fourth Commandment, or preached against the profanation of the Lord's day, a large class, estimated at 800, positively refused to pollute their lips with the utterance of the order, and were in consequence suspended, driven from their livings, excommunicated, prosecuted in the Court of High Commission, or forced to leave the kingdom.[2] Let one case show the manner in which that foolish and wicked edict, having an archbishop for its most zealous abettor and most effective executioner, if not its instigator, was employed as an engine of oppression and mischief against innocent men, and many of the best of England's ministers. It is the case of Thomas Wilson, A.M., minister of Otham, in Kent, so admirable a specimen of his class as might have drawn from any bishop possessed of a spark of religion or common sense, the aspiration as to his clergy, *O si sic omnes!* On declining to read the Declaration, Mr. Wilson was sent for to Lambeth, when he was examined on this among various charges: "You refused to read the King's Declaration for Sports on Sundays, and spoke disdainfully to the apparitor and officer of the Court." His reply was, "I said to the apparitor, 'Remember the Sabbath-day to keep it holy;' and I said no more. I refused to read the book, not out of contempt of any authority, being commanded by no law. The King's Majesty doth not in the book command or appoint the minister to

[1] Wilk. *Concil.* vol. iv. pp. 483, 484.

[2] Neal (1837), vol. i. pp. 561-564.

read it, nor it to be read, but published. And seeing there is no penalty threatened, nor authority given to any one to question those who refuse to read it, my refusal to read it was upon sufficient grounds of law and conscience ; which, for the satisfaction of this high Court, and to clear myself from contempt, I shall briefly express thus : His Majesty's express pleasure is, that the laws of the realm, and the canons of the Church, be observed in all places of the kingdom, and therefore at Otham, in Kent ; but this book, as I conceive, is contrary to both. It is contrary to the statute laws ; it is contrary to the ecclesiastical laws ; it is contrary to the Scriptures ; it is contrary to the Councils ; it is contrary to divines, ancient and modern ; it is contrary to reason." No sooner was this part of the defence concluded, than the Archbishop said, "I suspend you for ever from your office and benefice till you read it ;" and Mr. Wilson continued suspended for the space of four years.[1] It has been said of this excellent man : "What he preached on the Lord's day he practised all the week. He was a strict observer of the Sabbath, and eminently successful in promoting the same practice among his people at Maidstone, as well as at other places, one of the judges having publicly declared, that in all his circuit there was no town where the Lord's day was so well observed."[2]

The wrongs and sufferings of hundreds of Puritan ministers were not the only or greatest mischief of a Declaration, which, setting at nought the Sabbatic doctrine and law of the Church, and being, in fact, as it has been termed, a royal invitation to the people to give themselves up to dissipating, riotous, and intemperate diversions on a day sacred to sobriety, did incalculable damage to the religion and morals of the land. In the year of its publication, Richard Baxter, then a youth, resided at Whitehall with Sir Henry Newport, Master of the Revels, having been persuaded to try his fortune at Court ; but being entertained there with a play instead of a sermon on the Lord's-day afternoons, and hearing little preaching except what was against the Puritans, he found a month's experience of Court life sufficient, and retired with disgust.[3] His account is confirmed by the *Strafford Letters*,

[1] Brook's *Lives of the Puritans*, vol. iii pp. 174, 175.

[2] *Ibid.*

[3] Orme's *Life of Baxter*, p. 14.

where we have the following picture : "The French and Spanish Ambassadors were both at the King's mask, but not received as ambassadors. The French sat among the ladies, the Spanish in a box. It was performed on a Sunday night. My Lord Treasurer Juxon was there by command." [1]

When the Court and the clergy thus took the lead in breaking down the barriers of religion, what was to be expected but a general flood of impiety ? "I cannot forget," says Baxter, "that in my youth, in those late times, when we lost the labours of some of our conformable, godly teachers for not reading the *Book of Sports* and dancing on the Lord's day, one of my father's own tenants was the town-piper, hired by the year (for many years together), and the place of the dancing assembly was not an hundred yards from our door. We could not, on the Lord's day, either read a chapter, or pray, or sing a psalm, or catechize, or instruct a servant, but with the noise of the pipe and tabor, and the shoutings in the street continually in our ears. Even among a tractable people we were the common scorn of all the rabble in the streets ; and called Puritans, precisians, and hypocrites, because we rather chose to read the Scriptures, than to do as they did, though there was no savour of nonconformity in our family. And when the people, by the book, were allowed to play and dance out of public service time, they could so hardly break off their sports, that many a time the reader was fain to stay till the piper and players would give over. Sometimes the morris-dancers would come into the church in all their linen, and scarfs, and antic-dresses, with morris-bells jingling at their legs ; and, as soon as common-prayer was read, did haste out presently to their play again." [2]

Such was the baneful influence of a book, which, though replete with neither argument nor eloquence, yet, as the word of a king, had power. Scarcely, however, had "this practical part of the Sabbatarian difference" commenced, when the Government saw that authority must, if possible, be sustained by means of the press. Learned ecclesiastics were accordingly employed to write in vindication of the measures of the Court. And they were not slow to do the bidding of their superiors ; hence there

[1] Vol. ii. p. 148

[2] *Practical Works* (1838), vol. iii. p. 906.

rose up together, or in rapid succession, a class of authors whose writings perverted the doctrine, and gave a new tone to the literature of the Sabbath.

Among the foremost was the noted Dr. Peter Heylyn, who issued, in 1634, his already-mentioned translation of Prideaux's *Oration*, and, in 1635, his *History of the Sabbath*, which, though extending to 450 quarto pages, "was written, printed, and presented to the King in less than four months."[1] In this work the author traces the alleged Notices of the Institution from the 2d chapter of Genesis down to the Declaration of Charles I., gathering in his course proofs, as he presumes, that the Sabbath was unknown in the world till it was given to the Jews, who neither observed nor regarded it as a moral precept; that, at the destruction of their temple by the Romans, it was abrogated with other ceremonies; and was, by the few Gentiles who took notice of it, known only to be derided; while the Lord's day had no other authority than the voluntary consecration of it to religious uses by the Church, rose gradually, by means of edicts, canons, and decretals, to the esteem it enjoys, and may, when not employed in public worship, be spent in all such business and pleasures as are lawful in themselves, and not forbidden by the existing civil power.

In his *Life of Archbishop Laud*, Heylyn informs us that, while "the practical and historical part" was assigned to "Heylyn of Westminster, who had gained some reputation for his studies in the ancient writers," "the argumentative and scholastical was referred to the right learned Dr. White, then Bishop of Ely, who had given good proof of his ability in polemical matters in several books and disputations against the Papists."[2] Dr. White himself, who published his *Treatise of the Sabbath* in 1635, states in the Dedication to Laud, that he had, by his Grace's direction, obediently performed in the publication what was commanded by his sacred Majesty, whose will it was that a treatise should be set forth in counteraction of those principles, commonly preached, printed, and believed throughout the kingdom, on which Brabourne had grounded his arguments. It showed "method in their madness" that the authors and defenders of the *Book of*

[1] Vernon's *Life of Heylyn*, p. 88.

[2] Page 296.

Sports sought to cover their opposition to those generally received "principles," in other words, to the doctrine of Bownd and of the Homilies, under the pretext that such doctrine led, by necessary consequence, to opinions so extreme and unpopular as those of the Sabbatarian just named. While White has much in common with Heylyn, it is only just to him to say that he admits an obligation of "equity" on Christians in the Fourth Commandment, "argues the apostolical institution of the Lord's day from its immediate universal adoption," and states, that to devote it wholly to religion is "a work of grace and godliness pleasing and acceptable to God."[1] His Treatise has been called the most learned production of the time on its subject, yet, both in the work itself, and in a defence of it against an able anonymous reply, he deals so largely in undignified abuse as not only to evince very slender attainments in self-government, but to betray the fact and the consciousness that his cause was as weak in the moral, as it was strong in the physical force, by which it was supported. "I turned over the leaves both of the Bishop's and D. Heylyn's book," says "the pious and profoundly learned" Joseph Mede, writing to Dr. Twisse in April 1636, "when they came newly out, that I might see their principles and the way they went: further I am not acquainted with them; because I took no pleasure neither in their conclusions nor in their grounds, which, if they be urged, would overthrow a great deal more than they are aware of."[2]

Drs. Heylyn and Francis White were followed by Dr. Pocklington, whose *Sunday no Sabbath: a Sermon*, after passing, what was to him, the easy ordeal of the licenser, in the earlier part of 1635, was preached by the author in August of the same year, and, according to the copy before us, had reached its second edition from the press by 1636. In 1640, the Long Parliament committed a blunder, to say the least, when it condemned the Sermon, with the *Altare Christianum*, another product of the doctor's pen, to be publicly burnt in the city of London and the two Universities, by the hands of the common hangman—a fate inappropriate to performances which otherwise would have found their way to their native obscurity.

[1] *Treatise*, pp. 255, 256.

[2] *Works* (1672), p. 839.

It does not appear whether *A Sovereign Antidote against Sabbatharian Errors,* "by a reverend, religious, and judicious divine," printed in 1636, came out under the sanction of its author, Dr. Sanderson, who had written and sent it in a manuscript letter to a Mr. Th. Sa. of Nottinghamshire, in the year 1634. It has been published at different times with the name of the writer in his *Cases of Conscience.* From a comparison of this tract with previous and subsequent works of Dr. Sanderson, it should seem that his views of the subject fluctuated; and it has been supposed that, in his case as in that of Hammond, the influence of the primate prevailed over the judgment of the individual.[1] The following words of the tract in question give countenance to the latter view, and, at all events, show a truckling to the powers that were, unworthy of the man who wrote them: "In this matter, touching Recreations to be used on the Lord's day, much need not be said, there being little difficulty in it, and his Majesty's last Declaration in that behalf having put it past Disputation. Those Recreations are the meetest to be used, which give the best refreshing to the body, and leave the least impression in the mind; in which respect, shooting, leaping, pitching the bar, stool-ball, etc., are rather to be chosen than dicing, carding, etc."[2]

Two other works of similar views belong to the same year. One of them is *A Treatise of the Sabbath and the Lord's Day,* by David Primerose, minister of the Protestant Church at Rouen. It was "Englished out of his French MS." by his father, Dr. Gilbert Primerose, a Scotsman who had been for some time a minister at Bordeaux, but now presided over a French congregation in London. If among works of the class and time the Treatise of Bishop White excelled in learning, and Dr. Heylyn's History was a prodigy of energetic application, the publication of Mr. Primerose must be regarded as bearing away the palm for a thorough-going heartless determination to explain away everything that makes for a holy and beneficent Sabbath. The other work is *A Discourse of the Sabbath and the Lord's Day,* by Christopher Dow, B.D., who was willing, he says, it should see the

[1] James's *Four Sermons on the Sacraments and Sabbath,* p. 259.
[2] *Eight Cases of Conscience* (1674), pp. 16, 17.

light, "considering that the brevity of it might make it passe and find favour with some, and that being of a mean straine, it might better meete with common capacities than larger and more elaborate tractates." The writer, we trust, did not know, though he ought to have known, that this was the language of self-gratulation on the honour of contributing in any measure to the overthrow of one of the best bulwarks of Christianity and his country. When we add the *Seven Questions of the Sabbath*, by Gilbert Ironside, B.D., and Dr. Heylyn's *Brief and Moderate Answer* to Mr. Henry Burton, both printed in 1637, we nearly complete, so far as we know, the list of original publications in defence of the Declaration of Sports, that appeared from 1632 to 1638, or, we might say, to 1650, twelve years of that period being a blank in anti-Sabbatic literature.

It takes not a little from the credit of these champions of Sabbath amusements, that men of other views, many of whom were both able and willing, had no liberty, either from pulpit or press, to expound their opinions. For recommending from the pulpit, in opposition to the Treatise of Bishop White, the sacred observance of the Lord's day, Mr. George Walker, a London rector, was convened before the Primate, and received canonical admonition.[1] And his having spoken against the putting down of afternoon sermons on the Lord's day was one of a few, not more heinous, acts for which Mr. Henry Burton was condemned to imprisonment and horrible mutilation of his person. Apart from its danger, the publication of writings favourable to the Sabbath was impeded by difficulties almost insurmountable. Some two or three tracts by Prynne, one by Burton, and a new edition of Sprint's Propositions formed, accordingly, the amount of force which was brought to bear against the attacks of the numerous publications, great and small, on the other side. The authors of these publications were, in some instances, ungenerous enough to twit an unlicensed opponent, who some way or other was enabled to give his sentiments to the world through the press, with the contraband character of his literary wares; an argument feeble for every other purpose than to quicken the vigilance of the authorities.

[1] *Athen. Oxon.* vol. i. p. 480.

It was another material deduction from the glory of the anti-Sabbatic writers in question, and from the weight of their opinions, that they were bound together and to a common cause by the spell of one gifted, unscrupulous, and resolute spirit. The dedications, the courtly eulogies, and in some instances the avowal of royal command or of archiepiscopal authority, as their reason for writing, pointed to Laud as the ruling star. But this subject more fitly falls to be treated by a clergyman of the Church of England. "It will readily be believed, that the opinion which was adopted by the energetic mind of Laud, soon found other kindred spirits to support it: accordingly at this time there rose up an host of men, who will ever be ranked among our ablest divines, and who all seemed to follow his course: Bishops White and Bramhall, and Jeremy Taylor, and Sanderson, with Dr. Hammond, and, though last, perhaps not least, Dr. Barrow." The objection, he observes, is not to the statement of duty as made by these great theologians, but to their rejection of the ground on which it truly rests, all of them regarding the Fourth Commandment as a Jewish and temporary ordinance, and all, except White, denying the apostolical institution of the Lord's day. After attributing "this agreement in deviation from the generally-received opinion" in some measure to "the extravagance of the Sabbatarians," he thus proceeds: "Something, too, must be ascribed to the influence of friendship, and the mutual interchange of thought, if we consider how they were all connected together. Bramhall went into Ireland with his patron, Lord Strafford; White was the friend, Taylor the chaplain of Archbishop Laud, by whom also Sanderson was recommended to the royal favour; Hammond was the friend of Sanderson; and though Barrow was of a somewhat later day, in his early life distress occasioned by the civil war made him indebted for his education to the generosity of Dr. Hammond."[1] This line of remark may be extended to other less distinguished members of the fraternity. Dr. Heylyn, it is well known, was the *protégé* of the Primate. Drs. Pocklington and G. Primerose were king's chaplains. Christopher Dow, says even Wood, "was much favoured by Dr. Laud, Archbishop of Canterbury (whose creature and champion he was), and by him promoted to several ecclesi-

[1] James's *Four Sermons*, pp. 252 257.

astical benefices."[1] Primerose, the son, had been the admiring and admired pupil of Prideaux. Ironside, indeed, Wood informs us, was "never chaplain to any spiritual or temporal lord, or to any king or prince." His views, he himself says, were formed and declared many years before the King's declaration was published and his preferments to a prebend and bishopric, we may add, came after services rendered by him to the Government. But he, too, was a humble, if not a "hungry expectant of office," when, in dedicating the "Seven Questions" to Laud, he besought his Grace "to receive both the work and the author into his patronage and protection," and added a prayer for "our Aaron, as if the Jewish "high priest" and "saint" were a type in anything, except in the worship of the golden calf, of a person who, so far from being "a lover of good men," was the leader of a class whose deeds Sir B. Rudyerd thus described and denounced in Parliament:—"We have seene Ministers, their Wives, Children, and Families undone, against law, against conscience, against all bowels of compassion, about not dancing upon Sundayes. What doe these sort of men think will become of themselves, when the Master of the house shall come, and finde them thus beating their fellow-servants?"[2]

The Primate and his friends had now, as far as they could, reduced the Sabbatic institution to a nullity. And this was only one of many wrongs, which drove thousands of families to foreign shores, till, by an Act of the King and Council, even this relief from oppression was precluded to its victims. But the year 1640 came, and along with it the exhaustion of the country's patience under protracted misrule. The Parliament assembled in November, and declaring its sittings permanent, proceeded vigorously to its Herculean task of reformation. To the Sabbath it rendered some important services; bringing to light the melancholy extent to which clerical ungodliness and profligacy, Trentine errors, and the want of religious teaching, prevailed in the Church, whereby were demonstrated the folly and wickedness of Laud's Anti-Sabbatic policy; passing several Acts for enforcing existing Statutes relative to the observance of the Lord's day, the members consistently exemplifying the law in their own practice; securing for

[1] *Athen. Oxon.* vol. i. p. 840.

[2] *Speeches and Passages of this Great and Happy Parliament*, pp. 103, 104.

the friends of the day freedom to proclaim their views regarding it from pulpit and press without fear of the Star Chamber, the High Commission, imprisonment, confiscation of goods, or bodily mutilation; and calling together the Westminster Assembly, thus eliciting one of the clearest and most important testimonies ever borne to the Divine authority, perpetual obligation, and sacred character of the Weekly Rest.

Of their new-born liberty several learned and excellent men speedily availed themselves to pour out through the press their Sabbatic stores. No less than eleven treatises, for the most part of considerable extent, and of no ordinary ability, appeared on behalf of the institution in the course of 1641. Two of them—a reprint of the *Pattern of Catechistical Doctrine*, by Bishop Andrewes, and the *Theses De Sabbato*, by Bishop Lake—were posthumous. The authors of the other works were Hamon, son of Sir Hamon L'Estrange; Dr. George Hakewill, Rector of Exeter College, Oxford; Richard Bernard, the laborious Rector of Batcombe; Dr. William Gouge, the pious and accomplished minister of Blackfriars, London; John Ley, rector successively of various parishes, who, in *Sunday a Sabbath*, one of two treatises published by him, was assisted by the MSS. and advice of Archbishop Ussher; George Abbot, a member of the Long Parliament, as well as a minister of the gospel; George Walker, Rector of St. John the Evangelist, already referred to; and Dr. William Twisse, minister of Newbury, a native of its neighbourhood, and Prolocutor of the Westminster Assembly. *The Morality of the Fourth Commandment* is perhaps the ablest treatise of the year 1641, and one which deserves ever to rank high amongst works of its class. A profound thinker, and an accomplished debater, Dr. Twisse was no less distinguished as a Christian, who, there is good reason to trust, now enjoys the begun realization of his hope as thus expressed when he was about to die: "Now I shall have leisure to pursue my studies to all eternity." The value of his work, intrinsically great, is enhanced by the already-mentioned sententious and pithy performance of Bishop Lake, which is appended to it. This learned prelate concludes the *Theses* by saying, that while cherishing charity for those who differed from him, and desiring for all the sobriety of judgment commended in Rom. xiv., yet "seeing to fetch the authority of the Lord's day from God, and to keepe it with all reasonable strictnesse, maketh most for piety—in a doubtfull case I incline thither."

While the admirable testimony of the Westminster Assembly on the subject of the Sabbath, to be presented in another part of this volume, had not yet appeared, certain writers conceived that in the works which had been recently published, numerous and excellent though these were, justice had not been done to an institution so outrageously wronged by the measures of Charles I. and Laud.[1] In addition to the ingenious treatise of Irenæus Philalethes in 1643, and a work by John Lawson in the following year, there appeared one of the largest, ablest, and most satisfactory discussions which the subject ever received, belonging, the first volume to 1645, the second to 1652. The authors, Daniel Cawdrey and Herbert Palmer, were distinguished members of the Westminster Assembly, by whose order, it has been said, the *Sabbatum Redivivum* was written. Palmer having in 1647, "gone to celebrate the Sabbatism above," it was left to the other to "put the last hand and file" to the work. It is stated in the Preface that they had prepared their MS. when "nothing had appeared for, but all against, the Sabbath," and that they were dissatisfied with former writers for either regarding the Saturday Sabbath as literally enjoined in the Fourth Commandment, thereby "losing their cause and the commandment too," or not sufficiently confuting the opinion. Palmer and Cawdrey were followed by John White, "the Patriarch of Dorchester," in a valuable dissertation of 1647; by Hezekiah Woodward in 1648; and by Thomas Shepard (1649), whose excellent volume will fall to be again noticed.

The opponents of the Sabbatic doctrine of the Puritans and of the Homilies had now for thirteen years been mute on the subject,

[1] From the following views expressed by Charles, it may be inferred that the Anti-Sabbatic measures of Laud formed no exception to the matters in which, according to Echard and Clarendon, the prelate had the hearty concurrence of the king: "I conceive the celebration of this feast [Easter] was instituted by the same authority which changed the Jewish Sabbath into the Lord's day or Sunday. For it will not be found in Scripture where Saturday is discharged to be kept, or turned into Sunday; wherefore it must be the Church's authority that changed the one and instituted the other."—Morer's *Dialogues*, p. 58.

constrained to silence for the greater part of that time, probably, by a fear of the treatment which befel Pocklington and Bray.[1] But at length encouraged by the state of feeling and of parties that followed the death of Charles I., an anonymous writer, who afterwards gave his name as Edward Fisher, Esq., craved to be heard, affirming and proving that Christmas day and the Lord's day are institutions of equal weight and authority, and that it is no less sinful to work on the former than on the latter day. The performance gave rise to a full and learned vindication of the Sabbath by Giles Collier, Vicar of Blockley, against the attempt to degrade it to the level of a human appointment; and to a publication by John, afterwards Dr. Collinges of Norwich, exposing the error of raising Christmas to the dignity of a divine institution. After a remarkable tract by Thomas Chafie, Vicar of Nutshelling, reprinted in 1692 with a recommendation by Bates and Howe; an interesting practical work by Philip Goodwin, "Pastour of the publike congregation, Watford;" a learned Latin dissertation by Dr. Henry Wilkinson, and publications by Prynne and Pynchon, all in favour of the Sabbath, there appeared in 1657, *The Judgment* of Ussher on that and other points, in which we are favoured with a long and erudite letter of the Archbishop to Dr. Twisse, upholding the doctrine of the Irish Articles. To this work, edited by Dr. Nicholas Bernard, Dr. Heylyn replied in his *Petrus Respondet*, displaying in the renewed effort to destroy the institution all his old zeal, and more than his former subtlety. Regardless of the Doctor's sophisms, Pearson, afterwards Bishop of Chester, proclaimed, in his *Exposition of the Creed* (1659), the common-sense view of the Sabbath, which, when the dust raised by what was really a faction in the Church had been well-nigh blown away, was seen to be the general creed of Churchmen, as it was of Nonconformists, and as it has continued to be the faith of both classes to this day.

The prolonged discussion of the subject by the friends of the institution has been, in part, owing to the necessity for checking

[1] In 1641 "the Lower House ordained the Mayor to see them both [Pocklington's *Altare Christianum* and *Sunday no Sabbath*] burnt at Cheapside, and Bray, the licenser, to read out of a paper his condemnation of a number of errors which he had licensed. He did so with a great deal of feigned repentance, for the Lower House this year makes many hypocrites."—Baillie's *Letters* (1775), vol. i. p. 290.

desecrations of the Sabbath which have more or less prevailed. The evils of the *Book of Sports*, and of the writings by which it was defended, were not to be remedied in a day. There mixed, moreover, in the ranks of the truly good and earnest men of the Commonwealth not a few who were mere followers of the multitude, and whose overdone profession of religion excited only disgust and contempt in one class and pity in another. When such persons returned at the Restoration to their natural element of licentiousness, they swelled the tide of profligacy, which, setting in from the Court, overflowed the land. The immorality and profaneness of that period are notorious, and we are let into the knowledge of their leading cause by Evelyn's sketch of a Sunday scene, which he witnessed at Whitehall, and where figured the king, his concubines, twenty great courtiers, with other dissolute persons, at cards round a large table, and "a French boy singing love songs in that glorious gallery."[1] Dr. Heylyn had said that danger to England was to be apprehended from the superstitious observance, not from the profane neglect of the Lord's day. We know not what his feelings were in the two years that he survived the Restoration, when he had it in his power, by a comparison of the state of the country with what it had lately been, to estimate his gifts as a seer, and the moral value of his views and labours as an anti-Sabbatist. Referring, in 1760, to Heylyn's prophecy, Jephson says: "We have lived to see the contrary, and that the Lord's day is overrun by profaneness infinitely more than ever it was overflown by superstition."[2] Bishop Horsley preached his eloquent sermons on the subject towards the close of the last century, and mentions "the roads crowded on the Sunday, as on any other day, with travellers of every sort," and "the mingled racket of worldly business and pleasure going on with little abatement" in London, as "scandals calling loudly for redress." The Sunday press, Sunday excursions by steamers, and Sunday trading, especially in intoxicating liquors, were the metropolitan enormities which disgraced the earlier part of the present century. And in our own day, when the institution has more than at any former time been assailed by the press, when railway proprietors have multiplied travelling, and its atten-

1 *Memoirs* (1827), vol. iii. p. 137.
2 *Discourse on the Religious Observation of the Lord's Day*, Preface, p. viii.

dant dissipation, on the Sabbath, a thousand fold, and when a National League strains every nerve to have a continental Sunday legalized in England, the tendencies of such measures receive mournful illustration in the fact that five millions of our countrymen habitually forsake the assembling of themselves together on the day and in the house of God.

But controversy has been rendered necessary by the prevalence of wrong opinions of the Sabbath, as well as by the practical abuses, in which they have both their origin and their result. The notion that every day is alike, entertained with various meaning and object by Saltmarsh (after Hetherington and others), Porter, Belsham, and a party who claim to themselves the distinctive title of "The Followers of Jesus," though it has had too few and inconsiderable supporters to call forth any special refutation, has not altogether passed unnoticed by defenders of a periodical holy day. More fruitful of discussion have been the views of a class of men who, spread over a space of more than two centuries, have contended for the perpetuity of the seventh-day Sabbath against the Christian world. Traske and Brabourne have been followed by Ockford, Saller and Spittlehouse, Tillam, Chamberlain, Coppinger, the Stennets, the Bampfields, Philanthropos, Philotheos, Carlow, Elwall, Cornthwaite, Wyncup, Dawson, Burnside, Shenston, and W. H. Black. But by far the greater part of the Sabbatic controversy and literature of England during the last two centuries has been owing to the necessity for combating opinions adverse to a weekly rest considered as in all ages a divinely appointed and essentially identical ordinance. Among the principal writers who have concurred in rejecting the generally received doctrine of a Sabbath expressly given and prescribed by God to mankind "from Adam to his latest son" have been Jeremy Taylor, Hammond, Bramhall, Barrow, and Spencer, in the latter half of the seventeenth century; Grascome, Morer, Paley, and Ogden, in the eighteenth; Higgins, Whately, Bannerman (author of the *Modern Sabbath Examined*), Fearon, Powell, Arnold, Domville, and Reichel, in the nineteenth. Persons so different from each other in important respects, and even in their views of the institution, must be understood as now classified together simply on the ground of their common hostility to a primæval holy day, and to the obligation on

Christians of the Fourth Commandment. We would not confound the noble Arnold with the ignoble Higgins, of whom a reviewer favourable to his doctrine says, "he is destitute of every quality that gives respect to a writer;"[1] Bramhall, who pleads so excellently for the express appointment of the Lord's day by Christ, and Grascome, who holds the same views, with Whately, who grounds the institution on the authority of the Church; or Taylor and Barrow, who affirm, the former, that "the observation of the Lord's day differs nothing from the observation of the Sabbath in the matter of religion, but in the manner," the latter, that "Christians ought to consecrate as much or more time to religion and mercy than the Jews," with Powell, who deems it an unhappy and superstitious misconception to suppose that it is sinful to do on a Sunday anything which it is not sinful to do on another day, and who, by hailing "the inevitable rejection of the *historical* character of the Mosaic narrative as a marked feature in the theological and spiritual advance of the present age," announces a principle which goes to "destroy the foundations" alike of the Sabbath and of revelation. Nor would we identify the views of Paley and Ogden, who acknowledge the Lord's day to be of divine authority, and even repudiate certain practices thereon as unbecoming the public worship allotted to the day, with those of Morer, who places his church and himself in opposition to the doctrine that the institution is of divine right; of Spencer, who considers the whole Hebrew ritual, in which he includes the Sabbath, as of heathen origin; of Fearon, who accounts for the Christian rest in the same way; of Bannerman, who believes that Scripture requires an every-day Sabbath, while he would by no means set aside the political enactment of a weekly holy day; of Domville, who maintains that there is no warrant to be found in the Bible for believing that we are enjoined by divine authority to observe the Sunday either as a Sabbath or as a stated day of assembling for public worship and religious instruction; or, we may add, of Milton, who, already known on the authority of Dr. Johnson as having in his latter days discontinued the observance of public and domestic worship, was by his posthumous work of 1825 fully disclosed as an Anti-Sabbatist to the extent even of surrendering every autho-

[1] *Critica Biblica*, vol. iv. p. 200.

ritative claim of the Lord's day, except what it derives from ecclesiastical appointment.

The result of the persevering opposition to the true theory and due observance of the institution, has been, that from 1658 to the present time there have appeared no fewer than four hundred publications of every description, pleading for the divine authority, holy character, and devout observance of the Lord's day. In refutation of Sabbatarianism, works have been published by Hanson, Aspinwall, Warren, Ives, Baxter, Benn, Bunyan, Trosse, Dr. Wallis, Marlow, Keach, Fleming, Dobel, Herbert Jones, Edmonds, with others not expressly devoted to the subject. It was a compensation for the disturbances and separations which the propagation of the views opposed by such writers produced in churches and society, that the subject was in consequence more thoroughly studied, and noble defences of the first-day Sabbath were written. A work of Tillam, who had collected some followers in Colchester, gave occasion to a treatise in 1659 by Edmund Warren, minister of St. Peter's in that town—a treatise under the title, *The Jewish Sabbath Antiquated*—which, notwithstanding its advocacy of the dogma of George Walker and James Alting respecting the primitive Sabbath as posterior to the fall of Adam, and as grounded on the purposed redemption of Christ, contains a clear statement, a powerful defence, and a heart-thrilling application of the generally received truth. To the stimulus of Sabbatarianism we owe the *Modest Plea for the Lord's Day* (1669), by Dr. Collinges of Norwich; and to a statement of the argument for the seventh day rest by the benevolent Francis Bampfield, we are indebted for the excellent vindication of the Christian Sabbath (1672), by the eminently devout and philanthropic Mr. Benn of Dorchester. Baxter (1671) and Bunyan (1685) wrote their interesting defences of the Lord's day for relieving the perplexities with which some good people in their times were distressed in consequence of the proselyting zeal of Saturday Sabbatists. The work of Keach (1700), published for the same purpose, issued in the restoration of his distracted church to order and peace. And but for the lucubrations of Thomas Bampfield, counsellor-at-law, we should never have been favoured with the earnest treatise by George Trosse of Exeter (1692), who, like John Bunyan and John Newton, from being a profligate became a zealous minister, or with two tracts by the celebrated Wallis (1692, 1693), in which he has added to the evidence of the versatility of his genius, and of the important service that a mind cultivated by science can render to religion.

Much more numerous, however, have been the works which have been directed against more dangerous errors and against practical evils. The first instalment was of the latter class, consisting of publications by Nicholas Billingsley, Thomas Gouge, so distinguished by his munificent charities, William Thomas, William Bagshaw, and John Wells, all ministers of the gospel. The *Practical Sabbatarian*, by Wells (1668), is a voluminous, though far from dry detail of duties, accompanied by a learned statement of the argument. The acute and excellent George Hughes of Plymouth published his *Aphorisms*, "because fresh enemies had with old weapons new furbished assaulted the truth," and for the purpose of showing "whether we are beholding to God or to the bare courtesy of the Church for a Sabbath." Of the well-known treatise on the subject by John Owen (1671), we will only say that, undertaken at the request of some learned men in the United Provinces, for vindicating the doctrine of the Sabbath against the attacks of "sundry divines" in that country, who maligned it as the *Figmentum Anglicanum*, and designed also for the revival of the same "much despised" doctrine in England,[1] it is perhaps as masterly an exposition and defence of the institution as the world has seen. In the *Divine Appointment of the Lord's Day*, which, though aimed particularly against Sabbatarianism, controverts also other errors, Baxter discovers a mind and attainments of an equally high order, perhaps, as those of Owen, both when he so originally establishes his thesis from the New Testament, and copes so successfully in the field of history with Heylyn. If in the few pages, where he argues against the formal obligation on Christians of the law of Eden and Sinai, he becomes weak as other men, and exposes himself to defeat, as well as impairs the authority and practical rule of the institution, it is to be remembered how cordially, and, we may add, how misgivingly as to the correctness of that opinion, he commends the labours of Abbot and others who dif-

[1] Letter from Owen to John Eliot (Mather's *Magnalia*, 1702), pp. 178, 179.

fered from him on the point. Dr. Nathaniel Homes, in 1673, held that the Lord's day is a return from the Jewish seventh day to the Patriarchal first day of the week, and was confident enough to entitle his essay, *The Sabbath-day's Rest from Controversie.* In the same sanguine spirit Thomas Cleandon intended by his *Serious and Brief Discourse* of nine quarto pages (1674) to "decide and determine all controversies respecting the Sabbath-day." With the humbler view of inducing his own children to sanctify the day, Sir Matthew Hale uttered a few words which have done more to promote its observance than some elaborate volumes. Not to mention a number of writers, whose compendious testimonies on the subject belong to another part of this volume, we add, as supporters of the institution in the seventeenth century, Nicholas Smith, Waite, John Gregory, John Smith, Dr. Townson, Bishop Hopkins, and William Allein.

The eighteenth century opens with the defective doctrine of Keach and Grascome,[1] and the errors of Morer, but the remedy is at hand in the sound views of Archbishop Sharp, Ollyffe, Newcome, and Bingham. Practical evil is encountered by the seasonable efforts of Hammersley, Howell, Humphries, Nelson, Matthew Henry, and Bishop Beveridge. If the learned Wotton, in his *Miscellaneous Discourses* of 1718, and the scholarly Hallet, try to deprive us of the Fourth Commandment as a rule for our observance of the first day of the week, they yet maintain the divine appointment of the Sabbath for all the economies of religion, and their deficiencies as well as mistakes are compensated by the accomplished Dr. Samuel Wright, in his able volume of 1724 and 1726;[2] by Robert Hill, Rector of Stanhow, in his *Reply to Drs. Heylyn and Wallis;* by the celebrated Dr. Samuel Clarke, in a sermon; and by Alexander Jephson, Rector of Craike, who produced in 1738, and republished in 1760, an excellent treatise, enriched, like Wright's, with quotations from eminent authors. Dr. Watts, feeling that the abounding desecration of the Sabbath of which Jephson complains, and other evils, were preying on the vitals of Nonconformist churches, had asked them in an earnest

1 These writers, and Dr. Wallis, rejected the doctrines of a primæval and patriarchal Sabbath.

2 Battely's *Original Institution of the Sabbath* (1726) we have not seen.

appeal of 1731, *What do ye more than others?* and afterwards published on the subject of the Sabbatic institution, in his Sermons and *Holiness of Times.* His admirer, Dr. Doddridge, handles the same topic in his lectures. The learned Dr. Kennicott declares decidedly for a perpetual Sabbath, and in his dissertations of 1747 establishes the article on which that doctrine ultimately depends—the divine institution of the weekly rest at the creation. Dr. Gibbons, known by his many writings, the zealous Walker of Truro, and the excellent Bishop Gibson, write on the subject wholly in a practical strain. Bolton assails a particular form of Sabbath desecration, while Moses Browne, without the genius of Herbert, makes good verse tributary to the cause. Dr. Webster sketches the history of the institution with more of the Puritan spirit than Grascome, while Catcott and Parry defend its antiquity—all of them in sermons. Steffe in 1757 was the first to enlarge on the wisdom and policy of a weekly day of rest and worship, though the *Occasional Paper* of 1740 may have suggested the idea. The controversial blends with the practical in the writings of Drs. Ridgley, Chandler and John Taylor, Richard Amner, Job Orton, Archbishop Secker, Coetlogon, Bishop Pearce, Jeylinger Symons, Lewelyn, Bishop Porteus, Archdeacon Pott, and Samuel Palmer. The pamphlets of Lowe and Dr. Thomas Horne are practical. Dr. Priestley, in controversy with his brother Socinian, Evanson, supports the orthodox opinion, and even Chubb upholds the first against the seventh day of rest. We, of course, omit many authors in this century whose views, though favourable to a divinely appointed and permanent Sabbath, are only briefly expressed in works on other subjects.

In the nineteenth century, efforts on behalf of the Lord's day have been called forth to an unparalleled extent. One of the most effective assaults on the abounding desecration of the day proceeded from a meeting of the friends of the London Christian Instruction Society, held in 1829. To this was owing the publication of several useful works by Sherman, Clayton, and Burder, with a reprint of the Essays by Dr. Heman Humphrey of America. Bishop Blomfield printed in 1830 his Letter to the inhabitants of London, which led to important results. The matter was taken up in the pulpit; the press was employed; the Lord's-day Society was formed; the country was everywhere roused. Parliament became an arena of the controversy, and its discussions operated beneficially among the upper ranks and in foreign lands, while the evidence collected by its means, and through the exertions of Sir Andrew Agnew, has been and will remain an inexhaustible arsenal for supplying the means of defence and attack in the cause of a holy Sabbath.

The amount of authorship which has been elicited on behalf of the institution in this century is immense. When we have advanced in it some years we find the path covered with writings, "thick as autumnal leaves that strew the brooks in Vallambrosa." Many of them, though ephemeral, may have done much good in their respective circles. A few that appear to us the more important may be named. Bishop Horsley, as the late Dr. Wilson said, has "three noble sermons on the subject, in which he powerfully maintains the generally received doctrine," though, as the Doctor justly added, "he errs in considering the Sabbath more of a positive than moral character." Dean Milner presents both argument and practice with energetic brevity. *The Christian Sabbath* of Holden, notwithstanding some prolix digressions, is one of the best modern discussions of the subject. Dr. Daniel Wilson's volume is scarcely inferior to that of Holden. Of the treatise of Thorn, it is enough to say that it is recommended by men of note, including John Foster and Robert Hall, and that it had in 1830 reached its seventh edition. More or less complete publications—some of them bearing the impress of the well-known genius and scholarship of their authors—have been furnished by Gurney, Conder, Treffry, Charlotte Elizabeth, Drs. Croly and Richard W. Hamilton, the Woolwich Lecturers, Johnstone, Ball, and Hill, author of the prize essay, *The Sabbath made for Man.* Some have appeared to advantage in conflict with opponents of the common doctrine, as Hey of Leeds, in replying to Dr. Paley; Atcheson, to Mons. Beausobre; James of Cobham, to Dr. Heylyn; Cameron, Foster (Collon), Barter, and particularly Professor Samuel Lee and Archdeacon Stopford, to Archbishop Whately; Brooke, to Burnside and Bannerman; Bouchier, to H. Mayhew; a writer in the *London Quarterly Review*, to Powell; M'Guire, to Langley; and O'Neil, with others, to Reichel. Some have happily illustrated particular departments of the question, as Jordan, who has thrown light on septenary institutions in heathendom, and Baylee, who has usefully laboured in the fields of history and statistics. Others have effectually exposed certain errors and abuses, as a Layman, who ably assails the Sunday newspaper; Kingsmill, who impressively warns his countrymen against the attempts of Anti-Sabbatic writers, Leagues, and shareholders in railways and the Crystal Palace, to bring them under his charge as chaplain of a prison; Arthur, who exhibits with graphic power the evils of a French Sunday; Napier, who in Parliament eloquently deprecated the opening of the British Museum on the Lord's day; Baptist Noel, who applied his earnest spirit to the dispersing of Sunday music bands; and Henry Rogers, who exerted his great talents, that might have found still more fitting exercise on the whole question, to crush the fancy that access to places of public amusement on the Sabbath would be in any one shape a boon to our people.

The enemies of the divine and salutary law of a weekly holy rest, have, doubtless, by their principles and measures, done much injury, and to none more than themselves; but they have hitherto found it, as all who make the attempt will ever find it, impossible to effect its overthrow. Opposition has not only awakened profounder inquiry among many concerning its claims, but served to animate the zeal of Christian men on its behalf, and to bind them together in a phalanx, which, going forth under the leadership of the Lord of the Sabbath, may be expected to place the institution, in due time, above "the strife of tongues," and the rude foot of practical violation, thereby closing the history of Sabbatic controversies, if not also of Sabbatic literature, in England.

UNITED STATES.

It has been the happiness of North America that her foundations were to such an extent laid in religion, and that, destined to be the resort of persons of all characters and fortunes from the old world, she has at various times received into her territory many of the best of men, bringing with them, for the counteraction of her evils and the advancement of her prosperity, Christian principles, institutions, and manners. The earnest prayers and hallowed Sabbaths of her founders and settlers have entailed on her a rich and long-continued blessing, which it is to be hoped will prevail to the overthrow of whatever tends to cut it off.

One of the chief cares of the Pilgrim Fathers, as of those who preceded them from Holland, and followed them from England, was the due observance of the sacred rest. In the earliest records of the Dutch colonists in New York, there are decrees of the most stringent character, intended to guard the infant community against the demoralizing tendencies of Sabbath profanations.[1] There are still earlier records of attention on the part of the English setttlers to this subject. Whether they established themselves in New Plymouth, Salem, or Cambridge, they alike felt the sanctification of the Lord's day to be an all-important matter. Few will justify all the measures employed by them for enforcing the duty, but their reverence and regard for the institution were indubitable. It was not long, however, before roots of bitterness springing up troubled them. The most serious of their early trials is thus described by Samuel Rutherford :—"They were not well established in New England, when Antinomians sprang up among them, for the Church cannot be long without enemies. These were libertines, Familists, Antinomians, and enthusiasts, who had brought these wicked opinions out of Old England with them, where they grew under prelacy. I heard at London, that godly preachers were in danger of being persecuted by Laud for striving to reclaim some Antinomians. Divers of them became unclean, they had no prayer in their family, no Sabbath, insufferable pride, hideous lying."[2] But union is strength. A Synod was called. The errors were unanswerably refuted, and unanimously condemned. "And so the Lord," says Shepard, who was mainly instrumental in closing the career of Ann Hutchinson and her party, "within one year wrought a great change among us, having delivered the country from war with the Indians and Familists, who rose and fell together."[3]

1 *Decrees of Peter Stuyvesant*, 1647, 1648. *The Sabbath in New York*, p. 6.
2 *Spiritual Antichrist*, pp. 171, 180.
3 Albro's *Life of Thomas Shepard*, pp. cxxv. cxxvi.

But it was not so easy, especially by fines and the stocks, to rid the country of some other errors and evils in relation to the Lord's day. We find several ministers—Cotton, Hooker, and Cobbet—corresponding with Shepard, and stating arguments for the common doctrine,[1] as if the matter engaged their serious consideration, and had been or were about to be canvassed in the pulpit or through the press. The points on one or other of which certain persons had difficulties and doubts, were the morality and the day of the Sabbath.[2] Mr. Shepard, we know, did preach a course of sermons on the whole subject of the institution, which were "thrown into the form of theses or short propositions at the earnest request, and for the particular use of the students of Harvard College," and afterwards, in substance, published in 1649.[3] Dr. Albro, his American biographer, justly eulogizes the *Theses Sabbaticæ*, as "a masterly discussion of the morality, the change, the beginning, and the sanctification of the Sabbath." Thomas Shepard, who was obnoxious to Laud, retired to America in 1635, was first pastor of the first church, Cambridge, Mass., and is well known as the author of several practical works, particularly sermons on the Parable of the Ten Virgins, which, when preached, accomplished their object of contributing to put down the Antinomian heresy in New England. It was said of him, that he "scarce ever preached a sermon, but some one or other of his congregation was struck with great distress, and cried out in agony, 'What shall I do to be saved!"[4] And he himself, addressing some young ministers, said on his deathbed, "*First*, that the studying of every sermon cost him tears; he wept in the studying of every sermon. *Secondly*, before he preached any sermon, he got good by it himself. *Thirdly*, he always went up into the pulpit, as if he were to give up his accounts unto his Master."[5]

The Churches in New England, having, at a Synod in 1648, adopted the Westminster Confession of Faith as their doctrinal

1 Felt's *Ecclesiastical History of New England*, pp. 569, 604, 614.

2 *Ibid.* pp. 587, 614.

3 Besides the edition in his Collected Works (1853), there is one before us of the year 1650, and we have seen another which appeared in 1655.

4 *Life*, p. clxxx.

5 Mather's *Magnalia* (1702), p. 238.

creed, continued to maintain its Sabbatic as well as other principles. The accounts we have of their ministers, in the *Magnalia* and other records, show how holy they were, and how observant of the sacred rest. What they practised they inculcated. Thus John Eliot, the Apostle of the Indians, himself a man of distinguished piety and benevolence, brought his converts to engage that "they would remember the Sabbath-day to keep it holy as long as they lived." At a Synod held in 1662, the churches again professed their adherence to the doctrines of the Westminster Confession, with those of the Savoy Confession. And they were zealous to uphold the practice equally as the theory of the institution. In 1679, when various calamities had befallen the country, a Synod was convened to consider the reasons and remedies, when it was agreed that one of the causes of Providential frowns was the profanation by many of the Lord's day. Some years thereafter we find the churches solemnly renewing their covenant to "walk circumspectly," and declaring, as they did in like manner of various other practices, "It would be a great evil in us, if we should not keep a strict guard both on our own thoughts as well as words and works on the Lord's day; and also on all that are under our influence, to restrain them from the violations of that sacred rest." The scene somewhat resembles the remarkable one in Scotland at the meeting of the General Assembly of 1596. And it was more to promote objects of this practical nature than to combat error, that Increase Mather, and his son Dr. Cotton Mather—both valuable and voluminous writers—published, the latter, *A Discourse on the Observation of the Lord's Day*, in 1703, the former, *Meditations on the Sanctification of the Lord's Day*, in 1712; and that Samuel Willard, a minister in Boston, and vice-president of Harvard College, wrote so largely on the fourth commandment, in his *Body of Divinity*, which was printed in 1726.

The illustrious Jonathan Edwards follows. In his three sermons on the perpetuity and change of the Sabbath, he fully achieves his object, which is the establishment of two propositions. "*First*, It is sufficiently clear, that it is the mind of God, that one day of the week should be devoted to rest and religious exercises, throughout all ages and nations. *Second*, It is sufficiently clear, that, under the gospel dispensation, this day is the first day of the week." If he has not brought so much learning to bear on the question as did Owen, he has applied to it a mind even more acute and perspicacious ; and we must hold that propositions "sufficiently clear" to Edwards, Lord Bacon, Locke, and Burke, in common with the great body of Christian men, are not evident to others simply because they will not see. The sermons appear to have been written and preached within a few years after his ordination to the ministry, and the publication of them, with that of his *Journal*, and *Life of Brainerd*, must have contributed greatly to the sanctification of the Sabbath in America, as well as wherever these works have been read. It is worthy of remark, that a discourse preached by him in condemnation of the prevailing practice of devoting the evening of the Sabbath, and the evening after the stated public lecture, to visiting and diversion, was the means of originating the first remarkable revival of religion (1734), under his ministry at Northampton. A pupil of Edwards, and editor of his works, Dr. Samuel Hopkins, entertained views in common with him on this as on various other subjects, and has expounded the doctrine of the Sabbath at considerable length in his *System of Doctrine.*

Dr. Nathan Strong and Dr. Timothy Dwight had been class-fellows of equal merit, and were life-long friends. The former was "the learned and very useful" minister of a Presbyterian congregation in Hartford, Connecticut, and "distinguished for his discernment and knowledge of men." His two volumes of sermons, printed in 1798, include one on the Sanctification, and another on the benefits of the Sabbath, both exceedingly good, and worthy of the friend of Dwight. While Strong was engaged in the publication of his work, Timothy Dwight, the grandson of Edwards, had begun to deliver the course of sermons, the publication of which has given so much celebrity to his name. His contribution to the cause of the Sabbath amounts to five sermons on the Fourth Precept of the Decalogue, which form a considerable treatise, and must, during his more than twenty years' presidency of Yale College, have been pronounced once in the hearing of most of the young men under his care—in numbers that soon increased from one hundred and ten to three hundred and thirteen—producing convictions and impressions, of "the perpetuity, sacredness, and importance" of the institution, to be carried with them through life, and through them reproduced in thousands of other minds. And from the time of their publication, somewhere between 1817 and 1819, the eloquent prelections must have served in America and in this country to awaken similar convictions in multitudes of readers. The late Bishop of Calcutta, referring to the author, said, "This last name deserves especial notice. Dr. Dwight, as well as his illustrious countryman, Edwards, has honoured the American school of theology—rapidly increasing in importance—with a most convincing and able discussion of the question in all its branches, both theoretical and practical: they perhaps form the best of our modern treatises, though it would be unjust to Dr. Humphrey, of Amherst College, to withhold a tribute of applause from his excellent Essays."[1]

If America had produced no other works on the Sabbath than have been named, it would, her disadvantages and comparative youth considered, have been no small honour; but we have to add her more recent contributions to the argument and literature of the subject, which surpass previous exertions in number, if not in worth. There are the excellent *Manual* of Professor Agnew, with its able Introductory Essay by Professor Samuel Miller, and the very interesting *Reports and Permanent Documents* of "the American and Foreign Sabbath Union." Four of these Documents, reprinted by the American Tract Society, with the name of Dr. Justin Edwards, Secretary to the Sabbath Union, as author, form *The Sabbath Manual.* There are also works by Phelps, Drs. Stone and Barnes, which we have not seen. Drs. Emmons, Woods, and Wayland, the last avowedly borrowing from Gurney, devote portions of their able writings to the institution. The Rev. L. Coleman has brought his historical lore to the enforcement of Sabbatic claims and duties in his Christian Antiquities, and Historical Sketch of the Christian Sabbath in the *Bibliotheca Sacra* (1844). Dr. Stevens has eloquently pleaded the obligations and blessings of the Lord's day in a Sermon, and Professor Dabney has ably discussed "the Sabbath Controversy" in the *Southern Presbyterian Review.* The Tract Society has printed a

[1] Dr. Daniel Wilson's *Seven Sermons.* Preface.

number of useful publications on the observance of the institution, including valuable tracts by Drs. Plumer, Spring, Nevins, and Schmucker; and the Sabbath Committee of New York, amidst various zealous and successful exertions for checking Sabbath desecration, has issued, with the same view, some important documents. But among American publications of recent times, we have seen no abler defences of the weekly holy day than two articles which have appeared in the *Princeton Review*, under the titles, "Sunday Mails" (1831) and "Sunday Laws" (1859), the latter said to be from the pen of Dr. Charles Hodge.

We have little to state as to what has been written in America on the other side of the question. The Sabbatarians, whose Church membership is said to be 7000, have, by a magazine, a newspaper, and a Tract Society, endeavoured to raise bulwarks for the defence of the seventh-day Sabbath. We have before us a series of books and tracts, old and new, issued by the Society. There are two histories of the body—one by Clarke in 1811, recording its rise and progress in the States, the other by Mrs. Davis in 1851, embracing its annals in all ages and lands. But there have been and are more formidable opponents of the Christian Sabbath than the Sabbatarians. An American Review, now extinct, propounded some years ago the doctrine that the Sabbath was not originally a day devoted to the exercises of religion, and that it is now most appropriately kept by festivity and amusement. The article was headed Sunday Mails, and drew forth the able reply under the same title already mentioned. There appeared in 1853 a volume in which the question is discussed, Whether there is any authority for the Christian Sabbath?—the Rev. J. N. Brown supporting the affirmative, and W. B. Taylor contending for the negative. And we observe from the paper *Sunday Laws* that instances of the most daring opposition to the Sabbath have lately occurred in the country, in which a William Logan Fisher, and some imported Germans, have been conspicuous. At a meeting of the latter, it was resolved that "any attempt, direct or indirect, to exact the keeping of some holy day, enjoined, or supposed to be enjoined, by the Jewish or Christian Scriptures, as the first or seventh day of the week, is alike defiant of natural right and constitutional law." Fisher, in his *History of the Institution of the Sabbath-day*, contends against Sunday laws, his reviewer informs us, on the threefold ground, that the Bible is not the Word of God; that the Bible itself does not require such an observance of the Sabbath as our Sunday laws assume; and that, admitting the Divine origin of the Old Testament, and conceding that the observance of one day in seven as a holy Sabbath to God is therein enjoined, it was a purely Jewish institution, and is not binding upon Christians. "It is well for people to understand each other," says the reviewer, who concludes a very thorough exposure of the lawless liberty claimed by Fisher and the Germans, in these words of plainness and power: "This country was settled by Protestant Christians. They possessed the land; they established its institutions; they formed themselves into towns, states, and nation. From the nature of the case, regarding the Bible as the Word of God binding the conscience of every man with Divine authority, they were governed by it in all their organizations, whether for business or civil polity. Others have since come into the country by thousands; some Papists, some Jews, some Infidels, some Atheists. All were welcomed; all are admitted to equal rights and privileges. All are allowed to acquire property, to vote in all elections, made eligible to all offices, and invested with an equal influence in all public concerns. All are allowed to worship as they please, or not at all, if they please. No man is molested for his religion, or for his want of religion. No man is required to profess any particular form of faith, or to join any religious association. Is not this liberty enough? It seems not. Our 'Free Germans' and other Anti-Sabbatarians insist upon it that we must turn infidels, give up our God, our Saviour, and our Bible, so far as all public or governmental action is concerned. They require that the joint stock into which they have been received as partners, and in which they constitute even numerically a very small minority, should be conducted according to their principles, and not according to ours. They demand, not merely that they may be allowed to disregard the Sabbath, but that the public business must go on on that day; that all public servants must be employed; all public property, highways, and railroads should be used. They say we must not pray in our legislative bodies, or have chaplains in our hospitals, prisons, navy, or army; that we must not introduce the Bible into our public schools, or do anything in a public capacity which implies that we are Protestant Christians. Those men do not know what Protestant Christians are. It is their characteristic, as they humbly hope and believe, to respect the rights of other men, and stand up for their own. And, therefore, they say to all—Infidels and Atheists—to all who demand that the Bible shall not be the rule of action for us as individuals, and as a Government, you ask what it is impossible can be granted. We must obey God. We must carry our religion into our families, our workshops, our banking-houses, our municipal and other governments ; and if you cannot live with Christians, you must go elsewhere."[1]

That the sanguine hope of another American writer, as expressed in the following words, may be fulfilled, is devoutly to be wished : "If the wise, and good, and patriotic in our land persevere, and especially if ministers of the gospel generally bring the influence of the gospel to bear on this subject, the day, there is every reason to believe, is not far distant when, by the blessing of the God of the Sabbath, the greater part of our nation will be, at least externally, a Sabbath-keeping people."[2]

SCOTLAND.

It may to some appear out of place to introduce, under the head of controversies on the Sabbath, a country where we ought to look for the fruits of peace and sanctity rather than for the turmoils and desolations of war. And it is true that, from the Reformation to the present time, the Scottish Church has had but one doctrine on the subject ; and that for a long period general acclaim accorded to the nation a distinction above all others for a sacred regard to the Lord's day. But besides the aversion to holy restraints and duties common to human nature everywhere, the peculiar exposure of the Scots to foreign aggression against their worship and liberties, and the *perfervidum ingenium*, which led them to carry the war for truth and right into other lands, have

[1] *British and Foreign Evangelical Review* for January 1860.

[2] Dr Schmucker's *Appeal in behalf of the Christian Sabbath*, p. 15.

engaged them in Sabbatic contests not a few, and originated a Sabbatic literature equal in value, if not in amount, to that of any country.

For the greater part of three centuries has the institution encountered strong opposition from without. A Scotsman, James VI., from being a boastful admirer of Presbytery, became its avowed and bitter foe, and after his accession to the throne of England, speedily availed himself of his increased power to attempt the subversion of the religious polity and rights, including the Sabbath, of his native land. Charles I. was equally disposed, though less able, to carry on the nefarious work. The measures with the same view adopted in the reigns of Charles II. and James II.—measures dooming within a period of twenty-eight years no fewer than 18,000 persons to death, or to sufferings worse than death—have certainly, for folly and wickedness, been rarely paralleled in the history of any country. During such a time it was to be presumed that the Lord's day would be trampled under foot by one class, who, indeed, selected it as the season for their bloodiest deeds, and that it could not be observed by the other as they would. But the doctrine of its sanctity formed a part of the testimony, which they earnestly maintained, and for which they were willing to die. It has been well said, that the sacrifices of missionaries and of their supporters for the propagation of Christianity, so honourable to our times, are not for a moment to be compared with the expenditure of suffering and substance which its conservation cost our fathers. And more effectual than even persecution has been the influence of imported people and customs from England and Ireland for impairing the religion and Sabbath observances of Scotland. But evil has been to some extent the occasion of good, and it is a pleasing reflection that, despite the follies and cruelties of the Stuart kings, the deadening influence of prelacy and moderation, and, in our own day, the corrupting power of English wealth and Irish poverty, the popular belief and feeling of the country have, from the period of the Reformation down to the present time, been eminently Sabbatical.

Apart from the press, much has been done to secure for Scotland her hallowed day of rest. The Parliament from time to time passed Acts, for the most part suggested by the Church

Courts, which, according to the best authorities, amounted ultimately to a very complete legal provision for the protection of the Lord's day against open desecration. Still more numerous are the Acts of her supreme ecclesiastical court, which not only in 1566 and 1575 abjured all human holidays, but by its decrees, and the direct exercise of discipline, did much subsequently to maintain sound doctrine and right practice in reference to the weekly holy day throughout the nation. Three instances are worthy of particular notice. One of these occurred in 1596, when the members of the General Assembly were stirred to "great searching of heart" as to their treatment of the Fourth and other Commandments of the Divine Law, melted to genuine sorrow for sin, and warmed with a love which faithfully and boldly extended its care to his Majesty's household, the whole resulting in the spread of similar exercises and feelings, and in a general reformation over the land. Another belongs to the year 1638, when the Assembly, so celebrated for its connexion with the Second Reformation, excommunicated the greater part of the prelates for, with other grave offences, their shameless profanations of the Lord's day. The ratification of the Westminster Confession of Faith, with the full arrangement of the form of worship and discipline, by the General Assembly of 1647, which completed the Reformation, is the third instance.

The inferior courts were no less watchful over the interests of practical religion. The Synod of Lothian, for example, censured Spotswood, minister at Calder, afterwards the noted Archbishop, and Law, minister at Kirkliston, for playing at foot-ball on the Lord's day.[1] The Session records of the latter part of the sixteenth century and throughout the seventeenth, teem with proofs of the diligence with which ministers and elders sought to promote the piety and morals of the people, and especially their

[1] Mr. John Davidson, minister at Prestonpans, by whose powerful appeals the Assembly of 1596 was so deeply impressed, was Moderator of the Synod at the time, and urged that the offenders should be deposed, "but the Synod agreed not thereto; and when they were called in, he said, 'Come in, ye pretty foot-ball men—the Synod hath ordained you only to be rebuked;' and turning to the Synod, he said, 'And now, brethren, let me tell you what reward you shall get for your lenity; these two men shall trample on your necks, and the necks of the ministrie of Scotland.'"—Livingstone's *Memorable Characteristics.* Wod. Soc. *Sel. Biograph.* vol. ii. p. 296.

obedience to the Fourth Commandment. Burnet, when referring to the time immediately prior to the Restoration, says :—"They kept scandalous persons under a severe discipline : for breach of Sabbath, for an oath, or the least disorder in drunkenness, persons were cited before the church-session, that consisted of ten or twelve of the chief of the parish, who, with the minister, had this care upon them ; and were solemnly reproved for it."[1] Among the evils inherited from Rome, was the custom of performing comedies on the Lord's day, which continued for some years after the death of Knox, but was increasingly discountenanced, and ere long, through the influence of the sessions and magistrates, discontinued. In 1754, the sessions commenced the practice of employing individuals of their number to traverse the towns on Sabbaths and other seasons of public worship for the purpose of causing notice to be taken of such as should be found "vaging abroad upon the streets, and of having them cited before the session."[2]

But probably the faithful public ministrations, and the assiduous labours in private, of the excellent ministers, with whom Scotland has been more or less favoured in all periods of her reformed history, have contributed more than anything else to the formation and maintenance of her character as a Sabbath-keeping country. When we think of such a man presiding successively over the students of Glasgow and St. Andrews as Andrew Melville, who could in the Privy-Council pronounce Archbishop Bancroft a Sabbath-breaker ; of John Welch, on one occasion weaning an easy-minded minister from his "bow-butts and archery" on the Sabbath afternoon, by engaging him to spend that time with himself and his friends, John Stuart and Hugh Kennedy, in prayer, and, on another, declaring to a gentleman, with whom he had in vain remonstrated against the patronizing of foot-ball and other pastimes on the Lord's day, that he should be cast out from house and hold, words which the unhappy man had soon to confess were

[1] *Hist. of his Own Time* (1850), p. 102.

[2] The persons so employed were called Searchers. Principal Lee, in his evidence given before a Committee of the House of Commons in 1832, says, that the practice continued for a century and a half. But similar measures have been resorted to occasionally in later times.

verified; of Henderson, who, when Charles I. had attended the High Church in the forenoon of the Sabbath after his arrival in Edinburgh in 1641, but spent the afternoon in playing at golf, conversed on the enormity with his Majesty, who afterwards gave constant attendance, as he did also at family worship performed morning and evening in the palace by that faithful minister; and of William Guthrie, who, by giving an equivalent for the profits of each day's shooting, could prevail on a parishioner to exchange on the Sabbath the fowling-piece and the field, for the Bible and the Church, till he learned that godliness was its own sufficient reward, and became, as an elder, an auxiliary to his minister in winning men from evil; when we think of such individuals—specimens of the ministry of their time—we see how adapted the means were to make the Church of Scotland the "Philadelphia" portrayed by Kirkton and Burnet. And when we remember Halyburton's dying counsels to his boy David, "not to come near anybody that would swear, lie, speak what was bad, or break the Sabbath;" Boston's lasting penitence for a youthful violation of the Fourth Commandment; Ebenezer Erskine's searching words from the pulpit, "I am ready to judge that folk's acquaintance with God himself is known by the regard they show to his holy day;" Alexander Moncrieff's pungent answer to the man who demanded to know his right to advise him against a Sabbath excursion, "You will learn that at the day of judgment;" and Brown of Haddington's saying, by which he endeavoured to regulate himself and his family, that "conversation on the common affairs of life, or even on the more external and trivial matters of the Church, on the Lord's day, was unsuitable to the spiritual exercises of the day, and offensive to God;" when we remember such men, we recognise the worthy successors of the Scottish Reformers and Covenanters, and the fitting means of perpetuating among their countrymen the honours and blessings of the day of rest.

Nor has Scotland, amidst difficulties of no ordinary kind, merely maintained the Sabbath at home. She has furthered its interests abroad. She helped to equip Teellinck for his successful contest in Zealand. Her Welch, Boyd, Forbes, Dury, Andrew Melville, Brown, and Crawford, with others, exemplified, and in some instances publicly defended, their principles in reference to the weekly holy day, in various parts of the Continent. Livingstone, Blair, and their compeers, spread those principles in Ireland. The stand made by Scotland for her Church and freedom had no slight influence on the summoning of the Long Parliament, and on the assertion by Englishmen of their down-trodden Sabbatic and other rights—a struggle which she materially helped also to maintain. And though she failed to secure permanently for England an ecclesiastical constitution like her own, her efforts were not fruitless, as, to mention nothing else, they were eminently tributary to the production of that noble Confession of Faith, and kindred documents, which have been the means of lasting good, though chiefly to her own people, yet largely also to the inhabitants of other regions of the globe.[1] Rutherford entered the lists with Saltmarsh. But this brings us to the Sabbatic literature of Scotland, a goodly portion of which we owe to the efforts of her sons to vindicate their views of the Lord's day in foreign lands.

We have met with no very early specimen of Scottish authorship on the subject. Writers may be found—like Cowper in his *Holy Alphabet;* Malcolm, in his *Exposition of the Acts;* David Calderwood, in his *Altare Damascenum;* and John Weemse of Lathocker, in his *Christian Synagogue*—who briefly express the views of their country. The *Exposition of the Laws of Moses,* by the last-mentioned author, which appeared in 1632, is the first Scottish work, so far as we know, that treats with considerable fulness of the institution. The works of Weemse generally give evidence of "very considerable learning and information." In the *Re-examination of the Five Articles of Perth,* belonging to the year 1636, Calderwood has what may be called a *Treatise on the Sabbath,* in which he defends the commonly-received doctrine with learning and power. Dr. Guild, of Aberdeen, wrote in 1637 an earnest remonstrance against a particular form of Sabbath profanation in his neighbourhood. But the next writer, who, though he resided and published in England, was born and educated in

[1] I am informed that Mr. Henderson had a chief hand in drawing up the *Confession of Faith* and *Catechisms,* and particularly the *Directory for Worship and Ordination.*—*Wodrow Correspondence,* vol. iii. pp. 32, 33.

Scotland, calls for more particular notice, both as the work is one of special merit, and the author little known. In 1639, when the reign of terror in England was approaching its climax, Dr. Thomas Young, then vicar of Stowmarket, in Suffolk, issued an anonymous treatise in defence of the Lord's day. To do so at all in such circumstances proved his zeal and courage; and yet that the *Dies Dominica* appeared without the name of writer, publisher, printer, or the place where it was prepared or printed, was a sign of the times, and, along with the fact that no prosecution followed, showed that the author knew how to temper his ardour with the discretion which has been called the better part of valour. The volume having, thirty-two years after its publication, been commended by Baxter as "the moderatest, soundest, and strongest treatise on the subject that he had seen," many were led to inquire after it, and a translation of it, which a worthy knight had by him, was published in 1672. In a Preface to the translation, Baxter extols the author as a man "eminent in his time for great learning, judgment, piety, and humility; but especially for his acquaintance with the writings of the ancient teachers of the churches, and the doctrine and practice of former ages." Dr. Young was born at Loncarty, Perthshire, in 1587 or 1588, studied at St. Andrews, settled in London, or its neighbourhood, as a teacher,[1] was preceptor of John Milton, and, in succession, minister to the congregation of English merchants at Hamburg, vicar for thirty years of Stowmarket, minister of Duke's Place, London, and a member of the Westminster Assembly, and master of Jesus' College, Cambridge. From this last-mentioned situation, which he filled with great ability, he was ejected for refusing the engagement, or promise of fidelity to the Commonwealth as established without a King or House of Lords. He was one of the authors of *Smectymnuus*, having, according to Baillie, contributed "the most part" of it. The man who filled so many important offices with the highest reputation, and who impressed alike the experienced Baxter and the youthful Milton, with feelings of regard and admiration, the latter representing him as the half of his life, and as having inspired him with the love of poetry, must

[1] For these facts we are indebted to the researches of Masson.—See his *Life of Milton*, pp. 53, 54.

have been distinguished by intellectual gifts and moral excellence of no common order.[1]

Among the many other Scottish writers who did honour to their country and to the seventeenth century, and who asserted the Divine claims of the Sabbath, we are not aware of any one who wrote a separate treatise or tract on the institution except Brown of Wamphray, and Crawford, whose able works have been mentioned in connexion with the controversies in Holland. Some of them, however, handled the subject in their expositions of the Decalogue. William Colville, Principal of the University of Edinburgh, has devoted to the Fourth Commandment some seventeen pages of his *Philosophia Moralis Christiana*, which appeared in 1670. The views of the celebrated Leighton, successively Presbyterian minister of Newbottle, Principal of the University of Edinburgh, Bishop of Dunblane, and Archbishop of Glasgow, are more briefly, though not less decidedly, expressed. And the *Law Unsealed* of the eminent James Durham, published in 1675 by his widow, contains a very full and able discussion of Sabbatic doctrine and duty, and discovers the learning and deep piety which are evident in his other writings. It received the warm commendation of Dr. Owen, and its numerous editions attest the large measure of popular favour which it has won. Robert Barclay, the Quaker, dissented from the popular doctrine of the Sabbath, "knowing no moral obligation by THE FOURTH COMMAND, or elsewhere, to keep the FIRST DAY OF THE WEEK more than any other," but keeping it, nevertheless, for reasons of necessity, equity, mercy, and apostolic example. In the following century, while notices of the institution may be found, only a few contributions, in a separate form, or to any extent, were made to its argument and literature. Bishop Burnet devotes one of his Fourteen Sermons, and J. S[mall], "a Presbyter of the Episcopal Church of

[1] See Milton's *Elegia Quarta ad Thomam Junium*, and his *Familiar Epistles*, of which two are addressed to Dr. Young. In the Elegy the poet says:—

"Ille quidem est animae plusquam pars altera nostrae,
Dimidio vitae vivere cogor ego.
. . . .
Primus ego Aonios illo praeunte recessus
Lustrabam, et bifidi sacra vireta jugi;
Pieriosque hausi latices, Clióque favente,
Castalio sparsi laeta ter ora mero"

Scotland," a tract, to the subject in 1713, the latter being a defence of the morality of the Sabbath, in answer, particularly, to the arguments of Philip Limborch. There came out in the same or preceding year the well-known *Treatise* of Willison, his earliest work, which must, in its various editions, have been a blessing to his country. *The Sabbatism of the People of God*, by John Glas, appeared in 1747, and is to be found, with his *Three Divine Rests*, in his collected works. But nowhere is there to be found an account of the doctrines and duties of the Sabbath—clearer, more satisfactory, or more adapted for general usefulness—than is given in the second part of the *Synod's or Fisher's Catechism*, which appeared in 1760. The biographer of Mr. Fisher, referring to this exposition of the *Shorter Catechism*, says—"At the very first meeting of the Associate (Burgher) Synod, Mr. Fisher, along with Messrs. Ebenezer and Ralph Erskine, was appointed to carry forward a wise and important plan, which had been under the consideration of the Associate body in its undivided state."[1] Fisher was followed by Brown of Haddington in his *Christian Journal*, *System of Theology*, and other works. John Barclay, the Berean, having in 1776 published an Essay on the First Day of the Week, upholding its sacred claims, a reply by "a Christian Church," and affirming, with Edmund Porter, that Christ is the Christian's only Sabbath, came out in the same year. In 1778 we for the first time meet with a Scottish working man—"a tradesman of Montrose"—taking part in the controversy.[2]

But the present century has in Scotland, as in England, been peculiarly affluent in publications having for their object the illustration and defence of the weekly sacred rest. After an excellent anonymous pamphlet of 1800, there appeared Essays by James Mitchell (1802), Samuel Gilfillan[3] (1804), and Patrick M'Farlane (1805). The celebrated Poem of Grahame was given to the world in 1804, reaching its third edition in the following

[1] *Narrative of the Life of Rev. James Fisher*, by John Brown, D.D.

[2] The writer published a third edition of his *Treatise* in 1786, disclosing himself as "Alexander Jackson, silversmith," and in that year a resident in Alloa.

[3] The fact that this Essay, which in substance had appeared in the *Christian Magazine* towards the close of the preceding century, passed in the course of twenty years through fourteen editions, one of them in the Gaelic language, may perhaps justify us for offering no apology of filial partiality and gratitude for this special notice.

year, and its fourth in 1806. John Struthers, a shoemaker, and no ordinary man in head or heart, printed a small edition of his *Poor Man's Sabbath* in 1804, which was "received with such a degree of indulgent partiality as to induce him to offer a new edition thereof" in 1805. In 1809, Mr. (afterwards Professor) Duncan of Midcalder, contributed to the *Christian Magazine* two papers, illustrating with much ability a variety of positions on the subject, and after some time there followed at intervals publications by Wemyss, M'Beth (two editions), Glen, and Parker. Of a sermon by Dr. Chalmers, the late Bishop of Calcutta said, "It is in the most powerful and awakening manner of its author, and of itself settles the question."[1] Two very able and erudite papers, the one on "The Origin of New Year's Day Rites" (*Christian Instructor*, Feb. 1829), the other on "The Weekly Division of Time" (*Edinburgh Theol. Magazine*, Dec. 1829 and Jan. 1830), did great honour to the writer, the Rev. Alex. Nisbet, of the Secession Church, Portsburgh, Edinburgh, then a student of divinity.[2] Next in order were published *Letters, etc.*, to Dr. Robert Hamilton, combating his doctrines of an abrogated Sabbath and Decalogue, and works by Forbes, Gavin Struthers, M'Farlane, and Burns (Kilsyth). In 1832, Dr. Wardlaw gave to the world *Discourses*, than which no work has more logically and lucidly treated the theory, or more impressively enforced the duties of the institution. This volume was succeeded in the same year by an excellent tract, "*The Christian Sabbath Vindicated*, by William [afterwards Dr.] Innes, minister of the gospel." *Thoughts*, by Douglas of Cavers, only too few; and Dobie's Law of Scotland relative to the observance of the day, belong to 1833. Sermons by White, and Tracts by James Haldane and a clergyman of the Church of Scotland, bring us to 1840, when there was issued what is said in the title-page to be the seventh edition of "*Mistaken Views regarding the Observance of the Sabbath*, by Alexander Marjoribanks of that Ilk," who seems to have gained for himself

[1] Dr. D. Wilson's *Seven Sermons*, Preface. The Sermon referred to, *On the Christian Sabbath*, appeared in 1823. Striking and valuable though it is, two others, not less so, followed in subsequent editions of Dr. Chalmers's Sermons—the one, on *The Christianity of the Sabbath*, the other on *The Advantages of a Fixed Sabbath.*

[2] Reprinted in the author's *Remains* (1835), edited by the Rev. Dr. Taylor, then of Auchtermuchty.

the unenviable distinction of being one of the earliest Scottish writers who scoffingly assailed the institution. On the same side, though not identical in spirit or views, succeeded the lucubrations of Anti-Sabbatos, Taylor, H. C. Wright, Aytoun, Russell, two or three anonymous pamphlets, J. N. Paton, and Allan Clark, an elder of the Church ; and, on the other side, publications by Murray (Morton), D. T. K. Drummond, M'Farlane, Robert Haldane (two tracts), Bruce, Fairbairn, and Davidson, in 1842 ; Carson, in 1844 ; Lorimer, Bridges, Thomson (Leith), Nixon, Somerville, Thomson (Dr. A.), and James M'Beth in 1847.

We have now to mention two efforts on a large scale for promoting right views and practice in relation to the Lord's day—efforts suggested by the ingenious benevolence, and sustained by the munificent liberality of one individual. To John Henderson of Park, "the religious world is indebted for the origin and wide circulation" of "the tracts on the Sabbath," which were published in the course of the years 1847 and 1848, and of which in a collected form, two editions have appeared under the title, *The Christian Sabbath.* This work, which is the joint production of seventeen ministers, belonging to eight denominations of Christians, forms a remarkably complete and interesting treatise on its subject. To the same person we owe the conception and accomplishment of a measure which is without parallel in any department of literature. As the multiplication of railway and other travelling facilities on the Lord's day, was defended on the ground of its benefit to working men, he determined, towards the close of 1847, to appeal to them on the question, and offered three prizes for the three best essays upon *The Temporal Advantages of the Sabbath to the Labouring Classes.* In the short space of about three months, 1045 essays were received. The adjudicators awarded the first prize to John A. Quinton, journeyman printer, Ipswich ; the second, to John Younger, shoemaker, St. Boswell's Green ; and the third, to David Farquhar, machinist, Dundee. The measure obtained the patronage of the Queen and Prince Albert. His Royal Highness contributed five additional prizes. The British public made up the number to more than 100. The publication of the first three, and of many more essays, including *The Pearl of Days*, by a female, which was not admitted into the competition, has furnished a body of evidence, fit to form a supplement to the mass of facts collected by the House of Commons' Committee in 1832. The work of composition may have been the means of intellectual and moral improvement to one thousand and forty-five minds. And the dispersion of their writings in great profusion over the land,[1] was calculated to excite inquiry, reflection, and right feeling in many more. But with regret we add, that even a few of Scotland's working men proved false to the religion which had elevated their country and their class—false too, at a time, when their brethren were flooding the land with testimonies to the necessity and value of a weekly day consecrated entirely to sacred rest. In 1849, one of this stamp had so little of the spirit of a Scotsman, not to say a Christian, as to put forth his *Sabbath* versus *Sunday*, and another uttered in 1852 a sympathizing *Voice from the Workshop*. Happily, however, two or even ten of such writers bear a small proportion to the number of friendly essayists, among 700 of whom there were 225 resident, and many non-resident, natives of Scotland.[2]

The singular list of Scottish Anti-Sabbatic writers is closed with a copious defence of the Saturday Sabbath, by James A. Begg; a voluminous publication by Robert Cox; the novel impiety of a Sunday Steamer vindicated by its abettors; Dr. R. Hamilton's Reply to Professor Miller; a lecture by John Gordon; and *The Whole Doctrine of Calvin about the Sabbath and the Lord's Day*, a compilation by the already named Mr. Cox. We have to mention, on the other hand, as upholding the doctrine of their country,—Laing, in 1848; the author of *The Sabbath at Home and Abroad*, Pyott and Crease, who both write in poetic strains, with Rennison, in 1849; Lewis, Hunter, Dr. Greville, and the author of *An Address on the Evils of Sabbath Labour*, in 1850; D. C. A. Agnew and Oliver, in 1851; the writer of *The Christian's Sabbath*, and D. Gorrie, author of *The Sabbath, a Prize Poem*, in 1853; Professor Miller, Stewart, and Catherine Sinclair, in 1854; Pirret, and the authors of *The Claims of the Sabbath*, in 1855; M'Fie and Dr. Candlish, in 1856; Colvin, in 1857; J. M. Pollock, the writer of *The Love of God in the*

[1] To the number of 609,750 copies.—Jordan in *Religious Condition of Christendom.* (1852), p. 132

[2] *Ibid.* p. 131.

Sabbath, and Court against Langley, in 1858; and M'Naughtan, in 1859.

The marked contrast between the two classes of writers who have been enumerated, is significant. Those of them who have opposed the prevailing views of the institution number about twenty. They have flourished within the last quarter of a century. They include no name of note. And, except Begg and Cox, they have dogmatized on a matter which they been at no great pains to understand. It is otherwise with the authors who have maintained the doctrine of a Sabbath substantially the same from the beginning to the end of the world. They are upwards of a hundred. They extend over a period of about three centuries. They are for the most part known to have been qualified by education, character, and experience to write on the sacred theme. And not a few of them have been distinguished by their learning, talents, piety and beneficence, as Weemse, Calderwood, Young, Durham, Leighton, Brown, Burnet, Willison, the Haldanes, Duncan, Chalmers, Wardlaw,—not to name others, who still live among us, honoured for their acquirements, usefulness, and worth.[1]

Similar discussions to those that have been sketched have taken place in other countries, particularly in Germany and France. But we must pass them over. Dr. Hengstenberg has traced the German controversies on the subject, though we must say with a partial pen.

If we reflected on the moral condition of mankind, the discordant views which have been held in every department of knowledge, and the difficulty of arriving at certainty in many even of the simplest matters of fact, it would not surprise us that on the subject of the Sabbath there should have existed at any time a variety of sentiment. Nor will any mind that is sincere in the search after truth, allow a circumstance, common to so many things, to prejudice the particular one now under con-

[1] Of Scottish publications that have appeared since the preceding list was prepared for our first edition, we add for 1860, "A Few Observations on the Sanctification of the Sabbath," by James Young, an elder of the U.P. Church; for 1861, an article on Dr. Hessey's Bampton Lecture in the "North British Review," No. 67, and "The Sabbath Viewed in the Light of Reason," etc., by the writer of this note; and for 1862, "Our Scottish Sabbath," by Dr. A. Thomson.

sideration. Let it be remembered that the magnitude of the interests involved in the disposal of so large a portion of our limited and precious time, would warrant every exertion to reach a right decision, although the matter were much more difficult than it is—that the truth, after all, may be easily discovered by the honest inquirer—and that while the theories on the Sabbath, after they have been reduced to their proper categories, and estimated at their real worth, may be found neither so numerous nor so formidable as at first sight appeared, there has perhaps never been a topic on which a greater number of the wise and good have been agreed than the divine authority, the sanctity, and the value of a weekly day of rest and prayer.

These theories have to some extent been set forth in preceding pages. But it is desirable that the most important of them should be presented in a compendious form, so far as this can be done in a case in which so many writers, more or less agreed in certain views, have each some notion of his own. The general points in dispute concerning the institution have been its importance—its authority—its date and duration—the proportion and distribution of its time—the rule of its observance—and the manner in which it should be enforced. A weekly holy day is repudiated by some because they hold all days to be alike common—by others, because they hold all days to be alike sacred. The Sabbatarian affirms, that the seventh day of the week is the Divinely authorized, immutable Sabbath of all time, while the great majority of Christians maintain that "the obligation of that day ceased, together with the abrogation of [ceased together with] the other Jewish rites and ceremonies, at the death of Christ."[1] The claims of a weekly rest are admitted by various classes as a salutary arrangement of the State, or as a necessary ordinance of the Church, or as recommended by Jewish institution and apostolic practice—or as an express appointment of Heaven. Of those who believe in the Divine authority of the Lord's day, there are several classes. One class consider it as having no connexion with a Sabbath in Eden, which they deny to have had any existence, or with the Sabbath of Sinai, which, they assert, has been abrogated. A second class, conceding the primitive institution

[1] Tridentine Catechism on the Third [Fourth] Commandment.

of a Sabbath, view neither that nor the Jewish Sabbath—both, they say, having passed away with their respective economies—as constituting any formal reason for hallowing the Lord's day, the authority and sanctity of which, however, they strenuously maintain. And a third class plead, that the first day of the week has, by the ordination of Jesus Christ, succeeded to the seventh day Sabbath, not as the latter was applied according to the judicial and ceremonial laws of the Jews, but as it was appointed for man in Paradise, embodied in the Decalogue, and regulated by the fourth of its precepts. A variety of tenets, too, have been held with respect to the nature of the Sabbath law in the Fourth Commandment, some regarding it as a ceremony which has disappeared; others, as partly ceremonial and temporary, partly moral and enduring; a third class as simply positive; a fourth, as not positive at all, but throughout natural, moral, and unchangeable even as concerns the seventh day of the week; and a fifth, as natural, moral, and positive, or moral-positive. Some conceive that the Lord's day ought to be sacredly observed throughout all its hours, admitting, however, exceptional cases of necessity and mercy; others, that its demands of sacred service are satisfied by a few hours spent in public worship, the remaining time being available, in the opinion of one class, for such employments and recreations as do no violence to outward decency and decorum, but, in the view of others, for everything that may be lawfully done on any other day. A difference of sentiment on the manner in which the institution ought to be dealt with by the State has existed, but has excited little discussion—some believing that the Sabbath is a matter which lies beyond the sphere of civil enactments; others deeming it right that it should be protected, and certain outward violations of its requirements should be restrained and punished by the magistrate, either, according to one opinion, for political reasons, or, according to another, because Sabbath-breaking is, like murder, a transgression of the Divine law. To this enumeration of theories may be added that which interprets the days of God's working and rest at the creation as denoting, not common days, but periods of long duration, the dogma being employed by some to annihilate, by others, to favour, a primal and perennial day of rest.

That a weekly day of entire consecration to repose from secular labour, and to the immediate service of God, cases of necessity and mercy excepted, was at the creation of the world divinely appointed for man, was promulgated from Sinai in the Decalogue, and, being transferred by Jesus Christ from the end to the beginning of the week, was by Him recognised as an ordinance of the Christian dispensation, and as still under the rule of the Fourth Commandment,—is a doctrine which it is the object of this volume to uphold, illustrate, and recommend. And in endeavouring to accomplish this object, it is our purpose,—First, to adduce proofs from reason and experience of the excellence, value, and Divine origin of such a holy day. Second, to present the testimony of revelation to its Divine authority, its divinely-prescribed duties, and its divinely-estimated importance. Third, to exhibit from history evidence corroborative both of the proofs from reason and of the testimony of revelation on the subject. Fourth, to vindicate the institution against opposing theories, schemes, and arguments; and Fifth, to enforce its claims against practical perversions and neglect.

PROOFS FROM REASON AND EXPERIENCE OF THE EXCELLENCE AND DIVINE ORIGIN OF THE SABBATH

CHAPTER I.

PHYSICAL AND INTELLECTUAL ADAPTATIONS OF THE SABBATH.

"I feel as if God had, by giving the Sabbath, given fifty-two springs in the year."
COLERIDGE.

"I am prepared to affirm that, to the studious especially, and whether younger or older, a Sabbath well spent—spent in happy exercises of the heart, devotional and domestic—a Sunday given to the soul—is the best of all means of refreshment to the mere intellect."—ISAAC TAYLOR.

THE requisites to man's physical wellbeing may be comprehended under food, air, exercise, rest, sleep, cleanliness, and a cheerful state of mind.

Exercise is necessary, not only in many cases to the removal of disease, but in general to its prevention, and to the continued soundness and vigour of the entire animal system. To be beneficial, however, it must be moderate. Excess here is as fatal as defect. And it must be regular. There must be alternations of exertion and repose, the latter, particularly in the form of sleep, being needed for recruiting the nervous energy which labour has exhausted, and for abating the activity of the circulation which would else acquire a rapidity incompatible with life. Man ought to go forth to his work and to his labour until the evening, performing with regularity and without oppression his daily task under the eye of day. Those who work must work while it is day. They that sleep, sleep in the night. It is then that deep sleep falleth on men. Nature itself, in its vicissitudes of day and night, instructs us when to labour and when to indulge repose.

But in addition to the sleep and refreshment of night, there is need, from time to time, of a day of rest. "Although the night apparently equalizes the circulation, yet it does not sufficiently restore its balance for the attainment of a long life—hence one day in seven, by the bounty of Providence, is thrown in as a day of compensation to perfect by its repose the animal system."[1] By the periodical interposition of a day's respite from labour, a check is given to a course of toil, which would speedily destroy the workman, or, in other words, an opportunity is afforded for the rest which physiologists and physicians judge necessary for a season in many cases of disease, and recommend to be sought, at stated intervals, by all who would live long and see happy days. They tell us that the animal frame, whether in man or beast, can sustain only a certain amount of continuous exertion, and that the transgression of this limit, if persisted in, must, at no distant period, impair the constitution. "I believe," says Dr. Carpenter, "that it is the opinion of those who work many horses in coaching, etc., that it is better to work a horse (say ten miles a day) for four days, and to give him an entire rest on the fifth, than to work him eight miles a day for the whole five."[2] In the case of human beings, the earlier decay, the more prevalent diseases, and the briefer average life of working men than of the upper and middle classes of society, together with the uniform proportion which these evils bear to the amount of unremitting toil, confirm the conclusions of science. Taking the whole of the French population, human life, according to the estimate of M. Villerné, is protracted twelve and one-half years among the wealthy beyond its duration among the poor. In England, too, the difference is greatly in favour of the former class, as appears from the Report of the Poor-Law Commissioners for 1842, where thirteen cases are adduced, showing the average life of three classes to be as follows :—

	Gentlemen.	Tradesmen.	Working Population.
Town, ...	42	28	21
Country, . . .	50	44	35

[1] Dr. Farre in Evidence before a Committee of House of Commons (1832), p. 11[illegible].
[2] Letter to Mr. Grainger, *Woolwich Lectures on the Sabbath*, p. 53.

That a proportion of mortality so sad for the working classes is owing to a variety of causes, is not to be denied. Poverty, impure air, want of cleanliness, and vicious indulgence, contribute each its share of injury. But when we consider that unduly protracted labour operates with a twofold force, fostering these very evils as well as directly dilapidating the strength of its victims, we may well regard it as a principal cause of their physical deterioration. "My own opinion," writes Dr. Carpenter, "has long been very decided, that ten hours a day is the fullest amount that ought to be assigned to continued bodily labour, and where there is much mental tension, I should say that even this is too much." Mr. Grainger, who publishes this opinion, and affirms it to be concurred in by the highest medical and scientific authorities in this country, and confirmed by his own official inquiries in the manufacturing districts, adds, "If that limit be exceeded, the penalty must be paid in unnecessary sickness, in premature decay of the system, or, as constantly happens, in premature death."[1] Let the blame of these results be equitably distributed among those who, to gain their own ends, unwisely sacrifice the interests of their inferiors, and those who, with still more glaring folly, allow themselves, by vice and the neglect of Sabbatic rights, to be reduced to slavery.

There is another kind of labour—that of the mind—which more speedily and powerfully than merely animal exertion affects the physical condition, inasmuch probably as it calls into action the entire system by means of the brain, and its ubiquitous nervous energy. The moderate and regular exercise of the mental faculties and feelings is even conditional to the possession of the highest bodily health, while fitful and aimless employment of the mind, or incessant anxious thought on any one subject induces idiocy, or insanity, and death :—

> "But 'tis not thought (for still the soul's employed),
> 'Tis painful thinking that corrodes our clay."

No class of men enjoy better health, or attain more years, than those of calm studious habits. Persons, on the other hand, who overtask their mental powers, are prematurely sacrificed to their

[1] Letter to Mr. Grainger, *Woolwich Lectures on the Sabbath*, p. 53.

ardour or ambition. Few students are ignorant of the relief which some change, say a walk, the call of a friend, or a fresh topic of investigation, yields to the heated brain. Weber was aware of the effect and danger of intense uninterrupted thought, when he explained, "Would that I were a tailor, for then I should have a Sunday holiday!" By spending his evenings in soothing conversation with a friend after his daily labours on his great work, the *Synopsis*, Poole showed that he knew both his danger and the remedy.[1] Nor was the eminent Dr. Hope, of London, less considerate in dismissing every evening at eight o'clock all interest about his patients, a practice to which he was wont to attribute his long-continued life and health. "I do not think," says Dr. Carpenter, "that more than eight hours a day can be given to purely mental labour."[2]

Cleanliness has so close an affinity to morals as to have been classed among the virtues. It has, also, an intimate connexion with health, both as contributing to the purity of the atmosphere which we inhale, and as promoting the circulation of the blood, particularly over that membrane, the skin, which performs so important a part in the complex and delicate economy of life. It was no arbitrary law which required of the Jews frequent ablutions. It was one founded in the necessities of men, particularly in eastern countries, and calculated to have, morally and physically, a salutary influence on its subjects. It were easy to prove that a weekly holiday tends to foster habits of cleanliness. Let it be sufficient to refer to the appearance of church-going people in Scotland or England, as contrasted with the following state of things in France after its first Revolution: "The moroseness occasioned by the want of a Sabbath in France, has an effect on the cleanliness of young men engaged in manual labour; they pursue their daily drudgery in their dirty working dresses, and habit renders them at length averse to a change of linen and clothes."[3]

A cheerful mind is held by physiologists and medical men to be one of the causes of health. For want of this all means fail;

[1] Rose's *Biograph. Dict.* Article "Poole."
[2] *Woolwich Lectures*, p. 53.
[3] Jorgenson in his *Travels through France*, quoted *Edinburgh Review*, vol. xxviii. p. 382.

but by its aid the full benefit of exercise, air, food, and medicine is secured. One of the most striking illustrations of the influence exerted by the state of the mind on the bodily health is afforded by the fact, that the proportion of sick in an army is least after a victory, greater when it is quartered in a garrison during peace, increased in a campaign, and highest in the event of a defeat, although the circumstances otherwise be not unfavourable.[1] Rest itself, while not the only boon of a Sabbath, is one of its salutary provisions. Many who are utterly regardless of any Divine claim to a portion of their time are yet willing enough to have a day of leisure. The call for variety and repose is the voice of their nature. To that call the recurring day of rest is a gratifying response. They feel that the prospect of a period of vacation lightens and animates work, and that a change braces them for fresh efforts. Thus they go on hopefully and happily with their weekly task. Now, as labour to be favourable to health must be prosecuted voluntarily and with pleasure, it is impossible to calculate the sanitary advantage of a Sabbath-day to the many children of toil.

But there are other modes in which, by means of the pleasure it brings, the institution produces salutary effects. Its required subjects of thought are great, pure, and of surpassing interest; and its services combine, in a manner and degree peculiar to themselves, the means of mental elevation and social good, with those of rational and unalloyed delight. It is mainly thus that the Sabbath is promotive of a healthful cheerfulness of mind. Its engagements have a power of their own to turn back the current of anxious thought and distracting care, and to beguile the toils of the succeeding week.

Here, then, in the noblest sense, are "the intellectual, moral, and sympathetic enjoyments," which physiologists assure us are conducive to health, and which warrant the application to the conscientious Sabbath-keeper of these words, from the pen of Dr. Southwood Smith. "Enjoyment is the only condition of life which is compatible with a protracted term of existence. The happier a human being is, the longer he lives; the more he suffers, the sooner he dies; to add to enjoyment is to lengthen life;

[1] Chambers's *Information for the People*, vol. i. p. 670.

to inflict pain is to shorten the duration of existence."[1] It is allowed that to receive and give instruction relative to the Creator, Preserver, and Saviour of mankind ; to disburden the mind of its cares by supplication to the Father of Mercies ; to utter and hear "the songs and cheerful sounds" of praise ; to read, think, and converse about the glories of nature, redemption, and immortality, and to do good to the bodies and souls of their fellow-creatures, are to some professed friends of the Sabbath unpleasant occupations, and are conceived by its adversaries to induce in all who engage in them a gloominess such as they themselves, if so employed, would feel ; but the duties enumerated have in their own nature no such tendency, as, if we believe the testimony of the most truthful of men, confirmed by all the outward tokens of happiness, they most certainly in their own experience have no such result. Wilberforce was not a less joyous man than any of those contemporary statesmen who kept no Sabbath, nor would an actuary have regarded theirs as "better lives." And are our labouring men, who spend the seventh day in their ordinary work, or in idleness and amusement, really happier beings than their fellows who devote it to sacred use? We may with perfect confidence reply, the very reverse.

It thus appears that an occasional season of rest beyond that of night is of advantage to our physical nature, adjusting the measure of labour to the labourer's strength, and lightening its pressure by inspiring cheerfulness and hope, and that to this extent the Sabbath, while it makes provision for the inferior animals according to their more limited wants, is adapted to the necessities and to the wellbeing of man.

But why a whole day? and why a seventh day? To these important questions we proceed to offer some reply. The cravings of nature for periods of rest may, as regards the proportion of time that would be satisfying and beneficial, be considerably vague. Experience, however, soon convinces the individual that such seasons must be frequent and regular. Those who are habitually occupied in hard work would in general prefer for relaxation a whole day, though more rarely recurring, to portions of days at short intervals. It is well known to be a practice for

[1] *Philosophy of Health*, vol. i. p. 101.

artisans to labour some additional time each day that they may enjoy more leisure at the close of the week. Such persons, if in any degree observant, discover that a periodical day of rest tends to promote their comfort and health, provided they avoid those excesses of indulgence, and even of idleness, which frustrate the best provisions for human happiness. From whatever causes arising, certain it is that the seventh day was among ancient nations, and is in many countries still, observed as a season of abstinence from the ordinary business of life. Recent observations and experiments, moreover, have fully demonstrated that such is the allowance of time which man and even his beast of burden require for rest in order to the ease and safety of customary labour. Let us adduce evidence for the truth of this position.

We are not aware that much attention has been given to this subject by our eminent writers on Physiology and Health. Dr. Carpenter, indeed—and he is himself a host—writing to a friend in 1852, said, "My own experience is very strong as to the importance of the complete rest and change of thought once in the week."[1] But the matter has come under the consideration of not a few scientific as well as practical men, whose testimony with respect to it is entitled to credit, and appears to be decisive.

The evidence of J. R. Farre, M.D., on the point, has obtained considerable currency and fame. "All men, of whatever class," he says, "who must necessarily be occupied six days in the week, should abstain on the seventh, and in the course of life would assuredly gain by giving to their bodies the repose, and to their minds the change of ideas, suited to the day, for which it was appointed by unerring wisdom. I have frequently observed the premature death of medical men from continued exertion. I have advised the clergyman, in lieu of his Sabbath, to rest one day in the week: it forms a continual prescription of mine. I have seen many destroyed by their duties on that day, and to preserve others, I have frequently suspended them for a season from the discharge of those duties. The working of the mind in one continued train of thought is destructive of life in the most distinguished class of society, and senators themselves stand in need of reform in that particular. I have observed many of them de-

[1] *Woolwich Lectures on the Sabbath*, p. 53.

stroyed by neglecting this economy of life."[1] This testimony, important as that of an able and experienced physician, derives additional weight from the medical authorities in this country and in America, who have expressed their emphatic concurrence in its terms, or given forth a corresponding opinion. No fewer than six hundred and forty-one medical men of London, including Dr. Farre, subscribed a petition to Parliament against the opening of the Crystal Palace for profit on Sundays, containing the following sentence—"Your petitioners, from their acquaintance with the labouring classes, and with the laws which regulate the human economy, are convinced that a seventh day of rest, instituted by God, and coeval with the existence of man, is essential to the bodily health and mental vigour of men in every station of life."[2] Many medical men on the other side of the Atlantic—of whom we name only Drs. Warren of Boston, Smith of New York, Harrison and Mussey of the Ohio Medical College, and Alden of Massachusetts—are equally decided in entertaining the same views. We must content ourselves with the striking words of Dr. Mussey, Professor of Surgery in the above-mentioned institution, who affirms that "under the due observance of the Sabbath, life would, on the average, be prolonged more than one seventh of its whole period; that is, more than seven years in fifty."[3]

From medical authority let us turn to the views held by persons who, as masters and employers of workmen, or as otherwise having excellent opportunities of observing the condition of the laborious members of society, are competent witnesses in the cause. Dr. Humphrey mentions a case which has often been cited. "A contractor went on to the west, with his hired men and teams, to make a turnpike road. At first he paid no regard to the Sabbath, but continued his work as on other days. He soon found, however, that the ordinances of nature, no less than the moral law, were against him. His labourers became sickly; his teams grew poor and feeble; and he was fully convinced that more was lost than gained by working on the Lord's day. So true it is, that

[1] Report on the Observance of the Sabbath-day from Select Committee of House of Commons, etc. (1832), p. 119.

[2] *Association Medical Journal,* June 1853, p. 554.

[3] *Permanent Sabbath Documents* (Boston, U.S., 1844), No. 1, p. 30.

the Sabbath-day labourer, like the glutton and the drunkard, undermines his health, and prematurely hastens the infirmities of age and his exit from this world."[1] Let another out of many similar instances suffice. Two thousand men "were employed for years, seven days in a week. To render them contented in giving up their right to the Sabbath as a day of rest, that birthright of the human family, they paid them double wages on that day, eight days' wages for seven days' work. But they could not keep them healthy, nor make them moral. Things went badly, and they changed their course—employed the workmen only six days in a week, and allowed them to rest on the Sabbath. The consequence was, that they did more work than ever before. This, the superintendent said, was owing to two causes—the demoralization of the people under the first system, and their exhaustion of bodily strength, which was visible to the most casual observer."[2] When we advert to exertions of another description, we find that the result of everyday work is the same. It was remarked by the celebrated painter, Sir David Wilkie, that "those artists who wrought on Sunday were soon disqualified from working at all."[3] The editor of the *Standard* some years ago recorded the result of many years' observation in these words—"We never knew a man work seven days a week, who did not kill himself or kill his mind." And Wilberforce said that he could name several of his contemporaries in the vortex of political cares whose minds had actually given way under the stress of intellectual labour, so as to bring on a premature death.[4]

There is a third class who, from their experience of hard labour, either of mind or of body, are entitled to be listened to on this question. Manual labourers will be found nearly unanimous in the conviction that continuous toil is destructive to health; and we have seen upwards of one thousand of them publishing to the world their persuasion that a weekly day of exemption from toil, and yet spent not in total inaction or amusement, but in the duties of piety and benevolence, is indispensable to their physical welfare,

[1] *Essay on the Sabbath* (Lond. 1830), p. 60.
[2] *Permanent Sabbath Documents*, No. 1, p. 83.
[3] *The Sabbath at Home and Abroad*, p. 47.
[4] Venn in Scott's *Discourse on Wilberforce*, p. 32, note.

and even to the preservation of life. One of them remarks, that "on more than one occasion he has found that continued application to labour during six days in the busy season, and consequent long hours, was more than his constitution would bear, and that if he had attempted to dispense with the relaxation of the Sabbath, he should long since, he firmly believed, have retired to the rest and silence of the grave."[1] Another says, "Many a man would tell us that he could not support himself under his arduous toils, were it not for the periodical return of the Lord's day."[2] When persons who have attempted to work on the seventh, as on the other days of the week, have been compelled to resort to its rest, the evidence is even strengthened. A party of gold-diggers in California made trial of the former practice. The result is thus stated by Dr. Brooks, one of their number :—"After dinner we determined to rest till the next day. The fact is, that the human frame will not stand, and was never intended to stand, a course of incessant toil; indeed, I believe that in civilized, that is to say, in industrious communities, the Sabbath bringing round as it does a stated remission from labour, is an institution physically necessary. We have all of us given over working on Sundays, as we found the toil on six successive days quite hard enough."[3] The French, it is well known, had sufficient experience of both a seventh and a tenth day's rest; and that the change from the former to the latter had been, in respect of sanitary interests, found wanting, formed one of the reasons of their return to their ancient practice. Akin to the testimony just presented is that of persons who have been engaged in the more exhausting labours of the mind. A distinguished financier charged with an immense amount of property during the great pecuniary pressure of 1836 and 1837, said, I should have been a dead man had it not been for the Sabbath.[4] Similar was the experience of Wilberforce in another department of mental exertion. "I have often heard him assert," observes the Rev. John Venn, "that he never could have sustained the labour and stretch of mind required in his early political life, if it had not been for the rest of the Sabbath."[5] Dr. Farre, who has

1 *Prize Essays by Five Working Men*, p. 174. 2 *Ibid.* p. 42.
3 *Four Months among the Gold-finders in Alta California*, pp 58-60, 82.
4 *Permanent Sabbath Documents*, No. 1, pp. 27, 28.
5 Venn, in Scott's *Discourse on Wilberforce*, p. 32, note.

afforded us the benefit of his acquaintance with the human frame, may again be called to attest the influence of professional toils which may be considered as both mental and bodily. "I have found it essential to my own wellbeing," he says, "to abridge my labours on the Sabbath to what is actually necessary."

A very interesting department of our subject respects the benefit accruing from a weekly day of rest to certain of the lower animals. These creatures have in common with man physical natures, which are worn down by excessive labour and recruited by rest. They are observed to be amenable to laws of health and disease no less unerring, and in some instances even more appreciable, than those which apply to their masters. And it is found that such of them as are employed in our service require equally as we the rest of the seventh day. The statement made before a statistical society by Mr. Bianconi of Clonmel in Ireland, proprietor at the time of one hundred and ten vehicles which travelled from eight to ten miles an hour, is well known. He mentioned that none of the cars, except those connected with the mail, were run on Sunday; that he found it much easier to work a horse eight miles every week-day, in place of six miles, than an additional six miles on Sundays; and that by this plan there is a saving of thirteen per cent., adding, I am persuaded, that man cannot be wiser than his Maker.[1] Intelligent coach-proprietors have confirmed the views of Bianconi.[2] And an American writer, after adducing some interesting facts in proof of the necessity of the Sabbath's rest to man and beast, proceeds to say, "Great numbers have made similar experiments and uniformly with similar results; so that it is now settled *by facts*, that the observance of the Sabbath is required by a *natural law*, and that were man nothing more than an animal, and were his existence to be confined to this world, it would be for his interest to observe the Sabbath."[3]

That the Sabbatic institution is eminently calculated to promote the intellectual improvement of mankind, will appear from two considerations.

[1] See *Life of Sir A. Agnew*, p. 29.

[2] Report on the Observance of the Sabbath-day from Select Committee of House of Commons, etc. (1832), pp. 126, 127, 130.

[3] *Permanent Documents*, No. 1, pp. 40, 41.

First, it affords regularly the opportunity and facilities for desisting from pursuits which, if not so interrupted, are fatal to mental cultivation, and a season for employing the means of improving the mind, which, without such an institution, could not be provided.

Let us look at this consideration, in the first instance, as applying to persons whose occupations are of an intellectual rather than of a physical nature, men of science and literature, statesmen, financiers, merchants, and others. It is well known that the exertion of thought on any subject, if prolonged beyond a certain time, is detrimental to both body and mind. Health fails, and nothing is more unfavourable to mental vigour than physical exhaustion. The views become clouded; the power of attention is impaired; and the result of persistence in such a course must, as already remarked, be idiocy, insanity, or death. What would have prevented these evils? Nothing but a discontinuance of the customary mental exertion. It is not the activity of the intellect, but its activity as put forth in one uniform mode, that does the injury. The cure, or the preventive, as the case may be, must be sought for, not in total rest, which is not necessary, and is indeed, from the nature of spirit, impossible, but in variety of exercise. There must be, in fact, a regularly recurring day on which the current of thought shall flow in a new channel—a day neither too frequent nor too rare in its return. And it must be prescribed, not by physicians, or by any human law merely, but by an indisputable, over-awing authority, as well as be connected with engagements and sanctions fitted to absorb in themselves, and neutralize the most powerful attractions and propensities that bind men to their ordinary pursuits.

Let us next turn for a moment to the case of the far greater number who subsist by the work of their hands. To them a Sabbath is no less necessary, intellectually, than to the other class. Were there no such day, the continual drudgery to which they should be consigned would preclude every means of mental culture. Working men there must be; and it is manifest that if their toils were interrupted only by night and an occasional holiday, there could be no disposition, motive, or even time, for acquiring knowledge and otherwise improving their minds. While the every-day labour in many trades ought to be lessened, there must, moreover, be periodical seasons, and these at no great intervals, which the labourer can count upon and call his own—there must, in other words, be a weekly Sabbath.

But, *second*, the Sabbatic institution provides subjects and occupations fitted to stimulate and discipline the faculties of the human mind.

The period that can be allowed the great majority of men in a civilized country for cessation from their ordinary business, must necessarily be a small proportion of their whole time. It would, therefore, require to be well husbanded and laid out, so as most effectually to secure to intellectual labourers engagement on subjects the most important, and yet the most diverse from those that usually engross their thoughts, and to manual labourers the best nourishment and exercise for their spiritual nature. If so brief and precious a season be not thus spent, it might, in so far as mental profit is concerned, be as well not possessed at all. And to the mass of men there must in such a matter be prescription. To leave them in ignorance and uncertainty as to the manner of employing their leisure time, would be, in the far greater number of cases, to render the time useless, or rather a burden and a curse.

How fully does the Sabbath meet those demands! Its work, as well as its specific time, is appointed. In adaptation to our constitution, that work is not only different from the secular business of other days, but diversified in its parts, uniting the public, the domestic, and the personal—the pleasure and the profit of acquiring knowledge, by the various channels of reading, hearing, and reflection—and the opportunities of imparting instruction and administering comfort to our fellow-creatures. Such are the wise arrangements and determination of the work of the day.

Then what grander, more interesting, or more beneficial subjects can be presented to human inquiry than creation and its works—the world in its divine government and redemption—the Supreme Being in his infinite and glorious perfections—the relation of man to his Maker, to the present scene, and to a future state—the cause and results of his manifest depravation—and the knowledge, purity, and happiness which are the destined inheritance of a coming age! What engagements, too, can be more ennobling or gladdening than drawing near to the Eternal, offering him homage, investigating his character and works, and celebrating his praise? Intelligent on such topics, and stimulated by such exercises, what higher learning or better mental training can a man receive—to what other kind of knowledge or intellectual effort can he be either indifferent or inadequate?

There is one special means of favourably influencing the general mind, which may be considered as almost identified with the Sabbath, being a kindred institution that has sprung up with it, and shared its fortunes of prosperity or decay. We refer to the pulpit. One man has by previous training been prepared for the office of a preacher, and devotes himself to the collection of those stores of truth which he gives out on the first day of the week to hundreds or thousands, whereby he stirs dormant faculties, enlightens ignorance, and suggests topics of consolation and encouragement under the toils and trials of life. The work of one saves that of many, and as he profits by the exertions of the merchant, husbandman, and mechanic, so they receive the fruit of his studies without being subjected to his peculiar labours. When to these considerations we add the power of the living voice, the sympathies of associated hearers, and, above all, the magnitude of the themes illustrated and enforced, we venture to affirm that no means are more adapted to the constitution and improvement of the human mind, than the Christian pulpit. The fit occupant of so commanding a post must wield a mighty influence over the minds of his fellow-men. "The messenger of truth"—

> "Armed himself in panoply complete
> Of heavenly temper, furnishes with arms
> Bright as his own, and trains, by every rule
> Of holy discipline, to glorious war,
> The sacramental host of God's elect.
> Are all such teachers? Would to Heaven all were!"

There is another specific means of intellectual benefit connected with the institution—Sabbath-evening instruction—which may be ranked next in importance to the pulpit itself. By requiring from children and domestics an account of what they have heard from their ministers during the day, and by catechetical exercises on that evening, heads of families may largely promote their own improvement and that of their households. Where these duties are conducted with wisdom and affection, what an amount of information may be lodged in the memories, what an impulse given to the faculties, of teachers, and taught! Nor is this the only way in which the evening of a holy day can be turned to account in the communication of knowledge. Many are so circumstanced as to have it in their power to take charge of young persons who have no others to care for their welfare, and Sabbath-schools prove, like parental tuition and deeds of charity, the means of blessing both the givers and the receivers. If there were no such day, however, or if it were devoted to manual labour or to pleasure, the vast machinery of mental and moral education to which we have now referred could not exist.

But valuable as are the engagements of the day in these respects, we should not fully estimate their worth, if we did not take into account the means of instruction and mental improvement on other days, which they stimulate and maintain.

The Sabbatic institution stands related not merely to the public teaching of the preacher, but to the more frequent private ministrations of the pastor. The presence of such a man, educated as he ought ever to be and usually is, must be a light to his neighbours. By his conversation in company—by his official visits from house to house—by his attention to the young—by his encouragement of reading and education—and by the necessity laid upon him, in connexion with other office-bearers of the Church, to exclude the grossly ignorant from certain Christian privileges, he is perhaps more than any other single individual the instrument of awakening inquiry and diffusing knowledge.

While idleness, secular work, and frivolous or worse pursuits on the sacred day, give their corresponding tone to the mind in the progress of the week, the person who has been on that day conversant with highly intellectual and interesting themes will be constrained to follow out those trains of thought which such engagements have originated. One inquiry suggests another. Acquisitions are successively made. And thus from week to week the man advances in the highest, most comprehensive, most useful of all departments of knowledge—the knowledge of himself, and of the Being who alone presents an object that answers the demands of the human understanding, and satisfies the cravings of the human heart.

The observer of the Sabbath, moreover, is induced by its instructions, and by his own conscience and inclinations to practise, daily, certain duties than which no means can be conceived more subservient to intellectual profit. He who has on that day heard with proper earnestness and interest the public reading and exposition of portions of the sacred volume, must desire to repair to its pages for further information, and for testing the sentiments of the preacher. Every one knows the effect of persevering diligence in any pursuit. And what must be the expanding, assimilating power of a Book, containing confessedly the loftiest truths, the most perfect rules of morals, the finest poetry, the most ancient history, the most graphic pictures of nature, the profoundest views of man, the noblest strains of eloquence, over the mind of him who "gives his days and his nights" to its perusal? If the saying, "Beware of the man of one book," as intimating the intellectual prowess of such a reader, was ever in its fullest sense applicable to any one, it must have been to the student of the greatest and best of books—the Bible.

To the searching of the Scriptures, the friend of the Sabbath adds a service no less effectual for mental elevation. He holds intercourse by prayer with the All-wise and the Almighty. And if converse with the intelligent has the effect of informing and expanding the mind, how mighty the influence on the intellectual faculties of frequent communion with "the Father of lights!"

It is the practice of all heads of families who are marked by their reverence for the Lord's day, to convene their households morning and evening, when possible, for devotion, including praise, the reading of the word of God, and prayer. "This is a school of religious instruction. The whole contents of the sacred volume are in due course laid open before the members of the family. Every day they are receiving 'line upon line, precept upon precept.' A fresh accession is continually making to their stock of knowledge; new truths are gradually opened to their view, and the impressions of old truths are revived."[1] That this admirable discipline of the intellect is provided by the authority which appointed the day of sacred rest might be shown. It is sufficient, however, for our present purpose to state, that Sabbath observers feel both an obligation and a disposition to follow up their public services on that day with those of personal and domestic devotion. When David, King of Israel, had been employed in the public acts of religion, he "returned to bless his household." "Public exercises of religion, when properly conducted, have a happy tendency to prepare the mind for those of a more private nature. When the soul is elevated and the heart softened by the feelings which public worship is calculated to inspire, we are prepared to address the throne of grace with peculiar advantage: we are disposed to enter with a proper relish on such a duty, and thus to go from strength to strength."[2]

To the means of intellectual improvement furnished by the institution, may be added the useful reading, the rational conversation, and the meetings for religious conference, for secular instruction, and for other important objects to which the friends of the Sabbath are incited by its teachings and studies, and which, while indisposing for and precluding indolence and unworthy occupations, make them intelligent and acute on all subjects that concern their true interests. The desire of knowledge, awakened in reference to the momentous matters of religion, will "seek and intermeddle with all wisdom."

From the account of the educational provisions of the Sabbath which has thus been presented, it might be conclusively inferred that an institution so adapted to the constitution and improvement of the human mind must yield correspondent fruit; in other words, that individuals must be distinguished by intelligence, and communities by civilisation, in proportion as they have observed a weekly day of sacred rest. It ought to require no tedious process of reasoning, or long array of facts, to convince any one that a person who rests every seventh day from severe intellectual efforts, and refreshes his spirit for new exertions, will be more enlightened and more capable of adding to the stock of human knowledge than another who goes on in an unrelieved, unvarying, and there-

[1] Robert Hall's *Works*, 12mo. vol. v. p. 289. [2] *Ibid.* pp. 283, 284.

fore depressing and enfeebling course of application to the same studies. Argument and evidence ought still less to be demanded in support of the very obvious truth, that the man who spends fifty-two days of the year in dealing with the most intellectual and varied of all subjects, will be superior in mental capacity and acquirements to him who spends the same amount of time in unremitting bodily toil, or in mere recreation and amusement. In proportion as this is true of the individuals composing a society, it must be true of the aggregate body. The inveterate dislike to the institution, however, which has set many to the utmost stretch of their ingenuity for the purpose of perplexing and complicating a very plain matter, requires us to show that intellectual improvement, besides being among the adaptations, is everywhere the actual result of a hallowed Sabbath.

What Sabbath-observing nation, it has been asked, has ever been barbarous or ignorant? The lands of the Sabbath and of the Bible have always been the chosen abodes of knowledge, and the lights of the earth. The Jews were in possession of a literature when darkness covered all other people. Every nation that received the gospel and the Christian Sabbath found them to be the elements of learning and civilisation. Corrupted though Christianity soon became, it remained even in the dark ages in some measure an asylum of literature and a conservator of learned works. Whence that corruption? Rome perverted the Sabbath, discouraged the general reading of the sacred volume, and well-nigh quenched the light of the pulpit in spectacles, pageants, buffoonery, and the mysteries of the mass, and its life in pæans to Mary and curses against heretics, proving herself then, as she is still, an incubus on the progress of Europe to light and prosperity. But the Reformation, which liberated the sacred day from human impositions, raised it from the degrading level of unauthorized festivals, restored the Scriptures to unrestricted use, and elevated the pulpit to its place as the great instrument of unfolding and enforcing sacred truth and law, was everywhere the reviver of letters, and the nurse of a spirit of inquiry and intelligence. Let England and France, Scotland and Spain, Canada Upper and Canada Lower, the United States and Mexico, Ulster and Connaught, show how much intellectual character is affected by the presence or absence of a holy Sabbath. No country has continued so long to maintain its superiority in respect of the attainments of its learned men, and the general intelligence of its people, as Britain; and in no country has more regard been evinced to the Lord's day. Next in order to Britain comes America, advancing with rapid strides in "the march of intellect" as well as of religion, and already, perhaps, in the department of common education, outstripping its rival. Nor in their own mental supremacy merely, but in taking the lead of all others as propagators of knowledge and civilisation throughout the world, do these great nations exhibit the power of the principles which it is the business of the Sabbath to expound and conserve, to enforce and diffuse. Never was more done in defence of the institution, or more of its spirit felt, than from the middle of Elizabeth's reign to the Restoration, a period which a high authority pronounces to be unequalled in point of "real force and originality of genius" by any other age, those of Pericles, of Augustus, of Leo X., and of Louis XIV., being unworthy of comparison with it.[1] No less distinguished, as regards the body of the people, were the times in the history of Scotland when not only the claims and observance of the Lord's day were contended for, but efforts were successfully made to set up an adequate number of schools in every parish, as well as to raise a high standard of theological literature; and the times of those Puritans who settled in America, and who, the friends of a day of holy rest, were also educated and intelligent men, few if any of them being unable to read, and one of the first subjects of their attention being a suitable provision for the establishment of common schools and academies. In our own day, it is Sabbath observing parents who are most anxious to have their children educated; it is Sabbath-keeping artisans who are the most diligent readers of their class, as well as the most numerous pupils in our schools of art. The fact of one thousand and forty-five working men having written essays on the institution—all of them creditable to the writers—six hundred of them so respectable, as, in the opinion of a gentleman who had carefully examined them, to be worthy of appearing

[1] Francis Jeffrey. See *Edinburgh Review*, vol. xviii. pp. 275, 276; and Jeffrey's *Contributions to the Edinburgh Review*, vol. ii. pp. 38, 39.

in print, and a few such as would have done no discredit to the most practised pens, is indeed a phenomenon in the literary world, which nothing but the mighty power of the Sabbath and of its connected influences can explain. Many working men, however, have no weekly resting-day. Now, as one of the above-mentioned writers asks, "When did we ever meet with any one who from the nature of his employment is required to labour on the Sabbath as on other days, who has come out of his obscurity, and taken his stand as an author in literature, science, morals, or religion? Indeed," as he adds, "no one expects it; the bare supposition is ludicrous."[1] And yet these men are not inferior in natural capacities to other men. Their frequent efforts to obtain emancipation from their protracted hours of labour, that they might enjoy the rest of the seventh day, have evinced a desire of better things, as well as a deep conviction, that, while the cause of their degradation is the loss of that sacred season, its recovery is the main instrument for elevating their mental condition.

If the Sabbath had done nothing more than promote the intelligence and civilisation of the masses, it would be entitled to our high regards. But this is not its only intellectual triumph. It blesses in the same way all classes of minds that come under its influence. In the department of secular knowledge, it is a means of good to both foes and friends; to foes, who are trained in youth under its auspices, and afterwards feel the salutary impulse of its encompassing spirit; to friends, among whom may ever be discovered the most distinguished men in all kinds of mental endowments and exertion, with a few, such as Lord Bacon, Sir Isaac Newton, John Locke, and Jonathan Edwards, who, by general consent, occupy a pre-eminent place among the intellectually great. And there is another department of knowledge, the spiritual, belonging exclusively to true Christians, who, in proportion as they have maintained the integrity and honour of their religious institutions, have, by "rising from nature" to its Author, by searching after "the cause of causes," and in the range of their vision taking in the infinite and eternal, proved themselves to belong to a higher order of intelligences, and to possess far greater grasp and power of mind than those philosophers, scholars, and

[1] *The Universal Treasure*, p. 125.

sages, who are learned in the writings of men, but not in the Word of God; who have measured the distance of the stars, and told us what is contained in the bowels of the earth, but have not soared to the heaven above, nor sounded the hell below; who have calculated the period of an eclipse, but not the hour of death; who have explored the constitution of the soul, but considered not its accountableness or destination; who have wasted themselves in investigating the changes which this earth has undergone, without a single reflection on their concern in that great crisis, when "the earth and the works that are therein shall be burnt up."

CHAPTER II.

MORAL AND RELIGIOUS INFLUENCE OF THE SABBATH.

"A corruption of morals usually follows a profanation of the Sabbath."—BLACKSTONE.
"Il n'y a pas de religion sans culte, et il n'y a pas de culte sans dimanche."
MONTALEMBERT.

JOHN FOSTER describes the Sabbath as "a remarkable appointment for raising the general tenour of moral existence."[1] The saying, and that of Blackstone, as may afterwards appear, are abundantly verified by facts. Meanwhile, a brief inquiry into the *rationale* of the matter will discover grounds for accrediting the institution with the results uniformly seen to follow its observance—in other words, for identifying it as an essential instrument in their production.

First, then, if we view the weekly holy day as a periodical pause of labour, we shall find that it is conducive to the interests of morality. Its regular rest recruits the animal frame, and prevents some strong temptations to intemperance. Men must have either rest, or artificial means of enabling them to sustain an unnatural amount of effort. The Sabbath provides the former, intoxicating drink supplies the latter. The weekly season of freedom from toil and trouble secures also a regular opportunity for the cultivation of domestic intercourse, that powerful incentive to virtue. In the nature of things can virtue thrive, or vice fail to abound, among married persons who are deprived of the soothing, refining influences of home, and must not the unmarried be led by the same circumstances to forego the hope of honourable matrimony, and to resort to an unhallowed substitute? Incessant labour, moreover, renders moral improvement impracticable, as it allows no sufficient or regular time for attention to the matter. It op-

[1] *Evils of Popular Ignorance* (1839), pp. 47, 48.

presses and irritates the workman, and thus tempts him to save his exertions by a hurried unfaithful performance of his task, or by the still easier process of stealing or begging his bread. And from the contracting influence of one ever-present engrossing object, as well as from the controlling, assimilating power of scenes of impurity and discomfort, it not only prevents expansion of mind beyond the narrow sphere of his own fatigues and wants, and precludes any lofty aspirings to what is either good or great, but tends to sink the man in the animal—to brutalize him—to make him utterly selfish and savage, unless, as sometimes happens, it reduce him to so entire a prostration of spirit and energy as to render him incapable of doing much of either good or evil. Scarcely less immoral in its tendency is mental toil, absorbing as it does the mind in its one subject, so that no other can command its interest, and impairing the intellectual and physical powers, the health and vigour of which are so necessary to high moral attainments, and to sustained moral efforts.

But, *secondly*, we must consider the Sabbath as a day of instruction and worship in order to complete the evidence of its moral power.

The provision of respite from ordinary labour is but a part of the Sabbatic arrangement—a part of it, indeed, good in its place—capable of advantage, but convertible also to evil, and then only answering its whole design, as well as serving fully its end of rest, when it is made tributary to its sacred objects. It is as a day of holy rest that it is so powerful in promoting the physical well-being and mental improvement of mankind. And it will not accomplish much for their moral benefit, if the enjoyment of its rest be not conjoined with the right use of its means of religious knowledge and worship.

What the institution and observances are which are found to be connected with a high measure of morality in any case, we have already described in the preceding remarks on the arrangements which have been shown to be favourable to the improvement of the mind, and which might be proved to be equally so to that of the manners. It is necessary, in addition, merely to advert in a few words to the following characteristics of the Sabbath wherever it stands related to superior virtue among a people.

The most perfect rule of ethics, according to the confessions even of infidels, is expounded and studied on that day—a rule extending to the relations and circumstances of all mankind—uniting with this universality of reference, a wonderful conciseness, simplicity, and clearness—unassailably self-consistent—embracing the regulation of every outward act, and yet preferring its chief claims to a pure heart—and inculcating love to all men, founded on a paramount love to the Supreme Being. This rule is held forth under the authority of the Divine Creator and Governor of the Universe, who has declared the penalty of its violation to be eternal death. But along with these truths, it is announced that the Lawgiver himself, in compassion to his creatures, and yet resolved that the purity of his name and government shall receive no taint, has provided in the substitution and sacrifice of a Personage, at once Divine and human, an atonement for transgression. It is proclaimed, also, that he is willing to receive into favour all who repent and accept reconciliation through this medium, and that those who do so shall then come under the Divine law as divested of the condemnation and terror which the breach of it had caused, and shall find a course of obedience to it accompanied by abundant help, profit, and pleasure here, and followed by perpetual honour and happiness in a nobler state of being hereafter. It is impossible to conceive considerations more powerful than these for awing and melting human hearts, and for inspiring those feelings of penitence, fear, hope, joy, love, which bear irresistible sway over the minds of men. There is the highest moral discipline in the study of such themes. But to this are added the elevating approach to the Being of infinite greatness, purity, and love—the communion of fellow-men in circumstances so fitted to beget feelings of mutual sympathy and regard—the watchful care of faithful guardians over the temporal interests and moral condition of the people on every day—and the various influences of reading, reflection, example, instruction, and counsel, for which the Sabbath guarantees time and opportunity to those who hallow its sacred hours. We have to add that in connexion with such means of good there is imparted a celestial influence—the necessity of which human frailty proves, and the actual receiving of which the experience of the most virtuous men attests, disposing the individual to abandon the most vicious habits and to live soberly, righteously, and piously in the world.

Where, we may ask, can there be pointed out a similar provision for teaching and enforcing morality, or the laws of any society or country? The purest ethics of Greece and Rome were polluted by foul admixtures; wanted authority; were recommended by no perfect example in gods or men; relaxed law to accommodate human imperfection, instead of presenting means of vindicating the law by the punishment of the offence, and yet of restoring the offender to favour and purity; and contained no provision for securing influence to prompt and strengthen virtuous endeavour. Passing over other systems liable to equally fatal objections, we find those Protestants, who claim the right to abridge the time and to lower the obligation of the Christian Sabbath, stripping it of well-nigh everything that seems to constitute its moral power. To secularize the day in any form or degree does not appear a likely means of enabling a man to shake off the dust of earth, and to nourish his mental part, his immortal spirit. Nor do the services usually attached to such a Sabbath—the devotions engaged in as if they were a disrelished task, and cold prelections on virtue, with little or no reference to resources and commanding motives for its cultivation, and to the means of its acceptance above—give the best promise of moral fruit.

How a Sabbath, sneeringly called puritanical, but in reality regulated, as will be proved, by the law of its Author, should exert an influence on character so much more potent and salutary than that of any other scheme, it is not difficult to perceive. Some of the principles involved in the subject have been recognised by persons of the greatest name in ethical science, and in practical philanthropy. Sir James Mackintosh, when referring to the superior excellence of certain communities, observes, "Those who preached faith, or, in other words, a pure mind, have always produced more popular virtue than those who preached good works, or the mere regulation of outward acts."[1] The principle of faith, which, terminating on merely human testimony, is so controlling a power in the business of life, is, when its object is the Word of God, as much more operative as the evidence is more certain, and

[1] *Memoirs*, vol. i. p. 411.

as the truths and facts are immensely more important. Let men believe that they are under the eye of an omniscient, almighty, pure, and benignant Intelligence, to whom they are responsible for every thought as well as every action, and especially that "the same awful Being submitted to pay the forfeiture of sin in his own person," that they might not die for ever; and must not this belief "work by love," "purify the heart," and "overcome the world," so as that it shall be powerless to terrify or seduce from the path of rectitude? A philosopher, even more distinguished than the one just named, has borne a still fuller testimony to our principles. It is a well-known fact, for which they have often been vilified, that the advocates of a strictly observed Sabbath hold at the same time the necessity, if we would lead men to happiness and virtue, of the greatest prominence being given in its instructions to the doctrine of the Atonement as the means of reconciliation with Heaven. Dr. Adam Smith had the sagacity to see the truth and importance of this doctrine. "If man," he says, "would hope for happiness, he is conscious that he cannot demand it from the justice, but that he must entreat it from the mercy of God. Repentance, sorrow, humiliation, contrition at the thought of his past conduct, are, upon this account, the sentiments which become him, and seem to be the only means which he has left for appeasing that wrath which, he knows, he has justly provoked. He even distrusts the efficacy of all these, and naturally fears lest the wisdom of God should not, like the weakness of man, be prevailed upon to spare the crime, by the most importunate lamentations of the criminal. Some other intercession, some other sacrifice, some other atonement, he imagines, must be made for him, beyond what he himself is capable of making, before the purity of the Divine justice can be reconciled to his manifold offences. The doctrines of revelation coincide, in every respect, with these original anticipations of nature; and, as they teach us how little we can depend upon the imperfection of our own virtues, so they show us, at the same time, that the most powerful intercession has been made, and that the most dreadful atonement has been paid, for our manifold transgressions and iniquities."[1]

[1] *Theory of Moral Sentiments* (1759), pp. 205, 206. These and some other noble sentences are omitted in later editions.

Another characteristic of societies in which the Lord's day is regarded with peculiar respect is a watchful care over their members. Let us hear the words of the same writer, adducing evidence for the moral benefit of the practice only the more reliable that it plainly comes from no partisan. Referring to a person passing from his notoriety in a country village to the obscurity of a large town, where, unnoticed, he is very likely to abandon himself to every sort of lowest profligacy and vice, he adds, "He never emerges so effectually from this obscurity; his conduct never excites so much the attention of any respectable society as by his becoming the member of a small religious sect. He from that moment acquires a degree of consideration which he never had before. All his brother sectaries are, for the credit of the sect, interested to observe his conduct; and if he gives occasion to any scandal, if he deviates very much from those austere morals, which they almost always require of one another, to punish him by what is always a very severe punishment, even where no civil effects attend it—expulsion or excommunication. In little religious sects, accordingly, the morals of the common people have been almost always remarkably regular and orderly, generally much more so than in the Established Church. The morals of those little sects, indeed, have frequently been rather disagreeably rigorous and unsocial."[1]

While philosophy has thus appreciated some of the principles of our subject, philanthropy has borrowed others of them for the reformation of society. The effective exertions of Mrs. Fry, for the good of prisoners, proceeded on the principle that to reach the hearts of men, and to inspire them with the only morality worth the name, that which is of love and choice, you must treat them with kindness—a principle involved in the whole of Christianity; in its law, the sum of which is love; in its doctrines, which without omitting to influence the fears and to secure the respect of human beings, overpower the heart by their matchless exhibitions of benevolence and mercy; and in its institutions, not the least benignant of which is the day when man is recreated by bodily rest, and has the opportunity of coming under the discipline of a system so mighty for winning him from a wretched course of folly

[1] *Wealth of Nations*, B. v. ch. i. Art. iii.

to the path of purity and peace. But, in fact, as art has derived many of its finest designs from nature, so all classes have attested the excellence of religion, either by reverently and for good copying its measures, or by stealing them with the view of effecting different or hostile ends. Julian saw it necessary to adopt its system of preaching in support of his new faith. Its music has been imitated by those who would enliven their meetings for good or evil. Its festivals have led to the institution of days in honour of great men. Its means of circulating knowledge have been applied to the dissemination of error. And how much, to add no more, has its Sabbath been made use of by those who never cease to malign one of their chief boons!

Let us now endeavour to show that the Sabbatic institution is an indispensable means of religious good.

The necessity of a weekly day of rest to the prosperity and even preservation of religion in the world has been proclaimed by the almost universal voice of mankind. Jews and Christians have ever devoted a seventh day to holy uses. Mohammedanism has always appropriated Friday to public devotion and instruction. Paganism, holding sacred in many instances the same proportion of time, has in no instance dropped all periodical festivals, till its people have well-nigh lost the conception of an object of worship. That so many, in regions and periods widely remote from each other, have observed a Sabbath, or some analogous arrangement, is a strong testimony to its religious necessity. And the remaining members of the human family, by whom religion has been partially or altogether discarded, come in to complete the universality of the testimony. Jeroboam, king of Israel, renounces the worship of Jehovah; but finds it necessary to have some kind of worship, with its relative places, times, and priesthood. Julian abandons Christianity, but sees the advantage to his new religion of introducing into the temples of idolatry a system of public instruction after the model of that of the Christian Church.[1] The French, exchanging Popery for the religion of so-called Reason, must yet have their temples and decades for upholding and promoting their altered faith, and are soon obliged to furnish a

[1] Prideaux's *Connexion, etc.* Part i. p. 390.

stronger verdict on the subject by restoring their former worship and institutions such as they were. And in our own country various classes, who have rejected the authority of the Sabbath, have, notwithstanding, justified the appointment to the extent of appropriating the day to meetings for the advancement of their peculiar opinions. By approving of the Sabbath abstractly considered, and lauding it in this view as an admirable provision for rest, recreation, and mental culture, these classes unwittingly pronounce a judgment in favour of the religious institution, for they never saw or heard of a holy day entitled to such praise but the one which religion originated and has maintained. There is yet another way in which the wise are taken in their own craftiness, and, contrary to their intention, made to confess the religious power of the holy Sabbath. Whence the desire and attempt to destroy the day as a day of sacred rest and service? Whence but that in this character it is an adjunct and indispensable help to religion? The French were aware that, most summarily and effectually to put down religion, they must remove its weekly holy day. Despotic rulers have known well that to break down the Sabbath is to crush the spirit and the liberty which religious instruction and worship inspire. And when infidelity would liberate itself from the restraints of Christianity, it labours to reduce the Lord's day to the continental standard, convinced that a day devoted entirely to rest and piety is the chief barrier to the compassing of its designs.

Conclusive in favour of our position though evidence so ample and varied is, the necessity of a Sabbath to the prosperity and even existence of religion is a doctrine which derives even stronger support from the nature of religion itself, considered as a creed to be understood and believed, a ritual to be observed, and a rule of moral conduct to be obeyed.

First, Religion must have some time for its consideration and practice. This is surely a self-evident truth.

Second, Religion must have times free to be applied to its business. This proposition is scarcely less obviously true than the preceding. "The heathen men by the light of nature have seen that everything is then best ordered when it hath but one office—that is, whatsoever is done, it must be thoroughly done, it must be alonely done. The reason is, we are finite creatures ; and if two things be done at once, one part of our thoughts will be taken from the other : we cannot wholly intend two things at once."[1]

Third, Religion must have fixed times for its teachings and worship. In the ordinary affairs of life, should the time of any matter be left indefinite, there would be no provision for its being attended to at all. If without some peremptory arrangement, many things that are agreeable to us would be forgotten, what would be the fate of those to which we are disinclined or averse ? How constantly would the excuse be made, "Go thy way for this time ; when I have a convenient season I will call for thee ;" and how constantly would the convenient season fail to come ! It is of importance, therefore, that times for the duties of religion should be determined. If they had not their understood days and hours, certain religious services could not be performed at all.

Public worship is a becoming as well as prescribed homage to the Great King. It is a means of receiving blessings from heaven. It elevates, purifies, and gladdens human hearts. It is a proclamation of great truths to the world. It is a commemoration of great facts. But it must have its set times. The time and place are co-relative. If there were no common time, there could be no appointed place. "Ye shall keep my Sabbaths and reverence my sanctuary, I am the Lord," was an order once given from the court above. It was perfectly in keeping that when an atheistical people abrogated the day, they should proceed forthwith to desecrate the temples of religion.

We have, in the preceding chapter, adverted to the wisdom and power of the provision whereby the preacher applies the fruits of study to general advantage, and one living voice can reach the ears, and thrill the hearts of many. But without fixed times that voice could not be heard—those fruits could not be distributed—there could, in fact, be no public instruction.

Family religion is right and good. But we believe that there would be no such thing without a Sabbath. Such is the state of society, that this is the only day on which some are disposed, and others have it in their power to engage in family prayer. Take away the Sabbath, and while one class would be without the im-

[1] *The Moral Law Expounded,* by Bishop Andrewes (1642), p. 328.

pulse which the regularly returning sacred day gives to domestic piety, the greater number would be in the situation of the omnibus men in London, who, never seeing their children except when these are in bed, can have neither the inclination nor opportunity to worship with or instruct their families.

Religion consists greatly in the discharge of beneficent offices beyond the circle of home. But take away the Sabbath, and you absolutely preclude to tens of thousands the advantage and pleasure of doing, and to many more the profit of receiving, this species of good.

Personal religion is "the one thing needful." But its attainments and duties are next to impracticable without a Sabbath. How without this institution would men, oppressed with toil, and allured by temptations to drown their cares in sleep or intoxication, feel any disposition for communing with their own hearts, with their Creator, or with a future world? Is it not true that many do not call on the Almighty, or study the truths and facts of Christianity, because, keeping no holy day, they are continually immersed in business or in worldly pleasure? It is sad to think that those who might redeem one day in seven for attending to the claims of God, of their souls, and of a future existence, do not avail themselves of the opportunity. How much more melancholy were this, from the want of a Sabbath, the inevitable condition of all! The thought will intrude amidst the most incessant occupations and bustle of life, For what purpose all this labour? For what end these cares, or these gratifications? Whither am I bound? Where shall I be when a few years have passed away? Is it worthy of my nature to be ever looking down to this earth, or engrossed with the present? These thoughts do occur, and it is irrational to seek oblivion of them in mirth, or to dispel them by courting a different train of reflection. If the impulses of nature suggest repose, the dictates of conscience demand the trial of some means of genuine relief to remorse and apprehension. It is not enough to have the season of night for a pause in the perpetual iteration of engagements, for that requiring physical rest, admits of little speculation. There must be a Sabbath, unless one class are to be for ever bound to the chariot-wheel of labour, and another so continually whirled in the vortex of pleasure, as to render it no less easy for a camel to go through the eye of a needle than for the sons of men to enter into the kingdom of God.

Fourth, The time must regularly and frequently recur; in short, must be one day in seven. No subject can be properly studied, no art acquired, if application to them be interrupted during long intervals. Interest is impaired; lessons are forgotten; habits cannot be formed; and, after losing time and labour the professed learner has in the end accomplished nothing. The question then is, What is the necessary frequency of time for religion—the time, that is, which its more deliberate study, and its more public exercises statedly require? We answer, the greatest frequency compatible with the secular and spiritual interests of mankind—in other words, one whole day in every seven. This arrangement being, as we have seen, most adapted to the physical, mental, and moral nature of man, must be most consonant, also, to his religious character—determining the proportion of holy time which is most conducive to his temporal advantage, and which thereby enables him to bring the greatest amount of health, energy, leisure, and comfort to bear on his sacred studies and business.

It follows from the preceding statements in this chapter that religion and morality will flourish, fade, or die, according as a weekly holy day is observed, perverted, or lost. And if we show that such is, in point of fact, the relation of religious and moral character to the institution, the truth of our thesis is established.

Let it be remarked, then, that where the Sabbath is duly honoured and observed, religion and morality prosper. The facts that prove this position are too numerous to be particularized. They are to be found in the history of the early Christians; of the Waldenses; of the Puritans in England and America; of the Covenanters and Seceders in Scotland; of the evangelical parties in the English and Scottish Church Establishments, and of the converts to Protestant Christianity in heathen lands. In all these cases, without exception, a vigorous, purifying, elevating Christian influence has been exerted in connexion with a devout, sacred respect for the Lord's day.

Let it be observed, further, that in proportion to the perversion of the institution religion and morals decline. Hogarth, like himself, is true to nature, when, in one of the early plates of the Series of Industry and Idleness, he represents the idle apprentice, whose course ends at the gallows, as gambling on a Sunday upon a tomb-stone during Divine service. The downward movement in religious creed and character has substantially the same commencement. This is the acknowledgment of almost all criminals. It is the experience of many others not yet criminals in the eye of human law—the victims of a state of society which they cannot control, and which, unnecessarily and wickedly excluding them from places of worship, soon extinguishes the impressions of an early religious education. And good men confirm these testimonies to the danger of tampering with a benignant yet holy institute. "I have long found it a most important and beneficial rule," says Bickersteth, "to give the Sabbath to God as entirely as possible, and especially to spend at least an hour or two alone. I am sure, humanly speaking, all religion would soon be gone from me, if I did not adopt this plan."[1] The corruption of churches begins and proceeds in the same way. It might be shown that nothing has had more influence in debasing the Church of Rome than the holidays, feasts, and ceremonies, by which one after another of the associated observances, and simple benevolent provisions of the Lord's day have been supplanted and neutralized. If that one institution had been preserved in its integrity, and unique authority as a sacred day, and maintained in its proper accessories of a pure worship, a preached gospel, and a free Bible, it would have been impossible to uphold, if not to introduce, the domination of the priesthood, the idolatrous worship of the Virgin and of the mass, the abominations of celibacy and the confessional, the manifold enormities, in short, by which that Church has made religion an object of contempt and disgust, and filled the greater part of Europe with ignorance, poverty, and crime. The infidelity and other evils, which have so laid waste the Protestant churches on the Continent, have a close connexion with wrong views and practices in reference to the Sabbath. The Reformed and Lutheran Churches, particularly the former, were at first careful to maintain

[1] *Memoir of Rev. E. Bickersteth*, vol. i. p. 224.

the celebration of the day, but the example of Romanists and infidels around led to a gradual departure from this practice, which was abetted by certain unguarded expressions of the Reformers tending to lower the claims of the institution. "The evil once begun," says Fairbairn, "proceeded rapidly from bad to worse, till it scarcely left in many places so much as the form of religion."[1] The history of religion in England is rife with examples of similar unhappy effects of a disregarded or maltreated Sabbath.. From the Reformation downwards to the present time there have been two ecclesiastical parties, which have been distinguished by their different views and treatment of the Lord's day, and which have in consequence displayed an equal diversity in religious character and influence. They might be compared to two rivers—one foul, fierce, and desolating as the Aar; the other, "a pure river of water of life, having on either side the tree of life, whose leaves are for the healing of the nations." For a time the one or the other may almost disappear, or their waters partially intermingle, but in general they flow on in separate and parallel currents. The Puritans within and without the Church of England have been at once the warm friends of the Sabbath, the most decided Christians, and the best members of society. In Scotland, too, the periods distinguished by the profanation of the Lord's day have been precisely the periods in which the interests of religion and morality have sustained the greatest damage, and the abettors of the profanation have ever been identical with the ungodly and immoral.

Let it be observed, once more, that where no Sabbath is known, there is no religion or virtue at all. The following facts are sufficient to confirm the statement. The great majority of 100,000 men employed on the inland navigation of England are deprived of the blessings of the Lord's day, and are consequently, with their wives and children, generally speaking, in a state of deplorable ignorance of the gospel and of the power of religion.[2] Baror Gurney, when passing sentence of death on two boatmen at the Stafford assizes, said, "There is no body of men so destitute of all moral culture as boatmen; they know no Sabbath, and are

[1] *Typology*, vol. ii. p. 475.
[2] Baylee's *Facts and Statistics*, p. 65.

possessed of no means of religious instruction."[1] It has been said that no class of men are more frequently before the magistrates than the London cab and omnibus drivers, who are employed *every day* from thirteen to sixteen hours in their calling. Habits of intoxication and profane swearing prevail to a great extent amongst both classes; and the same characteristic attaches to them as to others who are deprived of the privileges of the Lord's day, namely, demoralization and degradation.[2] Mr. Edge, of Manchester, observes, respecting the London bakers, that "the low mental and moral condition of the trade generally in London at the present time is notorious."[3] Mr. Henry Ellis, a master baker, says of them, "Those good and moral impressions which they first received in their early days are entirely lost, from the continual practice of working on the Sabbath day."[4] The city and metropolitan police, numbering 5000, although guardians of the public peace, as a body live almost without regard to religion, or thought of another world.[5] In four years, 1849-1852, 54 of that body were convicted of offences, 970 were dismissed, and 524 were suspended; 2495 were fined, 64 were reduced in rank, 3151 resigned. The value of the property stolen during that period was £153,942, of which £34,032 was recovered.[6] The want of a day of rest and moral training is found to corrupt a class, who from their circumstances in life might be expected to rise superior to deeds of villany. We refer to servants in our post-offices, who number 14,000, and labour in many instances from six to ten or even twelve hours on the Sabbath. It is stated in a Report of 1843 by a Committee of the House of Commons, that, from January 5, 1837, to January 5, 1842, the immense sum of £322,033, contained in letters, was lost in passing through the post-office.

Whatsoever, therefore, impairs the authority of a sacred resting day tends to quench virtuous feeling, and to obliterate from the world the truths, laws, and blessings of religion. In referring to the public teaching of Christianity on the Sabbath, Dean Prideaux

1 Baylee's *Facts and Statistics*, p. 64. 2 *Ibid.* p. 84.
3 Quoted in *Address on the Evils of Sabbath Labour*, p. 11.
4 Evidence before the House of Commons' Committee in 1832, p. 159.
5 *London City Mission Report* (1845), p. 24.
6 *Christian Times* (1853), p. 370.

remarks, that "It is not to be doubted but that if this method were once dropped among us, the generality of the people, whatever else might be done to obviate it, would in seven years relapse into as bad a state of barbarity as was ever in practice among the worst of our Saxon or Danish ancestors."[1] If along with the pulpit the Sabbath itself were set aside, we should require to take a worse state of society than that to represent the woful result. The weekly day of rest and worship may in some imperfect form survive the extinction of Christianity, but Christianity has never existed without its Sabbath. Let this be lost to our country or to any land, and the religion which employs it for its own preservation and advancement must, with all the blessings of the highest civilisation, disappear along with it. And it is lamentable to reflect that so many of the inhabitants of Great Britain are employed in strenuous endeavours to pull down that fabric of religion, morality, and social happiness, which by means of the Sabbath has been reared and consolidated in these lands, and which has for centuries been no less the envy and admiration of the world than the blessing and glory of our people.

[1] *Old and New Testament connected, etc.* (1720), part i. p. 293.

CHAPTER III.

ECONOMY OF A WEEKLY HOLY DAY.

"If the Sunday had not been observed as a day of rest, but the axe, the spade, the anvil, and the loom had been at work every day, during the last three centuries, I have not the smallest doubt that we should have been at this moment a poorer people and a less civilized people than we are."—LORD MACAULAY.

IT is a remarkable fact, that, while the multiplication of holidays impoverishes individuals and communities, the opposite effect is produced by a weekly day of sacred rest. The labourer receives the same amount of wages for his six days' work that he would receive for the work of seven.[1] The institution, therefore, brings to the working classes once in the week a clear gain of a resting day, which they can apply to the husbanding of their strength, to the cultivation of their minds, and to the instruction of their families. By means of the wise and merciful appointment of a Sabbath, they are enabled to spend fifty-two days of the year most profitably to their own interests, physical, mental, and moral, and beneficially in various ways to their kindred and neighbours, not only without lessening the amount, but with the effect of enhancing the value of their marketable time.

That the Sabbath is a financial benefit is manifest from its sanitary power. The natural result of the more uninterrupted health and greater physical strength which it secures, combined with the pleasure and hope suffused by its rest over the engagements of the week, is an increased amount of human labour in every grade of society. Dr. Farre has told us that men of whatever class who must necessarily be occupied six days in the week would, in the course of life, gain by abstinence on the seventh. One class would by the increased vigour imparted, accom-

[1] "The workmen are aware, and the masters in many trades admit the fact, that were Sunday labour to cease, it would occasion no diminution of the weekly wages."—*Report on the Sabbath* (1832), p. 8.

plish more mental work.[1] Every student would find, like Hey of Leeds, that the complete suspending for one day in the week of all his secular pursuits would prepare him to "resume his studies with renewed ardour and alacrity."[2] The lawyer would experience a greater facility in transacting business on the Monday morning, and would feel the relief afforded by a weekly day of rest to be beneficial in every point of view.[3] And those who are called labouring men would, in like manner, do more work. To the sentence employed as our motto, Macaulay adds, "Of course I do not mean that a man will not produce more in a week by working seven days than by working six days. But I very much doubt whether, at the end of a year, he will generally have produced more by working seven days a week than by working six days a week, and I firmly believe that at the end of twenty years he will have produced less by working seven days a week than by working six days a week."[4] If a labourer had no regular day of rest, his ability for exertion would continually decrease. For a time he might do more in seven than in six days, but this, as a few facts will make certain, could not continue for a course of years, or even of months. Wilberforce, writing to Christophe, king of Hayti, October 8, 1818, and referring, besides other means for the welfare of his people, to the proper observance of the Sabbath, says, "I well remember that during the war, when it was proposed to work all Sunday in one of the royal manufactories, for a continuance, not for an occasional service, it was found that the workmen who obtained Government consent to abstain from working on Sundays executed in a few months even more work than the others."[5] Similar trials were made in the public service of the United States and of France, and the practice was abandoned in both instances because, from less work being done, it was not profitable to the state.[6] Mr. Bagnall, an extensive iron-master, discontinued the working of his blast-furnaces on the Lord's day, and in 1841, about two years after

[1] *Report on the Sabbath* (1832), p. 119.
[2] *Life of W. Hey, Esq., F.R.S.* 2d Edit. vol. i. p. 153.
[3] Evidence of James Bridges, Esq., in *Report on the Sabbath*, p. 201.
[4] *Speeches* (1854), pp. 450, 451.
[5] *Life of Wilberforce*, vol. i. p. 275.
[6] *Permanent Sabbath Documents*, No. I. pp. 33, 34.

the change had been adopted, stated to a committee of the House of Lords, "We have made rather more iron since we stopped on Sundays than we did before." After a seven years' trial of the plan, Mr. Bagnall wrote thus, "We have made a larger quantity of iron than ever, and gone on in all our six iron-works much more free from accidents and interruptions than during any preceding seven years of our lives."[1] Such facts as these prepare us for crediting a statement which has been made, that the amount of productive labour in France was diminished by the change from a seventh to a tenth day's rest,[2] and for rejecting the policy of Arkwright and others, which, in the spirit of the Egyptian taskmasters, and of slavery wherever found, and blind no less to the material than to all the higher interests of society, would cancel the Sabbath as if it were a day of idleness and loss, and condemn the great majority of mankind to one monotonous course of grinding toil.

The arrangement which thus secures to the workman every seventh day for rest and mental profit without any pecuniary loss, and to the employer a larger return for his capital, has this other great advantage to both, that it favourably affects the quality of labour. Work, in the circumstances which the want of a weekly day of rest supposes, must be carelessly and improperly performed. It is observed that at the close of a day's employment the men become less efficient, and the work is more imperfect. A falling off in excellence, as the consequence of exhaustion, has been noticed also in literary performances. When labour is continued over the Sabbath, the spirits and strength flag. A steamer on the Thames having blown up some years ago, the foreman and stokers laid the blame on Sabbath work, which "stupified and embittered them, made them blunder, and heedless what havoc they might occasion." Mr. Swan, the intelligent superintendent of machinery to the Eastern and Continental Steam Packet Company, states that when the engines were getting constantly damaged, the mischief was instantly repaired by giving the men the rest of each seventh day.[3] It is thus evident that we cannot

[1] Baylee's *Statistics*, pp. 88, 89.
[2] Spring's *Obligations of the World to the Bible* (Collins), p. 215.
[3] Memorial to the Chairman of the Company.

violate the laws of our constitution without doing injury to ourselves and to society. But, on the other hand, since in all labour there is profit, it is not difficult to see that the observance of the Sabbath—which, by its influence on the physical frame, enables labourers, with less rather than greater effort, to do better as well as more work than they could otherwise perform—must contribute largely to the increase of individual comfort and of the national wealth. One important item in the gains of such labourers is the saving effected by them in many instances of the expenditure which the feebleness and disease of the overtasked and the unrested infallibly entail.

A similar profitable result to that produced by the sanitary power of the institution might be expected from its ascertained tendency to promote intellectual improvement. "Knowledge is power," says Bacon; "wisdom is better than strength," says the wiser Solomon. It is the mechanic of superior intelligence who may be expected to obtain the most remunerative employment, and it is the men of highest acquirements who enjoy the best means of advancement in the learned professions.

We have yet to mention the economic benefit of the Sabbath through means of the moral and religious character which it does so much to form. The hand of the diligent maketh rich, while sobriety and care husband the gains of industry. Idleness, on the other hand, clothes a man with rags; and vice, the most unproductive of all labour, speedily scatters the fortune of the rich and the pittance of the poor. Nothing, however, secures a high and abiding morality but religion, and nothing is more necessary to the preservation and influence of religion than its weekly holy day. How much, to say no more, must the lessons of wisdom and the habits of order, that are learnt on that day, help to guide in the use of all time, and in the performance of every work! "I know from experience that persons who are in the habit of attending a place of worship are more careful in their pecuniary transactions, they are more careful in their language, they are more economical in their arrangements at home, they are more affectionate and humane, and in every respect superior beings by far than persons of contrary habits. Those who neglect a place of worship generally become idle, neglectful of their person, filthy in their habits, careless as to their children, and equally careless in their pecuniary transactions."[1] The want of the Sabbath in France prevented regular industry during the week; and employers in this country inform us that their servants who attend a place of worship are, generally speaking, honest and diligent men, "never losing an hour of their time," and that "they are very glad to get hold of such men;" but that morality is obliterated by Sabbath labour, and that they have been compelled to discontinue such labour in consequence of the state of the men, who, from their not having proper instruction, could not be trusted with anything.[2] Incessant toil of itself demoralizes its victims. The overtasked resort to stimulants, and the delays, interruptions, waste, and injury occasioned by intemperate habits, must involve immense loss in various ways to the employers, to the employed, and to society at large. And how can men subjected to undue labour be supposed to care for the interests of their masters, and to rise above the temptations to wrong in many forms those whom they are apt to regard as treating them with severity and injustice? But give these men their weekly resting day at least, and you remove some strong inducements to improper indulgences, to unfaithfulness, and to dishonesty. Let them be taught to respect and observe the Sabbath, and much more will be accomplished than the withdrawal of the occasions of vice and crime. They will become intelligent and virtuous, skilful, industrious, and efficient, temperate and economical; and in all these ways they will promote their own interest, benefit their employers, and add largely to the general amount of wealth.

On such grounds as these we are prepared to expect that a country will prosper, and individuals be well-to-do, or the reverse, according as they enjoy or want the enriching influence of a weekly holy day. Nor are we disappointed.

The Popish cantons of Switzerland, with their numerous festivals, are poor and depressed compared with the Protestant cantons. Italy is a poor country, swarming with beggars as with worse than useless priests. In Rome, every third man is a pauper. In Naples, out of a population of 380,000, there were lately 220,000 with-

[1] Evidence of Mr. J. S. Thomas, Superintendent of Police, in Report on the Sabbath, p. 89. [2] *Ibid.* pp. 46, 104, 126, 160.

out any fixed employment. In Spain, 3000 needy relations and dependants are maintained on the estates of the Duke of Arcos. Need we mention Ireland, where, so far as they are Roman Catholics, the people are as destitute of the comforts of life as they are of a hallowed day? Not long before the commencement of the late famine, "two-thirds of the population subsisted on potatoes, nearly one-third were out of work and in distress thirty weeks in the year, and one-eighth were paupers or on the verge of pauperism. The merchant was poorer than the English clerk; the farmer would have been thankful for the food which servants in England threw away."[1] Mayo, the most Popish, is also the poorest county in Ireland. How different from Italy, Spain, and Ireland are those communities which, seeking at the Divine command spiritual riches for fifty-two days in the year, have the "other things added thereto," in a wealth largely accumulated in particular instances, and widely diffused among the population. We see one example in the United States. And we have another in Great Britain, where the periods of most earnest attention to Christian institutions have been the seasons of general prosperity, and where the chief drawback to social comfort is to be found in the pauperism, losses, and public burdens, which are obviously, and according to their own frequent confession, caused by men—many of them not natives—who keep no sacred Sabbath.[2]

Let us now turn to the component parts of a community in which the Sabbatic institution is known. The inhabitants of Great Britain may be divided into those who more or less respect the institution, and those who utterly disregard it. We need not say to which of these classes the greater proportion of general worth and comfort belongs. When we view them again, as arranged under the higher, the middle, and the lower orders of society, and attend to their comparative regard for the Sabbath, we find that the intermediate are the most distinguished at once by their observance of the day, and by their prosperity. If we contemplate the population of our land according to their employments, we discover that those who to the greatest extent trespass

[1] Dill's *Ireland's Miseries*, p. 11.

[2] The average income of every person in Great Britain is fully three times as much as that of an inhabitant of France.—*Gold and the Gospel*, p. 232.

in their callings against the law of a weekly day of rest and worship are the least prosperous. "There is no trade that we are aware of that violates the Sabbath law by labour so much as the bakers do, and no trade has suffered so much in consequence. A rich master baker, who has got his wealth by the profits of his business, is a rare thing to be met with. There are more journeymen in the baking trade who are decayed masters than in any other."[1] If we compare persons in the same profession or trade, whether in America or in England, the result will not be different. "A distinguished merchant said to the writer of this—'There is no need of breaking the Sabbath, and no benefit from it. We have not had a vessel leave the harbour on the Sabbath for more than twenty years. It is altogether better to get them off on a week-day than on the Sabbath. It is about thirty years since I came to this city; and every man through this whole range, who came down to his store, or suffered his counting-room to be opened on the Sabbath, has lost his property.'" "An old gentleman in Boston remarked, 'Men do not gain anything by working on the Sabbath. I can recollect men, who, when I was a boy, used to load their vessels down on Long Wharf, and keep their men at work from morning to night on the Sabbath-day. But they have come to nothing. Their children have come to nothing. Depend upon it, men do not gain anything in the end by working on the Sabbath.'"[2] "Do you conceive serving on a Sunday is injurious to the pecuniary interests?—I see it by most tradesmen round, that those who shut their shops on the Sunday are the people that do the best."[3] In the case of working men the influence of the Sabbatic rest and duties, or the want of it, appears with like certainty. When it was stated before the Commons' Sabbath Committee in 1832, that certain characters, on being induced to respect the institution, began to procure for themselves better food, and to refuse aid from the poor-rates, the fact was not a rare one. There is not a Christian missionary employed in instructing the neglected inhabitants of our towns who cannot relate many instances of the improved funds, diet, and dress, that very speedily attend the

[1] *Address on the Evils of Sabbath Labour*, p. 11.
[2] *Permanent Sabbath Documents*, No. I. pp. 52, 55.
[3] *Report on the Sabbath*, p. 50

resumption of religious observances, while it almost as invariably happens, that when the claims of public worship and of sacred time cease to be regarded, there commences a process of deterioration alike in character and in condition. Many such facts might be presented, but we must limit ourselves to two other cases belonging to very different periods. It is recorded by Calderwood that in the congregation of Mr. David Black, St. Andrews, which numbered 3000 communicants, there was not a single beggar or Sabbath-breaker.[1] "There is not," says a working man, "a neighbourhood, village, or township that is notable for its profanation of the sacred day of rest, but is proverbial for its poverty and its crime. The writer is acquainted with one within his own immediate neighbourhood, where all the people make it a practice to bake their bread upon the Sabbath-day for the sake of 'saving time;' but it is questionable whether there is another village in England where the labouring classes have got so little bread to bake. Many have been transported and imprisoned within the last few years from this 'dirty poaching' village for the crimes of arson and other felonies."[2]

Simply, then, as a commercial or pecuniary matter, it is for the advantage of individuals and communities to observe a weekly day of rest. Let us again listen to the eloquent Macaulay: "Rely on it, that intense labour, beginning too early in life, continued too long every day, stunting the growth of the body, stunting the growth of the mind, leaving no time for healthful exercise, leaving no time for intellectual culture, must impair all those high qualities which have made our country great. . . . On the other hand, a day of rest recurring in every week, two or three hours of leisure, exercise, innocent amusement, or useful study, recurring every day, must improve the whole man physically, morally, intellectually; and the improvement of the man will improve all that the man produces."[3]

[1] *Altar. Damasc. Ep. Phil. Vindic.* p. 65.
[2] *Prize Essays by Five Working Men*, p. 160.
[3] *Speeches*, p. 451.

CHAPTER IV.

INFLUENCE OF THE SABBATH ON THE RESPECTABILITY AND HAPPINESS OF INDIVIDUALS.

"They who always labour can have no true judgment; they exhaust their attention, burn out their candles, and are left in the dark."—BURKE.

OUR attention has been occupied with the evidence which appears to demonstrate the peculiarly beneficial bearings of the Sabbatic institution on the interests of health, wealth, intelligence, morality, and religion. The testimony, however, of reason and experience to the practical value of the institution would be incomplete without some consideration of still further results which by means of these interests, and otherwise, it is fitted to secure—results in personal, domestic, and national good.

On the benefits that accrue to individuals let two remarks suffice.

First, The Sabbatic institution is a means of elevating them to true respectability and honour. Every deduction from physical evil, every accession to mental improvement, and especially every advance in piety and virtue—attainments, as has been shown, all dependent in a great measure on the Sabbath—are so many contributions to respectability of character and condition.

A man to be in his proper position must be free. It is certainly unworthy of their nature that human beings should be in the situation of the slaves of Cuba or the Carolinas, of the serfs in Russia, of "the puppets of the Pope," or of the men and women in this country who are doomed to excessive toil. But degraded above all is the man who, considering himself free, is the victim of his guilt and passions, of his prejudices and errors, of his fears and follies. Such a state of things is the source of all slavery. What but sin has ever made one class of men tyrants, and another, bondsmen? All attempts at human aggrandizement must fail where sin continues to condemn and rule human beings. Without peace with Heaven, and a heart that loves God and man, not only will a moral vassalage remain which no form of civil freedom can countervail, but its bitter fruits in abject dependence of all kinds will continually be reaped. And what has ever been found capable of giving liberty to such captives but the good tidings of Revelation?

> "He is the freeman whom the truth makes free,
> And all are slaves beside;
> . . . . he has wings, that neither sickness, pain,
> Nor penury, can cripple or confine.
> No nook so narrow but he spreads them there
> With ease, and is at large."

And what more than the Christian Sabbath is tributary to the knowledge and influence of the expanding, emancipating truth? This institution is an essential means of removing the cause of all bondage, and of thereby destroying or preventing the effects. In its absence or neglect there is no security against the power of one class, and the depression of another. How manifest is it from the principles and facts set forth in previous chapters, that if all possessed and rightly used the weekly holy day, neither the oppressor nor the oppressed could exist in any part of the earth! It is only when men want, or, like the Jews, despise the Sabbath, that they can be made captives, or at least so crushed as that the spirit of liberty shall not survive and struggle till it win for itself a complete deliverance. It is the men in our own land who have no regard for the institution that subject their brethren to the degradation of perpetual labour, and it is the workmen who despise their birthright that can be so degraded. The employer who values, cannot but allow his servants to enjoy, the rest of every seventh day, as he respects its authority, knows its advantages to himself, and has learned by its means to honour all men, and to do to them as he would be done by; and the labourer or mechanic who breathes the spirit and relishes the repose of the sacred season, who has been taught by its lessons to economize his earnings and respect himself, will be prepared to negotiate from a higher platform with the dispenser of work and wages.

Whatever promotes efficiency in the business of life contributes to respectability and honour. But he who obeys what he holds to be a Divine law will be dutiful to men; and he who has been physically refreshed by the rest, and morally braced by the instructions of the Sabbath, will proceed to the work of the week, "rejoicing as a strong man to run a race." The influences which operate so favourably from week to week on his whole nature and condition impart, as the united result, energy to his character and proceedings. Some of the most remarkable men have been thus formed, as, for example, Sir Isaac Newton, who said that if in anything he excelled others it was by virtue of his power of application, which, we know, was invigorated by the hebdomadal rest and worship; and Howard, Wilberforce, Clarkson, Chalmers, and Buxton, none of whom allowed anything to bend him from the great purpose of his life and soul, and all of whom highly valued the Lord's day. The early Christians, the Reformers, the Puritans, and the Covenanters sanctified the Sabbath, and they were the most resolute of men. And what but the collective might of many individuals, nurtured by the same institution, has imparted an activity, enterprise, and determination, beyond all modern nations, to Britons and Americans, whose energy may be read in reclaimed wastes, in extending commerce and civilisation, in national wealth and comfort, in the cultivation of science and letters, and even in the prowess of the battle-field?

The man who is the object of respect and confidence among his fellows has attained true elevation and fame. Need a word be said to show that the infidel, the irreligious, and the immoral inspire no such feelings in their own or any other class of minds? Voltaire, who must be allowed to have been free from temptation to traduce his own creed, confessed that he avoided the utterance of infidel sentiments in the presence of his servants, lest, adopting and acting on them, "they should cut his throat." No less well known and generally believed is the trust-worthiness of Christian men of all ranks who are observant of their own religious institutions.

Nothing more ennobles a human being than the combined disposition and power to be useful—to be one of the world's benefactors. Every one who "labours, working with his hands the thing which is good, that he may have to give to him that needeth," and every person of substance and influence who employs them for good, occupy stations which the general voice pronounces to be honourable. And these "posts of honour" are usually filled by the men who are distinguished by their religious observances. It might be expected to be so. The lessons of benevolence, of brotherhood, of economy, of obligation and responsibility, of which others do not avail themselves, are from week to week set before them, pressed on their attention, studied and wrought into their minds; and the convocations of the sacred day, which others abjure, bring them into stated impressive intercourse with their neighbours and families, give them a deeper interest in both, allay prejudices and animosities, and continually remind them of the circumstances and claims of those whom but for such associations they would but slightly regard, or entirely forget. These lessons and associations, in creating a desire of usefulness, contribute at the same time to a mental and moral character which is necessary to give one power over others. "The writer has seen a town and neighbourhood kept in peace and good order at a time of high political ferment by the influence and mutual co-operation of some half-dozen poor men who observed and kept holy the Sabbath."[1] If it were not for a day of disengagement from ordinary labour, millions would be precluded not only the means of having a spirit of benevolence formed and cherished, but every opportunity for its exercise in their own families and among their neighbours. Let the Sabbath cease, and even in one department of education the injury would be vast and irreparable. As the greater proportion of 250,000 Sunday-school teachers subsist by daily labour, their self-improving and self-elevating instructions would be no longer possible, multitudes of children would be destitute of their sole means of education, and it could not in future be true, that "thousands of the working classes, now moving in a respectable sphere of life, owe their position in society to their attendance at the Sabbath-school."[2]

Thus it is that the great ordinance of the Sabbath raises a man to his proper place in society. How peacefully, righteously, and surely does it accomplish the object! No violence, disturbance, or

[1] *Prize Essays by Five Working Men*, p. 142. [2] *Ibid* p. 87.

failure attends the application of this mighty lever. It is "the cheap" elevator of individuals as of "nations." Of all other schemes for advancing a person to respectability and honour it may be said that they are either unrighteous, or, without this one, incompetent. Secular education may do much, but mainly as the handmaid of moral principle. The economy and industry which are not guided by benevolence and wisdom, will either fail to secure wealth, or amass it to the hurt of its owner. There are many who attempt to raise themselves by illegitimate means, but they cannot, as they ought not to succeed. Such are our gamblers of various classes; our professional men who deviate from their line, and make haste to be rich by foolish speculations; our fraudulent tradesmen, and those working men who squander their earnings on their appetites, subject themselves to continual toil, or attempt to force the price of labour. The disappointments and woes that have ever followed such measures are incalculable. Among the working classes how disastrous, for example, has been the last-named expedient! The strike of the Glasgow cotton-spinners in 1837, when, besides other unjust proceedings, they appointed "a persecuting committee, to persecute to the utmost" their recusant brethren, lasted for seventeen weeks and five days, and ended in their "giving in," not, however, without involving unspeakable hardships to many families, a fearful increase of immorality, crime, and disease, and a useless expense of £194,540. Similar were the termination and effects of the Preston strikes of 1836 and 1854 (the latter causing a total loss to the community of £533,250); of that among the Lanarkshire colliers in 1837, and of others too numerous to be specified. Let us attend to the wise words of a working man, whose remarks might well be pondered by persons of every rank: "We have listened to every nostrum, and tried every scheme that has been propounded by every demagogue, and set forth by every scribe; we have witnessed great changes in the State; we have seen the House of Commons reformed; the fiscal code revised, and restrictive laws repealed; we have expected much from all and from each of these great changes and many others. But our hopes have not been realized. The social condition of the working classes is still deplorable. . . . There are no evils to which we are subjected but the blessed God has provided a remedy. That remedy is the universal obedience to his laws, one of the most emphatic of which is, 'Remember the Sabbath-day to keep it holy.'"[1]

Second, The Sabbath is eminently conducive to personal happiness. The reverse has been maintained by those who are ignorant of the true nature of the institution, and prejudiced or inadvertent in regard to the condition of its friends. But what is there in the institution to make its friends unhappy? Ministering to repose and health, elevating the mind by connecting it periodically with the grandest subjects of thought, purifying the moral feelings and taste, fostering pious sentiments and emotions, affording opportunities of beneficence, promoting personal prosperity, and cherishing the domestic intercourse and virtues, the Sabbath, so far from being the cause of any unhappiness, appears to include in itself all the elements of the highest enjoyment.

When we consider the pursuits of those who contemn the day of sacred rest, we shall perhaps discover another reason for concluding that their opinions on this subject must be erroneous. They seek after secular knowledge, health, pleasure, fame, and wealth, respectively, without a primary regard to what will "minister to a mind diseased," or satisfy the cravings for an infinite and enduring good. How is it possible that any human being can be happy without the possession of blessings that will never be exhausted, and never be taken away? He who attends to the votaries of such pursuits as are circumscribed in extent, and limited by time, or who has reflected on his own feelings in following the same course, must perceive that the pleasure enjoyed has a sting, is feverish, and demands for its maintenance constant excitement, and the oblivion of certain objects and questions that have not been duly considered. It in fact proceeds on a great delusion. It cannot stand adversity. It withers under the look of death. Its possessor is fain to banish recollections and forebodings by bustle, movement, company, sleep, inebriety, and not rarely by suicide. This, however, is the pleasure generally of the men who neglect or trample upon sacred institutions. That they should conceive the Sabbath to be a gloomy appointment, and its friends to be unhappy, is not wonderful. They have formed their views of plea-

[1] *Prize Essays by Five Working Men*, pp. 130, 131.

sure by the low standard of their own desires, appetites, and tastes, and according to a common deception in moral optics, transferred to others the misery which exists only in their own spirits.

We are not, however, left to principles and reasonings as the sole means of deciding whether the institution be conducive or not to personal happiness. The tree is known by its fruits. So happy, according to all our observation, are the majority of our acquaintance and friends who keep the Sabbath, that we are disposed to impute the very few exceptions either to disease or to a want of religion. And the observation is in harmony with the history of the class, ancient and modern. Unhappiness is the exceptional case, which ought not to be considered as the exponent of Sabbatic tendencies. No class were happier beings than the early Christians, and their Sabbath was their most joyful day. Asceticism was of Pagan origin,[1] and gained ground among Christians in proportion as their doctrines and institutions were corrupted by foreign admixtures. The Reformers were not gloomy men; nor were the Puritans as a body, although they have been so maligned. They received treatment at one time enough to drive less resolute spirits to distraction, and at another they had an Augean task to perform requiring stern severity. But we venture to affirm that, where that assumed its harshest features, it was among the pretended friends of the new dynasty, who bounded so suddenly to the opposite extreme of licentiousness at the Restoration. We may estimate the character of the Puritans with considerable accuracy from that of their leading men. The following is the account given of Owen:—"He was very affable and courteous, familiar and sociable; the meanest persons found easy access to his conversation and friendship. He was facetious and pleasant in his common discourse, but with sobriety and measure. He was of a serene and even temper, neither elated with honour, credit, friends, or estate, and not easily depressed with troubles and difficulties."[2] What superiority to the depressing influence of adversity must he have attained who could compose his noblest and most laborious works amidst the turbulent elements of the Commonwealth, when concealing himself for safety, or when racked

[1] Neander's *Church History*, vol. i. p. 375.

[2] *Life of Owen*, by Orme, pp. 349, 350.

with the stone ![1] Rogers thus describes Howe—"He had nothing either of the anchorite or ascetic in his composition; dignified but not austere, he was grave without moroseness, and cheerful without levity."[2] "The benevolence of Charnock," says Calamy, "was universal, and his love took in whatever person or thing had anything lovely in it."[3] Who can doubt that Charnock must have been a happy man? It is mentioned by the same writer that Bates's "wit was never vain or light, but most facetious and pleasant."[4] Of Gouge, who went about continually doing good, Baxter said, "He never saw him sad, but cheerful."[5] It was the remark of a heathen philosopher, that no man could be called happy before death. The biographies of many of the Puritans record their blessedness not only during life, but in the immediate prospect of dissolution. Among Baxter's last words were these—"I bless God I have a well-grounded assurance of my eternal happiness, and great peace and comfort within." "Almost well."

These were some of the most noted of the Puritans at the time to which the charge in question has been chiefly applied. Many more of the same class of men who lived then and previously might be cited in proof that their religion did not "make their pleasures less." Their friends, who emigrated to America at different times, were persons of the same pious and cheerful spirit. Such also were the descendants of these expatriated Puritans. After remarking the sobriety, the industry, the suppression of crime, the total absence of beggary, the general diffusion of education, and the patriotic spirit, which distinguished New England towards the close of the seventeenth century, Grahame observes —"Yet this state of society was by no means inconsistent either with refinement of manners, or with innocent hilarity. Lord Bellamont was agreeably surprised with the graceful and courtly demeanour of the gentlemen and clergy of Connecticut, and confessed that he found the aspect and address that were thought peculiar to nobility, in a land where this aristocratical distinction was unknown. From Dunston's account of his residence in Boston in 1686, it appears that the inhabitants of Massachusetts were at

[1] *Life of Owen*, p. 352.
[2] *Life of John Howe*, by Henry Rogers, pp. 494, 504.
[3] Abridgment, vol. ii. p. 56.
[4] *Ibid.* vol. ii. p. 49.
[5] *Ibid.* vol. ii. p. 11.

that time distinguished in a very high degree by the cheerfulness of their manners, their hospitality, and a courtesy, the more estimable that it was indicative of real benevolence."[1] Were it necessary, the connexion between a strictly observed Sabbath, and every appearance of true peace and joy, might be traced down to the present day, in the lives and deaths of such men as Henry, Hervey, John Newton, Bickersteth, with many others, who all proved, by the alacrity with which they performed the duties of religion, and by their whole deportment, that they experienced wisdom's "ways to be ways of pleasantness, and all her paths to be peace."

Let us present the following beautiful tributes of two eminent men to the character of Wilberforce. "I never," says Sir James Mackintosh, "saw any one who touched life at so many points; and this is the more remarkable in a man who is supposed to live absolutely in the contemplation of a future state. When he was in the House of Commons, he seemed to have the freshest mind of any of those there. There was all the charm of youth about him, and he is quite as remarkable in this bright evening of his day, as when I saw him in his glory many years ago." "I never," says Southey, "saw any other man who seemed to enjoy such a perpetual serenity and sunshine of spirit. In conversing with him you feel assured that there is no guile in him; that if ever there was a good man and a happy man on earth, he was one." "There is," the same individual remarks, "such a constant hilarity in every look and motion, such a sweetness in all his tones, such a benignity in all his thoughts, words, and actions, that you can feel nothing but love and admiration for a creature of so happy and blessed a nature."[2]

The strictest views and practice in regard to the Sabbath are thus found to be compatible with pleasure, and so commonly associated with it as to warrant us in regarding them as cause and effect. This conclusion derives confirmation from the biographies of many ardent friends of the institution, which exhibit them as persons, not only of happy temperament, at all times, but especially so on the first day of the week. Venn, author of *The Complete*

[1] *History of the Rise and Progress of the U. S. of N. America*, vol. i. pp. 504, 505.
[2] *Life of Jay*, 2d edition, p. 321.

Duty of Man, says, "My Sabbaths are sweet to my soul."[1] Hey of Leeds informs us that in early life his Sabbaths were his happiest days, and that in later life he conceived that this day should be begun, carried on, and concluded with holy cheerfulness.[2] Philip Henry would sometimes at the close of the Sabbath-day duties remark, "Well, if this be not the way to heaven, I do not know what is."[3] That day must have been "a delight" to Wilberforce. "O blessed day," he says, "which allows us a precious interval wherein to pause, to come out from the thickets of worldly concerns, and to give ourselves up to heaven and spiritual objects. And, oh! what language can do justice to the emotions of gratitude which ought to fill my heart, when I consider how few of my fellows know and feel its value and proper uses. Oh, the infinite goodness and mercy of my God and Saviour!"[4] Of Henry Martyn it is said, that "the Sabbath, that sacred portion of time set apart for holy purposes in paradise itself, was so employed by him as to prove frequently a paradise to his soul on earth, and as certainly prepared him for an endless state of spiritual enjoyment hereafter."[5] Another thus writes, "Every day was a day of tranquil satisfaction, in which we had little to wish and much to enjoy: but the Sabbath presented us with peculiar consolations. We saluted every return of that holy day with undissembled joy, cheerfully laying aside all our usual studies and employments, except such as had a manifest tendency, either to enlarge our acquaintance with, or to advance our preparation for, the kingdom of God."

After quoting from Gilpin's *Monument of Parental Affection* the beautiful passage, of which the preceding words are a part, a writer asks, "Where shall we find in scenes of worldly mirth or amusement anything that can furnish such a rational and exalted source of enjoyment, and which will so well bear the retrospect, as in this?"[6] Certainly not among those of the upper classes to whose round of gaieties the day of rest brings hardly any inter-

1 *Life of Venn*, 4th edition, p. 468.

2 Life, 2d edition, vol. i. p. 153, and vol. ii. p. 64.

3 Life, by his Son, ch. viii.

4 Life, vol. iii. pp. 96, 97.

5 Memoir (1828), p. 479.

6 Dr. Innes (*Tract for the Times*, p. 9), himself an example of cheerful piety throughout a long life.

ruption, for *ennui* is their own common and appropriate name for their feelings; nor among those of the middle and lower ranks, who work every day, or spend the first day of the week in amusement; for their languid appearance, their abbreviated lives, their sullenness, irritability, and frequent resort to stimulants, tell a very different tale. There have been many such confessors as Colonel Gardiner, Gibbon, and Lord Byron. Colonel Gardiner said that when he appeared to his boon companions to be the most joyous of men, he was in reality so miserable as to wish he were the dog under the table. Byron, we presume, "held," as was his wont, "the mirror up to nature," when he wrote these words in *Childe Harold*:—

"It is that weariness which springs
From all I meet, or hear, or see:
To me no pleasure Beauty brings;
Thine eyes have scarce a charm for me.

"It is that settled, ceaseless gloom
The fabled Hebrew wanderer bore;
That will not look beyond the tomb,
But cannot hope for rest before."

And Gibbon, after referring to the "autumnal" as by some deemed the happiest season of a literary life, has this sad reflection —"But I must reluctantly observe that two causes, the abbreviation of time and the failure of hope, will always tinge with a browner shade the evening of life." (*Life*, 1837, p. 117.) How different the Christian! Religion proves its superiority to nature and philosophy by painting its bright bow in the clouds of adversity in the noon-tide of his day, and by fulfilling to him at its close the words, "at evening time it is light."

"I may not tread
With them those pathways—to the feverish bed
Of sickness bound; yet, O my God! I bless
Thy mercy, that with Sabbath peace hath filled
My chastened heart, and all its throbbings stilled
To one deep calm of lowliest thankfulness." [1]

[1] *Sabbath Sonnet*, Mrs. Hemans' Works (1839), vol. vii. p. 288.

CHAPTER V.

DOMESTIC BENEFITS OF THE SABBATH.

"A peculiar blessing may be expected upon those families where there is due care taken that the Sabbath be strictly and devoutly observed."—JONATHAN EDWARDS.

THE diversities in the domestic life of various countries and times have generally turned on the place assigned to woman. Her equality to man in all that is most important and enduring entitles her to his companionship, and while her feebler frame calls for his protection, her gentler and more patient spirit qualifies her for rendering to him the sympathy and help which he requires.

"When pain and anguish wring the brow,
A ministering angel thou!"

But although thus fitted to be his associate and friend, and belonging to a sex nearly as numerous as his own, it is but rarely that she has obtained her just rights, and that the world has fully availed itself of her salutary influence. It is only in the Bible that her claims are clearly and authoritatively ascertained; it is only as the Bible is known and believed that these claims are practically recognised, and that Milton's glowing lines are seen to be a picture of life:

"Hail, wedded love, mysterious law, true source
Of human offspring; sole propriety
In paradise of all things common else
By thee, adulterous Lust was driven from men
Among the bestial herds to range: by thee
Founded in reason, loyal, just, and pure,
Relations dear, and all the charities
Of father, son, and brother, first were known.

Far be it, that I should write thee sin, or blame,
Or think thee unbefitting holiest place,
Perpetual fountain of domestic sweets."[1]

In countries, accordingly, where justice and kindness rule the relation of the sexes, we discover, in beautiful combination, pure religion and morals, high intelligence and civilisation, general wealth, and a large amount of happiness. Wherever, on the other hand, that relation has been superseded by prevalent polygamy, or other substitutes, and wherever influences have extensively operated tending to relax and sever what ought to be a secure and life-long tie, the laws of nature, reason, and justice have been violated, woman has been degraded, and man in all his interests, physical, intellectual, moral, and social, has necessarily sunk along with her. The family, that sanctuary of infancy, that earliest and best school of piety, wisdom, and virtue, that retreat of toiled and weary man, that dearest asylum to the sorrowful, the sick, and the dying, has been dissolved, or never known. There is wanting the "humble hearth-stone, which is the corner-stone of the temple; and the foundation-stone of the city." Whatever, therefore, serves to form or to uphold the true family institution must be an unspeakable boon to the world. To this object the Sabbath conduces, and is even indispensable, as will appear, we conceive, from the following statements of facts and principles:—

1. We shall look in vain for a true and happy home in those places where no weekly holy day exists, or where its advantages cannot be enjoyed. In the lands of Paganism, the relation of the sexes has been debased by polygamy in some instances, by the facility and frequency of divorce in others, and by the depression of woman in all. What the domestic circumstances of the Greeks and Romans latterly were may be conceived from the fact, that in Athens and Rome "impurity was considered neither as an offence nor as a dishonour." China is honourably distinguished by the filial reverence and attachments of its people, to which may possibly be owing the "long life" and comparative "prosperity" of the empire; but deplorable must be the state of families in a country where the wife is the victim of the husband's caprice and tyranny, where concubinage is permitted, and where the father has

[1] *Paradise Lost,* Book iv.

power over the life of his child. The history of slave colonies, and the condition of many servants amongst ourselves, show that the Sabbath may have a place in the laws and calendar of a nation, and yet to certain classes bring no pause of toil, and yield no benefit. In slave colonies, the demand of every-day labour, the neglect to legalize marriage, and the most unrestrained licentiousness, have gone hand in hand,[1] while among certain classes of servants, as the cabmen of London, who labour on all days for sixteen or eighteen hours, it is found that not a few live with the lowest class of females in an unmarried state, and that their abodes are ordinarily scenes of wretchedness and destitution.[2] To the wellbeing of the family, therefore, some Sabbath appears to be indispensable.

2. Nor is domestic life virtuous or comfortable where the weekly day of rest stands connected with a false or an impure religion. The people of Guinea dedicate one day in the week to the honour of their idols. But what avails for their domestic advantage a day which is associated with demon-worship, with human sacrifices, and with the belief that women are slaves, who must compensate by their labour for the price of their purchase? The Mohammedans and the Mormons, in common, keep a Sabbath, follow impostors, add to the Bible a so-called new revelation from heaven, debase woman, and practise polygamy. The fruits, in both cases, are, accordingly, licentious manners and social degradation, the former class being sunk in "apparently irremediable barbarism," and the latter obviously ripening for destruction. Popery has freely imitated Paganism, but it has surpassed its prototype in this, with other particulars, that, corrupting the wife and dishonouring the husband, it has humbled both. Let French writers say how it is with the family in France. One relates that "six hundred and twenty thousand girls are educated by nuns, under the direction of the priests, and that these girls will soon be women and mothers, who, as far as they are able, will deliver their sons and daughters into the hands of the priests," adding, "Young man, you must ask of the priest the hand of the maiden before applying to her parents. . . . Poor man! you will have

[1] *Negro Slavery, C. Observer* (1826), p. 679.
[2] Baylee, p. 81, and Tenth London City Mission Report, p. 18.

a wife minus her heart and soul; and you will learn by experience that he who gave her to you on such terms, knows well how to resume his sway over her."[1] Another remarks, "In France we are obliged to use a periphrase, as if we were strangers to the thing: the *home* of England and the *chez-soi* of France."[2] It is not long since some of the leading men in that country, alarmed at the effects of the prevalent profanation of the Lord's day among the people, united in an attempt to stay the plague. One of them, Baron Augustin Cauchy, a member of the French Institute, wrote on the occasion in these strong terms: "Wherever a nation fails to keep this commandment [respecting the Sabbath], Christianity ceases to exist. There would then be an end to domestic life, to family ties; and civilisation would soon be succeeded by barbarism."[3] In Spain, there is no holy Sabbath. The first day of the week is the great day for the theatre, and particularly for the bull-fight, which is patronized by royalty, the nobility, and the priesthood.

> "The Sabbath comes, a day of blessed rest;
> What hallows it upon this Christian shore?
> Lo! it is sacred to a solemn feast:
> Hark! heard you not the forest monarch's roar?"

The poet proceeds to describe the scene, where

> "Yells the mad crowd o'er entrails freshly torn,
> Nor shrinks the female eye, nor ev'n affects to mourn."

And adds:

> "Such the ungentle sport that oft invites
> The Spanish maid, and cheers the Spanish swain.
> Nurtured in blood betimes, his heart delights
> In vengeance, gloating on another's pain.
> What private feuds the troubled village stain!"[4]

In harmony with such amusements, such a Sunday, and such a priesthood, is the disorganized state of the family and of general society in Spain, where every man must wear a weapon; where the most petty journey requires the preparation of a warlike en-

[1] *Priests, Women, and Families* (1846), pp. 61, 62.
[2] Roussel, *Catholic and Protestant Nations*, vol. ii. p. 80.
[3] Letter, in *My Connexion with the Sabbath Movement in France*, by C. Cochrane.
[4] *Childe Harold*, cant. i. st. 68-80.

terprise ;[1] and where "every town has its *Casa de Expositos*, that of Seville alone (seven-tenths or seven-ninths of whose inhabitants are entire strangers to religious ordinances) having nearly 1100 poor infants thrown upon its care every year, to which must be added that the mortality of that class is tremendous, and the real amount of infanticide, owing to the general licentiousness of the people, is incalculable."[2] But we must revert for a moment to France, which at one time exchanged Popery for Atheism, the Sabbath for the Decade. The experiment showed that infidelity was, even more than a corrupt religion, detrimental to the family. What the institution suffered from the worship of a strumpet let the following facts declare :—The National Convention enacted a law permitting divorce, of which there were registered, within about a year and a half, 20,000 cases ; and within three months, 562 cases, or one to every three marriages, in Paris alone. Well might the Abbé Gregoire exclaim, "This law will soon ruin the nation." But this was not all. "Infancy was committed to the tender mercies of State nurseries, in which nine out of ten died ; a system which, by infanticide and disease, had, in fifty years, reduced by one half the population of the Sandwich Islands, and were it to be universal and permanent, would, in a few centuries, nearly depopulate the earth."[3] The worship of the Goddess of Reason, who had been able to bestow nothing of that endowment on her votaries, was abolished, and the law of divorce was modified and then repealed ; but Popery, which is still, as we have seen, laying waste the family of France, was not able when restored to counteract the mischief produced by infidelity, for writers in the earlier part of this century said of the country : "A chilling egotism has dried up all the springs of sentiment. The domestic affections are extinct. No one any longer enters into those valuable and wise connexions by which the present generation is united to the generations which are to come." "Domestic crimes, parricides, the murder of husbands by their wives, and wives by their husbands, are almost as common as larcenies were wont to be."[4]

[1] Irving's *Alhambra* (1832), vol. i. p. 7.
[2] Rule's *Mission to Gibraltar and Spain*, pp. 237-239.
[3] Beecher's *Perils of Atheism*, p. 86.
[4] Dr. Esquirol and Mennais, in *Boyle Lectures for* 1821, by Harness, vol. ii. pp. 110, 111.

3. The family deteriorates under a neglected or profaned Christian Sabbath. "The Reformed faith," it has been remarked by a Roman Catholic writer, "is particularly favourable to family affection."[1] We accept the confession, which is not only honourable to the writer, but just. We shall find, however, in the countries of the Reformation too many examples of Sabbath desecration, and of slackened or even sundered family ties, because all Protestants are not sincere or consistent holders of their professed creed. Manifold influences—pride and fashion, avarice and the love of pleasure, by their exaction of untimely or interminable labour from tradesmen and servants; intemperance, by its neglect, brutal treatment, and beggaring of families; and licentiousness, by its "vile" adulteries, heartless seductions, and base patronage of "the Social Evil"—unceasingly operate to the overthrow of a holy Sabbath, and to the ruin of domestic sanctities, enjoyments, and hopes. But "what are the high places of Judah? are they not Jerusalem?"

> "The seventh day this; the jubilee of man.
> London! right well thou know'st the day of prayer."

In Lord Byron's time "the day of prayer" was known by many "a spruce citizen," "washed artisan," and "smug apprentice," only as a day of play—a day on which they might "gulp their weekly air," and indulge themselves "with draught and dance till morn." Since the noble poet's time, the evil has gone on and increased. A million of Londoners have abandoned church-going. An unprecedented number pour themselves by railways into the country. Amusements are provided for loiterers at home. And efforts have been made to have the Crystal Palace and other public resorts thrown open on the Lord's day, and thus to introduce a wholesale desecration of sacred time. The evil spreads from the capital over England, Scotland, and Ireland. That five millions of people in the United Kingdom abjure the claims of the Sabbath and the sanctuary is, in other words, to say that one million of families are without the benefits, physical, intellectual, moral, religious, and economical, which these institutions convey. Let those who know England better than we, speak

[1] Viel-Castel, in Roussel, vol. ii. p. 81.

to its consequent domestic condition. As for Scotland, we know that its home virtues and comforts have, in not a few instances, degenerated. The excessive competition in all kinds of trade has been injurious to personal and social religion, and the wages earned have gone into "a bag with holes." When families are formed in our cities and towns, it is too frequently forgotten to erect an altar—the protection, blessing, and glory of a house. Even in rural scenes, it is not so common as formerly

"To hear the song
Of kindred praise arise from humble roofs."

Our agricultural servants are in many instances detached from the families of their masters, and yet precluded the means of forming their own domestic circles—whence rudeness, wickedness, and crime. Intemperance has committed many ravages on household piety, peace, and order, and this, like other evils, from the very want of that Sabbatic strictness to which it has been so untruly and preposterously imputed. In short, objects of gain, education, and even benevolence, have occasioned removals of children from the care of parents, or parents from the society of their children, to the weakening of the foundations of the family and the church.

4. And yet it is certain that the family flourishes wherever the Christian Sabbath is rightly observed, and nowhere more than in Great Britain and America, which, with all their faults, are proverbially superior to other nations as Sabbath-keeping communities. There, ancient custom, law, and, what is better, the deep convictions and feelings of the majority of the people, are arrayed on the side of the institution. It is to these countries, accordingly, that several intelligent writers, Roman Catholic as well as Protestant, assign the palm for domestic virtue and happiness. "Nowhere," says Madame de Staël, "can be seen such faithful protection on one side, and such tender and pious devotedness on the other, as in married life in England. Nowhere do the wives share with so much courage and simplicity the troubles and dangers of their husbands, wherever the duties of their profession may call them." Baron D'Haussez observes, "All things considered, *ceteris paribus*, thanks to the influence

of the manners, the married state in England is happier than in any other country." In equally laudatory terms do M. de Tocqueville and M. Michel Chevalier write of the marriage tie and conjugal happiness as they exist in America.[1] Of Scotland, Dr. Currie remarks, "A striking particular in the character of the Scottish peasantry is one which it is hoped will not be lost—the strength of their domestic attachments. The privations to which many parents submit for the good of their children, and particularly to obtain for them instruction, has already been noticed. If their children live and prosper, they have their certain reward, not merely as witnessing, but as sharing in their prosperity. Even in the humblest ranks of the peasantry, the earnings of the children may generally be considered as at the disposal of their parents; perhaps in no country is so large a portion of the wages of labour applied to the support and comfort of those whose days of labour are past. A similar strength of attachment extends through all the domestic relations."[2] That France owes its low domestic state not to its soil, not to the mental or physical character of its people, but to its want of a holy Sabbath and a pure Christianity, might be largely shown from facts in the history of its Protestant Church. Let one case suffice, in reading which the Christian will recognise the leading features of his religion, and the Scottish Christian, in particular, might conceive that the scene is laid in his own land, instead of Africa. "Towards the end of the seventeenth century, there were about three thousand French refugees established at twelve leagues to the north of the Cape, in a fertile valley, which bears, to the present day, the name of French Valley. . . . There is a fourth village, the most considerable of all, that of La Perle, whose inhabitants, exclusively devoted to agriculture, are the richest in that Old Dutch Colony, now belonging to the English. This population has not forgotten the rigid principles and fervid piety of their ancestors. The traveller who crosses their hospitable threshold invariably finds upon the table one of those great folio Bibles which the French Protestants were wont to hand down from father to son, as a sacred patrimony and inestimable trea-

[1] See, for all these testimonies, *Roussel*, as before, vol. i. pp. 57, 58; vol. ii. p. 80.
[2] *Life of Burns*, Prefatory Remarks.

sure. The date of birth and the names of all the members of the family are invariably inscribed in it. Sometimes, too, one finds pious books in their houses, such as the Psalms put into verse by Clement Marot. An affecting custom has been preserved amongst these simple and austere men. Night and morning the members of each family assemble for prayer. There are no formalities or pompous ceremonies; they content themselves with praying with all their hearts, and with reading the Bible. Every Sunday, at sunrise, the farmers set out in their rustic vehicles, covered with hides or with coarse cloth, to attend Divine service, and at night they return peaceably to their homes. Gambling is unknown amongst them, and the refined corruption of European civilisation has not reached them. The useful arts and practical instruction are all they care for and cultivate. They seek to diffuse them among their former slaves, whom they have always treated with kindness, and they willingly devote much time and pains to the propagation of the gospel amongst the idolatrous races that surround them."[1]

5. When Sabbath observance is begun or resumed by any family or people, the sure and speedy consequence is an improvement in their domestic character and condition. The proof of this averment may be found in every report of Protestant missions, home and foreign. We give two or three of the more recent examples. The Report of the London City Mission presents the following among the statistics of the good effected by the Society during the year 1859-1860: "Shops closed on the Lord's day, 293; persons who have become communicants, 1236; backsliders restored to church communion, 253; drunkards reclaimed, 1102; fallen females rescued, 524; unmarried couples induced to marry, 300; family prayer commenced, 587."[2] A mission was begun in Aneiteum, one of the islands of the New Hebrides, in 1848. Formerly bigamy, polygamy, and repudiation of wives prevailed there. Female infanticide was frequent. Widows were strangled, and cast into the sea along with their husbands. In 1860, the Sabbath is as well observed as in any part of Scotland. Family worship is universally observed every morning and evening; in each of fifty or sixty districts, into which the island has been

[1] Roussel, vol. ii. pp. 205, 206. [2] *News of the Churches*, vol. vi. p. 162.

divided, there is a teacher, with his wife, and Christianity has in twelve years saved the lives of upwards of 100 females, widows, and infants. "I have married," says Mr. Inglis, one of the missionaries, "about 160 couples during the last six or seven years, and, with very few exceptions, they are enjoying as much domestic happiness as could reasonably be looked for."[1] Scarcely less interesting is the change that has passed over another island in Polynesia, which, from the excessive ferocity of its inhabitants, was by Captain Cook named Savage Island. The people retained the same character for sixty years after his time, but consented eleven years ago to receive missionaries, and now all of them, being 4300, are Christian, with the exception of some ten, who still stand aloof. In the days of heathenism there had been a fearful destruction of children, but now the natives, in whose cottages the voice of prayer and praise is daily heard, are "a loving and grateful people."[2] We may add, that the respect for the Lord's day which began to be entertained by the slaves in Jamaica and other colonies was connected with the observance of the law of marriage, and with a greatly improved morality in all respects.

6. Families in contiguous countries, districts, or villages, are strikingly distinguished from one another in respect of morals and comfort according to their treatment of the Sabbath. Such contrasts are frequently to be met with in town and country, at home and abroad. In Belgium, for example, "the population, fond, like the French, of pleasure, may be seen at the theatres, gardens, and all places of public resort," while in Holland, where, "it is said, no person wishing to retain a decent character in society, can absent himself on Sundays from the place of worship to which he belongs," "the chief pleasure is found at home, and the family circle furnishes the truest happiness."[3] A writer, describing two villages in the south of England, inhabited by fishermen, supplies another striking contrast. "Although but a mile and a half apart from each other, there is a great difference between the character and habits of the people of Mousehole and those of Newlyn. There is much more recklessness in the latter than in the former. The

[1] *Reformed Presbyterian Magazine* for September 1860.
[2] *Evangelical Magazine* for August 1860.
[3] Thorn *on the Sabbath* (1830), p. 273. Roussel, vol. i. p. 280.

men of Newlyn do not drink on board, but they drink a good deal on shore. A tipsy man is scarcely ever seen in Mousehole. This great reform is the work of the last few years. There were formerly five public-houses in the village, and now, although it has a population of about 1500, it does not afford sufficient custom to support even one. The habits of the people are in all respects superior to those of Newlyn. No fisherman from Mousehole will take to the sea on a Sunday. Every one of them attends some place of worship or other on that day. They are generally Methodists. They are also well educated according to their circumstances. The village school is a very efficient one. As indicative of their energy, I may here mention that the fishermen of Mousehole have, at a cost of £1400, built for themselves a pier, which, with the breakwater built many years ago by the Government, forms their little harbour. To construct it, they raised £1200 on their own joint bond, which they are paying off by instalments, each boat being put under a yearly contribution for the purpose."[1]

A third illustration, embracing eleven families, and extending over three generations, is even more important and conclusive than that of the two villages. In New Hampshire there are two neighbourhoods—one of six families, and the other five. The advantages of the two were nearly equal, except that the five families were about three miles farther from church, and had to pass one of those mountain ridges so common in that vicinity, called "Governor's Hill." The six families were fond of social intercourse, and used to spend their Sabbaths in visiting from house to house—never visiting the sanctuary. Some of them totally disregarded the Sabbath, and all eventually formed the habit. In the course of years, five were broken up by the separation of husband and wife, and the other by the father becoming a thief, and fleeing to parts unknown. Eight or nine of the parents became drunkards, most of whom have found a drunkard's grave. One committed suicide, and nearly all have suffered for want of the comforts of life. Of some forty or forty-five descendants, about twenty are known to be notorious drunkards, jockeys, or gamblers. Four or five are or have been in the State's prison. One fell in a duel. Some entered the army, and have never been

[1] Labour and the Poor, *Morning Chronicle*, Nov. 21, 1849.

heard from; others have gone to sea and never returned; and only a small number remain within the knowledge of their friends. Some are in the alms-house. Only one of the whole is known to have become a Christian, he having been "plucked as a brand from the burning" after having pursued a vicious miserable course from his youth; and he is the only one who has a competency of property, or the confidence of his neighbours. But how has it fared with the other five families, by whom, it is stated, no work was done nor visits made on the Sabbath, but who were all sure to be seen, riding or walking, on the way to the House of God; not without occasional taunts from their Sabbath-breaking neighbours? They all lived in peace, and were prospered in their labours. A large number of their children were reared up around them, numbering now, with their descendants, from two to three hundred. Eight of ten of the children are members of the Church, and adorn their profession. In only one instance has there been committed by any of the descendants a crime, which was followed by a speedy and deep repentance; and but one is known to be intemperate. Some of them are ministers of the Gospel. One is a missionary to China. Numbers are supporters and officers of churches. There has been among them no separation of husband and wife, except by death, and no suffering for want of the necessaries of life. The heads of these families lived to a good old age, and with a score or more of their descendants have gone down to the grave in peace, most of whom have left evidence that they died in the Lord. The homestead of a number of the families is now in the hands of the third generation. A colony has been planted by the descendants on the prairies of the West, maintaining the institutions of their fathers, and now reaping the benefits of their Sabbath-keeping habits and principles. These facts, say the narrators, speak a language not to be mistaken, and they come to you from the hand of the descendants of the five families.[1]

7. Thus it is invariably found, that where the Sabbatic institution is in force, the domestic institution flourishes; and that where the former is in abeyance, the latter is disorganized. The connexion of the one with the other, therefore, cannot be arbitrary.

[1] *Puritan Recorder*, quoted in *Christian Treasury* for 1850, p. 549.

There must be something in the Christian Sabbath that is necessary to the family. The influence, indeed, is reciprocal. It has been said that "none but married parents build churches, support ministers, or frequent the worship of God."[1] The head of the house is appointed in the Decalogue a custodier, teacher, and propagator of the Sabbath law. On the other hand, the Sabbath, or rather the pure religion, of which a day of sacred rest is an essential part, gives existence, stability, and prosperity to the family. The mighty agency operates by promoting all the interests—physical, mental, moral, and economical—of the person by whom the weekly holy day is respected, so that if each inhabitant of a house were to rest and worship in a Christian manner on that day, the various beneficial tendencies of the practice would concur to secure for him a large amount of good, and "the resultant" of the improved character and circumstances of the individual members would be the general welfare of the household. The same agency operates, also, by means of the instructions and laws which require a Sabbath for their promulgation and study, and by which persons are taught that marriage is a Divine ordinance; that it is the voluntary union of one man and one woman only, a union which nothing but the death or infidelity of one or other of the parties can lawfully dissolve; that husband and wife are bound to love each other, the former giving honour to the latter as being an heir with him of the grace of life; that parents and children, masters and servants, have their respective rights and obligations; and that, while multiplied evils must be awarded to all who trample on or neglect, many blessings are pledged to all who perform, their relative duties—truths, lessons, and sanctions, that no one can credit without recognising the importance of every human being, and abhorring both tyranny and insubordination in the family and everywhere else. And Christianity by its Sabbath favourably influences domestic life in yet another way. On that day the members of a household who are in many cases necessarily separated on other days, can, and do meet together, when mutual acquaintance, affection, and sympathy are cultivated; children and domestics are instructed; and family ties are strengthened, hallowed, and blessed by family prayer. Who that has participated in the pious,

[1] Dwight's *Theology*, Ser. 119.

rational, benevolent engagements and tranquil enjoyments of such a society, can, without doing violence to the strongest convictions, prefer the portion here and hereafter of the votaries and victims of delusive "pleasure," to

> "Finding in the calm of truth-tried love,
> Joys that her stormy raptures never knew?"

Thus it is that many acquire the views of married life, with the domestic habits which prevail in this, and some other countries, where, according to the confession of foreigners, are realized the highest idea and the best blessings of home.

If, therefore, "My dear, my native soil" would not allow those scenes to depart, from which

> "Old Scotia's grandeur springs,
> That makes her loved at home, revered abroad;"

if England would retain and brighten her

> "Domestic happiness, the only bliss
> Of Paradise that has survived the Fall;"

if Britain and America would not forfeit but increase their greatness; if France would "let the fire-side regain its influence," so that her "tottering edifice of religion and politics might acquire both tone and power;" if, in fine, the earth would shake from her the abominations of polygamy, concubinage, adultery, causeless divorce, and "the social evil," with all their present horrors, and their preparation of myriads for everlasting degradation and woe, —there must be a sacred remembrance in the church, the world, the house, the heart, of that indispensable auxiliary and safeguard of liberty and law, of the Bible and the school, of the sanctuary and the hearth—the Sabbath-day.

CHAPTER VI.

ADVANTAGES OF THE SABBATH TO NATIONS.

"I have lived long enough to know what at one time I did not believe—that no society can be upheld in happiness and honour, without the sentiments of religion." —*Words of* LAPLACE, *not long before his death, to Professor Sedgwick.*

"The Sabbath, as a political institution, is of inestimable value, independently of its claims to Divine authority."—ADAM SMITH.[1]

"WEALTH," says a popular writer on Political Economy, "is but one among a number of causes which conduce to the happiness of a people. Social happiness is the result of a pure religion, good morals, a wise government, and a general diffusion of knowledge."[2] Let us consider these and other elements which enter into national prosperity, with the view of ascertaining how much they are dependent for their existence and power on the Sabbatic institution.

The welfare of a country is in no small degree promoted by its wealth, provided this be not limited to a few, but, while possessed in a larger share by some, be diffused in a competent measure among all classes. It is in such circumstances that nations are more industrious, and have more leisure as well as inclination for the improving and refining pursuits of science, literature, and general knowledge. These circumstances remove society farther away from the evils of disorganization and barbarism. The augmented capital and the higher standard of enjoyment connected with such a state of

1 "The baronet's next undertaking was a quarto essay against what he then considered a too strict and puritanical observance of the Sabbath in Scotland, but with singular conscientiousness he destroyed the whole manuscript on hearing this remark from his friend, Dr. Adam Smith, which was the more memorable as coming from the apologist of David Hume: 'Your book, Sir John, is very ably composed; but the Sabbath, as a political institution, is of inestimable value, independently of its claims to Divine authority.'"—*Memoir of Sir John Sinclair*, by Chambers.

2 *Conversations on Polit. Econ.*, sixth edit. p. 24.

things supply increased stimulus to trade, and multiply the products of industry. And while a general plenty is a blessing, the affluence of individuals is a fund which can be drawn upon for large and expensive undertakings, and for any emergencies that may arise from unpropitious seasons or from prevailing disease. It has been remarked, that the kingdom of Judah was in all respects in its best state when its commerce was most extended, and its wealth most plentiful. A prevailing poverty, on the other hand, is in various ways injurious to society. It is one cause of the crime that destroys confidence, and entails a vast expense on a nation. It directly absorbs much of the capital of a country to the oppression of the industrious, and the prevention of many useful applications of money. It in many cases induces, invites, and localizes disease, whereby terror and death are spread all round. Of thousands thus made widows and orphans every year, the greater portion become burdens to the country, while the loss in productive labour by sickness and funerals, is immense. Add to this the destruction of property to which many in these circumstances are impelled, who are not under the control of intelligence and moral principle. And the evil ends not with one generation, but goes down to a sickly and degenerate posterity.

The riches, which prevent so much injury, and secure so much good to a nation, are the fruits, in abundant amount, of its productive labour. The persons who labour and economize, are benefactors of their country,—the idle and the wasteful diminish its wealth. It has been shown in a previous chapter, that incessant toil is detrimental to the commercial interests of a community in the diminished amount and depreciated quality of its material and mental products, as the consequence of its demoralizing tendency, and the physical exhaustion of the workmen; while, on the other hand, every kind of labour becomes, by the interposed rest of the Lord's day, more valuable, and therefore more remunerative. Connected with that day's rest, there are, we have seen, some remarkable provisions for benefiting both the labourers and the State. And it has appeared, that in point of fact the wealth of nations graduates according to the measure in which the day is religiously respected and observed.

Akin to the element of wealth is another—a spirit of improvement and useful enterprise. Of this spirit, although on a small scale, a happy illustration has been supplied by the Morning Chronicle Commissioner, in the case of the Sabbath-respecting and energetic fishermen of one of the contiguous villages, mentioned in the preceding chapter. The same cause produces the same effect, and as in that village, so everywhere it will be found that the Sabbath well kept promotes a desire for social improvement. And it produces the effect in two ways, directly on its friends, and indirectly on their neighbours who are cold or hostile to its claims. So powerful is the institution that it operates beneficially, not only on its own adherents, but through them on individuals and communities that to a great extent disregard its authority. Many of our principal inventions, discoveries, and arrangements, our steam-engines, our railways, and telegraphs, our schools of art, our agricultural, manufacturing, and postal improvements, take their rise in Britain or America, those lands of the Sabbath; and other lands follow in their wake. France, indeed, sends over her contributions to our civilisation; but they abound in the frivolous and the effeminate, and when substantial, are much helped by foreign impulse. Italy excels in the fine arts, and we are sufficiently willing to learn of her in that department, but we cannot forget that Rome, the seat of a government which ought, from the assumed infallibility of its head and church, to be the most enlightened and advanced on the face of the earth, is nevertheless found, as to all that is of the greatest importance to a country, lagging ingloriously behind. It will drain no marshes. It will introduce no subsoil plough into its Campagna di Roma. It abjures winnowing machines and iron bridges. It would form no railways, and strongly resisted the proposals of foreigners to introduce improved light into its dismal streets, and only the other day yielded to the pressure of universal opinion and example in these matters of obvious utility. Every attempted improvement, indeed, originated with English skill and capital. And "so effectually has the Pontifical Government developed its influence, as to have all but annihilated trade in the Papal States." In the other states, if we except Lombardy, matters are not much better, and even that fertile, well-watered portion of Italy is far behind in the march of improvement. We have seen that considerably more than a half of the inhabitants of Naples are without any fixed employment, yet the Neapolitan territory, which miserably maintains a population of between seven and eight millions, is capable of yielding abundant food for at least twenty millions of people, or three times the present amount.

As with Italy, so in many respects it is with all other countries which are burdened with an exacting superstition, that yields no compensating return, and are encumbered with a multitude of holidays,[1] without feeling the refreshing and animating influence of a weekly day of repose and religious instruction. These countries, however much they profit by the indirect influence of the institution coming upon them from other lands, and stimulating them by means of commerce to the exertions by which their natural capabilities are turned to some account, are yet low in the scale of material prosperity, for want of the direct impulse of the institution in exciting a spirit of improvement among the people. While the manufactures of Portugal are inconsiderable, its agriculture is the worst in Europe. How lamentable is the state of Spain, where the great body of the people are abandoned to idleness and vice,—where, with a climate and soil admitting in some spots of three or four crops in the year, not above a fourth part of the surface of the country is applied to any useful purpose, and where, with excellent facilities for commerce, the exports are less than those of some of our leading commercial towns.[2] "The Protestants of the United States," as Macaulay remarks, "have left far behind them the Roman Catholics of Mexico, Peru, and Brazil; the Roman Catholics of Lower Canada remain inert, while the whole continent round them is in a ferment with Protestant activity and enterprise."

It is so much easier for human nature to do evil than good that it is not wonderful that the Protestants on the Continent

[1] It has been estimated that the sum lost to Spain every holy-day or feast-day by the suspension of labour is £166,666, 13s. 4d., making an annual loss of nearly seven millions.—Bell's *Geography*, vol. ii. 272, note.

[2] *Christian Treasury* (1846), p. 379. The writer informs us that 400,000 quarters of grain, on an average, need to be imported every year to prevent multitudes from perishing by famine.

of Europe should, under the influence of Rome and of infidelity, have departed from the strict observance of the Sabbath which was for a long period maintained both in the Lutheran and Calvinistic churches. But when we bear in mind that this deviation, while at no time universal, has never proceeded to the same desecration of the institution as has prevailed among Romanists, and that those churches have always enjoyed in connexion with the Lord's day the means of Christian instruction, together with freedom from the burden of numerous holidays, we are prepared for the state of things which actually exists, a measure of enterprise inferior to that of British and American Protestants, and yet beyond that of their Roman Catholic neighbours.

In Switzerland what an improvement in every respect strikes the eye as you pass from Valais to Vaud, or from Lucerne to Zurich! And how spiritless appears the town of Lucerne with its alternate shops of *bijouterie* and cigars, compared with the bustling Zurich, so like our Birmingham or Belfast, or with thriving Geneva, although all the three have the common advantage of being situated near noble rivers and lakes! "The Cantons of Zurich, Basle, Geneva, Neuchatel, Glarus, and Outer Appenzell, which are all Protestant, are distinguished above the rest by their industry. One circumstance is remarkable, namely, that almost all the manufacturing industry of Switzerland is found in the Protestant part of it, while the Catholics possess little or none. Very often, as in Appenzell, the line of demarcation is quite sharply drawn. Manufactures and Protestantism cease at once, and give way to the herdsman and the shepherd; and that, not because there is any sudden change in the natural features of the country, for the little Canton of Glarus, for instance, is a high mountain land, and yet it abounds in industrial activity. But the people of Glarus are Protestants; they have fewer fast-days and holidays; and Protestantism awakens the powers of the mind, abates the influence of the priesthood, and teaches men to rely on their own exertions."[1] The writer observes that the same remark applies to Germany, where "of two villages close together, the Protestant community will be clean, industrious, and prosperous, while their Catholic neighbours

[1] Mugge's *Switzerland in* 1847, vol. i. pp. 202, 203.

will remain always poor and dirty."[1] "Crossing St. Maurice's Bridge, our passports are inspected, and so we are free to enter Switzerland again from Savoy: the religion, Protestantism, seems at once to make all things cleaner, happier, and more prosperous; never was a change more remarkable. English-looking breadth of tillage, vines and maize, and walnut groves and pleasant villages have succeeded to all their opposites and absences; and so these go on improvingly all through the Canton de Vaud."[2] Turning from the Continent to our own country, we see Ireland, possessed of every advantage in soil, climate, minerals, rivers, and harbours, for agriculture, manufactures, and commerce, and yet surpassed considerably in the amount of national revenue, and in its shipping, by somewhat smaller, and far less populous Scotland, while her people, though remarkable for their shrewdness and vivacity, are in the mass characterized by ignorance, sloth, filth, a general state of mind bordering on the savage, and a social condition continually approximating to destitution and famine. But you require not to go out of Ireland to be convinced that the blame rests on its prevalent religion, for passing from the south or west into the north, "you cannot but feel that Ulster is at least fifty years ahead of its sister provinces in all the true elements of national progress; and in its general aspect so much more resembles Britain than Ireland, that one could almost fancy some physical convulsion to have severed it from the one island, and attached it to the other."[3] This is the language of an Irishman, who also states that "in 1846, the Tidal Harbour Commissioners pronounced Belfast the first town in Ireland for enterprise and commercial prosperity. The revenue of its port increased during 1786-1850, from £1500 to £29,000." Of the comparative progress of the principal ports in Ireland we may judge from the following figures:—

		1797.	1842.
Belfast, ...	Tons	13,062	136,747
Londonderry, . .	,,	2,856	33,299
Cork, ...	,,	13,424	87,925
Dublin, . . .	,,	33,485	61,257

[1] Mugge's *Switzerland*, vol. i. p. 203.

[2] *Diary*, by Paterfamilias (1856), p. 220.

[3] Dill's *Ireland's Miseries*, pp. 30, 32.

There is, however, a higher species of activity than any that respects only our own material comforts. There is the enterprise that aims at the general good of society, and particularly its mental and moral improvement. It is necessary only to say here that no system has accomplished much good in this department, except in so far as it has reflected the light and radiated the heat which by means of the Sabbatic institution it has received from Revelation.

The reason of all this spirit-stirring effect of the Christian weekly festival is no mystery. Its observance withstands the depressing influence of toil. It is a protection against the pleasures which dissipate mental energy, and enfeeble moral purpose. It introduces men into the encouraging and animating fellowship of their fellow-creatures. And above all, it places them, consciously, under the Divine eye, which stirs into a correspondingly pure and benevolent activity every feeling and faculty of their being.

No country can in the highest sense prosper without such a government as, by good laws faithfully administered, and consistently exemplified by its rulers, discourages on the one hand injustice and oppression, and restrains on the other the encroachments of a lawless liberty. And it would be impossible to name an expedient better adapted to prevent the extremes of despotism and weakness in a government than the Sabbatic institution. The Sabbath is a constant memorial and safeguard to the rulers and the rich to keep them from forgetting their duty and responsibility. It is a perpetual bulwark for all the sons and daughters of toil against the undue exaction of labour, and against encroachment on their property of a seventh part of their time. And effectual as it is for producing popular intelligence and virtue, there must spring up in the country that respects it those lawgivers and magistrates who will consult the rights and the welfare of high and low, rich and poor, and who, strong in their own character, as well as in the support of a sound public opinion, will be able to repress the risings of turbulence and disorder. How strikingly does history confirm these views! In the days of Solomon, when the Jewish religion, including its Sabbaths, was in full operation, Judah and Israel enjoyed abundant comforts and great prosperity, and the account of this state of things is followed by the significant words, "And Judah and Israel dwelt safely, every man under his vine and under his fig-tree, from Dan even to Beersheba, all the days of Solomon." "And Solomon's wisdom excelled the wisdom of all the children of the east country, and all the wisdom of Egypt."[1] To the Sabbath did England in no small degree owe a government so puissant and beneficial as that of Cromwell, the happy domestic influence of which is admitted by Bishop Burnet, while its foreign aspect is eulogized by a no less unbiassed judge, Sir Walter Scott, who says, "Perhaps no government was ever more respected abroad."[2] To the Sabbath, as a principal cause, was Britain indebted for such a reign as that of William III., Prince of Orange, and for the superiority of our present constitution to the governments of Russia, France, and Italy, where the people are in chains, which the expansive spirit of a nation imbued with the influence of Christian truth and institutions, if we could suppose it thus fettered, would calmly break in pieces. The policy of those rulers, who amuse their subjects with frivolous objects on the Lord's day, that they may not by serious thought be led to discover that they are men and deeply injured men, may be cunning and successful for a time, but it is not wise, since its purpose is as short-sighted as it is unjust. The convulsions on the Continent in 1848 furnished impressive illustrations of this truth. It is a fact that these convulsions were more destructive in Roman Catholic kingdoms, where there was nothing entitled to the name of a Sabbath, than in Protestant communities, where the institution, inasmuch as it brought along with it the opportunities of a more rational worship and of better instruction, had not suffered so much deterioration. No Protestant prince lost his throne. And it is especially worthy of grateful remembrance that Britain, where, above almost all countries the Lord's day receives its meed, though far from its due meed of honour, stood firm and unscathed in all its interests amidst the shakings of the nations of Europe. "I see," says the Chevalier Bunsen, personating Hippolytus, "that you have erected most wonderful factories and cotton mills; but you do not make the poor

[1] 1 Kings iv. 20-34.
[2] *Tales of a Grandfather*, 8vo. (1848), p. 211.

people, men, women, and children, work in them on Sundays, as the Gauls [the French] do in their country. . . . You have known how to unite freedom with order, popular rights with a national aristocracy and hereditary monarchy, which union, our great heathen prophet Cicero said, would, if ever it could be brought to pass, form the most perfect of governments."[1]

The prevailing tranquillity which is maintained by a wise and just government is of the greatest moment to all the enjoyments and interests of a country. Spain, Italy, and Ireland, might be pointed to as presenting obvious contrasts to such a state of things, and reference too might be made to those occasional scenes of outrage and bloodshed in countries usually peaceful, which enhance to the inhabitants their prevailing advantages. In Scotland, 1800 soldiers suffice to keep the peace, while Ireland required, for the eight years preceding 1852, troops numbering at an average more than 25,000. Of these troops, scarcely 3000 are found in Ulster, and except in its southern counties, even these are wholly unnecessary. Not a soldier is stationed between Belfast and Derry, a distance of seventy miles, embracing two most populous counties, and various large towns. Of the 13,000 police in Ireland, the number stationed in Ulster in 1851 was 1901, little more than a seventh of the force for a third of the population.[2] What says M. de Montalembert, in name of a Commission reporting to the French Parliament in 1850 on Sabbath Observance? After remarking that the Almighty conferred success and security on human labour in proportion as nations respect the Lord's day, he refers in proof to England and the United States, and says, "Witness that city London, the capital and focus of the commerce of the world,[3] where Sunday is observed with the most scrupulous care, and where two and a half millions of people are kept in order by three battalions of infantry, and some troops of guards, while Paris requires the presence of 50,000 men."[4]

The connexion thus observed to subsist between a Christian

[1] Bunsen's *Hippolytus and his Age*, vol. ii. pp. 16, 17.
[2] Thom's *Statistics*, quoted in Dill, pp. 74, 8?.
[3] "O thou, resort and mart of all the earth.' —COWPER.
[4] *Rapport*, etc. (1850), pp. 37, 38.

institution and social order is not a matter of accident. From the whole preceding discussion in these pages, it follows that a Sabbath-keeping community will be healthy, intelligent, moral, and comfortable to the extent in which the influences of the institution are permitted to operate. Those who enjoy such blessings can have no interest in turmoil, or in mere change, and only the direst necessity would make them revolutionists, when all their feelings are in favour of peace and quiet. These men, too, can appreciate and make allowance for the difficulties of rulers, and their attempts at reformation will be rational and discreet. The meetings once a week of rich and poor prevent selfish insulation, remove ignorant prejudices, smooth asperities, cherish kindliness of feeling, create a mutual interest, teach lessons of civility, and promote refinement of taste and courtesy in manners. "The keeping one day in seven holy," says Blackstone, "as a time of relaxation and refreshment, as well as for public worship, is of admirable service to a State, considered merely as a civil institution. It humanizes, by the help of conversation and society, the manners of the lower classes, which would otherwise degenerate into a sordid ferocity and savage selfishness of spirit. It enables the industrious workman to pursue his occupation in the ensuing week with health and cheerfulness; it imprints on the minds of the people that sense of their duty to God, so necessary to make them good citizens; but which yet would be worn out and defaced by an unremitted continuance of labour without any stated times of recalling them to the worship of their Maker."[1] He might have extended his remarks to other classes of society. There are those besides the lower orders who can be selfish and disorderly, noted for family broils, and for their breaches of the public peace, but a truthful biography of such characters would let us see that those who do such things neither relish the business, nor experience the tranquillizing pleasures of a sacred resting day. The saying of Burke, that "whatever alienates man from God, must needs disunite man from man," holds good of all classes. Let us again borrow a few sentences from Bunsen's *Hippolytus.* After remarking, as already quoted, that our manufacturing people are not, like the Gauls [the French], condemned to Sunday labour, he thus proceeds: "You

[1] Blackstone's *Commentaries*, vol. iv. p. 63

have, like them, labourers and mechanics, aspiring to better their condition; but yours prefer working, and quietly associating together, to the making of revolutions, and plunging others and themselves into misery. You have ragged children; but you clothe and educate them for useful work, instead of enlisting them as soldiers to kill their fellow-citizens; and they like learning to read and to work, rather than making an attempt to convulse society by their votes, and to subvert order by arms. . . . You have just shown to the world the practical effect of the principle on which your social arrangements are based. People on the Continent believed (or tried to make others believe) that the gathering of so many hundreds of thousands of your working and labouring men around the spectacle of the Great Exhibition would be the signal, if not of famine and pestilence, certainly of revolution and bloodshed. But I have seen them surround their Queen with respectful affection: and far from any disturbance taking place, good-will and good-humour and plenty never have reigned more paramount anywhere than during these months among you. Now when I ask myself, since what time you have possessed this liberty and enjoyed this peace and tranquillity, I cannot help remarking that you owe it all to that godly reform you began to make of Christianity about three hundred years ago."[1]

The occasion, however—although ever to be deprecated—may call for the defence of a land against domestic or foreign foes. And who are the men best prepared in such a crisis to stand by their sanctuaries and hearths? The very persons who have by means of the Sabbath been disciplined not less to energy, enterprise, self-reliance, and physical strength, than to all the finer and gentler feelings of humanity. Macaulay describes Cromwell's army as one that never found, either in the British Islands or on the Continent, an enemy who could stand its onset—as startling and delighting Turenne by its fearless energy; and mentions a brigade, outnumbered by foes and abandoned by allies, which nevertheless drove before it in headlong rout the finest infantry of Spain. He lets us into the secret of all this power, when he says, "But that which chiefly distinguished the army of Cromwell from other armies was the austere morality, and the fear of God which per-

[1] Bunsen's *Hippolytus*, vol. ii. pp. 16-18.

vaded all ranks. It is acknowledged by the most zealous royalists that in that singular camp no oath was heard, no drunkenness or gambling was seen, and that during the long dominion of the soldiery, the property of the peaceable citizen and the honour of women were held sacred."[1] Thus "the people that do know their God are strong and do exploits." It was ever so in the history of the Jews, down to the time of the Maccabees. When they forgot their religion and its Sabbaths they became weak and dastardly, and were finally reduced to a condition of abject dependence and servitude. In France as compared with Britain, in Spain as compared with Holland, in South as compared with North America, we find proofs that the people whose character, mental, moral, and corporeal, has been deteriorated by ignorance, superstition, and the pursuits of frivolity and pleasure, are surpassed in energy and prowess by the men who have, through the Scriptures and the institutions of Christianity, imbibed the spirit of faith and courage, and had their intellectual and physical powers trained to activity and endurance. And who are those that at the close of a war return to their homes and ordinary avocations, without having been corrupted by the life of a camp or the excitements of the battle-field, and blend again in general society without the slightest disturbance of its order and peace? The men who, like Cromwell's warriors, have learned by the lessons of the Sabbath that war is not a matter of desire or taste but a painful necessity, and that "the post of honour is a private station." The historian proceeds to record the following remarkable facts connected with the disbandment of the army whose virtue and bravery in the campaign he had eulogized. "Fifty thousand men, accustomed to the profession of arms, were at once thrown on the world; and experience seemed to warrant the belief that this change would produce much misery and crime, that the discharged veterans would be seen begging in every street, or would be driven by hunger to pillage. But no such result followed. In a few months, there remained not a trace indicating that the most formidable army in the world had just been absorbed

[1] Macaulay's *History of England*, vol. i. p. 122. How different from the following: "No woman's honour is safe in any village through which a French detachment happens to be passing." Letters from Turin.—*Daily Express*, June 22, 1859.

into the mass of the community. The royalists themselves confessed that in every department of honest industry, the discarded warriors prospered beyond other men, that none was charged with any theft or robbery, that none was heard to ask an alms, and that if a baker, a mason, or a waggoner attracted notice by his diligence or sobriety, he was in all probability one of Oliver's old soldiers."[1]

When a society is characterized in its successive generations by a growing measure of health and longevity, it is generally regarded as in an improving condition. And what sound-minded person can doubt that the cultivation of the virtues of respect for life, industry, temperance, and providence, together with the improved physical comforts which such a condition implies, not to mention the pleasures of health itself, must presuppose as well as contribute to national wealth, energy, and happiness? When we compare the present state of our own country with that of degraded and short-lived savage tribes, with that of half-civilized China, where so many of the young are left to perish, or even with that of Europe, in those times when fell diseases created so much alarm and calamity, we have an impressive illustration of the blessings included in the increasing duration of human life. But England teaches us the same lesson in another way, for while "the value of life is greater there than in any country in the world,"[2] with all other elements of greatness and prosperity in proportion, she presents over-against these honours the spectacle of life in its lowest form of discomfort and abbreviation. We see a large class destroyed for lack of knowledge of the simplest sanitary rules, of the plainest principles of political economy, and especially of those intellectual and moral subjects which, above all other means, dignify, bless, and prolong the life of man. We see a vast number the victims of crimes, which not only in many instances entail capital punishment, but as connected with imprisonment and other sufferings, are equivalent to 30 years' tear and wear of life, the criminal of 35 years being 65 years old in constitution, and by imprisonment itself increase exactly fourfold the chances of death.[3] And we see tens of thousands ruined by vice,

1 Macaulay's *History of England*, vol. i. p. 154.
2 Dr. S. Smith's *Philosophy of Health*, vol. i. (1851), p. 147.
3 *Ibid.* p. 108.

avarice, vanity, ambition, luxury, indolence, intemperance, and other abettors of the claims of the grave. "The death-rate in Great Britain," said Mr. Chadwick, at the recent Social Science Congress in Glasgow, "may be stated in round numbers altogether at half-a-million annually. On an analysis of the causes of death with a knowledge of the present state of sanitary science, it is declared by others than myself that one-half may be prevented, and that, too, not by rudimentary, but by tried and well-ascertained means." Who can compute the moral, physical, and social evils involved in so many deaths with their foregoing sufferings,—the guilt of so many human sacrifices to human passions,—the lamentation, mourning, and woe of the sufferers and survivors,—the destitution to which so many widows and orphans are reduced, and the irreparable injury to society from lost labour, superadded burdens, increased disease, and multiplied crimes?

Science teaches us that many of such evils are preventible, and that, though there are bounds to life which cannot be passed, human beings might be so circumstanced, and might so act as to fill up happily the measure of their days. In confirmation of this position, it points to the higher average life attained by some nations and classes than by others, and to cases of countries, districts, and towns, where comparative health is enjoyed by all orders of the population. It is deeply to be regretted, however, that writers on sanitary reform, not fully applying the Baconian principle of gathering truth from a sufficient induction of particulars, have failed in so many instances to discover the root of the prevailing evil to be impiety, and to learn that all appliances which are not guided by this fact are mere palliatives, not remedies.

To one sanitary expedient this objection does not apply, for if there be any expression which the amplest evidence has proved to indicate more comprehensively than another the instrumentality by which so much waste of life is to be prevented, and the benefits of general and prolonged health are to be secured, it is to be found in the words, "Remember the Sabbath-day to keep it holy." For that evidence we refer to the preceding pages, and to a few statements now to be submitted, with the view of showing that the condition of large classes of men, in respect of health, bodily vigour, and longevity, according as they have laboured or rested on the Sabbath, is actually such as from the physical adaptations, and salutary effects in particular instances of the institution, might have been anticipated.

The countries of Europe where the duration of life varies most widely are England and Italy, and it will be admitted that no two countries differ more in their treatment of the day of sacred rest. While, as already remarked, the value of life is in no part of the world higher than in England, "the proportion of deaths to the whole number of inhabitants is greater in Italy than in any country of Europe."[1] It does not affect our conclusion, that this excessive mortality is owing in good part to undrained marshes and swamps. Let the refusal of Rome to accept the offer of Englishmen to remove the causes of fatal malaria set aside the apology, and show, moreover, what a change of religious institutions would do for the health of Italy. The intermediate rates of mortality in Russia, Austria, Sweden, Belgium, and Holland, and France, are not at variance with the results which their religious observances would lead us to expect. According to a census presented to Parliament, the proportion of sickness in the different provinces of Ireland was as follows: Ulster, 1 in 47·36; Leinster, 1 in 22·63; Connaught, 1 in 20·19; and Munster, 1 in 11·78. The lowest average life, in short, is to be found among savage men, criminals, prisoners, and slaves, who either have no knowledge of a holy Sabbath, or recklessly disregard it, while "the best lives" are to be found in Great Britain, and there among the "multitude that go to the house of God, that keep holy day." It has been said, that among the humbler provident classes who enrol themselves members of friendly societies in this country, there is experienced a prolonged duration of life above all others.[2] Not to mention how much the existence of a Sabbath in a land, and its observance by many, influence all classes to some extent, and contribute to the formation of such societies, we believe it will be found that the members who generally compose them are at the same time members of Christian churches. And it is indeed one of the glories of Christianity and its Sabbath,

[1] *System of Universal Geography founded on the works of Malte Brun and Balbi*, p. 562.
[2] Burton's *Polit. and Soc. Econ.* (1849), pp. 76, 77.

that a class of men are thereby elevated from circumstances which depress and cut short the earthly existence of their fellows, to a degree of comfort and a measure of life equal to those of their wealthier brethren, and proper to their rank as men.

In the same way would health and length of days become, much more than they are at present, the inheritance of society at large. Most certainly, if ignorance were generally enlightened, if crime and vice were everywhere suppressed, if labour were in all cases regulated by a due regard to human strength, and if people had comfortable dwellings, sufficient food, pure air, and cleanly persons, that happiness of individuals and nations arising from a pleasurable and protracted life would be realized which is thus with exquisite beauty described—"There shall be no more thence an infant of days, nor an old man that hath not filled his days; for the child shall die an hundred years old. And they shall build houses, and inhabit them; and they shall plant vineyards, and eat the fruit of them. For as the days of a tree are the days of my people, and mine elect shall long enjoy the work of their hands." Let us mark the closing words of the magnificent account—"And it shall come to pass, that from one Sabbath to another, shall all flesh come to worship before me, saith the Lord."[1]

On the importance of a prevailing morality to the welfare of a State it would be superfluous to enlarge. Let falsehood be general, and all confidence would be subverted. Abounding idleness would be abounding penury. If crime were unrestrained, where would be the security for property, the inducements to industry, economy, and improvement, or the opportunity for cultivating science and literature? A community corrupted by luxury and vice is always regarded as ready to become the prey of some powerful neighbour, or to waste away under poverty and disease. The greatest empires and many petty kingdoms have perished, the victims of their own wickedness. But for the check of a public morality, society generally would in due time reach the crisis of those tribes which have cast themselves out of the pale of civilisation and law; might become right, industry discarded, the land uncultivated, war and plunder the chief occupations, famine, pestilence, and death following in the train of sloth, igno-

[1] Isaiah lxv. 20-22; lxvi. 23.

rance, and rapacity, and the scene enacted in many places which was witnessed in a Polynesian island, where the three or four survivors of an exterminating war contended who should be king. But where is the security for a morality, which, not merely arresting decay, will impel society onward in a course of continual improvement? Let us learn from the dissolute manners of the Babylonians; from "the private debauchery and public profligacy in which the Greeks and Romans were steeped;" from the impure and cruel rites of idolatry; from the powerlessness of Islamism to preserve its adherents from vice, and its countries from degradation; from the incapacity of a corrupt Christianity, as in Spain, Italy, and Ireland, to stay the plague of moral evil, and to throw off the gangrene of political decline; and from the inroads of infidelity and immorality on continental and British Protestantism,—let us learn from all these facts that there is no sure provision for a conservative and elevating national virtue in science, literature, the arts, or in any religion that is without a weekly day devoted exclusively to rest and to the occupations and pleasures of a rational earnest piety. That the Sabbath as thus observed is the security for the morals and consequent preservation and advancement of nations, appears not only from the failure of all other expedients to secure these results, but from the uniform success in attaining them, which has distinguished the institution. The authorities in France, civil and ecclesiastical, began a few years ago to perceive that something better than a continental Sabbath is required, as was evinced in the efforts of M. de Montalembert, and of the Archbishop of Paris, to expose and correct its enormities. It would be well that foreigners who are desirous of promoting the observance of the Lord's day, would ponder the peculiarities which have imparted to the practice in this country a salutary influence such as they have not failed to observe and acknowledge, and that those Englishmen, too, who sigh for a continental license in this matter, would weigh the same subject in connexion with the failure of holidays in neighbouring countries to secure the morality of the people, and the prosperity and stability of States. Let both classes reflect on what constitutes the power of an institution which has done so much to make Britain a great country, and which is the means of raising up every year thousands from among those whom their own Sabbath-breaking and that of others have sunk in the lowest moral and social degradation, to the dignified position of virtue, usefulness, and comfort. Let them remember that there must be some admirable contrivance and energy in an instrument which has without an exception been employed in producing those remarkable changes of character, from a slothfulness hardly admitting of the moderate exertion necessary for cooking food to diligence in cultivating the soil, building comfortable dwellings, and engaging in commerce; from a total recklessness of life to feelings of mercy towards man and beast; from the desire of plunder to respect for property; from lawless libertinism to conjugal affection and fidelity,—which have crowned missionary efforts in heathen lands, and been among the glories of our age. If they considered these things, and drew the necessary inference that what has accomplished such results among all classes of men must be capable of accomplishing them universally, they could not but feel the obligation imposed upon them to cease from the suicidal, unpatriotic, unphilanthropic policy of ridiculing and opposing the sacred Sabbath, and to unite with its friends in maintaining its sanctity and extending its blessings.

Another element in social prosperity and happiness—one on which political economists place much reliance, and which has existed, as well as been beneficial in its operation, precisely in proportion to the observance of the Christian Sabbath—is a generally diffused intelligence. Knowledge is the parent and nurse of those arts which abridge human labour, multiply our comforts, and embellish and refine society. There are two great evils to which it is in no small degree an antidote. It is well ascertained that disease prevails and destroys in many cases where intelligence on the part of its victims would have arrested its progress, or even prevented its attack; that for want of the due exercise of the mental faculties whole tribes of human beings physically degenerate, and that from ignorance many others prematurely perish. Let men be properly instructed; and aware of the causes of injury to health, they will avoid them as they now eschew poison. For poverty, also, a principal remedy is to be found in the general information of the people. Impart instruction to an individual, and he acquires a self-respect which will make him unwilling to depend on the bounty of others, and he will therefore strive against sinking into penury. Intelligence will suggest to him reasons for providence and plans of economy. It will induce a readiness to discern the symptoms of a decaying trade, or of a threatened scarcity of employment, with a promptitude in turning to some other means of support, and the ability to meet the demands for a superior kind of work. Agricultural labourers in some parts of this country have, it is alleged, been prevented from going in quest of employment by "profound ignorance of everything connected with the countries whither they would be sent."[1] "The labour of the foolish wearieth every one of them, because he knoweth not how to go to the city." It is the peculiarity of work of every kind, as a writer observes, that a small addition to the expertness makes a large addition to the remuneration, and that the higher the grade the more marked is this difference. The superior education of the Scotsman, accordingly, gives him an advantage wherever he goes. His "knowledge is power" to adapt himself to circumstances, and to do what others cannot do; power, therefore, to raise himself above want, and to get on in the world. And what is thus for the benefit of the individual is for the common good. We find employers attesting that "educated workmen turn out the greatest quantity of the best work in the best manner;" that "the educated and cultivated workpeople of all ages are decidedly the best; more valuable as mechanics, because more regular in their habits, and more to be relied on in their work;" and that "their best servants are those who have been taught in their youth." The importance of intelligence on the part of those servants on railways, and in other situations, to whom in our day so great and dangerous powers are intrusted, it is impossible adequately to estimate.

1 This has been said of labourers in the south of England. The following furnishes both a contrast and a counterpart:—"I am old enough to remember the Highland tenantry of Scotland driven in multitudes from a soil to which their race had for ages been attached, nearly in a state of serfage, to make room, as is the case in Hungary, for sheep; and I had afterwards the happy opportunity of seeing the poor Highlanders attaining the means of independent living amidst the wilds of America; but the wretched serfs of Hungary have neither the intelligence nor the means to find so blessed an asylum."—*Austria and the Austrians*, vol. i. p. 19.

There remains to be noticed one more requisite to social prosperity—a pure religion. The conviction that the public recognition of a Supreme Being is indispensable to the good of society has been all but universal. The exceptions are like the monstrosities in nature, which do not disprove the existence of pervading general laws. When a Berkeley affirms the impossibility of matter, and a Hume fancies himself to be constituted, as described in four lines suggested for inscription on his monument—

"Within this circular idea,
Called vulgarly a tomb,
The impressions and ideas rest,
That constituted Hume"—[1]

such paradoxes are regarded as no more affecting the common rule of faith in the existence of matter and mind than any *lusus* does the ordinary course of nature. So the rare and unnatural appearance of a man who discards all religion proves nothing against it, if it does not strengthen, as exceptions do a rule, the evidence in its favour. The extravagance of opinion occasionally uttered on such a subject may be fitly compared to the aberrations of the person who conceives himself made of glass, or of the beggar who imagines himself a king, with this difference, that the views of the sceptic admit not of the apology of mental hallucination, but have originated, as the recantations of infidelity have afterwards proved, in some criminal passion. Mankind from Numa Pompilius downwards have been convinced that society cannot go on without religion. Even Robert Owen, who said so much against it, and did so little without it, was constrained at last to call in the aid of a supernatural element.

This general consent is itself a strong proof of the importance of religion to social prosperity, but it is impressively confirmed by the miserable situation, verging on dissolution, of all those communities in which the religious element has through neglect or violence been almost or altogether extinguished. It has been supposed that some savage tribes have no notion of a God, as they have no name for him in their language. Among the Esquimaux and the aborigines of New Holland, the impression of

[1] Lines by Mr. George Barclay. *Christ. Mag.* (1813), p. 311.

a Supreme Being was too feeble to inspire any religious worship. There was a class of the Tambookies, an African tribe, who disregarded what their parents said of Tixo, the Creator and Preserver of all things, considering them old and ignorant people, and said to the Moravian missionaries, "As we left off believing in God, you came to instruct us and to tell us more than our fathers and ancestors knew." All these may be said to belong to the very lowest class of human beings, and prove that man's descent as a religious being,. and his prostration as a rational and social creature, are in melancholy coincidence and proportion. Nor will civilisation protect against decline or anarchy the nations that have been smitten with a prevailing infidelity. Witness Greece before its loss of liberty, Rome at the wane of the republic, Italy amidst the corruption of its Church and State, and France before its first revolution.[1] The most remarkable of these is France, which is perhaps the only country that infidelity ever conquered to its views, and which amidst the reflected light of sixty centuries, and the blaze of civilisation, ventured on the tremendous experiment of proclaiming independence of Heaven; at one fell swoop abrogating the Sabbath, abolishing worship, and abjuring the faith of immortality and of a God! The results are well known —the disruption of all social bonds, the opening of the floodgates of immorality and crime, and an incalculable amount of misery, all tending to the sure and speedy ruin of the nation. Meanwhile the very mimicry of religion in their decades, in their goddess and temples of reason, in their orations and hymns in honour of their deities, was a tribute to the necessity of rest, instruction, and worship of some sort—the counterfeit confessing the felt need of the real—the new expedients, so grotesque and pitiful, while they betrayed man's helplessness without all religion, showing how shallow and idiotic his schemes are to contrive and provide a substitute. And the testimony in favour of religion received its full triumph, when the forced return of a proud people to their ancient faith, such as it was, attested that the civilized no less than the barbarous require a God, a religion, and a Sabbath, and when by the earliness of the return it was demonstrated that the reins of government could not even for a brief space

[1] Douglas's *Truths of Religion*, p. 12.

be intrusted to the hands of Atheism without involving general ruin, any more than Phaeton could for a day attempt to guide the steeds and chariot of the sun without setting the world on fire.

Although, however, infidelity has been tried and found wanting, it does not follow that every system claiming the name of religion should be adapted for much good to society. It is a pure religion which statesmen and political economists affirm to be important to social prosperity. We must judge of systems by their fruits. It is hardly necessary to say that the religions of savage nations will not stand this test. The New Zealanders had the idea of a Great Spirit, who thundered, brought the wind, and was the cause of any unforeseen loss of property or life, but they were nevertheless cannibals, and as far advanced in 1642 as they were a century later. The Polynesian nations without an exception entertained the belief of a Supreme Being, and yet their notions of the Deity were too gross and absurd to prevent exterminating wars and wasting licentiousness. Such are all savage tribes, except those who have sunk to the still lower depth of utter depression, which some have mistaken for simplicity and innocence. When we turn to nations of a superior grade, we shall find that none but those that have embraced Christianity have ever reached a complete civilisation. The religions of Egypt, Greece, and Rome, the most perfect ancient faith, failed to banish the most cruel customs, to humanize the upper classes, or to enlighten and elevate the great body of the people. And the creeds of Confucius, Mohammed, Brahma, and Boodh, have for ages down to the present day held multitudes of the human race in abject bondage, general poverty, and deep depravity. The difference, in short, of Europe and North America from the other regions of the earth, is the exponent of the superiority of the Christian to every other faith.

But the name Christian itself has been claimed by a variety of sects, entertaining opinions very dissimilar, and requiring us to apply the test by which we discriminate Christian from non-Christian systems,—their practical results. The chief of these parties are the Roman Catholic, Greek, and Protestant churches. There must be some superior vitality common to the creed of those Churches, to account for the superior social condition of their members to that of the whole world besides, but there must also be more life in Protestantism than in the other systems, in the ratio of its more salutary influence on the countries where it prevails. Roman Catholics themselves will admit, with one of their own journalists, that "unquestionably since 1789, the balance of power between Catholic and non-Catholic civilisation has been reversed." The evidence of history, much of which has been already presented, would support a more unqualified confession. But it is sufficient to add that, while Protestant missions have raised men of every clime from the lowest condition to all the decencies, and to many of the comforts of civilized life, Rome has signally failed here, and for the reason assigned in the following words,—a reason no less applicable to its comparative inefficiency at home: "The Church of Rome represses independent judgment and action, keeps its heathen neophytes submissive and in fetters, keeps them as it finds them, children. In Paraguay, in India, in every place where they have planted the cross, this has been a result, and never in a heathen country have we seen any national progress, social or religious, grow out of the propagation of the faith."[1]

But amidst the various creeds of nominal Protestants—some of them "wide as the poles asunder"—we have to inquire for the specific faith which most favourably influences the state of society. That Unitarianism is not entitled to this honour might be presumed from the closeness of its approximation to infidelity, and actually appears from its tried incapacity to propagate and maintain itself. We are saved the necessity of leading a proof of the former assertion by the admission of the great champion of the system, Dr. Priestley, who, in writing to Mr. Theophilus Lindsey respecting President Jefferson, said: "He is generally reported to be an unbeliever, but if so, you know he cannot be far from us."[2] The other assertion is established by the history of Unitarianism. Let the following facts speak for the rest. In Massachusetts, the stronghold of the system in America, while the Puritans were successfully employed in forming a Christian community in the

[1] *Quarterly Review*, vol. xciv. p. 184.
[2] Robert Hall's *Works*, vol. v. p. 134.

Sandwich Islands, which would on the whole bear advantageous comparison with that of the best regulated societies of the old world,[1] their Socinian neighbours were utterly indifferent to the claims of the Pagan world. While, according to Dr. Pierce, one of themselves, their settled ministers had, in the course of the years 1812-1846, decreased from 138 to 124, those of orthodox opinions had in the same period increased from 197 to 417. A writer who quotes these statistics remarks that Unitarianism had made little progress in the other States,—that its professors show little interest in propagating their faith,—and that during the years to which Dr. Pierce refers, evangelical Christianity had given existence to the Home and Foreign Bible and Tract Societies, and had covered the entire West with churches, academies, and schools, while Unitarianism had maintained a kind of dying life almost exclusively within a single State.[2] The want of diffusive and moral power in the creed as held in this country, was fully exposed by Hall and Fuller, till its friends, probably provoked by such strictures, and constrained by surrounding example, were led to make some feeble attempts to extend their views. Altogether it appears that Unitarianism is a parasitic plant which, having no hold of the soil, has struck its roots into other plants, and thence derives its scanty nourishment and feeble growth. Where would have been its fruits, such as they are, if it had not been for the trees of life and their healthful atmosphere, from which it has received aliment and support?

Nor is the Protestantism which steers a middle course between the Socinian and Evangelical schemes fitted to make much head against social evils. We refer to the creed intended by Sir James Mackintosh, when he represents those who preached works, or the mere regulation of outward acts, as having comparatively failed to make a favourable impression on public morals.[3] This creed has been fully tried in Protestant countries on the Continent as well as in England and Scotland, for both abroad and at home there have been predominant classes who have avowed and defended it, notwithstanding that they have subscribed another and a better. And we have only to look to the extensive symbolizing

1 *Quarterly Review*, vol. xciv. p. 91.
2 *Christian Times*, Jan. 27, 1854.
3 *Memoirs*, vol. i. p. 411.

of continental Protestantism with Romanism or with infidelity, and to the utter inefficacy of High Churchism in England, and of Moderatism in Scotland to leaven our people, not to mention foreigners, with Christian principle and character, to be convinced that "the pure religion" which the best interests of society demand has yet to be named.

That "pure religion" is principally to be found where the doctrines of the Reformation are in good faith embraced, as they are by many on the Continent, by the evangelical clergy and people of the established churches of England and Scotland, by far the larger proportion of the dissenters of both countries, and by great numbers in North America, to whom might be added our Protestant missionaries to a man. It is by the men of these views that all our great institutions for the circulation of the Scriptures, for Christianizing the heathen, and for the religious instruction of the neglected of all classes at home, have been originated and are sustained. In almost every scheme for promoting the temporal good of society, it is men of these views that take the lead and the labour. And it is persons of this class who, fully maintaining and carrying out the principles, most largely experience the blessings of the Sabbatic rest as these principles and blessings are thus associated: "If thou turn away thy foot from the Sabbath, from doing thy pleasure on my holy day; and call the Sabbath a delight, the holy of the Lord, honourable; and shalt honour him, not doing thine own ways, nor finding thine own pleasure, nor speaking thine own words: then shalt thou delight thyself in the Lord; and I will cause thee to ride upon the high places of the earth, and feed thee with the heritage of Jacob thy father; for the mouth of the Lord hath spoken it."[1]

[1] Isa. lviii. 13, 14.

CHAPTER VII.

APPLICATION OF PRECEDING PRINCIPLES AND FACTS IN PROOF OF THE DIVINE ORIGIN OF THE SABBATH.

"If this counsel or work be of man, it will come to nought; but if it be of God, ye cannot overthrow it."—GAMALIEL.

FROM the principles and facts set forth in the immediately preceding part of this volume, it appears that a weekly holy day cannot be dispensed with, if health, intelligence, religion, virtue, and happiness be of importance to mankind. There are some, however, who accord to the institution no slight measure of the credit due to it as an instrument of good, without yielding up their minds to the faith of its Divine authority. Such persons, it seems to us, neglect to follow out the light of evidence to its legitimate conclusions, and thus subject themselves to the imputation of inconsistency. Let us, following that light, attempt to show, that the considerations which evince the excellence and utility of the weekly rest, concur with other things in attesting that it is the contrivance, appointment, and charge of Heaven.

"Paley has deduced an argument, for this world being the work of an intelligent cause, from the relation of sleep to night. He says, 'It appears to me to be a relation which was expressly intended. Two points are manifest; *first*, that the animal frame requires sleep; *secondly*, that night brings with it a silence, and a cessation of activity, which allows of sleep being taken without interruption, and without loss.' . . . But what the rest of sleep is to the body, the repose of the Sabbath is to the soul. An argument less apparently demonstrative, because more refined and intellectual, might be deduced from the appointment of the Sabbath, that God is the Author of revelation" [and of the Sabbath], "as well as that He is the Author of nature from the relation of sleep to night. The body demands, by the necessity of its nature, a certain period of relaxation from toil ; but the mind, ever active, though not always active to [good] purpose, requires a positive rest, prescribed to it, in order that, by interrupting the ordinary chain of its thoughts, it may profit by a cessation of its usual cares ; and, since it cannot cease to think, may at least have a complete change of thought, at fixed intervals, which is its proper repose. Nor by this cessation or interchange of labour is the work which it is pursuing delayed. The mind reverts with a new energy to the object which for a season it has ceased to pursue. These pauses are common in the development of all organized beings."[1]

The Sabbath must have been the suggestion of infinite benevolence. Human beings are naturally selfish, but the selfish think only of themselves, and are neither inventive nor ready, neither exuberant nor painstaking, with expedients for relieving the misery or promoting the happiness of others. Many, indeed, of the race have become truly benevolent, but we have no evidence that they acquired the character in any other way than through the religion of the Sabbath. It is only in countries where that religion has existed that benevolent institutions have been known.[2] It is in the lands, at least, in which the Sabbath flourishes that charity abounds. It is the classes and individuals of these lands who reverence the institution that are pre-eminent for beneficence. The selfishness of man would not originate the benignant arrangement ; the benevolence of man came too late to contrive what already existed. But other considerations decide the matter not only against human, but against all creature claims. The Sabbath embraces in its provisions too large an extent of good for creatures to have imagined, evolves in its course beneficial tendencies which no finite mind could have foreseen, and attains its objects with an unfailing certainty which no dependent being could have commanded—proving itself to have had its source in the deep thoughts and warm feelings of a Divine heart.

The adaptations of the institution proclaim it to have been the device of Divine wisdom. The schemes and works of man, after

[1] Address by Douglas of Cavers on Slavery, Sabbath Protection, etc., pp. 35-37.

[2] China has been lately held to be an exception to the remark, but on grounds which require further elucidation.

the greatest care and labour have been expended on them, exhibit palpable marks of imperfection, but the Sabbath has never needed improvement. Human legislation, regulated as it is by endlessly diversified and continually changing peculiarities of place and time, must frequently be enlarged, modified, or abrogated, but the Sabbath has for ages stood out from week to week a reproach to all earthly ordinances—a glorious monument of unerring legislative skill. While other regular divisions of time—as day and night, the month and year—were made to man's hand in nature, there was nothing of this kind, nothing in the revolutions of the heavenly bodies, to guide him to the adoption of the seventh day for any purpose, but, nevertheless, the week, including in not a few instances a sacred day, has prevailed in many parts of the world from a remote antiquity. No people without a Sabbath have ever of their own impulse introduced it. After a long-continued experience of its value in some countries, there are numerous instances in which persons show sometimes by their language, more frequently by their conduct, that they account it a burden and a curse. Notwithstanding all the regard which many have ever entertained for it, its excellence is still far from being fully understood and appreciated even by the wise and good. How much light has but lately been thrown on its importance to the welfare of society! That a seventh day of sacred rest renders the labour of six days more remunerative than would be that of seven under a system of unremitting toil, and that it interposes a barrier against the enslaving of mankind, are proofs of the profound wisdom of the institution which it was reserved for recent times to bring into clearer view, if not entirely to discover. It is one thing, moreover, to see and unfold the merits of a discovery, and altogether another thing to make it. To the origination, in short, of an institution, proved to be adapted to the whole constitution and circumstances of mankind, there was indispensable so large a measure of knowledge, as to make it manifest that the claim by the Author of the Sabbath to omniscience itself would be no arrogance, and His exercise of the attribute no difficulty.

The sanctity of the Sabbath is a further evidence of its Divine original. The ordinance is too sacred for human beings to desire or even to think of. They could have imagined and wished a day of rest, but judging from the views and feelings of those who slight or scorn the present Sabbath (and the formation of a different character is one of the results and triumphs of the institution), there is in it, as a day of worship and holy rest, a class of qualities the reverse of those which man esteems and loves. But "of thorns men do not gather figs, nor of a bramble-bush gather they grapes. An evil man out of the evil treasure of his heart bringeth forth that which is evil." The Sabbath was evidently made for man, but not by man. Its author must have been divinely holy, as well as divinely benignant, intelligent, and wise.

Our position is established also by the justice of an arrangement which shows no respect of persons, prescribing the same duties and securing the same privileges alike to rich and poor, kings and subjects.

The preceding proofs respect the Sabbath as a contrivance, to the conception and origination of which, as has been shown, only a Divine being was competent. But to be of any avail, the institution must be adopted and employed by those for whose benefit it was designed. That they would never have appropriated the gift in its full extent without an external and controlling influence exerted on their minds and hearts, is manifest not only from the dislike which men feel to a holy day, but from the ignorance and pride by which they are led into the greatest divergences of opinion and practice on all sorts of subjects. The Sabbath must be socially as well as personally received and observed. And what but Divine power could bring so many various individuals, with all their supposed conflict of interests as masters and servants, employers and employed, sovereigns and subjects, to agreement respecting the propriety, the time, and the engagements of such an institution, or what but Divine authority could secure for it an unquestioning submission? Without that commanding influence, the discrepancy of sentiment on the matter must have produced a Sabbath of so endless a diversity of season and observance as to contain the elements of its speedy dissolution, or rather must have prevented the introduction of a Sabbath altogether. The remarkable harmony, however, among men of many ages and countries with respect to the proportion of time, the day, and the duties of a periodical rest—a harmony which has frequently awed its enemies into respect—points not only to Divine wisdom as contriving the institute, but to Divine power and authority as giving it establishment. Since writing these remarks we are happy to find that we can confirm and adorn the views expressed in them by the eloquent words of Dr. Croly. "The divine origin of the Sabbath might almost be proved from its opposition to the lower propensities of mankind. In no age of the world, since labour was known, would any master of the serf, the slave, or the cattle, have *spontaneously* given up a seventh part of their toil. No human legislator would have proposed such a law of property, or, if he had, no nation would have endured it. . . . The Sabbath in its whole character is so strongly opposed to the avarice, the heartlessness, and the irreligion of man, that, except in the days of Moses and Joshua, it has probably never been observed with due reverence by any nation of the world."[1]

In the awe with which, as just remarked, the institution inspires the hearts of its enemies, we discover another testimony to its superhuman ordination and character. The inconsistency is not in our statement, but in the person's own mind, when we say that the same individual may feel a consciousness, and utter a confession of the excellence of an object to which he once had, and may still have a dislike. Ovid has described no uncommon case :

"I see the good, and I approve it too—
Condemn the wrong, and yet the wrong pursue."

There are many, indeed, who profess a superiority to the fears and convictions which haunt evil-doers, and especially Sabbath-breakers, affecting to regard such feelings as mere superstition, and who in the midst of their pleasures would seem to be at ease as respects responsibility to a superior Power. But certain facts indicate that an inward disquiet lies at the root of their apparent indifference or joy. It has been said, that the disasters which frequently befall the profaners of the Lord's day, are owing in part to a sense of guilt, which so enervates and confounds them in the hour of danger as to deprive them of their usual power to employ the means of escape. Not unfrequently, too, persons who have lived in the neglect of religious ordinances and laws change

[1] *Divine Origin and Obligation of the Sabbath* (1850), p. 17.

their views and conduct, and then divulge the truth, that under all their seeming gaiety they have been wretched men. But justice overtakes others in their profligate career, and they become amenable to the outraged laws of their country. In these circumstances, as has often been observed, the confession is very commonly made, that their fall and ruin are traceable, in particular, to one great error—that of contemning the sacred day. The acknowledgment is entitled to all credit. It has not been bribed or wrung from them. It has been given spontaneously, and at a time when there is no possible temptation to falsehood. Why those persons uniformly fix on the desecration of the Lord's day as the primary cause of their undoing can be explained only on these two suppositions—that what they utter is true, and that there is a potency of evil in their conduct proceeding from the despite of no ordinary blessing, from the infraction of no human law.

Finally, the preservation of such an institution in such a world as ours affords evidence of an inward vitality, and an external guardianship, that are more than human. That it should have been continued in the decayed state in which we find it in some heathen countries, is a testimony to its original power, and to its deep seat in the wants and consciences of men. But that it should for many centuries have been maintained, as in other cases it has been, in its pristine vigour, is a fact which nothing can explain but its having been planted and cared for by a Divine husbandman. The Sabbath has had to contend with many adverse elements sufficient to have long ago withered any production reared and tended by human hands. There is the desire of change. There is the aversion to holy duties. There is the love of unrestrained pleasure. There is a grasping avarice. There is the strong passion for worldly eminence and fame. Under the influence of some one or other of these feelings, many pervert the institution—one class spending the day in amusement and revelry—another, in merchandise—a third, in prosecuting their literary or scientific studies. Many, again, compel those who are under their authority to ply their exhausting labours that they themselves may be enriched, though at the expense of the ruined health and neglected minds and morals of their servants. All this, which has nearly obliterated a holy Sabbath over the entire continent of Europe, shows how little patronage such a day receives from the world, and sufficiently accounts for the deterioration which in any instance it has suffered. Whence is this state of matters not universal? Whence has it never been universal? Whence is it that the institution flourishes in some places, and is seen springing up in others where it had been trodden down? The only answer is, it is a tree which has been planted, and is under the care of the superintending Providence,—of Him who, while in justice He removes it from the hands of violence, is in mercy disposed not utterly to take away, but even to cherish and restore what is so medicinal to the nations. In our motto we have applied to the Sabbath the words of the sagacious Gamaliel, uttered 1800 years ago. According to him, Christianity must have long ago perished if it had been of men. It has not been overthrown. Neither has the Sabbath. Let his warning be pondered by all who set themselves against the friends of either: "Refrain from these men, and let them alone; lest haply ye be found even to fight against God."

TESTIMONY OF REVELATION TO A SACRED AND PERPETUAL SABBATH.

CHAPTER I.

DIVINE INSTITUTION OF THE SABBATH AT THE CREATION, AND ITS OBSERVANCE BY THE PATRIARCHS.

"The Sabbath was made for man."

THE evidence for a weekly day of rest and devotion is of great variety and amount. Geography points to traces of the institution in almost every region of the globe. History records its early existence, its course of many centuries, and its remarkable preservation amidst the countless changes and hostile influences of society. Physiology concedes its sanitary power. Mental philosophy proclaims its intellectual adaptations. Ethics, law, and biography, together attest its importance to man as a moral and religious being; and economic science acknowledges its intimate connexion with individual comfort and social prosperity. Contributions such as these are of no slight value to the cause which they favour. They are, independently, capable of showing that the distribution of our time into six days of labour and one of holy rest is an arrangement too long-lived, too wide-spread, too wise, pure, and benevolent, to have "sprung of earth." They echo the announcements of Scripture. They ought thus to confirm the faith of the Christian, and induce unbelievers to bow to claims which so many witnesses concur without collusion to establish. It is no depreciation, however, of the evidence supplied by reason and experience on behalf of the institution, to say, that the Sabbath derives its best support and defence from the sacred Scriptures, which in its turn it so eminently serves to make known. It is in the testimony of revelation that perfect confidence as to the Divine origin and authority of the ordinance finds its inspiration and strength, and it is there alone that we discover the infallible rule, which must be followed, if we would rightly discharge the obligations, and fully receive the blessings of the day of rest.

The testimony of revelation concerning the Sabbatic institution may be comprised under three heads—its Divine obligation on mankind in all time, its Duties, and its Importance. Following this order, we proceed, in the first instance, to the illustration of a series of propositions on the subject of the Divine, universal, and permanent obligation of the institution.

FIRST PROPOSITION.—THE SABBATH WAS INSTITUTED BY GOD AT THE CREATION.

In the Book of Genesis, after his beautifully simple but magnificent account of the creation of the heavens and the earth, the sacred historian proceeds as follows :—" Thus the heavens and the earth were finished, and all the host of them. And on the seventh day God ended his work which he had made ; and he rested on the seventh day from all his work which he had made. And God blessed the seventh day, and sanctified it : because that in it he had rested from all his work which God created and made."[1]

No improvement in the translation would affect the substantial meaning of these words, which are generally admitted to be a faithful version of the original language. A critical examination of the terms employed, and the light of parallel texts, would only confirm the views of the passage which a first reading at once ascertains.

Without dwelling on the superlative value of the information here and in the preceding chapter for the first time recorded respecting the original of the world and of man, let us mark the leading facts as they bear upon our subject.

God rested on the seventh day from all his work which he had made. As the Almighty " fainteth not, neither is weary,"

[1] Gen. ii. 1-3.

and as "the Father worketh hitherto" in the production of human spirits, and in the sustentation and government of the universe, his rest on this occasion is obviously to be understood in a sense compatible with the constant activity and worthy of the majesty of the Creator—as a rest not from all work, but from the one work specified—a rest of cessation and satisfaction, not of languid repose.[1] He who afterwards on renewing the face of the earth rejoiced in his works, did, after making heaven and earth in six days, rest on the seventh, and "was refreshed,"[2] regarding with complacency and delight his completed creation.

While the Creator pronounced all the works of the six days to be very good, he reserved his benediction for the day of rest. "And God blessed the seventh day." When human beings utter words of blessing, they are only helpless petitioners. But it is the practice, as it is the prerogative, of the Divinity to impart the good which he pronounces with his lips. And he blesses creatures variously according to their natures; men, by bestowing favours which rational beings can alone relish and enjoy; the lower animals, agreeably to their limited capacities, opening his hand and satisfying the desire of every living thing; and "things without life," by making them the means of benefit and pleasure to intellectual and sentient creatures. In this last-mentioned form did he bless the seventh day. In no other mode could unconscious, insensible time be blessed. That day was distinguished above the others by being constituted a season and means of peculiar advantage and happiness.

The seventh day was devoted to sacred use, "God sanctified it." The radical idea in "sanctify," as the word is employed by the inspired writers, is separation from a common to a holy purpose, consecration to the Divine service.[3] Like blessing, sanctification is predicated of beings according to their natures. As all days are God's, and ought to be spent in his work, the sanctify-

[1] Shabath, as in 1 Sam. xxv. 9; Job xxxii. 1, "signifieth not such a rest as wherein one sitteth and doeth nothing, as the word Noach doth, but only a resting and ceasing from that which he did before."—Leigh, *Critica Sacra, sub. voc.* "It implies resting from, not in work."—*New Translation*, by De Sola, etc.

[2] Ex. xxxi. 17.

[3] "Ab usu et statu communi ad peculiarem et sacrum separare."—*Eichhorn.* "Usibus divinis accommodavit—a communi et profano usu segregavit in usum sacrum—ad cultum Dei destinavit."—*Kirch. Concord.*

ing of the seventh in particular would be a meaningless expression, unless it indicated a special appropriation of the day to the worship and glory of the Creator.

The benediction and sanctification of the seventh day had respect to the Divine rest as their reason or cause. "God blessed the seventh day and sanctified it, because that in it he had rested from all his work which God created and made," or, as we have it in the Decalogue, "In six days the Lord made the heaven and the earth, the sea and all things therein, and rested the seventh day, wherefore the Lord blessed the Sabbath-day and hallowed it."[1] The holy day recalls its occasion. They are linked together. Nor is the association incidental. It is designed. It was manifestly the purpose and arrangement of the Author of nature, that the day which saw the creation finished should be set apart in honour of the great work, or rather of himself as its Architect.

The institution thus appointed at the creation was designed to be a law, right, and blessing to mankind in all time. There is every indication of universality in the primæval arrangement. The example of the Almighty in working and resting was inscribed as it were on the creation itself, and partook of the extent and durability of the workmanship of his hands. It was an example addressed to the father of mankind, and through him to all his posterity. That would have been no blessing to Adam himself, and none to any other, which should light and expend itself on one solitary day. The blessing was pronounced on that day as the first-fruits of all sacred time. It applied as truly as the blessing of marriage to Adam's descendants. The seventh portion of time was hallowed for all ages, when the earliest instalment was sanctified. Having been prior to all special dispensations of religion, the Sabbatic institution is not liable to perish with any. The appointment is couched in terms that prove its capacity of incorporation with every economy. Its "sound went into all the earth, and its words unto the ends of the world," calling upon every human being to remember his Creator, and to enjoy the liberty and rest which He has provided for all who are willing to receive them. Who has any reason or authority for

[1] Ex xx. 11.

affirming that the law has become obsolete—that it does not remain in full force on the human family? And who may not, on the best grounds and with perfect confidence, say, "Here is an indefeasible right on which I take my stand against every attempt to deprive me of the seventh part of my time—here is a boon which, as divinely conferred, no man can justly or with impunity take away?"

SECOND PROPOSITION.—WHILE NO FORMAL NOTICE OF THE INSTITUTION OCCURS IN THE SUBSEQUENT HISTORY TILL THE CHILDREN OF ISRAEL HAVE DEPARTED FROM EGYPT, AND COMMENCED THEIR JOURNEYINGS IN THE WILDERNESS OF ARABIA, CIRCUMSTANCES ARE RECORDED, WHICH, BUT FOR THE ANTECEDENT INSTITUTION AND CONTINUED OBLIGATION OF A SACRED SEVENTH DAY, COULD NOT HAVE BEEN MENTIONED, OR EVEN HAVE EXISTED.

Although desirous to reserve controversy as much as possible to a subsequent stage of our discussion, and meanwhile to present simply the evidence for a permanent Sabbath, we cannot in justice to the latter object avoid reference here to the opinion maintained by Dr. Heylyn, Dr. Paley, and others, that notwithstanding the early notice in Scripture of the sanctification by the Creator of the seventh day, its actual institution as a Sabbath did not occur till twenty-five centuries thereafter. It appears a remarkable psychological fact that the mind which so acutely detected and so skilfully collated the indications of design in nature, and the coincidences between the Acts and the Writings of the apostles, should have seen no appointment of a day of rest in the narrative of the Divine proceedings at the creation of the world, and not even the slightest allusion to such a day in the remaining history for so many years. Had the eye been as morally single—as purged from prejudice in favour of a theory as it was intellectually penetrating, might it not have discovered the materials for a *Horæ Sabbaticæ*, scarcely less interesting and convincing than the *Horæ Paulinæ*?

One of the circumstances that could not have occurred but for the primæval institution of the Sabbath is the narrative itself of the event, considered in its manner and place. No one can suppose that the sacred writer is there describing what was not to take place till many years after the creation, without imputing to him either incompetency to write history and to express his own thoughts, or a disregard of truth, inasmuch as he has introduced a fact in such a connexion and in such terms as naturally and necessarily to lead us into the serious mistake that it was contemporaneous with the Creator's rest from his work of six days. That an inspired man should so write is an impossibility. The interpretation, therefore, must be false. How, after the light which the transactions of Sin and Sinai had in the view of Israel shed on the Sabbath, the words describing it should appear where they are at all, is to be explained only by the fact and importance of its early institution.

A second circumstance that presupposes the primitive appointment of the weekly holy day is the respect which began soon after to be shown for the septenary number. Let it be observed that it was the Creator himself, in denouncing "sevenfold" vengeance against the person that should take the life of Cain,[1] who first employed the number as a synonym of completeness or perfection, and that by the same authority it continued to be signalized in the arrangement that the beasts and fowls should be selected by sevens for preservation in the ark, in the allotted periods of plenty and scarcity in Egypt, in the prohibition of leavened bread for seven days in the passover, and in many other intimations of the Divine will down to the time when the Apostle John had in Patmos his vision of the seven golden candlesticks, and of one in the midst of them like unto the Son of man. This use, then, of the number was no superstitious practice of human device. It was Divine speech, and it had an important meaning. But that meaning could not consist in any intrinsic value of the number above others, for it had no such value. The first mention of it in a new application stands in almost immediate connexion in the sacred history with the seventh day on which God rested from the work of creation, and that application is not arbitrary, the "sevenfold" vengeance being a vengeance which completes its

[1] Gen. iv. 15.

purpose, sheaths the sword, and is satisfied, even as the Creator finished his work, rested, and was refreshed. The language addressed to Cain had a meaning, and was intended to be understood by all readers; but where is the signification of "sevenfold" to be found, if not in the preceding context? The meaning was the same to Cain as to them. And he and they are presented by the historian as having their eyes turned to the same great fact of a day of rest, blessed and sanctified when the world was made. Nor is this all. That a marked respect for the septenary number has, by the Divine example and sanction, been evinced alike in the Pentateuch and in the Apocalypse is a proof that the Creator will have his name remembered, and a seventh day hallowed in all generations.

No less significant in its bearing on our subject is the observance by the patriarchs of the weekly division of time. Noah "stayed seven days" three several times before he "sent forth the dove out of the ark."[1] The friends of Job sat down with him, in token of their sympathy, seven days and seven nights.[2] We read of the "week" in the days of Laban and Jacob.[3] And Joseph made a mourning for his father seven days.[4] But whence this regard to periods of seven days? There was nothing in nature to suggest or recommend it for adoption any more than there was some peculiar excellence in the number "seven" to secure for it a preference above other numbers. If there had, it would have been even more generally observed than it is. No human being would independently have conceived of such a notation of time—no number of human beings could have given it prevalence or perpetuity. The history, however, leaves no room for speculation. It informs us that the week was appointed at the creation, not by any provision made on the fourth day in the lights which were to be "for signs and seasons for days and years," but by the example of the Creator, who occupied six days in making the world, rested on the seventh, blessed and sanctified that day—not the eighth, or following days, on which he alike rested from creative work; and thus prescribed to us the same distribution of time, and of its work and rest, no less certainly or impressively, than if he had written the law on the phenomena of nature.

[1] Gen. viii. [2] Job ii. 13. [3] Gen. xxix. 27, 28. [4] Gen. l. 10.

From these facts we are led to infer what the week was which Noah and others observed, and why they so regulated their time. The week, as defined by the Creator, consisted of six days for work and a day of rest—of sacred rest; and such also must have been the week of the patriarchs. It is possible, indeed, for this cycle of time to be observed in some form after its Sabbath has ceased, but if the seventh day was and still is connected with sacred rites among heathen nations, is it conceivable that Noah could have forgotten or disregarded so important an alliance? His own piety, the language of God announcing to him that in *seven days* he would cause it to rain on the earth, and the warrant which the historian has given us for tracing a connexion of cause and effect between the week as originally appointed, and the week as observed by the patriarch, all forbid the supposition that he did not work for six days, and rest and worship on the seventh.

The prevalence of public worship, with its various accessories, necessarily implies the obligation and observance of a Sabbath. Religious assemblies are convened. Cain and Abel come together for Divine service. They were not the only persons present, as appears from Cain's postponement of his murderous deed till he and his victim were out of the sight of others in the field. This is the first recorded instance of public worship, if we may apply that epithet to a convocation and exercises on the small scale of an infant society. In the time of Seth "men began to call on the name of the Lord;" not that they for the first time professed or practised religion, as the history proves, but that, whether they were then called by, or invoked the name of the Lord, their profession and practice had become more public. Twice are we told in the Book of Job that "the sons of God came to present themselves before the Lord," and that Satan, as he has often since done, "came also among them." The services on such occasions are mentioned. There were sacrifices and offerings, which formed so important a part of ancient worship. Cain and Abel bring offerings. Noah, Abraham, Isaac, and Jacob erect altars, and devote victims thereon to Jehovah. Bishop Patrick, in expounding the account of the offerings of Cain and Abel, observes that the Hebrew word for *brought* is used never in reference to private and domestic sacrifices, but always of such as were in the times of the Jewish polity brought to the dooi of the tabernacle of the congregation. The friends of Job were divinely instructed to offer up for themselves a burnt-offering of seven bullocks and of seven rams. Instruction, too, was communicated in the assemblies for worship. Job had "instructed many and strengthened the weak hands," and where though not exclusively he had done so is intimated in his words, "I stood up and I cried in the congregation." Noah was a preacher of righteousness. We read also of the sacraments of circumcision and the passover—and of a priesthood with tithes for its maintenance. As there was a law for the consecration of property and of a certain proportion of it to the service of God, it is to be presumed that there would be one for the consecration of a certain amount of time to the same purpose. For all this worship understood places of convocation were requisite. Cain and Abel "came together into one place." It is chiefly the scene of public ordinances that is favoured with the presence of the Lord, from which Satan is said twice to have gone forth, and Cain once and for ever. And even more necessary must have been appointed places of worship when men began on a large scale to call upon the name of the Lord. But set times were also indispensable. Order and fixed places demanded them. If the sons of Job had their days for feasting, we cannot reasonably doubt that the sons of God had their days for worship. And it was so. "There was a day when the sons of God came to present themselves before the Lord." It was "in process of time," or rather, in the end of days, that Cain and Abel brought their offerings unto the Lord. We might plead that the time, like the age of a very young child, "an infant of days,"[1] admitted of reckoning not by years, months, or weeks, but by days. But it is sufficient for our purpose that the language unquestionably means an appointed season. We are informed in the Epistle to the Hebrews that Abel was accepted because he offered in faith, consulting the Divine will in regard to the matter, circumstances, and principle of the service. Cain was blamed, not for error as to the time or place, but for the state of his mind, and the bloodless nature of his offering. We can conceive him overawed by the appointed day of rest and worship, and induced by the customary

[1] Isa. lxv. 20.

suspension of labour into a compliance with the law and the custom, but we cannot conceive of so secular a character leaving his farm on working days for the purpose of appearing at the altar of God. And the historian here again has warranted the conclusion that the time of these offerings was the seventh day. He has recorded the consecration of that day to rest and holy use, and must have known that, in proceeding soon after to mention the first case of social worship, nothing was more natural than for his readers to take for granted that on this occasion the day so set apart would be applied to its appropriate purpose. Aware that such was the inference which would be drawn from his manner of writing, has he not sanctioned that inference?

Our position is confirmed by the remarkable instances of piety and virtue which distinguished the period under review. Is it requisite to name Enoch, Noah, Melchizedek, Job, Abraham, Isaac, and Jacob, Joseph, Moses, and Aaron? It was by the grace of God, and in the observance of religious institutions, that they became what they were. That the Sabbath must have been a principal means in fostering the faith, by which those "elders obtained a good report," appears from the felt and proved necesity of a periodical day of rest and worship to the religion of present days. We have already cited the acknowledgment of one of the best men whom our age has produced—Edward Bickersteth—that, but for a weekly day given as entirely as possible to God, religion would soon have abandoned him. And all who in any measure resemble that excellent individual will readily indorse the remark. To conceive that the patriarchs, who were men of like passions, men exposed to like temptations, toils, and sufferings, with others, could maintain for centuries a holy and happy life, without the stimulus and refreshment of the Sabbath, is to suppose a case which, if true, would prove the uselessness of the institution in any circumstances, but which, in fact, is a simple impossibility and a mere dream.

The long life and prosperity attained by good men in primitive times utter the same language. It was the arrangement of Providence, for important ends, that those men should live "many days," and "see good." But we have no reason to believe that their longevity was miraculous, or their success achieved independently of their own efforts. Both blessings were bestowed in connexion with their diligence, temperance, and care—both are divinely pledged to a race yet to come, and to them as sacredly observant of the weekly rest. What has been said in this volume of the necessity of the institution to health, prosperity, to mental, moral, and religious culture, while it applies to the present and the future, must have been equally true of the remote past.

Once more : there are incidents in the history of Israel in Egypt which give indication of a pre-existing Sabbatism. Moses and Aaron, by the direction and in the name of Jehovah, asked of Pharaoh to let the Hebrews go, that they might hold a feast unto God in the wilderness. What the feast was appears from the answer of the King of Egypt to their demand : "Wherefore do ye, Moses and Aaron, let the people from their works ? Get you unto your burdens. Behold, the people of the land now are many, and ye make them rest [sabbatize] from their burdens ;" and more decisively from the fact, that no sooner had the people gained their liberty than they celebrated "the rest of the holy Sabbath unto the Lord," feasting on the bread of heaven. Before this time, and on the very eve of the Exode, the Passover was instituted, where the Sabbatic circumstances of "seven days," "resting from all manner of work," and "holy convocations,' are all mentioned as matters with which it is taken for granted that they were well acquainted.

The doctrine of a paradisiacal and patriarchal Sabbath does not depend on the circumstances now reviewed, but however imperfectly they may have been stated, we venture to call for this verdict from our readers, that but for the antecedent institution and continued observance of a sacred seventh day these circumstances could not have existed.

CHAPTER II.

THE SABBATH PROMULGATED FROM SINAI AS ONE OF THE COMMANDMENTS OF THE MORAL LAW.

"Remember the Sabbath-Day to keep it holy."

WHEN we pass from the Patriarchal to the Jewish dispensation of religion, we discover increasing evidence that the Sabbath was designed to be a law and blessing to mankind. That under an economy so different in many respects from that which preceded it, and providing so many additional seasons for worship, the aboriginal holy day was not superseded, but retained with superadded tokens of respect, was a circumstance which gave promise of its continuing to hold a place among the laws and ordinances of heaven while the world itself should last.

THIRD PROPOSITION.—THE SABBATH, AS INSTITUTED AT THE CREATION, HAD A PLACE ASSIGNED TO IT IN THE MORAL LAW GIVEN FROM SINAI.

When the Almighty gave forth the Law of the Decalogue with his own voice from Sinai, one of the utterances was, "Remember the Sabbath-day, to keep it holy. Six days shalt thou labour, and do all thy work; but the seventh day is the Sabbath of the Lord thy God; in it thou shalt not do any work, thou, nor thy son, nor thy daughter, thy man-servant, nor thy maid-servant, nor thy cattle, nor thy stranger that is within thy gates; for in six days the Lord made heaven and earth, the sea, and all that in them is, and rested the seventh day: wherefore the Lord blessed the Sabbath-day, and hallowed it."[1]

[1] Ex. xx. 9-11.

That the Decalogue was not even as a code prescribed to the Jews only, or abrogated along with the other laws of Moses, but epitomizes the duty of human beings in all places and times, appears from the distinction conferred in Scripture on its precepts above the other commandments delivered to the Jewish people—from the catholic nature of the precepts themselves, and from their declared obligation on mankind.

1. The Scriptures have in various and unequivocal forms done special honour to the law of the ten commandments.

Its promulgation was heralded by solemn preparations. "Moses went up unto God, and the Lord called unto him out of the mountain." He is instructed to inform Israel of the Divine condescension and kindness about to be shown to them in the covenant to be established between God and them, and the necessity of holy obedience on their part, that they might be a peculiar treasure unto him above all people. He intimates these things to the people, and "returns their words unto the Lord." For two days they must sanctify themselves, that they might be ready on the third day, on which Jehovah was to come down in the sight of all the people upon Mount Sinai. Death was to be the penalty of going up into the mount, or touching the border of it. "And it came to pass on the third day, in the morning, that there were thunders and lightnings, and a thick cloud upon the mount, and the voice of the trumpet exceeding loud, so that all the people trembled. And Moses brought forth the people out of the camp to meet with God: and they stood at the nether part of the mount. And Mount Sinai was altogether on a smoke, because the Lord descended upon it in fire: and the smoke thereof ascended as the smoke of a furnace, and the whole mountain quaked greatly."[1]

In these circumstances of glory, grandeur, and terrible majesty, which made Moses himself say, "I exceedingly fear and quake," did Jehovah proclaim with his own lips the ten commandments. And thus, not only by priority of promulgation, but by the august solemnities attending it, did he distinguish these commandments above the civil and ceremonial statutes which were afterwards privately communicated to Moses. "These words the Lord spake

[1] Ex. xix. 16-18.

unto all your assembly in the mount, out of the midst of the fire, of the cloud, and of the thick darkness, with a great voice, and he added no more." But in reference to "the law of commandments contained in ordinances," it is said: "But as for thee stand thou here by me, and I will speak unto thee all the commandments, and the statutes, and the judgments which thou shalt teach them, that they may do them in the land which I give them to possess it."[1]

Nor was this all. It is possible for ingenuity, under a partial bias, to make too much of the following circumstances; but to deny that they impressively teach us the distinction of the Decalogue above the other laws of the Jews would seem to be "a refusing of him that spake on earth." The law of the ten commandments, uttered by "the great voice" of God, was also written by his own finger. It was too holy and glorious to be spoken "with the tongues of men and of angels," or to be taken down from the Divine lips by any human amanuensis. The Lawgiver must proclaim his eternal law with his own mouth, and indite it with his own hand. Twice was it so written. It was inscribed on tablets of stone, and in this form deposited in the ark, with all the security which incorruptible shittim-wood, and gold overlaid within, without, and above, could provide, and under the overshadowing cherubim, and inviolable Shechinah. But no Divine voice is heard announcing the laws of a temporary polity, or of a shadowy ritual; they are uttered in the ears of Moses alone. No Divine finger traces their written characters; for this the hand of Moses is deemed adequate. They are committed to no secure and precious casket; but placed beside the ark, as things warranting less reverence and care, and ready to be removed. In all these honours of the ten "words," the fourth commandment fully shared. Prefaced by the same solemnities, attended by thunders and lightnings, articulated by the Divine voice, all its words engraved by the Divine finger, and intrusted to the sacred keeping of the ark, who could have any reason to imagine that the Sabbath was a Jewish rite, belonging entirely to a covenant which was to decay, wax old, and be ready to vanish away?

[1] Deut. v. 22, 31.

The language in which the laws of the Jews are respectively mentioned in several parts of Scripture concurs with the circumstances now mentioned in discriminating them from each other. Not that the transitory rules of their politico-ecclesiastical state are ever absolutely depreciated. They are included in "the right judgments and true laws, the good statutes and commandments," "which were given them by the hand of Moses." The neglect or transgression of them was held to be an act of contempt to the Divine Lawgiver and King, and was visited with severe retribution. The loss of them in the Captivity was deplored as one of Israel's chief calamities; their recovery is promised as one of their greatest mercies. But there are several statements which indicate the inferiority of these privileges to others. Thus it is written in Hosea, "For I desired mercy, and not sacrifice; and the knowledge of God more than burnt-offerings;"[1] and in Jeremiah, "I spake not unto your fathers, nor commanded them in the day that I brought them out of the land of Egypt concerning burnt-offerings and sacrifice; but this thing I commanded them, saying, Obey my voice."[2] We have similar statements in the New Testament: "Woe unto you, scribes and Pharisees, hypocrites!" says our Lord, "for ye pay tithe of mint, and anise, and cummin, and have omitted the weightier matters of the law, judgment, mercy, and faith: these ought ye to have done, and not to leave the other undone."[3] How different the terms in which two of the apostles speak of the law of ceremonies and the law of morality! In referring to the former, the apostle Peter asks, "Now, therefore, why tempt ye God, to put a yoke upon the neck of the disciples, which neither our fathers nor we were able to bear?"[4] while the apostle Paul says of another law—plainly that of the Decalogue—"Wherefore the law is holy, and the commandment is holy, just, and good. We know that the law is spiritual; I delight in the law of God after the inward man."[5] And when mentioning the "advantage"—the profit which belonged to "the Jew"—to "circumcision," largely and "every way," the writer does not fail to give the preference to this one of their privileges, "that unto them were committed the oracles of God." Compar-

[1] Hos. vi. 6. [2] Jer. vii. 22, 23. [3] Matt. xxiii. 23.
[4] Acts xv. 10. [5] Rom. vii. 12, 14, 22.

ing these passages with each other, we arrive at the conclusion that the law of the Decalogue was honoured above the other laws.

2. When from the manner in which the laws of the Jews were delivered, and from the language of the sacred writers respecting them, we turn to the laws themselves, and consider their nature and designs, we discover further proofs of their diversity, and that they fall under two distinct classes.

One class, consisting of ceremonial and political regulations, were, like some of the ordinances of Christianity, manifestly provided, not for all time, but for the period of the particular economy to which they were attached and adapted. As the Lord's Supper would not have been appropriate to the circumstances of the Jews, so neither would the Passover have been congruous to those of Christians. And what is true of the Passover is true of the whole Jewish polity and ritual, which were suited exclusively to a certain spot of earth, as well as to a people that stood in special relations to the Almighty, and had extraordinary functions to fulfil. With the enlargement of the church beyond its former pale, the cessation of the theocracy, and the accomplishment of the objects that were to be attained by the severance of Israel from other nations, the authority of their rites and political code came to an end. This fact we read in the utter inapplicability of the ancient priesthood and sacrifices to a period when the substance of these shadows has been realized, and in the impossibility that a system which demanded a periodical resort to Jerusalem for worship, the suspension of agricultural industry at certain times, and various other peculiarities, should be practised by men scattered over the globe, and having no miraculous means of defence, guidance, or support. And yet these transitory rules were as really binding while their occasion lasted as any of the most enduring commandments. They were founded on the one great law of love to God and man, in which our Lord has summarily expressed all human obligations. They involved in them the undying principles of truth and righteousness. The Mosaic ritual was another form of the everlasting gospel. Circumcision and the Passover pointed to the most momentous facts and blessings, as do still our baptism and eucharist. And the judicial law was distinguished by its perfect equity, and by its merciful regard to the stranger, the widow, the fatherless, and even the lower animals. The change which befell these institutions was the annulling, not of principles or of essential law, but of certain applications of them, or of subsidiary arrangements, when the object of such bye-laws had been gained.

The other class of laws—those of the ten commandments—are evidently of such a nature as to be adapted and necessary not to the Jews alone, but to men of all countries and times. If it was right for the Jew to have no god but the one living and true God; to employ no images in his worship; to serve Him in spirit and in truth; to spend one day in seven in resting from ordinary work and in sacred engagements; to honour parents; to have respect to the life, purity, property, and reputation of himself and others, and to shun all covetous desire,—the same things must be right for the Gentile. If these commands were holy and just, and could not be violated without sin and injury as regarded the former, they are plainly as holy and just, and the transgression of them as truly deserving of blame and punishment in the case of the latter. If they were good to the one, it is impossible to conceive how they are not good to the other. They are, in fact, the laws of nature and of God to every human being. All this, indeed, is generally admitted as to nine of these commandments. The only question respects the fourth, which some hold to be only one of a number of Jewish rites, and doomed to share their fate.

But what is there in the law of the Sabbath to make it an exception? It provides rest from labour. Its very name signifies a ceasing from work. Other days are in contradistinction from it called working days. "Six days shalt thou labour, and do all thy work: but the seventh day is the Sabbath of the Lord thy God: in it thou shalt not do any work, thou nor thy son nor thy daughter, thy man-servant nor thy maid-servant, nor thy cattle nor thy stranger that is within thy gates." But for six thousand years man and beast have been subject to exhausting labour, and it would be no easy task to show how the Jews needed a day of rest more than many others both in ancient and in present times, or to prove that Christianity is less merciful to toiling man and his weary beast than was any preceding dispensation of religion. That the law of rest contemplated a much wider range of application than the people of Palestine appears from the little labour which for forty years after the proclamation of the law from Sinai they had to perform, and from their miraculous exemption during many years of their subsequent history from much of the toil of other men.

The Sabbath was also an appointed season of mental improvement and spiritual good. And was the soul more precious, or its salvation and improvement more important in Judea than in any other part of the world—in the days of Moses than in those of Abraham or of Christ? A more spiritual economy would rather imply the necessity of higher mental cultivation, and of greater attention to "the things that belong to our peace." But how would it be possible for the majority of our people to acquire the one and do the other without a Sabbath? It is easy to talk of the freedom from restraint, and the liberty secured by Christianity; but unless we have a set day and place for religious duties, they cannot fail to be neglected. Christians, as much as the good men of a former economy, have found that a day for a periodical dismissing from their minds of all secular business and cares, and for directing their thoughts and regards to "the things that are above," is indispensable to their preparation for a future world.

The Sabbath, in short, was a stated day of sacred service in honour of its almighty and gracious Author. Having rested from his work of creation, God blessed and sanctified the Sabbath-day. But the creation of the world by Jehovah is a fact which respects, not one nation only, but mankind, and the belief of which is fundamental to all true religion. If it was the duty of the Jews to remember their Creator, no less was it the duty of the patriarchs, and no less is it the duty of men now. If the one stood in need of the knowledge of God as the maker of all things, and required a Sabbath as the means, equally were these blessings indispensable to the others. If the Sabbath in old time was marked more than ordinary days by typical shadows of a coming Saviour, is it reasonable to conceive that there should be no day to remind us, by its returning rest and meditations, of the great Redemption—a work which, like the creation, concerns men of every time and class, and is much more glorious than any other work or deliverance of the Almighty? How comprehensive in itself, and how decisive of this, as of other questions on the subject, is the maxim of our Lord, "The Sabbath was made for man!"

3. But the proof of the permanence of the Decalogue is completed and sealed by the fact of the declared obligation of its precepts under all economies.

Formally given from Sinai, it had been the rule of man's conduct from the beginning. In the history recorded in Genesis we find traces of the knowledge of all the ten commandments. The offerings of Abel, Noah, and others, and the language to Abraham, "I am the Almighty God, walk before me, and be thou perfect," prove that these persons were acquainted with the obligation to worship and serve the one living and true God. That the use of images in worship was forbidden appears from Jacob's exhortation to his family to put away strange gods. The reverential regard to the Divine name which is required in the third commandment is implied in the practice of administering an oath, and in the prevalent respect for promises thus solemnized. The honour due to parents was acknowledged in the conduct of Noah's sons, as also in their father's prophetic intimation of its consequences, in the obedience of Isaac to Abraham, and in other instances. Cain was condemned for taking the life of his brother, and was conscious of his guilt, while at the commencement, again as it were, of the world, after the flood, the law subsequently forming the sixth in the Decalogue was impressively renewed. The indignation of Jacob's sons on account of the dishonour done to their sister, the father's resentment of the cruelty by which they avenged the deed, and the conduct of Joseph, with his words, "How can I do this great wickedness, and sin against God?" showed the authority of the seventh as well as of the sixth. The protest of Joseph's brethren against the charge of theft indicated that both parties were acquainted with the precept which says, "Thou shalt not steal." The same knowledge on the part of Laban and Jacob is proved in the matter of the stolen images. The ninth precept was known even to Pharaoh, the contemporary of Abraham, as was manifested by his remonstrance with the patriarch for not adhering to truth in representing his wife as his sister. And kings are recorded to have been punished for their covetousness. It might be reasonably concluded from the preceding instances of respect for nine of the commandments that the Sabbatic law was in force ; but we are not left to this inferential mode of ascertaining the fact, there being none of the precepts of the Decalogue presented in so full detail as the fourth is presented in the narrative of the original appointment of the day of sacred rest.

But not only were the patriarchs under Divine law,—the same law which after their time was *formally* given to their descendants. The heathen who never had any communication with the children of Abraham, and who were not within hearing of the thunders of Sinai, and "the great voice" of the Lawgiver, were under law to God. The apostle Paul in the Epistle to the Romans classes them with the Jews, as composing that "world" which is throughout "guilty before God," and charges them with every variety of sin. But where no law is, there is no transgression. Yet they knew that "they who commit such things" as "unrighteousness, fornication, wickedness, covetousness, maliciousness, hatred of God, pride, disobedience to parents," and other sins, "are worthy of death." "For when the Gentiles, which have not the law, do by nature the things contained in the law, these, having not the law, are a law unto themselves : which show the work of the law written in their hearts, their conscience also bearing witness, and their thoughts the meanwhile accusing or else excusing one another." They are indeed said to be "without law." They were destitute of the knowledge of the will of God as contained in the sacred oracles, or, according to the language of these oracles, "He showeth his word unto Jacob, his statutes and his judgments unto Israel. He hath not dealt so with any nation." "What advantage hath the Jew ? or what profit is there of circumcision ? Much every way : chiefly, because that unto them were committed the oracles of God." In the Law and Gospel known to the Jews, the one more clearly than to other nations, the other exclusively, both classes were alike concerned, else where would have been the alleged advantage of the Jew ? The Gentiles and the Jews are supposed by the apostle to be under the same law, known, indeed, in different degrees, but so known by both as that the former who have not the law are said when obedient to do by nature the things contained in *the law*, and to show the work of *the law* written in their hearts, while the Jews are said to "do the same" as the Gentiles when both transgress it. And it is when the apostle has proved that Jews and Gentiles are all under sin, that he thus declares the result of their trial by the everlasting rule of righteousness: "Now we know that what things soever the law saith, it saith to them who are under the law: that every mouth may be stopped, and all the world may become guilty before God."

It is not questioned that the Jews were under the law of the Decalogue. It only remains, then, to inquire whether we have evidence that its obligation descends to Christians.

In more than one respect is it true that they are delivered from the law given to Israel. With the political part of that law as a directory, except as regards its principles and maxims of eternal morality, they have no concern. They are freed or rather exempted from any obligation to observe the Levitical ceremonies. And there is a sense in which they are delivered from the Decalogue itself, but delivered in a manner that binds them the more strongly to its requirements. The law of the ten commandments, proclaimed from Sinai, was, as it had been since the fall of man, a law of condemnation and curse as well as a law of liberty. It is so under the dispensation of the Gospel. Thus the apostle Paul says, "Cursed is every one that continueth not in all things written in the book of the law to do them;" and thus the apostle James, "Whosoever shall keep the whole law, and yet offend in one point, he is guilty of all." No one was more stern in preaching the terrors of the law than the Saviour himself. And what was the purpose of all this? It was that sinful men might be delivered from the condemnation and curse of the law, and brought to obey its precepts, the very precepts for transgressing which they were condemned, but which are still their rule, as unbending as ever, yet rendered practicable and attractive by the Saviour's atonement, love, and grace. "We are delivered from the law, that being dead wherein we were held, that we should serve in newness of spirit, and not in the oldness of the letter. What shall we say then? Is the law sin? God forbid. The law is holy, and the commandment holy, just, and good. I delight in the law of God after the inward man."

That Christians are under the law of the ten commandments is the doctrine of the New Testament. "Think not," said Christ, "that I am come to destroy the law or the prophets: I am not come to destroy, but to fulfil. For verily I say unto you, Till heaven and earth pass, one jot or one tittle shall in no wise pass from the law, till all be fulfilled. Whosoever, therefore, shall break one of these least commandments, and shall teach men so, he shall be called the least in the kingdom of heaven: but whosoever shall do and teach them, the same shall be called great in the kingdom of heaven."[1] That our Lord here, under the expression "the kingdom of heaven," refers to the Christian dispensation, is certain. He and John the Baptist announced that dispensation under the same phrase, "the kingdom of heaven is at hand." And that he speaks of the law of the Decalogue is manifest from the immediately subsequent words of his sermon, in which he proceeds to expound and enforce some of its precepts, vindicating them from the perversions and limitations by which the Jews had corrupted them. He does not specify every one of the commandments; but a general proposition respecting a law, illustrated by a few examples, must be understood as involving a principle applicable to all the particulars of that law. The Sabbath is not mentioned, neither is the Fifth Commandment. Our Lord, however, takes other opportunities of freeing both from Jewish additions and abuses—the Fifth, in the case of the person who, that he might be exempted from the duty of applying his property in aid of his parents, called it "corban," or something devoted to God; and the Fourth in numerous instances. It is a striking confirmation of our views that our Lord never does honour to any ceremonial or judicial enactment by redeeming it from the false glosses of the scribes and Pharisees.

On various other occasions did our Lord so speak and act as beyond all doubt to teach us the continued obligation of the Decalogue. Thus, when the young man asked what good thing he should do that he might have eternal life, Jesus replied, "If thou wilt enter into life, keep the commandments;" and then,

[1] Matt. v. 17-19.

in answer to another question inquiring what these were, said, "Thou shalt do no murder, Thou shalt not commit adultery, Thou shalt not steal, Thou shalt not bear false witness, Honour thy father and thy mother: and, Thou shalt love thy neighbour as thyself."[1] Here five of the ten commandments are specified, and affirmed to be binding. Our Lord's purpose was to show the individual his true character, and it was sufficient for this end to set before him a part of the law. But by this selection he has attested the authority of the whole Decalogue.

Our Lord teaches the same doctrine to the lawyer who asked which was the great commandment in the law, when he said, "Thou shalt love the Lord thy God with all thy heart, and with all thy soul, and with all thy mind. This is the first and great commandment. And the second is like unto it, Thou shalt love thy neighbour as thyself. On these two commandments hang all the law and the prophets."[2] As in his language to the young man, he had summed up the precepts of the second table in love to our neighbour, so here he comprehends the whole Decalogue in love to God and man, declaring as plainly as language could express it that every one of the ten commandments continues in all its ancient authority.

The language of the apostles, in like manner, recognises the permanence of the Decalogue. In applying the Fifth Commandment to the children of Christian parents, and enforcing it by its ancient promise of long life,[3] the apostle Paul has no idea that the language *in the land* made the precept a merely Jewish one, as originally given, but clearly regards it as one which embraced the Gentiles as well as the Jews—the time to come as well as the time then present. How indubitably does the same apostle recognise the obligation of the ten commandments in the Epistle to the Romans, when he says, "Do we make void the law through faith? God forbid; yea, we establish the law"—when he declares "the law" to be "holy, and the commandment to be holy, just, and good;" and when he expressly enjoins specific precepts of the law.[4] The apostle James, also, thus writes respecting the law of the ten commandments: "Whosoever shall keep the whole

1 Matt. xix. 16-19.
2 Matt. xxii. 37-40.
3 Eph. vi. 1-3.
4 Rom. iii. 31, vii. 12, xiii. 9.

law, and yet offend in one point, he is guilty of all. For he that said, Do not commit adultery, said also, Do not kill. Now, if thou commit no adultery, yet, if thou kill, thou art become a transgressor of the law."[1] The principle here implied would warrant equally the statement, "He that said, Honour thy parents, said also, Remember the Sabbath-day to keep it holy. Now, if thou do no dishonour to thy parents, yet, if thou profane the Sabbath, thou art become a transgressor of the law."

[1] James ii. 10, 11.

CHAPTER III.

THE SABBATH, UNDER A CHANGE OF DAY, A CHRISTIAN ORDINANCE AND LAW.

"And it shall come to pass, that from one Sabbath to another shall all flesh come to worship before me, saith the Lord."

FOURTH PROPOSITION.—A VARIETY OF CIRCUMSTANCES CONCURRED TO JUSTIFY THE CONFIDENT EXPECTATION, THAT THE SABBATIC INSTITUTION WAS TO BE PERPETUATED UNDER CHRISTIANITY.

WHEN this last and best dispensation of religion was introduced the world stood as much as ever in need of a Sabbath. The physical nature and necessities of mankind remained the same as they had been. A time had been predicted when "the thousand natural shocks that flesh is heir to" should be removed or abated, but it has not yet fully come, and when it shall come, there is no reason for conceiving that it will bring with it the entire cessation of fatiguing exertion. "They shall labour," but "not in vain;" they shall build houses and inhabit them; plant vineyards and eat their fruit. The absence of all labour would be a curse and not a blessing. Far advanced as we are in the nineteenth century of Christianity, we see man and beast still wearied with toil, and still requiring the rest of night and of every seventh day.

When men became Christians, they continued to have mental and religious wants. All of them needed for the improvement of their intellectual faculties a weekly change of employment, and for their moral and spiritual welfare a frequently returning season of rest from their ordinary business, and of instruction, reflection, and devotion. Many of them had scarcely any other means of mental improvement, or any other opportunity of deliberately attending to their own eternal interests, and those of their children, than a Sabbath afforded. And there is still no possibility that human beings can live piously, morally, and happily, without a day of sacred rest. To imagine that Christianity would, in these unchanged circumstances of man, be without its holy day, would be to suppose that it would be less wise, pure, and benevolent, than preceding economies, or rather, that it would be so different a system as to be no religion at all.

There remained also the irrevocable obligation of worship in all its parts—personal, domestic, and public, and how any human being in the present condition of society could observe that worship in a manner becoming the claims of its great object, and with any satisfaction or advantage to himself, or rather how he could observe it at all, it is for them who would improve on the plans of Divine wisdom and benevolence to show.

Besides the existence of the same necessity for the Sabbath, such an institution was capable of yielding the same advantages as ever, and it was to be presumed from the promises of a happier era that Divine blessings, instead of being restricted, would be continued and even increased.

The statute of the primæval rest, too, was unrepealed. All along from the time of its institution to the departure of Israel from Egypt—even though it were true that in a brief history it is not alluded to—it remained a standing rule for the world. When next expressly introduced, it is in the form not of a revocation, but of a revival. Immediately thereafter, it is solemnly recognised in a law promulgated for mankind. Had the proceedings in Sin, or at Sinai, issued in an appointment that contravened or superseded the original enactment, there would be a plea for the opinion that the Sabbath of Paradise had ceased. But what plea of this nature can be preferred where that institution is made the basis of legislation, and its ancient reason, character, and sanction, only in expanded form and more solemn manner, renewed?

The law given from Sinai, in like manner as that given in Eden, remained in full force. Christ was careful to clear it from Jewish corruptions, and if there was any precept more particularly vindicated by him and honoured than another, it was that requiring the Sabbath-day to be kept holy. It is not the practice of a wise man to repair a house which he is about to pull down.

Add to such reasons for expecting a Christian holy day the fact, that the hope was cherished by Old Testament predictions and promises, which declared that the Sabbath would exist, be honoured and blessed under the reign of Messiah. In more than one part of this volume are the prophetic and gracious intimations on these points quoted and considered. Let us only, after referring our readers to the fifty-sixth and fifty-eighth chapters of Isaiah, where there are glowing representations of the coming dispensation with its Sabbatic blessings for men of all classes, and its house of prayer for all people, advert for a moment to the last sentence but one in the writings of that prophet. It is this: "And it shall come to pass, that from one new moon to another, and from one Sabbath to another, shall all flesh come to worship before me, saith the Lord."[1]

It is not the meaning of these words, that a time is coming when every day will resemble the day of the new moon and the Sabbath-day, that is, when its holier service of God will be like a worship all the month and week over. It is true that the Word of God holds out the prospect of a time when the labours of our race in procuring what is necessary for food and defence will be diminished, and when their opportunities for attending to the soul will be multiplied. But it is not said that they shall come from day to day, but from month to month, and from week to week. In the language of Scripture as well as in common speech, what is done from year to year, as in the case of the command of Israel to keep the passover from year to year, is done annually—what is done from month to month, or from week to week, is done monthly or weekly. Nor is it the meaning of these words, that the stated Jewish days—new moons and Sabbaths—should be continued or revived in future times. The Scripture must be expounded in consistency with itself. If there are to be the Jewish times, there must also be priests and Levites, and an actual repairing of "all flesh" to the literal Jerusalem. If on the other hand, the priests and Levites of a preceding verse denote

[1] Isaiah lxvi. 23.

the office-bearers of the Christian Church, and if Jerusalem signify the church itself, then the new moons and Sabbaths must only refer to the seasons of public worship under Christianity whatever these seasons may be. In no other way could the prophet have made himself understood than by mentioning religious observances as they then prevailed. All that we are warranted, therefore, to draw from the verse before us is, that as the people of Judea at set times repaired to Jerusalem to worship, and as they observed their new moons and Sabbaths, so in a future age all flesh, or men of every land, shall connect themselves with the church of God, and engage from month to month, and from week to week, in "its stated observances and solemn forms."[1]

FIFTH PROPOSITION.—WHILE A VARIETY OF CIRCUMSTANCES HELD OUT THE PROSPECT OF A PERENNIAL HOLY DAY, THERE WERE OTHERS THAT TENDED TO PREPARE THE MINDS OF MEN FOR SOME CHANGE IN THE INSTITUTION.

It had already undergone changes in its relations and bearings. From being a simple rule of duty it became a part of the condition on which depended man's happiness. It passed into the provisions of the covenant of grace. It was received into the Jewish economy, and in that connexion was a memorial of the deliverance of the children of Israel from Egyptian bondage, as well as of the world's creation—a political regulation and a ceremonial type, as well as a moral law. These were precedents which indicated that there might be future changes in the application, which should not affect the substance, of the institution.

A dispensation so important, and in some respects so new as that of Christianity, might be presumed to require, in adaptation to its own character and purposes, some alterations in the Sabbath. It might be expected, for example, that the work of redemption would have a prominent niche and statue in this monumental institute. The Scriptures had presented this work as one that should cast all preceding works into shade. They had told us of a new creation more glorious than the old, and therefore more

[1] Alexander's *Prophecies of Isaiah*.

entitled to remembrance ; of a redemption more precious far than the rescue from Egyptian thraldom, and therefore much more worthy to be immortalized. If the material creation merited a memorial, still more the moral ; if the temporal deliverance of a single nation deserved to have an institution enacted in its honour, incalculably more the spiritual and eternal salvation of a multitude that no man can number.

Nor were there wanting intimations of what the necessary change would be. The seventh was an important day under the Mosaic economy, but various instances occur in which the eighth was honoured. Circumcision, a seal of the righteousness of the faith which Abraham had yet being uncircumcised, was to be administered on the eighth day. On the eighth day were the first-born of cattle to be offered to the Lord, and the sheaf of the first-fruits to be presented and accepted. On that day the consecration of Aaron and his sons, and the sanctification of the Temple, were completed. These and similar transactions were shadows of things to come, but the body is of Christ. And where shall we find an eighth day signalized by any doings or blessings of Christ correspondent with those types except the day on which He rose from the dead ? There is one typical representation in particular that calls for remark. It occurs in Ezekiel's vision of the Temple. That this vision was not realized in the building of the second temple appears from, besides other facts, the differences in its worship from that prescribed by the law of Moses ; and that there will be no literal fulfilment of it at a future day, is obvious from several considerations, one of which is sufficient, and is, that sacrifice is for ever abolished by Christ, so that to attempt its revival would be to deny *His* sacrifice. The only supposable accomplishment of the vision is in the condition of the Christian Church : And what is there that fulfils the following prediction, if not the first day of the week and its Christian worship ? "And when these days are expired, it shall be, that upon *the eighth day, and so forward*, the priest shall make your burnt-offerings upon the altar, and your peace-offerings ; and I will accept you, saith the Lord."[1]

[1] Ezek. xliii. 27.

SIXTH PROPOSITION.—THE FACTS RECORDED IN THE NEW TESTAMENT, AS REGARDS BOTH THE PERPETUITY AND BLESSINGS OF THE SABBATH, AND THE CHANGE OF ITS DAY, HAVE FULFILLED THE PREDICTIONS AND REALIZED THE TYPES, OF THE OLD.

The obligation of observing the seventh day as the Sabbath has ceased. This is conclusively established by a variety of evidence.

It appears from several passages in the New Testament that on the introduction of Christianity attempts were made by certain converts from among the Jews to impose upon Gentile believers the observance of the law of Moses, particularly circumcision, the distinction of meats, and sacred seasons. Such attempts were repeatedly resisted by the apostles. We have the judgment of the apostle Paul on the subject, as regarded the days of the old ritual, in these words to the Colossians : "Let no man judge you in meat or drink, or in respect of an holy day, or of the new moon, or of the sabbath-days : which are a shadow of things to come ; but the body is of Christ."[1] In the preceding verses the apostle had referred to the privilege enjoyed by the Christians at Colosse, of freedom from the obligation to observe Jewish ceremonies. They had been circumcised, indeed, but it was with "the circumcision made without hands." "The handwriting of ordinances, which was contrary" both to them and to the apostle, had been "taken out of the way by Christ, who nailed it to his cross." And then, in the words before us, they are told that no man ought to judge or condemn them in reference to meat or drink, a holy day or festival, the new moon or Sabbath-days. The word in the original for Sabbath-days is plural, and always in that form has the sense of the Jewish Sabbath in the New Testament. In its singular form it is employed with the same meaning, only two exceptions being pleaded for in which it is supposed by some to denote the Christian Sabbath,[2] and which will again come under our notice. Whether, then, we consider the relation of the words to the apostle's subject and purpose, the connexion of confessedly Jewish ceremonies with the Sabbath-days in the verse, or the meaning of this term itself, we must believe that the Colossian

[1] Col. ii. 16, 17. [2] Matt. xxiv. 20 ; Acts xiii. 42.

converts, and, by parity of reason, all Christians, were by this sentence of the apostle exempted from the obligation of keeping the seventh-day Sabbath, as really as they were from that of paying regard to the distinctions in food, the festivals, and new moons of the preceding economy. The same, or at least a corresponding truth, is taught in the words addressed to the Galatians (iv. 9-11): "But now, after that ye have known God, or rather are known of God, how turn ye again to the weak and beggarly elements, whereunto ye desire again to be in bondage? Ye observe days, and months, and times, and years. I am afraid of you, lest I have bestowed upon you labour in vain." But as it is not said that Christians were raised above the necessity, or deprived of the advantage and enjoyment of meat and drink, so neither is it intimated that they were to have no set day of sacred rest and service. The text must be adhered to, and it relates to ritual matters alone—to Sabbaths, as, like new moons and holidays, forming a part of the Jewish ceremonial. Beyond the application of the term to what was common in Sabbath-days with distinctions in meat and drink, and with the festivals and new moons of the Jews, we have no warrant to go in interpreting the apostolic decree. Let us recollect, besides, that the apostle is writing at the distance of thirty years from the date of our Lord's resurrection, and at a time when the assembling of Christians for public worship on the first day of the week had become an established practice. The Colossians must, therefore, have understood him, not as setting aside all sabbatical observance which, without dropping a hint of discouragement, he was aware prevailed under a change of day, but simply as discharging from obligation on conscience a day which every one knew to be the last of the week. While, moreover, his words discard the days of Judaism, they touch not the authority of the ancient statute of Paradise, and in undermining ceremonial rites, leave unshaken the moral foundation on which rests the prescription, "Remember the Sabbath-day to keep it holy."

However they may be conceived to differ, the earlier decision on the subject of the observance of particular days in the Epistle to the Romans, is in unison with that in the Epistle to the Colossians, and furnishes additional evidence that the obligation of observing the seventh day as a sacred day had been annulled. The apostle addressing the church at Rome, which was composed partly of converted heathen, and partly of converted Jews, and in which a diversity of view existed in reference to the keeping of certain days, says, "One man esteemeth one day above another; another esteemeth every day alike. Let every man be fully persuaded in his own mind. He that regardeth the day regardeth it unto the Lord; and he that regardeth not the day, to the Lord he doth not regard it."[1] As the design of the whole Epistle is to show that the way of salvation through Christ is opened alike to Jews and Gentiles, Jewish rites and ceremonies being superseded, and as abstinence from certain meats is adduced along with days, as the subject of difference on which the apostle decides, it is obvious that the days in question are the Mosaic holy days. The class who had been Jews had a special regard for these days; the class who had been heathen attached no importance to them. In this case they were not to condemn each other, but to act on their respective conscientious convictions. Was this the language appropriate to the fact of the continued obligation of the seventh day? The sacred observance of that day had at one time been the solemn duty of the Jews, frequently pressed on their attention, and enforced by the promise of valuable blessings to those who discharged it, as well as by denunciations of calamity against the disobedient. Now, however, to adhere to what was formerly so indispensable, places the person in the very different position of the weak though well-meaning object of forbearance.

The fate of the seventh-day Sabbath is in accordance with the apostolical decisions. Silence here is very different in its import from the silence that followed the birth of the institution. There is this difference, with others, that in the latter case the silence was broken, while in the former it remains undisturbed. Amidst the circumstantial details of the early Christian Church, we never after his resurrection find the followers of Jesus assembling for sacred services on the seventh day. Nor was it the manner of the Saviour during his stay for forty days on earth to go as formerly into the synagogue on that day. He honours the meetings of his disciples, but it is no longer on the seventh day. Frequently do the apostles and Christians "come together," but

[1] Rom. xiv. 5, 6.

in several instances the first day of the week is expressly mentioned as the set time, while the old day of the Sabbath is never said to be selected for such assemblies. It affects not the truth of our statement, that the apostle Paul repeatedly met with the Jews on that day,[1] and "reasoned with them out of the Scriptures, as his manner was." This practice did not in his case involve agreement with them in their adherence to the day, or in any of their peculiarities, else he must be supposed to have also fraternized with pagans by preaching in the Areopagus, thereby defeating his avowed purpose not to sanction but to revolutionize the views and customs both of Jews and heathens on all such occasions. His philanthropy impelled him to go about, like his Master, doing good—doing good as he had opportunity to all. It was in particular his heart's desire and prayer for his kinsmen according to the flesh, that they might be saved; and in acting on this feeling he was guided by the Master's arrangement, to which he thus refers when addressing the Jews at Antioch in Pisidia: "It was necessary that the word of God should first have been spoken to you." To fulfil these benevolent wishes to the utmost it was obviously wise and necessary that he should embrace the favourable opportunities of access to his brethren and fellow-men afforded by the scenes and seasons of their wonted and largest concourse. Where it did not compromise truth or duty, he was ready to go farther than this—even to become all things to all men, that he might save some. He could keep the passover, circumcise Timothy, purify himself according to a Jewish rite, call himself a Pharisee, own Ananias as high-priest—such conformity being allowed to a Jew in tenderness to his brethren, that they might not be driven from Christianity, but be gradually won over from an abrogated ritual. And yet in perfect consistency with these concessions, he taught the doctrines that the Mosaic ceremonies were virtually displaced, that it was a denial of the Messiah to attempt their revival as necessary to salvation, and that no man was to judge those Gentiles who refused to submit to them, while practically he would have withstood the apostles to the face, if they had attempted to compel a Titus, or even a recusant Jew, to be circumcised. The subsequent history of the seventh-day Sabbath, while it illustrates

[1] Acts ix. 20; xiii. 14-16; xvi. 13; xvii. 1-3; xviii. 4.

the wisdom of this policy, confirms our doctrine of its authoritative abolition. Regard for it died out, and another day rose gradually and peacefully to ascendency. For a time the former continued as a subordinate season of worship, but for some fifteen or sixteen centuries it has been, except by the Jews and a very small sect of Christians, altogether disregarded. Is it within the limits of moral possibility that a day which has for so long a period failed to secure the respect and observance of the Christian Church is entitled to the claim of Divine authority?

The first day of the week was divinely appointed to be the Christian Sabbath.

Let it be remembered that no new institution required to be enacted. The law prescribing a day of rest after six days of labour had been from the beginning. It was given in Paradise, impressively recognised in the wilderness of Sin, and solemnly announced from Mount Sinai. Promises of blessing to its friends, and proclamations of calamity to its enemies, were from time to time sounded in the ears of the Jews by the prophets. The primæval appointment and the fourth commandment remaining unrepealed and irrevocable, with their unchanged and unalterable reasons, the hopes of the ancient church were at the same time pointed to a permanent day of rest and worship with adaptations to the new and more glorious creation. Our Lord had confirmed all these views of the institution, and these hopes of men. He declared that the Sabbath was made for man, and yet that man was not made for the Sabbath. He claimed to be the Lord of the Sabbath. He cleared its law and the other moral precepts from misrepresentation. And while he thus taught the importance and value of a weekly holy day, he rebuked the superstitious regard for a particular day (the design of which had been accomplished), and prepared the minds of men for a change. If Israel in the wilderness of Sin, as Henry expresses it, so "readily took the hint" of a Sabbath there given, much more might it be supposed that there was abundant light reflected from the glorious resurrection of the Saviour to indicate to his disciples the day which should henceforth be devoted to sacred rest and service. And how inexcusable are we if his marked selection of a particular season for his visits to them, and for sending them the

Holy Ghost—their use of the same season in their public celebration of his praise and ordinances, and the name given to it by which he asserted and they admitted his claim to it as his own,—if these facts do not carry ample evidence to our minds that the time referred to, the first day of the week, is by his authority constituted the Sabbath of Christianity.

The resurrection of our Lord from the dead was both the indication and the cause of the transference of the Sabbatic day from the end to the beginning of the week. All the evangelists record the fact that the former event took place on the first day of the week; but one of them more concisely and directly: "Now when Jesus was risen early the first day of the week, he appeared first to Mary Magdalene." It was not by accident that the Redeemer rose from the dead on that day. There are reasons for the times of much less important events. Circumstances might have been so arranged as that Jesus should have risen on the seventh day of the week; but it was not so ordered. That on this day he should lie in the dust of death was a plain token that it was no longer to be "a delight"—a day of joyful commemoration. The day of His resurrection was the first day of the Saviour's rest, and the analogy, to say nothing more, to the Divine procedure in creation required that the day on which He rested from a transcendently more glorious work should be the season of rest and celebration in His kingdom. "There remaineth therefore a rest," the keeping of a Sabbath, "to the people of God. For he that is entered into his rest, he also hath ceased from his own works, as God did from his."

In proof that the day of His own rest was to be the season of rest and prayer to His followers, our Lord met with His disciples on the very day of His resurrection. After favouring individuals of them with His presence and instructions, so that their hearts burned within them while he talked with them by the way, and opened to them the Scriptures, He appeared in the midst of the assembled eleven, and other friends, and said unto them, "Peace be unto you. Why are ye troubled? and why do thoughts arise in your hearts? Behold my hands and my feet, that it is I myself."[1] The scene is thus described by another evangelist:

[1] Luke xxiv 36, 38, 39

"Then the same day at evening, being the first day of the week, when the doors were shut, where the disciples were assembled, for fear of the Jews, came Jesus, and stood in the midst, and saith unto them, Peace be unto you. And when he had so said, he showed unto them his hands and his side. Then were the disciples glad when they saw the Lord. Then said Jesus to them again, Peace be unto you : as my Father hath sent me, even so send I you. And when he had said this, he breathed on them, and saith unto them, Receive ye the Holy Ghost. Whose soever sins ye remit, they are remitted unto them ; and whose soever sins ye retain, they are retained."[1] It is added that "Thomas was not with them when Jesus came," and that when informed by the other disciples that they had seen the Lord, he said, "Except I shall see in his hands the print of the nails, and put my fingers into the print of the nails, and my hand into his side, I will not believe."

The establishment of the first day of the week as the Christian Sabbath still further appears from the time and incidents of our Lord's second visit to his assembled followers. "And after eight days, again his disciples were within, and Thomas with them. Then came Jesus, the doors being shut, and stood in the midst, and said, Peace be unto you. Then saith he to Thomas, Reach hither thy finger, and behold my hands ; and reach hither thy hand, and thrust it into my side : and be not faithless, but believing." Here we have plainly a stated day of religious convocation, and that the first day of the week. From another part of the narrative it appears that the disciples had returned to their accustomed manual labours. Their dependence on these labours for their subsistence required that they should attend to their secular calling, the more so that their time had lately been occupied, and their thoughts absorbed by the events that preceded and attended the crucifixion. They needed, however, as before, a weekly holy day. They could not and would not observe two Sabbaths. The resurrection of their Lord had prescribed the proper day, and this, with His visit, taught them to expect His presence on the first day of the week. Accordingly, "after eight days again his disciples were within." And on His

[1] John xx. 19-23.

part our Lord shows his regard to the day. He absents Himself from the disciples for a whole week, and by appearing among them a second time on the first day of the week, and in the scene of public worship, expresses, in the most emphatic manner, his approval of "the order," both as respects the time and the engagements of this infant Church. Thus, too, the apostle Paul and his friends tarried at Troas seven days, and yet the first day of the week is the only one mentioned on which the disciples came together to break bread, or on which the apostle preached to them.[1] We may presume that it was in like manner to hold public fellowship with the Christians in Tyre, and to preach the gospel, that his sojourn there too was for the same period, as thus related: "And finding disciples, we tarried there seven days: who said to Paul through the Spirit, that he should not go up to Jerusalem. And when we had accomplished those days, we departed, and went our way."[2]

The sacred observance of the first day of the week extends over a wider space than Jerusalem, and to a later time than that of the events there that have been mentioned. We alluded to the apostle Paul's conduct at Troas as a case in which other days are allowed to pass unnoticed, and public religious services are postponed till the first day of the week should come round. But his whole proceedings there, with those of the Church, are justly regarded as very clearly pointing to the first day of the week as the recognised Christian Sabbath. The narrative is as follows: "And we sailed away from Philippi after the days of unleavened bread, and came unto them to Troas in five days, where we abode seven days. And upon the first day of the week, when the disciples came together to break bread, Paul preached unto them, ready to depart on the morrow; and continued his speech until midnight. And there were many lights in the upper chamber, where they were gathered together. And there sat in a window a certain young man named Eutychus, being fallen into a deep sleep: and as Paul was long preaching, he sunk down with sleep, and fell down from the third loft, and was taken up dead. And Paul went down, and fell on him, and embracing him, said, Trouble not yourselves; for his life is in him. When he, therefore, was come up again,

[1] Acts xx. 7.
[2] Acts xxi. 4, 5.

and had broken bread, and eaten, and talked a long while, even till break of day, so he departed. And they brought the young man alive, and were not a little comforted."[1] Let these facts be adverted to in addition to that already noticed. The Christians at Troas "came together," or assembled together, the common phrase for church-meetings in the New Testament. As Peter talked with Cornelius, "he went in, and found many that were *come together*."[2] "Now in this that I declare unto you I praise you not, that ye *come together* not for the better, but for the worse. For first of all, when ye *come together* in the church, I hear that there be divisions among you."[3] "If therefore the whole church be *come together* into one place, how is it then, brethren? when ye *come together*, every one of you hath a psalm, hath a doctrine, hath a tongue, hath a revelation, hath an interpretation. Let all things be done unto edifying."[4] "Not forsaking *the assembling of yourselves together*, as the manner of some is."[5] Further, they came together "to *break bread*." That similar language in Acts xxvii. 35 refers to an ordinary meal, appears from the previous advice of the apostle to his fellow-voyagers, who had fasted for fourteen days, to take some food, as it was for their health; from the words, "Then were they all of good cheer, and they also took some meat;" and, indeed, from the occasion and the persons so employed. Nor do we doubt that in one or two instances, besides, the reference in such language is to the same thing. But when it is said, "They continued in the apostles' doctrine and fellowship, and breaking of bread and prayer," and when they "came together to eat bread," there can be no question that the observance of the Lord's Supper is to be understood. It was a meeting for the public celebration of Divine ordinances at which the apostle was present and preached. In a word, this coming together was the ordinary practice of the disciples at Troas. The use of a common expression for Christian worshipping assemblies determines this, while it is to be observed in corroboration of the view, that it is not said that the apostle, as he did in the case of the elders at Ephesus, called the members of the church together, but that "upon the first day of the week, when the disciples came together to

[1] Acts xx. 6-12. [2] Acts x. 27. [3] 1 Cor. xi. 17, 18.
[4] 1 Cor. xiv. 23, 26. [5] Heb. x. 25.

break bread, Paul preached unto them, ready to depart on the morrow." If the case now described does not intimate that the Christians at Troas at least were in the custom of keeping holy the first day of the week, and that one of the apostles sanctioned that custom by everything that could express sympathy and fellowship in their meeting and engagements, we know not what the narrative can mean, or what other terms could more clearly convey the facts. The statement is the more conclusive that the incidents are so natural in their character and expression. And what different custom from that at Troas—prevalent as it was at so great a distance from Jerusalem, and well-nigh thirty years after the date of the first Christian assembly—can we suppose to have then prevailed in any other part of the Christian world?

Let another case embracing a number of churches supply the answer. In the First Epistle to the Corinthians it is thus written: "Now concerning the collection for the saints, as I have given order to the churches of Galatia, even so do ye. Upon the first day of the week let every one of you lay by him in store, as God hath prospered him, that there be no gatherings when I come."[1] The first day of the week is never before mentioned but as the day of the Redeemer's resurrection, and of religious assemblies and business. These are its only distinctions—the only marks by which it is discriminated from the other days of the week, and by which we are to know its character. We are fully warranted by this history, therefore, to regard it as a sacred day. And here we are made acquainted with the important fact—not the less certain that it required no formal declaration—that it was well known in this its only character by the Corinthian and Galatian churches, if not also by "all that in every place call upon the name of Jesus Christ our Lord, both theirs and ours," to whom, with the Christians at Corinth, the epistle is addressed. The writer takes it for granted that all Christians observed it as a holy day. The prescription of benevolent contributions to be made on it—not once or twice, but constantly—is only in harmony with its nature. The seasons of worship were anciently sanctified by such gifts and offerings.[2] Our Lord asserted the doing of good as an appropriate duty of the Sabbath-day. The frequent periodi-

[1] 1 Cor. xvi. 1, 2. [2] Deut. xvi. 10.

cal return of such a day—its facilities for calm reflection and the cultivation of social affections—its bringing the rich and poor together, and equalizing them in the Divine presence—its sacred recollections, services, and hopes—all tend to promote beneficence, to impart principle and regularity to its exercise, and at once to prevent undue pressure on the resources, and to swell the ultimate amount, of liberality.

The expression, "Lord's day," in Rev. i. 10, is justly regarded as a decisive testimony to the Christian Sabbath. "I was in the Spirit," said the apostle John, "on the Lord's day." This latter expression corresponds with the phraseology of the Old Testament, "A Sabbath to the Lord," "The Sabbath of the Lord thy God," and still more with the Saviour's language, "The Son of man is Lord even of the Sabbath-day."[1] The designation of "Lord" in the New Testament is usually to be understood of Jesus Christ. We read of the word of Christ—the ministers of Christ—the Lord's table—the cup of the Lord—the body and blood of the Lord—the Lord's supper—the Lord's death—so we read of the Lord's day. He has appropriated a day to himself; but as his word, his ministers, his table, his death, are for the benefit of men, to be applied, however, in securing that end, according to his prescription,—so is it with his day. Which day of the week that is, cannot be reasonably questioned. The apostle refers to it as well known to the churches of Asia. He knew that the first day of the week was the day of the resurrection and visits of his Lord—the day held as sacred by the churches of Troas, Corinth, and Galatia—and by the simple mention of its name as the Lord's, he, or rather the Spirit of God, has authorized us to conclude that "the first day of the week" and the "Lord's day" are expressions which denote the same day. His testimony, moreover, proves that the day was not only honoured by the Christian churches and by himself, after the lapse of nearly a century from the time of the Redeemer's advent, but honoured under the name and sanction of the Lord Jesus Christ.

[1] *Κύριος καὶ τοῦ σαββάτου—τῇ Κυριακῇ ἡμέρᾳ*, a different expression from the day of the Lord, *ἡ ἡμέρα Κυρίου*.

SEVENTH PROPOSITION.—IT IS IMPOSSIBLE THAT THE FIRST DAY OF THE WEEK SHOULD HAVE COME TO BE THUS GENERALLY RECEIVED AND OBSERVED AS A HOLY DAY, OR RATHER AS *the weekly* HOLY DAY, WITHOUT DIVINE AUTHORITY.

And this for the following reasons :—

First, The existing prepossessions in favour of the seventh day. It was natural that the Jews should have strong attachments to the whole Mosaic system, which was of Divine appointment, which was that of their fathers, and hallowed in their minds and hearts by its antiquity, glory, and so many tender recollections. How difficult, accordingly, was it for the apostles to believe that all distinctions between Jews and Gentiles had ceased ! The apostles had to bear much with their converted brethren, and to make concessions to their prejudices. And yet, while they were permitted for a time to respect the former distinctions of meats and days, we do not find any evidence in the New Testament that they refused to keep holy the first day of the week. Many of them, at all events, with the apostles at their head, sanctified that day. That this should take place in the case of any, and eventually to the exclusion of regard for the seventh day, in that of almost all, can, we conceive, be accounted for only on the ground that they had sufficient evidence and the clear conviction that the change of day was of God.

Second, The regard which Jehovah has to his worship, and his rejection of human interference in its appointment and regulation. Of this, we have ample evidence in the second commandment ; in the charges repeatedly given to add nothing to his words ; and in the condemnation and punishment of such persons as Nadab and Abihu for offering strange fire on his altar, Jeroboam for devising a religious feast of his own heart, the antichristian power that should "think to change times and laws," Ananias and Sapphira, and others. That the apostles and early Christians should of their own accord abandon the seventh day, and institute the first as a day to the Lord, would be to suppose that their Master had permitted them to violate the order of His own house, and to teach for doctrines the commandments of men.

Third, The abundant provision made for regulating all the observances of religion. Jesus had before his ascension "given commandments through the Holy Ghost unto the apostles," and commissioned them to "teach" mankind "all things whatsoever he had commanded them." And the words of the apostle Paul to the Thessalonian Christians show the authority under which he acted in his preaching and writings: "We beseech you, brethren, and exhort you by the Lord Jesus, that as ye have received of us how ye ought to walk and to please God, so ye would abound more and more. For ye know what commandments we gave you by the Lord Jesus."[1] From several parts of the New Testament, we learn that in acting and ordering as we have seen one of them did in reference to the first day of the week, they are to be regarded as ruling our conduct, their ordinances and commandments being those of their Master and Lord.[2] How was it possible, therefore, for them to appoint the churches to assemble for worship on that day, to encourage the practice, or to induce believers to follow it, if they had not received of the Lord how to teach and act in this most important matter?

Fourth, The apostolic censure of the observance of days. The Galatians were remonstrated with for this conduct: "But now, after that ye have known God, or rather are known of God, how turn ye again to the weak and beggarly elements whereunto ye desire again to be in bondage? Ye observe days, and months, and times, and years. I am afraid of you, lest I have bestowed upon you labour in vain."[3] Now it is impossible that inspired men should both condemn the observance of days, and yet observe them themselves, and countenance by their words and deeds the practice, unless the two things were distinct—unless, while other days were set aside, the first day of the week had come into authorized and sacred use.

Fifth, The prophetic intimations of a Christian Sabbath. If the consecration of the first day of the week be not the fulfilment of these intimations, they have failed of accomplishment, for that was for centuries the only recognised Sabbath, and still is the Sabbath of nearly the whole Christian Church.

[1] 1 Thess. iv. 1, 2.
[2] Acts xv. 24, 28, 29; Luke x. 16; 1 Cor. xiv. 37; 1 John iv. 6.
[3] Gal. iv. 9-11.

Sixth, The events and blessings which have attended this day. If the ancient Sabbath was attested by extraordinary occurrences, not less the new. The day of the Redeemer's resurrection was a day of marvels. It was also a day of blessing, when he announced peace, breathed on His disciples the influences of the Spirit, gave them their commission, and held with them the most condescending and endeared intercourse. It was on the first day of the week that He removed the doubts of one of their number. It was on the first day of the week, when the Christians were all with one accord in one place, that the Holy Ghost came down, an event so great in itself, and so fraught with good to mankind. On this day the first Christian sermon was preached; thousands were converted, the Church was fully formed, and the Lord's supper publicly celebrated. It was on the Lord's day that the apostle John was in the Spirit, heard a *great voice* as of a trumpet, saw the glorified Saviour in the midst of the churches, and was commanded to write the things which he had seen, the things that then were, and the things that should be thereafter. And it has been on the Christian Sabbath ever since that the greatest good has been done to mankind, by that Word and Grace which have covered so many regions of the earth with moral beauty, and prepared so many human beings for heaven, and which shall, in yet more auspicious times, reclaim a revolted world to the service and enjoyment of its Maker.

What, then, is wanting to the evidence that the day on which Christians cease from labour, and worship their Divine Saviour, is truly the Sabbath of God, the Lord's day? We have seen the first day of the week to be coæval with the second and more glorious rest of God, sanctified by His example and word, and blessed with His favour, presence, and grace from the beginning till now. If not "the day which the Lord hath made," it is surely its morning and meridian too. If not the consummation of "the rest which remaineth to the people of God," it is certainly the season of a Sabbatism of which heaven will be, in more perfect form, and more unceasing flow, the prolongation for ever.

CHAPTER IV.

DUTIES OF THE SABBATH.

"Six days shalt thou labour, and do all thy work; but the seventh day is the Sabbath of the Lord thy God: in it thou shalt not do any work, thou, nor thy son, nor thy daughter, thy man-servant, nor thy maid-servant, nor thy cattle, nor thy stranger that is within thy gates."

NOTHING is more certain than that any portion of time, however in itself valuable, or capable of being turned to profitable account, is in fact a blessing or a curse according to the purposes to which it is appropriated, and the way in which it is spent. The excesses that have usually attended the festivals of idolatry, and the abuse of holidays by many of our own people, are sufficient confirmation of the remark. To estimate the Sabbatic institution aright we must view it complexly, not as an abstraction, or even as so much time measured off for any use that men may prefer, but in its concomitants of sacred design, appropriate instructions, fitting observance, and the blessing of its Author; and its importance must be understood to consist in the opportunity which at proper intervals it affords not only of rest from secular labour, but of attending to objects and of being acted on by influences which mould into their own elevated and pure character the nature of man, and which without such an arrangement could not be to the same extent, if at all, available.

One of the designs of the Sabbath has ever been to afford rest from labour, with a view to the refreshment of the animal nature, and its invigoration for the work of the six days.

The Almighty himself, who is never weary, rested from the six days' work of creation as a pattern to man. He "rested and was refreshed." And He blessed the seventh day, setting it apart as a day of repose to human beings. The first man, while untainted by sin, had these things in common with us, that he partook of food, had an employment which demanded the exertion of his bodily energies, and was capable of sleep—all involving the means of maintaining the existence and ministering to the well-being and pleasure of his physical nature. As these things were compatible with perfection in excellence and happiness, not less so were the rest of night and the rest of the seventh day. It will be admitted that had he not fallen from purity, he, with his race, would have remained under the law of the Sabbath, and enjoyed its blessings. It may be conceded, on the other hand, that had he, like the angels that sinned, been abandoned by his Maker, his Sabbath would have ceased as irreconcilable with a scene where the inhabitants "rest not day or night." But we are ill qualified to affirm what on certain suppositions might be the procedure of an infinite Being. Man, however, neither persevered in obedience, nor was hopelessly cast off. As he is the object of forbearance and mercy, it does not appear that he is placed beyond the pale of the blessings, or exempted from the obligations of a day of holy and happy rest. There is no intimation that the statute was cancelled, or its benefit withdrawn. It was given to man as a creature consisting of body as well as soul, and placed in a material world. It is plainly so expressed as to be adapted to all dispensations. If man in innocence needed a weekly resting-day, no less certainly was the provision required by himself and his posterity after their transition to the state involved in the sentence : "Because thou hast hearkened unto the voice of thy wife, and hast eaten of the tree, of which I commanded thee, saying, Thou shalt not eat of it : cursed is the ground for thy sake ; in sorrow shalt thou eat of it all the days of thy life. Thorns also and thistles shall it bring forth to thee ; and thou shalt eat the herb of the field. In the sweat of thy face shalt thou eat bread, till thou return unto the ground."[1] Accordingly, while we find him precluded access to the tree of life, and driven from Eden, nothing is said implying that the Sabbath has been set aside. Cain and such as he went out from the presence of the Lord—that is, voluntarily forsook the scene of sacred privilege, of worship, and of Sabbaths, that, like many of our own day,

[1] Gen. iii. 17-19.

they might uninterruptedly prosecute their worldly views and pleasures. That such men as Enoch and Noah, who walked with God, were without the benefit and happiness of the Sabbatic rest, it is on various grounds unreasonable to conceive. If a brief life as ours were insupportable without a weekly day of repose, how impossible for the patriarchs to pass their eight or nine centuries thus! All their interests of mind and body, time and eternity, demanded such a day. It might be the hard lot of Israel, when borne down by Egyptian bondage, to be deprived partially or wholly of this blessing, but on their arrival in the wilderness of Sin, they are put in full possession of the great charter of human liberty and rights, and begin to enjoy it, none making them afraid.

The law, as given from Sinai, sets forth the same design of the institution—rest from labour: "Six days shalt thou labour, and do all thy work; but the seventh day is the Sabbath of the Lord thy God: in it thou shalt not do any work, thou, nor thy son, nor thy daughter, thy man-servant, nor thy maid-servant, nor thy cattle, nor thy stranger that is within thy gates; for in six days the Lord made heaven and earth, the sea, and all that in them is, and rested the seventh day: wherefore the Lord blessed the Sabbath-day and hallowed it."[1] The work, of which there must be a cessation, is the work of our calling or business. This must all be done in the six days. On the seventh there must not be any such work. Nothing can be plainer than the prohibition. And the only reason why it could be necessary to illustrate its meaning is that the human mind can pervert the clearest law to its own sinister purposes. Hence it is that we are furnished with Divine comments on this law. The prophet Isaiah informs us, that it is against the law of the Sabbath to do our own ways, or to speak our own words, or to find our own pleasure on that day. The terms of the law imply all this—for its object is rest from all secular work—and how can he fulfil this object who busies himself with action, or word, or thought about such work? But, on the other hand, no one could reasonably suppose from this commandment that a sheep was not to be lifted from a pit, that the diseased must not be cured, or that the hungry must not be fed. Actions necessary for the preservation

[1] Exod. xx. 9-11.

of life or the relief of distress do not constitute ordinary secular work. It was to clear the law from such mistaken views of it that our Lord condescended to teach the Jews that works of piety, necessity, and mercy, might be done on the Sabbath, which they themselves knew might be done, and did not object to till they had a purpose to serve. As Jesus was "Lord of the Sabbath," he knew best its design and requirements, and therefore all these works must have been accordant with both. He repeatedly asked whether such actions were not agreeable to the law, and his enemies themselves could not say that they were not. Yet our Lord did not make a practice or labour of healing on the Sabbath ; nor did he authorize his disciples to adopt a custom of plucking and bruising ears of corn ; nor command a systematic preparation of appliances for providing against the possible accident of an animal falling into a pit. It is deeds of mercy to the suffering—deeds essential to the duties of piety—deeds of necessity, incapable of being provided for beforehand or postponed, that he practised and recommended.

And when we examine the narratives of the New Testament, we find nothing, after the introduction of the Christian dispensation, done by Christ, or his apostles, or the churches, that was contrary to the old commandment of resting one day in seven. We have seen that the institution is permanent, and what would it be without rest? And the testimony of Christian writers after the time of the apostles is most harmonious as to the observance of the Lord's day as a season of abstinence from labour.

As rest, then, has been the law of the Sabbath in all periods of its recognition in Scripture, it is the law now as really as ever. Now as formerly it is a duty to cease from our usual business. The plough must stand—the counting-house and sale-room and workshop must be shut—the artisan must suspend the use of his implements—the transactions of buying, selling, and getting gain must be discontinued—the author and scribe must drop their pens—the man of literature and science must lay aside his ordinary reading and investigations. We have said, all this *must* be, or *ought* to be ; but what is thus imperative, is at the same time so reasonable and good as should be felt to be freedom and pleasure.

Nor are our usual avocations all that ought to be suspended on the Sabbath of God. We are not to do any secular work; we are not to do our own ways, or speak our own words, or find our own pleasure. All that does not involve sacred service must be laid aside, as without this there is not rest. Suppose, for example, the day to be spent in unnecessary thoughts about the business of the world, it would not gain its object of rest to the body, as continual thought about one set of matters is destructive to those material organs which the mind employs, and thus to the whole system. The statesman, equally as the man who is constantly engaged in manual labour, has a short life. Suppose, again, that the day were devoted to recreation, amusement, or convivial indulgence. All observation and experience show that these afford no proper rest to body or mind. Such occupation converts the day into a working-day of the worst description. He who knows our frame, and all whose ordinances are adapted to its wants and welfare, has prescribed rest from our own pleasures, and from our own words (which are in one sense actions, and bring no repose to the spirit) as well as from our own works and ways.

To fulfil this purpose of rest, the whole day must be so spent. A Sabbath-day is just as long as another day. We find the Saviour rising early on the first day of the week, and it was not till the Sabbath's sun had set that he proceeded to heal the multitudes of sick that were brought to him.[1] The hours allowed for repose are, especially in the case of the great majority of mankind, too precious to admit of being alienated from their great purpose. One infraction of the law has its injurious effect. Many smaller deviations constitute a large total of injury. The smaller leads on to the greater. And admit the principle that one hour of the day of rest may be sacrificed, where shall the admission and the practice stop, short of the abandonment of the whole day? Here, too, the Author of the Sabbath has evinced his wisdom and his goodness in exactly defining and peremptorily requiring a certain time—a day of rest. So important is the object of this part of the arrangement, the distribution of all time into that of work and that of rest, that no encroachment must take place on the smaller proportion allotted to the latter object. A portion is

[1] Luke iv. 18-41.

rather allowed to be taken from the greater and added to the less. The obligation of labour on the six days is as binding as rest on the seventh, but not in the same measure. Secular days may be applied in certain circumstances otherwise than in the work of our callings, but we have no liberty to throw away any part of the seventh day. One abstraction from ordinary time which is allowed and required, is the portion of it that is necessary to preparation for the day of rest. The children of Israel gathered and prepared the Sabbath's manna on the preceding day. If we are fully to enjoy our rest, it is necessary, when the time of it arrives, that we be as completely disengaged as possible from disturbing work and cares, and this can be accomplished only by despatching business so that no violent transition is required.

But rest for bodily refreshment and invigoration is not the only or chief design of the Sabbatic institute. Another and higher purpose of its rest was, that it might give man facilities for sacred engagements. The law is, "Remember the Sabbath-day to keep it holy," and the example of Jehovah is set forth as our pattern. But what was His procedure? He rested from one class of works, but not from all working. In like manner we are to rest from the works appropriated to the six days, but not from all activity. This would be the rest of a mere animal, not of a man. It would be an impossibility. The spirit of man, like its Maker, is from its very nature incessantly active. And this very activity is compatible with continued mental vigour and bodily health. Variety of exercise both of body and mind is, under certain conditions and limitations, the repose and refreshment of both. The person who has toiled with his hands during the week finds it rest, not only to cease from such labour, but to exercise his mind on intellectual subjects. The other person who has laboured mentally during the week finds his spirit refreshed by a change of theme. Nor must we forget what is the chief ingredient in the felt rest of both—the change from the unsatisfying and distracting things of earthly pursuit to intercourse with those tranquillizing and gladdening objects of a spiritual and holy heaven, to which man's nature was originally adapted, and without which it can never be in its proper state of health, order, and happiness.

It is a great truth that the Sabbath was made for man, both for the health of his body and for the good of his mind. But when this oracle was uttered, it was to overthrow the idea that man was made for the Sabbath, not the idea that the Sabbath was made for God. Man himself was made for the Divine service and glory, and this is the highest end of the Sabbath as of all things.

> " That as the world serves us, we may serve Thee,
> And both Thy servants be." [1]

The glory of Jehovah required a day on which man should be more fully than on other days engaged in serving Him—on which rent should be paid to the Proprietor, tribute to the Government—on which the sons of God should come together and swear fealty to their Master—on which subjects should wait on their King, and testify their reverence and loyalty—on which the head of the lower creation should offer the collected homage of all his charge to the universal Lord. The Sabbath is "the Sabbath of the Lord thy God"—it is "the Lord's day." It is designed for man's benefit subordinately, but it is not man's day, and therefore not a day for man's business. It is God's day, and therefore a day for God's work. And it is beneficial to man just in the measure in which it is applied to its chief object, the serving and honouring of its Author.

The God of the Sabbath has prescribed its business. In all ages there has been a service appointed for that day. It would appear that Adam himself had a special work to perform on it. While his thoughts and desires were all holy in the engagements of the six days, it is not inconsistent with his perfect excellence to suppose that his mind required once a week a day of more immediate fellowship with his Maker. The holiness of an angel is that of continual immediate consecration to God. The holiness of an embodied spirit is that of a creature devoted to the service of God in secular occupations for one period of time, and in direct homage for another period of time. Man is finite, and while engaged in the former cannot attend with equal intensity to the latter. And while necessary to his own full happiness, it was

[1] Herbert.

requisite as a duty to his Maker that innocent man should offer a special weekly homage to his Creator, Benefactor, and King.

But passing from this period of man's history, as to which our information is scanty, and looking to the subsequent accounts of Sabbath observance, we find increasing light thrown on this subject.

It is a principal part of the duty of the Sabbath to attend the house of God, and engage in its services of praise, prayer, and religious instruction. Early in the history of mankind are Cain and Abel mentioned as bringing their offerings unto the Lord. This was "in process of time," or at the end of days. As the Sabbath was a divine ordinance, Abel, a good man, must have observed it, and Cain, who had not yet cast off all religion, must have been, as formerly remarked, too engrossed with the world to have any other day to spare for his worship. In the acceptance of Abel's offering and in the rejection of Cain's, we see the Divine approbation of worship that was according to appointment, and the Divine disapprobation of a service that wanted authority. The stated day and place had been attended to by Cain, else there would have been a will-worship which would be condemned, as well as his want of an offering of blood. Cain soon after went out from the presence of the Lord—not from God's presence absolutely, but from his gracious presence—the scene of Sabbaths and worship, and therefore of Divine favour. While men were few, the services of the Sabbath were comparatively private and domestic. But in course of time, it is said, "Then began men to call on the name of the Lord"—that is, more publicly to profess or invoke the name of the Lord. Under the Mosaic economy, there was the public worship of the tabernacle, temple, and synagogue on the Sabbath. And under Christianity, the followers of the Saviour are found meeting together on his day for sacred service.

Of the services connected with the house of God under both economies it will be proper here to present a brief enumeration.

Prayer was so much the practice of the ancient church that the house of God is called the house of prayer; and prayer was no ceremonial service which has passed away, for that house of prayer was to be for all people, and the first Christian churches "continued in prayer." Praise was another part of the public worship. "Praise waiteth for thee, O God, in Zion." "Enter his gates with thanksgiving, and his courts with praise." Christ sang a hymn with his disciples after the institution of the Supper. And his first followers "were continually in the temple, praising and blessing God." The reading and preaching of the Word are ordinances common to the Jewish and Christian Churches. In the former, "the prophets were read every Sabbath-day" (Acts xiii. 27), and "Moses of old time hath in every city them that preach him, being read in the synagogues every Sabbath-day" (Acts xv. 21). This, like praise and prayer, being a part of the worship of the synagogue, and not of a ceremonial character, is properly continued in the Christian Church; and we find Paul giving charges for the reading of his Epistles in the churches (1 Thess. v. 27; Col. iv. 16). Ezra not only read the Scriptures but gave the sense. When Christ ascended on high He gave pastors and teachers for the edifying of His body, the Church. The apostles preached on the day of Pentecost, at Troas, and wherever they went, on the Lord's day, though not exclusively on that day. One of them solemnly charges Timothy to preach the Word, and instructs him to commit this trust to faithful men who should be able to teach others. It is unnecessary to enlarge on an ordinance of which the Scriptures are so full. The offering of their substance for the service of God is another duty of the assembled worshippers on the Sabbath. By such contributions were the priests, and the poor, and the expenses of religious institutions provided for under the law. The Israelites were not to appear before the Lord empty, and Paul gives instructions to the churches to perform on the first day of the week a similar service. In the Christian Church baptism was to accompany instruction, and the Lord's Supper was administered on the Lord's day.

All these ordinances supposed not only persons to dispense them, but persons to wait on the dispensation and enjoy its benefits. In ancient times he was pronounced blessed who waited at the posts of Wisdom's gates. In New Testament times, it is said, "How shall they believe in him of whom they have not heard?" "Not forsaking the assembling of yourselves together, as the manner of some is; but exhorting one another, and so much the more as ye see the day approaching. For if we sin wilfully after that we have received the knowledge of the truth, there remaineth no more sacrifice for sins." The same danger was incurred at the very outset of religion. Cain's going out from the presence of the Lord led not only to his own ruin, but to that universal corruption of manners among his descendants, which, infecting also the descendants of Seth, brought on the flood that swept not merely all save one family from the land of the living; but millions, there is reason to fear, into the place of woe. And all indifference to the public means of grace and worship, evinced by total desertion of the sanctuary, or by occasional unnecessary absences, is an act of contempt to the great King of the Church, and proves that apostasy from the truth and from the ways of God has taken one of its most decided steps. The evil is the more criminal and injurious that, besides involving a personal neglect of the Creator and Redeemer, it is an omission of an important testimony to the world on behalf of religion. How becoming and profitable when "the whole Church comes together!" And there are those who are ever so regular in this matter that nothing but dire necessity prevails to make their seats empty. These are the persons who are likely to profit by the means of grace, and who, as far as this goes, strengthen the hands and encourage the hearts of the ministers of religion, rear orderly families, and build up the Church of God. One thing ought to be added as of no small importance. We refer to punctuality in keeping appointments with God, the want of which is surely very like an evidence of indifference to His service. They were men of a different spirit, of whom one of their number could say, "Now, therefore, are we all here present before God, to hear all things commanded thee of God."

> "Sundays observe; think when the bells do chime,
> 'Tis angels' music, therefore come not late:
> God then deals blessings. . . .
> Let vain or busy thoughts have there no part;
> Bring not thy plough, thy plots, thy pleasures thither.
> Christ purged His temple, so must thou thy heart."[1]

[1] Herbert's *Temple*.

CHAPTER V.

DUTIES OF THE SABBATH.

"I was in the Spirit on the Lord's day."

THE Sabbath is a day appropriated to the services of domestic piety. "It is the Sabbath of the Lord your God in all your dwellings."

Family worship is one of its duties. It is not the only day for that interesting and profitable service, for it is not the only day on which families stand in need of, and receive blessings from above; it is not the only day, therefore, on which it is proper and necessary for them to acknowledge their Benefactor. But certainly the Sabbath is a day on which it would be peculiarly inexcusable and criminal to omit such a duty, and on which it ought to be performed with special interest and care. The daily sacrifice under the law was doubled on the seventh day, and in the temple service of Ezekiel was to be tripled.[1] The fourth commandment is specially directed to heads of families, requiring them, as such, to keep the day holy. On that day "it is a good thing to show forth God's loving-kindness in the morning, and his faithfulness every night." Reason itself dictates this as the duty of every morning and evening. The heathen had their household gods. The members of families salute their head as they part at night and meet in the morning, and can they retire and assemble without any recognition of Him from whom their being and blessings are all derived? "The ox knoweth his owner, the ass his master's crib." "If I be a father, where is mine honour? If I be a master, where is my fear?" A service, so evidently to reason itself a duty and a privilege, required not

[1] Ezek. xlvi. 4, 5. Hence perhaps the practice, at one time more common, than, we presume, it now is, in Scotland, of the observance of worship in families three times on the Lord's day.

so much prescription, as directing and animating examples, promises to encourage its observance, and warnings to deter us from its omission. And we have all these. We see Job offering sacrifices continually for his children; Abraham, Isaac, and Jacob, as they journeyed with their families, building altars wherever they went; David, after engaging in public worship, returning to bless his household; Esther fasting with her maidens;[1] Daniel going into his house, and kneeling down and praying three times a day, as he had done aforetime, which was family prayer, since otherwise it could not be known, as it was, to be his custom; Cornelius fearing the Lord with his house, and praying in his house or with his household; above all, our Lord praying with his family of disciples, and teaching them how to pray. These are examples, and we have the following promise and warning: "If two of you shall agree on earth as touching anything that they shall ask, it shall be done for them of my Father which is in heaven." "Pour out thy wrath upon the families that call not on thy name." The worship of a family includes, with prayer, the melody of praise, and the devout reading of a portion of the sacred volume. "The voice of rejoicing" was heard of old "in the tabernacles of the righteous." Paul and Silas did not omit to sing praises to God even in a prison. Christians are thus commanded: "Let the word of Christ dwell in you richly in all wisdom; teaching and admonishing one another in psalms and hymns and spiritual songs, singing with grace in your hearts to the Lord." The religious instruction of families is the business of every day. It was no ceremonial rule which enjoined parents to speak of the Divine law to their children day by day, as they rose up and sat down, in the house and by the way—and to train up a child in the way it should go. This is the law of Christ in all ages. "Ye fathers, provoke not your children to wrath; but bring them up in the nurture and admonition of the Lord." "I know him"—Abraham—"that he will command his children and his household after him." Solomon bears testimony to his father's care, and walks in his steps.[2] Hezekiah appears to have had three great objects in view for his remaining life on recovery from

[1] "Fasting is always connected with prayer in Scripture."—M'Crie's *Esther*, p. 129.
[2] Prov. iv. 1-4.

sickness—walking humbly, the praise of God in the temple, and making known divine truth to his children. Timothy is congratulated on his unfeigned faith which dwelt first in his grandmother Lois and his mother Eunice, and on his having from a child known the holy Scriptures—by whom he was taught them it is unnecessary to say—"which were able to make him wise unto salvation through faith which is in Christ Jesus."[1] This "delightful task" cannot be too regularly and diligently performed during the week, and when thus attended to, answers the important end of showing the young that religion is a matter for every day. One day's instruction, too, would do little comparatively to inform the mind—one day's training would do little to check inclinations to evil, and to form habits of goodness. But the Lord's day presents more abundant time, leisure, opportunity, and calm for calling a family together, and ascertaining and promoting their progress in Divine knowledge. The sacredness of the day and its associations give additional impression to what is taught on it. It is worthy of notice that, after preaching to the multitude, our Lord taught his disciples in private.[2]

Conversation on "the great things of God's law" is another duty of a family on the Lord's day. The primitive Christians saluted each other every first day of the week with the words, "The Lord is risen." The conversation of Christ and his disciples related almost entirely to such subjects, even on common days. And on all the Sabbaths and Lord's days which the Redeemer spent on earth, and the conversation of which is recorded, his discourse, except a sentence or two relating to matters of necessity, bore on the things that concerned salvation and eternity, so that men were constrained on one of these days to wonder at "the gracious words that proceeded out of his mouth;" on another to say, "Blessed is he that shall eat bread in the kingdom of God;" and on a third to exclaim, "Did not our hearts burn within us, while he talked with us by the way, and while he opened to us the Scriptures?" And can that be restraint or bondage which the benevolent Saviour has taught us by his example? or can we be wrong when we walk in his steps? If the mind that was in him be in us, in proportion as it is so will grace, as it was with him, be

1 2 Tim. i. 5; iii. 15. 2 Mark iv. 34.

poured into our lips, for "out of the abundance of the heart the mouth speaketh." We err in not speaking more on common days of the subjects on which the Saviour delighted to expatiate. How mean are all our secular matters compared with the interests of the soul, the things of God's law, the great salvation, and a momentous eternity! David invited all that feared God to come near and he would tell them—about his wars, his prowess, and wealth? —no, but what God had done for his soul. To a commonplace question from a king, Jacob returned a pious and an instructive answer. Moses and Jethro sanctified their meeting by sacrifice. The men in Malachi's time who "spake often one to another," must have spoken of the name on which they "thought." Christ and Moses and Elias spake (some conceive that the day of the transfiguration was the Sabbath-day) of the decease which Jesus should accomplish at Jerusalem. "A word about Christ," said Ussher to a friend, "ere we part." And if this should be the most delightful, as it is incomparably the most important and glorious subject for every-day converse, how especially should the Sabbath be felt to be its appropriate season! Brainerd says of those who talked on the Sabbath of secular affairs, "Oh, I thought what a hell it would be to live with such men to eternity." And again, in reference to some irreligious characters: "All their discourse turned on the things of the world, which was no small exercise to my mind. Oh, what a hell it would be to spend an eternity with such men! Well might David say, I beheld the transgressors, and was grieved. But adored be God, *heaven* is a place into which no unclean thing enters."[1]

Personal devotion, and attention to the means of spiritual improvement in private, form a congenial work of the Lord's day. The study of God's word, communing with our own hearts, reflection on our past lives, the remembrance of our Creator, the consideration of the work of redemption, the anticipation of death, judgment, and eternity, and the pouring out of the soul in prayer to God, these are duties of every day, and specially of a day that affords so many facilities and reasons for such occupations. Said a good man, "O how I love thy law! it is my meditation all the day." To quote a psalm or song for the Sabbath-day: "It

[1] Edwards' *Works* (1839), vol. ii. pp. 334, 337.

is a good thing to give thanks unto the Lord, and to sing praises to thy name, O Most High. For thou, Lord, hast made me glad through thy work: I will triumph in the works of thy hands. O Lord, how great are thy works! and thy thoughts are very deep." The feelings of good men in anticipating and reflecting on the public services of the sanctuary are thus indicated: "I was glad when they said unto me, Let us go into the house of the Lord." "A day in thy courts is better than a thousand." "When I remember these things, I pour out my soul in me: for I had gone with the multitude; I went with them to the house of God, with the voice of joy and praise, with a multitude that kept holy day." The Sabbath, "the holy of the Lord," was to be called "honourable" and "a delight;" and as the command was that persons were on that day not to do their own ways or find their own pleasure, the ways they were to do were God's ways, and the pleasure they were to find was pleasure in him and in his service.

No pretence of personal or family duties can exempt from the obligations of public worship. But neither must public interfere with domestic, nor either with personal duties. If there is one class of engagements that are more than another an evidence to a person himself of his own piety, it is the class of personal duties, secret prayer, meditation, self-examination, and the study of the Scriptures, and of other holy books. And yet it is not the observance of certain practices that shows the character so much as the spirit in which they are performed. How is it with us in this respect? Are we seen by Him who seeth in secret retiring from society on the Lord's day, that we may converse with our spirits, and with their great and gracious Father and Redeemer? Alas! if it be not so, it is too certain that we are not "spiritually minded, which is life and peace, but carnally minded, which is death." Our attendance in the house of God in this case is a mere self-righteous task, instead of a work of gratitude and love; a cloak to hide us from ourselves, instead of a gratification and a profitable discipline of the heart.

It is in accordance with the nature and designs of the Sabbath to devote a portion of it to works of benevolence and mercy. And our Lord, who hath left us an example that we should walk in his steps, calls us by his own practice to these labours of love. On the Sabbath he cured a demoniac, and healed Simon's wife's mother of a fever. We find him afterwards restoring to strength on that day the man who had for thirty-eight years been impotent, and commanding him to take up his bed and walk. He next vindicates his disciples against the cavils of persons who had censured them for plucking some ears of corn, and rubbing them in their hands, for the purpose of satisfying their hunger. He further heals a man whose hand was withered, and gives sight to another who had been born blind, having previously prepared clay and applied it to the man's eyes. He looses from her infirmity a woman who had been for eighteen years bowed together by Satan, and cures a man of the dropsy. The apostle Paul, who says, Be ye followers of me, *even as I am of Christ*, and who remembered that God will have mercy and not sacrifice, abruptly ended his discourse at Troas, that he might employ means for restoring to life the young man, Eutychus, who, overpowered with sleep, had "fallen down from the third loft, and was taken up dead." "Pure religion and undefiled before God the Father" consists greatly in this, "to visit the fatherless and the widow in their affliction." "As we have opportunity," we are to "do good," temporal and spiritual, "unto all, especially to them who are of the household of faith." And what day is more seasonable for "doing well" than the day which was appointed to be a blessing to man, provided we, like the Saviour, attend to its claims on us personally, and do not unnecessarily postpone to the Sabbath-day what may and ought to be done before?

The law of the Sabbath requires more than the work which is limited to the day itself. It takes in all our time. It says, "Six days shalt thou labour, and do all thy work." Not that we are bound to spend the whole six days in secular work. Commands of moderation, of regard to health, and of daily acts of devotion and beneficence, come in to claim their share of attention, and to regulate a labour which becomes criminal and injurious by excess.[1] The importance of redeeming time in general, and of diligence in all our business, is frequently recognised in Scripture.

[1] Affirmativa ligant semper, sed non ad semper, negativa ligant semper et ad semper.

"Be thou diligent to know the state of thy flocks, and look well to thy herds." "Seest thou a man diligent in business? he shall stand before kings; he shall not stand before mean men." "Even when we were with you, this we commanded you, that if any would not work, neither should he eat." And besides many other important reasons for such conduct, it is necessary to the sanctification of the Sabbath. The more diligent and regular we are in the business of the preceding week, the more prepared are we for that day: prepared in having all despatched in such time as not to encroach on sacred hours, and prepared in a free mind, a clear conscience, and in that full, satisfactory exertion of body and spirit in the matters of this life, which stimulates a desire for a holy rest. "He that is not faithful in his calling, will never care to keep the Sabbath; and he that keepeth the Sabbath, will be diligent in his calling. Those two are like the two cherubim whose faces looked one towards another."[1]

Nor is this the only preparation necessary for gaining the object of the Sabbath. This day fits us for the work of the others; but the others do not so much fit us for the work of this. An abridgment of the labour of the six days, while necessary to the full enjoyment of the seventh even as a day of rest, is no less essential to the complete attainment of its end as a day of holy service and happiness. To be immersed in worldly cares and pleasures, up to the last hour of Saturday, is incompatible with a right observance of the first day of the week. In like manner, if the design of the Sabbath is to be fully answered, we must not immediately when it is over plunge into those occupations and pleasures which destroy the impressions, and prevent the benefit of the engagements of the day.

Another important duty connected with the Sabbath, and not confined to the day, is our promotion of its observance by others. "Thou shalt not do any work, thou, nor thy son, nor thy daughter, thy man-servant, nor thy maid-servant, nor thy cattle, nor thy stranger that is within thy gates." It is the duty of doing good in this particular respect to our neighbour and brother; it is the duty of "not suffering sin," the sin of breaking the fourth commandment, "upon our neighbour."

[1] Weemes's *Works*, vol. ii. p. 223.

In concluding this exposition of Sabbatic duties, we must advert briefly to two additional topics.

First, It is only through faith in Jesus Christ that we can be safe, obedient, or happy under this law. By the law, including this as well as other precepts, is the knowledge of sin. The apostle says, without excepting the fourth commandment, "We know that the law is spiritual," reaching to the thoughts, desires, and aims of the mind equally as to the words and acts of the life. Tried by this one statute, who is not convicted by it of sin in heart and in conduct? But the wages of sin is death. "Cursed is every one that continueth not in all things written in the book of the law to do them." "Christ Jesus," however, "came into the world to save sinners." "There is salvation in no other." "By him all that believe are justified." And not until we are united to Him by faith, pardoned and renewed in the spirit of our minds, can we have any pleasure in His law and day; not until we have his grace given to us shall we be disposed to keep any one of the Divine commandments. "How deeply sensible," says the Rev. Henry Venn, referring to the Sabbath, "should we be of our own inability to observe the day according to the will of God." Faith works by love, and, believing, we rejoice with unspeakable joy; love to the person and law of Him who died for us and rose again; joy on account of His atonement, resurrection, and glory, and in the assurance thereby inspired of a blessed immortality. This spirit was attainable and attained in ancient times. Right-hearted men calling the Sabbath a delight, the holy of the Lord, honourable, received the promise, "Then shalt thou delight thyself in God;" and seeing, like Abraham, the day of Christ, the day of His advent and reign, afar off, were glad; or beholding, like others, the stone which the builders rejected become the head of the corner, raised these notes of praise, "This is the day which the Lord hath made; we will rejoice and be glad in it."

Second, The Sabbath law is as sacred amidst the liberties of Christianity as it was under a severer economy, and enforced by yet more impressive sanctions. That its circumstances should be different was to be expected. They were not the same after the fall as they had been in Paradise, and they changed again when the seed of Abraham, from being only families and wanderers, had become a settled and numerous people. The Sabbath could no longer be a type when the things shadowed by it had come. It could no longer be sanctioned by a penalty of temporal death, because Christianity was not a theocracy. It could not offer rewards in the land of Palestine, for it is now part of a system, of which the field is the world. As time had made progress, and the natural had been succeeded by the moral creation—the deliverance from Egypt followed by the redemption from sin—it could now enter into relation to an event greater than even those of all preceding ages, and in adaptation to this event might be transferred from the seventh to the first day of the week,—to the day when the Redeemer rose from the dead, and entered on his glorious rest. None of these changes could affect the nature of the Sabbath as a day of rest—a day of holiness and service to the Lord. As the sun is the same orb that shone on the world yet unvisited by sin and unblasted by the curse, and now enlightens it as a revolted and blighted province of the universe—the same when rising brightly in the east, then enveloped in clouds, and then breaking forth in all its glory—so it is the same Sabbath which has cheered mankind in their conditions of original purity and subsequent depravation, and which, after varied fortunes, is now risen to its highest earthly honour. The Sabbath, like the sun, has never essentially changed. In ancient times, as really as now, it was a delight, and combined mercy with sanctity. Now, as well as then, it is not a day of idleness, or worldly business, or worldly pleasure. Has the removal of its penalty of death made its profanation less criminal than idolatry and disobedience to parents, which also no longer incur the forfeiture of the offender's life? Is redemption less holy and spiritual a subject of remembrance than creation? Because we are brought nearer to heaven, are we permitted to become more worldly—more occupied with amusements and vanities—less obliged to meditate, pray, and praise on the day which now more than ever borders on and resembles the days of eternity? This would be to say that God's moral law is mutable; that Christ came to relax it, to destroy foundations, to make man less just as to God's time, less holy in his service, and therefore less happy. What saith the New Testament? "That He would grant unto us, that we, being delivered out of the hand of our enemies, might serve Him without fear in holiness and righteousness before him all the days of our life." "Wherefore, receiving a kingdom which cannot be moved, let us have grace whereby we may serve God acceptably, with reverence and godly fear: for our God is a consuming fire." He is a consuming fire—a holy God—and His jealousy burns still round His sanctuary and His day. "For this cause," saith the apostle, referring to want of reverent regard to a Divine institution, "many are weak and sickly among you, and many sleep." "Not forsaking the assembling of yourselves together, as the manner of some is. For, if we sin wilfully after that we have received the knowledge of the truth, there remaineth no more sacrifice for sin, but a certain fearful looking for of judgment and fiery indignation which shall devour the adversaries."

CHAPTER VI.

DIVINE ESTIMATE OF THE IMPORTANCE OF THE SABBATH.

"And call the Sabbath a delight; the holy of the Lord, honourable."

THE importance of the Sabbath has been very fully considered as it appears in the light of Reason and Experience, but we have still to view the subject in the clearer light of Revelation.

First, A precedency of rank has been accorded to the Sabbatic institution under all the economies of religion. It appears to have been the earliest provision of a sacred kind made for the benefit of our first progenitors, preceding, even, the establishment of the covenant of life. It was, as Jeremy Taylor observes, the first point of religion that was settled after Israel came out of Egypt. It had a place assigned it, not only in the Decalogue, and thus above all political and ceremonial regulations, but in the first table of the law, which—summed up in love to God, "the first and great commandment"—lies at the foundation of all morality, and transgressions of which are more aggravated as subversive of all justice, order, and good in the universe; and as involving a more immediate aggression on the authority and person of the Lawgiver[1]—a ground on which idolatry and the desecration of sacred time are alike forbidden. Elevated thus highly by its place in the first table, the fourth commandment is honourable even as compared with the preceding three, not merely as connecting them with those of the second table, but as "the only commandment," to use the words of Dr. Winter Hamilton, "that *affirmatively* and *directly* requires duty to God." And as the original institution was contemporaneous with the completion of creation, so when the

[1] 1 Sam. ii. 25.

Saviour rose from the grave He by this act at once proved the perfection of the atonement, and reared its monument in a day consecrated to His service.

Second, No institution has been more frequently promulgated than the Sabbath. It is announced at the Creation. It is again stamped with the Divine authority in the sight of assembled Israel in the wilderness of Sin. In a few weeks thereafter—and that was certainly of no small moment which must so soon be repeated—we hear it proclaimed in thunder from Sinai. And once more does it come forth from the excellent glory with altered day and name, and with superadded purpose and honour, but in all its substantial import, when Christ rests after a consummated redemption. This frequency of formal intimation has never been accorded to any other statute of ancient or modern times. Was it thus cared for and protected as being a chief bulwark of religion, and yet a law the importance of which was not so obvious to the human mind, or the sacredness of which was peculiarly repugnant to the human heart? Whatever may be the reason, certain it is that its Author has taken special care to provide the means of securing to Himself the glory of His own day, and to man its blessings.

Third, The terms of legislation in reference to the institution have been unusually copious and explicit. All the commandments are expressed with a Divine comprehensiveness and perspicuity. But the fourth has some remarkable peculiarities. It is the largest and fullest of them all. It alone is prefaced by a solemn memento. Unlike the rest, it is presented in two forms, first positively, stating what we are to do, and then negatively, stating what we are not to do. Unlike all but the tenth, it is minute in the specification of the persons whom it concerns. The other precepts are not so enforced—most of them containing no arguments, and none of them so many as the fourth. No law could be stated more unequivocally, as none has been more frequently set forth. For all this particularity there was occasion. There is nothing that man feels to be a greater restraint on his sinful inclinations than a day devoted to God. There is nothing which he is more ready to abuse to the purposes of a lawless liberty under the pretence of its grant of a right to rest. There is nothing which has been more assailed and mutilated than the law of the Sabbath. And there is nothing so surely detrimental to a true religion as the success of its enemies in secularizing throughout a country, and wresting from men the day which has been provided as a principal means of guarding Divine truth, and advancing human piety.

Fourth, The Sabbath has been honoured by its relation to peculiarly important facts. The Creation was a great event—great in itself as the work of Divine wisdom, goodness, and power—and great as the theatre of other works no less wondrous. In honour of the Deity as the Author of this mighty work was the day of sacred rest appointed. Had man not sinned, Creation would have been, it is probable, the chief means of declaring the glory of the Divinity. In his fallen state, it does teach him those doctrines of the Divine existence and attributes which lie at the foundation of all religion. How important the institution which was designed and fitted to be to innocent man a perpetual remembrancer of his Maker, especially as a regularly recurring season for the more immediate contemplation of His perfections, and which is equally suited, as, from the want of all evidence of the revoking of the destination, it is obviously intended to answer the same purpose to man guilty and depraved! In the present condition of human beings, who dislike to "retain God in their knowledge," a weekly festival with religious instruction, is, still more than it was in their first estate, needed by them, that the Creator may not be forgotten in these His own dominions, and by us His own offspring.

There is another event of extensive and abiding importance—an event greater than the Creation, as it reveals more of the character of the Supreme Being, and secures a higher and more enduring, even an eternal happiness to man. Compared with Redemption, all other works are unworthy to "come into mind." To this completed work the Lord's day has been indissolubly linked.

Creation and Redemption are facts wherein Jehovah is seen in His full glory, and which it is most of all things for man's good to know and remember. What a sacred and benign lustre is thrown over the Sabbath by its association with such facts! how important the institution which has their memory intrusted to its keeping! With what reverence and interest should that day be regarded which brings us so immediately into the presence of the Almighty and the All-merciful!

Fifth, The manner in which the institution has been appointed and at different times proclaimed, is no less significant of its peculiar importance. The solemnities of Sinai did not signalize the law of the Sabbath more than the other nine commandments, but it says not a little on its behalf that it partook equally with the others of the awful and impressive testimonies which that occasion supplied to the glory of the moral law. But there were demonstrations of the sacred excellence of the institution which belonged exclusively to itself. What an august occasion for the expression of the Divine will when man had just come into being, and when his ears were saluted with the voice of his Maker calling him to remember his Creator on the first day of his youth, while the morning stars were singing together, and all the sons of God were shouting for joy! How stupendous the work which had just been finished! How noble the argument—Jehovah is resting from His work, and invites thee by His example to enter into His Divine rest! Then, looking forward over a space of two thousand and five hundred years, we see the Author of the Sabbath not only overcoming the evil of mistrustful men by giving them food from heaven, but glorifying His own day by miraculous works. Nor was this the wonder of a day. For forty years the uncorrupted manna gathered on the sixth day for the following day's use, and the preservation of the portion laid up beside the ark, gave special attestation and honour to the Sabbatic institution. Let us only add, that the manner in which the Lord's day was introduced, though more in accordance with a kingdom that "cometh not with observation," had a moral sublimity more truly august and impressive than had been the thunders and lightnings of Sinai. The Lord of glory, after condescending to suffer and die for men (what infinite love was this!) stepped from the tomb, and sanctified the day of His resurrection to be the Sabbath of Christianity, and a monument of His finished redemption. He too, as God did, rested from His work—appropriated the day as His own—and taught us by His example, and by His appearances in the midst of His disciples, that there still remained a rest to the people of God.

Sixth, The means which the Author of the Sabbath still more directly employs to maintain its authority and to enforce its observance, demonstrate its eminent sanctity and value.

The frequency and solemnity of His commands on the subject show how momentous the keeping of the day of holy rest was in the view of God. He had scarcely uttered His charge by Moses to Israel, that "no man was to go out of his place on the seventh day," when He pronounces in tones of thunder the law, "Remember the Sabbath-day, to keep it holy," which is soon followed up by large and repeated commands to the same effect: "Verily my Sabbaths ye shall keep—ye shall keep the Sabbath, therefore, for it is holy unto you—ye shall keep my Sabbaths and reverence my sanctuary—keep the Sabbath-day to sanctify it, as the Lord thy God hath commanded thee."

He remonstrates and complains, as well as enjoins. "How long refuse ye," were his words to Moses at the descent of the manna, "to keep my commandments and my laws?" "Then I contended with the nobles of Judah, and said unto them," were the words of Nehemiah from God, "What evil thing is this that ye do, and profane the Sabbath-day? Did not your fathers thus, and did not our God bring all this evil upon us, and upon this city? yet ye bring more wrath upon Israel by profaning the Sabbath." "Notwithstanding, the children rebelled against me—they polluted my Sabbaths."

He appeals to the dignity, reasonableness, and value of the institution. It is the holy Sabbath—a Sabbath to the Lord—a delight, the holy of the Lord, honourable—the Sabbath of the Lord thy God—the Lord's day. It is one day in seven. "See, for that the Lord hath *given* you the Sabbath." "Moreover also I *gave* them my Sabbaths, to be a sign between me and them, that they might know that I am the Lord that sanctify them—but my Sabbaths they greatly polluted." The Son of man is Lord *even* of the Sabbath.

He condescends to vindicate and interpret His law. He does so by the prophets. He does so especially by Jesus Christ. What clearer evidence could have been given of the Divine regard for the institution than the means employed to free it from the additions and corruptions by which man had disfigured and perverted the simple and gracious ordinance of heaven? "We may collect," says Howe, "there is an awful regard due to the Sabbath-day. When our Lord justifies the cure now wrought on their Sabbath only on this account, that it was an act of mercy toward a daughter of Abraham; by the exception of such a case he strengthens the general rule, and intimates so holy a day should not, upon light occasions, be otherwise employed than for the proper end of its appointment. Though our day be not the same, the business of it, in great part, is."[1]

He warns by words of threatening and acts of retribution. The law which assigned death as the punishment of Sabbath-breaking was obligatory only during the time and within the local limits of the theocracy. Nor was this the only offence which incurred among the Jews the awful penalty. Adultery, murder, and stubborn disobedience to parents were capital crimes. The transgression even of certain ceremonial requirements involved the forfeiture of life. But, while this punishment of the Sabbath-breaker teaches to all ages and places the lesson that his sin was no trifle, there is something in the enactment of the law in the matter, and in the only recorded instance of its execution, which serves to impress our minds with the conviction that a peculiar enormity attached to the infraction of the fourth commandment. "Ye shall keep the Sabbath, therefore, for it is holy unto you. Every one that defileth it shall be put to death; for whosoever doeth any work therein, that soul shall be cut off from among his people. Six days may work be done; but in the seventh is the Sabbath of rest, holy to the Lord, whosoever doeth any work in the Sabbath-day, he shall surely be put to death."[2] "And while the children of Israel were in the wilderness, they found a man that gathered sticks upon the Sabbath-day. And they that found him gathering sticks brought him unto Moses and Aaron, and unto all the congregation. And they put him in ward, because it was not declared what should be done to him. And the Lord said unto Moses, The man shall be surely put to death: all the congregation shall stone him with stones without the camp. And all the

1 On Luke xiii. 16. *Works*, Lond. (1836), p. 1010.

2 Ex. xxxi. 14, 15.

congregation brought him without the camp, and stoned him with stones, and he died; as the Lord commanded Moses."[1] Whether similar cases occurred we are not informed. But death under the direction of the judicial law was not the only way in which the punishment of offences against the Sabbath was threatened and visited. That law contemplated, with the remarkable exception of the case of suspected conjugal infidelity, only overt acts. Israel, however, were under other laws, which took cognizance of the heart, and of many actions which, though not amenable to the civil jurisdiction, subjected offenders to the Divine displeasure, expressed in various forms of calamity. And no sin appears to have called forth more comminations and judgments than that of contemning sacred institutions, particularly the Sabbath. Jehovah is represented as lifting up his hand to that people in the wilderness, that he would not bring them into the land which he had given them, flowing with milk and honey, which is the glory of all lands, because they despised his judgments, and walked not in his statutes, but polluted his Sabbaths, for their hearts went after their idols. This determination was fulfilled in the case of many, but his eye spared others, so that he did not make an end of them in the wilderness. When, after renewing his covenant with them, and charging them to hallow his Sabbaths, they proved disobedient, and polluted his Sabbaths, he said he would pour out his fury upon them to accomplish his anger against them in the wilderness; but withdrew his hand, and wrought for his name's sake that it should not be dishonoured in the sight of the heathen, in whose sight he had brought them forth. And again, he lifted up his hand in the wilderness, that he would scatter them among the heathen and disperse them through the countries, because they had not executed his judgments, but had despised his statutes, and polluted his Sabbaths, and their eyes were after their fathers' idols. This last threatening, which had been uttered in the days of Moses, had begun to be carried into effect when the prophet Ezekiel thus recorded it. To these attestations of the solemn importance of the Sabbath, let us add another from the Old Testament Scriptures. It appears, from a passage in the prophecies of Jeremiah, that the welfare and even the continued existence of

[1] Numb. xv. 32-36.

the Jewish State were suspended on the observance by the people of that institution; for he declares, that if they hallowed it, and did no work therein, the nation should in the highest measure prosper, and the city remain for ever, but that if they would not hearken unto God to hallow the Sabbath-day, and not to bear a burden, even entering in at the gates of Jerusalem on the Sabbath-day, then should he kindle a fire in the gates thereof, which should devour the palaces of Jerusalem, and not be quenched. Although we had no evidence of the fulfilment of this denunciation, its utterance might suffice to convince us that the institution must have been precious in God's sight, which was so fenced round against its foes by the terrors of devouring fire and of national ruin. But the words of the prophet were verified in the destruction of Jerusalem by the Romans, with fire, and on the Sabbath-day.

Nor are equally solemn proofs of the Divine respect for holy seasons and appointments wanting under Christianity. This benignest form of true religion was introduced with "just judgments on wicked men." As it advanced, the abuse of a Divine institution was followed by sickness and death. It was to avowed Christians that the warning was addressed: "Not forsaking the assembling of yourselves together, as the manner of some is; but exhorting one another; and so much the more as ye see the day approaching. For if we sin wilfully after that we have received the knowledge of the truth, there remaineth no more sacrifice for sins, but a certain fearful looking for of judgment and fiery indignation, which shall devour the adversaries. He that despised Moses' law died without mercy under two or three witnesses; of how much sorer punishment, suppose ye, shall he be thought worthy, who hath trodden under foot the Son of God, and hath counted the blood of the covenant, wherewith he was sanctified, an unholy thing, and hath done despite unto the Spirit of grace? It is a fearful thing to fall into the hands of the living God."[1] These dread words proclaim that Christianity has its penalties no less than had Judaism—penalties the more fatal that they are spiritual and lasting; that "our God is a consuming fire," who will be sanctified in "them that come nigh" him, as certainly as when for offering strange fire the sons of Aaron "died before the

[1] Heb. x. 25-31.

Lord," or when he swore by his excellency that he would not forget their works who in the time of Amos wearied of his Sabbath, but would send them a famine of his word, with other calamities; and that he is as resolved to assert the claims of his forsaken institutions and assemblies now as when the uncircumcised were doomed to excision from their people. It is extremely wicked for poor mortals to judge their fellow-men, to deal out disaster according to their own views and passions, and not to unite charity and mercy towards others with severity against their own misdeeds. But it would, on the other hand, be a base betrayal of truth, and a cowardly shrinking from duty, to evade the perception and avowal that peculiar retributions are in our own day awarded to the profaners of the Sabbath. It *must be* so, unless God has ceased to rule the world, and to maintain the authority of his law. It *is* so, for although there is no death by the laws of nations to such men, they themselves, in untold numbers, have confessed that their sin has found them out, and brought them to this doom. It *is* so, for although no voice from heaven says to particular classes or individuals as to the Jews, "I will visit you with this or that penalty for contempt of my day;" or, after the infliction, "This was owing to your profanation of the Sabbath," yet the principles of the Divine government remain the same—the Divine menaces against the offence are still on record—the same causes produce their wonted effects—the practice abounds, and two classes of facts are manifest—the one, calamitous events which point as with the finger to their guilty cause; the other, those natural consequences of the sin—the increased irreligion, the immorality, the abbreviated life, and other evils which it requires a considerable portion of this volume to present even in an imperfect outline, and which have there been proved to prevail to a large extent in the measure of a personal, domestic, and national disregard for the Sabbatic institution. And let it not be presumed, because no injury seems to attend such a course in the present state, that the Divine word, and the evidence for the importance of the institution, have in any degree failed. For there is reserved a perfect retribution to individuals in a future world, and the words lately cited direct our thoughts to a consummation of punishment there, which completes the proof from the penal sanctions of the Sabbath, that no "common thing" is trampled upon, and no venial fault committed, when men forsake the assembling of themselves together on the day, and for the worship, of the Almighty.

But the Sabbath is recommended by promises of good as well as guarded by penalties. Its Author, at its original institution, pronounced on it a benediction which He has never recalled, but again and again renewed. This benediction was repeated in the most impressive manner from Sinai. And prophets were commissioned to unfold the boon. "Thus saith the Lord," by Isaiah, "Keep ye judgment, and do justice: for my salvation is near to come, and my righteousness to be revealed. Blessed is the man that doeth this, and the son of man that layeth hold on it; that keepeth the Sabbath from polluting it, and keepeth his hand from doing any evil. Neither let the son of the stranger, that hath joined himself to the Lord, speak, saying, The Lord hath utterly separated me from his people: neither let the eunuch say, Behold I am a dry tree. For thus saith the Lord unto the eunuchs that keep my Sabbaths, and choose the things that please me, and take hold of my covenant; even unto them will I give in mine house, and within my walls, a place and a name better than of sons and of daughters: I will give them an everlasting name, that shall not be cut off. Also the sons of the stranger, that join themselves to the Lord, to serve him, and to love the name of the Lord, to be his servants, every one that keepeth the Sabbath from polluting it, and taketh hold of my covenant; even them will I bring to my holy mountain, and make them joyful in my house of prayer: their burnt-offerings and their sacrifices shall be accepted upon mine altar; for mine house shall be called an house of prayer for all people."[1] The same prophet is directed to describe the duties of the Sabbath, and the happiness and honour which the performance of them insures, in these remarkable terms: "If thou turn away thy foot from the Sabbath, from doing thy pleasure on my holy day; and call the Sabbath a delight, the holy of the Lord, honourable; and shalt honour him, not doing thine own ways, nor finding thine own pleasure, nor speaking thine own words: Then shalt thou delight thyself in the

[1] Isaiah lvi. 1-7.

Lord; and I will cause thee to ride upon the high places of the earth, and feed thee with the heritage of Jacob thy father: for the mouth of the Lord hath spoken it."[1] Similar is the testimony of the prophet Jeremiah: "And it shall come to pass, if ye diligently hearken unto me, saith the Lord, to bring in no burden through the gates of this city on the Sabbath-day, but hallow the Sabbath-day, to do no work therein; then shall there enter into the gates of this city kings and princes sitting upon the throne of David, riding in chariots and on horses, they, and their princes, the men of Judah, and the inhabitants of Jerusalem, and this city shall remain for ever. And they shall come from the cities of Judah, and from the places about Jerusalem, and from the land of Benjamin, and from the plain, and from the mountains, and from the south, bringing burnt-offerings, and sacrifices, and meat-offerings, and incense, and bringing sacrifices of praise, unto the house of the Lord."[2] And judging from such promises, made to individuals and to classes—to Gentiles and Jews—the following character of the most glorious era in the history of this earth is to be viewed as not the least of the causes of that glory: "And it shall come to pass, that from one Sabbath to another, shall all flesh come to worship before me, saith the Lord."[3]

Finally, The Sabbath is distinguished by its antiquity and duration.

It is nearly as old as the creation. On the sixth day of time that work was completed, and its Author stamped the following day with his signature, in perpetual memory of Himself as the Being by whose underived wisdom the vast undertaking was devised—by whose uncaused power it was achieved. Adam awoke from his first sleep to behold the light of the earliest Sabbath-day. Almost contemporaneous with the appointment of marriage, it might be said of the corrupters of the one as it was to the perverters of the other, "From the beginning it was not so." Age, indeed, does not consecrate evil or magnify a trifle, but it imparts interest to what is innocent, and venerableness to what is great and good. We are commanded to ask for the old paths; and where shall we find older paths than the law of the Sabbath, and the way of salvation through the seed of the woman? The hoary

[1] Isaiah lviii. 13, 14. [2] Jer. xvii. 24-26. [3] Isaiah lxvi. 23.

head is a crown of glory when found in the way of righteousness. Our Magna Charta is an ancient guarantee of civil rights, but neither in antiquity, nor in its own nature and extent, can it for a moment vie with the world-old and world-wide charter of a free seventh day, which the Creator hath given to the human race for all time. How many changes and catastrophes has it survived! Kingdoms have, in multiplied instances, risen and fallen. Systems of opinion on all subjects have succeeded each other in constant succession. The institutions of man have perished one after another. Religious ordinances themselves have fulfilled their temporary destinies and disappeared. But the Sabbath, like the perpetual hills, has outlasted the patriarchal altars, witnessed the decay of all other sacred monuments, survived the tabernacle, temples, and sacrifices of a gorgeous ritual, and, after the various fortunes of eighteen Christian centuries, is still as full of vitality and vigour as at any former period of its history. And we have reason to believe that, like the ordinances of heaven, it will live through all the ages of time. Nor will it end when the sun has ceased to run its course. Then, indeed, it will no more bless the men who shall be found to have preferred death to life—a lawless freedom to a holy rest. But there will "remain a rest to the people of God," and for them the Sabbath will begin a brighter career, as the one day—the unchanging holy day of eternity.

CHAPTER VII.

THE SABBATISM OF HEAVEN.

"There remaineth therefore a rest to the people of God."

In the preceding part of this volume, the Sabbath has been considered as a law and ordinance belonging to the present state. It is solely in this point of view that writers for the most part regard it. The Sabbatism of a future world, however, is a doctrine which is not only favoured by the analogy of the Divine procedure hitherto, but revealed in the Holy Scriptures.

First, we have the doctrine announced in the words of our motto, which occur in Heb. iv. 9. In this chapter, according to the learned and profound Owen, three periods, with three great works, having each its Divine rest and its memorial day for men, are mentioned. The first is the time when the Almighty finished His work of creation, rested and was refreshed, and sanctified and blessed the seventh day. The second is the period when He redeemed the children of Israel from Egyptian bondage. Of this work it is said: "I am the Lord thy God, that divided the sea, whose waters roared: the Lord of Hosts is his name. And I have put my words in thy mouth, and I have covered thee in the shadow of mine hand, that I may plant the heavens and lay the foundations of the earth, and say unto Zion, Thou art my people" (Isa. li. 15, 16). On that occasion, too, Jehovah rested, saying, "This is my rest, and here will I dwell," and though some of those who were invited to enter into His rest, fell short of it and died in the wilderness, others participated in the Divine blessing, enjoying the inheritance of the promised land. The day selected for the celebration of the rest of God in this case was the old seventh day. "The time for the change of the day was not yet come, for this work was but preparatory for a greater." The third period was coincident with the accomplishment by Jesus Christ of human redemption. The work itself, the rest of the Saviour, and the consequent resting-day for men, are all expressed in these words : "There remaineth therefore a rest"—the keeping of a Sabbath—"to the people of God. For he that is entered into his rest, he also hath ceased from his own works, as God did from his." The rest into which the Redeemer entered was not His lying in the grave, for this was part of his humiliation and subjection to the curse of the law, but His rising from the dead on the third day, for then He began to rest from His labours, and to receive the reward of His work—and that third day—the first day of the week—fitly became the day of celebration in His kingdom. But this is the kingdom of heaven—the kingdom not only of grace, but of glory—an everlasting kingdom. And "there remaineth therefore a rest to the people of God"—a Sabbatism suited not only to the church on earth, but to the church in heaven.

Accordingly, second, the happiness of a future state, as unfolded in the Word of God, includes the great elements of a Sabbath day.

Rest is one of these elements. At death the spirits of the just "rest from their labours"—they "enter into peace." But the rest of a spirit can neither on earth nor in heaven be inaction. It is, in the case of a holy being, rest, as opposed not to activity, but to hurry, distraction, toil, uneasiness. There is accordingly service—the immediate service of God—as well as rest. "His servants shall serve him." They "rest not day and night, saying, Holy, holy, holy, Lord God Almighty, which was, and is, and is to come." There is the commemoration of the same works as on earth. Creation is celebrated. "The four-and-twenty elders fall down before him that sat on the throne, and worship him that liveth for ever and ever, and cast their crowns before the throne, saying, Thou art worthy, O Lord, to receive glory, and honour, and power ; for thou hast created all things, and for thy pleasure they are, and were created." Redemption is eminently the subject of remembrance and praise. "The four living creatures and four-and-twenty elders fell down before the Lamb, having every one of them harps and golden vials full of odours, which are the prayers of saints. And they sung a new song, saying, Thou art worthy to take the book, and to open the seals thereof: for thou wast slain, and hast redeemed us to God by thy blood out of every kindred, and tongue, and people, and nation; and hast made us unto our God kings and priests: and we shall reign on the earth." One great end of a day of rest is to afford the means of public worship. Such is the worship which everywhere pervades the record of celestial occupations. The leisure of the weekly holy day was designed also to enable us to receive religious instruction, and to engage in sacred studies. And in another world there appears to be required the opportunity of a perpetual Sabbath for the same object. It seems impossible to bring a created being to a state of perfection in knowledge at which it could be said that further he could not advance. It seems necessary to the very nature of a rational creature to grow, whether it be in good or in evil. God alone is unchangeably and absolutely perfect in intelligence. The angels, who have ever beheld the face of God, are still learners. It was the one desire of a good man to dwell in the house of the Lord all the days of his life, that he might behold His beauty and inquire in His temple. His confident hope was thus expressed, "As for me, I will behold thy face in righteousness: I shall be satisfied, when I awake, with thy likeness." And one object of the Saviour's desire that His followers might be with Him in heaven was, that they might behold His glory. If when they behold in a glass the glory of the Lord they are changed into His image from glory to glory, much more when they see no longer through a glass darkly, but face to face. His servants shall serve Him, and they shall see His face. The performance of benevolent acts is peculiarly appropriate to the day of rest, and is even enjoined in Scripture (1 Cor. xvi. 1, 2). The law of earth, "Thou shalt love thy neighbour as thyself," is also the law of heaven. Charity or love is greater than either faith or hope, and never faileth. And in the heavenly state it must express itself, though not in reproof, or in words of condolence, or in acts of relief, yet in the benignant eye, in the affectionate voice, in the animating song, in the communication of intelligence, in offices of kindness and friendship. The penitence of a sinner, the conversion of the kingdoms of this world into the kingdoms of Christ, the casting out of the great dragon, that old serpent, called the Devil and Satan, and the destruction of Babylon, are represented in the sacred volume as spreading joy and inspiring songs of praise among the inhabitants of heaven. The seraphim do not indulge solitary and selfish joys, but cry one to another, Holy, holy, holy is the Lord of hosts : the whole earth is full of His glory. And in the same spirit the nations of them that are saved rejoice in a common salvation, and above all things, rejoice in the highness of their Lord and Saviour. The Sabbath-day on earth is a time consecrated entirely to God, and such, as appears from words already cited, is the Sabbath of heaven. And as there is one service in particular in which Christians feel themselves on the Lord's day to be brought to the gate of heaven, we find that if one thing more than another is the distinction of the engagements and happiness of eternity, it is the celebration of the decease which was accomplished at Jerusalem.

Third, the Sabbath remaining substantially unchanged, attains its highest honours in the world above. There it must in all time have been known and prized as an instrument of good on earth, but its value in this aspect will then only be fully seen when its services, as a means of bringing many sons to glory, have been completed. When a building has been finished, the scaffolding is taken down and forgotten. It is not so when the copestone is laid on the house of God. The great means of its erection was the obedience unto death of Jesus Christ ; and this, we find, divides the interest and the praise of heaven with the agency of Him who sitteth upon the throne (Rev. vii. 10). Even creatures themselves, although only serviceable as they have received grace and blessing from the Divine Saviour, are acknowledged and rewarded as the instruments of turning many to righteousness. And the Sabbath, too, receives an honour which is not conferred on merely positive institutions, inasmuch as it is received into the economy of heaven—the service of eternity. The Sabbatic good to which Dr. Croly in the following sentence refers, may be expected to be in a large measure attained in a golden age awaiting the earth, but its perfect realization is reserved for the new heavens and the new earth : "As the full possession of providential blessings is given only to the completeness of human obedience, it is probable that neither the natural results nor the full knowledge of the Sabbath have ever yet been enjoyed by the fallen race of mankind."[1]

In the glorious rest of the Saviour, the people of God participate when they sit down with Him on his throne. Let these words suffice to describe their condition : "God shall wipe away all tears from their eyes ; and there shall be no more death, neither sorrow, nor crying neither shall there be any more pain : for the former things are passed away. There shall be no more curse. There shall be no night there ; and they need no candle, neither light of the sun ; for the Lord God giveth them light : and they shall reign for ever and ever" (Rev. xxi. 4 ; xxii. 3, 5).

Their worship is perfect. They are without fault. "These are they which came out of great tribulation, and have washed their robes, and made them white in the blood of the Lamb. Therefore are they before the throne of God, and serve him day and night in his temple : and he that sitteth on the throne shall dwell among them" (Rev. vii. 14, 15). It has been said that praise on earth is the chief emblem of the occupations of eternity.

> "All that we know o' the saints above,
> Is that they sing and that they love."

Reading, preaching, prayer in some of its parts, and certain other forms of devotion, are superseded, but praise remains—that disinterested, delightful employment of the angels, and of every man who has had the enmity and selfishness of his heart thawed by the Divine grace and love, and been formed in this way to show forth God's praise. "The ransomed of the Lord shall return and come to Zion with songs and everlasting joy upon their heads." The following incident gives some idea of what praise should be :—A prayer-meeting in the south of Scotland was scattered by persecution, which consigned some to the horrors of Dunnottar Castle, and banished others to foreign parts. At the Revolution, the survivors re-assembled for prayer, and began the devotions of the evening with the Psalm—

> "Had not the Lord been on our side,
> May Israel now say ;
> Had not the Lord been on our side,
> When men rose us to slay ;

[1] *Divine Origin and Obligation of the Sabbath*, p. 3.

They had us swallowed quick, when as
Their wrath 'gainst us did flame:
Waters had covered us, our soul
Had sunk beneath the stream."

A person who was present on that occasion, a relation of my informant, declared, "Such singing I never heard before, and expect never to hear again till I get to heaven." Praise must have been a chief part of the devotion of Paradise, and would, we may conceive, have been the employment of unfallen men for ever. But how superior the praises of a countless host to those of Eden, and how has redemption, with its superadded themes, its new songs, and, we may add, the higher tone of sentiment which it has inspired, improved the melody! The account of the universal anthem (Rev. v. 9-14) is unspeakably sublime; but for a still nobler swell of praise we must look forward to the day of complete redemption. Who would not desire to hear that music? rather—for to hear it from hell would but add to our misery—who would not wish to "bear some humble part in that immortal song?"

Heaven's commemoration of great events is all that God would have it to be. Here material objects are employed and are necessary to conduct our thoughts and feelings to the Unseen, and to preserve the remembrance of redemption. Bread and wine must be used. And these emblems are few, simple, and expressive. But there is no need of such things in a spiritual temple, where God is seen face to face, where stands "a Lamb as it had been slain," and where the perfected understanding, memory, and heart are delightfully and exclusively devoted to the highest subjects. The glass is unnecessary when we clearly see the object—the streams are superseded when we are at the fountain. How undistracted, spiritual, and pure must be the devotions and celebrations of heaven, when perfect minds will be directly employed on Divine and eternal things!

The investigation of truth is not peculiar to the final condition of "the people of God," but it is then conducted under the best auspices. The first man had the garden to keep and dress, and was thus prevented from devoting himself entirely to the contemplation of spiritual objects. He had not God as the object of direct vision, or Christ as the manifestation of the Divine perfections to behold, or the whole universe to study, or the immediate teaching of Him who is the Light of the world. The redeemed, again, had on earth many disadvantages for inquiry, in an encumbering body, which required so much attention, and by its frailty and cares interrupted the exercises of the mind—in evil propensities, which diverted the spirit from its proper engagements, and darkened its views—in the many surrounding things which often unprofitably occupied the time—and in a thousand avocations which exhausted the strength without having any connexion with the improvement of the intellectual faculties. The spirits of the just themselves are inferior in this matter to those who after the resurrection inhabit the heavenly world, in not having the glorified organs of sense by which to communicate with their appropriate objects, and in having neither the completed mystery of God, nor the full assembly of holy beings to call forth and sustain their noblest energies. From all this we may see how abundant are the advantages which men who are delivered in soul and body from all evil must have for prosecuting the search of truth in the eternal world. And how superior their pursuits to all others, even to many that were laudable and necessary in this life! They themselves were in many instances, through their connexion with the earth, and from an impaired bodily constitution, subjected to employments which are not congenial to the high faculties and sanctified desires of the mind. Much of their time and strength was expended on the body, on the acquisition of food and raiment, health and perishing objects—engagements which, though necessary, and when properly attended to profitable to men, and honouring to God, are yet peculiar to a state of things induced by sin, and are not in themselves worthy of the origin and capacities of a spiritual and immortal being. But now they rest from all such labours, and are entirely occupied with services suited to their powers and characters—services such as angels engage in, and tending to bring them near to God, as well as to assimilate their nature to His. The pursuits of the philosopher are despised by the ignorant, and by the men who place all value in houses and lands, trade and money. But as mind is more excellent than matter, and as it is from the former that all other things receive direction, improvement, and importance, so are the labours of the philosopher worthy and useful above those of the merchant, husbandman, and mechanic. Still higher in the scale are the studies and aims of the man of God. So thought David when he longed to appear before God, preferred a day in His courts to a thousand, and would have rejoiced, as we have already remarked, to spend all the days of his life in the house of God, beholding His beauty and inquiring in His temple. So judged the apostle Paul, who counted everything but loss for the excellency of the knowledge of Jesus Christ his Lord. So decided the Son of God when He showed His preference of Mary's devout attention to His instructions above Martha's bustling care about His personal comfort, and pronounced the object of Mary's choice to be the good part—the one thing needful. And from the brief but pregnant notices furnished in the Scriptures respecting the studies and tastes of holy, happy angels, and glorified men, we find their spirit to be in unison with that of David, that of Paul, and that of their Lord—in other words, that they have none in heaven but God, that there is none upon earth that they desire beside Him, that He is their portion for ever, and that whether they study, converse, or sing, or whatsoever they do, they do all to His glory.

The holiness and benevolence of heaven are of the most exalted order. The Sabbath is "the holy of the Lord"—a day which is to be kept holy—on which we are required to honour Him, not doing our own ways, or finding our own pleasure, or speaking our own words, a day for the exercise of loving-kindness, and to be called a delight. In heaven, the day is sacredly observed by the inhabitants. They are in the fear of the Lord all the day long. How deep were their reverence of Him and their humility even on earth—Isaiah and Job for example! But how much more purely and powerfully, though without any consciousness of vileness, do these feelings operate in the hearts of the redeemed before the throne, who know so much of the sanctity and majesty of God! They fall down before Him! They cast their crowns before the throne. Then what ardent love and fervent gratitude! When the day of judgment has fully disclosed the destinies of mankind, and heaven has received the whole company of the blessed; when the work of redemption in all its parts is finished, Christ will be glorified in his saints, and admired in all them that believe. To sit down at the feast of eternity, a feast prepared from the foundation of the world, and prepared at such an expense—a feast enjoyed in security, while many are "without," exposed to all the fury of the tempest of Divine indignation—how glowing must be their love and gratitude to the Father who chose them, to the Son who bought them, to the Spirit who qualified them for these everlasting joys! Their enlarged knowledge and deepened humility have increased their sense of obligation, and their growing intelligence and lowliness of mind will increase it for ever. Every recollection of sin, every thought of the misery of the lost, every new view of the greatness and purity and goodness of God their Saviour will impart additional warmth to the ardour of their love and to the fervour of their thankfulness.

It is God who is the judge of what is the most honourable employment for His rational creatures, and it is to the highest and last state of His servants as appointed and made known by Him that we are to look for a model. It is heaven that should give law to earth, not earth to heaven. "Thy will be done on earth even as it is done in heaven," is a petition which Christ has taught us to offer at the throne of grace. The exercises of patience, of contrition, of well-doing to the ignorant, the poor, the afflicted, the dying, noble as they are on earth, are superseded in heaven, but this impairs not the glory of heaven's occupations. It will be better even here when one shall not need to say to his neighbour, Know the Lord. The celebration of victory is better than the battle. Who but a fool would wish the times of temptation, ignorance, and conquest to return? Who but a mere animal would desire the Elysium of paganism or the paradise of Mohammed? Who but a poor self-seeker, an earth-worm, would consider an existence spent in accumulating lore or money to be the glory or happiness of man? Who but a devil would deem it "better to reign in hell than serve in heaven?" The service of heaven is itself to reign. "His servants shall serve him"—and "they shall reign for ever and ever." To serve—by loving supremely Him who is altogether lovely—by increasing in the knowledge of Him who comprehends in Himself all that is true, great, and good—and by praising Him who alone is excellent, and the Author of all being and happiness—this is the high end of man's existence attained—this is liberty, this is honour, this is blessedness, this is perfection.

It is a characteristic of the Sabbath that it is the means of manifold blessings, and this distinction is eminently displayed in heaven. The institution, as has been amply shown, strewed its earthly path with every variety of good, and would have conferred a much greater amount of benefit but for mistaken friends who misrepresented its character and detracted from its authority—but for real enemies who rejected the doctrine of its Divine origin and obligation, or disobeyed its law. Even on earth it was the means of forming a character and bestowing a happiness, of which the holiness and bliss of heaven are the consummation. And its rest, worship, commemorations, studies, and employments *there* will yield, in continually growing amount, the fruits of righteousness and joy. For all this it has facilities formerly unknown—facilities in the perfect unanimity of the inhabitants respecting its claims and character—in the absence of all internal and outward hinderances to its observance—in the place itself, where, dwelling on high and in a quiet habitation, they enjoy perfect security and peace—and where they not only have the instructive, animating society of all the holy angels and all good men, but walk in the light of that temple of which it is said, "The glory of God did lighten it, and the Lamb is the light thereof."

But it crowns the glory of the Sabbath in heaven, that it is eternal. This is that greatest Sabbath which has no evening.[1] Its rest, its worship, its society, its commemorations, its advancing knowledge, holiness, and happiness, are to be without end. Spirits replenished with Divine influence, and having bodies endowed with undecaying health and strength, will be occupied in services which produce no weariness, and enjoy pleasures which never pall. The thought, beyond expression great, is gloomy to "men of the world, who have their portion in this life," but transporting to such as David, who expected to "dwell in the house of the Lord for ever," and to "sing praises to God while he had any being,"—to such too, as the apostle, who felt that he could administer no stronger consolation to sorrowing Christians than to say,—"and so shall we ever be with the Lord."

1 *Sabbathum maximum, non habens vesperam.*—August. *De Civit. Dei*, cap. 30.

EVIDENCE FROM HISTORY FOR A WEEKLY DAY OF REST AND WORSHIP.

TRACES OF SEPTENARY INSTITUTIONS AMONG PAGAN NATIONS.

There are certain observances which have prevailed to a wide extent, as well as from an early period, in the heathen world, and which, as bearing an affinity greater or less to the Sabbatic institution, may be considered as affording striking testimony to its primæval origin. These are threefold : the appropriation of periodical days to religion and rest from ordinary labour—the division of time into weeks—and the ascription of special importance to the septenary number.

Traces of sacred days of some sort, though varying in frequency in different countries, may be discovered in many Pagan nations, the exceptions being limited to certain tribes sunk, like the aborigines of New Holland, to a very low point in the social scale.

The Phœnicians, according to Porphyry, "consecrated the seventh day as holy."[1] Before Mohammed's time, the Saracens kept their Sabbath on Friday, and from them he and his followers adopted the custom.[2] It is stated by Purchas, that the natives of Pegu had a weekly day on which they assembled to receive instruction, from a class of men appointed for the purpose.[3] The Pagan Slavonians held a weekly festival.[4] In the greater part of Guinea, the seventh day—Tuesday—is set apart to religious worship.[5]

[1] Euseb. *Præpar. Evang.* lib. i. c. 9. [2] Purchas's *Pilgrimage*, p. 264. [3] *Ibid.* p. 574.
[4] Helmoldus, cited by Ussher. *The Judgment of the late Archbishop of Armagh*, pp. 79, 80.
[5] Hurd's *Religious Rites*, etc. (1812), p. 423. Bell's *Geography*, iv. 30.

It would appear that the Chinese, who have now no Sabbath, at one time honoured the seventh day of the week.[1]

Among the ancient Persians, the eighth was the festal day, the calendar of the Magi having this day marked in it as holy.[2] The old Roman week consisted of eight days, and every eighth day was specially devoted to religious and other public purposes, under the name Nonæ or Nundinæ, so called from the Roman practice of adding the two nundinæ to the seven intervening and ordinary days; in the same way as in Germany and in our own country, the expression, "eight days," is used for a week, and as the French and Italians call a fortnight *quinze jours*, and *quindici giorni*, respectively.[3] The people of Old Calabar observe an eighth-day Sabbath, termed Aqua-erere.[4] Humboldt refers to an ancient law which required the Peruvians to work eight consecutive days, and to rest on the ninth.[5]

The Burman feasts are held at the full and change of the moon.[6] According to another authority, the quarters are also observed as festivals.[7] A sacrifice was celebrated by the Mexicans every month, at the period of the full moon, in a public place, to which, in every village, the high road led from the house of the chief of the tribe.[8] The inhabitants of Madagascar and of Senegambia, on the other hand, preferred the time of new moon for their devotions.[9] One of the principal stated festivals in the South Sea Islands—the *pae atua*—was held every three moons.[10] The Babylonians solemnized, with great magnificence, five days of the year. Twice every year, at the winter and summer solstices, the Emperor of China, in his character as high priest of the nation, offers prayer and sacrifice to Shang-Te, the Supreme Being.[11]

1 In a work ascribed to Fuh-he, who is supposed to have lived considerably more than four thousand years ago, the following remarkable sentence is to be found:—"Every seven days comes the revolution"—that is, of the heavenly bodies, as generally explained by Chinese scholars; and it is a singular fact, that in the Chinese almanacs of the present day there are four names applicable, during the course of each lunar month, to the days which answer to our Sundays.—Gillespie's *Land of Sinim*, pp. 161, 162.

2 Hyde *De Relig. Vet. Pers.*, pp. 189, 190.

3 Smith's *Dict. of Gr. and Rom. Antiq.*, words *Calendarium* and *Saturnalia*.

4 Communication by Rev. H. Goldie, of Old Calabar, to the writer.

5 *Researches*, i. 285.

6 Knowles's *Life of Mrs. Judson*, p. 98.

7 Crawford's *Embassy*.

8 Humboldt's *Researches*, ii. 123.

9 *Scott. Miss. Register*, i. 230. Bell's *Geography* (1849), iv. 6.

10 Ellis's *Polynes. Researches* (1831), i. 350.

11 Gillespie's *Land of Sinim*, p. 166.

Annual seasons of worship, also, have prevailed in many countries. Besides their daily offerings and frequent ablutions, the Hindus have a grand annual sacrifice.[1] In China, in addition to the worship constantly performed by the priests at the temples, and numerous occasions, when the gods receive special honour, there is "the festival of the New Year," which is observed in the month of February of our year, as a season of idolatrous worship and general festivity; and is the only season, during the whole twelve months, of universal gaiety, and total cessation from business.[2] The conclusion of the year—called its "ripening"—was celebrated in Huahine, one of the Society Islands, with a festival, which was regarded as a kind of annual acknowledgment to the gods.[3] Of the Saturnalia, which, with the Opalia and the Sigillaria, occupied seven days once a year, Macrobius affirms that it was a festival older than Rome itself.[4] The anniversary of Bel or Baal (Beltein), lately lingered, if it does not still linger, in some parts of Scotland.[5] But it were endless to enumerate examples of annual festivals, as these, particularly on the first day of the year, have been common in almost all countries.

While it will be admitted that the instances adduced of weekly holy days have a direct bearing on our subject, it may be asked, What relation have octonary, monthly, quarterly, or annual observances to a seventh day of rest and worship?

Our first answer to this question is, that such observances exemplify the Sabbatic principle, so far as regards stated seasons of devotion, and of exemption from ordinary labour. This labour is discontinued, and homage is rendered to some deity, at certain periodical times. Cases of Sabbatism, to this extent, are frequent. The people of Calabar were wont, on their Sabbath, to approach the Supreme Being (Abasi) in prayer; and though they now observe the day merely as a holiday and in merry-making, they abstain from labour in the fields, and suppose, that if they did not so abstain, their labour would be unprofitable, and some evil would befall the labourers.[6] The Ashantees on their sacred day,

[1] *Encyclopædia of Religious Knowledge*, p. 623.
[2] Gillespie's *Sinim*, pp. 67, 73.
[3] Ellis's *Polynes. Researches* (1831), i. 351, 352.
[4] *Saturnal*, lib. i. cap. 7.
[5] Stewart's *Sketches of the Highlanders of Scotland*, i. 9.
[6] Communication of Mr. Goldie.

worship their fetiches, and circumcise their children.[1] In Guinea, generally, similar practices have prevailed. Purchas says of the people, "The seventh day they leave working, and reckon that to be their day of ease and abstinence from work, or their Sunday, which they call Dio Fetissos. They hold it on Tuesday. That day the fishermen go not to the sea for fish, etc. They have a priest or fetissero. He, upon their Sabbath-day, sits upon a stool in the middle of the market, before the altar or place whereupon they sacrifice unto their fetisso, and then all the men, women, and children come and sit round about him, and then he speaketh unto them, and they sit still to hear."[2] A recent account states, that the negroes of Guinea desist on the seventh day from the labour of fishing, though no other occupation is interrupted, and that every man dedicates to the honour of his tutelar divinity one day in the week, on which he drinks no palm-wine till sunset.[3] The only religious service in Pegu was one of public instruction. The preachers rose early, and by the ringing of a bason, called together the people to their sermons.[4] The Peruvians, we have seen, were to rest every ninth day. On the days of the Burman feasts, all public business is suspended—the people pay their homage to Gaudama at the temples, presenting to the image, rice, fruits, flowers, candles, etc. Aged persons often fast during the whole day. Some visit the colleges, and hear the priests read portions of the Boodhist writings.[5] The purpose of the Mexican monthly, and of the Hindoo annual, festival, was the offering of sacrifice. In Senegambia, both the Kafirs and Mohammedan converts, at the appearance of the new moon, give vent to an ejaculatory address to the Deity, thanking him for his goodness during the month that has elapsed, and imploring a continuance of his favour during the month that is commencing.[6] The quarterly feast of the South Sea Islanders was observed with religious rites, followed by an entertainment; and on occasion of the annual festival in Huahine, there were prayers at the Marae (temple), and a banquet, after which each individual returned to his home, or to his family

1 Hurd, 423.
2 Purchas's *Pilgrimage*, book 7, ch. 2, sect. 4.
3 Bell's *Geography* (1849), iv. 30.
4 Purchas's *Pilgrimage*, p. 574.
5 Knowles's *Life of Mrs. Judson*, p. 98.
6 Bell's *Geography*, iv. 6.

marae, there to offer special prayers for the spirits of departed relatives.[1]

Such, too, were the Sabbatical observances of ancient times. The Persians worshipped the sun: in allusion to which practice, Tertullian says, *Æque si diem solis lætitiæ indulgemus, aliâ longè ratione quam religione solis*—"If we spend Sunday joyfully, as well as they, it is for a very different reason from the worship of the sun."[2] The Greeks and Romans, according to Aretius, consecrated Saturday to rest, conceiving it unfit for civil actions and warlike affairs, but suited for contemplation; and a day, therefore, on which the Divine patronage was to be implored against dangers and misfortunes.[3] The following lines of the old annalist, Lucius Accius, quoted by Macrobius, inform us that the Greeks, in town and country, especially in Athens, celebrated the feast of the Saturnalia in honour of Saturn, masters and servants feasting together:—

"Maxima pars graiûm Saturno; et maxime Athenæ
Conficiunt sacra, quæ Cronia esse iterantur ab illis.
Cumque diem celebrant, per agros, urbesque fere omnes
Exercent epulis læti, famulosque procurant
Quisque suos: nostrisque itidem et mos traditus illhinc
Iste, ut cum dominis famuli tum epulentur ibidem."[4]

"The manner in which all public *feriæ* were kept," to quote again from one of the best works on Greek and Roman antiquities, "bears great analogy to our Sunday. The people generally visited the temples of the gods, and offered up their prayers and sacrifices. The most serious and solemn seem to have been the *feriæ imperativæ*, but all the others were generally attended by rejoicings and feastings. All kinds of business, especially law-suits, were suspended during the public *feriæ*, as they were considered to pollute the sacred season."[5] The author proceeds to give specimens of decisions by Roman pontiffs, in cases of doubt, as to the kinds of work that might be done on the *feriæ*; and when we mention that the works pronounced lawful were such as had refer-

[1] Ellis's *Polynesian Researches*, i. 351, 352.
[2] *Apol. v. Gent.* xvii.
[3] *Problem loc. de Sab. Observ.*
[4] *Saturnal*, lib. i. cap. 7
[5] Dictionary, article *Feriæ*.

ence to the gods, to the supply of the urgent wants of human life, to circumstances in which injury or suffering would be the result of neglect or delay, as of a tottering house, or of an ox falling into a pit, we must admit the striking resemblance, in some respects, of the *feriæ* to the Sabbath of Revelation.

But the question of the relevancy of heathen holidays to our subject requires a further answer. There is good reason to believe that these holidays are corruptions of the Sabbatic institution, as respects both its proportion of time, and the nature of its engagements. The curtailing of its time has been the result, in some instances, of a process by which septenary have gradually passed into less frequent, because thus more congenial observances; and in others, of the violent and crafty measures of rulers, who have been known summarily to transfer the stated rest from the seventh day to a tenth, or to expunge all but a yearly sacred day from the national calendars. Such facts as Jeroboam's substitution of his one feast of the eighth month for the Jewish feasts—the reducing of the seasons of worship in Persia by Yezdegerd to that of Nauruz, or New-Year's Day—and the institution of decades in France, prepare us for more readily assenting to a statement made by some of the Fathers, to the effect that, at a very early period, the place of the weekly Sabbath was usurped by an annual religious festival. And the revolutionized object and rites, as well as day of the French worship—the weekly prayers of Calabar succeeded by mere rest and merriment—the desecrated Sabbath of the Jews, at various periods of their history, and of many professed Christians, still, with the entire disappearance of a seventh sacred day in China, if not also in the islands of Polynesia—are proofs how possible it is, that a holy day may not only become a day of revelry and wickedness, but ultimately be absorbed in the current of ordinary time.

The distribution of time into weeks, is another observance which appears to have a close connexion with a septenary day of rest and sacredness. The antiquity and extensive prevalence of this practice might be established by ample historical details. Let it suffice, however, in a matter on which there is so general an agreement, to present the words of four eminent writers :—" The septenary arrangement of days," says Scaliger, " was in use among the Orientals from the remotest antiquity."[1] "We have reason to believe," observes President de Goguet, "that the institution of that short period of seven days, called a *week*, was the first step taken by mankind in dividing and measuring their time. We find, from time immemorial, the use of this period among all nations, without any variation in the form of it. The Israelites, Assyrians, Egyptians, Indians, Arabians, and, in a word, all the nations of the east, have in all ages made use of a week, consisting of seven days. We find the same custom among the ancient Romans, Gauls, Britons, Germans, the nations of the north, and of America."[2] According to Laplace, "the week is perhaps the most ancient and incontestable monument of human knowledge."[3] We add a sentence from Humboldt, venturing, however, to premise, that the Peruvian ninth day of rest seems to prove a former notation of time by weeks even in America. "It appears," he remarks, "that no nation of the New Continent was acquainted with the week or cycle of seven days, which we find among the Hindoos, the Chinese, the Assyrians, and the Egyptians, and which, as Le Gentil has very justly observed, is followed by the greater part of the nations of the Old World."[4]

The respect shown to the septenary number is a third pagan observance of a Sabbatic character, which calls for notice. However much certain numbers, as three, four, ten, and others, might be prized, none appears to have been honoured with so permanent and general an estimation as the *numerus septenarius*. There is no species of subject, religious or secular, divine or human, spiritual or material, which it has not been employed to illustrate and magnify. And it has been in use for these purposes by peoples the most diversified in condition, and the most remote from each other in place and time. It has been consulted in the construction alike of Egyptian pyramids and cities, Assyrian and Arabian temples, and Indian pagodas. It has been sacred equally to Saturn and to the planets, to the sun-god of Persia, and to the elements and week-gods of Scandinavia. It has determined the number of the seasons of mourning, and the days of expiation—of the wonders of the world, and the wise among men. It directed the

[1] *De Emend. Temp.* lib. i.
[2] *The Origin of Laws* (1761), vol. i. p. 230.
[3] *Œuvres*, tom. vi. (1846), liv. i. ch. 3.
[4] *Researches*, vol. i. p. 283.

heating of Nebuchadnezzar's furnace. It ruled the retinue of the court of Shushan. It has sounded the depths of slavery. It has measured noble deeds. Ajax bore his shield covered with seven hides. Boreas ruled in his sevenfold, many-celled cave. The classes of the Polynesian areois, supposed to be a society of divine original, were seven. The chosen conductors of the great annual sacrifice offered by the wild Indians were seven. The priests who prepared the more solemn feasts in ancient Rome were seven. Seven was the complete number of sacrificial victims with Deiophobe as with Balaam—in Athens as in the land of Uz. Seven ewe-lambs sealed the covenant between Abraham and Abimelech. Agamemnon's peace-offering to Achilles included seven tripods and seven maids. Seven ages were the gift of the gods to Tithonus; and according to Shakspere,

> "All the world's a stage,
> And all the men and women merely players:
> They have their exits and their entrances,
> And one man in his time plays many parts:
> His acts being seven ages."

And taking a loftier flight than our poet, the Hindu, not unlike the Mohammedan, whose expected paradise is seven heavens, imagines a sidereal ladder, through whose seven gates his soul is to ascend to the residence of Brama—its own pristine as well as last abode of bliss.

In accounting for facts so diversified, and yet having so much in common, we must resort to some powerful variable force, not to a physical or natural law. If, for example, there had been anything, as there was not, in the revolution of the moon, or in the peculiar excellence of the number "Seven," to originate septenary observances, the observances would have been found whereever the course of the planet was seen, or the number known. We must, moreover, trace the facts to a cause operating at a remote fountainhead of nations. Laplace assigns to the week a high antiquity, and its existence among all successive generations is held to be "a proof of their common origin."[1] The septenary enumeration of the planets, and Jewish example, came too late to

[1] *Œuvres*, tom. vi. liv. i. chap. iii.

produce the first instances of the week in heathendom. Finally, the greater prevalence of this division of time in the East seems to point to its origin in that direction.

All these conditions are fulfilled by the account in the Pentateuch, the oldest of books, which relates, that the Creator having made the world in six days, rested on, blessed, and sanctified the seventh; and which, after repeated notices of worship, and of respect for the number seven, as applied to time as to other things, acquaints us with the dispersion from Shinar, into all countries, of the descendants of the only family that had survived the desolating flood. By them were the creation, the week, the state of innocence, the fall, the deluge, and other subjects—all recorded afterwards by Moses, and found pervading and partially redeeming so many heathen mythologies—made known throughout the world. In the relation of septenary observances to religion, creation, and the flood, aided by the proverbial power of customs derived from ancestors, we find the moral force adequate to the conveyance of these observances, despite of many hostile influences, over thousands of years. But a momentum, depending upon fading traditions, must decrease; and hence changes have come over the week and Sabbath of Paganism, while in countries enjoying a written revelation, they have remained in their integrity and power.

If philosophy, which disclaims the fanciful and the intricate, when she has found the simple and the satisfactory, be listened to, it will be admitted that the traces of pagan rites confirm the Mosaic record, and the doctrine of a primal, Divine Sabbath, by an amount of evidence which, in a matter involving no fierce antipathies, would command an unhesitating and unqualified belief. "Many vain conjectures have been formed concerning the reasons and motives which determined all mankind to agree in this primitive division of their time. Nothing but tradition concerning the space of time employed in the creation of the world, could give rise to this universal, immemorial practice."[1]

[1] President de Goguet. *Origin of Laws*, vol. i. p. 280.

THE SABBATH OR LORD'S DAY IN THE FIRST THREE CENTURIES OF CHRISTIANITY.

A statement of the evidence for the authority and value of the Sabbath would be incomplete without some account of its history. The Word of God, indeed, is the standard of all religious faith and practice, but we must be indebted to the annals of the world, and especially of the Church, for help in ascertaining the canon of revelation, in interpreting its language, and in verifying its declarations and prophecies, its promises and warnings. In the aid derived from these annals our subject largely shares. The manifold vestiges of the Sabbatic institution, traceable in the written remains of heathen nations, strikingly confirm the doctrine of its primæval and Divine appointment. And as we follow its track in Christendom, we find that ecclesiastical records render, in various forms, still more important service.

The history of the earlier centuries of Christianity throws light on the meaning of certain Scripture terms which have been the occasion of a vexed question among controversialists. In designating what is now known amongst us as the Christian Sabbath, the Fathers make use of names which they never apply to any other day of the week. With them "the eighth day," "the day of the Sun," "the first day of the week," and "the Lord's Day," signify one particular day and no other. Barnabas, or whoever was the author of the Catholic Epistle ascribed to him, mentions "the eighth day" as that on which "Jesus rose from the dead," and which the Christians of his time observed as a festal day.[1] We are informed by Justin Martyr, that the Christians of the second century assembled on "the day of the Sun," and that they did so, "because on this first day God made the world, and Jesus Christ our Saviour rose from the dead."[2] The same Father affirms, that "Christ rose from the dead on the eighth day," which, he adds, "may be called the eighth and yet remains the first."[3] In the third century, Cyprian represents the eighth day as both "the first after the Sabbath, and the Lord's Day."[4]

[1] Epist. c. 15.
[2] *Apol.* 1, *ad finem.*
[3] *Dial. cum Tryph.* c. 41.
[4] Epist. 64.

When we compare these passages with each other, we find that "the eighth day," "the day of the Sun," or Sunday, "the day of the Redeemer's resurrection," "the first day of the week," and "the Lord's Day," are, according to the combined testimony of Barnabas, Justin Martyr, and Cyprian, the same day. Were it not that we are limited by our theme to a certain period, we might enlarge the proof from the language of Hilary, Ambrose, Chrysostom, and Augustine. Theorists, who affirm that the Jewish seventh day continues the day of the Christian Sabbath, and others, who assert that there is no evidence in the New Testament for the Divine appointment of a day of sacred rest under Christianity at all, have thus one of the chief grounds of their opinions swept away—the ground, that the expressions, "the first day of the week," and "the Lord's Day," do not denote the day to which in our time they are usually applied. There is the most satisfactory proof in Scripture itself, that the designations must be so understood; but when Christian writers—some of whom were conversant with persons that might have seen and heard the apostle John—agree with the great body of Christians in their views of such phraseology, not a shade of doubt ought to remain as to the correctness of the interpretation.

It is otherwise, as respects uniformity of meaning, with the word "Sabbath," which is not in the writings of the Fathers employed to indicate exclusively one day. The earlier Fathers appear always to express by it the "seventh" day, while they designate by some one or other of the above-mentioned terms the distinctive season of Christian worship. As "the Sabbath" had been for so long a time the well-known title of the weekly holy day among the Jews, it was obviously needful for preventing mistake, that the institution which had passed to a new day should have a new name. But as time advanced, and may not we add, as the Lord's day came to be no longer in danger of being confounded with the Jewish Sabbath, the old name was gradually resumed and attached to the Christian holy day. The earliest instance of the restoration of the word to its ancient honour, that we have discovered, occurs in a passage of Irenæus (A.D. 178), where, after showing that Christ in healing the sick did nothing "beyond the law of the Sabbath-day," he draws the conclusion, that "the true sanctification of the Sabbath consists in doing works of mercy."[1] He is followed by Clemens Alexandrinus, who holds the eighth day "to be properly the Sabbath, but the seventh a working day;"[2] and by Origen, who says, "Leaving the Jewish observances, let us see how the Sabbath ought to be kept by a Christian;" concluding his description with the words, "This is the observance of the Christian Sabbath."[3] Examples might also be given from the writings of Gregory of Nyssa, Jerome, Augustine, Rufinus, and Chrysostom, but they belong to a later date. Several instances, doubtless, exist in which Augustine and others employ the word "Sabbath" in its original acceptation. But this they do when they have occasion to mention and discriminate the Jewish and Christian weekly days of rest; and, even in this case, they sometimes say, "the Jewish Sabbath." On other occasions, they feel that there is no need of any explanatory or qualifying epithet when they call the Lord's day the Sabbath; a fact which is only in harmony with the conviction, everywhere manifest in their writings, that the Sabbatic institution had, besides specific relations to the Mosaic and Christian economies, a generic rest and sacredness common to all times. The Fathers might conceive, as many since their days have done, that there is something in a name, and that though circumstances required them for a time to restrict themselves to certain expressions, they could not, in justice to ancient rights, or dutifully to the immutable Decalogue, surrender a word so significant of their privileges and obligations as "the Sabbath."

There is a particular instance of the employment of the word "Sabbath-day," in the New Testament, as to the reference of which, whether to the seventh-day or to the first-day Sabbath, there has been some controversy. It has occurred to us that a solution of the difficulty may be found in the following remarks. Jerusalem was taken and destroyed by Titus in A.D. 70. Our Lord had, in reference to that event, said to his disciples, "There shall not an hair of your head perish. When ye shall see Jerusalem compassed with armies, then know that the desolation thereof is nigh. Then let them which are in Judea flee to the

1 *Adv. Hæres*, lib. iv. c. 19. 2 *Strom.* lib. vi. c. 16.
3 *Hom.* 23, in Num.

mountains, and let them which are in the midst of it depart out" (Luke xxi. 18, 20, 21). In fulfilment of these words, both of promise and command, the Christians had escaped and taken refuge at Pella.[1] From the tactics employed by the Roman general, we learn what day was intended in another command of our Lord to his disciples: "Pray ye that your flight be not in the winter, neither on the Sabbath-day" (Matt. xxiv. 20). We are nowhere informed of the precise time at which the Christians left the city. It is only in general terms stated by Eusebius that they did so after the war had commenced under the conduct of Titus. It has often been affirmed that they left the city at the time of the retreat of Cestius Gallus, when, according to Josephus, many of the most eminent of the Jews swam away from the city as from a sinking ship.[2] But the departure of the Christians is not mentioned by that historian as having then occurred, nor does the supposition agree with the language either of Eusebius or of the evangelists, the latter defining the time as that when Jerusalem was to be encompassed with armies, and the abomination of desolation should stand in the holy place (Matt. xxiv. 15; Mark xiii. 14; Luke xxi. 20). The military ensigns were the chief objects of Roman idolatry, and when these were brought to the temple, and sacrifices were offered to them, "the abomination of desolation stood in the holy place." This was the signal for flight to the followers of Christ. The season was summer, and the day was not the Lord's day,—for on that day Titus made his attacks,—but a Jewish Sabbath-day, when, knowing that the inhabitants would not desecrate the time by any military or other work, he employed himself in constructing machines, and making his preparations for the active prosecution of the siege on the other days.[3] Saturday was the most convenient, if not the only possible day, on which the Christians could leave the city. In their situation, it is not conceivable that they could forget their Lord's command to them to pray. Their supplications were heard as

[1] Euseb. *Hist.* lib. ii. c. 5. [2] *Wars of the Jews*, B. ii. ch. 20.

[3] Titus employed the Sabbath-days in constructing machines, etc., previous to his attacks on the following Sundays. His first assault was on Sunday, April 22, A.D. 70. Part of the lower city was taken, Sunday, May 6; the temple was burnt, Sunday. August 5; and the upper city was taken and destroyed, Sunday, Sept. 2.—Kitto's *History of Palestine*, vol. ii. p. 756.

regarded the season. They must have been heard also as to the day. If we are right in conceiving that the day of their escape was a Saturday, the Sabbath-day referred to in Matt. xxiv. 20 was not, as some contend, the last, but the first day of the week.

We have abundant evidence that a stated day was sacredly observed by the Christians in the first three centuries, and that this was the first day of the week.

Clement of Rome (68-70), in writing on behalf of the Church there to the Church of Corinth, says : "We ought to do in order all things which the Lord hath required us to observe at stated times. The offerings and sacred services, which it is our duty to render, he hath commanded to be presented neither carelessly nor irregularly, but at appointed times and hours."[1] The writer here intimates, as a fact known to both churches, that Christ had prescribed seasons for divine worship. The want of reference to any particular season by name implies the notoriety of the matter.

We have followed the transactions of the second century for only a very few years, when we light upon a record of sacred usage in Bithynia, the more satisfactory in some respects that it comes from a hostile quarter. We refer to the celebrated letter of Pliny the younger, written to the Emperor Trajan. As lieutenant of the emperor in Pontus and Bithynia, he had been ordered to employ the severest measures against the Christians under his authority, but judged it prudent, before proceeding to the utmost rigour, to represent their case to his master. He says, that after being examined, "they affirmed that the whole of their fault or error lay in this, that they were wont to meet together on a stated day, before it was light, and sing among themselves by turns a hymn to Christ as God, and to bind themselves by an oath, not to the commission of any wickedness, but not to be guilty of theft, or robbery, or adultery, never to break a promise, or to deny a pledge committed to them when called upon to return it. When these things were performed, it was their custom to separate, and then to come together again to a meal, which they ate in common without any disorder ; but this they had forborne

[1] *Epist.* sect. 40.

since the publication of my edict, whereby, according to your commands, I prohibited assemblies."[1] How extensively the religion, which Pliny calls "the superstition," of these good and peaceful members of society, had spread, appears when he adds: "Many of all ages, and every rank, of both sexes likewise, are accused and will be accused. Nor has the contagion of the superstition seized cities only, but the smaller towns also, and the open country. Nevertheless, it seems to me that it may be restrained or corrected. It is certain that the temples, which were almost forsaken, begin to be more frequented, and the sacred solemnities, after a long intermission, are revived. Victims, also, are everywhere bought up, whereas for some time there were few purchasers."

From this time, for a period of some thirty years, we find no trace of the Lord's Day. But the circumstantial account of the manner in which the Christians spent their holy day, as given by Justin Martyr, in his first Apology (A.D. 138 or 139), fully compensates the preceding blank. "On the day called Sunday," he writes, "there is a meeting in one place of all who reside whether in the towns or in the country, and the memoirs of the apostles, and the writings of the prophets are read. The reader having concluded, the president delivers a discourse, instructing the people, and exhorting them to imitate the good things which they have heard. Then we all stand up together, and engage in prayer, after which bread is brought in, with wine and water. The president offers up, according to his ability, prayers and thanks a second time, to which the people express their assent with a loud Amen. Then follow a general distribution and participation of the things for which thanks have been given, and a portion is conveyed to the absent by the deacons. The more affluent contribute of their substance as each is inclined, and the remnant is intrusted to the president, wherewith he relieves the orphans, widows, etc. We all assemble together in common on Sunday, because it was on this first day that God having changed darkness and chaos, made the world, and because on the same day Jesus Christ our Saviour rose from the dead. For he was crucified the day before that of Saturn, and on the day after that of

[1] *C. Plin. C. Sec.* lib. x. ep. 97.

Saturn, which is the day of the Sun, he appeared to his apostles and disciples, and taught them what we now submit to your consideration."[1]

After a lapse of another period of thirty years, we are again furnished with ample testimony to the continued life and vigour of the institution. In A.D. 170, the Lord's day is known at Sardis, for Melito, bishop of the church there, writes a book on the subject, and Eusebius, who supplies the information, and who attests the character of the weekly holy day in his own time, must be considered as intimating the identity of the sacred season in Sardis and Cæsarea. Of the same date is the evidence of Theophilus, bishop of Antioch, who appeals to the observance of the Lord's day as a custom in the churches, and of Dionysius, bishop of Corinth, who, in writing to the Romans, and to Soter, their bishop, and after commending them for their liberality to their brethren and to other churches, which had distinguished them during their whole history, remarks, "We have passed (or kept) the Lord's day and perused your epistle, which we shall hereafter read continually, as we do that of Clemens, that we may be replenished with precepts and wholesome instructions."[2] Already, we see, had a practice been introduced different from that described by Justin Martyr, who says nothing of any reading in the church but of the sacred writings. The words of Dionysius, however, while they clearly certify the regular observance of the Lord's day at Corinth, imply a common understanding and interest in the subject there and in Rome, and also suggest what must have been "the appointed times," referred to in the epistle which Clement had written from the church of the latter city to that of the former a hundred years before.

The words of Irenæus and Clemens Alexandrinus (A.D. 178) on the subject, are more appropriate to a subsequent page. It is enough at present to say, that the language of both writers indicates the general respect for the Lord's day which was entertained at the period when they flourished.

Like Pliny and Justin Martyr, but with still more detail, Tertullian sets forth the manner in which Christian worship was conducted in his time. Although he does not mention the day in

[1] *Apol.* 1, *ad finem.*

[2] Euseb. *Eccl. Hist.* lib. iv. c. 22.

the description itself, he has, in a preceding chapter of the same work, declared, that the Christians solemnized "the day of the Sun," "the day after Saturday, in distinction from those who call this day their Sabbath." The passage is too long for insertion, but the following is, we trust, a faithful translation of so much of it as bears upon our subject:—"We Christians, incorporated by our common faith, worship, and hopes, meet for prayer, in which we as it were take the kingdom of heaven by a violence grateful to God, not forgetting to offer up supplications for emperors, and all in authority, for the prosperity and peace of the state, and for the delay of the final doom. We assemble, also, for receiving instruction, warning, and exhortation from the Divine Word, whereby we nourish our faith, animate our hope, establish our confidence, and stir up ourselves by every argument to the practice of good works. On these occasions discipline is administered with all solemnity, and the censures pronounced on offenders are regarded as anticipating the judgment to come. Every one puts something into the public stock once a month, or when he pleases, and according to his ability and inclination, for there is no compulsion; these pious deposits being applied, not to the indulgence of appetite, but in aid of the poor, orphans, the aged, the shipwrecked, the persecuted, and for burying the dead. Then follows a supper, a love-feast, not an entertainment for the sensual, but a refreshment to the hungry and the needy. To this supper we do not sit down till we have previously tasted the pleasure of prayer to God; we sup in the recollection that God is to be worshipped in the night season, and we converse with the consciousness that He hears us. Praise succeeds, and the whole is concluded with prayer, when we depart; not for the purposes of dissipation, licentiousness, or violence, but with the same regard to purity and moderation as in our coming together, like men who have been enjoying a spiritual banquet rather than a common supper."[1] Thus, for another century, notwithstanding a variety of influences tending to its injury, has the Lord's day continued to maintain its pre-eminence, and to be kept with sacred care. And it is important to remark the connexion of a well-observed holy day with the general excellence of the Church, since it was at this time that

[1] *Apol.* c. 39.

the beautiful panegyric was extorted from her enemies, "Behold how these Christians love one another!"[1]

In the third century, amidst various internal sources of weakness to the Church, and assaults against her from without, the weekly holy day continued to be held in honour. "On a solemn day," says Minucius Felix, referring to the day of public worship, and of the love-feast which followed, "persons of both sexes, and of every age, assemble at a feast with all their children, sisters and mothers."[2] The writings of Origen show that the Lord's day was observed at Alexandria, and that he was careful to instruct his flock in the duties of the day.[3] Cyprian of Carthage has a single sentence on the subject, afterwards to be quoted, which is the more important that it expresses the views of a Council held in A.D. 253, and which implies the unchallenged recognition in his time of the institution itself. And the evidence of Commodian (A.D. 270), who mentions the Lord's day, and of Victorine (A.D. 290), who says, "It is our custom then [on the seventh day] to fast, lest we should seem to observe the Sabbath of the Jews;"[4] was only wanting to complete the proof that the lapse of three centuries, with the assaults of heathen and Jewish persecution, and the growing corruption of the Church, has left to a great extent in its primitive simplicity and sacredness, the ordinance of a weekly season of rest and devotion.

The history of the period under review, besides throwing light on the names and observance of the Sabbath, acquaints us with the doctrinal views entertained by the early Fathers in reference to the institution. We indeed have the same Scriptures to determine our creed on the subject as they had; but when a doctrine is apparently consonant to that supreme authority, our confidence in the conviction that we have read the document correctly, is strongly confirmed by the coincidence of our opinions with those of good men, especially of such of them as lived within a comparatively short time of the apostolic age. Tertullian, Origen, and Cyprian, uncontradicted by any early Christian writers, held, that the Sabbath was of primæval appointment. Little has been said

[1] *Ibid.* Tertullian mentions (*Adv. Psyc.* c. 13), that the psalm most frequently sung by the Christians was the 133d.
[2] Octavius, c. 9.
[3] *Contr. Celsum*, lib. 8. Hom. 5. in Isa. ii.
[4] Holden *on the Sabbath*, p. 306.

on the theory of the institution by the Fathers who preceded Tertullian. He states, "that Christ himself made the Sabbath-day more holy by his well-doing on it, which by the blessing of the Father was made holy from the beginning;"[1] and declares, that this view of the antiquity of the day was entertained by the Jews of his time.[2] Origen expresses the opinion, that Job observed a seventh day, and regards the narrative in Genesis ii. 1-3, as intimating the institution of the Sabbath when the work of creation was finished.[3]

The Fathers of the first three centuries believed that the Jewish Sabbath-day had been set aside. To Trypho's assumption of the permanence of the seventh-day rest, Justin Martyr replies, "There was no need of the Sabbaths, nor festivals, nor oblations, before Moses; so now, in like manner, there is no need of them, since Jesus Christ the Son of God, was, by the determinate counsel of God, born of a virgin, of the seed of Abraham, without sin."[4] Clemens Alexandrinus regards the seventh day as no longer entitled to be called the Sabbath, but as having taken the place of a working day.[5] The same doctrine is held by Tertullian, who says, in name of Christians, "We have nothing to do with the Sabbaths, new moons, and feasts in which God at one time took pleasure."[6] He affirms, and enlarges on the statement, that the seventh day was "a temporary Sabbath."[7] Additional illustrations will occur under our next remark.

According to the early Fathers, the first day of the week has been by Divine authority appointed the day of rest and worship for Christians, in place of the seventh, the day of the Jewish Sabbath. Clement of Rome, as we have seen, urges attention to the seasons of worship which Christ had commanded to be observed. Barnabas, disclaiming the old Sabbath-day, declares the eighth day to be its acceptable substitute.[8] Justin Martyr, too, not only condemns the Jews for adhering to the former day, but describes the worship of the Christians in his time as observed on the day of the sun, and states that they assembled for that pur-

[1] *Adv. Marcion*, lib. iv. c. 12. [2] *Adv. Jud.* c. iv.
[3] Kennicott's *Two Dissert.* p. 169, note. Origenis *Con. Cels.*, lib. 6 (Cantab. 1658), p. 317, et in *Mat. Tract*, p. 20. [4] *Dial. cum Tryph.* sect. 23. [5] *Strom.* lib. vi. c. 16.
[6] *De Idolatriâ*, c. 14. [7] *Adv. Jud.* lib. iv. [8] *Epist.* c. 15.

pose on the first day, as it was the day on which God made the world, and Jesus Christ our Saviour rose from the dead.[1] "This commandment," says Clement of Alexandria, "informs us that the world was made by God, and that he gave us the seventh day for rest on account of the sufferings and afflictions of life; and the eighth day," he adds, "appears rightly to be named the seventh, and to be the true Sabbath, but the seventh to be a working day."[2] The writings of Tertullian abound in testimonies to his faith in the Divine authority of the Lord's day, some of which will fall to be noticed under another head. Cyprian testifies to the same belief. In writing to Fidus, one of the clergy of Carthage, who held that infants ought not to be baptized before the eighth day, and informing him of the decision against him of a council called to consider his opinion, he says, that the practice of observing circumcision on the eighth day was a type fulfilled in Christ, and adds, "For because the eighth day, that is the first after the Sabbath, was to be the day on which the Lord should rise, quicken us, and give us the circumcision of the Spirit, this eighth day or the first after the Sabbath, and the Lord's day, was foreshown in the figure, which figure ceased with the realization of its import, and the bestowal of the spiritual circumcision."[3] Unlike some modern writers, the Clements, and others, do not arrogate to the Church the appointment of the weekly holy day. Let us hear Tertullian, "The apostles introduced nothing at their own discretion, but faithfully assigned to the people the discipline which they had received from Christ."[4]

It was the creed of the Fathers, that the Lord's day ought to be wholly spent in sacred rest and service. All ordinary work was to be discontinued on that day. Tertullian, in remarking on the words, "Thou shalt do no work," asks, "What work?" and answers, "Thine own, doubtless. For it follows that he should take away those works from the Sabbath, which he had previously indicated to belong to the six days. Thine own—that is, human and customary works."[5] The same writer, in contending for the honours of the Lord's day, and after mentioning that it was the practice of a very few to abstain from kneeling in prayer on

[1] *Apol.* I. *ad fin.* [2] *Strom.* lib. vi. c. 16. [3] *Epist.* 64.
[4] *De Præscript. adv. Hæret.* c. 6. [5] *Adv. Marcion,* lib. ii. c. 21.

Sabbath—that is, Saturday, says, "But we ought, according to the doctrine received by us, to beware on the Lord's day alone, not of that only"—kneeling in prayer—"but of all anxiety, deferring even business, lest we should give place in any degree to the devil."[1] Like-minded as to the duty of entire rest from work was Origen, who remarks, "Leaving the Jewish observances, let us see how the Sabbath ought to be observed by a Christian. That Sabbatism, mentioned Heb. iv. 9, is the observation of the Sabbath, on which no worldly actions ought to be done."[2] Not that the Fathers supposed that sacred time was profaned by labour in cases of necessity. When Tertullian has shown, as already quoted, that we are not to do our own works, he adds, "But to carry about the Ark, that is, round the walls of Jericho, can seem neither a daily work nor a human, but a rare and holy work, and therefore by the very commandment of God divine."[3] "The priests," says Irenæus, "in kindling a fire and slaying beasts on the Sabbath-day, were not guilty of any sin."[4] That worldly pleasures were to be shunned, while frequently inculcated by the later Fathers as one of the duties of the Lord's day, is plainly involved in the language already quoted. The proper business of that day, be it further remarked, was, in the view of these excellent men, the service of God in works of piety and benevolence. Origen not only excludes secular work from the engagements of the Sabbath, as in the words formerly adduced, but completes the description of a sanctified day thus: "If, therefore, you cease from all worldly works, and execute nothing worldly, but give yourselves up to spiritual exercises, repairing to church, attending to sacred reading and instruction, thinking of celestial things, solicitous for the future, placing the judgment to come before your eyes, not looking to things present and visible, but to those which are future and invisible—this is the observance of the Christian Sabbath."[5] But works of benevolence are to be added. Irenæus shows that Christ in healing the sick did nothing beyond the law, which did not prohibit cures upon the Sabbath-day, or even caring for cattle; and then draws the conclusion, "That the true sanctification of the Sabbath consists in doing works of

[1] *De Orat.*, c. 23. [2] *Hom.* 23, in Num. [3] *Adv. Marcion*, lib. ii. c. 21.
[4] *Contr. Valent.*, lib. iv. c. 19. [5] *Hom.* 23, in Num.

mercy."[1] To the same effect is a chapter in Tertullian's work against Marcion.[2]

Let us, under this topic, add, that the Fathers, while they sufficiently disclaimed the Jewish ceremonies, have occasionally avowed their faith in the substantial sameness of Sabbatic obligations under the Jewish and Christian dispensations, and that several of them, earlier and later, have, without dissent so far as we have seen on the part of any, recognised the Fourth Commandment as the abiding rule of the Christian holy day. Thus Irenæus: "Preparing men for a life of holiness, the Lord Himself with His own voice spake the words of the Decalogue alike to all: these commandments, therefore, continue with us, extended and enlarged, not abolished, by his coming in the flesh. But the ordinances of bondage he gave to the people separately by the voice of Moses; as Moses himself says, 'And the Lord commanded me at that time to teach you statutes and judgments.' These, then, which were given as a yoke of bondage, and as a sign to them, he has blotted out by the new covenant of liberty."[3] Clemens Alexandrinus held the continued authority of the Decalogue, from his exposition of the fourth precept of which we have already extracted a remarkable sentence on the Sabbatic institution. Let us add another remark, which is, that the Fathers, with all honest men, recognised in a day devoted to the Divine service, a whole day. The ancient tithes consisted of a tenth part of a person's substance, which was consecrated to a religious use. In like manner, when a seventh day was set apart to God, it was one entire day out of the seven. The sacred half-days—the *intercisi* of the heathen, had an analogy to some of the Mosaic holy days, but not to the weekly Sabbath. When Dionysius of Corinth said that he and the Church had kept the Lord's day, his language means that they had kept the day throughout. Sabbaths, in the estimate of Irenæus, were whole days. Origen upbraids those "who gave one or two hours of the day to God, and came to church to prayers, or heard the Word of God in passing, but expended the remaining portion of it on the world and their appetites."[4]

[1] *Contr. Valent.*, lib. iv. c. 19.
[2] Lib. iv. c. 12.
[3] *Adv. Hæres.*, lib. iv. c. 31.
[4] *Hom.* in Num.

There is yet another part of the Sabbatic creed, held by the early Christians, which deserves a concluding brief notice. We refer to their high estimate of the Lord's day. They called it the first of days, the chief of days, a day of gladness. They honoured it by standing in prayer, and by not fasting. They rose early and sat late, that they might redeem their holy time. Persecution could not cool their ardent regard for "the Lord's solemnities." And Tertullian recommends to those who could not celebrate the day and its worship with sunshine, to meet for that purpose in the night season, which would be "illumined by the light of Christ."

THE SABBATH IN CENTURIES IV.-XV.

The first three centuries of ecclesiastical history furnish the most valuable support to the claims of the weekly holy day. But the subsequent periods are not wanting in scarcely less important aid to the same cause. The history, as it advances, multiplies the tests of prophetic truth relative to the promised preservation, prevalence, and blessings of the institution. We therefore proceed, though necessarily in a somewhat perfunctory manner, with the annals of the Sabbath.

THE TERMS, "FIRST DAY OF THE WEEK," "LORD'S DAY," AND "SABBATH."

It has already been stated, that persons of widely different opinions on the question have contended for an exegesis of the above-mentioned names, which militates against the generally received doctrine of the Christian Sabbath. Having produced some of the earlier Christian writers as witnesses against such misinterpretations, let us confirm their testimony by that of their most distinguished successors. Jerome, who will be admitted to have been no mean proficient in the knowledge of the versions and style, to say the least, of the sacred writings, explains the words, "the first day of the week," by the words, "the Lord's day."[1]

[1] "Per unam Sabbati, hoc est, in die dominico." Quoted by Beza, *Annot.* in 1 Cor. xvi. 2.

In expounding the verse, "And upon the first day of the week, when the disciples came together to break bread," Chrysostom observes, "It was then the feast of Pentecost, and the Lord's day."[1] At a much later time, the venerable Bede interprets the phrase as meaning the same day. "The Sabbath," says Augustine, "is the seventh day, but the Lord's day, coming after the seventh, must be the eighth, and is also to be reckoned the first. For it is called the first day of the week (una Sabbati)."[2] These words while they confirm the general belief in the identity of the time indicated by the first, eighth, and Lord's day, show that the word Sabbath continues to be made use of when it is necessary to distinguish the first day of the week from the Jewish Sabbath-day. But various Fathers in the fourth century, including Augustine himself, repeatedly apply the word, as Irenæus and Origen had done, to the weekly sacred season of the Christian Church. Instances will occur in subsequent quotations. Let two, meanwhile, suffice. "We enjoy," says Hilary, A.D. 354, "the festivity of a perfect Sabbath on the eighth, which is also the first day of the week."[3] To these accord the words of Gregory Nyssen: "Behold the Sabbath, blessed for thee from the beginning; mark by that Sabbath, the Sabbath of the present day, the day of rest which God hath blessed above other days."[4] Alexander of Hales might have taken higher ground than that in the following sentence: "Because the Sabbath-day, taken indeterminately, is called the day of rest, or vacation to God; after this manner the Lord's day may be called the Sabbath-day, without any prejudice of the Christian name, or scandal of Christians."[5]

DOCTRINES.

Dr. Paley, proceeding to answer what he calls the main question involved in the controversy on our subject, which is, "Whether the command by which the Jewish Sabbath was instituted, extend to us?" says, "If the Divine command was actually delivered at the Creation, it was addressed, no doubt, to the whole human species alike, and continues, unless repealed by some subsequent revela-

[1] *Hom.* in Acts xx. 7. [2] In Ps. cl. [3] *Prol.* in Ps.
[4] *Orat.* 38. [5] Cited in Dr. Young's *Dies Dominica*, p. 25.

tion, binding upon all who come to the knowledge of it. This opinion precludes all debate about the extent of the obligation."[1] That opinion, or rather truth, of a primal Sabbath, is so transparently presented in the Sacred Volume, as to have gained the general assent of Christian men. We have to include the Fathers of the fourth and following centuries in the number. On this turning point they are at one with each other, and with Tertullian, Origen, and Cyprian. Thus writes Lactantius, "God completed the world, and this admirable work of nature, in the space of six days, and then consecrated the seventh, from which he had rested from his works. This is the Sabbath-day."[2] Athanasius expresses the conviction, that the things which Moses taught, the same Abraham observed, and Noah understood very well.[3] "The first Sabbath," says Epiphanius, "from the beginning decreed and declared by the Lord in the creation of the world, has revolved in its cycle of seven days from that day till now."[4] In the preceding section, the words of Gregory Nyssen to the same effect have been quoted. Augustine, in his *City of God*, dates the Sabbath of eternity from the creation of man.[5] The intimation of a weekly holy day is, in a sentence afterwards to be produced, regarded by Chrysostom as having been divinely made "from the beginning."[6] And Theodoret says, "When God had made all things, instead of creating on the seventh day, He bestowed on it a blessing, lest, of the seven, that day only should be without honour."[7] As the doctrine continued to pass current down to the sixteenth century, when it was cordially embraced by Luther, Calvin, and the other Reformers, it is unnecessary any further minutely to mark its traces in the history.

In the Christian Church, from the fourth to the sixteenth century, it was the prevalent belief that the use of the seventh day as a Sabbath was set aside with the dispensation to which it had belonged. Whatever regard was shown to Saturday, the feeling was never among Christians of a kind to compete with their veneration for the Lord's day. This has been demonstrated in the

[1] *Mor. Phil.* book iv. ch. 7.
[2] *Divin. Instit.* lib. vii. c. 14.
[3] *De Sab. et Circ.*
[4] *Panar. Hær.* 51.
[5] Lib. xxii. c. 30.
[6] *Hom.* 10, in Ge.
[7] *Quæst.* 21, in Ge.

learned works of Milton's tutor and Bingham.[1] When attachment to the seventh day was tending to the dishonour of the first, the Council of Laodicea interfered to repress the indignity by enacting as follows :—" Christians ought not to act as Jews, and rest from labour on the Sabbath [Saturday], but should work on that day. And, giving pre-eminent honour to the Lord's day, they ought then, if they can, to rest from labour."[2] When it is considered that the canons of this assembly were received by the Sixth Œcumenical Council into the general law of the Church, it will be allowed that the abrogation of the Jewish Sabbath has been an extensively-received doctrine among professed Christians. It is, besides, recognised in subsequent councils, in the legislation of the period, and in the works of the Fathers. No small part of these works are devoted to the overthrow of the synagogue and all its peculiarities. " The disciples of Christ," says Epiphanius, when contending against the Ebionites, who kept both the Sabbath and the Lord's day, " knew very well from his conversation with them, and from his doctrine before his passion, that the Sabbath was discharged."[3] And both Chrysostom and Theodoret consider " days," in these words, " Ye observe days, and months, and times, and years ; I am afraid of you, lest I have bestowed upon you labour in vain," as signifying Jewish Sabbaths in contradistinction from the Lord's day of Christianity.[4] But this position will receive further confirmation from the illustration of the following.

That the Lord's day had, by Divine authority, been constituted the weekly day of rest and devotion under Christianity, is another of those doctrines which were generally received in the period under review. According to statements of the Fathers already quoted, the cycle of seven days still revolves, and " God hath blessed the Sabbath of the present day above other days." Eusebius thus writes : " The Word [Christ], by the new covenant, translated and transferred the feast of the Sabbath to the morning light, and gave us the symbol of true rest—the Lord's day, the first of the light, in which the Saviour obtained the victory over death."[5]

[1] *Dies Dominica*, p. 37, etc. ; *Antiq.* B. xx. ch. 3.
[2] *Can.* 29, *Concil. per Ruel et Hartman.* vol. iii. p. 254.
[3] *Contr. Ebion. Hær.* xxx. c. 32. [4] In Gal. iv. 10. [5] *Comment on* Ps. xci. (xcii)

Referring to our Lord's appearing to his disciples when they were met together after his resurrection, Cyril draws this conclusion: "By right, therefore, are holy assemblies held in the churches on the eighth day."[1] The Lord's day is by Gregory Nazianzen called "God's own day."[2] Augustine declares that "the Lord's day was established by Christ," that "there is one Lord of the Sabbath and of the Lord's day," that it is "called the Lord's day because the Lord made it," and that it "seems properly to belong to the Lord."[3] According to Chrysostom, "God from the beginning intimates to us the doctrine, that within the compass of a week one whole day is to be set apart to spiritual works."[4] In the fifth century, Maximus, Bishop of Turin, Sedulius, and Leo I., Bishop of Rome, testify to the same truth. We quote the words of Sedulius:—

"Cœperat interea post tristia Sabbata felix
Irradiare dies, culmenque nominis alti
A Domino dominante trahit, primusque videre
Promeruit nasci mundum, atque resurgere Christum.
Septima nam Genesis cum dicit Sabbata, claret
Hunc orbis caput esse diem, quem gloria regis
Nunc etiam proprii donans fulgore tropæi,
Primatum retinere dedit."[5]

The testimonies of writers in the sixth century—of Anastasius Sinaita, Gregory of Tours, and Isidore, Bishop of Seville—harmonize with the preceding. It is sufficient to quote the last: "The apostles ordained the Lord's day to be kept with religious solemnity, because on it our Redeemer rose from the dead, which was therefore called the Lord's day.[6] To A.D. 601, belongs Hesychius, Bishop of Jerusalem, "author of several productions," particularly a commentary on Leviticus, in which he says, "Following their (the apostles') tradition, we set apart the Lord's day to Divine assemblies;" and expresses the generally received opinion, that the day of the descent of the Holy Spirit on the apostles was the Lord's day.[7] And the venerable Bede, who adorned the eighth century, holds that "the rest of the seventh day, after six

[1] In Joan, lib. xii. c. 58.
[2] *Hom.* 1, in Pasch.
[3] Epist. 86, Young's *Dies Domin.* p. 71.
[4] *Hom.* 10, in Ge.
[5] *De Resur. Carmen.* lib. v.
[6] *Opera* (1617), p. 396.
[7] In Levit. lib. ii. c. 9.

days' working, was always wont to be celebrated, and that the Lord's day was the memorial of the Lord's resurrection."[1] It was in the ninth century that Charlemagne called five councils for remedying the prevailing disregard of the Lord's day, with other evils of the Church, and said, in his edict, "We do ordain, as it is required in the law of God, that no man do any servile work on the Lord's day," but that "all come to the church to magnify the Lord their God for those good things which on this day He bestowed upon them."[2] His son, Louis the Pious, several Popes, Alfred the Great, and Leo the Philosopher, testified, in the same century, to the Divine authority and sacred character of the day. These views, as appears from the writings of Bernard, Theophylact, Anselm, P. Alphonsus, Alexander de Hales, Aquinas, Wycliffe, from the decrees of councils, from the edicts of princes, and the Constitutions of bishops, continued to prevail in the following centuries. Our space will admit of only two or three examples. "The Lord's day," according to Anselm, "signifies that true rest which He who rose from the dead on the Lord's day now secures and promises to the saints, and therefore we do rest on that day from labour."[3] "The vacation of the Lord's day," says the irrefragable doctor, "is the moral part of the Decalogue in the time of grace, as the seventh day was in the time of the law;" and again, "The observance of a day indeterminately, that at some time we should attend on God, is moral in nature and immutable; but the observance of a determinate time is moral by discipline—by the adding of Divine institution. When that time ought to be, is not for man to determine, but God."[4] We have to add, that the Waldenses and Bohemian Brethren, who bore testimony against the growing errors and corruptions of the Church, acquiesced in her creed as regarded the weekly rest. Thus, in an explanation of the Ten Commandments, dated by Boyer A.D. 1120, the Fourth is held to be the rule of the Lord's day to Christians.[5] The Taborites—the remnant of whom, afterwards joining with a party from the Calixtines, took the name of Bohemian Brethren—maintained that the faithful are not bound to keep any festival but the

[1] Beda, *Lib. de Offic.*

[2] Morer *On the Lord's Day*, p. 261.

[3] *Opera* (1612), *Enar. in Apoc.* i. 10.

[4] Cited in Young's *Dies Domin.*, p. 46.

[5] Blair's *Hist. of Waldenses*, vol. i. p. 220.

Lord's day.[1] After that union, the Brethren took advantage of a respite from persecution, about A.D. 1471, for regulating their government and discipline, when they declared "the observance of the Sabbath to be of moral obligation ; because the seventh day was sanctified at the Creation, the Ten Commandments enjoined the Sabbath, and in the days of the apostles the Lord's day was appointed instead of the Jewish Sabbath, and therefore was not ceremonial."[2]

PRACTICAL TEACHINGS.

On the important subject of the manner in which the Lord's day ought to be spent, the latter coincide with the earlier opinions of the Christian Church. Eusebius, after mentioning the transference of the Sabbath and its duties to the first day of the week, observes, "These duties more appropriately belong to this day, because it has a precedence, is first in rank, and more honourable than the Jewish Sabbath." He continues, "It is delivered to us that we should meet together on this day, and it is ordered that we should do those things announced in this Psalm."[3] We see what idea of the sacredness of the day Athanasius entertained, when he described "a multitude of soldiers with arms, drawn swords, bows, and spears, proceeding to attack the people, though it was the Lord's day."[4] Cyril thus addressed his hearers : "Manual labour is forbidden on a feast-day, that you may exercise yourselves more entirely in Divine matters."[5] The Council of Laodicea, while they repudiated the regular cessation of work on Saturday, enjoined abstinence from labour on the Lord's day. In unison with these sentiments is the language of Chrysostom in the following exhortation to his flock : "You ought not, when you have retired from the church assembly, to involve yourselves in engagements contrary to the exercises in which you have been occupied, but immediately on coming home read the sacred Scriptures, and call together the family, wife and children, to confer about the things that have been spoken, and after they have been

[1] M'Crie's *Miscell. Writings*, p. 162.
[2] Blair's *Waldenses*, vol. ii. p. 109.
[3] In *Comment.* on Ps. xci. (xcii.)
[4] *Histor. Tracts* (Oxford, 1843), p. 192.
[5] Lib. viii. c. 5, in Joan.

more deeply and thoroughly impressed upon the mind, then proceed to attend to such matters as are necessary for this life."[1] The last clause has, in the absence of better arguments, been eagerly laid hold of to show that the preacher approved of a return to worldly business after the public and private duties of religion had been discharged. Not to mention the incompatibility of such a recommendation with the moral object aimed at in the homily, if not even with the physical powers of his hearers, Chrysostom has elsewhere stated enough to satisfy us that he had no such meaning. In other passages of his works he says, "The Lord's day hath rest and immunity from toils;"[2] and holds abstinence from worldly affairs on the day to be "an immovable law."[3] To these might be added a variety of statements by the Fathers, which imply their conviction that worldly pleasures were to be shunned at the times sacred to heaven. We cite two or three in which that conviction is clearly expressed. "The sanctification of the Sabbath," says Gregory Nazianzen, "consists not in the hilarity of our bodies, nor in the variety of glorious garments, nor in eatings, the fruit whereof we know to be wantonness, nor in strewing of flowers in the way, which we know to be the manner of the Gentiles, but rather in the purity of the soul, and the cheerfulness of the mind, and pious meditations, as when we use holy hymns instead of tabors, and psalms instead of wicked songs and dancings."[4] Opposed though Augustine was to secular work, he was still more averse to the indulgence of worldly pleasure on the Lord's day. His saying, "It is better to plough than to dance," is well known. It occurs in connexion with a reference to the Jews, as in his time spending their Sabbath in idleness and pleasure: "They are at leisure for trifles, and spend the Sabbath in such things as God forbids. Our rest is from evil works, theirs from good works. For it is better to plough than to dance."[5] But it was still better, in his view, to abstain from both, and to act in the spirit of his own words, "Let us show ourselves Christians by keeping holy the Lord's day."[6] The same spirit breathes in the words of Basil, Gregory Nazianzen, and Chrysostom. The Bishop of Cæsarea, having given as a

1 *Hom.* 5, in Matt.
2 *Hom.* 43, in 1 Cor. xvi. 1.
3 *Hom.* 5, in Matt.
4 Quoted by Twisse in *Mor. of the Fourth Commandment*, p. 173.
5 In Ps. xcii.
6 *Ad Casul.*, Epist. 86.

reason for the practice of standing in prayer on the Lord's day, not only that Christians are risen together with Christ, but that the day seems in some measure an image of the world to come, adds: "The Church instructs her disciples to offer their prayers standing, that by being from day to day reminded of the life that will never end, we may not neglect to make provision for the change of habitation."[1] In a similar spirit writes his friend of Nazianzum: "But we who worship the Word should find our only pleasure in the Scriptures, in the Divine law, and in narrating the events relative to the feast."[2] "The Sabbath," remarks Chrysostom, "is not a day of idleness, but of spiritual action."[3] In its duties, as in other things, the weekly holy day has ever been in substance the same institution. The objection, that Moses and Christ had different doctrines, Augustine does not hesitate to repel with the assertion, "The doctrine was the same, the difference respected only the time."[4] Passing to later centuries, we find that such views continued to be held. Cæsarius, Bishop of Arles, rebukes the impiety of Christians who do not entertain the reverence for the Lord's day which the Jews appear to have for their Sabbath."[5] The testimony of Columba is specially interesting, as it expresses the feelings of the heart at a moment which tests the sincerity of faith, and the value of a creed: "This day," he said to his servant, "in the Sacred Volume is called the Sabbath, that is, rest; and will indeed be a Sabbath to me, for it is to me the last day of this toilsome life, the day on which I am to rest (sabbatize) after all my labours and troubles, for on this coming sacred night of the Lord (Dominicâ nocte), at the midnight hour, I shall, as the Scriptures speak, go the way of my fathers."[6] According to Isidore of Spain, "the observance of the apostolic institution, with religious solemnity," is to "rest on that day from all earthly acts, and the temptations of the world, that we may apply ourselves to God's holy worship, giving this day due honour for the hope of the resurrection we have therein."[7] Aquinas held that "such a day was appointed not for play, but for praise and prayer."[8] And in harmony on this subject, with good men of

[1] *De Spirit. Sanct.* c. 27.
[2] *Orat.* 38.
[3] *De Laz. Conc.* 1.
[4] *Contr. Faust*, lib. xvi. c. 28.
[5] *Hom.* 12.
[6] *Life*, by Adamna (1857), p. 230.
[7] *Opera*, p. 396.
[8] *Opusc. de Præc.*, 10.

every age and clime, was Wycliffe, who, in his *Exposition of the Decalogue*, remarks on the precept concerning the Sabbath-day, that this day should be kept by "three manners of occupations, 1*st*, In *thinking*,—how God is Almighty, All-knowing, All-good, All-just, All-merciful—and thinking, that creation was completed on that day, that Christ rose from the dead on that day, that knowledge and wisdom came to the earth by the descent of the Holy Spirit on that day, and that on that day, as many clerks say, shall be doom's-day, for Sunday was the first day, and Sunday shall be the last day." He concludes an exhortation to his reader, to "bethink" him of redemption, with the words, "It should be full sweet and delightful to us, to think thus on this great kindness, and this great love of Jesus Christ." 2*d*, In *speaking*,—speaking in confession of sin to God, in "crying heartily to God, for grace and power to leave all sin, and ever after to live in virtue," and in urging neighbours to better living. 3*d*, In carefully *attending public worship*,—preparing for it by endeavouring to bring to it pure motives, and by avoiding indulgence in the pleasures of the table, that the mind may be in its best state for performing the duties of the day, and following up the services of the house of God, by visiting the sick and the infirm, and relieving the poor with our goods. "And so," he adds, "men should not be idle, but busy on the Sabbath-day about the soul, as men are on the week-day about the body."[1]

ECCLESIASTICAL MEASURES.

The means employed by the Church in centuries IV.-XV. for restraining the abuse and promoting the observance of the Lord's day, though liable to exception in several particulars, concur with contemporary writings in showing that the institution continued to be generally regarded as of Divine appointment and sacred obligation. Minute detail here would not be necessary, were it practicable. It is sufficient to refer to the leading facts.

From a list before us, admitting, probably, of considerable enlargement, it appears that, during the above-mentioned centuries,

[1] *Tracts and Treatises of John de Wycliffe*, pp. 4-6.

no fewer than about seventy councils and synods recognised the weekly holy day as a Christian ordinance, most of them adopting canons on its behalf. These conventions extended over the whole period, there having been no century in which some assemblage of the clergy did not express respect for the Lord's day; and they were spread over the then known world, particularly Europe. They were attended by the most eminent ecclesiastics, and from the number as well as from the character of the members, their canons may be considered as among the best means of ascertaining the state of opinion at their respective dates. To these collective indications of the general doctrine respecting the institution, and to the united measures adopted to promote its better observance, we have to add the services rendered in both respects to its cause by the ministers of religion in their several charges, by the Fathers, as Ambrose, Augustine, and Chrysostom, and by such men as Ecgbright, Egbert, and Alcuin.

Both councils and individuals exerted themselves from time to time to remedy *indolent neglect* in reference to the Lord's day. The twenty-first canon of the Council of Eliberis (A.D. 305) ordained that, for absence from church three successive Lord's days, a layman should be temporarily excluded from communion. In 347, the council of Sardica decreed that no bishop should be permitted to be absent from his church for more than three weeks; and the Council in Trullo (A.D. 691), combining the two canons, enacted that a clergyman, unnecessarily absent from his own church more than three Lord's days, should be deposed, and a similarly negligent layman cut off from communion.[1] One great object, indeed, of the councils, and of bishops in their respective spheres, was to secure the attendance of the people in the house of God; and in their canons and constitutions they sometimes descended to such particulars as that the hearers should remain to the close of the service.

Secular labour on the Lord's day was inhibited. Husbandry

[1] Our facts have been derived from several works on the councils; but to save a multitude of references, we may state, that in Neale's *Feasts and Fasts*, and Morer *on the Lord's Day*, may be found the chief heads of what relates to our subject, with the authorities.

in its various operations, all mechanical works, merchandise, and unnecessary travelling, were forbidden. Legal proceedings must "cease and determine." No folkmote or political assembly must hold. Marriages were not to be solemnized, criminals were not to be executed. In a word, persons, of whatever country or quality, were required to forbear servile work, that they might have leisure for the worship of God.

Worldly amusements, moreover, were condemned. We meet with frequent denunciations against the exhibitions and encouragement of theatrical shows and dancings, as well as against hunting and various pastimes, on the sacred day. When the Bulgarians sent questions on this and other matters to Pope Nicholas, in A.D. 858, his reply was, "That they should desist from all secular work and carnal pleasure, or whatever contributed to defile the body; and do nothing but what was suitable to the day." Dunstan, Archbishop of Canterbury, did himself honour by issuing a special order, that "King Edgar should not continue to hunt on the Lord's day."

Such things were enjoined as *included* or *furthered the positive duties* of the day. Instruction by regularly officiating incumbents in churches, or, in their indispensable absence, by substitutes, was provided. All vicars were required, even at so late a time in mediæval history as 1360, to read the word of God to the people in their own language. Repeatedly do we find more frequent communicating urged as a means of promoting Sabbatic observance. With the same view, councils defined the time of holy rest, and exhorted the people to be present at the public worship of Saturday. One peculiar arrangement was, that "the archdeacon, or some other dignitary, should take special care that all prisoners, every Lord's day, might be well relieved in what their necessities called for." The following is a specimen of a synodical decree on the manner of observing the day. The bishops assembled at Friuli, in Italy, thus resolved: "That all people shall with due reverence and devotion honour the Lord's day, beginning on the evening of the day before, and that thereon they more especially abstain from all kinds of sin, as also from all carnal acts, and secular labours: and that they go to church in a grave manner, laying aside all suits of law and controversies, which might hinder their praising God's name together."

The good men of those days were urgent, if not always wise, in *the arguments and inducements* employed by them for the accomplishment of their object. In not a few instances they properly confined themselves to their own spiritual province, the administration of the truth, law, and discipline of Christ. But in too many others, they called in the help of the weapons that are carnal. Pecuniary fines were exacted. The man who used his cattle in customary work forfeited an ox or a team. Stripes constituted, in certain cases, the punishment of the Sabbath-breaker. Nay, the partial loss of patrimony, and degradation to slavery, were inflicted according to circumstances. These were mistaken awards of clergy and councils to the violaters of Christian institutions and laws. But the men who thus punished offenders, proved at least their conviction of the enormity of the offence. It is more pleasant to mark "the more excellent way" of religious argument and appeal, when the authorities refer the people to "the law of God," as demanding the sanctification of the Lord's day, when they entreat their observance of it by a regard to "the reverence and rest of the Lord's resurrection," when they remind them of the Divine example, and when, with Bishop Riculphus, they complain "That some people made no conscience of going to market, and doing such other things on the Lord's day as all laws human and Divine forbade them to do," and like him decree, that "All imaginable care shall be taken to redress and put a stop to those ungodly courses, as being a great folly and shame, that any Christian should so overlook the day which is the memorial of Christ's resurrection, and our redemption by him, and so eagerly pursue his worldly gain at a time when he ought to be employed in holy offices for God's honour, and the good of his own soul, and theirs belonging to him."

Nor was it forgotten to warn Christians against a *formal and superstitious Sabbatism.* While they were to abstain from rural works, and this world's and their own pleasures, "they were to be filled with spiritual joys, and busily vacant with all their heart in unwearied praises." When some had conceived that no work whatever was to be done, they were reminded that it was lawful to ride, to dress victuals, and to do what concerned the neatness of the body or of the house. How remote from superstition and mere form, and yet how true and just the representation of Theodulph, Bishop of Orleans: "Such is the sanctity of the Lord's day, that nothing should be done in it except religious and necessary exercises; for if liberty be given of sailing and travelling, it must only be in cases of necessity, and so as not to interfere with public worship. Every Christian should go to the house of God, early and late, and avoid improper conversation on the way. We should have leisure only for God, in holy exercises and benevolence, and in the praises of the Lord with our friends. As for our feasting, it is to be spiritual with our neighbours and with strangers."

LEGISLATION.

In March, A.D. 321, Constantine issued a decree that all should rest on the venerable day of the Sun, with the exception of those engaged in husbandry, who were allowed to attend to the work of their calling. In June of the same year he renewed the order, with the additional exception, of such actions as concerned the liberation of prisoners, and the manumission of slaves. The Lord's day was to be consecrated to prayer. Christian soldiers were allowed freely to frequent the churches, and there without molestation offer up their prayers to God. Others of the army "who had not tasted the sweetness of Divine knowledge," he commanded to repair to the fields, and join together in acts of devotion. He even prescribed a form of prayer, which he required all his soldiers to use on the first day of the week, and in their daily worship. Governors of provinces were instructed to observe the Lord's day. All were likewise enjoined to honour other holidays and feasts of the Church; but the same abstinence from labour was not made imperative on such occasions.

It may in this place be remarked, that important evidence in favour of the institution can be extracted from edicts of the civil powers, as also from the canons of councils, while both may have been connected with objectionable measures. When Constantine could not be neutral as to the Lord's day—when for him not to hold and obey the Sabbatic law must have involved the rejection and transgression of a Divine commandment, and the refusal of a provision essential to the well-being of the empire—it was right and good that he determined to recognise and protect the weekly holy day. But this proceeding on his part, and as followed in other cases, may be pleaded as a strong testimony to the value and necessity of the institution, by those who hold that the magistrate has no right to sanction holy days of human appointment, to permit agricultural or other secular labour on the day of rest and worship, or to compel his subjects to perform those devotional services which lie out of the legitimate reach and power of civil authority.

Constantine died in A.D. 337. After the intervening reigns of his three sons, his nephew, Julian, ascended the throne, and proceeded to restore idolatry. Even he, as we have had repeated occasion to remark, gave evidence, however unwittingly, in favour of Christianity and its weekly holy day, by introducing into his Pagan system improvements borrowed from the Christian worship. The following emperors—Valentinian, Gratian, Valentinian II., and Honorius, in the west, with Valens, Theodosius the Great, Arcadius, Theodosius II., in the east—issued edicts, designed respectively to prohibit certain law proceedings, and to put an end to theatrical exhibitions on the Lord's day. In one of these laws the words occur, "the day of the sun, which our fathers rightly called the Lord's day." From another we cite the following sentence : "Nor let any man think himself obliged in honour and reverence to us"—when the anniversaries of his birth and accession to the throne happened to fall on such days—"to neglect the sacred religion and business of the day, and apply himself to public diversions ; for let him not doubt, that we look upon ourselves as then best served and honoured when the excellencies of the great God and his mercies to mankind are most devoutly celebrated." The Emperors Leo and Anthemius (A.D. 460) prohibited worldly pleasures, as well as law proceedings, on the Lord's day, under the penalty that the offender, if having a place under government, should lose it, and forfeit his estate. There followed enactments by Theodoric the Great, several kings of France, Ina, king of the West Saxons, and Withred, king of Kent, all having for their object to prevent the desecration of the day of rest by secular business or labour. Charlemagne, benefiting by the advice of Alcuin, evinced special zeal in calling councils for the reformation of abuses connected with the Lord's day ; and it is worthy of remark that, though he punished the disturbers of worship with death, he on several occasions affixed no penalty to the neglect of religious ordinances or to the desecration of sacred time, leaving these offences to be dealt with by the ecclesiastical power. In his edict calling five councils, in A.D. 813, he has these words : "We ordain, as it is required in the law of God, that no man do any servile work on the Lord's day,"—of which a variety of examples are given,—but that men and women "come all to the church to magnify the Lord their God for those good things which on this day he bestowed on them." His son, Louis the Pious, walked in his steps ; and, aware how much depended on the example of persons in superior station, put forth the following decree : "It is necessary that, in the first place, priests, kings, and princes, and all the faithful, should most devoutly exhibit a due observance and reverence of this day."

Alfred the Great was the ornament of the closing years of the ninth century, as Charlemagne was the distinction of its commencement, and of the latter part of the preceding. One of his laws, in 876, while appointing penalties for offences on the Lord's day and certain holidays, declared that "among the festivals, this day ought more especially to be solemnly kept, because it was the day wherein our Saviour, Christ, overcame the devil." In the same century was issued the well-known edict of the Emperor Leo, "the Philosopher," which, after mentioning that the Lord's day was to be honoured with rest from labour, and that he had seen a law (Constantine's) which, restraining some works but permitting others, did dishonour to the day, proceeds as follows : "It is our will and pleasure, according to the true meaning of the Holy Ghost, and of the apostles by Him directed, that on that sacred day, whereon we were restored to our integrity, all men should rest themselves and cease from labour, neither the husbandman nor others putting their hand that day to prohibited work. For if the Jews did so much reverence their Sabbath, which was only a shadow of ours, are not we, who inhabit light and the truth of grace, obliged to honour that day which the Lord hath honoured, and hath therein delivered us both from dishonour and from death? Are not we bound to keep it singularly and inviolably, sufficiently contented with a liberal grant of all the rest, and not encroaching on that one which God hath chosen for his service? Nay, were it not a reckless slighting and contemning of all religion to make that day common, and think we may do thereon as we do on others?"[1] Athelstan and Edgar, Edward the Elder, and the Emperor Otho, in the tenth century; Ethelred, Canute, and Edward the Confessor, in the eleventh; Manuel Comnenus and Henry II., in the twelfth; the Parliament at Scone and Henry III., in the thirteenth; Edward III. in the fourteenth; and Henry VI., with Edward IV., in the fifteenth,—are all recorded to have employed their authority to maintain the observance of the weekly rest. An order issued in the fifteenth century by Catworth, the Lord Mayor of London, in concurrence with the Common Council, was more worthy of the cause than some royal decrees. Referring only to the Lord's day, it required "that no manner of commodities be within the freedom bought or sold on Lord's days, neither provision nor any other thing; and that no artificer should bring his ware unto any man to be worn or occupied that day."

ASCENDENCY.

The history of Christendom, from the beginning of the fourth to the close of the fifteenth century, presents a variety of facts illustrative of the peculiar importance which continued to be attached to the first day of the week.

One of the evidences of this feeling is discovered in certain things which were to be done on that day. If the Church made too much of the circumstance of posture in prayer, her insisting that on the Lord's day her members should stand up in performing the duty, proved the honour in which the day was held as a memorial of a completed and accepted redemption. Early in the fourth century (A.D. 306), Peter, Bishop of Alexandria, informs us, that the Christians did not kneel in prayer on the Lord's day, as

[1] Heylyn's *Hist. of the Sab.*, Part ii. p. 140.

that was a day of rejoicing, because on it Jesus Christ was raised from the dead.[1] The celebrated Council of Nice (A.D. 325), attended by no fewer than 318 bishops, and by Athanasius, pronounced against kneeling in prayer on that day. This, too, was eminently and usually the day of the communion. It was also the day on which Easter was, after some time, universally celebrated, as well as the sentence of excommunication pronounced.

Another token of special respect for the first day of the week, is to be found in the exclusion of certain other things from the services of the day. Abstinence from labour came to be required on holidays as well as on the Lord's day; but it is worthy of notice, that this practice was not enjoined by any eastern law for the first seven centuries, though in the west it was otherwise.[2] Fasting, which, so far as we have observed, was not forbidden to be practised on holidays, and was excluded from Saturdays in the east, though required in the west, was held to be dishonouring to the Lord's day, and frequently declared to involve the severest censures of the Church. The guilty person, if a clergyman, was to be deposed,—if a layman, to be excommunicated. "Let him," it is said "be anathema." The west and east agreed in excepting the Lord's days from the period of fasting, whatever might be its length.[3] Litanies, also, fixed for a particular day, were deferred when that day was a Sunday.

We see in the preparations that were to be made for the proper observance of the day, how sacredly it was regarded. Thus, in a Council at Croy, in Spain, it was agreed that 'all Christians should be admonished every Saturday evening to go to church by way of preparation for the Lord's day." Directions are repeatedly given to begin the observance of the day on the previous evening. Kings and councils, in a number of instances, decreed that the weekly rest should extend from noontide of Saturday to Monday morning.

The manifold and persevering exertions put forth for the upholding and observance of the weekly holy day, declare the esteem in which it was held. It employed, we have seen, the care of many councils and synods. The dignitaries of the Church were

[1] Dupin's *Eccl. Writers*, vol. ii. p. 26.

[2] Neale's *Feasts and Fasts*, p. 101.

[3] *Ibid.* p. 311.

often engaged in framing canons for its better observance. Authors commended it to their readers. The pulpit poured out eloquent tributes to its excellence, and urgent appeals on its behalf. Princes and inferior magistrates acknowledged its Divine claims, and felt its value as a beneficent institution. That was regarded as no common or trifling matter, for the neglect and contempt of which men were deposed from the ministry, expelled from the church, subjected to corporal chastisement, deprived of patrimony, or reduced to serfdom. And we have to add, that the resort to more remarkable, if less injurious measures in the cause, was significant of the importance supposed to belong to it. The story of an apparition said to be seen by Henry II. of England, and charging him to have no servile work done throughout his dominions on the Lord's day, except what concerned the provision of meat and drink, that so he might succeed in all his affairs, and of his misfortunes in consequence of neglecting the mandate, has a meaning and use to the extent of indicating the opinion, that the day was the charge of Heaven, and that its sacred observance was connected with human prosperity and happiness. The same lesson is taught by the case of Eustachius, Abbot de Flay, in the following century. This ardent person preached from city to city, and from place to place, throughout England, forbidding the holding of markets on the first day of the week. Many entered into his views, but their undue zeal in overturning the booths and stalls of those who persisted in the practice, led the king and council to cite and fine them for disorderly proceedings. The Abbot, then, produced what he called a mandate from Heaven for the strict observance of the Lord's day, in which various calamities were denounced on those who did not keep that day and the festivals of the saints. The same warrant was produced and read in a Scottish Council of A.D. 1203, when the King, with consent of his Parliament, passed it into a law, that Saturday from noon was to be counted holy, and that the people were to engage in holy actions, going to sermons and the like, from that time till Monday morning, or be subjected to a penalty. It appears, however, that a relaxation of this law, so far as regarded fishing, was made by Alexander III. in a Parliament at Scone in 1214, and confirmed afterwards by James I., the prohibition of such work being limited to the time between the evening of Saturday and sunrise of Monday.

We have been pleading certain facts as, notwithstanding the enthusiasm and other evils mixed up with them, contributing to prove that the Sabbatic institution has a testimony in the heart even of a degenerate Christian society. And we will take the liberty of making use of another fact for the same purpose. Holidays have no warrant in Scripture, and have contributed sadly to foster superstition and immorality. And yet, usurpers though they are of Sabbatic rights, and detrimental to Sabbatic objects, they had their origin in the recognised authority and felt benefit of the only true holy day. It was in the more advanced stage of human festivals and feasts that a class arose, who made use of them for upholding despotism and an overbearing hierarchy, and for attempting the subversion of the Lord's day. In the earlier days of the Church, Christians, desirous of recalling the various facts in a religion which they reverenced and loved, and finding spiritual profit and pleasure in the duties of a stated season of worship, sought, in the multiplication of memorial times, and of their attendant devotions, to do honour to the birth, death, and ascension, as had been done to the resurrection of Christ, and to augment their own spiritual advantage and pleasure. This was well meant, but it involved the great error of being wise above what is written—the evil of being righteous overmuch. It was a testimony, however, to the heavenly and good institution, as the counterfeit is to the genuine and valuable coin.

The doctrine of Divine judgments, as attending the violation of Divine laws, has frequently been supposed to be the peculiarity, and merited reproach of the Puritans. The history of the Church, however, reveals it as a doctrine of Fathers, Prelates, and even of Popes. It was held by Gregory of Tours.[1] Pope Eugenius, observing that certain persons, especially women, spent their time in dancing and singing, gave directions to a Synod, held, about A.D. 826, at Rome, "That the parish priest should from time to time admonish such offenders, and desire them to go to church and offer prayers, lest otherwise they might bring some great calamity on themselves and others." The Pope had a conviction

[1] Heylyn's *Hist. of the Sab.*, Part ii. pp. 113, 114.

that the neglect of Divine institutions exposed men to disasters. Nor was the conviction rare. At a Provincial Council held at Paris, about A.D. 829, under Louis and Lotharius, Emperors, the prelates complained that the Lord's day was not kept with the reverence becoming religion and the practice of their forefathers; "which," they add, "was the reason that God had sent several judgments on them, and in a very remarkable manner punished some people for slighting and abusing it." In confirmation of this statement, they refer to cases known to many of them, and heard of by others, of several countrymen following their husbandry on this day, who had been killed with lightning, or had miserably perished under convulsions, "whereby it is apparent how high the displeasure of God was upon their neglect of this day." We adduce these views and instances, not as showing that profanation of the Lord's day is sometimes visited with remarkable expressions of the Divine wrath, though of this position there is ample proof, but as another evidence of the solemn importance which, in the times to which the facts belong, was attached to the institution.

We have to mention the language in which the Lord's day is spoken of as yet another proof of our position. The frequent application to the first day of the week, in the writings and enactments of the time, of such expressions as "the venerable day of the sun," "the chief of the festivals," "the feast of feasts," "the beginning of our life," "the primate," "the queen," "the first and chief" of days, "the regal day," "the day which is better than all other days, common or festive," evinces the high and peculiar regard which was entertained for the sacred season. The Emperors Leo and Anthemius speak of the Lord's day as "ever honourable and worthy of veneration;" and Alfred the Great, we have seen, declares, in a law on the subject, that among the festivals the Lord's day more especially ought to be solemnly kept, because it was the day wherein our Saviour, Christ, overcame the devil. It is the "sacred day," says Leo the Philosopher, "whereon we were restored to our integrity,—the day which the Lord honoured by rescuing us from the captivity of death," the day "which God hath named for his service, and which it were a reckless slighting and contemning of all religion to make common."

OBSERVANCE.

Of the means employed in the period of our present survey for securing honour and respect to the Lord's day, more is recorded than of the successful results. It would be wrong, however, to draw the conclusion, that the measure of practical regard to the institution is to be estimated by the space which it occupies in history. "It is not necessary, that those things which are constantly done should be noted in history, but those things which are rarely done." The preaching, writings, and other labours of such men as Athanasius, Ambrose, Chrysostom, and Augustine must, among their happy effects, have been instrumental in forming many to so essential a character as that of willing subjection to the Fourth Commandment. The diligence and zeal of councils in prosecuting the same object could not be in vain. But when the eminent Fathers of the fourth and beginning of the fifth century disappeared from the scene, so many impediments to the advance of Sabbath profanation were removed. The spirit, which in other times made that day to be a delight, gave way to one which regarded it as a form and a burden; and the new appliances of fines and bodily chastisement to restrain its abuse, showed that open violation and slothful neglect of the sacred rest had become more prevalent. One token of good, however, was the desire shown throughout the sixth century to stay the progress of the evil. The succession of efforts employed for this purpose by twenty councils, and the views of the institution entertained, proved how excellent it is in itself, and how it commends itself to the reason and convictions of mankind. In the following century, we have accounts of the general observance of the day; one of them by Cummianus, an Irish Abbot or Bishop, of the year 640, and another by Theodore, Archbishop of Canterbury, both in the same terms. "On the Lord's day," says the latter, in his *Pœnitential*, "the Greeks and Romans neither sail nor ride on horseback; they do not make bread, nor travel in a carriage, except to church only, nor do they bathe." The Emperor Charlemagne having been desired by the clergy to provide for the stricter observation of the day, "he accordingly did so, and left no stone unturned to secure its honour, and restrain his subjects from abusing it.

His care succeeded, and during his reign the Lord's day bore a considerable figure. But after his decease it put on another face."[1] This relapse, however, served to rouse the friends of the institution to greater exertion. Councils were convened at Paris and Aken (Auchen, Aix la Chapelle). Bishop Jona and others set themselves against the evil. And when we take into account, also, the efforts of Leo, the Philosopher, and Alfred the Great, we are not surprised at the remark of an historian as respects Christendom generally in the ninth century : "We are now prepared to allow that there is considerable truth in the statement, that during the contests concerning image-worship, society was strict in all religious observances, and great attention was paid to Sunday."[2] It was a part of the creed of the Waldenses, "that the observation of the Sabbath, by ceasing from worldly labours and from sin, by good works, and by promoting the edification of the soul through prayer and hearing the word, is enjoined" in the law of God.[3] We are furnished with information respecting their morals by Reinerus Sacco, an apostate from their church, and a Jacobin inquisitor, who wrote a book against them about 1254, and whose testimony is above suspicion. Besides mentioning, "that they work on feast days, and disregard the fasts of the Church, dedications, and benedictions," and referring to their churches and schools, he says, "They are composed and modest in manners. They do not multiply riches, but are content with necessaries. They are also chaste, especially the Leonists. They are temperate in eating and drinking. They do not go to taverns, nor to dancings, nor to other vanities. They restrain themselves from anger. . . . They avoid scurrility, detraction, levity of conversation, lying and swearing."[4] We may conceive what their deportment on the first day of the week would be, from the circumstance, that, when a barbe or minister was appointed, an oath was administered to him before the assembled barbes, in this form, "Thou, such a one, swearest on thy faith to maintain, multiply, and increase our law, and not to discover the same to any in the world, and that thou promisest not in any manner to swear by God, and that thou observe the Lord's day, and that thou wilt not

[1] Morer *On the Lord's Day*, pp. 270, 271.

[2] Finlay's *Byzan. Empire*, vol. i. p. 311.

[3] Blair's *Waldenses*, vol. i. p. 220.

[4] *Ibid.* vol. i. pp. 408, 412.

do anything to thy neighbour which thou wouldst not have him to do to thee, and that thou dost believe in God who has made the sun and moon, the heaven and the earth, the cherubim and seraphim, and all that thou seest."[1]

The practice of the Bohemian Brethren in relation to the Christian weekly holy day, which, we have already seen, they held to be appointed instead of the Jewish Sabbath, was the following: "The brethren rested from all secular employments. Their domestics and cattle also rested. They strictly avoided drunkenness, gambling, dancing, idle conversation, lounging, and the like; and spent the day in singing God's praise, reading the Bible, and attending four or five services at church."[2] Besides several days for commemorating events in the history of Christ, and others relating to Mary, the Apostles, and the martyrs, but on which every one after the public services returned to his work, they kept fasts four times a year, and on occasions of remarkable calamities, or of the exclusion of an individual from the Church.[3] They made a distinction between the Sabbath and the other days; the former being considered by them as of inviolable obligation, the others observed with Christian liberty, for recalling important facts, and for giving opportunities of useful admonition, that, "after preaching and prayers are over, they may apply themselves to their ordinary works as on other days."[4]

From the facts set forth in this and two preceding sections, it appears that for fifteen centuries the first day of the week was, under various names, recognised throughout Christendom as a divinely-appointed day of worship and sacred rest; that it was regarded as the old ordinance of paradise and Sinai, adapted by extrinsic changes to the New Economy; and that many writings, canons, edicts, and other measures, attested the concern of good men for its observance, and their conviction of its high dignity and excellence. It is not necessary to the evidence for the Sabbath, which the history of that long period supplies, that the language used respecting it, the measures employed on its behalf, and the performance of its duties, should have been immaculate. There have been writers—Dr. Heylyn, for example—who

[1] Blair's *Waldenses*, vol. ii. p. 157.
[2] *Ibid.* vol. ii. p. 109.
[3] *Ibid.* p. 110.
[4] Bruce's *An. Secul.* p. 202.

have subjected this evidence to a process of disingenuous, unjust, and naughty criticism, which shows a disposition to bear down rather than to discover truth, and under which, as generally applied, no document, no testimony, no man on trial for life, no interest, however important, could be safe. The marvel is, that amidst the growing corruption of a great part of that period, there was such a unanimity of opinion respecting the Lord's day, and that the day did not cease to exist. Nor let it be said that the prevailing evil betrayed any inefficiency in the ordinance. From two causes at least—from endlessly multiplying holidays, which obscured its authority, and diluted its strength, and from the ever increasing neglect and perversion of its essential agencies of instruction and worship—it was not allowed its full and proper influence. In all cases in which the Sabbath has been dissociated from enfeebling, demoralizing festivals of human device, and been joined to its natural allies of sound religious instruction, and a simple, pure worship, it has evinced itself to be the power of God in stemming the tide of error and immorality, and in making communities pious, virtuous, and happy. And that must be a mighty institute which has been found to live and bless mankind under manifold disadvantages, and which, in the case before us, crippled though it was, not only maintained its ground amidst such elements of destruction, but for so long a time prevented the entire overthrow of the religious and social edifice.

THE SABBATH AT THE REFORMATION.

In the controversy respecting a weekly holy day, parties have eagerly sought support for their respective opinions in the writings of the Reformers. These eminent men have, on the one hand, been represented as holding the common creed of Christians on the subject, although it is admitted that their language in several instances is not in seeming accordance with such views, and have, on the other, been considered as denying the Divine obligation of a stated day of sacredness and rest. Of late years scarcely a volume or tract in defence of the latter notion has appeared, which has not "bristled" with the names of Luther and Calvin as the advocates of liberty from all Sabbatarian impositions. Much, indeed, as

Luther, Calvin, and their associates, are entitled to our admiration for their learning, piety, and zeal, and to our gratitude for the services which they rendered to all the interests of mankind, it must be recollected that their sentiments do not on this or on any other point amount to a test of truth. It is not, however, inconsistent with the great principle, that no man is our master in such matters, to feel a desire to have the sanction of the Reformers for our interpretation of the sacred oracles. The friends of the Sabbath, in particular, would be gratified by the persuasion, that such men had vindicated for themselves a place in the "great cloud of witnesses" for the Divine origin, perpetual sacredness, and indispensable value of that blessed institution. Let us, therefore, inquire what were the views on this subject of the distinguished persons by whose instrumentality our deliverance from Papal bondage was accomplished.

The following remarks and illustrations will, we trust, present in a just light the views of the Reformers on the subject of the Sabbatic institution :—

1. They regarded the weekly day of rest and worship as a most reasonable, useful, and indispensable arrangement. In the Confessions of Augsburg, Saxony, and Helvetia, we find such expressions as these applied to the institution : "It was requisite to appoint a certain day, that the people might know when to come together."[1] "Natural reason doth know that there is an order ; and the understanding of order is an evident testimony of God ; neither is it possible that men should live without any order, as we see that in families there must be distinct times of labour, rest, meat, and sleep ; and every nature, as it is best, so doth it chiefly love order throughout the whole life."[2] "Although religion be not tied unto time, yet it cannot be planted and exercised without a due dividing and allotting out of time unto it. . . . . Except some due time and leisure were allotted to the outward exercise of religion, without doubt men would be quite drawn from it by their own affairs."[3] These passages teach us that the Lutheran and Reformed Churches were agreed as to the propriety, and the necessity to the ends of religion, of certain times being set apart for its exercises and study. The Reformers individually apply these

[1] Hall's *Harmony of Confessions*, p. 401. [2] *Ibid.* p. 402. [3] *Ibid.* p. 382.

principles to specific seasons. Thus Luther says, "It is good and even necessary that men should keep a particular day in the week, on which they are to meditate, hear, and learn, for all cannot command every day; and nature also requires that one day in the week should be kept quiet, without labour either for man or beast."[1] On two occasions we find him utter his earnest desire for the abolition of holidays, and on both, with the express exception of the "*Dies Dominicus.*"[2] On the worth and absolute need of the weekly Sabbath, Calvin is still more explicit. It is as requisite now as it ever was: "While the day has ceased as the figure of a spiritual and important mystery, there are other and different ends for which it is set apart; and in respect of the duty of resting from all earthly cares and employments, and applying to spiritual exercises in public and private, the necessity of a Sabbath is common to us with the people of old."[3] The observance of it comprises in it all religion: "Under the observance of the Sabbath is comprehended the sum of all piety."[4] The neglect of it indicates the destitution and the contempt of Christian blessings: "And hereby it appears what affection we have towards all Christianity, and towards the serving of God, seeing we make that thing an occasion of withdrawing ourselves further off from God, which is given us as a help to bring us nearer unto him; and be we once gone astray, it serveth to pull us quite and clean away—and is not that a devilish spite of men?"[5] Such neglect not only is an act of indignity to religion, but renders every part of it ineffectual and valueless: "He who setteth at nought the Sabbath-day, has cast under foot all God's service, as much as is in him; and if the Sabbath-day be not observed, all the rest shall be worth nothing."[6] The observance of it, on the other hand, brings happiness to the individual, and secures protection to the state. "The Sabbath, or rest of God—le repos de Dieu,—is not idleness, but true perfection, which brings along with it a calm state of peace."[7] "The city will be safe, if God be truly and devoutly worshipped, and this is attested by the sanctification of the Sabbath."[8] We add the words of

1 Quoted in Fairbairn's *Typol.*, vol. ii. p. 467.
2 See p. 17 of this vol., *note* 4.
3 *Comment.* on Exod. xx. 8-11.
4 *Comment.* on Exod. xvi. 28.
5 Ser. 34 on Deut. v.
6 On Deut. v. Ser. 34.
7 On John v. 17.
8 On Jer. xvii.

Bucer: "It must needs be a very great contempt of God, not to bestow one day in the whole week in the knowing and serving of our Creator, of whom we have received ourselves and all things else that we enjoy."[1]

2. The sacred observance of the first day of the week was a duty which the leaders of the Reformation were careful to enforce. "Farel's first experiments in discipline," as Dr. Henry informs us, "had proved very distasteful. Among the things forbidden were games of chance, swearing, slandering, dancing, the singing of idle songs, and masquerading. The people were commanded to attend church, to keep Sunday strict, and to be at home by nine o'clock in the evening. These laws were proclaimed with the sound of a trumpet, and with threats of severe punishment against transgressors. Four preachers and two deacons were appointed, and a school was established. Farel published a short formulary of belief, consisting of twenty-one articles, and was probably associated in this with Calvin, who published a catechism in French."[2] What a disciplinarian Calvin was, and how he laboured by unwearied preaching and writing to enlighten and reform the Genevese, while on him "came the care of all the churches," we need not say. But he has not received the credit due to him as a friend of the Sabbath. Partial extracts from his notices of the subject have been industriously circulated, while care has not been shown to set forth such passages as the following: "It is for us to dedicate ourselves wholly to God, renouncing our feelings and all our affections; and then, since we have this external ordinance, to act as becomes us, that is, to *lay aside our earthly affairs*, so that we may be entirely free to meditate on the works of God."[3] "The Sabbath is the bark of a spiritual substance, the use of which is still in force, of denying ourselves, of renouncing all our own thoughts and affections, and of *bidding farewell to one and all of our own employments*, so that God may reign in us, then of employing ourselves in the worship of God."[4] "Every man," he remarks, as a reason why Christians should not go to law upon the Lord's day, "ought to *withdraw himself from everything but the consideration of God and His works*, that all men may be

[1] On Ps. xcii.
[2] *Life and Times of John Calvin*, vol. i. p. 112.
[3] Ser. 34, Deut. v.
[4] *Ibid.*

stirred up to serve and honour Him."[1] And as he excludes secular labour, so also worldly recreations : "If we employ the Lord's day to make good cheer, to sport ourselves, to go to games and pastimes, shall God in this be honoured ? Is it not a mockery ? Is not this an unhallowing of his name ?"[2] Peter Viret, his colleague, was like-minded : "One end of bodily rest on the Sabbath," he says, "is that men might attend upon the ministry and service of God in the church, and that we might meditate upon the works of God, and be occupied in the duties of charity to our neighbours."[3] The friend of Calvin, as well as of Luther, Bucer, referring to the service of God as required on the Lord's day above all others, gives utterance to these earnest words : "Let our manners show it, let the holiness of our lives testify to it, let our works prove it ; for who will believe that he has been present at the assemblies of the Church, and has heard the word of God with a sincere heart and a true faith, who bestows the remainder, not only of that day, but of his life ; not only more vainly, but more wickedly ?"[4] Zuinglius, Bullinger, who succeeded him in his pastoral charge, Œcolampadius, Peter Martyr, and Zanchius, have written to the same effect. Thus also taught Luther and his friends. "Although the Sabbath," Luther says, "is now abolished, and the conscience is freed from it, it is still good and even necessary, that men should keep a particular day in the week for the sake of the word of God, on which they are to meditate, hear, and learn, for all cannot command every day ; and nature also requires that one day in the week should be kept quiet, without labour either for man or beast."[5] Even when, in the vehemence of his zeal against a return to Judaical observance, he rashly orders persons to trample on the institution rather than pervert it in that form, he does not forget to say, "Keep it holy for its use' sake, both to body and soul."[6] In treating of the Third [Fourth] Commandment, Melanchthon mentions, among the breaches of it, the neglect of the public ministry of the church. Bucer says, "It is our duty to sanctify one day in each week for the public service of religion : that there be one day in the week on which the people may have nothing else to do than to go to church, there

[1] Ser. 93 on Deut. v.
[2] Ser. 34 on Deut. v.
[3] On Fourth Commandment.
[4] In Matt. xii. 11.
[5] Fairbairn, as before.
[6] Coleridge's *Table Talk*, ii. 315.

to hear God's word, to pour out their prayers, to confess their faith, to give thanks, to make oblations, and to receive the holy communion: hence the Lord's day was consecrated to these by the very apostles."[1] Let us add Chemnitz, who, though he belongs to a later time, was an able and learned expounder of Lutheran doctrine, and has been brought forward against us. In his view, "the Sabbath is violated chiefly by those who abuse that time of rest unto pleasures, lightness, surfeiting, drunkenness, and all other kind of wickedness; whereby it cometh to pass, that commonly God is upon no day more offended than upon those which are specially appointed unto his worship and service."[2] And again, "Christ by his example doth show how the time between the public assemblies ought to be devoted to spiritual improvement, for after he had taught in public, and the assembly was dismissed, he privately examined and further instructed his disciples."[3] These last words remind us that the Reformers, like the Fathers and all "good Christians," regarded the Lord's day as lasting beyond the hours of public worship, as having the same extent with any other day, and as a day to be sanctified throughout. "Let us bear in mind," says Calvin, "that this day is not appointed for us only to come to the sermon, but that we might employ the rest of the time in praising God;" and, as he afterwards remarks, "in digesting the good doctrine, that by this means we may be so formed and fashioned as that during the week it may cost us nothing to raise our hearts to God."[4]

3. The lessons which the Reformers taught on this subject were by them and by their flocks conscientiously practised. We have seen no account of Luther's more private deportment on the day of rest; but, from the character of the man, and from his more deliberate utterances regarding the sacredness and importance of the institution, we may presume that his Sabbath-keeping would be such as became one so pious and prayerful as he was. The same conclusion seems to be warranted by the habits which he was the means of forming in others. For it appears that such Sabbath desecration as became general in later times, was for a considerable period unknown in the Lutheran Church. Plitt, of

[1] *De Reg. Christ.*, lib. i. c. 11.
[2] *Exam. de Diebus Festis.*
[3] *Exam. de Diebus Festis.*
[4] On Deut. v. Ser. 34.

Bonn, who mentions this fact, at the same time states, respecting the Protestants who held the Calvinian creed, that "of old the Reformed Church specially maintained a strict Sabbath celebration in accordance with the law of God."[1] On this subject Calvin remarks, "I am obliged to be a little more prolix here, because in our day some unquiet spirits make an outcry about the Lord's day. They complain that the Christian people are nursed in Judaism because some observance of days is retained."[2] "When our shop windows," he observes in another publication, "are shut on the Lord's day—when we travel not, after the common order and fashion of men—this is to the end we should have more liberty and leisure to attend on that which God commandeth, that is, to be taught by His word, to meet together, to make confession of our faith, to call upon His name, to exercise ourselves in the use of His sacraments—the purpose which this order ought to serve."[3]

4. The Reformers believed the Sabbath to have been appointed by God at the creation. In explaining Gen. ii. 3, Luther says, "It therefore follows from this place, that if Adam had abode in innocence, he should yet have kept holy the seventh day—that is, he should have instructed his descendants concerning the will and worship of God, and rendered to Him praise, thanksgiving, and offerings. On other days, he should have cultivated the soil and tended his flocks. Nay, after the fall he sanctified that seventh day; in other words, he instructed his family on that day, as is testified by the offerings of his sons, Cain and Abel. Wherefore, the Sabbath was from the beginning of the world set apart to Divine worship."[4] According to *The Confession of Saxony*, which was drawn up by Melanchthon, and expresses the views of Luther and his friends, "There hath been at all times, even from the beginning of mankind, a certain order of public meetings. There hath been also a certain distinction of times, and of some other ceremonies, and that, without doubt, full of gravity and elegancy, among those excellent lights of mankind, whenas in the same garden or cottage there sat together Shem, Abraham, Isaac, and

[1] In *Relig. Condit. of Christendom* (1852), p. 465.

[2] *Instit. on Fourth Commandment.*

[3] Ser 34, on Deut. v.

[4] *Lutheri Opera* (M.D.L.), tom. v. p. 23.

their families; and whenas, that sermon which Shem made concerning the true God, the son of God, the distinction of the Church and other nations, being heard, afterward they together used invocation."[1] Melanchthon, in his *Commentary on Genesis*, remarks, when considering ch. ii. 3, that the seventh day, as the word sanctify denotes, was appropriated to the Divine service. In expounding Exodus xx. 8, Calvin has these words: "Unquestionably, when he had finished the creation of the world, God assumed to Himself, and consecrated the seventh day, that He might keep His worshippers entirely free from all other cares when engaged in considering the beauty, excellence, and glory of His works." On the 11th verse of the same chapter, he remarks, that the prohibition to gather manna on the seventh day, seems to imply the received knowledge and use of the Sabbath, and that it is incredible that, when God delivered the rite of sacrifice to the saints, the observance of the Sabbath could have been neglected. Let us add a sentence from his notes on Genesis ii. 3: "God, therefore, first rested, then blessed this rest, that *in all ages it might be sacred among men*; in other words, He consecrated every seventh day to rest, that His *own example might be a perpetual rule*." According to Peter Martyr, the fourth ranks in antiquity with its associated requirements in the Decalogue: "This commandment of the Sabbath was no more then first given when it was pronounced from heaven by the Lord, than any other of the moral precepts."[2] Of the Sabbath, Bullinger, commenting on Rom. xiv. 5, says, "As it was in the beginning of the world, so it must continue to its end." Beza, in his annotations on Rev. i. 10, observes, that "the seventh day having stood from the creation of the world to the resurrection of Christ, was exchanged by the apostles, doubtless at the dictation of the Holy Spirit, for that which was the first day of the new world." And Ursinus, in his Catechism, after mentioning the reasons for the institution, remarks, "As these relate to no definite period, but to all times and ages of the world, it follows that God would have men bound from the beginning of the world even to its end to keep a certain Sabbath."

5. With such views of a primal Sabbath, the Reformers could not but regard it as in substance perpetuated in the Jewish weekly

[1] Hall's *Harmony of Confessions*, p. 402. [2] On Gen. ii.

holy day. While they agreed with all Christians that God commanded the Jews to sanctify one day in seven, they had no conception of its dating from the 2500th year of the world, but considered the transactions of Sin and Sinai as the recognition of a world-old institution. And on two grounds—its origination in the example and command of Jehovah at the creation, and its renewal in the Decalogue—they held it to be of Divine authority.

6. In like manner, their views respecting the early appointment of the weekly day of rest fully committed the Reformers to the doctrine of the Divine authority of the Christian Sabbath. This they knew had been the holy day of the Church from the time of the Redeemer's resurrection. They themselves had regularly observed it as such. In this and in no other day they saw their idea of a primitive and permanent weekly rest realized. They were therefore shut up to the conclusion that the Lord's day, being the continuance of a heaven-born institute, must necessarily be an ordinance of God.

But sufficient though this evidence is, it is not the only ground on which we can rest the assertion, that the Reformers maintained the doctrine in question. Let us adduce the following additional proofs. These men are found to reject certain practices which had been customary in the Church, for the express reason that they were not sanctioned by the word of God. "The fast of Lent," says the latter Helvetic Confession, "hath testimony of antiquity, but none out of the apostles' writings; and therefore ought not, nor cannot, be imposed on the faithful."[1] In the same Confession it is declared, "As for Popish visiting with the extreme unction, we have said before that we do not like of it, because it hath many absurd things in it, and such as be not approved by the canonical Scriptures."[2] On the fast of Lent, the Confession of Würtemburg harmonizes with that of Helvetia, as these words show: "It is manifest that Christ did not command this fast; neither can the constitution of our nature abide it, that we should imitate the example of Christ's fasting, who did abstain full forty days and forty nights from all meat and drink."[3] We have seen, in an early part of this volume, that holidays were entirely rejected by the Scottish Reformers, because they "had no institu-

[1] Hall's *Harmony of Confessions*, p. 383. [2] *Ibid.* p. 385. [3] *Ibid.* p. 403.

tion ;" that they were ousted from Geneva, first by Farel and Viret, and a second time by the Council ; that there was none in reformed Strasburg ; that the Church of Zurich discarded twelve feast-days ; and that Luther and the Belgic churches would have banished them if it had been in their power. Henry, in his *Life of Calvin*, remarks, "The Bernese, after accomplishing the expulsion of the ministers"—Calvin, Farel, and Courad (or Couralt),—"had re-established in Geneva the following festivals :—the circumcision, the annunciation, the ascension, and Christmas-day. These the Genevese now at once abolished, and by so doing highly incensed their allies. Calvin, to whom this movement was generally attributed, did not think it necessary to take any steps against it, recollecting, probably, that the observance of holy days is nowhere expressly enjoined in Scripture."[1] In another part of the work, the author unnecessarily laments the sacrifice in the Protestant Church of "that joyous life which was connected with the Catholic festivals, and which Zwingle, Farel, and Calvin, so disturbed by their abridgment of the holidays. Thus, while the Lutheran Church retained even the least of the festivals in the ecclesiastical year, the Reformed Church could with difficulty retain the four high festivals, the preachers not even alluding to the rest in their discourses. Calvin was neither in favour of, nor absolutely against, the festivals ; but was obliged to yield to the common wish of the people." The writer introduces here this note : "In the register of December 19, 1554, we find the following notice :—'Christmas-day shall be celebrated as usual, though Calvin has represented to the Council that it would be as well to dispense with this festival as with the other three ;'" and proceeds thus : "He was slanderously accused of wishing to abolish the Sabbath : against this statement he defended himself, and showed, in a letter to Haller, how the report arose.[2] Farel and Viret had at first pursued the practice of noticing the festivals which had occurred in the week on the following Sunday. After the expulsion of the ministers, these festivals were celebrated on the original days. On Calvin's return, and when he was strenu-

[1] Vol. ii. p. 115.

[2] John Haller, "of the illustrious family of that name," was pastor of the Bernese Church.—Bonnet, in his *Letters of Calvin*, vol. ii. p. 235, *note*.

ously endeavouring to establish his reformation according to the Gospel, he appointed, though regarding the observation of the festivals as a matter of indifference, certain hours for prayer on those days, and during which the shops were to be kept closed. At noon every one was to return to his usual occupations. Christmas-day was the only festival retained. The Council, however, without asking him, abolished, in 1551, all the attendant solemnities."[1] Although, then, particular expressions have been conceived to imply the contrary, the facts that have just been adduced prove that the Reformers considered the Lord's day as belonging to a very different category from holidays. They reduced the number and altered the observance of holidays—in some instances, wholly excluded them—and, if they had had their wish, would in every case have done so. In no instance was it ever attempted, or even proposed to them, to displace the Lord's day. The charge preferred by Barclay against Calvin, that "he had a consultation once as to transferring the Lord's day observances to Thursday," had nothing to support it but the word of a man who lived in the Court of James I., as a spy in the interest of the Queen-Mother of France, and who, says Dr. Twisse, "if he could not prove true and loyal to his natural prince, could not be expected to carry himself truly and honestly towards John Calvin."[2] A charge, which was not even attempted to be sustained by a particle of evidence, and yet still figures in anti-Sabbatic works, merits no refutation, but we may state that it is disproved by the uniform respect for the day which Calvin expressed in his words and by his life.

There are, besides, direct references by the Reformers to the Christian Sabbath which establish the position, that they held it to be a Divine ordinance. They believed, we have seen, that nature and order demanded some time to be set apart in every age to rest and religion, and that a seventh day for these purposes was prescribed at the creation for the human race in their successive generations. They, at the same time, believed that all obligation to observe Saturday as a Sabbath had ceased. The question, then, to be determined was, On what other day are we to enjoy the indispensable rest and worship of a weekly holy day

[1] Vol. i. p. 418.

[2] *Moral. of Fourth Com.*, p. 35.

—on what day are we to be favoured with the provisions, and to fulfil the enduring appointment of Paradise? That appointment, and the moral part, as they called it, of the Fourth Commandment, they believed to be still in force. They might have seen that, nothing more than some indication of the particular day was required. They did say, that there is no express command in the New Testament declaring, "Thou shalt keep holy the first day of the week." The conclusion to which some suppose they came was, that the early Christians were left at liberty to take the day which they might agree to prefer. Such a conclusion, it might be shown, was utterly unwarranted. Nor could they hold it consistently with what they themselves thus declare respecting the manner in which the Lord's day was appointed. In the Confession of Saxony we find these words: "We thank God, the everlasting Father of our Lord Jesus Christ, who, for His Son and by Him, gathered an eternal Church, for that even from the first beginning of mankind He hath preserved the public ministry of the gospel and honest assemblies; who Himself also *hath set apart certain times for the same;* and we pray Him that henceforth He will save and govern His Church."[1] "The general rule," as we read in the Confession of Augsburg, "abideth still in the moral law, that at certain times we should come together to these godly exercises; but the special day, which was but a ceremony, is free. Whereupon *the apostles* retained not the seventh day, but did rather *take the first day of the week for that use*, that by it they might admonish the godly both of their liberty, and of Christ's resurrection."[2] We add a sentence from the same Confession, "The true unity of the Church doth consist in several points of doctrine, in the true and uniform preaching of the gospel, and *in such rites as the Lord himself hath set down.*"[3] Let us compare two sentences, the one in the former, the other in the latter Helvetic Confession: "Even the Lord's day itself, ever since the apostles' time, was consecrated to religious exercises, and unto a holy rest; which also is now very well observed of our churches, for the worship of God, and increase of charity."[4] "The which [the true] Church, though it be manifest to the eyes of God alone, yet is it not only

[1] Hall's *Harmony of Confessions*, p. 435.
[2] *Ibid.* p. 430.
[3] *Ibid.* p. 217.
[4] *Ibid.* p. 382.

seen and known, by certain outward rites, *instituted of Christ himself*, and by the Word of God, as by a public and lawful discipline; but it is so appointed, that without these marks no man can be judged to be in this Church, but by the special privilege of God."[1] "Consecrated since the apostles' time," in the former of these sentences, points to the inspired means by which the will of Christ was made known. "It was meet," says Melanchthon, "that the apostles should on this account"—the resurrection of Christ—"have changed the day."[2] Bucer observes, "The Lord's day was consecrated"—as a day on which the people might have nothing else to do than engage in religious services—"by the very apostles."[3] "The Sabbath," according to Bullinger, "is ordained of God not for rest in itself, for he nowhere alloweth idleness; therefore the rest of the Sabbath is commanded for another end, namely, for the diligent study of religion, for it is therefore commanded to rest from manual labour, that we may spend this whole day in the exercise of religion."[4] The apostles must have been Calvin's "ancients" in the following words: "It was not without reason, that the ancients substituted what we call the Lord's day in the room of the Sabbath. For when the true rest, which the old Sabbath symbolized, had its fulfilment in the resurrection of Christ, by that very day which ended the shadows, Christians are warned not to cleave to the shadowy ceremonial."[5] If Calvin had represented Christians as substituting the Lord's day for the Sabbath, he would, in contradiction to his own solemn protest, have justified one of the pretensions of Rome, that of affecting power to change times and laws. Such a power is greater than that of prescribing a single duty of the first day of the week; and yet for this the word of an inspired apostle was required, for, as Calvin says, "It was for this use"—the peace (the good) of Christian society—"that the Sabbath was retained in the churches planted by him" (the apostle Paul), "for he appoints that day to the Corinthians, whereon to collect their contributions in aid of their brethren in Jerusalem."[6] We have found Beza affirming, that the first day of the new world

[1] Hall's *Harmony of Confessions*, p. 217.
[2] Wells' *Practical Sabbatarian*, p. 612.
[3] *De Reg. Christ.* lib. i. c. 11.
[4] On Rom. xiv. 5.
[5] *Instit. Fourth Commandment.*
[6] *Ibid.*

was adopted by the apostles in place of the seventh day, "*doubtless at the dictation of the Holy Spirit.*" In words similar to those of Beza, both Gallasius (Nicolas des Gallars), one of the ministers of Geneva, and Faius, a successor of Calvin, ascribe the change of day to the Holy Spirit.[1] The latter adds, "The observance of this day, therefore, is not to be accounted a matter of mere indifference, but to be carefully attended to as a perpetual apostolic tradition."

In yet another way did the Reformers show their faith in the doctrine of a Divine and permanent Sabbath. They considered the Lord's day as coming under the authoritative direction of the Fourth Commandment. They erred, indeed, as we conceive, by regarding this commandment as partly ceremonial, an error which has involved some of their other statements in confusion, if not contradiction, and has been turned to bad account in anti-Sabbatic opinion and practice, both on the Continent, and in this country. But the ceremonial part of the precept they believed to have passed away, leaving the moral part to sanction the Christian Sabbath and guide its observance. Thus Luther, after telling us that "this commandment, literally understood, does not apply to us Christians," says, "But in order that the simple may obtain a Christian view of *that which God requires of us in this commandment*, observe that we keep a festival." He then refers to two objects of the institution applying to our times, the provision of rest for the children of toil, and of time and opportunity to men in general, such as they could not otherwise have, for attending to religion.[2] The ideas of Calvin on the subject are thus expressed: "The ancients are accustomed to call the fourth precept shadowy, because it comprehended an external observance of the day, which at the coming of Christ has along with other figures been abolished, which, indeed, is by them expressed justly." But he adds, "This gives only the half of the truth. Whereupon a higher sense has to be sought, and there are three reasons to be considered why this command is to be observed." He then proceeds to state and enlarge on the reasons, and adds, "The sum is, as the truth was delivered to the Jews under a figure, so it is commanded to us without shadows: *First*, that we aim at a per-

[1] In Exod. xxxi. *Disput.* 47, *in* 4 *Legis Præcept.*

[2] In his *Larger Catechism.*

petual resting from our works during the whole of life, that God may work in us by his Spirit. *Again*, that every one should diligently exercise himself in private in the pious recognition of the works of God, as often as he has leisure; then also that all may together observe the lawful order of the Church established for hearing the Word, for the administration of the sacraments, and for public prayers. *Thirdly*, That we may not inhumanly oppress those placed under us."[1] The following words of the same individual are clear and decided: "Most certainly what was commanded concerning the day of rest must belong to us as well as to them [the Jews]. For, let us take God's law in itself, and we shall have *an everlasting* rule of righteousness. And, doubtless, under the ten commandments, God intended to give *a rule that should endure for ever*. Therefore let us not think that the things which Moses speaks respecting the Sabbath-day are needless for us: not because the figure remaineth still in force, but because we have the truth thereof."[2] We need add nothing more than that the Reformers were all pledged by the Formularies which they had subscribed, and by their expositions of the Ten Commandments in their Treatises and Catechisms, to the doctrine, that though the Mosaic ceremonies were repealed, and though the curse of the law was to all believers abrogated, the Moral Law, including the Fourth Commandment, is "a perpetual rule to mankind."[3]

But it remains that we listen to a few words from two distinguished men, whom we have not yet heard on any part of the subject; from Zwingle, one of the most learned of the Reformers, and John Knox, whom an able writer has lately characterized as "perhaps, in an extraordinary age, its most extraordinary man." The former, after declaring that Christ hath freed us from the Sabbath in so far as it was ceremonial, says, "But as far as regards the spirit of the law, which always remains, it eminently respects us. The spirit of the law is to love God supremely, and to love our neighbour. Now to hear the Word, to meditate on God's mercies, and to assemble for public prayers, belong to the

[1] *Institut.* on Fourth Prec. [2] Ser. 34, on Deut. v.

[3] See Statements in Hall's *Harmony*; of latter Helvetic Confession, p 109; of French, p. 113; of Belgian, p. 114; and of Augustan, p. 178.

spirit of the law, and then that our family and their works may rest concerns the love of our neighbour. For although we are not bound to a certain time, we are bound to the glory of God, to his Word, to the celebration of his praise, and to the love of our neighbours. Love, therefore, will teach us, when to labour, when to keep holy day. For love never fails."[1] In another place, referring to persons who betray their folly and ignorance by "babbling about ceremonies," and "affirming that the Sabbath is one of them," he says, "The Sabbath is established by the first two and chief commands of God, which constitute the foundation and basis, as it were, of all laws and of the prophets. The authority of the first command, or love to God, conjoins with it the Sabbath, and affirms and approves it, because this is the time when men are wont to meet to hear the Word of God, by the guidance of which, as far as can be attributed to doctrine, we are led into the true knowledge of the Lord himself, as the apostle Paul says in Romans x. 14. The Sabbath, therefore, is not a ceremony, nor ought to be classed with ceremonies. So the second command, the love of our neighbour, confirms the use and religious obligation of the Sabbath. For equity demands that some rest and recreation of the body should be allowed to our servants. We render it ceremonial by a Jewish observance."[2] The following words show how he conceived the day should be spent: "The observance of the Sabbath is here so carefully taught us by God, that we may cease and rest from sins, and withdraw our foot from evil (Isa. lviii.), and that we may apply ourselves to Divine things, to the reading of the law, to the Word of God, to thanksgiving, to prayers, to the recollection of Divine blessings. In fine, God having a regard to our good, has appointed a rest for our wearied bodies (for which reason the night also has been made for the use of men), for that which is without alternate repose is not enduring."[3] It is to be regretted that Knox, than whom no Reformer had a clearer or more logical head, should have written so little respecting the Sabbath. What his views of it were, however, may be certainly known from the *Confession of Faith*, and the *First Book of Discipline* which were drawn up by him and five other minis-

[1] In *Epist. ad Coloss.* c. ii. tom. iv. p. 515.
[2] *Oper.* tom. i. pp. 253, 254.
[3] In Matt. xii. tom. iv. p. 59.

ters; from the Acts of the General Assembly, at which he was usually present; and, indeed, from the proverbial views and habits in the matter of the Scottish people, on whom he has exercised so powerful and salutary an influence. The summary of the "most just, most equal, most holy, and most perfect law of God" given in the Confession, though the duties not the precise words of almost any of the commandments are given, and the rejection of everything in religion and in the worship of God that "has no other assurance but the invention and opinion of man," prepare us for two things in the *First Book of Discipline*: First, the decisive condemnation of festivals in these words, "The holy days invented by men, Christmas, Circumcision, Epiphany [and so forth], we judge utterly to be abolished forth of this realm, because they have no assurance in God's Word;" and second, the following injunction relative to the observance of the only holy day recognised by the Reformers of Scotland: "The Sabbath must be kept strictly in all towns, both forenoon and afternoon for hearing of the Word; at afternoon upon the Sabbath, the Catechism shall be taught, the children examined, and the baptism ministered. Public prayers shall be used upon the Sabbath, as well afternoon as before, when sermons cannot be had." In the third Assembly, which met in June 1562, the year in which the English Convocation agreed to adopt and publish thirty-eight of the now thirty-nine Articles, and the enlarged *Book of Homilies*, it was resolved "that supplication be made to Queen Mary for the punishing of Sabbath breaking, and of all vices commanded by the law of God to be punished, and yet not commanded by the law of the realm," and the Queen was again petitioned to the same effect in the Assembly of June 1565, while articles were prepared to be sent to her Majesty, one of which mentions "manifest breaking of the Sabbath day," among "the horrible and detestable crimes" which ought to be punished. It was in the Assembly of December 1566 that the Helvetic Confession was approved, with the express exception of the part that tolerated festival days. On all these occasions probably—at the meetings of 1562 and 1566 certainly—Knox was present, and must have been, as he was in everything that respected the welfare of the Scottish Church, the leader in the proceedings.

Were we to imitate certain anti-Sabbatic writers, we should be satisfied with having presented only such statements on this subject as favour our own dogma, and with leaving our readers to the unqualified impression that the Reformers were consistent advocates of a permanent Sabbath. It is not easy, indeed, to conceive how men, who held opinions and maintained the practice which have been represented in their own words, could have afforded occasion to any for claiming their patronage of a very different creed. But as our cause appears to us too good to expose us even to the temptation of withholding any part of the truth, we intend to produce in a following chapter certain expressions of the eminent men in question which have been considered as hostile to our doctrine. If it should be found that the result does not deprive us of their names as friends of the Sabbath, we take out of the hands of its enemies a weapon of which they have made an unsparing and injurious but unwarranted use. If they should be seen to be inconsistent with themselves, their influence on either side is neutralized. If it turn out that the scale preponderates against us, the question is where it was, to be decided not by authority but by evidence.

Before concluding our notices of the Sabbath at the Reformation, let us turn for a moment to the Church of Rome, and see how the institution then fared within her pale. The Council of Trent was convened by Pope Paul III. in 1545, professedly for the purpose of correcting the ecclesiastical disorders of which many so loudly complained. In its canons and decrees there are a few references to the Lord's day and holy days as seasons to be devoutly and religiously celebrated, and to be taken advantage of by bishops and preachers for instructing the people in the Scriptures and in the mysteries of the mass. The Catechism put forth by the Council devotes a chapter to the Third (our Fourth) Commandment. There we find it stated that the Sabbath dates from the time of the Exodus; that, while the other commandments of the Decalogue are precepts of the natural and perpetual law, the third, as regards the time of observing the Sabbath, belongs not to the moral but ceremonial law, in which sense the obligation to observe it was to cease with the abrogation of the other Jewish rites at the death of Christ; that it, however, comprises something that appertains to the natural and moral law—in other words, the worship of God and practice of religion; that the apostles therefore resolved to consecrate the first day of the seven to worship, and called it the Lord's day; and that, in order to their knowing what they are to do and abstain from on this day, it will not be foreign to the pastor's purpose to explain to the faithful word for word the whole precept. The Catechism further represents the Jewish Sabbath as a sign of a spiritual and mystic, and also of a celestial rest. It then, with Rome's usual art, glides into language which identifies the Apostles with the Church: "It hath pleased the Church of God, in her wisdom, that the religious celebration of the Sabbath-day should be transferred to the Lord's day. By the resurrection, on that day, of our Redeemer, our life was called out of darkness into light, and hence the Apostles would have it called the Lord's day." Proofs from the Scriptures and the Fathers are produced for a number of these statements, but none is alleged for the following: "From the infancy of the Church, and in subsequent times, other days were instituted by the Apostles and by our holy Fathers, in order to commemorate with piety and holiness the beneficent gifts of God." The way is thus prepared for placing the Sabbath and Feast-days in close connexion, and finally, as in the following words, for putting them on the same level: "There are many other things which our Lord in the Gospel declares may be done on Sundays and holidays, and which may be easily seen by the pastor in St. Matthew (ch. xii. 1, *et seq.*) and St. John" (v. 10, *et seq.*; vii. 22, *et seq.*) Thus Rome, faithful to her policy, seeks to neutralize truth by error, and to gain the purposes of error by fortifying and dignifying it with an alliance to truth. She finds in Cardinal Tolet, Sir Thomas More, and others, defenders of her assumed power over sacred times, and in the civil authorities the means of enforcing it, for already (in 1538) had three or four men of Stirling suffered death "because they did eat flesh"—meats which God hath created to be received with thanksgiving—"in Lent," at a marriage; and even while the Council is sitting, a poor man, for working on a holy day, that his family might not starve, is consigned to the flames.

THE SABBATH AFTER THE REFORMATION.

The period now to be surveyed brings to the Lord's day no improvement of position or observance in the church or countries of the Papacy. It is something, however, that a portion of its sound doctrine is contained in the creed of the former, and its statute embodied in the laws of the latter, both the doctrine and the statute bearing their silent testimony against the thoughtless folly by which they are reproached, and the foul deeds by which they are continually defied. Who can say that there have not been some in every age of that church who have been its devout observers? It is not long since the friends of the Sabbath were surprised and gratified by the zeal of the Archbishop of Paris, and the courage of M. de Montalembert on its behalf, and by the welcome with which many of the people of France hailed the labours of Cochrane for the same object.

The free spirit, on the other hand, inspired by the Reformation, has prompted inquiry; and, accordingly, the Sabbath has, with other subjects, been the matter of earnest consideration and discussion. Two facts are worthy of remark. First, The institution has continued for three centuries to be a law of the Protestant nations of Europe. It has not been the spirit of the Reformation, but the spirit of Popery that has ever endangered that law. It was this latter spirit that produced the *Book of Sports.* The following anecdote derives credibility from the whole circumstances of that celebrated publication. The subject of the recovery of England to Popery was considered in a conclave of cardinals at Rome, and after various modes of effecting this desirable consummation had been suggested, a wily member of the fraternity said, "Take away England's Sabbath, and your object is gained." Not long after, the Declaration of Sports appeared.[1] Second, The agitation of the subject has led to clearer, more settled, and more salutary opinions respecting it. The controversies about ceremonies in England led to the more satisfactory form in which the doctrine of the Sabbath was set forth in the Homilies than it had assumed in Cranmer's

[1] Related at a public meeting in Islington a good many years ago by the Rev. Dr. Wilson, son of the late Bishop of Calcutta.

Catechism and other authorized documents. Similar controversies between the ministers of the Church of Scotland, and those who thrust upon that country the Articles of Perth, confirmed Scotsmen in their early view of the Sabbath, and prepared Henderson and his brethren for the prominent and effective part which they took in framing the Westminster formularies. It has been said, too, that the Sabbatic strifes in Holland contributed to the lucid statements on our subject in the same formularies. In this last case, the discussions must have operated more by warning than by example, as the doctrine of the Assembly at Westminster was a decided improvement on that of the Synod of Dort, and was in fact the same doctrine as Robinson and Teellinck had carried from England and Scotland to the Netherlands.

In following the remaining course of Sabbatic history, which runs most strongly and clearly in English and Scottish channels, we begin with the views of a weekly holy day which have been embodied in the formularies of our several churches.

DOCTRINE OF OUR CHURCHES.

The Sabbatic doctrine of the Church of England is to be found in her Articles, Liturgy, and Homilies. Her seventh Article recognises the continued obligation of the Ten Commandments thus : " Although the Law given from God by Moses, as touching ceremonies and rites, do not bind Christian men, nor the civil precepts thereof ought of necessity to be received in any commonwealth, yet, notwithstanding, no Christian man whatsoever is free from the obedience of the commandments which are called moral." In " the Order of the Administration of the Lord's Supper," it is required that " the priest, turning to the people, rehearse distinctly all the TEN COMMANDMENTS ; and that the people still kneeling shall, after every commandment, ask God mercy for their transgression thereof for the time past, and grace to keep the same for the time to come." The words of this prayer are set down for them in the *Prayer-Book*. When the " minister," for example, has recited the Fourth Commandment, the " people" are directed to say, " Lord, have mercy upon us, and incline our hearts to keep this law." In the ministration of both public and private baptism of children, the sureties are enjoined to provide that those who have been baptized shall be taught to learn the Creed, the Lord's Prayer, and the Ten Commandments, in the vulgar tongue; and in the form of public baptism they are farther required to take care that the children be brought to the Bishop to be confirmed by him, so soon as they can say these lessons. Accordingly, in "the Order of Confirmation," it is said, "The Church hath thought good to order, that none hereafter shall be confirmed, but such as can say the Creed, the Lord's Prayer, and the Ten Commandments; and can also answer to such other questions, as in the *Short Catechism* are contained: which order is very convenient to be observed; to the end, that children, being now come to the years of discretion, and having learned what their god-fathers and god-mothers have promised for them in baptism, they may themselves, with their own mouth and consent, openly before the Church, ratify and confirm the same." One of the things promised for them, and which at their confirmation they take it upon them to perform, is, "I will endeavour obediently to keep God's holy will and commandments, and walk in the same all the days of my life, God being my helper."

Referring to pp. 40-42 of this volume for the consentaneous doctrine of the Homilies on the subject, let us now present the views held by the Westminster Divines, as they are expressed in the *Westminster Confession of Faith*, and in the words—to many more familiar and endeared—of the *Shorter Catechism*:—

"As it is of the law of Nature, that, in general, a due proportion of time be set apart for the worship of God; so, in his Word, by a positive, moral, and perpetual commandment, binding all men in all ages, He hath particularly appointed one day in seven for a Sabbath, to be kept holy unto him: which, from the beginning of the world to the resurrection of Christ, was the last day of the week; and, from the resurrection of Christ, was changed into the first day of the week, which in Scripture is called the Lord's Day, and is to be continued to the end of the world, as the Christian Sabbath."

"This Sabbath is then kept holy unto the Lord, when men, after a due preparing of their hearts, and ordering of their common affairs beforehand, do not only observe an holy rest all the day from their own works, words, and thoughts about their worldly employments and recreations; but also are taken up the whole time in the public and private exercises of His worship, and in the duties of necessity and mercy."[1]

"Which is the Fourth Commandment?

"The Fourth Commandment is, Remember the Sabbath-day, to keep it holy. Six days shalt thou labour, and do all thy work; but the seventh day is the Sabbath of the Lord thy God: in it thou shalt not do any work, thou, nor thy son, nor thy daughter, thy man-servant, nor thy maid-servant, nor thy cattle, nor thy stranger that is within thy gates. For in six days the Lord made heaven and earth, the sea, and all that in them is, and rested the seventh day: wherefore the Lord blessed the Sabbath-day, and hallowed it.

"What is required in the Fourth Commandment?

"The Fourth Commandment requireth the keeping holy to God such set times as he hath appointed in his Word; expressly one whole day in seven, to be a holy Sabbath to himself.

"Which day of the seven hath God appointed to be the weekly Sabbath?

"From the beginning of the world to the resurrection of Christ, God appointed the seventh day of the week to be the weekly Sabbath; and the first day of the week ever since, to continue to the end of the world, which is the Christian Sabbath.

"How is the Sabbath to be sanctified?

"The Sabbath is to be sanctified by a holy resting all that day, even from such worldly employments and recreations as are lawful on other days; and spending the whole time in the public and private exercises of God's worship, except so much as is to be taken up in the works of necessity and mercy.

"What is forbidden in the Fourth Commandment?

"The Fourth Commandment forbiddeth the omission or careless performance of the duties required, and the profaning the day by idleness, or doing that which is in itself sinful, or by unnecessary

[1] *Confession*, ch. xxi. sects. 7, 8.

thoughts, words, or works, about our worldly employments or recreations.

"What are the reasons annexed to the Fourth Commandment?

"The reasons annexed to the Fourth Commandment are, God's allowing us six days of the week for our own employments, his challenging a special propriety in the seventh, his own example, and his blessing the Sabbath-day."[1]

Such was the clearly and scripturally stated doctrine of the Sabbath that proceeded from one of the most learned and pious assemblies ever convened, including a Lightfoot, a Gataker, a Twisse, a Henderson, a Rutherford, a Wallis, and a Reynolds, and such ever since, as it was more or less before, has been the faith of the best men of Scotland, England, and the continents of Europe and America, the only drawback being that too many have risen up to counteract such views by perverse disputings or by ungodly practice.

The Independents, who formed a small minority in the Westminster Assembly, though they differed from the other members on certain points, took no exception to the general opinion on the subject of the Sabbath. No fewer than a hundred ministers and messengers of their denomination, including Dr. Owen, met in a Synod held in 1658, and drew up a Confession of their Faith, of which, as compared with that of the Westminster divines, Neal remarks, "The difference between these two Confessions, in points of doctrine, is so very small, that modern Independents have in a manner laid aside the use of it in their families, and agreed with the Presbyterians in the use of the Assembly's Catechism."[2] The general doctrine of this admirable summary of Divine truth, which is substantially that of the Thirty-nine Articles and Homilies of the Church of England, was cordially held by the evangelical members of that Church, and, with few exceptions, by the English Non-Conformists, till the rise of Methodism, when, while Whitefield and his friends adhered to the old creed, Wesley and his numerous followers in some important respects departed from it. No class, however, have been more zealous abettors of a holy Sabbath than the Wesleyan Methodists. From England, the Westminster Formularies were imported into Scotland, which, having suggested and

[1] *Shorter Catechism.* [2] *History of the Puritans* (1738), vol. iv. p. 191.

materially contributed to their production, adopted them, with the valuable addition of her own Directory for Family Worship, to be henceforth and eminently her inheritance. She had been familiarized by her Reformers with a Sabbath, attended by no competing holidays, and strictly observed, but she gladly welcomed the fuller testimony on the subject supplied in the Confession of Faith, Directory, and Catechisms. Nor have the separations from her Church of some considerable parties diminished the Sabbatic teaching and practice of the land. These parties have both retained the old zeal for the Lord's day, and given an impulse to the feeling in the society from which they sprang. The Secession Church, including the Erskines, the Moncrieffs, Adam Gib, and Brown of Haddington, Drs. Young of Hawick and Lawson of Selkirk, Drs. Jamieson of Edinburgh and Waugh of London, Drs. Ferrier of Paisley and Dick of Glasgow,—the Relief Church, represented by Gillespie, Thomas Bell, and Dr. Struthers,—the Reformed Presbyterian Church and its leaders, Macmillan and the Symingtons,—the Independents and Baptists, headed the one by Glas, Greville Ewing, and Dr. Wardlaw, the other by the Haldanes and Dr. Innes,—the United Original Seceders, who rejoiced in such spiritual guides as Drs. M'Crie, Paxton, and Stevenson,—and the Free Church, of which Dr. Chalmers was the *facile princeps*,—all held, as their successors to a man still hold, the Sabbatic doctrine of the Confession of Faith. From some of these Churches have proceeded independent and able declarations and defences of that doctrine, which, but for overcrowding our pages, we should have been happy to introduce in this place.[1]

One other doctrinal statement may suffice. It is "The Primary Address" of the Society for Promoting the Observance of the Lord's Day—a manifesto which was written by Dr. Daniel Wilson, late Bishop of Calcutta, and not only expressed the views of the members of the society, many of whom belonged to the Church of England, but was unanimously assented to in 1855 by the Metropolitan Committee, composed of "many ministers of religion of

[1] We refer, in particular, to "The Testimony of the United Associate Synod of the Secession Church," and "The Testimony to the Truths of Christ, agreed to by the United Original Seceders,"—the former drawn up by Dr. Stark, Dennyloanhead, and Professor Duncan of Mid-Calder—the other, by Drs. M'Crie and Stevenson (Ayr).

various denominations :"—"That the dedication of one day in every seven to religious rest and the worship of Almighty God is of Divine authority and perpetual obligation, as a characteristic of revealed religion during all its successive periods ; having been enjoined upon man at the creation—recognised and confirmed in the most solemn manner in the Ten Commandments—urged by the prophets as an essential duty, about to form a part of the institutions of the Messiah's kingdom—vindicated by our Divine Lord from the unauthorized additions and impositions of the Jewish teachers—transferred by Him and his apostles, upon the abrogation of the ceremonies of the Mosaic Law, to the first day of the week, in commemoration of the resurrection of Christ, and on that account called 'The Lord's Day'—and finally established in more than all its primitive glory as an ordinance of the spiritual universal Church of the New Testament, and a standing pledge and foretaste of the eternal rest of heaven. And that this meeting believes that every person in a Christian country is bound in conscience to devote this seventh portion of his time to the honour of God, by resting from the business of his calling ; by abstaining altogether from the pursuit of gain, and from ordinary pastimes and recreations ; by guarding against every worldly avocation and interruption ; and by spending the entire day in the public and private duties of religion, with the exception of such works of necessity and charity as our Saviour by his example was pleased to allow and command : so as to designate this one day of rest and Divine service, after six days of labour, as a more distinguished privilege of the Christian, than it was of the Patriarchal and Jewish dispensations."[1]

PERSONAL TESTIMONIES.

It is only a few of such testimonies—which might be indefinitely multiplied—that our space allows us to record. But these few are sufficient to show how individuals of various times, stations, and other circumstances, are at one as to the authority and value of the weekly rest. Let Lord Bacon be our first witness in the cause. "A Christian," he says, "thinks sometimes

[1] Baylee's *Hist. of the Sabbath*, pp. 219, 220.

that the ordinances of God do him no good, yet he would rather part with his life than be deprived of them." "In the distribution of days, we see the day wherein God did rest and contemplate His own works was blessed above all the days wherein he did effect and accomplish them." "It is an easy thing to call for the observance of the Sabbath-day; but what actions and works may be done on the Sabbath, and what not,—to set this down, and clear the whole matter with good distinctions and decisions, is a matter of great knowledge and labour, and asketh much meditation and conversing in the Scriptures, and other helps, which God hath provided and preserved for instruction."[1] Sir Matthew Hale's name as a friend of the institution is familiar, but the following sentence from his writings is not so commonly cited as some others:—"And thus you have the reason of the obligation upon us Christians, to observe the first day of the week, because by more than a human institution, the morality of the fourth commandment is transferred to the first day of the week, being our Christian Sabbath; and so the fourth commandment is not abrogated, but only the day changed, and the morality of that command only translated, not annulled."[2] "The very life of religion," says Archbishop Leighton, "doth much depend upon the solemn observation of this day; consider but, if we should intermit the keeping of it for one year, to what a height profaneness would rise in those that fear not God; which are yet restrained (though not converted) by the preaching of the Word and their outward partaking of public worship; yea, those that are most spiritual would find themselves losers by the intermission."[3] The Archbishop's contemporary, Bishop Pearson, has these words in his *Exposition of the Creed*: "From this resurrection of our Saviour, and the constant practice of the apostles, this first day of the week came to have the name of 'the Lord's day;' and is so called by St. John, who says of himself in the Revelation, 'I was in the Spirit on the Lord's day' (Rev. i. 10). And thus the observation of that day, which the Jews did sanctify, ceased, and was buried with our Saviour; and, in the stead of it, the religious observation of that day on which the Son of God

[1] *Works* (1855), vol. ii. p. 230; (1852), vol. i. p. 175; (1730), vol. iv. p. 429.
[2] *Contemplations* (1676), vol. i. pp. 483, 484. [3] *Works*, vol. iv. p. 14.

rose from the dead, by the constant practice of the blessed apostles, was transmitted to the Church of God, and so continued in all ages."[1] Passing over the similar views of Dr. H. More, Bishop Hopkins, Drs. John Scott (author of the *Christian Life*) and Littleton, we come to the following interesting words—the more so as proceeding from such a man: "Besides his particular calling for the support of life," says John Locke, "every one has a concern in a future life, which he is bound to look after. This engages his thoughts in religion; and here it mightily lies upon him to understand and reason right. Men therefore *cannot be excused* from understanding the words and framing the general notions relating to religion right. THE ONE DAY IN SEVEN, besides other days of rest, allows in the Christian world time enough for this (had they no other idle hours), if they would but make use of these vacancies from their daily labour, and apply themselves to an improvement of knowledge with as much diligence as they often do to a great many other things that are useless."[2] To the judgment of Locke we add that of Addison: "I am always very well pleased with a country Sunday, and think, if keeping holy the seventh day were only a human institution, it would be the best method that could have been thought of for the polishing and civilizing of mankind."[3] Lord Kames, Adam Smith, and Burke are names of great weight, as those of men eminent for talent, knowledge, and sagacity. The first-mentioned says: "The setting apart one day in seven, for public worship, is not a pious institution merely, but highly moral; with regard to the latter, all men are equal in the presence of God; and, when a congregation pray for mercy and protection, one must be inflamed with good-will and brotherly love to all. In the next place, the serious and devout tone of mind, inspired by public worship, suggests naturally self-examination. Retired from the bustle of the world, on that day of rest, the errors we have been guilty of are recalled to memory: we are afflicted for those errors, and firmly resolve to be more on our guard in time coming. In short, Sunday is a day of rest from worldly concerns, in order to be more usefully employed upon those that are internal. Sunday, accord-

1 Edit. of 1845, p. 415.
2 *Conduct of the Understanding*, sect. 8.
3 *Spectator*, No. 112.

ingly, is a day of account; and a candid account every seventh day is the best preparation for the great day of account. A person who diligently follows out this preparatory discipline will seldom be at a loss to answer for his own conduct, called upon by God or man. This leads me naturally to condemn the practice of abandoning to diversion or merriment what remains of Sunday after public worship, such as parties of pleasure, gaming, etc., or anything that trifles away the time without a serious thought, as if the purpose were to cancel every virtuous impression made at public worship. Unhappily this salutary institution can only be preserved in vigour during the days of piety and virtue. Power and opulence are the darling objects of every nation; and yet, in every nation possessed of power and opulence, virtue subsides, selfishness prevails, and sensuality becomes the ruling passion. Then it is that the most sacred institutions first lose their hold, next are disregarded, and at last are made a subject of ridicule."[1] The words of Smith, already employed as a motto, deserve to be again presented. "The Sabbath," he said, "as a political institution, is of inestimable value, independently of its claims to Divine authority." And, in his *Letter to a Member of the National Assembly*, Burke gave utterance to these memorable sentences: "They who always labour can have no true judgment. You never give yourselves time to cool. You can never survey from its proper point of sight the work you have finished before you decree its final execution. You can never plan the future by the past. These are among the effects of unremitted labour, when men exhaust their attention, burn out their candles, and are left in the dark. *Malo meorum negligentiam, quam istorum obscuram diligentiam.*" Next in order is Cowper, who, in a letter to the Rev. Wm. Unwin, thus fully propounds his Sabbatic views:—"With respect to the advice you are required to give to a young lady, that she may be properly instructed in the manner of keeping the Sabbath, I just subjoin a few hints which have occurred to me upon the occasion; not because I think you want them, but because it would seem unkind to withhold them. The Sabbath, then, I think, may be considered, first, as a commandment, no less binding upon modern Christians than upon ancient Jews;

[1] Creech's *Fugitive Pieces*, p. 182.

because the spiritual people amongst them did not think it enough to abstain from manual occupations on that day, but, entering more deeply into the meaning of the precept, allotted those hours they took from the world to the cultivation of holiness in their own souls; which ever was, and ever will be, a duty incumbent upon all who ever heard of a Sabbath; and is of perpetual obligation both upon Jews and Christians (the commandment therefore enjoins it, the prophets have also enforced it, and, in many instances, both scriptural and modern, the breach of it has been punished with a providential and judicial severity, that may make bystanders tremble): *secondly*, As a privilege which you well know how to dilate upon, better than I can tell you; *thirdly*, As a sign of that covenant, by which believers are entitled to a rest which yet remaineth; *fourthly*, As the *sine qua non* or necessary part of the Christian character; and, on this head, I should guard against being misunderstood to mean no more than two attendances upon public worship, which is a form complied with by thousands who never kept a Sabbath in their lives. Consistence is necessary to give substance and solidity to the whole. To sanctify the Sabbath at church, and to trifle it away out of church, is profanation, and vitiates all! After all, I could ask my catechumen one short question, Do you love the day, or do you not? If you love it, you will never inquire how far you may safely deprive yourself of the enjoyment of it. If you do not love it, and you find yourself obliged in conscience to acknowledge it, that is an alarming symptom, and ought to make you tremble. If you do not love it, then you wish it was over, because it is a weariness to you. The ideas of labour and rest are not more opposite to each other, than the idea of a Sabbath, and that dislike and disgust with which it fills the minds of thousands, to be obliged to keep it. It is worse than bodily labour." "Sir John Shore," afterwards Lord Teignmouth, "neglected not, amidst the toils and cares of empire, those literary pursuits which were ever congenial to his taste, and which he cultivated in the society of his friend, Sir W. Jones, who, like himself, was the son of a widowed mother, whose maternal solicitudes were amply repaid by their auspicious results. On the death of that unrivalled Oriental scholar, Sir John Shore succeeded to the chair of the Asiatic Society, and pronounced an elegant and luminous eulogium on his predecessor." It is added, in a note, "How anxiously he felt in after years upon the subject of the observance of the Lord's day may be seen by a paper from his Lordship's pen, which he addressed to us for insertion in our volume for 1803, p. 537, signed 'Sunday.' His Lordship makes Sunday complain of the grievous neglect shown to him, in this professedly Christian and Protestant country. His Lordship did not view the Christian Sabbath as the mere creature of ecclesiastical authority; but, on the contrary, makes it 'derive all its title to consideration from its Divine origin.' He mentions many of the ways of idleness, business, and pleasure—the last he calls "the devil's allurements'—in which the day is too often violated, both by the rich and the poor. We quote one passage, which deserves to be seriously considered at the present moment: 'I remark many of the poorer classes who find the respect which they pay to me (Sunday) most amply rewarded, not merely by an exemption from their daily labours, but by a composed frame of mind, which is the natural consequence of a due attention to me. With many, it is the only consolation they enjoy; and I cannot but therefore deprecate that more than common species of cruelty which would endeavour to deprive these poor people, not only of bodily rest, but of spiritual consolation. Of this cruelty every man who, by example, encouragement, or authority, endeavours to degrade me in their estimation, is most palpably guilty; and whatever he may think, incurs by it a most awful responsibility, which he will be called upon one day to answer.'"[1] It would not be easy to find a more comprehensive or more beautiful tribute to the Day of Rest than the following by the biographer of Knox and Melville, the late Dr. M'Crie:—"The Sabbath is the wisest and most beneficent, as well as the most ancient, institute of heaven; the first gift which God conferred on our newly created parents, and by which he continues to testify at once his care for our bodies and our spirits, by providing relaxation for the one, and refreshment for the other; the joint memorial of creation and redemption; the token of God's residence on earth, and the earnest of man's elevation to heaven; an institute which blends together, like the colours of the rainbow,

[1] *Christian Observer* (1834), pp. 264, 265

—itself a sacred emblem,—recollections of the innocence of our primeval state, and the grace of our recovery, with anticipations of the glory to which we are called; an institute in the observance of which we feel ourselves associated, not only with all who 'in every region, yea, on every sea,' believe on the same Saviour; but also with holy men, apostles, prophets, and patriarchs, in every age since 'men began to call on the name of the Lord;' nay, in which we are raised to communion with the Father of our spirits; and, by resting with Him on the seventh day, receive his sacrèd pledge, that in labouring and doing all our work on the six days, we shall have that blessing which alone maketh rich, and addeth no sorrow."[1] Let the eloquent words of Principal Forbes close these testimonies: "One result of a due economy of time, is a due amount of relaxation. He whose waking hours are well occupied, need not grudge himself a good night's rest. His very holidays are part of his economy; and the seventh day sheds its invigorating influence over the other six. By earnestness in your studies during the week, I advise you to reap the enjoyment of that beneficent provision of the Almighty, and by a sedulous abstinence in thought, as well as in act, from your occupations, to restore the tone of your minds and the capacity for vigorous exertion. None who have not made a strong effort are aware of the admirably tranquillizing influence of twenty-four hours studiously segregated from the ordinary current of thought. Monday morning is the epoch of a periodic renovation."[2]

CIVIL ENACTMENTS.

The late clerical secretary of the Society for Promoting the due Observance of the Lord's Day has thus summed up the Sabbath laws enacted in England from the year 1604: "In the reign of James I., trading in boots and shoes on the Lord's day is prohibited by law; and by an act passed in the first year of the reign of Charles I., it was found necessary *to restrain by a law assemblages of persons from various parishes* on the Lord's day.

[1] *The Witness*, Aug. 28, 1861.
[2] Rev. D. C. A. Agnew's *Occasional Papers on Sabbath Observance.* No. 12.

And in the second year of the same king, *travelling of carriages is prohibited.* We can easily conceive how inconsistent with such legislation must have appeared to his subjects the re-issuing, on the part of the king, of the Book of Sports of his father, which virtually encouraged what the Act of the first year of his reign pronounced unlawful. The Act of the 29th Ch. II. c. 7, is a very important one, still in force, and needing only some amendments, chiefly as regards an increase in the amount of the penalties, to render it efficient. It *prohibits the following of ordinary callings*, and enjoins upon all, publicly and privately, to exercise themselves in the duties of piety and true religion. The Act 21 Geo. III. c. 40 has proved a highly beneficial law, in *preventing places of amusement being opened for payment of money* on the Lord's Day. Bishop Porteus was the first who suggested the necessity of an Act of this nature, in order to suppress assemblages of an immoral and irreligious tendency on the Lord's day. The Act, though stringent and efficient for its purposes, is evaded with impunity in London, persons being admitted to public gardens by means of refreshment tickets purchased on the ordinary days of the week. In the reign of George IV., and subsequently at different times, Acts were passed *regulating inns, taverns*, etc., on the Lord's day. It is to be hoped the day is not far distant when the law will require them to be closed wholly on the Lord's day, with such exceptions as charity may require ; for it is now an established fact, that crime increases in the same degree in which public-houses are allowed to be opened on the Lord's day. The Act 3 and 4 William IV. is deserving of special notice. It *enables the election of officers of corporations, formerly required to be held on the Lord's day, to be held on Saturday or Monday.* It is the Act of the late Sir Andrew Agnew, and was passed in 1833. The bill was drawn up by Mr. George Rochfort Clarke ; the preamble of it is important, for it *asserts it to be the duty of the Legislature to remove as much as possible impediments to the due observance of the Lord's day.* Imperfect as is our legislation on the subject of the Lord's day, yet it has proved a mighty barrier to keep out the tide of profanation of the day with which the love of gain and of pleasure, more than of God, would otherwise have inundated us ; it has also proved highly protective to society in general, in securing to a population the most active, industrious, and hard-worked in Europe, the privilege of one day in seven for religious instruction and rest."[1]

Of the civil enactments in Scotland relative to the Sabbath, and belonging to the years 1661, 1672, 1693, 1695, and 1701, the late Lord President Blair said, in 1823, "By these Statutes, every person guilty of *profaning the Sabbath-day in any manner whatever*, is made liable in a pecuniary penalty, *toties quoties*, to be recovered, by prosecution before sheriffs, justices of peace, or any other judge ordinary. And the minister of every parish, the kirk-session, or the presbytery, or a person named by them, is entitled to prosecute. There appears, therefore, to be no defect in the law as it stands, if duly executed."

ECCLESIASTICAL COUNSELS.

Turning to the practical teachings on our subject with which this nation has been blessed, we begin with a few sentences taken from the Homily "Of the Place and Time for Prayer:" "God's obedient people should use the Sunday holily, and rest from their common and daily business, and also give themselves wholly to heavenly exercises of God's true religion and service." "God's people hath always, in all ages, without any gainsaying, used to come together upon the Sunday, to celebrate and honour the Lord's blessed name, and carefully to keep that day in holy rest and quietness, both man, woman, child, servant, and stranger." "Wherefore, O ye people of God, lay your hands upon your hearts, repent and amend this grievous and dangerous wickedness [profaning the day by riding, marketing, labour, rioting, and excess], stand in awe of the commandment of God, gladly follow the example of God himself, be not disobedient to the godly order of Christ's church, used and kept from the apostles' time until this day. Fear the displeasure and just plagues of Almighty God, if ye be negligent and forbear not labouring and travelling on the Sabbath-day or Sunday, and do not resort together to celebrate and magnify God's blessed name in quiet holiness and godly reverence."

[1] *Hist. of the Sab.*, by the Rev. John Baylee, pp. 134-136.

The following are the more copious instructions of the Westminster Assembly on "the Sanctification of the Lord's day:"—

"The Lord's day ought to be so remembered beforehand, as that all worldly business of our ordinary callings may be so ordered, and so timely and seasonably laid aside, as they may not be impediments to the due sanctifying of the day when it comes.

"The whole day is to be celebrated as holy to the Lord, both in public and private, as being the Christian Sabbath. To which end, it is requisite, that there be a holy cessation or resting all that day from all unnecessary labours; and an abstaining, not only from all sports and pastimes, but also from all worldly words and thoughts.

"That the diet on that day be so ordered, as that neither servants be unnecessarily detained from the public worship of God, nor any other person hindered from the sanctifying that day.

"That there be private preparations of every person and family, by prayer for themselves, and for God's assistance of the minister, and for a blessing upon his ministry; and by such other holy exercises, as may further dispose them to a more comfortable communion with God in his public ordinances.

"That all the people meet so timely for public worship, that the whole congregation may be present at the beginning, and with one heart solemnly join together in all parts of the public worship, and not depart till after the blessing.

"That what time is vacant, between or after the solemn meetings of the congregation in public, be spent in reading, meditation, repetition of sermons; especially by calling their families to an account of what they have heard, and catechising of them, holy conferences, prayer for a blessing upon the public ordinances, singing of psalms, visiting the sick, relieving the poor, and such like duties of piety, charity, and mercy, accounting the Sabbath a delight."

In adopting the preceding document, the General Assembly of the Church of Scotland added to it a "Directory for Family Worship." "On the Lord's day, after every one of the family apart, and the whole family together, have sought the Lord (in whose hands the preparation of men's hearts is), to fit them for the public worship, and to bless to them the public ordinances, the master of the family ought to take care that all within his charge repair to the public worship, that he and they may join with the rest of the congregation : and the public worship being finished, after prayer, he should take an account what they have heard ; and thereafter, to spend the rest of the time which they may spare in catechising, and in spiritual conferences upon the Word of God : or else (going apart) they ought to apply themselves to reading, meditation, and secret prayer, that they may confirm and increase their communion with God : that so the profit which they found in the public ordinances may be cherished and preserved, and they more edified unto eternal life."

The United Secession Church, which has since coalesced with the Relief body, under the name of the United Presbyterian Church, gave forth along with her statement of principles a warning against practical evils, which thus deals with the evil of Sabbath desecration : "Another indication and form of impiety, is the lamentably extensive profanation of the Sabbath,—by parties of pleasure, by unnecessary travelling, by the transaction of business, and by devoting the day to mere bodily recreation. To what devices do many resort for the purpose of evading the laws which have been wisely and justly enacted to secure its external observance ! and how is the authority of the Divine precept disregarded by those who privately appropriate this sacred portion of time to the assorting of accounts, writing letters of business, and other arrangements as to secular affairs ! The precept is as really, and sometimes as grossly, violated by the carnal, and altogether unbecoming conversation too prevalent among those who make other and higher professions. We cannot too strongly reprobate the practice of limiting the observance of the Sabbath to the hours of public worship, and forthwith, as if no further obligation existed, indulging in feasting, visiting, walking, amusements, the reading of profane authors, and of newspapers, and the prosecution of secular studies. Ought religion to be deemed a labour to be as slightly undergone, and as speedily dispatched as possible ? How criminal every attempt to rob the Most High of what, in a liberal grant to man, he hath appropriated to himself ! No recreation can be lawful on the Sabbath, but what accords with the principal design of the day, which is manifestly to rest with God in the delighted contemplation of his glory as displayed in the works of nature, but especially in the mystery of redemption; and to render to him the homage he requires. It is thus only we are fitted for returning to the business of life, under pious impressions, and prepared for that Sabbath, when bodily recreation shall be no longer needful. So far from tolerating the least encroachment on that sacred day, the Scriptures condemn the very disposition to say, 'What a weariness is it, when will the Sabbath be over,' that we may return to our secular employments? Amos viii. 5; Mal. i. 13, 14. Both spiritual and temporal prosperity are, by the promise of Him who alone can bestow them, connected with due respect to the Sabbath. Isa. lvi. 2-7; lviii. 13, 14."[1]

From the Laws and Regulations of the Wesleyan Methodists, in which there are several directions concerning the observance of the Lord's day, we select one addressed to the Chairmen of Districts: "Let us earnestly exhort our societies to make the best and most religious use of the rest and leisure of the Lord's day: let us admonish any individuals who shall be found to neglect our public worship, under pretence of visiting the sick or other similar engagements: let us show to our people the evil of *wasting* those portions of the Sabbath, which are not spent in public worship, in visits or in receiving company, to the neglect of private prayer, of the perusal of the Scriptures, and of family duties, and, often to the serious spiritual injury of servants, who are thus improperly employed, and deprived of the public means of grace; let us set an example in this matter, by refusing for ourselves and for our families, to spend in visits, when there is no call of duty or necessity, the sacred hours of the Holy Sabbath; and let us never allow the Lord's day to be *secularized* by meetings of mere *business*, when such business refers only to the *temporal affairs* of the Church of God."[2]

[1] *Testimony*, pp. 167, 168.
[2] Warren's *Digest of the Laws and Regulations of the Wesleyan Methodists*, p. 77.

PRACTICAL MEASURES.

It has been too characteristic of the Continental churches and people to allow their Sabbatic doctrine, and laws to slumber in their Confessions and statute-books. This has been too much the case at home, but still more abroad. In England, there have always been men who have endeavoured to carry out their principles into measures for promoting the observance, and remedying the desecration of a day which they reverenced and loved. The Puritans ; their evangelical successors within and without the pale of the Church ; and the Methodists, have been the means of preserving true religion, including the sanctification of the Sabbath, in the land. They have employed for this purpose the pulpit and the press, and in their families and neighbourhoods, private instruction, and the silent influence of holy example. Scotland has been no less favoured with the practical measures by which her creed has been prevented from becoming a dead letter. John Knox gave the impulse, which the Melvilles, Welch, and others, carried on and increased.[1] The immediate successors of the great reformer, and the Covenanters struggled, as did the Puritans, for Sabbatic rights and privileges in times of danger and persecution. The number of Acts passed by the General Assembly on this subject is very great, says the Rev. Dr. M'Farlane, who supplies instances, from 1638 to 1708, and adds, "From these specimens of Acts of Assembly, it will be seen how the Church availed herself of the aid which the laws afforded for the suppression of gross breaches of the Sabbath. To show, however, that these venerable fathers of the Church, and chief framers of the habits of our country depended not merely, or even chiefly, on police regulations, for carrying their ends into effect, we have only now to turn to the means which they employed for the suppression of profanity [profaneness] in general."[2] The means urged for this purpose were that

[1] See *Booke of the Universall Kirk of Scotland*, p. 344, for evidence of the faithfulness of the General Assembly in calling to account certain nobles of the land on the subject of Sabbath-breaking, and of the gratifying success which attended their measures. At a later period, the session-records of Ayr bear testimony to the vigilant care of John Welch to have the institution sanctified in that town. We trust, that a satisfactory "life" of this remarkable man, which has employed the *con amore* labours of our friend, the Rev. James Young of Edinburgh, will be forthcoming at no distant date.

[2] *Treatise on the Christian Sabbath*, pp. 258, 262.

ministers should be "much in prayer and supplication on account of these evils," that they "preach plainly and faithfully against" them, that they "deal earnestly and much with the consciences of evil-doers," that "Church judicatories do faithfully exercise church discipline against all such scandalous offenders," that "ministers and elders take care that the worship of God be performed in each family" under their care, and that "all prudence and meekness of wisdom, along with fidelity, be shown" in the use of the various expedients for the reclamation of the erring. The churches that at various times disconnected themselves from the Church of Scotland, while, as we have already seen, they retained her doctrine respecting the Sabbath, have strenuously sought to secure for it due regard and honour.

In the present century the friends of the Sabbath, imitating the example of the promoters of Bible circulation and of missions, have resorted to the new form of associated effort outside the walls of their respective churches for vindicating the claims, and advancing the interests of an institution, in regard to the Divine authority and indispensable importance of which they were agreed. In 1831, the Society for promoting the due observance of the Lord's day was formed in London. "In all the movements in reference to the Sabbath, which have been made since its formation, it has taken a prominent," and we may add, an energetic "part." "The continually increasing desecration of the Lord's day in Scotland led to the formation," in 1847, of the Sabbath Alliance, designed to embrace the whole of that division of the United Kingdom, and having for its basis, "the Divine authority and universal and perpetual obligation of the Sabbath, as declared at large in the Word of God, and more formally and particularly in the Fourth Commandment of the Moral Law." By its publications, public meetings, the visits to the country of its agents, its exertions against Sabbath profanation, by means of railways, the post-office, the traffic in liquor, baking, and other practices, it has rendered important service to the cause of religion. A society in Glasgow having the same object has also been successful. When the appeal, as mentioned in pp. 167, 168, was responded to by 1045 working men, who competed for the prizes offered to their class for the three best essays on the "temporal advantages of the Sabbath," seventy of the writers were Glasgow men. These seventy met in the year 1849, and formed themselves into "The Glasgow Working Men's Sabbath Protection Association." Their object was to defend the Sabbath against all unnecessary encroachments on its sacred time, and, in the prosecution of this object, they were to avail themselves of every means sanctioned by Christian principle, especially sermons, lectures, addresses at public meetings, and the circulation of tracts and pamphlets bearing on the subject. They have laboured assiduously to prevent or remove various forms of Sabbath desecration connected with railways, the post-office, the Sydenham Palace, the British Museum, the employment of cabs and carriages, the opening of shops for the transaction of ordinary business, Sunday steamers, and the liquor traffic. We have much pleasure in quoting a sentence or two from a letter, addressed in 1858, by their President, at that time Mr. James Lemon, in name of the Association, to Lord Stanley, when a petition of certain *savans* prayed the Government to open various places of amusement for public exhibition on the Lord's day: "We beg most respectfully to state that aggressions such as these which your Lordship is attempting to make on the day of rest have been the very means of banding us together for the protection of our inalienable birthright to rest one day in seven; and it pains and alarms us when we hear of a peer of the realm endeavouring to annihilate the very principles which his ancestors in the worst of times so nobly defended. And we consider that we are in duty bound at this crisis, to remonstrate with your Lordship, by declaring that we repudiate all systematic and predetermined labour, however amusing it may be, if it enslaves our neighbours on the Sabbath day, inasmuch as all such labour undermines the Word of God, the grand basis of Sabbath preservation, and tends to foster principles which sap the foundations of domestic virtue, true piety, and national prosperity." Various other associations, in England and Scotland, have contributed to the advancement of the great cause of Sabbath observance; but they are too numerous for specific mention.

No one who truly regards the weekly holy day himself, will be indifferent to its desecration, or unwilling to employ his influence for remedying the evil. But there are individuals, who from their better opportunities, their greater ability, or more fervent zeal, have rendered a wider or more enduring service to the institution than others have accomplished, and who are therefore entitled to our special grateful commemoration. Such men have been a Knox, a Greenham, a Bownd, a Twisse, a Young, an Owen, a Durham, a Willison. Such too, have been Bishop Porteus, Holden, Bishop Blomfield, Dr. Wilson, Mr. Joseph Wilson, Sir Andrew Agnew, the Rev. William Leake and the Rev. John Davies, the Earl of Shaftesbury, John Henderson, Esq., of Park, and Mr. Peter Drummond of Stirling.

OBSERVANCE.

The sanctification of the Sabbath in the family is one of the best evidences of the influence of its doctrine, and yet is itself one of the most effectual measures for extending its beneficial power, a measure second only to that which is wielded from the pulpit. Let us present a brief account of instances in which the Sabbath has shed its purity and peace in the dwellings of our people.

From a number of contemporary examples we select one from a situation in life very far from being favourable to a holy rest. Lord Harrington died at the early age of twenty-two in 1613, only a few years before the issuing of the *Book of Sports.* This young nobleman "usually rose every morning at five, and sometimes at four. When he first waked, his constant care was to cultivate communion with God, by offering up the first-fruits of the day and of his thoughts to the uncreated Majesty. So soon as dressed, he endeavoured to put his heart in tune for family worship, by reading a portion of Scripture; after which, he prayed with his servants. This duty concluded, he spent about an hour in reading some valuable book, calculated to inform his understanding, and to animate his graces. Calvin's Institutions and Mr. Rogers's Treatise were among the performances which he highly esteemed, and which he carefully studied. Before dinner and before supper his family were called together to wait on God in reading, singing, and prayer. After supper, prayer was repeated." . . . On the Lord's day, "after evening sermon, two of his servants repeated in the family, before supper, the substance of that and the morning discourse, from notes which they had written at the times of preaching; and so great was his memory, that he himself would usually repeat more than they had committed to writing. He then entered the heads and principal passages of each sermon, in a plain paper book which he kept for that purpose, and afterwards dismissed his domestics with prayer, in which he had a very extraordinary gift."[1]

The same spirit reigns half a century thereafter in the domestic circle at Broad Oak, and in many families about that time, both while they were in the Church of England, and when they had been ejected from its communion. The distinguished commentator, Matthew Henry, has given the following interesting account of the manner in which the Sabbath was spent in his father's house. "The Lord's day he (the Rev. Philip Henry) called and counted the queen of days, the pearl of the week, and observed it accordingly. The Fourth Commandment intimates a special regard to be had to the Sabbath in families: 'thou and thy son, and thy daughter, etc.' 'It is the Sabbath of the Lord in all your dwellings.' In this, therefore, he was very exact, and abounded in the work of the Lord in his family on that day. Whatever were the circumstances of his public opportunities (which varied, as we shall find afterwards), his family religion was the same: extraordinary sacrifices must never supersede the continual burnt-offering and his meat-offering, Num. xxviii. 15. His common salutation of his family or friends on the Lord's day in the morning, was that of the primitive Christians: 'The Lord is risen, he is risen indeed;' making it his chief business on that day to celebrate the memory of Christ's resurrection; and he would say sometimes, 'Every Lord's day is a true Christian's Easter-day.' He took care to have his family ready early on that day, and was larger in exposition and prayer on Sabbath mornings than on other days. He would often remember, that under the law the daily sacrifice was doubled on Sabbath days, two lambs in the morning, and two in the evening. He had always a particular subject for his expositions on Sabbath mornings, the harmony of the evangelists several times over, the Scripture prayers, Old Testament prophecies of Christ, 'Christ the

[1] Toplady's *Works*, (1837), pp. 469, 470.

true treasure' (so he entitled that subject), 'sought and found in the Old Testament.' He constantly sung a Psalm after dinner, and another after supper on the Lord's days. And in the evening of the day his children and servants were catechized and examined in the sense and meaning of the answers in the catechism, that they might not say it (as he used to tell them) like a parrot, by rote. Then the day's sermons were repeated, commonly by one of his children when they were grown up, and while they were with him; and the family gave an account what they could remember of the word of the day, which he endeavoured to fasten upon them, as a nail in a sure place. In his prayers on the evening of the Sabbath, he was often more than ordinarily enlarged, as one that found not only God's service perfect freedom, but his work its own wages, and a great reward, not only after keeping, but (as he used to observe from Ps. xix. 11) in keeping God's commandments—a present reward of obedience in obedience. In that prayer he was usually very particular, in praying for his family and all that belonged to it. It was a prayer he often put up, that we might have grace to carry it as a minister, and a minister's wife, and a minister's children, and a minister's servant should carry it, that the ministry might in nothing be blamed. He would sometimes be a particular intercessor for the towns and parishes adjacent. How have I heard him, when he hath been in the mount with God, in a Sabbath evening prayer, wrestle with the Lord for Chester, and Shrewsbury, and Nantwich, and Wrexham, and Whitchurch, etc., those nests of souls, wherein there are so many that cannot discern between their right hand and their left in spiritual things, etc. He closed his Sabbath work in his family with singing Ps. cxxxiv., and after it a solemn blessing."[1]

Another half-century elapses, and the excellent Dr. Doddridge is found walking in the steps of Philip Henry: "The Lord's day was most strictly and religiously observed in his family; and after the public and domestic services of it, he often took them [his pupils] separately into his study, conversed with them concerning the state of religion in their souls, and gave them suitable advice. Often on the Lord's-day evening he discoursed seriously with them [his servants] by themselves, and prayed with them."[2]

[1] *Life of Mr. Philip Henry*, pp. 74-76. [2] *Life*, by Orton, pp. 98, 132.

Dr. R. W. Hamilton has in eloquent strains described the old Puritan Sabbath with its domestic devotions morning and evening —and its public assemblies and worship. Of the latter, he says, "Sermons full of thought and powerful in application, having much unity and closeness, with *doctrine raised* and *improvement enforced*, repaid the long-exacted attention. They knew not our miscellany of vocal praise, but breathed their gratitude and adoration through the strains of the sweet singer of Israel. Public prayer was systematic, still various, abounding in intercession, such as the minister's closet had indited, and his heart had already made his own." Referring to the Sabbath evening counsels of a father and the instructions of a mother, to the catechism heard and the preaching reviewed, he observes, "That made their generations strong. . . . Thus were they trained and formed. . . . In the change of all this we are weak." He adds, "Some of us knew the likenesses well. We have seen the counterparts. These customs had come down to us. Such were the families to which birth added us. Such were our fathers, and such the mothers who bore us. We declaim no inventions, we draw no pictures, we speak no unknown things. In them was reflected the Puritan race. In them those saints revived and stood up once more. In this resemblance but little degenerated, we may measure their worth, and as by a personal observation, fully know their doctrine, manner of life, purpose, faith, long-suffering, charity, patience."[1]

We have quoted, in p. 226, part of a description of an English Sabbath, as it was passed at a later period, for the purpose of showing that a sacred weekly day holily spent is not a day of gloom. We now give a few more sentences. "It was a day truly honourable in our eyes, and marked as a season of sacred delights. Its various exercises, whether public or private, produced an exhilarating effect upon our minds, and never failed to set us some paces nearer the object of our supreme desires. It was a kind of transfiguration-day, shedding a mild glory upon every creature, and enabling us to view the concerns of time in connexion with those of eternity. . . . Many a joyful Sabbath have we thus spent together, especially during the latter years of our Joshua's continuance with us. And now when his mother

[1] *Horæ et Vindiciæ Sabbat.* pp. 183, 185, 187.

and I are disposed, on the return of these sacred seasons, to look with regret towards his vacant place, we endeavour to animate each other with the hope of shortly following our dearest son to the celebration of that eternal Sabbath above, of which we have enjoyed so many sweet anticipations here below."[1]

It is said of the late Princess Charlotte and her husband, Prince Leopold, "Their whole domestic habits were marked by sobriety and virtue. Respect for the Lord's day formed a prominent feature in their domestic arrangements. Divine service was regularly attended; and the evening hours of the sacred day were employed in the perusal of pious writings, or in other exercises suited to its design."[2]

We add a few illustrations of a domestic Sabbath, as it once existed, and still exists in Scotland. Ruddiman, the distinguished grammarian, printer, and librarian of the Advocates' Library, "was frugal of his time, and moderate, both in his pleasures and amusements. His day was usually employed in the following manner. He rose early, and devoted the morning to study. During the sitting of the Court of Session, he used to attend the Advocates' Library from ten till three. He commonly retired from dinner at four, except when it was necessary to show respect to friends. His evenings were generally spent in conversation with the learned. During the decline of his age, when an amanuensis became requisite, his day was spent somewhat differently. His first act of the morning was to kneel down, while his amanuensis read prayers. He lived chiefly in his library. A basin of tea was brought him for his breakfast; he dined about two o'clock; and tea was again sent in to him a little after four. His amanuensis generally read to him seven hours a day, Sunday alone excepted, which, in the presence of his family, and with the help of the Rev. Mr. Harper, was dedicated to the service of God."[3] Of Professor Lawson of Selkirk it is said by Dr. Belfrage, "So different was his conduct from the common practice of indulging longer in sleep on the Sabbath morning than on others, that he rose earlier, and made his family do so. His domestic instructions and prayers

[1] Gilpin's Monument of Parental Affection, quoted in Gilfillan's *Essay on the Sanctification of the Lord's Day* (9th Edit.), p. 124, etc.

[2] *Sermon* by Dr. John Campbell of Edinburgh (1817), p. 14.

[3] *Life*, p. 276.

were never hurried over, but discharged as a duty, felt to be pleasing as well as solemn. Of Fisher's Catechism he had a very high opinion, made his young people read portions of it again and again with great care, and meditate on them, and he then examined them as to their conceptions of its meaning, and the impressions which it should produce. There was a circumstance in his family instruction which showed his admirable skill, and which rendered it most delightful to the young; with his questions and counsels he mingled appropriate anecdotes, exhibiting the pleasures of religion, God's care of His saints, the beauty of early piety, the happiness of the family whose God is the Lord, how the fear of God operates as a preservative from sin, what God has done in honour of His own day, and what consolations and hopes the promises of the gospel have yielded in sickness and death."[1] "To the deep tone of his piety," says the biographer of the late Rev. John Jameson of Methven, a man at once of high genius, the most saintly character, and the warmest, tenderest heart, "may be ascribed that calm delight, combined with solemn concern about his public work, which were so visible in his very countenance on the Lord's day. On that day he rose early, seemed in haste to realize it as a day of rest from the labours of the week; was often heard to say, 'What a blessing is it, after all, that on this day God does not require us to waste our thoughts on earth-born cares!' He seldom spoke with his family, beyond inquiring after their welfare, till his public duties were over; and to those in whom he chose to confide, he accounted for this by saying, that, when his family were all in health, he could not even think of them till he had done what he could; so heavily did the work of God press on his spirit. But after the public services of the day were over, he delighted in having his family all about him, and would often speak on for a long time, with great ease and cheerfulness, about those passages of Scripture which circumstances happened to suggest to him. For some time before his death, his mind on these occasions turned very frequently to the doctrine of the resurrection; and at one time, with the view perhaps of apologizing for this, he spoke nearly as follows:—'My children, I never like to dwell long on the thought of death; *that* is a

[1] *Memoir* prefixed to Dr. Lawson's *Discourses on David*, p. xxi.

gloomy subject; my mind is always for bounding off to the bright morning of the resurrection, a morning so full of life, and peace, and joy. Ah! that is the morning which will vanquish death, and swallow up in perfect victory all the ill it has ever done to this poor heart of mine, by tearing asunder the finest ties which bound it to the earth, and sending some of our fairest flowers to the dull cold grave. Why should death hold so many, all their days, in the bondage of its fear? What is it to die, but just to wink and to be with Christ?' This last thought seemed to dwell in his mind, and to yield him much enjoyment. When, not long before his death, a Christian friend spoke to him rather despondingly of the long and weary ages that the body must lie in the grave, he replied, in his usual hearty way, 'It is just to-morrow morning; you never think the night long when your sleep is sound.'"[1]—Of Mr. John M'Lelland, a "Christian farmer," it is said, "Indeed, from the account sent me by one who remains on the farm, and was with him for several years, and from what I knew otherwise, it does appear as if his Sabbath work alone was more than he was able to perform. His general rule, after returning from the place of public worship, five miles distant, was to visit one workman's family, and join with them in reading, expounding Scripture, and prayers—to gather all the children who could or would come into his own house for instruction—and afterwards to take his own children by themselves, and his female servants by themselves, and close up the employments and enjoyments of the day by family prayers. It is well to work while it is day, for the night cometh when no man can work, and to him it was drawing nigh."[2]

We have yet to notice the public respect which the Sabbath has received in the United Kingdom, to an extent, especially in Scotland, which is paralleled elsewhere only in the United States of America. Its fortunes, indeed, have from various causes been considerably chequered, but in none of its descents has it ever reached the same depression as in other countries, and it has sometimes culminated to a point of honour somewhat corresponding with its standard and its final triumph. A writer on the subject thus describes some of its palmy days in England: "As we do not

[1] *Remains, with Memoir*, by the Rev. D. Young, D.D., Perth, 3d edit., pp. 19-21

[2] *The Christian Farmer*, by the Rev. J. Towers, Birkenhead, p. 42.

find any other Reformed Church hath either so clearly maintained the doctrine of the Sabbath as ours, both in the Homily of the Time and Place of Prayer, and in so many authorized writers for more than sixty years; or so solemnly observed it by command of laws, injunctions, and canons, and the conscientiousness of governors of families and private Christians; so we find a special ratification of the promised blessing, both in spiritual and temporal respects."[1] For nearly the twenty years from 1640 to 1660, the Sabbath was allowed to maintain its benignant sway. The Revolution improved its condition after a sad reverse. And the revival of religion through the labours of Romaine, Whitfield, and Wesley, was the life of all Christian institutions. "A number of the converts of Wesley and Whitfield," says Jay of Bath, "were yet living when I began to appear in public, and some of them I knew intimately; and they made too deep an impression upon me to be forgotten. . . . . Their attachment to the means of grace was intense; nor would they suffer distance or weather, or slight indispositions to detain them. The Sabbath was their delight, and they numbered the days till its arrival. And as to the poorer of them—

'Though pinched with poverty at home,
With sharp affliction daily fed;
It made amends, if they could come
To God's own house for heavenly bread.'

Nor were these services only pleasing to them in the performance, they were remembered and talked over for weeks after. For the sermons they heard, if not highly polished, left effects which were as goads, and as nails fastened in a sure place by the hand of the Master of assemblies. They also seemed to have more veneration for the Scriptures, and to peruse them with more directness, simplicity, and docility,—for the Bible, as yet, had not been turned into a work of science rather than of faith, and of everlasting criticism rather than of devotion, nor were thousands of tutors and multitudes of volumes found necessary to explain a simple book designed for 'the poor,' and the 'common people' by the only wise God Himself."[2] Methodism still leavens a portion of

[1] *Sab. Redivivum*, by Cawdrey and Palmer (1645). Epist. to the Reader, pp. 4, 5.
[2] *Autobiography* (second edition, 1855), pp. 175-177.

the masses, and though multitudes of working men have in our day forsaken the house of God, their places are increasingly supplied from the middle and higher ranks. If in Scotland the Sabbath was for some time after the Reformation not so well observed as afterwards, this was owing to no want of zealous efforts on its behalf, but to the rooted customs of Romanism; and that very period was the seed-time, when the Reformers were sowing in tears what was to be reaped in joy. The Covenanters were distinguished by their ardent love to the Sabbath. This was well known by their persecutors, some of whom, when in pursuit of an intended victim, and hearing him chant, in lively strains, some Scottish air, passed on, saying, "That, at least, is not Alexander Brown; he would not sing songs on the Sabbath-day."[1] Sir Walter Scott, employing the cant term of a certain class, has charged their mode of keeping the day "as Judaical." The charge has been repelled by two writers, than whom few were more qualified to pronounce on the point. "We do not know," remarks Dr. M'Crie, "what our author means, and we are not sure that he has himself any distinct idea of what is meant by a Judaical observance of the Sabbath. We know of no peculiar strictness on this head exacted by our Presbyterian forefathers, above what is practised by the sober and religious part of the inhabitants of Scotland to this day. And whatever he may be pleased to think of it, there are many of as enlightened minds, and of as liberal principles, as he can pretend to, who glory in this national distinction; and one reason why we will not suffer our ancestors to be misrepresented by him, or by any writer of the present times, is the gratitude which we feel to them, for having transmitted to their posterity a hereditary and deep veneration for the Lord's day."[2] Principal Lee, when under examination, in 1832, by a Committee of the House of Commons on the Observance of the Sabbath, was asked, "Can you say, from your knowledge of history, whether the description given by a celebrated novelist of the period of the Covenanters is historically correct, and whether their precise manners were as strongly marked in contrast to the other party as that ingenious writer would have us to suppose?" His answer was, "Most cer-

[1] Simpson's *Traditions of the Covenanters*, 1844, Series First, p. 225.

[2] *Miscellaneous Writings*, p. 276.

tainly that description is not historically correct ; there never was such gloom attending the observance of the Sabbath in Scotland as that celebrated writer alleges. The Sabbath, though observed with the greatest reverence, was a day rather of sober and cheerful piety, than of any painful restraint. It may be, as the question has been asked, not improper to state, that the greater part of the description applying to the religion and morals of that class of persons in Scotland who are known by the name of Covenanters, must have been supplied almost altogether by the imagination of the writer." The Principal then specifies some instances of glaring ignorance on the part of the accuser of these good men, and concludes thus : "I refer to these particulars merely as specimens of the inaccuracy of the descriptions which have probably made an impression not easily effaced, though it has done great injustice to the characters of an oppressed and persecuted race, who, derided as they have been as feeble-minded fanatics, did more than any other body of men both to maintain the interests of religion, and to secure for their posterity the enjoyment of civil liberty."[1] When we consider that it was not till the Revolution that the Scottish people of that time had "rest round about," for keeping the Sabbath, and carrying out their principles and wishes, we are prepared to admit the consistency of the admitted high regard for the institution on the part of the Covenanters with the following statement of Dr. Lee : "I have great reason to think that the Sabbath was observed with the greatest strictness and solemnity in Scotland, soon after the period of the Revolution of 1688, till about the year 1730," a fact, which he ascribes "to the very great vigilance, faithfulness, and zeal with which both ministers and elders performed their duty towards those who were placed under their charge, and more, perhaps, than to any other cause, to the universal practice of Bible education."[2] About the time, however, when the institution began to wane in the Church of Scotland, a new society was about to take its rise—the Secession—in which the Sabbath has for more than a century been peculiarly

[1] *Minutes of Evidence*, pp. 272, 273. It is right to state that Sir Walter Scott made some, if an inadequate, reparation of his error, and bore a testimony to the truth, in the more favourable representation which he gave of the Covenanters in his subsequent novels and in his *Tales of a Grandfather*.

[2] *Minutes*, p. 269.

respected, and by which an impulse was given to religion in the Mother Church, that has led, through the zeal of those who have been disrupted from her communion, and the improvement of those who have remained in it, to the greatest good in this and other lands.

What conclusions are we warranted to draw from the whole history in the preceding pages ? These two propositions, at least, seem to follow from the facts : that a taste and practice opposed to the hatred of restraint, and to the love of selfish, worldly indulgence, which are naturally so strong in man, must have had their origin and support from a Supernal source ; and that the Sabbath, which the human heart has been brought by a Divine hand to relish, must itself, like every good and perfect gift, have come down from the Father of lights, with whom is no variableness, neither shadow of turning.

THE SABBATH DEFENDED AGAINST OPPOSING ARGUMENTS, THEORIES, AND SCHEMES.

CHAPTER I.

ALLEGED ANTI-SABBATISM OF THE REFORMERS.

The Reformers, as was shown in a former chapter, believed the Sabbath to be of Divine and perpetual obligation, regarded it as of supreme importance, and enforced as well as exemplified its sacred observance. It is not denied, however, that they sometimes expressed themselves respecting it in terms which have given occasion and some plausibleness to the charge of hostility to the institution. This is the more to be regretted that their unguarded language must have often been recited, as certainly it has repeatedly been printed, unaccompanied by their better utterances on the subject, and that many, in such a case, do not trouble themselves to inquire into the circumstances, so as to understand the proper import and value of the words employed. It is the opinion of Dr. Fairbairn, who has fully and carefully examined the whole matter, that they were substantially sound upon the question, in so far as concerns the obligations and practice of Christians, and it will be a satisfaction to us, if, under the following heads, we can advance any facts or considerations for confirming the opinion.

In the first place, let it be understood on both sides, that whatever were the views of the Reformers, their name does not decide the controversy between the friends and the opponents of a Divine, sacred, and permanent Sabbath. It is too evident that the latter have employed that name as if it ought to silence every plea for such an institution—and we will not affirm that the former may not have been too anxious to have men of such repute on their side. Both classes in such a case forget the example which the Reformers have set them, and, what is of much more consequence, the law of Christ, which says, "Call no man master." Men may err, but not the Word of God.

Second, If we duly weighed the circumstances of the Reformers, we should be disposed to moderate our estimate of the value of their judgment in this matter. They had, for example, but limited means for examining and discussing the subject. The Great Apostasy has ever been a perversion, not an open renunciation of Christianity—"a noble vine," not rooted up, but "turned into the degenerate plant of a strange vine." Rome, professing to retain, has yet corrupted every doctrine, institution, and law of Jesus Christ—recognising, for example, the Mediator between God and men, but associating with Him many other intercessors; avowing adherence to the Scripture, but to the Scripture as supplemented and made void by the writings and traditions of men; and, in short, without discarding the Lord's day, adding a number of encumbering holidays, giving them in many instances an honour equal and even superior to God's own day, and claiming for "the Vicar of Christ" lordship "even of the Sabbath." It was thus with arrogant claims, and gross abuses, affecting the Lord's day, not with the open denial of its authority, or rejection of its sacred character, that the Reformers had to grapple. The latter subjects formed no part of their controversy with Rome, and, indeed, had never come under discussion to any extent in the Church. Their circumstances did not call them particularly and critically to consider the general question, and, judging from the small space allowed to the weekly holy day in their works, as well as from their occasional manner of writing respecting it, the institution appears to have received less than most other points in theology of their careful attention. They knew it in their Christian love and practice more than as a doctrine. The heats, besides, and the turmoils of a great revolution, were not the most favourable state in which calmly to weigh and adjust a system of truth. And when long-continued, deep-seated, and wide-spread evils had to be remedied, much of the work of reformation was necessarily left by the originators to those who should come after them. Such considerations might guard us against the mistake of supposing that Luther and Calvin had clearer views of the Sabbatic institution than its friends in later times, and of attaching the whole weight of honour acquired by them in other fields of labour and prowess, to their sayings and doings on an arena where they had not put forth their might. Another circumstance was, the state of the institution in the Church which they sought to reform. It was the confession of Roman Catholic writers themselves, that the Church had, in the beginning of the sixteenth century, reached a measure of corruption which rendered her incapable of bearing either her disorders or the remedies. One of her intolerable disorders was that of holidays, which, begun early, was now nearly at its worst. Pious, but misguided zeal, as we have already seen, introduced stated feasts and fasts. In Constantine's tampering with the Fourth Commandment, by permitting agricultural labour on the Lord's day, and ordering the observance of certain holidays, we discover the germ of bolder assumptions afterwards made by the Papacy when it sought to change the times and laws of the Most High. The greater festivals were promoted to the rank of Sabbath-days. Then, as by Bernard, all other holy days were held, equally with the only true holy day, to be grounded upon the Divine law. The next step, of which we have an instance in an edict of Edward IV. of England, was to sink in the general class of such days the Lord's day. In the same century (the fifteenth) the seasons of rest from labour had so multiplied, and been the occasions of so much profligacy and riot, as to excite the alarm and remonstrances of thoughtful men, only, however, to be disregarded by the Popes, who "did not only keep the holidays, which they found established, in the state in which they found them, but added others daily as they saw occasion."[1] "The third part of the year," in consequence, "passed away in idle festivals."[2] The Sabbath, than which, as in a former part of this volume has been shown, nothing tends more to the moral and monetary good of society, was prostituted into a means of general demoralization

[1] Heylyn's *Hist. of the Sab.*, Part ii. p. 168.
[2] Beza, *On Song of Solomon*, Ser. 8 on ch. iii.

and poverty. That day, designed and fitted to be a season of worship and religious instruction, was, from its uncongenial connexion with so many unhallowed festivals, compelled to serve in the cause of profaneness, infidelity, and vice. It was found easier and more pleasant, by priests and people, to spend a multitude of consecrated days in attending on processions and the mass, than in the labours of teaching and learning Divine knowledge. What was worse, holidays came to be regarded as the whole of man's salvation and sanctity. They were considered as holy in themselves, and as rendering sacred what was done on them. The doctrine of grace, according to the Augsburg Confession, "is almost wholly smothered by traditions, which have bred an opinion, that, by making difference in meats, and such like services, a man must merit remission of sins and justification. In their doctrine of repentance there was no mention of faith, only these satisfactory works were spoken of; repentance seemed to stand wholly in these. Secondly, these traditions obscured the commandments of God that they could not be known, because that traditions were preferred far above the commandments of God. All Christianity was thought to be an observation of certain holy days, rites, fasts, and attire."[1] Ochin says, "If thou wouldest ask at what time God ought to be loved, they [the Papists] will answer, on the Sabbath and festival days." "For observing the first and chiefest commandment of the law, it is sufficient that, at the least the twinkling of an eye, upon the Sabbath-day, we have in us some act of love towards God, with exalting Him above all things; and that this, through our most [*sic*] and mighty free will, is always in our power."[2] Men's minds were thus turned away from the means of salvation, and from the study and practice of true religion, into the endless and perplexing labyrinth of a vast system of casuistry relating to meats, drinks, days, and "the putting on of apparel;" and "many fell into despair, some murdering themselves because they could not keep the traditions."[3] The design of the Papacy in the whole matter was to promote its own ascendency, and to fill its

1 Hall's *Harmony of Confessions*, p. 397.
2 *Sermons*, quoted in James's *Sermons on the Sacraments*, pp. 218, 219.
3 Hall's *Harmony of Confessions*, p. 398.

coffers, "the monks daily heaping up ceremonies, both with new superstitions, and also with new ways to bring in money." And to bind down and perpetuate these burdens on the minds and consciences of men, it was taught and believed, that "Christ gave the charge of devising new ceremonies, which should be necessary to salvation, to the apostles and bishops."[1] From this the transition was easy to the daring, blasphemous dogma, that the bishops, by virtue of this authority, had "dispensed with a precept of the Moral Law, and changed the Sabbath into the Lord's day."[2] Such, while the institution was professedly maintained and honoured, were the evils by which its rights were invaded, and its influence was impaired. Trained under such a system, how could it be supposed that the Reformers should retain no taint of its errors? and yet, exasperated at the enormities which they had discovered, how could they be expected to avoid every extreme in the opposite direction? Such views would imply them to be more than human.

Third, The views of the Reformers on the subject of the Sabbath have not been fairly presented. It is possible that on both sides of the controversy there may be writers who, in searching for passages that favour their own views and wishes, unintentionally omit those of a different description. Such a method of leading evidence, if it cannot be pronounced in their case to be wrong in morals, and indefensible in logic, unless we are sure that it was knowingly resorted to, betrays at least a carelessness which proves their unfitness for their task. We are willing to place in this category a number of works of recent date, in which certain strong and peculiar statements of the Reformers appear, while much clearer and more decisive declarations, containing nearly all the received doctrines on the Sabbath, are excluded. It is especially painful to find Dr. Hengstenberg chargeable with this conduct, the more so that the influence of his name imparts greater currency and power to the injury and wrong.

Fourth, The words of the Reformers have been in some instances misunderstood. Let us give an example from a passage in the *Institutions* of Calvin, who says, "Nor do I so value the septenary number as to bind the Church to its servitude, nor shall I

[1] Hall's *Harmony of Confessions*, p. 401. [2] *Ibid.*

condemn the churches which observe other days for their meetings, provided they avoid superstition, which they will do if they only observe the day from regard to discipline and good order. . . . Thus vanish the trifles of false teachers who have in former days imbued the people with Judaical notions, alleging that only what was ceremonial in this commandment was abrogated, that is, the appointment of the seventh day, and that what was moral, or the observance of one day in seven, remained. But that is nothing else than to change the day in reproach of the Jews, and yet to retain the same holiness of a day, forasmuch as there continues among us the same mystery in the meaning of days that prevailed among the Jews. And verily we see what they have made by such doctrine who adhere to their constitutions, and thrice surpass the Jews in the gross, carnal superstition of Sabbatism, so that the rebukes of Isaiah (Isa. i. 13; lviii. 13) are no less applicable to the men of our day than to those whom he censured in his own time."[1] That when he said he would not restrict the Church to the number seven, or condemn the churches which observed other days for their meetings, he meant that he would not diminish but increase the opportunities of worship, and would add to, not change, the day of the hitherto observed Sabbath, is manifest from his very words, not to say from his practice, and from all that he elsewhere advances respecting a perpetual seventh day of rest, the duties divinely assigned to it, and its vast importance. He will admit of superadded days of worship, but not superstitious holidays. In the second part of the quotation, he has been erroneously supposed to deny the morality of a septenary rest. This supposition would make him contradict what he has repeatedly affirmed of the Divine example of resting at the Creation as a perpetual rule, and of the Fourth Commandment as an everlasting law of righteousness to mankind. In the words referred to, however, he assails not a seventh day, but a fancied change of one seventh day of Jewish observance into another seventh day of Jewish observance; a change made under colour, that by keeping the proportion of time they honoured the morality of the institution, while, in fact, they carried along with them the ceremonial character of the old Sabbath. To substitute the first for the

[1] *On Fourth Commandment.*

seventh day in such circumstances was merely to put a slight on the Jewish day, not to turn Jewish into Christian practice. He concludes his remarks thus: "But the general doctrine is principally to be maintained, lest religion should fall or languish, that sacred assemblies are to be diligently observed, and attention given to the external aids which foster the worship of God." The amount of the whole is, that the seventh proportion of time is not to be regarded as something in itself holy, or to be observed with superstitious feelings and forms, but to be employed in spiritual exercises, and for furthering piety as the business of the whole life.

Our remark applies also to a few expressions which, common to the Reformers in general, sound strangely to ears trained to the distinct sounds emitted on our subject by the Puritans of England and the Reformers and Covenanters of Scotland. "It was not without a reason that the ancients substituted what we call the Lord's day for the Sabbath." (Calvin in *Institutions.*) "The Church did appoint the Lord's day, which day for this cause also seemed to have better liked the Church, that in it men might have an example of Christian liberty, and might know that the observance neither of the Sabbath, nor of any other day, was of necessity." (Augsburg Confession.) "For we believe neither that one day is holier than another, nor that rest by itself is acceptable to God, but yet we keep the Lord's day, not the Sabbath, by a voluntary observance." (Helvetic Confession.) "They did not desist from manual labour on the ground of its interfering with sacred study and meditation, but from a sort of religious obligation, because they dreamed that by ceasing from work they revived mysteries which were at one time authorized." (Calvin, *Institutions.*) It is manifest, not only from the doctrines already shown to have been held by the Reformers, as well as from their whole conduct, but also from their plain statements already adduced, that the liberty claimed by them as to times was a freedom not from the keeping of a day of holy rest, but from the yoke of ancient ceremonies, from that yoke particularly, as wreathed round the necks of Christians by Rome, and held necessary to be worn by them if they would be saved; and that when they say, "The Church chose a day," or "such a thing liked the Church;" they are not to be understood as denying the appointment of the Lord's day to have been made by Christ. Thus, in words already quoted, the Augsburg Confession says, "The general rule abideth still in the moral law, that at certain times we should come together to these godly exercises; but the special day, which was but a ceremony, was free." But did Christians determine what day they were to sanctify? Let the Confession declare that Luther and his friends had no such idea, for it adds: "Whereupon the apostles retained not the seventh day, but did rather take the first day of the week for that use, that by it they might admonish the godly both of their liberty and of Christ's resurrection." While the Helvetic Confession states: "We keep the Lord's day, not the Sabbath, by a voluntary observance," and "every Church chooses for itself a certain time for public prayer and the preaching of the gospel," it declares, "that the Lord's day was devoted to religious meetings and sacred leisure, even as early as the times of the apostles, and that it is not left free to every one capriciously to overturn this arrangement of the Church."

John Knox himself—whose love and reverence for the Lord's day are written in the First Book of Discipline; in the Acts of the early Assemblies of his Church, which repudiated holy days, and testified against the desecration of *the holy day;* and in three centuries' history of his country—has been represented as conceiving "the Sabbath to have been an exclusively Jewish institution, and never meant for this advanced dispensation;" and this on the grounds, that there is no express mention of the sanctification of the Sabbath in the Confession of Faith, which he with others drew up [the substance, however, is there], and that the Duke of Châtellerault and the English Ambassador supped with him on a Sunday evening. Our preamble to this charge, and our statement of the charge itself, are its refutation, and we draw the conclusion to which every considerate and candid mind will come, when we add, It is a pure fancy. It is true indeed, as alleged, that the Duke of Châtellerault supped with the Reformer, but we leave it to our readers to judge from the following words whether there was anything in the matter inconsistent with the most sacred respect for the institu tion : "Upon Sondaye at night, the Duke supped with Mr. Knox, wher the Duke desired that I shold be. Thre speciall pointes he hathe promised to perform to Mr. Knox before me : the one is never to goe for any respecte from that he hath promised to be, a professor of Christ's worde, and setter forthe of the same to his power : the nexte, alwayes to shewe hymself an obedyent subjecte to his sovereigne, as far as in duetie and in conscience he is bounde : the thyrde, never to alter from that promes he hathe made for the mayntenance of peace and amytie betwene both the realmes. I had of hym besides thys, manie good wórds myselfe touchinge thys latter poynte."[1]

Again, the Reformers, in their zeal against superstition, made use of strong language which ought not to be interpreted literally, or viewed apart from the other sayings, and from the practice of its authors. Such is the character of the expressions of Zuinglius, who said that man was lord of the Sabbath ; of Tyndale ; and of his convert, Frith (pp. 35, 36 of this volume). It is remarked of Tyndale and Frith, "These excellent men (cut off before the Reformation had made much progress in England, Frith in 1533, Tyndale three years afterwards), wrote at the time when the evil of the number of the Romish holidays, and the superstitious observance of them by the people, was so strongly felt, as to call for a check even from those who had not then embraced the opinions of the Reformers. Yet we should notice that they both speak of Sunday, as made the day of public religious instruction, instead of the ancient Sabbath ; and though Tyndale somewhat extravagantly considers the change of any other day for it still in the power of the Church, his friend Frith represents the change as having been made by the apostles ; for St. Paul certainly was among those forefathers in the beginning who abrogated the Jewish Sabbath."[2] We may add, that none of these men ever attempted to carry his vehement words into effect, and that Tyndale, as noted page 36, was evidently a devout observer of the Lord's day. But Luther was still more given to such paroxysms of zeal. "The law of Moses," Dr. Hengstenberg re-

[1] Letter from Randolph (English Ambassador) to Cecil, in Wright's *Queen Elizabeth and her Times*, vol. i pp. 114, 115.
[2] James's *Four Sermons*, pp. 221, 222.

presents him as saying, "belongs to the Jews, and is no longer binding upon us. The words of Scripture prove clearly to us that the ten commandments do not affect us; for God has not brought us out of Egypt, but only the Jews. We are willing to take Moses as a teacher, but not as our Lawgiver, except when he agrees with the New Testament, and with the law of nature."[1] Hotter still he becomes, according to Coleridge, who treats us, in *Table Talk*, to the following explosion: "Keep it holy," are the words of the Reformer, "for its use' sake, both to body and soul! But if anywhere the day is made holy for the mere day's sake, if anywhere any one sets up its observance upon a Jewish foundation, then I order you to work on it, to ride on it, to dance on it, to feast on it, to do anything that shall reprove this encroachment on the Christian spirit and liberty."[2] "As for the Sabbath or Lord's day," he remarks, "there is no necessity for keeping it; but if we do so, it ought to be not on account of Moses' commandment, but because nature teaches us from time to time to take a day of rest, in order that men and animals may recruit their strength, and that we may attend the preaching of God's word."[3] On other occasions, however, he declares that "it is *good and necessary* that men should keep a particular day;" speaks of what "*God requires* of us in this [the fourth] commandment," and holds that, "because the Lord's day has been appointed from the earliest times, we ought to keep to this arrangement." It so far explains the two modes of expression to suppose, that the Reformer objects only to a superstitious regard for a day; but the full verification of the saying, "Luther is to be interpreted by Luther," must, in the present instance, be sought for by comparing Luther less cool and informed, with Luther calm and instructed. He himself would not thank us for attempting to make him at one with himself, for he says, "If at the outset I inveighed against the law, both from the pulpit and in my writings, the reason was, that the Christian Church at the time was overladen with superstitions, under which Christ was altogether buried and hidden, and that I yearned to save and liberate pious and God-fearing souls from this tyranny over the conscience. But

[1] *Lord's Day*, p. 61. [2] *Table Talk*, vol. ii. pp. 315, 316.
[3] Michelet's *Life of Luther*, Book iv. chap. ii.

I have never rejected the law." "He who pulls down the law, pulls down at the same time the whole framework of human polity and society. If the law be thrust out of the Church, there will no longer be anything recognised as a sin in the world, since the gospel defines and punishes sin only by recurring to the law."[1] And again, "Let us leave Moses to his laws, excepting only *the Moralia*, which God hath planted in nature, as 'the Ten Commandments.'"[2] When, accordingly, John Agricola Islebius, the founder of the Antinomian party (1538), represented the Reformer as holding the doctrine, that the law was abrogated, the latter, in an epistolary exposure of the opinions of the party, said, "And truly I wonder exceedingly how it came to be imputed to me, that I should reject the law or ten commandments, there being so many of my own expositions (and those of several sorts) upon the commandments, which also are daily expounded and used in our churches, to say nothing of the Confession, and Apology, and other books of ours. Add hereunto the custom we have to sing the commandments in two different tunes, besides the painting, printing, carving, and rehearsing them by children, both morning, noon, and evening; so that I know no other way than what we have used, but that we do not, alas! as we ought, really express them in our lives and conversation."[3] As an evidence how sensible he was that his opinions were far from being infallible, we find that when a friend informed him of some persons in Belgium, who were offended at certain parts of his writings, his reply was, "When you meet with anything of no worth, delete it, delete it."

Further, it is due to the Reformers to give prominence and weight to the latest expression of their sentiments. We have not seen any express indication on the part of Luther of "compunctious visitings" for his language respecting the Sabbath, yet we cannot but accord with a Lutheran writer in the conviction, that his commentary on Genesis, written not long before his death, and expressing the formerly quoted, clear, decided views of the primitive appointment of the institution, with his hymns on the Decalogue, which he wished to be sung in the Church while he lived and

[1] For this and preceding quotation, see Michelet as above, chap iv.

[2] Luther's *Table Talk*, No. 271.

[3] Rutherford's *Spiritual Antichrist*, p. 71.

after he was gone, represented his latest Sabbatic opinions.[1] One of these hymns, composed in 1525, runs :—

> "Honour my name in word and deed,
> And call on me in time of need:
> Keep holy too the Sabbath-day,
> That work in thee I also may."

And the other of the previous year, has the words :—

> "Hallow the day which God hath blest,
> That thou and all thy house may rest:
> Keep hand and heart from labour free,
> That God may have his work in thee."[2]

Lastly, it may even be allowed that the Reformers erred to some extent in regard to the weekly holy day, while it is held that they did not thereby forfeit their claim to be ranked among the friends of the institution, inasmuch as the truth decidedly outweighs the error. Calvin, Luther, and, indeed, all the principal men of the Reformation except Knox, were of the opinion of Augustine and others of the Fathers, that the fourth was distinguished from the rest of the commandments by being partly of a ceremonial character. They seemed not to know how the transference of the sacred rest from the last to the first day of the week could be reconciled to the doctrine of a moral, unchangeable precept, and therefore adopted the theory of a double aspect of the commandment, one part being ceremonial which has passed away, the other being moral and enduring. The distinction is as unnecessary as it is untenable. The Second Commandment might as well be supposed to have a twofold character, inasmuch as the means of worship, which it rules, have been changed from Jewish to Christian ordinances. The alteration in both cases was in the circumstances of the law, provided for by positive appointment and special revelation, not in the law itself. The Sabbath had a ceremonial or typical character under the Levitical economy, but not so its royal precept. This was the distinction that ought to have been made by the Fathers and Reformers, but their adopting another, though an error, did not originate in a low estimate

1 Brunsman, *Sab. Quies*, par. 215, 219.

2 *Geistliche Leider*, Lond. (1845), pp. 53, 56, and Massie's Translation, etc., pp. 53, 55.

of the day of rest, which they regarded, the typical aspect having disappeared, as still the charge of a moral statute. The error, however, had the effect of perplexing their views on the subject, and leading to the use of certain expressions, which have exposed their respect for the institution to suspicion, and the cause itself to practical injury. Another matter in which all the Reformers, with the exception again of Knox, appear to us to have more or less fallen into error, was that of holidays. We have seen that some would have removed such days entirely, which in fact was done in Geneva, and at Strasburg, and that the number of them in several instances was reduced. But none of the Reformers was so decided in opinion and practice on the subject as Knox. Even Calvin treated the question as one of comparative unimportance. Whatever was the cause, Luther's early desire for the abolition of holidays was not fulfilled. The prejudice in favour of some of them was strong, as we learn from the feelings of the Bernese, of the Belgian magistrates, and of a few in Scotland, who continued to observe certain feast-days for some time after the Reformation. These observances were restored in Geneva, and have been permanently disregarded among Protestants only by the Puritans of England, and the Presbyterians of Scotland, with their descendants in America and other countries, and by the missionary churches which they have planted in various lands. But the failure of the good men of the Reformation to carry into effect Luther's desire for the disbanding of the holidays, while to be regretted, does not appear a sufficient ground for questioning their respect for the Lord's day, which, though in some instances it was classed by them as if it were only the chief in a series of such days, they repeatedly declared to be an express appointment of Heaven, and indispensable to the welfare of the church, withholding, at the same time, that honour from other days of rest and worship.

Having endeavoured to present the Sabbatic opinions of the Reformers in the light of truth and facts, we venture to claim on their behalf from our readers a verdict of "not guilty" of the offence of hostility or even indifference to the institution. They erred, it is allowed, in some of their expressions and proceedings. They unhappily failed to distinguish between the Sabbath as it stood in the Decalogue, and the Sabbath as connected with the judicial and ceremonial appendages of Judaism, and to eradicate what some of themselves called "the useless and hurtful practice of holiday keeping." Theirs, however, were the mistakes of ardent friends of piety and good morals, who in eagerly opposing enormities fell into some errors, and in checking the gross abuse of the external and preceptive, as well as in aiming at a high measure of the spiritual and the voluntary in religion, did not sufficiently adjust the claims of the outward and the inward, of liberty and law. Knox avoided their mistakes. In 1547, he adopted, as the result of independent inquiry, the great principles, which guided his future career, and by which he was honoured to effect the most thorough of the salutary revolutions accomplished at the Reformation. In that year he taught at St. Andrews the doctrine that everything in religion ought to be regulated, not by the pleasure and appointment of men, but according to the Word of God, and in the same year maintained in a public disputation, that the church has no authority, on pretext of decorating Divine service, to devise ceremonies, and impose upon them significations of her own. Row, referring to the six ministers, including Knox and himself, who were employed to draw up the *First Book of Discipline*, says, "They took not their example from any kirk in the world; no, not from Geneva; but drew their plan from the sacred Scriptures." It was in this way, we believe, that Knox formed those views of the Sabbath, which were afterwards so fully expounded by the Puritans, and to which his country owes so much. That the Puritans were indebted to him on the subject, we do not affirm. We know that he took some part in revising the Articles of the English Church, effected some alterations in her service-book, had much influence with the authorities, and produced great impression by his preaching, while from 1549 to the end of 1553 he resided in England; and we should conceive it more likely that the Puritans borrowed from him, than, as has been supposed, he from them. But it is not necessary to suppose either case, as the more that men make the Scriptures their study and their rule, the more will they "see eye to eye."

CHAPTER II.

MILTON AND OTHER EMINENT MEN.

We are not done yet with the argument which arrays against a holy Sabbath a few great names. Although it has failed as respects the Reformers, those who advance it have other names in reserve, of which the greatest is John Milton. True it is, that even after the Puritan training which he had received from his learned and idolized tutor, and after uttering as with "the tongues of angels" the praises of Him who

> "From work,
> Now resting, blessed and hallowed the seventh day,
> As resting on that day from all his work"—

Milton did indeed, by his latterly abandoning public and domestic worship, and by a posthumous attack on the authority of the Christian Sabbath, lend his influence to opinions subversive of three kindred institutions, to which in his youth and manhood he owed the direction and impulse that issued in his noble prose writings, and in his yet nobler poetry. "In the distribution of his hours," as Dr. Johnson in his Life of the Poet observes, "there was no hour of prayer, either solitary or with his household; omitting public prayers, he omitted all." In such circumstances, the less that is said of Milton's hostility to us the better. The melancholy change of religious practice, to which his biographer refers, not merely neutralizes his anti-Sabbatic influence, but is a potent argument for his former and against his latter creed. We would recommend to our opponents to say nothing of another remarkable man, Selden, who has written more learnedly than satisfactorily respecting the Sabbath in his *De Jure Naturali et Gentium*. For they will be reminded that this prodigy of lore was a member of the Westminster Assembly, did not appear to intimate at any of its meetings dissent from its doctrine on the Sabbath, and subscribed the Solemn League and Covenant, while in the following words he takes a middle course between the tenets of the Confession of Faith, and those of the anti-Sabbatists: "Why should I think all the Fourth Commandment belongs to me, when all the Fifth does not? What land will the Lord give me for honouring my father? It was spoken to the Jews with reference to the land of Canaan, but the meaning is, if I honour my parents, God will also bless me. We read the commandments in the Church service, as we do David's Psalms; not that all concerns us, but a great deal of them does."[1] It is affirmed of Selden that he "seems to have been often led by the current of circumstances to act against his personal convictions." He, therefore, is not a man of such religious and moral weight as to turn the scale against the perpetual obligation of a weekly day of entire rest and worship. Exceptions might also be taken to others of the class, who are relied on as authorities against us.

Were the question to be decided by mere names, the friends of the Sabbath would have no reason to shrink from the trial. But they disclaim such means of settling it. They bear in mind that no human being is infallible or to be held entitled to prescribe a creed to his fellow-creatures, that their duty is to try the spirits and prove all things, and that the greatest, wisest, and best of mankind fall into errors, which tend to recall us from confidence in men, to entire trust only in the Infinite. They yet, consistently with all this, believe that they ought to despise no man, that much importance may justly be attached to the opinions of the learned, and particularly of those who combine goodness with intelligence, and it becomes us to consider well before we dissent from views which have been entertained by persons of the greatest mental and moral excellence, and, especially, on which the Catholic Church has uttered all but a unanimous voice. Before, then, we agree to follow Milton, let us hear what other oracles have uttered, and then bring all to the oracles that are sacred and Divine.

[1] *Table Talk*, 1819, p. 169.

In questions that concern our physical frame, we naturally apply for information, and appeal for judgment, to persons who have made the human body their study, or by reason of their occupations in life have had better means than others of knowing the effects of labour and rest. Dr. Carpenter, who stands at the head of physiologists, has said, "My own experience is very strong as to the importance of the complete rest and change of thought once in the week;" and Dr. Farre's well-known testimony to the necessity of the weekly Sabbath as respects health, has been corroborated by many physicians of this country and America, without having, so far as we have observed, been contradicted by any. "He could, as an old soldier," said Major-General Anderson of himself, at the recent annual meeting of the Sabbath Alliance, "give an emphatic testimony in favour of the Sabbath. For a good many years before he gave up his last command, his duties were of a more arduous nature than fell to the general lot of men, particularly during the Crimean war, when latterly he knew not, from an early hour in the morning till a late hour at night, what it was to have an hour's rest. He looked forward with most anxious desire for the rest of the Sabbath, and felt on the Saturday as if he could not have gone on longer. But for the Sabbath, he hesitated not to say that he would have sunk under the protracted and incessant toil to which he was exposed. God blessed the Sabbath-day to his poor, exhausted frame; he was strengthened, and, he trusted, refreshed also in spirit, so that he was able to discharge his duties till the close."[1] The sighs and groans of animal nature in man and beast, wherever oppressed by unbroken labour, proclaim the indispensable need of a Sabbath.

Another valuable class of witnesses on this subject are our hard students, our philosophers, who are well acquainted with the laws of mind or matter; our philologists, who are versed in languages and criticism; and our men of historical research, who, in the successes and failures of the past, see rules and beacons for the present and future. Let the laborious Principal Forbes, Isaac Taylor, and Henry Rogers, express the value of the Sabbath to students. Lord Bacon, Sir Isaac Newton, Dr. Wallis, John

[1] *Daily Review*, February 11, 1862.

Locke, and Sir David Brewster, shall guarantee the philosophy of the institution. Archbishop Ussher, Drs. Owen and Kennicott, Sir William Jones, Dr. Jamieson, Dr. Pye Smith, and Professor S. Lee, have proved by their Sabbatic opinions—some of them by their researches on the subject also—that profound erudition has accepted and justified the commonly-received doctrine of the weekly rest; while Principal Lee and Lord Macaulay, thoroughly versant in the annals of our country, have shed some vivid rays on our national obligations to the institution.

Magistrates, statesmen, judges, divines, and moralists ought to be competent to say how far a Sabbath is valuable to the moral or the economical interests of a State. Oliver Cromwell and Washington knew well what was necessary to the defence and prosperity of a country, and the Sabbath was in their view essential to a virtuous and flourishing people. No judge has excelled Sir Matthew Hale, or lawyer, Blackstone, and they pleaded earnestly for a sanctified Sabbath. Lord Kames was both a judge and a philosopher, and his words were, "Sunday is a day of account, and a candid account every seventh day is the best preparation for the great day of account." No moral writer has surpassed Addison for simplicity and elegance, Johnson for power and vigour, and Foster for originality and depth, and they appreciated and commended the weekly rest. The most classical and beautiful writer of the English language, and one of the most impressive of pulpit orators, Robert Hall, was a conscientious observer of the Lord's day. The clear-headed, logical, and persuasive Wardlaw defended a careful attention to Sabbatic duties. Henry, "the prince of commentators," and Bunyan, the author of the finest allegory in any language, pleaded for and practised the sanctification of the first day of the week. And the institution has been venerated by Howe, Bishop Hopkins, Lightfoot, Burnet, Stillingfleet, Tillotson, Doddridge, Dean Prideaux, Dr. Samuel Clarke, Rev. Thomas Scott, Dr. Dwight, Dr. M'Crie, Dr. Paxton, Dr. Dick, Dr. John Brown, and many others of the greatest name in theological literature.

Men of rank form a peculiar class, among whom temptations to vice are many and great, and any voice that proceeds from such a quarter calling for a weekly restraint on their own pleasures, and a general pause of labour to servants and working men, is entitled to respect. Such persons have been a Lord Harrington, a Lord Dartmouth, who could "wear a coronet and pray," and Lord Gambier; and such are some of our nobility in present times. "Whether at sea or on shore," it is said of Lord Gambier, "our departed friend duly and devotedly observed the day of the Lord, that day which is so awfully desecrated in this Christian land. During the thirty years that I had the happiness to number him in my congregation, his attendance in the sanctuary was uniform. Whoever was absent, he was there, as long as the state of his health would admit. Nor did he think it sufficient to come once to worship on the Sabbath: this pious servant of God made conscience of attending both the morning and evening services; and whenever the Lord's Supper was administered, he was a regular guest at the sacred table."[1] Nor have there been wanting instances of crowned heads, like our late King George III. and the Protector, who have not been ashamed to "Remember the Sabbath-day to keep it holy."

It is not unimportant to have the testimony of persons of superior talents and sagacity adduced in favour of a cause of which they are not partisans or plighted supporters. Let those who would sneeringly impugn the sacred observance of the Lord's day, ponder the words of Sir Walter Scott, who was placed in early life under a religious training as strict as any Covenanter or Puritan, and who, though no Sabbatarian, said, "Give to the world one-half of Sunday, and you will find that religion has no strong hold of the other." How far another mind, worthy of a station near the greatest, was indebted to the lessons and discipline of a Sabbath, we are not aware. Dr. Sprague informs us that the *Practical View* had, according to the statement of Mr. Wilberforce, the author, the cordial approbation of Burke, who must have uttered his opinion in the year that he died. We know that the great statesman and orator sought his chief solace in the bosom of his family. We might presume also, from his language in condemning the sittings of the National Assembly of

[1] Ward's *Funeral Sermon for Admiral Lord Gambier*. He refers to his devout and fervent manner in worship,—and his piety as not confined to stated seasons of devotion, but hallowing and gladdening his whole life.—*Christian Observer* (1833), 507.

France on the Lord's day, that he had experienced its rest to be a benefit to his ardent and active spirit, which, fully knowing the injury of great tension of thought, could therefore prize the value of a stated interval of repose and relief to its overtasked powers. Dr. Adam Smith was still more exempt, we suspect, from Sabbatic prepossessions than either Sir Walter Scott or Mr. Burke, and yet we find him attesting the importance of religious institutions to the welfare of society in his *Wealth of Nations*, and in his already cited words addressed to Sir John Sinclair.

We have more than once adverted to Milton in connexion with the institution; in one place as "surrendering every authoritative claim of the Lord's day, except what it derives from ecclesiastical appointment,"[1] and in another as having discontinued the observance of public and private worship. Let us now see how the Sabbath was regarded by a few others, who, like him, by general acclaim, occupy a pre-eminent place among the intellectually great. Of Lord Bacon, it was said by Ben Jonson, that he seemed to him "one of the greatest men and most worthy of admiration that had been in many ages;" and the lapse of time has detracted nothing from, but rather confirmed the eulogium. He erred, but who has not? and the following words may be regarded as the language at once of the penitent, and of the friend to Christian institutions: "I have loved the assemblies, I have delighted in the brightness of thy sanctuary. . . . Thy creatures have been my books, but thy Scriptures much more. I have sought thee in the courts, fields, and gardens, but I have found thee in thy temples."[2] Laplace, a fitting judge, has observed that the discoveries and profound views presented in *The Principia*, "will insure to it a lasting pre-eminence over all other productions of the human mind;" and it is deeply interesting to connect with this signal tribute to the genius of Sir Isaac Newton, the statements of his biographer, that his observance of the religious institutions of his church was irreproachable, and that the book which he read with the greatest assiduity was the Bible.[3] In the same order of minds as Bacon and Newton, although he has not attained their high reputation, or exhibited their variety of

[1] Page 143.

[2] *Works* (1852), vol. ii. p. 405.

[3] *Life* (Tract Society), p. 82.

gifts, some have been disposed to rank President Edwards, of America, whose powers Hume, Mackintosh, Stewart, and Chalmers have alike honoured, and whom Robert Hall characterized, somewhat extravagantly indeed, as the greatest of the sons of men. "Never," says Henry Rogers, "was a triumph of genius more decisive than that of Jonathan Edwards. By the concurrent voice of all who have perused his writings, he is assigned one of the first, if not the very first place, among the masters of human reason."[1] Now, Edwards was eminently a nurseling, as well as an unanswerable defender of the Sabbatic rest and influences; and "his observation of the Sabbath was such as to make it throughout a day of real religion; so that not only were his conversation and reading conformed to the great design of the day, but he allowed himself in no thoughts or meditations which were not of a decidedly religious character."[2]

More important far, however, than worldly rank, scholarship, talent, or genius, is moral excellence; and it is one of the chief glories of the Sabbath that it has ever been the object of veneration and regard to the men who have risen to the highest point in the scale of piety, or been the most ardent in benevolent exertion and philanthropic enterprise. Where shall we find the fire of devotion and love burn more intensely than in the breasts of Baxter, Rutherford, Leighton, Brainerd, Simeon, Bickersteth? or bowels of compassion for suffering humanity yearn more tenderly and constantly than in Howard, Clarkson, Wilberforce, Buxton? or zeal for the glory of God, and desire for the eternal good of men glow more strongly than in Eliot, Martyn, Carey, Chalmers?—all of whom felt the Sabbath to be a delight, and esteemed the holy of the Lord, honourable. And some there have been, as Jonathan Edwards, in whom it is hard to say whether the powers of intellect, or the religious affections, were the more transcendent. It is a memorable saying of Dr. Chalmers: "We never, in the whole course of our recollections, met with a Christian friend, who bore upon his character every other evidence of the Spirit's operation, who did not remember the Sabbath-day to keep it holy;"[3] and the fervent M'Cheyne asks, "Can you name one godly minister, of

[1] Essay on the Genius and Writings of Jonathan Edwards, prefixed to *Works* (1839), p. 1. [2] *Works* (1839), Life, p. ccxxv. [3] *Works*, vol. ix. p. 265.

any denomination in all Scotland, who does not hold the duty of the entire sanctification of the Lord's day? Did you ever meet with a lively believer in any country under heaven—one who loved Christ, and lived a holy life—who did not delight in keeping holy to God the entire Lord's day?"[1]

It is recorded of Eliot, the missionary, "His observance of the Sabbath was remarkable. He knew that our whole religion fares according to our Sabbaths; that poor Sabbaths make poor Christians; and that a strictness in our Sabbaths inspires a vigour into all our other duties. Hence, in his work among the Indians, he brought them, by a particular article, to bind themselves, as a principal means of confirming them in Christianity, 'To remember the Sabbath-day to keep it holy, as long as we live.' For himself, the sun did not set the evening before the Sabbath till he had begun his preparation for it. Every day was a sort of Sabbath to him; but the Sabbath-day was with him a type and foretaste of heaven; nor would you hear anything drop from his lips on that day but the milk and honey of that country, in which there yet 'remaineth a rest for the people of God.'"[2]

Howard thus writes, "*Turin, Nov.* 30, 1769.—My return without seeing the southern part of Italy was on much deliberation, as I feared a misimprovement of a talent spent for mere curiosity at the loss of many Sabbaths, and as many donations [to the poor] must be suspended for my pleasure."

"Hoping," he said, at a later period, "I shall be carried safely to my native country and friends, and see the face of my dear boy in peace, remember, O my soul, to cultivate a more serious, humble, thankful, and resigned temper of mind. As thou hast seen more of the world by travelling than others—more of the happiness of being born in a Protestant country, and the dreadful abuse of holy Sabbaths—so may thy walk, thy Sabbaths, thy conversation, be more becoming the Holy Gospel. Let not pride and vanity fill up so much of thy thoughts; learn here [in Rome] the vanity and folly of all earthly grandeur; endeavour to be a wiser and better man when thou returnest. Remember many eyes will

[1] *Memoir and Remains* (1846), pp. 561, 562.
[2] *Missionary Register*, vol. ii. (for 1814), p. 310.

be upon thee, and, above all, the eye of that God before whom thou will shortly have to appear."

"As will have been gathered from the foregoing, Sunday was with Howard a sacred day—a section of times not belonging to this life or to this world. He never travelled, nor did any manner of work on it. When on the road, he rested the Sabbath over in whatsoever place the accidents of the journey might have conducted him to. If no opportunities offered for attending public worship, he retired for the whole day into his secret chamber, and passed it in pious services and spiritual self-examinations."[1]

[1] Dixon's *Life of Howard* (second edition), pp. 107, 119, 120.

CHAPTER III.

THEORIES TRIED BY THE PRINCIPLES OF THE DIVINE GOVERNMENT.

IT is intended to apply in some following chapters certain tests derived from both Reason and Revelation, to the leading opinions that have been entertained on the subject of the Sabbath, with the view of adjudicating on their conflicting claims. As we proceed, occasion will be afforded for adverting to the more important arguments which have been advanced, and to several schemes which have been propounded, in reference to the institution. The test to be applied in this chapter is furnished in those principles of the Divine government, which are discovered in its history, and more plainly in the inspired volume.

1. One of such principles is unity of plan. In proving "the unity" of God from "the uniformity" observable in the physical universe, Dr. Paley has truly and beautifully said, "We never get amongst such original or totally different modes of existence as to indicate that we are come into the province of a different Creator, or under the direction of a different will."[1] In confirmation of this statement, he refers, among various facts, to the one law of attraction carrying all the planets about the sun, one atmosphere investing and connecting all parts of the globe, one moon influencing all tides, and one kind of blood circulating in all animals. What is true of the material is no less true of the moral world in all its known provinces and eras. In physical nature we observe an endless variety of bodies and phenomena under the uniform regulation of great common principles, and in like manner, amidst a diversity of circumstances and forms, we discover a pervading unity in the laws of the moral government of God. We find the same benevolence, sovereignty, and love of righteous-

[1] *Works, Nat. Theol.* ch. xxv.

ness reigning in the Divine procedure; one Saviour for Jew and Gentile, one method of justification, and one indispensable requisite of regeneration, in all ages; one kind of worship substantially offered, and one moral code obeyed, by Adam, Abraham, Moses, David, and Paul; and one Church, which, in obedience to the Divine call—"Enlarge the place of thy tent, and let them stretch forth the curtains of thine habitations" (Isa. liv. 2)—has passed from a circumscribed into an extended economy. In holding that the great Master has ever regulated the time of his servants—that the King of kings has never been without his appointed seasons for receiving the petitions and homage of his subjects, the theories that maintain a permanent and universal Sabbath preserve the consistency of the Divine administration. But the other theories violate this harmony when they suppose that for many centuries there was no Sabbath at all, and then, for many more, a Sabbath rigidly ruled, and when they countenance either the entire abolition of the sacred day, or the new appointment of a partial one, a *dies intercisus*, or the opinion that the arrangement of resting and holy time has been left entirely to human discretion. We confidently ask whether, in passing from the Patriarchal to the Jewish, and then to the Christian manner of religion and life as represented by these theories, we do not find ourselves amongst so original and totally different modes of existence as to indicate that we *are* come under the direction of a different will?

2. It is at the same time a character of the Divine government that its plans are progressive in their development; that, while the great outlines are in all ages the same, there is a gradual filling up of the scheme. Paley and others imagine a transition from no Sabbath to one whose rules were of the most stringent description, a view implying not only a violent change utterly unlike the usual method of the Divine procedure, but the introduction of an entirely new principle, of which we have no parallel case in the history of the moral government of God. We may indeed be reminded of the Incarnation as an unprecedented fact, peculiar to the latest dispensation of religion, but this fact did not burst on an unprepared world; it was intimated in the first promise, it was more clearly made known in the prophecies that followed, it was shadowed by frequent appearances of the Divinity

in human form, and its benefit was really enjoyed by all believers in ancient times. It is like the Atonement, which, though not actually made till thousands of years had elapsed, was from the beginning a declared principle and felt blessing of religion. The objection from the Incarnation would be in point, if the Sabbath had been anticipated and its good realized long before it came into existence. This, however, could not be. Advantage may and does spring from a future moral fact, but not from a prospective institute. Nor is the theory which restricts the Sabbath of Christianity to the old day less opposed to the principle of progress. While Paley introduces an element so new in its nature, and so abrupt in its entrance, as to disturb the orderly and equable march of the Divine government, this altogether arrests it, and stays progress and improvement. It stereotypes a moral precept on a mere accident. It is an attempt, however undesigned, to perpetuate Judaism. It reverses the command to forget the things which are behind, and to reach forth to those which are before. How much more consonant that any of these theories, to an identical and yet advancing scheme, is that of a Sabbath which, as the same holy and benignant institution in all time, presents a history, not of unnatural stagnation or of violent transitions, but of harmony with the unfolding plans of its Author, subserving the piety and bliss of paradise; then sustaining the hope of a coming Saviour, as well as faith in the Creator; now commemorating, along with the ever-to-be-remembered fact of a finished creation, the more glorious fact of a perfected redemption, and offering a more immediate and satisfying foretaste of heavenly joy; and, finally, receiving its highest and most lasting honour at the consummation of all things, when, entirely transferred to the world above, it will be the sole measure of the eternal life!

3. A regard to order is a manifest feature of the Divine rule. "God is not the author of confusion." He who requires that all things should be "done decently and in order," is Himself the perfection and pattern of His own law. The Great Master "gives authority to His servants, and to every man his work." In correspondence with this principle of order which pervades the Divine administration, and which prevails in every well-regulated society

among men, is the theory which affirms a perpetual Sabbath; which affirms, in other words, that the Ruler of the world has never failed to legislate on one of the most important affairs of His Court and Kingdom—the days when He will confer favours on His people, and receive their homage. But how strange and anomalous are the views supposed by other theories that, while mankind in general have had their distribution of time for secular work and sacred service, the only possessors of a true religion should for many generations have been without such arrangement; that while "gods many and lords many" "which are yet no gods," have received the tribute of periodical holy days, the only living and true God should have been without this order and honour, and should have introduced the custom only after it had been practised by idolaters and outcasts from His favour; that He who regulates the time for all other things, for daily labour and nightly repose, for sowing and reaping, for the migrations of the swallow and the fall of a sparrow equally as for the removal of kings and the destruction of empires, in short, "for every purpose," should have, in any instance, omitted the prescription of a season for His own immediate service, and what is especially remarkable, that He should appoint such a season for the Jews and not for the Patriarchs or for Christians! Such views involve a charge of disorder, derogatory to the perfection of that "kingdom which ruleth over all." And yet the notion of a rigid adherence to one day, the seventh, while it seems a tribute to order, may in reality be an imputation to the Divine Government of a human frailty which so often amongst us perverts a noble virtue into the vice of a slavish punctiliousness. The Disposer of time is not under its control. "He changeth the times and the seasons." "The Son of Man is Lord even of the Sabbath." He who commanded Israel on their coming out of Egypt to commence their year in a different month, and who abolished the years, months, and days of the Jewish ceremonial, has it no less in His power to say, "It is my will that henceforth the first instead of the last day of the week shall be the day of rest to the world, and the day of my special worship." Such a change would only be agreeable to the authority which the God of order claims and has repeatedly exercised over man's time, while not to exert it in this case might be to transgress the higher order of assigning to Redemption its proper precedency among the Divine works.

4. Among the excellencies of the Divine government is that "goodness which endureth continually." If we refer to providence, Scripture and facts assure us that "the Lord is good to all," and that "his tender mercies are over all his works," while He is peculiarly kind to "them that love him, and are the called according to his purpose," to whom "all things work together for good." If we turn to the scheme of redemption, we find that it has uniformly combined with saving mercy to some, a bountiful proffer of its blessings to all. Now it is not in accordance with either the general philanthropy or the special love of God to conceive that the Sabbath is not a provision for all time. It is contrary to His benevolence to suppose that many centuries had passed away ere mankind were favoured with an institution which has been proved to be in all respects so conducive, and even indispensable, to their wellbeing; and it is especially contradictory to that peculiar regard which the God of salvation entertains for His own obedient children, to imagine that He should have withheld so great a boon as the Sabbath from such men as Enoch, Noah, and Abraham. Christianity is, still more than preceding dispensations, distinguished by its catholicity and benevolence; and how incongruous the idea, that it has entirely set aside a law which provides a periodical rest for man and beast, or that, beyond two or three hours for public worship, it has made no appointment for the still more important interests of the soul! And what shall be said of their views who, admitting the benignant character, and expediency of the institution, maintain nevertheless that there is no express authority for the Lord's day? No express authority for a day which is essential to the welfare of men and the lower animals! The notion, on other grounds untenable, is a reflection on the love and care of the universal Ruler, and equally on the grace of the Author of Christianity, as it implies that the former could cease to preserve man and beast, and that the latter would abandon His friends to perpetual and perplexing uncertainty respecting the seasons of Divine worship. A better theory, however, not only leaves unimpeached, but glorifies the goodness of God, since it teaches the doctrine of a Sabbath instituted for man from the beginning, and

destined to continue to the end of time, a Sabbath, too, which would have been universally and uninterruptedly possessed, had men not cast off its salutary but for them too holy restraints and demands, and which the good have never failed to be favoured with, to prize, and to enjoy. That there is no want of express authority for the Christian Sabbath is obvious, not at present to mention still more convincing considerations, from the remarkable harmony among true Christians in the matter, from their readiness in general to recognise the obligation of the institution without feeling any doubt or difficulty in regard to the path of duty, and from the profit and pleasure received by them in proportion as they devote a whole day in seven to holy rest. And would not that small minority of Christians who honour the Divine goodness by holding in common with their brethren the perpetuity of the Sabbath, still more honour it if they were brought to see that in checking a superstitious fondness for mere times, and in magnifying the new creation by the transference of the ordinance from the day of a preparatory economy, to that which ushered in the better covenant, it has won for itself not the least of its benign glories?

5. The Divine Ruler must regulate His subjects by laws. Without these there could be no good government. A state of things in which every one is allowed to do what he pleases, is identical with disorganization, disorder, and all evil. Better far any government than none. The reign of Jehovah is a reign of law. Even among those who have not liked to retain Him in their knowledge, His law is recognised by their consciences. And where He has favoured any of the human race with the revelation of His merciful designs towards man, whether immediately after the fall, or after they had lost sight of them, there He has at the same time made known His will as to all that they should do in His service. The patriarchs and the Jews had the means of directing them in their conduct. And so have Christians. They "are not without law to God, but under the law to Christ." And what the excellence of the law of God is we are abundantly informed. It is perfect, exceeding broad, spiritual, holy, just, and good.

But certain theories of the Sabbath appear to be irreconcil

able with this character of the Divine government, by detracting from the excellence, if they do not even set aside the obligation, of the law of God. For many centuries, according to several of them, there was no rule for a Sabbath; during the period of the Mosaic economy, there were very definite, and full, and solemn regulations on that subject; and, under Christianity, there is no authorized day for rest and worship, say some, and none, say others, beyond the appropriation of a day to rest, and of a few of its hours to Divine service. And yet the supporters of all these theories regard the Sabbath as a great and indispensable blessing. But such views exhibit Divine legislation as at one time complete and at another imperfect, wholly or in part overlooking the provision of an acknowledged necessary boon and direction relative to the important matter of the seasons in which the social worship of God is to be observed; in other words, as a matter of partiality and fluctuation. Nor is this all. These theorists set aside from being a law to us not only the Fourth Commandment, but the other nine as given from Sinai. The laws of the New Testament, according to them, are our only rule of conduct. Thus we are without law. For the New Testament has no law of its own. It is a commentary, not a law.

The doctrine of a perpetual Sabbath, on the other hand, recognises the Divine law as, like its Author, perfect and immutable; as holy and impartial, prescribing the same distribution of time for men of all ages and nations—as good, setting forth the Divine will in clear and unequivocal terms, and providing a day of rest and worship adapted for all. Let it not be considered as a satisfactory reply to this view, that some things were required of the Jews that are not required of us, and that many such changes have taken place under the government of God. It is true that the ancients were to offer sacrifice in *anticipation* of a Saviour, while we are to observe the Lord's Supper in *memory* of a Saviour; that there is a wide difference between heathen men and Christians, in respect of the measure of obligation and responsibility; that the Jews were to observe certain feasts, annual and monthly, as well as the sacred rest of the seventh day of the week, while we are to observe only one stated day, and that, the first day of the week. *The varieties in all these cases are in the circumstances of man-*

kind, not in the law. These circumstances determine the application of the one law, without altering it by a single jot or tittle. To imagine, however, a change from no Sabbath to a Sabbath, and then from a Sabbath to none at all, or to one that is limited to two or three hours, is to imagine a change not in the circumstances but in the essential principles of law and government, since one day of rest and worship in the seven is a statute founded on the Divine example at the Creation of the world, and on the demonstrated demands of the human constitution : moreover, be the matter what it may, we are not legislators, but subjects bound in everything to obey our Divine Sovereign, who has given us a rule that embraces all our thoughts, words, and actions. And whatever changes may take place in the circumstances of the Sabbath, it is not conceivable that these can ever be in the direction of diminishing its value or the amount of its time. The new fact of a finished redemption, and the increased privileges entailed by it, only serve more clearly to show the importance of the institution, and to supply motives for its more spiritual and earnest observance ; while, instead of subtracting from its allotted and necessary time, they direct our views, and approximate us more nearly to the eternal period when the condition of man no longer requiring the labour of six days for the supply of his bodily wants, his whole time shall be sacred time ; his exclusive occupation that of keeping a Sabbath.

We deny not to those friends of the institution who cling to its ancient day the credit of a conscientious respect for the law of the Ten Commandments. But we conceive that their scheme and pleadings do, in fact, misrepresent and dishonour that law. It is right to ascertain and vindicate its real meaning. But assuredly the Lawgiver must be the best interpreter of His own law. Now, we find two things done by His apostles, who must have acted in both by His authority, else their writings are not a part of the Word of God, nor their example, though expressly declared to be so, a rule for us. The Jewish Sabbath-days are repealed, as "a shadow of things to come," and yet on the first day of the week, worshipping assemblies are repeatedly declared to be held by the apostles and the Christian churches. While it would be as absurd to infer from these facts a change in the fourth commandment as it would be to suppose that the fifth is no longer binding on those who are not resident in "the land" to which it primarily referred; on the other hand, it would be no less absurd, in opposition to inspired interpretation, to construe the former as binding us to the observance of the seventh day. Let it be observed, in a word, that an opinion which insists on such a meaning of the expression, "the seventh day," as brings the statute into collision with apostolic appointment and practice, when the language admits of another and harmonious explanation, and which lends a perpetual glory to a day no longer, according to a sacred writer, to be gloried in, strikes, in one blow, at the authority of the New Testament, of the Sabbath law, and of the entire Decalogue.

6. In close connexion with the principle of an administration by law, is another principle in the government of God, that of an exclusively Divine legislation. It is the prerogative of the Most High to frame and authorize the rules by which His worship and service are to be conducted. According as this right is recognised in Sabbatic theories may we estimate their truth.

Theorists have not been satisfied with shaping Divine laws to their own views and wishes, but, to complete the dishonour done to the Lawgiver, they have fancied man himself rightfully vaulting into the seat, and seizing the reins of government. The Church, say some, has the power of enacting a weekly holy day. The State has it, say others. Every man, says a third class, is in this matter a law to himself. The advocates of a Sabbath appointed by the Supreme Ruler for all time, while recognising, as we have seen, the existence and perfection of the Divine law, acknowledge also the authority of its Author as exclusive, admitting of no co-ordinate rule, and leaving no legislative power in the hands of creatures.

The civil power may undertake too much, and burden itself with matters which would be better left to individual discretion and private arrangement. And yet were the surveillance perfect, there would be reason rather for satisfaction than for complaint. It is because private associations and individuals know best how to promote their own interests, and are in this way larger benefactors of the State, that a redundancy of law is an evil. But the legislation of infinite intelligence, justice and goodness, cannot be too comprehensive and supreme.

There is but "one Lawgiver," and His law is "exceeding broad." In instituting the ancient worship, everything, down to the smallest vessel and pin, was embraced in His prescriptions. How frequently are we told that this and that part of the work in the construction of the tabernacle, and this and the other particular in its connected service, were done "as the Lord commanded Moses!" And the temple as well as the tabernacle was built and furnished according to a Divine pattern. Nor, in settling the affairs of the Christian economy, was the Head of the Church less mindful of His prerogative, or of the good of men. "Moses was faithful in all his house as a servant, but Christ as a Son over His own house." The sole Lawgiver still rejects from the rule of His Church, "the commandments of men." The apostles enacted no laws, instituted no ordinances. Their business was to "teach all things whatsoever their Master commanded them." They disclaimed "dominion over the faith" of their disciples. And their instructions have been deposited in the New Testament as the complement of Revelation, that volume which is not to be altered, and by which all the teachings of individuals, and all the dogmas of councils are to be tried.

It is, as with other things, so with the appropriation of time. As to this also we are under a complete and exclusive law. He who has appointed to every thing its time, and who "changeth the times and the seasons," has ever refused to give this "glory to another." In the instance even of ritual observance, Elijah shall wait for, and Gabriel respect, the time of the evening sacrifice, and the man "who made Israel to sin" is held forth to execration for "devising of his own heart" the day of a religious feast. It is an antagonist of "the Most High and of His saints," an anti-Christian power, that is predicted as "thinking to change times and laws," as, in other words, "presuming to alter the appointed seasons and the law."[1] And the Lawgiver is as "jealous" as ever of His prerogative: "For the Son of man is Lord even of the Sabbath." When do we find Him surrendering this Divine right, and conveying it to any man or number of men? Among His last words

[1] Wintle's Version.

on earth were: "All power is given unto me in heaven and in earth." When, therefore, the Pope ventured to substitute "festivals"[1] for the "Sabbath-day," in the Fourth Commandment, and otherwise to claim a power over the institution, he perpetrated not the least of the enormities of that usurped authority by which he conceives himself at liberty to suspend, alter, or abrogate Divine laws, and serves himself heir to the names and to the doom of "the opponent of the Most High," and "the man of sin." Closely did they follow in his track who devised, proclaimed, and patronized "The Book of Sports." And to plead, as Archbishop Whately does, for the right of the Church, and, as others do, for the right of the State, to institute a Sabbath, are surely errors of the same description, and, however plausibly presented, infringements as real of His prerogative, who is Head of the Church and Lord of the Sabbath.

And let not those who maintain that all days are now alike, and nevertheless observe a weekly Sabbath from mere considerations of its utility, or of its former or present prevalence, imagine that their views escape the charge of interference with the Divine prerogative. These views tend to the conclusions, that the Deity has abdicated his dominion over the times of worship, and abandoned men in that matter to anarchy and confusion. They hold that sacred days have been abrogated, and yet they keep them,—in other words, they institute an ordinance, and make a law, "of their own hearts."

Nor can the theory which maintains the continued obligation of the seventh day stand the test of the principle now under consideration. If the Sabbath be in all respects simply moral, it must also be to that extent immutable. That the appropriation of *a seventh* day to rest and worship is moral, positive, and, on earth, unchangeable, we admit. It is not more conceivable that this law of Creation and of Sinai could be repealed in the present state than that the whole economy of nature could be subverted. It is as impossible that the consecration of one day in seven to sacred service should be set aside in this world as that

[1] Ricordati di Santificare le Feste—Remember to keep holy the festivals.—*Dottrina Cristiana, etc.*, p 24 (composed by Bellarmine, by order of Clement VIII., and approved by the Congregation of Reform).

the second or the fifth precept should be obliterated from the Decalogue. The continued demand for such a day, at once by the physical wants and by the spiritual necessities of man, is an additional evidence of its moral character and of its permanence. But the Lord of the Sabbath not only refused to impose the observance of the Jewish "sabbath-days" on His Gentile followers, but after His resurrection paid no respect to them in His own practice, met with His disciples on the first day of the week, and was imitated in His regard for the latter by all the Christian churches of whose assemblies for worship there is any account. Circumstances, as we have already seen, are mentioned, showing that arrangements were made for it as the stated and understood day of such meetings. It follows that there was something in the old Sabbath which could be changed, that the institution admitted of transference from the last to the first day of the week; and as it has appeared that various theorists have asserted for human beings the power of appointing a Sabbath, it is now as manifest, that there are others who refuse to accord to the Divine Lawgiver that prerogative of "changing the times and the seasons," which He has challenged for Himself, and which His own proceedings, and the practice of the apostles proved Him to have exercised.

CHAPTER IV.

THEORIES TRIED BY THEIR TENDENCIES AND RESULTS.

Reason itself might and frequently does decide on such questions as are now under trial, by pronouncing certain opinions to be sound or the opposite according to their manifest operations and effects. The character of the Divine government as revealed in Scripture leads to the same conclusions, for it is a government of truth and righteousness which by its constitution, and demands on mankind, proves itself favourable to whatever is just, true, and good, and hostile to "the unfruitful works of darkness." In like manner, the Word of God expressly declares the fruits of dogmas to be a test of their merits, and connects the evidence for the truth of its predictions respecting the ultimate prevalence of Christianity with the benign influences of Christian institutions, and the virtues of Christian men. Let us therefore apply this test of good tendency and results as a means of enabling us to judge between the contending pretensions of theories on the subject before us.

We must here class together the "no Sabbath" and the "every-day Sabbath" opinions, as, how different soever in their professed moral objects, they are agreed in their antagonism to *a periodical* holy day. For illustrations of the influence of the former creed, we refer to the most degraded parts of the heathen world, to the worst characters of European society, and to France after she had discarded her weekly Sabbath. If Scotsmen or Englishmen, who are favoured in temporal things beyond all other nations, and those of them who are blessed above many of their own countrymen, long to be reduced to the condition of savages, slaves, devils incarnate or their victims, let them retire from a country which they dishonour, and establish a Sabbathless community, but let them not suppose that their views will influence any one whom reason and common sense have not forsaken. And as it is a fact, that nothing great or good has ever sprung up in a land entirely destitute of sacred time, so it is equally true that a region of the earth in which all time was alike holy has never been witnessed, a fact, which is itself a proof that neither the great Ruler nor the mass of mankind have ever approved of the introduction on earth of an arrangement which is adapted only for the constitution and circumstances of the inhabitants of heaven. Some approach has indeed been made to it in the manifold holidays of the Church of Rome; but a church which has done so little comparatively for the religion or for any interest of the world is not a model to be copied by patriots or philanthropists. And looking to the few who have at any time embraced the theory, we shall admit that aiming at too much they have lost all, and exposed themselves to the charge thus caustically expressed :—

> "Shrewd men, indeed, these new reformers are!
> Each week-day is a Sabbath, they declare:
> A Christian theory! the un-Christian fact is,
> Each Sabbath is a week-day in their practice."[1]

The professed believers in all other mistaken theories declare that they maintain the usefulness, or even necessity of a weekly day of rest. We must reason with them on this their own avowed principle; and, if it can be proved that they cannot hold both the principle and their theories, they ought to renounce the latter, and give their influence to an institution which they admit to be salutary or indispensable to the good of mankind.

The class of theorists who have entertained the doctrine of the perpetual seventh-day Sabbath have been so few, and so surrounded by the influences of more prevailing sentiments, as to afford but limited means of enabling us to judge respecting the religious and moral character which the system contributes to form, or the good of any kind which it tends to diffuse. The very fact of the limited extent to which the theory has prevailed is unfavourably significant, and fatal, we conceive, to its claim of being the Sabbath of God or the Sabbath for man. The cause of truth, indeed, has sometimes been intrusted to a few hands, as when the witnesses for true religion are represented as being only two, while the world wondered after the Beast. But that in times alike of

[1] Washington Irving.

prosperity and of adversity, of a reviving and declining religion, so few holding the doctrine in question should be found in any part of the world, is surely a proof that it is possessed of little vital power, and not destined to regenerate and bless the world. What, for instance—as, judging from the limited observance of the last day of the week, we may be permitted to ask—would have become of the Sabbath itself, the instrument of so much good, if other views of it had not prevailed? The same unanswerable objection applies to the dogma which would convert the days of creation into millenary cycles—and confound, to borrow an expression of Bishop Horsley, the writing of a history with the composition of riddles.

The view which confines the ground of the Sabbatic institution to apostolic practice and appointment virtually sets aside a day of sacred rest. On the supposition of a previously-enacted and still-existing law providing for such a day, the language and proceedings of the apostles are all that the new dispensation required. But they are not complete or sufficient as an independent authority for an entirely Christian institute. The apostles, in their mention of the first day of the week, say nothing of its design and observance beyond those of public worship, and contributions of our substance to the poor; nothing of further rest from secular labour; nothing, in short, of the way in which the greater part of a whole day, and that "the Lord's day," is to be spent. Whether, then, we consider the divine manner of clearly defining the purposes and duties of religious ordinances, or the uselessness of any law that is indefinite and doubtful, we are shut up to the conclusion, which other considerations no less demand, that we must seek in the Old Testament as well as in the New—in primitive institution and in Sinaitic legislation, as well as in Apostolic instruction and example—for the obligations and characters that complete the Christian Sabbath. It is well for the institution and for mankind that few of the best friends of both have adopted a theory which rejects the Divine and only adequate security for a periodical day of rest to man and beast, and secularizes all but a few hours in the week, thus frustrating both the moral and physical ends of sacred time, and exposing its tiny spark to extinction on an ocean of worldly business, pleasures, and cares.

Those who call in question the primæval origin of the Sabbath are chargeable with doing an injury and a wrong to the institution. They would remove one of its main pillars—the evidence, afforded by its appointment at so early a period, to prove its destination for the race. They would take away from its venerableness ; they would disprove, if they could, its necessity. Their theory says, "The patriarchs lived and died without a Sabbath, attaining long life and high measures of moral excellence independently of its aid ; and what they could dispense with so may we." And who would care to contend for a Jewish ceremony which the experience of the patriarchs has proved to be a local and temporary expedient, useless to men in general,—nay, if useless, an encumbrance and an evil ?

Certain theorists, by grounding the institution on human authority, ecclesiastical or civil, place it on a foundation of sand. The conscience is not reached. The law must vary with every latitude and every reign. Independence and caprice, allowed exemption from the immediate control of a Supreme Being, declare "that they will not be trammelled where the Creator has left man free." The love of pleasure or of gain says, "I will take such a law into my own hands, and spurn enactments which stand in the way of my interest and gratification." Thus made supreme in a matter in which the feelings are opposed to restraint, how can it be conceived that man's submission to Sabbatic law can be either hearty or lasting, or that the law itself can stand ?

We have yet to compare, in respect of adaptations and effects, the creed on which the Christian Sabbath is founded with that of not a few who would improve on it. The latter and their nostrums may be thus described. There are men who seem to be deficient in the capacity of knowing when it is well with them in any situation, and consequently to be wanting in the wisdom that would direct them to "let well alone." It is worse still when any one is ignorant of his highest mercies, "the things that belong to his peace." Those who quarrel with the day of rest combine both kinds of folly. Not content with the worry of six days, they must prolong it into the seventh, and, grudging the pause and respite of one day in the week, they will not, on the one hand, avail themselves of it as an indispensable means of preparation for the "rest that remaineth to the people of God ;" or on the other, take the full use of its facilities for mere repose of mind and body, as some compensation for the coming long future when they can have no rest day or night. It is such men, we believe, who are satisfied neither with the outer nor with the inner peace of the Sabbath, and would have a sacred day mutilated or abolished. It is not to be supposed that, with such blindness to their own weal, they should be fully aware of the true reason for their wishes respecting the institution. They have, however, ventured to assign a reason, involving a fiction as great as ever was invented, or attempted to be palmed on human credulity—the notion that a carefully observed Sabbath injures health, and genders and fosters vice. For these evils they propose as a remedy the removal of their supposed cause, and the substitution for a day of sacred rest of one devoted, in part at least, to recreation and amusement, or to the study of science and of the arts. We have already abundantly established the physical, intellectual, and moral adaptations, blessings, and even necessity of a holy Sabbath; but to make "assurance doubly sure," let us confront the old with the new expedients, and show that the latter are as insufficient as they are unnecessary for their alleged purpose.

If we look, in the first instance, to the scheme which proposes an entire or partial holiday, or day of amusement and pleasure, we shall see that it is condemned by all experience, alike by that of a sacred and by that of a merry-making day. The necessity of a weekly day of rest to the physical welfare of men is admitted even by those who are unfriendly to a holy Sabbath. "The infidel," says one, "can have no interest in revoking its blessings, or accelerating its ruin. He may laugh at the ravings of fanaticism, or sneer at the fears and reasoning of inflamed zeal; but the *substantial* benefits of the Sabbath he is as anxious to preserve as any."[1] "There is no one," observes another, "who denies that a day of repose and relaxation from labour once a week is for the benefit of the working classes, and there is no one who would wish to do away with that usage. It is nearly the only breathing-time in a life of toil which the poor man enjoys."[2] We accept these statements as in so far a testimony, and, coming from such quarters, an important testimony, in favour of a Sabbatical institution. But

[1] *A Voice from the Workshop*, p. 15. [2] Speech of James Aytoun, Esq., 1847, p. 4.

when we are told, as we are by the former writer, and by others, that in advancing proofs of the physical advantages of the institution we only "beat the winds," we must crave liberty to dissent from the opinion, and to say that such a task, so far from being bootless, as merely establishing a dogma generally received and plainly true, is one that is called for, just because it is fitted to produce the convictions which the quotations now given express, and to lead their authors and others to the further knowledge and conclusions on the subject which it is evident they have not yet reached. Let it be remarked, that certain views may not be rejected, and yet not be sufficiently influential on the conduct, and that it is on this account requisite frequently to reproduce, illustrate, and enforce them, that they may take more of the shape of living, practical principles in the minds of those by whom they are professedly held. But we confidently deny the allegation of a universally existing belief as to the utility of the Sabbath, viewed even simply as a day of rest. Who does not know that many voluntarily labour on that day, and that many require such labour from their servants? Is it possible that these persons are convinced of the physical necessity of a weekly day of rest? Who, again, does not know that the call of so many for a Sabbath of amusement and pleasure, either in whole or in part, is in reality the demand of such a mode of spending its hours as must subject multitudes to continual labour and its fatal results, that others may enjoy rest and indulgence? Do those men sincerely believe that a Sabbath-day is desirable as a season of respite from the toils of life, who plead for "a system, which providing for the gain of some, and the recreation, the amusement, and the vices of others, at the expense of their fellows, has a direct tendency to undermine health, exhaust the strength, and shorten the lives of those who are its victims?"[1] On the supposition, so contrary to all experience, that no vice were indulged, it is an unanswerable objection to Sunday excursions by trains and otherwise, and to all public amusements on that day, that the health of thousands, employed in affording the means of pleasure to others, is necessarily sacrificed. The superiority of a day of sacred rest to that which some would put

[1] Petition of 641 Physicians and Surgeons in London against the opening of the Crystal Palace on Sabbath.

in its place appears in this, as in other respects, that its tendency, like the mission of its Lord, is not to destroy but to save life. According to its wise and benevolent provisions, families may have all that is conducive to health and happiness without the drawback of slavery and pain to any one, and hundreds may have the means of public instruction and enjoyment at the cost of a measure of exertion on the part of one individual, which, judging from the longevity of his class, *necessitates* no bodily harm. There is another great mistake or fallacy in the language employed on this subject by those who profess to be satisfied as to the physical necessity of a Sabbath, which they would nevertheless alienate from what they are pleased to call puritanical practices. They speak and write in seeming ignorance or forgetfulness, that the principal, if not almost the entire evidence in favour of such a day goes to prove the importance of *a Christian* Sabbath, while we have no evidence of the sanitary benefit of a day consumed in idleness, in recreation, or even in the study of nature or science. Whence have those persons almost any idea at all of a Sabbath but from the observance around them of the Sabbath of Christianity? Whence, especially, have they much proof of the utility of such a day but from facts connected with that observance? Let them do justice to the truth, and own that they have derived the very conception of a weekly day of rest from Revelation, or from its friends, and that they know little or nothing of its physical advantages, except in so far as these have appeared in its contrasted honour and neglect as a religious institute. In the absence of evidence that a weekly day of rest is capable of yielding greater or even equal benefit to health by being wholly or partially severed from religion, they are not authorized to affirm, as some confidently do, that the separation would be productive of any such effect. They are still less warranted to employ the facts which demonstrate its beneficent influence as a Christian appointment, for the purpose of evincing its excellence in any other character. Until we have some assurance that a community, or any portion of it, could be persuaded to spend a seventh day in *harmless* amusement, or in listening to lectures on science and art, with the result, too, of a larger accession to health than arises from a religiously employed Sabbath, it would, simply on grounds of expediency, be extremely foolish to part with a present real for a future imaginary good. This experiment would be the more unwise that we already have enough in ascertained principles and facts to enable us to predict its complete failure. The continental Sabbath is precisely such an institution as many in our land seem ambitious to set up. But we have yet to learn that the Sabbath abroad has achieved more for the physical nature of Frenchmen or Germans than the Sabbath at home has done for that of Scotsmen or Englishmen. Let Paris under its first Revolution warn us of the health-consuming and life-destroying orgies that would attend the worship of Nature and Science, as surely as they waited on the rites of the Goddess of Reason. Let the wasting profligacy which followed the republication of the *Book of Sports* tell us what would be the effect of reviving a Sabbath of pleasure. In the intemperance, the jaded appearance, the reluctant, tardy return to work, of Sunday pleasure-seekers, we have already specimens of the wider-spread evil which would ensue, if the religious occupations of the day were generally exchanged for the delights of the rural excursion or the excitements of the tea-garden. "Physiologically considered," to employ the words of Dr. Farre, "power saved is power gained, and the waste of power from every kind of excitement defeats the purpose of the day. So that on the Sabbath the labouring man is expending the powers of his body, instead of husbanding them for the following week, and chiefly if he be engaged in drinking,"[1] Take away the religion of the Sabbath, and you remove the chief if not the only barrier in such a country as this against the encroaching covetousness of one class and the perpetual slavery of another—evils of which the least enormity is, that they prey upon the flesh, blood, and bones of their victims. "If," says the *Times*, "the sacred character of the day be once obscured, there would not remain behind any influence strong enough to keep a thrifty tradesman from his counter for twelve hours together. A man who would observe the day as a Sabbath would retrench it as a holiday, and thus competition and imitation would at length bring all to the common level of universal profaneness and continuous toil."[2] And the amplest experience will

[1] Report on the Observance of the Lord's Day (1832), p. 118.
[2] Editorial Article, July 14, 1848.

be found to confirm the following statement of men well acquainted with the human constitution : "While they are most especially called to minister to the physical sufferings of their fellow-creatures, your petitioners cannot overlook the close relation subsisting between moral and physical disease, or entertain the hope that any plans which do not make full provision for their spiritual as well as their physical necessities will effect any great or permanent improvement in the health or habits of the labouring population."[1]

But, in the second place, it is said that all the intellectual benefit which a religious Sabbath is supposed to yield might be attained by means still more consonant to the constitution of the human mind, and more effectual for its elevation. "You boast," it is affirmed, "of the power of your day of preaching and prayer, but is there not the alternative of a Crystal Palace, or of lecture-rooms supplied with facilities for the study of science and the arts, and would not this be a much better means of informing and invigorating the intellect, as well as of promoting health, than the immuring, dull, and deadening engagements of a day devoted to religion ?" We might satisfy ourselves by referring to the observations already made, on the "Intellectual Adapations of the Sabbath," as a sufficient reply, so far as principles are concerned, to these questions. If the views there advanced be just, they ought to satisfy the propounders of a weekly day of literary and scientific instruction as a substitute for a religious Sabbath, that such a scheme could not for any considerable period be maintained or even come into general observance, for want of some adequate authority to impose on the world a common time for any species of secular studies ; that it would fail of adaptation to all classes, since it would afford no relief from customary toil to at least two large portions of society,—to the many servants whose physical labour would be required for the carrying out of its designs, and to the cultivators of science, literature, and the arts, who would be without the change of thought so essential to the refreshment and renovation of their powers, and to their energy and success in the education of their fellow-men ; and that its topics and business would exert but a feeble influence over the public mind compared with religion, having no similar response in the human

[1] Petition of 641 Physicans and Surgeons.

conscience, and no text-book like the Bible, which, never yet either falsified or improved by the results of inquiry, or by the progress of discovery, has remained for ages down to this hour the most instructive, interesting, and powerful of all books. The allegation of dulness as attaching to a day spent in the duties of religion has been disposed of in a former part of this work (pp. 222-227). We will further say of it only, that it could be hazarded by no man who had not coloured the day and its observers with the dark shade of his own spirit. But the questions admit of reply from the testimony of experience, and if we examine for a little the comparative claims of the proposed expedient and of that which it is intended to displace, we shall find not only that the former is utterly inadequate for its purpose, but that proof has been accumulated of the pre-eminent adaptation of the latter to the constitution and improvement of the human mind.

Looking then, first, at *the practicability* of the measures under consideration, we find the evidence to be decisive in favour of a sacred day. It is an important circumstance that there never has been an instance of a Sabbatic institution apart from some kind of religion. This has not been owing to the want of opportunities, of endeavours, or even of partially successful efforts to found such an institution. In this country, and in many others, no man is compelled to keep a sacred Sabbath; any one may not only abstain from going to a place of worship, but may employ the day in the study of science, either individually or socially. Such things have been done. The French converted their churches into temples of so-called Reason, where public affairs were descanted on, moral orations pronounced, and political hymns sung. The Socinians in London had "several debating clubs established among them in the metropolis on the Lord's day."[1] There have been rejecters of Christianity who have had their assemblies on the first day of the week for their edification in unbelief. And yet the supporters of these and similar schemes, with the idea and all the details of the working of a Sabbath before their eyes, with the convenience of a day in general observance on which to attempt their supposed improvements, with the influence of man's aversion to what is sacred in favour of their designs, and with all

[1] *Works of Robert Hall* (1839), vol. 7, p. 130

their concessions, moreover, to the religious convictions and customs of society, have never been able to secure more than a very partial and temporary adoption of a weekly day for instruction, whether in infidelity or in any merely secular matter. Avarice and the love of animal pleasure have ever proved more than a match for such devices. It is religion alone that has provided a Sabbath suited to all men, established it against the opposition of the strongest human passions, and maintained it in all ages. From the earliest period of authentic history to the present time, the world has never wanted its seventh-day festival. Wherever Christianity has prevailed, it has carried its Sabbath along with it. And we have only to examine the records of modern missions to be convinced how admirably adapted the institution is to men in every clime; how speedily and effectually it displaces the old customs when its religion has been embraced, and how firm a lodgment it effects in the consciences and affections of the converts. On the score, then, of practicability, it has the decided evidence of experience in its favour, while all such evidence pronounces the proposed substitute to be a hopeless project.

Let us now turn to another criterion of the intellectual adaptation of a seventh day, according as it is employed in religious services, or in other means of mental improvement; we mean *power or efficiency*, and let us see what facts disclose on this point. If it be said that the religious institution has so preoccupied men's minds as to preclude a fair trial of other expedients which have but rarely been invested with a formal appointment, we reply, that considering the facilities and favourable feelings for a change already mentioned, we can see nothing in all this but a testimony to the efficiency of a sacred, and the imbecility of a secular Sabbath. That surely which is too feeble to struggle into general use, or to maintain its ground, promises no good should it by any possibility be brought into full operation. That, on the other hand, which, with the whole tide of human immorality set in against it, has nevertheless prevailed in the world, proclaims thereby its power to reign. But it is not true that the former has not had a sufficient trial. It was the subject of experiment, under a formal appointment, for ten years in France, the result of which was that it had to take refuge in religion. There are many in our own land engaged in the pursuit of knowledge who never keep a religious holiday, and who enjoy the freedom from interruption in their studies which such a day secures. This state of things has long existed, and is to be found in other countries as well. In all Popish lands the Lord's day is, for the most part, free to be applied to mental exercises or to anything else, and will be taken advantage of for the former purpose by some of each community. Add to these cases that of the far greater proportion of mankind who have been without the restraints of a sacred day, and who therefore have had more time for making acquisitions in learning. It appears, therefore, that the proposed and other methods of intellectual discipline which have been deemed worthy to supplant the Christian Sabbath have been sufficiently tried to enable us to judge of their merits. And we are willing to accept the history of the latter, circumscribed and abated though its proper influence has been by the keenest opposition, as furnishing the means of deciding on its fitness as an instrument of mental improvement. To that history, as formerly presented in a summary form, we add only the comprehensive words of Jortin: "To whom are we indebted," asks the learned writer, "for the knowledge of antiquities, sacred and secular, for everything that is called philology or polite literature? To Christians. To whom for grammars and dictionaries of the learned languages? To Christians. To whom for chronology, and the continuation of history through many centuries? To Christians. To whom for rational systems of morality and of natural religion? To Christians. To whom for improvements in natural philosophy, and for the application of these discoveries to religious purposes? To Christians. To whom for metaphysical researches carried as far as the subject will permit? To Christians. To whom for jurisprudence and political knowledge, and for settling the rights of subjects, both civil and religious, upon a proper foundation? To Christians."[1]

We have yet, thirdly, to show that the reason alleged for measures which would abridge or even supplant a carefully sanctified Sabbath has no foundation in fact. It is the weekly holy day as observed in this country that is affirmed to be immoral in its ten-

[1] Jortin's *Sermons*, vol. vii. pp. 373, 374.

dency, and it will be a sufficient answer to the charge if we can show that it finds a thorough refutation in certain moral contrasts furnished by our country's annals. In briefly tracing these contrasts we shall see enough to justify Foster's eulogium, that "the Sabbath is a remarkable appointment for raising the general tenor of moral existence," and the words of Blackstone and Pollok: "A corruption of morals usually follows a profanation of the Sabbath;"

"Sure sign, whenever seen,
That holiness is dying in a land,
The Sabbath was profaned and set at nought."

How dissimilar was England when above one hundred murders had been committed in the kingdom by ecclesiastics, of whom not one had been punished so much as with degradation, the punishment enjoined by the canons, to England in the time of Queen Elizabeth! What an alteration in the other direction followed the publication and republication of the *Book of Sports*, which opened the flood-gates to all kinds of licentiousness! Mark the improvement which was the result of a change of measures. Never were the claims of the Lord's day more ably defended and enforced from the pulpit and the press, or more zealously complied with in the practice of the people, than during the times of the Commonwealth and of the preceding struggles. "You might walk the streets [of London] on the evening of the Lord's day," as Neal observes of "the people in the Parliament quarters," "without seeing an idle person or hearing anything but the voice of prayer or praise from churches and private houses."[1] He further says that there were no gaming-houses nor houses of pleasure, nor was there any profane swearing nor any kind of debauchery to be seen or heard in the streets.[2] Referring to the period when the monarchy had been overturned, he remarks: "In the midst of all these disorders there was a very great appearance of sobriety both in city and country; the indefatigable pains of the Presbyterian ministers in catechising, instructing, and visiting their parishioners, can never be sufficiently commended. The whole nation was civilized, and considerably improved in sound knowledge."[3] Compare with these years some later periods

[1] *History of the Puritans*, ii. 591. [2] *Ibid.* 594. [3] *Ibid.* iv. 18.

when the Sabbath law was not so obeyed; the time, for example, of Charles II., when "religion, which had been the fashion of the late times, was universally discountenanced, those who observed the Sabbath, scrupled profane swearing, etc., being branded as fanatics, and the exorbitant vices of the Court spread over the whole nation, and occasioned so general a licentiousness as to require the king's notice of it in addressing the Parliament;"[1] and the days of Walpole, when corruption was so notorious as to elicit from that statesman the saying, that "every man had his price;" and when London itself was infected with banditti, so that many gentlemen were robbed and even murdered on the public streets in open day. Let us observe the opposite effect of a continued respect for the institution among the Puritans who were driven from their country, as well as among their descendants. The Pilgrim Fathers took refuge in Holland. But, as Mather, in his *Magnalia*, says, "they saw that, whatever banks the Dutch had against the inroads of the sea, they had not sufficient ones against a flood of manifold profaneness; they could not with ten years' endeavour bring their neighbours particularly to any suitable observation of the Lord's day, without which they knew that all practical religion must wither miserably."[2] So they resolved to leave Holland. What character they maintained while in that country may be known from the testimony of the magistrates of Leyden, who, while reproving the Walloons, say, "These English have lived now ten years among us, and yet we never had any accusation against any of them, whereas your quarrels are continual."[3] After this noble race had been settled for one hundred years in America, they are found persevering in a dutiful respect to the Sabbath and its sacred services, and in a course of practical morality becoming their principles and profession of religion. The same alternations of good and evil, arising from the same causes as are presented in the history of England, appear in that of Scotland. The interval between her first and second Reformations was marked by a very efficient system of Christian instruction, and by the "very healthful moral condition of her people,"[4] the efforts of the bishops who were

[1] *History of the Puritans*, iv. 354, 355.

[2] Mather's *Magnalia*, p. 5.

[3] Mather's *Magnalia*, p. 6.

[4] Chalmers's *Works*, vol. xvi. p. 289.

introduced by the Court, in propagating their views of religion, and in attempting to bring the observance of the Sabbath into conformity to that encouraged by royal proclamation, serving to stimulate the zeal and exertions of the faithful ministers of the land. The period, again, from the second Reformation to the Restoration of the Monarchy was even more distinguished by the religious and moral elevation of the country. Kirkton's account of its concluding years is well known. We give a portion of it: "In the interval betwixt the two kings, religion advanced the greatest step it had made for many years. Now, the ministry was notably purified, the magistracy was altered, and the people strangely refined. No scandalous person could live, no scandal could be concealed in all Scotland, so strict a correspondence there was betwixt ministers and congregations. At the king's return every parish had a minister, every village had a school, every family almost had a Bible, yea, in most of the country all the children of age could read the Scriptures, and were provided of Bibles, either by the parents or their ministers. I have lived many years in a parish where I never heard an oath, and you might have ridden many miles before you heard any. Also, you could not for a great part of the country, have lodged in a family where the Lord was not worshipped by reading, singing, and public prayer. Nobody complained more of our Church government than our taverners, whose ordinary lamentation was, their trade was broke, people were become so sober."[1] In this state of things Charles II. ascended the throne. This event was soon followed by an attempt to enforce Episcopacy upon the Scottish nation, which gave rise to a war of about twenty-eight years' duration. The act for the establishment of parochial schools was repealed. Three hundred and fifty ministers were ejected from their parishes, and forbidden to preach even in the fields, or to approach within twenty miles of their former charges. In their place were appointed men whom Burnet describes as "mean and despicable in all respects, the worst preachers he ever heard, ignorant to a reproach, and many of them openly vicious."[2] With these men, and their persecuting, profligate, and profane

[1] Kirkton's *History of the Church of Scotland*, pp. 48, 49, 64, 65.
[2] *History of his own Times* (Edit. of 1850), p. 103.

supporters, compare the Covenanters, whose attachment to the weekly holy day, though, alas! to them no day of security and rest, we have already seen: "It is ascertained," as Principal Lee deposed before the House of Commons' Committee on the Sabbath in 1832, "that in the time of the Covenanters, which I believe to have been a period of great religious light, and of great strictness and purity of morals, there was scarcely an individual in the lowlands of Scotland who could not read, and who was not in the habit of reading the Bible; and scarcely a family in which the worship of God was not regularly performed, both by celebrating the praises of God, reading the Scriptures and prayer."[1] The Revolution, indeed, put an end to persecution, rescinded the acts establishing a form of religion opposed to the wishes of the people, and led to the restoration of the parochial schools. But it is not surprising that the evils which had been inflicted by a tyrannical government, a brutal soldiery, and a clergy sunk in sloth, ignorance, and vice, should not cease with their causes, particularly as hundreds of these clergy were retained in their charges. So late, accordingly, as 1698, ten years after the Revolution, there were, according to Fletcher of Saltoun, 200,000 people who subsisted by begging from door to door, and the half of whom were vagabonds, living without any regard or submission either to the laws of the land, or even those of God and nature; robbing, murdering, and at country weddings, markets, burials, and on other public occasions, to be seen, both men and women, perpetually drunk, cursing, blaspheming, and fighting together. But how improved the times when Scotland had begun to recover from the effects of political oppression and of anti-Sabbatic influences, and to feel the reforming power of its religious faith and institutions! "After the Revolution, I find from the accounts of the schools in towns and lowland parishes, some of which I have in my possession, that in the periodical examinations which took place, there are regular returns of the numbers of the children who were reading different books, some of them the New Testament, but the greater part reading the entire Bible; and that was the period certainly when the Sabbath was most strictly observed, and when, according to all the

[1] Minutes of Evidence, p. 271.

accounts that can be best relied upon, the morals of the people were likewise the most healthy."[1] Defoe writes thus of the state of Scottish morality in 1717 : "The people are restrained in the ordinary practice of common immoralities, such as swearing, drunkenness, slander, fornication, and the like. As to theft, murder, and other capital crimes, they come under the cognizance of the civil magistrates, as in other countries ; but, in those things which the Church has power to punish, the people being constantly and impartially prosecuted, they are thereby the more restrained, kept sober, and under government, and you may pass through twenty towns in Scotland without seeing any broil or hearing one oath in the streets ; whereas, if a blind man was to come from there into England, he shall know the first town he sets his foot in within the English border, by hearing the name of God blasphemed and profanely used even by the little children on the street."[2] The same contrasts may be seen at other times and even in our own day. We shall be told, indeed, of particular vices which have brought a stigma upon the best Sabbath-keeping country in the world, and on some of its most God-fearing cities. No little exaggeration, it has been proved, has been employed on the subject—a natural resource of those who envy a high reputation, and hate a holy institution. Without enlarging on this part of the question, for which we cannot afford space, let a few facts relative to the morals of the cities referred to, and of a country parish, at different periods, serve to show that it is the neglect, not the observance of the Lord's day, that accounts for any real deterioration in the character of the people.

Mr. Creech, well known in his day, and still remembered as an author, bookseller, and Lord Provost of Edinburgh, contributed to the Statistical Account of Scotland some remarkable sketches, which were afterwards published in his *Fugitive Pieces*, of the modes of living, trade, manners, etc., of that city, as these appeared in the years 1763, 1783, 1793. The following are a few specimens :—"In 1763 it was fashionable to go to church, and people were interested about religion. Sunday was strictly observed by all ranks as a day of devotion, and it was disgrace-

[1] Principal Lee—Minutes of Evidence, p. 271.
[2] *Memoirs of the Church of Scotland* (1844), p. 353.

ful to be seen on the streets during the time of public worship. Families attended church with their children and servants, and family worship was frequent. The collections at the church doors for the poor amounted yearly to £1500 and upwards. In 1783 attendance on church was greatly neglected, and particularly by the men. Sunday was by many made a day of relaxation, and young people were allowed to stroll about at all hours. Families thought it ungenteel to take their domestics to church with them. The streets were far from being void of people in the time of public worship, and, in the evenings, were frequently loose and riotous, particularly owing to bands of apprentice boys and young lads. Family worship was almost disused. The collections at the church doors for the poor had fallen to £1000. In no respect were the manners of 1763 and 1783 more remarkable than in the decency, dignity, and delicacy of the one period, compared with the looseness, dissipation, and licentiousness of the other. Many people ceased to blush at what would formerly have been reckoned a crime.

"In 1763, masters took charge of their apprentices, and kept them under their eye in their own houses. In 1783, few masters would receive apprentices to stay in their houses, and yet from them an important part of succeeding society is to be formed. If they attended their hours of business, masters took no further charge. The rest of their time might be passed (as too frequently happens) in vice and debauchery, hence they become idle, insolent, and dishonest. In 1791, the practice had become still more prevalent. Reformation of manners must begin in families to be general or effectual.

"In 1763, the clergy visited, catechised, and instructed the families within their respective parishes, in the principles of morality, Christianity, and the relative duties of life. In 1783, visiting and catechising were disused (except by very few), and since continue to be so. Nor, perhaps, would the clergy now be received with welcome on such an occasion. If people do not choose to go to church, they may remain as ignorant as Hottentots, and the Ten Commandments be as little known as obsolete Acts of Parliament. Religion is the only tie that can restrain, in any degree, the licentiousness either of the rich or of the lower ranks; when that is lost, ferocity of manners and every breach of morality may be expected.

> 'Hoc fonte derivata, clades
> In patriam populumque fluxit.'

"In 1763, house-breaking and robbery were extremely rare. Many people thought it unnecessary to lock their doors at night. In 1783, 1784, 1785, 1786, and 1787, house-breaking, theft, and robbery were astonishingly frequent, and many of these crimes were committed by boys, whose age prevented them from being objects of capital punishment. In no respect was the sobriety and decorum of the lower ranks in 1763 more remarkable than by contrasting them with the riot and licentiousness of 1783, particularly on Sundays and holidays. The king's birthday, and the last night of the year, were, in 1783, devoted to drunkenness, folly, and riot, which in 1763 were attended with peace and harmony.

"In 1763, young ladies (even by themselves) might have walked through the streets of the city in perfect security, at any hour. No person would have interrupted or spoken to them. In 1783, the mistresses of boarding-schools found it necessary to advertise, that their young ladies were not permitted to go abroad without proper attendants. In 1791, boys, from bad example at home, and worse abroad, had become forward and insolent. They early frequented taverns, and were soon initiated in folly and vice, without any religious principle to restrain them. It has been an error of twenty years, to precipitate the education of boys, and make them too soon men."[1]

"In 1763, the question respecting the morality of stage-plays was much agitated. By those who attended the theatre even without scruple, Saturday night was thought the most improper in the week for going to the play. In 1783, the morality of stage-plays, or their effects on society were not thought of. The most crowded houses were always on Saturday night. The custom of taking a box for the Saturday night through the season, was much practised by boarding mistresses, so that there could be no choice of the play, but the young ladies could only take what was set before them by the manager. The galleries never failed to

[1] *Edinburgh Fugitive Pieces*, pp. 100-112

applaud what they formerly would have hissed, as improper in sentiment or decorum.[1]

"In 1763, hairdressers were few, and hardly permitted to dress hair on Sundays; and many of them voluntarily declined it. In 1783, hairdressers were more than tripled in number; and their busiest day was Sunday. In 1763, the revenue arising from the distillery in Scotland amounted to £4739, 18s. 10d.—in 1783, to £192,000."[2]

In the same work there is an account of a country parish as it was in the years 1763 and 1783. We give an extract. "In 1763, all persons attended divine worship on Sunday. There were only four Seceders in the parish. Sunday was regularly and religiously observed. In 1783, there is such a disregard of public worship and ordinances, that few attend divine worship with that attention which was formerly given. Ignorance prevails, although privileged with excellent instructions in public sermons, in examination, and in visiting from house to house by the pastor. When the form of religion is disregarded, surely the power of it is near dissolution. In 1763, few in this parish were guilty of the breach of the third commandment. The name of God was reverenced and held sacred. In 1783, the third commandment seems to be almost forgotten, and swearing abounds. I may say the same of all the rest of the ten, as to public practice. The decay of religion and growth of vice, in this parish, is very remarkable within these twenty years."[3]

Let us now take the case of Glasgow, where, after allowing for over-statement, it is admitted that a rapidly accumulating population, including vast hordes of immigrants from various parts of the world, are in many instances regardless of the laws of sobriety. There was a time, however, when our western capital, and Scotland at large, were eminent not only for temperance, but for general moral excellence. An Englishman, who sojourned in Glasgow in 1703, testifies that "all the while he was there he never saw any drunk, nor heard any swear, and in all the inns of the road to that part of Scotland they had family worship performed."[4] Another Englishman, Defoe, as we have seen, bears a remarkable

1 *Edinburgh Fugitive Pieces*, p. 113. 2 *Ibid.* pp. 78, 79. 3 *Ibid.* p. 142

4 *Works* of Matthew Henry (1853), vol. i. p. 585.

attestation to Scottish morality in 1717. It will surely not be pretended that the Sabbath is better observed or better enforced in 1862 than it was in 1703 and 1717—years comprehended in the period which, according to Principal Lee, was the halcyon time of Scotland's weekly holy day. The reverse is the fact. What then has the Sabbath to do with the immorality of Glasgow? The commercial metropolis of Scotland "flourished" once "by the preaching of the Word," but she has deteriorated in our day because so many refuse to hear the Word. Vice has kept pace, not with the observance, but with the neglect of the Lord's day. But there is another contrast which must not be forgotten in this argument—that between the distinguished excellence of the many who honour the day, and the moral and physical degradation of the too numerons class who despise it. Intemperance and profaneness are both cause and effect. Sabbath-breakers and drunkards are usually one and the same class of men; while it is true everywhere that the men who most respect the institution are not only the most temperate members of society, but the most moral in all respects in their conduct, and almost the only persons who do anything in their localities for promoting sobriety and every virtue among their neighbours. It is among those that devoutly regard the sacred day in our large cities that we find the individuals who dive into the darkest, filthiest, and most dangerous haunts of wickedness, with the view of reclaiming the inhabitants from ignorance, wretchedness, and crime, or who, while most of others care not for the neglected and profligate except to scowl upon them as they cross their path, patiently labour in the self-denied and arduous work of instructing the young that they may rescue them from ruin, and guide them in the way of purity and happiness. It is from among them, too, that those go forth who brave the hazards, or suffer the privations of a residence in unpropitious climes and among savage tribes, solely for the spiritual good of their fellow-creatures. What scheme, indeed, for enlightening the ignorant, reforming the immoral, relieving poverty, abating disease, and comforting sorrow, has not among its principal patrons, and most active auxiliaries, the very men who are charged as demoralizing their fellow-citizens for no other reason than their fidelity to the Divine and benignant law of the Sabbath, and so charged by the persons who owe it to the Sabbath-keeping and other excellences of the objects of their abuse that they are preserved and in peace amidst the elements of destruction. Is it possible that a law which produces such fruits of mercy and kindness can be a bad law? The imputation of hypocrisy to men who are the friends of such a law, and bright illustrations of its moral excellence, is itself a confirmation of our views, for certainly, if those who prefer such a charge had enjoyed the mental discipline of the Sabbath, or had imbibed its spirit, they could not have been so ignorant of language and character, so wanting in courtesy and candour, or so destitute of prudence and self-respect, as to apply to the most upright and useful members of society a term so notoriously, wickedly, and stupidly inapposite.

But we feel that we have said more than enough of these accusations and their fabricators—and we conclude the chapter with a passage relating to Sweden, which not only adds to the proof of the fallacy of the views that we have been combating; but gives a striking warning against the slightest countenance to "doing evil that good may come:" "We have frequently of late been told by a certain class of philanthropists," says the Rev. James Lumsden, "that our Scottish habits of Sabbath observance are the main cause of the intemperance of our land, and that the true and effectual method of promoting sobriety is to give facilities and encouragement to our hard-working artisans, to escape from their homes by railway and steam-boat on Sunday afternoons and enjoy the healthful atmosphere and instructive landscapes of the country. It is well to inquire what success this experiment of employing Satan 'to cast out Satan,' has had in a country where it has been carried on for a period of satisfactory length, and in circumstances peculiarly favourable, in a climate very similar to our own, among a people of the same race, and free from the disturbing element of the Sabbatarian denunciations of the pulpit and the press. And what has been the effect of this holiday Sabbath upon the sobriety of the nation? Why, that by the confession of the Swedes themselves, their nation is the most intemperate in Europe;[1] that in a country where manufacturers have not drawn a promis-

[1] As a proof of this, the recent Parliament has increased the duty on the manufacture of ardent spirits two-and-thirty fold

cuous population into over-grown villages and crowded towns, where incentives to vice, arising from high wages, rapid prosperity, and commercial bustle and over-working, are absent, where the people are almost as thinly spread as in our Highlands, the rate of consumption of ardent spirits is higher than in this country; and that a region, where primitive purity as well as primitive quiet might be supposed to have found a refuge, is pervaded by the intemperance of our neglected lanes and luxurious cities."[1]

[1] *Sweden; its Religious State and Prospects*, 1855, pp. 12-14.

CHAPTER V.

THEORIES AND ARGUMENTS TRIED BY THE DOCTRINE AND LAW OF REVELATION.

WHEN it has been already proved, on the one hand, by the amplest evidence of Reason, Revelation, and History, that the Sabbath, according to one of its theories, is of Divine original and authority, and an indispensable blessing to mankind, and, on the other, that rival theories and schemes, as tested by the principles of the Divine Government, and by experience, are destitute of worth, power, and benefit, it may seem superfluous to prosecute the contest. But our opponents endeavour to find in Scripture support for opinions which have failed to gain the suffrages of the greatest and best of men, or to supply any satisfying credentials of their success. To Scripture they appeal, and to Scripture the very tower of our strength, it can be no disadvantage for us to go.

But the most conflicting doctrines and practices have been held to be scriptural—and it is possible for persons of any party to come to the Word of God, and because they are proud, to be sent empty away. If we would derive instruction and guidance from that Word, we must understand its meaning, and for that purpose follow the rules according to which it demands to be interpreted, and which commend themselves to the reason and common sense of mankind. Let us, therefore, enunciate some of these Scriptural, rational, and common-sense rules, and apply each rule as we proceed for enabling us to decide on the claims of various theories and arguments, which have been put forth on our subject. We do not profess to dictate to others, but we cannot, in this part of the volume, argue with those who appeal to Revelation, if they nevertheless reject its authoritative prescription of the manner in which its meaning is to be ascertained.

First Rule.—It is necessary that we recognise the Old and New Testaments as alone constituting the Word of God. No writing, besides those in the Protestant canon, and no oral tradition, have any claim to be received as parts of Divine revelation. Whatever, therefore, Rome advances from tradition to justify her assumed right to change the day of the Sabbath, or to appoint holy days of her own, has to us nothing of the character of "proofs of holy writ."

Second Rule.—We must receive the Word of God, thus defined and complete in its parts, as a Revelation divinely perfect in its whole character. It is true of the Old Testament as of the New, that it is "given by inspiration of God, and is profitable for doctrine, for reproof, for correction, and instruction in righteousness; that the man of God may be perfect, throughly furnished unto all good works."[1] To neglect either division of the Bible, or to magnify it at the expense of the other, would betray so utter a misconception of the whole book, as must preclude the discovery of truth on every one of its great subjects. Let this treatment be shown to a volume of human production, and the injustice no less than the folly of such procedure would be seen and condemned by all. But in deciding with respect to the Sabbath and other matters, there are those who are chargeable with this partiality, so directly in opposition to the demands of Scripture and of reason, and who, therefore, must fail of arriving at the knowledge of the Divine mind and will. These persons conceive that the selection of a particular people to be the objects of Divine favour, and the depositaries of the Divine oracles, is a circumstance with which we have nothing to do, further than as a matter of curiosity or of historical interest. How many regard the people of Israel as if they had been the inhabitants of another planet, and their system of religion as if it had almost nothing in common with the Christian! How many look upon the Old Testament as an obsolete part of Divine revelation, which it is unnecessary to read for instruction of life and manners—whose Psalms are not to be sung—whose principles apply not to us—

[1] 2 Tim. iii. 16, 17.

whose worthies are no models—whose spirit is unchristian! Nothing could be more remote from the truth—nothing more daringly impious if it were not so vastly ignorant. Judaism was a Divine, wise, holy, good, sanctifying, saving system of religion—substantially one with the Christian. It was a local and stationary, not like Christianity a moving, circulating light, but it was the means of preserving religion in the world, and it steadily bore testimony to the existence of the one living and true God, the God of mercy and salvation, while its privileges were open to all Gentiles who abandoned idolatry, and acceded to the profession of the true faith. Considered even as to their transitory peculiarities, the Jews were appointed to serve great ends with respect both to the surrounding world and to future ages. But, more than this, the Jews were men who, in common with others, stood in need of a Saviour, and of a law to guide them as rational and immortal beings. To them, accordingly, a Saviour was made known by typical representations and the preaching of the prophets—to them a moral law was given. There are, doubtless, matters in the Old Testament that are not a rule for us, but so are there in the New. There are many things in both that directly concern all, and there are many things of this universal application in each that are not in the other. That we may know the whole of our faith and duty, we must repair to both, and along with other parts of doctrine and practice search for the true character and obligations of a weekly rest in the earlier as well as in the later revelation. We have as much to do with what Genesis testifies respecting the Sabbath as we have to do with what it declares concerning the institution and law of marriage. What was moral in Judaism is as truly binding upon us as it was obligatory upon the Jews. This rule of interpreting Scripture, therefore, while it sanctions the perpetual obligation of a seventh day's rest and worship, sets aside the notion that the institution of the Sabbath in Paradise, and its promulgation at Sinai, had no respect to mankind in general, or if they had respect to us, that it was only by way of an analogy which directed but did not bind.

The perfection of Revelation has other bearings on our subject. It teaches inquirers that, as its thoughts and reasonings have come forth from infinite wisdom, and as its very words are "the words of the Lord, which are pure words, as silver tried in a furnace of earth, purified seven times," they must be reverently examined, not wrested, not instructed by the reader, but listened to, that he may receive whatever instruction and impression they are designed to impart. If we would not defeat the great end of language, which is the transmission of thought, and if we would not dishonour a Divine composition, which, as in everything else, so in adaptedness to its design of conveying salutary and indispensable information to "the common people," and to the poor as well as to the learned and the rich, must transcend the literature of earth, we ought to be persuaded that holy men, speaking as they were moved by the Holy Ghost, could not utter unintelligible words, or express one thing when they meant another. And yet how confidently do some who give evidence that they have not attentively considered what they profess to have read, pronounce on this and that passage of Scripture, and how deliberately do others assert a particular view of a text to be just, when they ought to know that they are forcing it into the service of a favourite theory! One of the most remarkable instances of the bold freedom with which certain writers have treated the sacred text, is furnished in the attempt to set aside the idea of a primitive Sabbath, by the notion that the mention of it in Genesis antedates the institution by thousands of years. Let us again present the beautifully simple and clear words of the record:—"Thus the heavens and the earth were finished, and all the host of them. And on the seventh day God ended his work which he had made; and he rested on the seventh day from all his work which he had made. And God blessed the seventh day, and sanctified it; because that in it he had rested from all his work which God created and made."[1]

It might be presumed that no one could come to the perusal of this earliest notice of the Sabbath, with the view of transferring the meaning of the words to his mind, rather than of imparting his own previous impressions to the words, without learning that the consecration and observance of the seventh day were immediate consequences of the Divine rest. So plain a matter is this to all who read only for instruction, that one would feel as if an

[1] Gen. ii. 1-3.

apology were needed for the apparent childishness of elevating into a formal proposition so obvious a truism. But certain writers have so insulted the understandings of mankind, and so trifled with the sacred page, as to affirm that a space of 2500 years intervened between the day of rest, and the actual appointment of the institution by which it was to be commemorated, the order of time being departed from for the sake of the connexion of subject; and have on this mere assertion, so gratuitous and wild, built theories and systems for guiding the faith and conduct of the world in some of the most important duties and concerns of men. The view which the words as clearly indicate as language ever expressed thought or fact, and which has commended itself to the common sense of the generality of readers, is to the effect that the seventh day on which God rested, was the identical day which he blessed and sanctified, its transactions being as immediately consecutive to those of the sixth day as these were to the proceedings of the fifth. If the Creator performed the works of the six days on these days, He must have rested, sanctified, and blessed the seventh day on the seventh day. If the acts of the seventh day were not done on the seventh day, neither were the acts of the six days done on the six days. In other words, there was neither creation nor Sabbath till the children of Israel had encamped in the wilderness of Sin! What is the conclusion to which the theory in question would shut us up? It is, that a sacred writer has expressed himself in such terms as necessarily to lead us into error, from which there is no escape but into the domain of absurdity. How low those conceptions of the character of holy writ, which could inspire the proleptic dream, or how forlorn the hopes of a cause which has driven its friends to an expedient so foolish as well as so allied to the irreverent and profane!

Let us offer a second example of the forced and unnatural construction which has been perpetrated on the narrative of creation. We refer to the interpretation which makes the six days of the Creator's working denote periods of long duration. The good sense of its most ingenious defender, Faber, led him ultimately to discard an opinion, which, however unintentionally on the part of its supporters, is in reality a libel on the simplest and most perfect style of historical writing. It is true that the term "day" is employed in Scripture in different meanings, some of which occur within the compass of a few sentences in the account of the creation, but in none of the cases is the sense at all obscure. "And God called the light Day, and the darkness he called Night. And the evening and the morning were the first day." Each of the days of creation being defined to include the light and the darkness must therefore have been a period of twenty-four hours, the time on which the earth performs one revolution upon its axis. The seventh day, though wanting the definition given of the others, yet as belonging to a numbered series having the same common name of day, must, as nothing is said to the contrary, have been of the same duration as its predecessors. And when the sacred writer, having informed us that the heavens and the earth were finished in six of those periods, adds, "These are the generations of the heavens and of the earth, in the day that the Lord God made the earth and the heavens," where the word comprises six common days, there is no difficulty in distinguishing "day" in the summary, from "day" in the details, and in perceiving that it denotes generally a time. "In what manner the creation was conducted," says Bishop Horsley, "is a question about a fact, and, like all questions about facts, must be determined, not by theory, but by testimony; and if no testimony were extant, the fact must remain uncertain. But the testimony of the sacred historian is peremptory and explicit. No expressions could be found in any language, to describe a gradual progress of the work of six successive days, and the completion of it on the sixth, in the literal and common sense of the word 'day,' more definite and unequivocal than those employed by Moses; and they who seek or admit figurative expositions of such expressions as these, seem to be not sufficiently aware, that it is one thing to write a history, and quite another to compose riddles. The expressions in which Moses describes the days of the creation, literally rendered, are these: When he has described the first day's work, he says—'And there was evening, and there was morning, one day;' when he has described the second day's work, 'There was evening, and there was morning, a second day;' when he has described the third day's work, 'There was evening, and there was morning, a third day.' Thus, in the progress of his narrative, at the end of each day's work, he counts up the days which had passed off from the beginning of the business; and, to obviate all doubt what portion of time he meant to denote by the appellation of 'a day,' he describes each day of which the mention occurs as consisting of one evening and one morning, or, as the Hebrew words literally import, of the decay of light and the return of it. By what description could the word 'day' be more expressly limited to its literal and common meaning, as denoting that portion of time which is measured and consumed by the earth's revolution on her axis? That this revolution was performed in the same space of time in the beginning of the world as now, I would not over confidently affirm; but we are not at present concerned in the resolution of that question: a day, whatever was its space, was still the same thing in nature—a portion of time measured by the same motion, divisible into the same seasons as morning and noon, evening and midnight, and making the like part of longer portions of time measured by other motions. The day was itself marked by the vicissitudes of darkness and light; and so many times repeated, it made a month, and so many times more a year. For six such days, God was making the heaven and the earth, the sea, and all that therein is, and rested on the seventh day. This fact, clearly established by the sacred writer's testimony, in the literal meaning of these plain words, abundantly evinces the perpetual importance and propriety of consecrating one day in seven to the public worship of the Creator."[1] To these remarks of an eminent scholar, we add the words of an able geologist as well as theologian:—"We have then six days, which I conceive there is good reason to regard as six natural days, six rotations of our globe upon its axis, each in about twenty-four hours."[2]

Third Rule.—In examining particular passages of Scripture, we must consider them in connexion both with their context and with other passages relating to the same topics. Such a process of induction is due even to the humblest of writers. And it is due still more to inspired men, whose words, purer and more precious than gold, we must carefully gather and generalize if we would know what the great Teacher would have us believe and

[1] Sermon xxiii.
[2] Dr. J. Pye Smith in "Course of Lectures to Young Men" (1838), p. 18.

do. We must compare spiritual things with spiritual. Of the extent to which the testimony of Revelation on the subject before us has been misrepresented by the disregard of this undoubted canon, the following are illustrations :—

A noted case occurs in the attempt to set aside the primæval Sabbath on the ground, that after the notice in the second chapter of Genesis no further mention of a hallowed day is made by the historian till he has proceeded to record the miraculous provision of the manna. "If the Sabbath had been instituted at the time of the creation, as the words in Genesis may seem at first sight to import, and if it had been observed all along, from that time to the departure of the Jews out of Egypt, a period of about two thousand five hundred years ; it appears unaccountable that no mention of it, no occasion of even the obscurest allusion to it, should occur, either in the general history of the world before the call of Abraham, which contains, we admit, only a few memoirs of its early ages, and those extremely abridged ; or, which is more to be wondered at, in that of the lives of the first three Jewish patriarchs, which in many parts of the account, is sufficiently circumstantial and domestic."[1]

It is not for man to decide on the manner in which a Divine Revelation should be made. It belongs to him to examine the actual revelation, under the conviction that both in its matter and in its mode, it must be perfect. Instead, therefore, of indulging in uncertain speculations on such a circumstance as that referred to, and we must say, exaggerated, by Dr. Paley, we ought to have recourse to the light, if any, that has been shed upon it by other parts of Scripture. If we would do justice to the character of Manasseh, we must read not only of his monstrous wickedness, as recorded in the second book of Kings, but of his penitence and reformation, as related in the second book of Chronicles. It would be an unwarranted inference from the biography of Solomon if we conceived that his sun had gone down under a dark cloud of apostasy, for, turning to the Ecclesiastes, we see the luminary setting in cloudless and mild glory. If we did not trace the sacred history far beyond the close of the Pentateuch, we should not be aware that the true law of marriage, which, from the hardness of

[1] Paley's *Works*, 18mo, vol. iv. pp. 290, 291.

Jewish hearts, had been for four thousand years in abeyance, was finally re-asserted in its original purity and obligation.

In the passage which we have cited, the eminent author has not entirely neglected to compare one part of Scripture with another. But his induction is both faulty and incomplete.

It is faulty. He has examined the history in Genesis, but he has inverted the universally admitted order of procedure in comparing the separate parts, having employed the obscure to define the clear, the negative to illustrate the positive, or having, in other words, instead of interpreting the subsequent silence of the historian by his simple narrative of the Creation, interpreted the narrative by a silence, his construction of which is *a mere conjecture.* If the terms in which the alleged appointment is couched had been dark and doubtful, the omission of reference to it afterwards might be an element in determining their import, but the fact of the appointment has been put on record in the clear and indubitable language of inspiration, and no such omission can alter a fact, which must stand for ever. Had the author of Genesis never more mentioned the Sabbath, although this circumstance could not have annihilated the fact of the appointment, it would have afforded a plausible ground for the doubt whether the evidently instituted day of rest and worship had not been permitted to expire. But the silence was ultimately broken, faintly by the still small voice of the descending manna, and soon after, effectually, by the thunders of Sinai. The true meaning of silence, therefore, in this as in many other instances, is consent. It intimates that nothing had transpired from which it could justly be inferred that the conveyance of a Sabbatic boon had been withdrawn, or that the imposition of Sabbatic obligations had been cancelled. It conveys even more than this, and emphatically, as on numerous occasions, implies the superfluousness of utterance.

But Dr. Paley's induction is also incomplete. Had his survey been more comprehensive, and had he thus performed a simple act of justice to the inspired writers and to truth, he would have found that the circumstance made use of by him to abridge the pedigree, limit the extent, and weaken the authority, of a confessedly benignant institute, which every friend of morals and humanity should desire to see surrounded and fortified by every Divine sanction, is in entire agreement with the history of other great enactments and facts, and with the general history of the Sabbath itself.

How fares it with various institutions, laws, and events? Of the Fall of man nothing is said for the period during which the Sabbath receives no particular notice. That momentous event is traced only in the sins and miseries of the race, just as the appointment of the weekly rest is seen in *its* results—in the prevalent regard to the septenary number, and distribution of time, and in the indications of social religion, with its priesthood, tithes, set places and seasons of worship; circumstances which were the natural sequences of the Creator's working and rest, and which cannot be accounted for but on the supposition of that prior Divine example and arrangement. Was the account of the Fall in the beginning of Genesis the mere intimation of a destined or prospective event, as it is alleged the account of the Sabbath was? An affirmative answer would be as reasonable in the one case as in the other. The announcement of Redemption was indeed a prediction, but in harmony with other facts we find that the greatest of all events, after an early and obscure notice, is hardly again mentioned for the long period of two thousand five hundred years. "Although particular instances of the observance of the Sabbath by the old patriarchs, could not be given and evinced, yet we ought no more on that account to deny that they did observe it, than we ought to deny their faith in the promised Seed, because it is nowhere expressly recorded in the story of their lives."[1]

How scanty the references in Genesis to the creation if we except the first and second chapters! The observance of the ordinance of circumcision is never once alluded to between the times of Joshua and John the Baptist. There is no notice of the Passover from the date of Deuteronomy xvi. 2, to the days of Isaiah. We have already adverted to the long-continued omission of any assertion of the true law of marriage. The Sabbatical year is during a space of nine hundred years passed over in silence. And not one of the laws of the Decalogue except the sixth, is ever formally announced till they are promulgated from Sinai, although we have

[1] Owen on *Sab.*, *Exerc.* 3d., sect. 37.

evidence that they were obligatory and known. "Excepting Jacob's supplication at Bethel, scarcely a single allusion to prayer is to be found in all the Pentateuch; yet, considering the eminent piety of the worthies recorded in it, we cannot doubt the frequency of their devotional exercises."[1] How "unaccountable" on Dr. Paley's principle, such intervals of neglected reference, if the institutions and laws were really appointed and observed, and if the events actually took place! But notwithstanding the silence of history, we know that these were all veritable transactions. And such also must have been the early institution of a day of sacred rest.

The obscurity which for a time rested on the fortunes of the Sabbath is, moreover, in coincidence with its own general history. In the account of the time from Moses to Elisha, when the Jewish ritual and laws were in all their vigour, and the record of events was so full, "no mention of" the institution, "no occasion of even the slightest allusion to it," occurs. And yet, as Archdeacon Stopford observes, "That was a much longer period of history than we have of the patriarchal age."[2] Dr. Paley is satisfied with the evidence in the New Testament for a Christian Sabbath, but that evidence does not consist in the number of notices or even allusions on the subject, which are few and scattered. It is only, indeed, in such cases as the introduction of new economies, or the necessary exposure of flagrant perversions, neglects, or desecrations of the sacred rest by the professors of the true religion, that the mention of it is at all particular, as at the Creation, the descent of the manna, the giving of the Law, the charges preferred against Israel by the prophets, the predictions by the same persons of the nature and glory of the Christian dispensation, and the vindication by our Lord of the Sabbath law from the abuses of Jewish tradition and superstition. Unless there are such demands for specific remark, it is the practice of the inspired writers to maintain an entire abstinence on the subject, as, for example, in the time following the transactions of Sinai, or to make those incidental references to it, as in 2 Kings iv. 23, which the relation of other facts renders necessary. That there are circumstances throughout the history of the period from the Creation to the

[1] Holden on the *Christian Sabbath*, p. 37. [2] *Scripture Account of the Sabbath*, p. 43.

Exodus, which imply the appointment of a Sabbath, has already been adverted to; but even on the supposition of the absence of all allusion to any such institution during that long period, the method of Revelation, comprehensively viewed, precludes the inference that it is unnoticed, either because it had been abrogated, or because it had never been appointed.

The argument, therefore, of Dr. Paley is disproved, as it leads to conclusions which, besides being contrary to "the seeming import," as he allows, "of the words in Genesis," or, as ought rather to be said, to their only possible meaning, are discountenanced by the analogy in Scripture of cases in which the existence of Sabbatic and other institutions and laws is unquestionable, and which would, in fact, be as fatal to their authority as to the claims of a primæval day of rest. The argument, in other words, by proving too much, is utterly useless for its purpose, and forms another evidence of the weakness of the cause which it is brought to support.

Rather let the blank in the history of the Sabbath, of which so much has been made, be permitted to remain "unaccountable," than be explained by wresting from its true meaning a sacred narrative of surpassing simplicity and clearness. May it not, however, be accounted for in a legitimate way? In some preceding remarks it has been traced to a principle or rule in revelation, that there is for inspired as for other men, "a time to keep silence and a time to speak." But this rule itself has reasons, which it discloses in the instances in which it is applied to regulate both the omissions and notices of the Sabbath. In circumstances such as those of Cain, who went out from the presence of the Lord, and became the father and founder of a godless race, it is unnecessary to specify the disappearance of any particular institution, when all have been swallowed up in the vortex of a general irreligion. It is different with a people like the Jews, who were banished to Babylon on account partly of their neglect of Sabbatic privileges, and of whom it is natural to record both Jerusalem's "remembrance, in the days of her affliction and misery, of her pleasant things in the days of old," as contrasted with her Sabbaths now mocked, her sanctuary violated, and her bread taken away, and Jeremiah's lamentation over the forgotten solemn feasts and Sabbaths in Zion. When, on the other hand, the institution is generally respected by a pious race, like the descendants of Seth, it would be as superfluous to relate the fact as it would be formally to announce the continued shining of the sun ; and where individuals obey the law of the Sabbath in their hearts and in the privacies of their homes, a chariness in the disclosure of such matters is only in keeping with the character of good men who are not forward to divulge their religious experience, and with the spirit, too, of the sacred penmen, who usually draw a veil over such scenes, choosing, except in a particular case, as of David, who must sacrifice in the Psalms his private feelings for the public good, to present their worthies in the attitude rather of public action for God and man than of personal devotion. That the sacred writers dwell on certain matters of truth and conduct still more than on the weekly rest, and refer to the observance of it and of other institutions as of no avail without the faith and love of the heart, and the obedience of the life, are clear indications that it is only a means to the higher end of salvation and moral excellence. And yet that they do not thereby prejudice the institution itself is no less manifest. Isaiah and our Lord, who unsparingly denounce the substitution of ordinances and forms for faith and holy character, are careful to assert the authority and true designs of the Sabbath. When the spirit of the world encroaches on its limits and duties, it is seen that piety and morals are endangered in another form, and it is now the time for an Amos to sound the alarm to those who long for the cessation of its brief hours that they may return to the congenial occupation of "setting forth wheat." The mention of it in the first and last books of Scripture, and in intervening ones of various dates, the particularity with which it is noticed at the introduction of all the great changes in the forms of religious polity, and the ancient predictions of its prevalence in the last days, all proclaim its great and permanent importance. And when we add that it is frequently referred to incidentally, and that its names occur nearly a hundred times in the Bible, it will appear that it has not been without a proportionate share of attention in a volume which is not large, and comprehends the records of some four thousand years, with predictions extending to thousands more.

CHAPTER VI.

THEORIES AND ARGUMENTS TRIED BY THE DOCTRINE AND LAW OF REVELATION—*continued.*

Let us now apply the rule which Dr. Paley has overlooked, and we shall find that there are references in various parts of Scripture to a primitive Sabbath which not only confirm the common view of the narrative in Genesis ii. 1-3, but, by the incidental way in which they are made, show how unnecessary the sacred writers deemed it to unfold and fortify the obvious meaning of the historian.

1. One of the references is to be found in the account of the giving of the manna. The children of Israel had, in their journeying from Egypt, reached the wilderness of Sin, when they charged Moses and Aaron with bringing them into so inhospitable a region for the purpose of "killing them with hunger." God informed Moses that He was to "rain bread from heaven," that the people should gather a certain rate every day, that on the sixth day they should prepare what they brought in, and that it should be twice as much as they gathered daily. The rulers having reported to Moses this double quantity as "an accomplished fact," he replied, "This is that which the Lord hath said, To-morrow is the rest of the holy Sabbath to the Lord." It is impossible that this last expression could have been employed if there had been no preceding institution of the Sabbath, for in this case there would have been no idea in the minds of the rulers that corresponded with the word "Sabbath," and no fact in their memories of any such observance as is intimated in the phrase, "the rest of the holy Sabbath." The rulers, however, ask no explanation, and Moses gives none either then or next day, when he says, "To-day is a Sabbath unto the Lord." The ordinance,

therefore, existed before this time, and its name must have been a household word. Let us now look at the arrangement of this and the preceding history as it appears to readers in all subsequent time. They have seen, in the beginning of the second chapter of Genesis, a notice of the seventh day as sanctified and blessed, and also the next express mention of such a day in the sixteenth chapter of Exodus. They have found the latter pointing to a pre-existent institution, and have turned to the former as the only account of such a thing in the previous history. They have identified the two. If this be a mistake, they have of necessity fallen into it, not only from the want of any words to guard them against the error, but from the manner in which the historian has arranged his materials and expressed his ideas. The mistake, accordingly, is general, only a few learned men, who had a purpose to serve, having escaped it. If we would not impute to a sacred writer literary inability or intentional deception, we have no alternative but to believe that the Sabbath was instituted at the creation.

2. Within a few weeks after the transactions in the wilderness of Sin,—for the weekly reckoning of time had not been lost in Egypt,—the following words were uttered from Sinai: "Remember the Sabbath-day to keep it holy." The language reduplicates on the earliest notice of the seventh day's rest, and in two distinct forms establishes the antiquity of the institution. It refers to a previously appointed and understood holy day, the only account of the origin and object of which is given in Genesis ii.; and it determines the duty of observing it to have been binding from the beginning, for it is not said, as it would if the obligation had been new, "Wherefore the Lord blesseth the Sabbath-day and halloweth it," but "Wherefore the Lord blessed the Sabbath-day and hallowed it." It is the Sabbath-day, therefore, not merely as observed and confirmed at the giving of the manna, and mentioned abruptly, and without explanation or reasons in Exodus xvi., but as originated at the creation and described in Genesis, that is commanded to be kept in sacred remembrance.

3. We arrive at the same conclusion respecting the original of the Sabbath by comparing the words of Genesis with a passage in the Epistle to the Hebrews. The writer of that Epistle has

been warning the Christian converts from Judaism against the unbelief which excluded their fathers from the rest in the promised land, and which would make them fall short of another rest promised to themselves. This could not be the rest of Canaan, which was now past. Nor could it, he says, be the rest of the seventh day, because this rest immediately followed the creation, and could not therefore remain to be entered into: "For we which have believed do enter into rest, as he said, As I have sworn in my wrath, if they shall enter into my rest: although the works were finished from the foundation of the world. For he spake in a certain place of the seventh day on this wise, And God did rest the seventh day from all his works." "There remaineth therefore a rest to the people of God. For he that is entered into his rest, he also hath ceased from his own works, as God did from his." Without recurring to the service otherwise rendered to the cause of the Christian Sabbath by the argument and language of the apostle which has already been considered, let it suffice in this place to say, that they could have no bearing or meaning, if the rest of the seventh day had not subsisted and been enjoyed from the beginning of time.

4. The self-evident sense of the history in Gen. ii. 1-3 is confirmed by our Lord, when he says, "The Sabbath was made for man."

Let another of those expedients to which the opponents of a primæval Sabbath have been driven in support of their cause, be exhibited for a little in the concentrated light of Scripture. Some have maintained, that the appropriation by Jehovah of the seventh day to beneficent and sacred use contemplated His own good and His own observance, not a benefit to be enjoyed and a service to be performed by man. That He rested on the first seventh day, and was refreshed or satisfied with His work of creation, and that the work and the rest were designed for the ultimate and highest end of His own glory, we readily acknowledge. But the direct purpose of the whole was the good of human beings. For man was all this done, and "for our sakes, no doubt, this is written." This purpose of the Divine procedure neither excluded the benefit of other creatures as a subordinate design, nor interfered with the ultimate end of the Creator's glory, for which man himself and all other beings were made, but was rather tributary to both. As to the Sabbath, the connexion of the words in the narrative of the creation ought to leave no one in doubt that the immediate design of its appointment was the happiness of mankind. When we consider that the work of the six days consisted in the providing of a residence for man, with everything in it to supply his wants, as well as bright luminaries hung over it to give him light, to be for signs and for seasons, for days and for years, and that to man was given dominion over every living thing that moved on the earth—a grant renewed in some respects to Noah and his sons, when, as the representatives of the race, they took possession of the renewed world—we cannot avoid the obvious conclusion, that the proceedings of the seventh day were in like manner designed for the direction and good of human beings. The sanctifying and the blessing of the day must have respected the same being, a being sentient as well as capable of having a time set apart for him ; but Jehovah needed not a day for His own holy use, and could receive no blessing from such a day. And when we extend our induction beyond the words in Genesis—when we consider the great things recorded in other parts of Scripture as done by the Almighty for our race—in the donation to them of the earth—in the co-operation of all events "for good to them who love" Him—in His preference before all temples, before that even of the whole material universe, of "the upright heart and pure"—in the preparation for every one who faithfully serves Him in this world, of a seat with Himself on the throne of heaven—in writing to us the great things of His law—above all, in His manifesting Himself in human nature for man's redemption,—it appears to be only like Himself,—having occupied six days in a work which He could have performed in an instant of time, to rest on the seventh, as an example of order, activity, and repose to us, and to appoint a day of special blessing and sanctity for human happiness and guidance. To this meaning of the Creator's conduct, so transparent in itself, and so entirely in harmony with all His other procedure, the Redeemer has set His seal in the words of the Fourth Commandment, and in His memorable saying, "The Sabbath was made for man."

Our rule, in like manner, satisfactorily disposes of certain philological objections which are advanced against the authority of the Lord's day. The friends of the seventh-day Sabbath, by dwelling so much on certain idiomatic expressions in the original text of Scripture, show how much they regard their explanations of these phrases as among the strongholds of their system. In order to get rid of the Lord's day, they endeavour to show that the expression *μία σαββάτων*, rendered in our Bibles "the first day of the week," cannot refer to this day, but signifies "one of the Sabbaths," or "one day of the week." But what Mark and the other evangelists call *μία σαββάτων*, the former designates *πρώτῃ σαββάτου*, thus determining the meaning of both expressions to be the same, the first day of the week. The females who designed to embalm the body of Jesus did not proceed to fulfil their intention till after the Sabbath, or seventh day, was over, for it is said, "They rested the Sabbath day, according to the commandment,"[1] and "in the end of the Sabbath, as it began to dawn toward the first day of the week, came to see the sepulchre,"[2] when they found Jesus was not there. It was, therefore, on the day after the seventh day, or, in other words, on the first day of the week, that his resurrection occurred. "You say," observes the eminent mathematician, Dr. Wallis, in his controversy with Mr. Thomas Bampfield, "the Greek word *μία* signifies *one*, and *εἷς μια ἑν* is rendered (not *the first*, but) *one*, about an hundred times in our translation of the New Testament; and *μία σαββάτων* (which we translate *the first day of the week*) you render by *one of the Sabbaths.* Now, 'tis very true that *μία* in Greek doth signify *one* (and it may be so translated, for ought I know, as often as you say). But if you were so good a critic as to correct the translation, you might have known that *μία σαββάτων* cannot signify *one of the* Sabbaths, for then it should have been *ἓν σαββάτων*, because *σαββάτα* is the neuter gender. Would you think *una Sabbatorum* to be good Latin for *one of the* Sabbaths? And you do not much mend it when you say, *one of the week*, meaning *one day of the week;* for if by *one*, you mean *some one*, it should then be *τὶς ἡμέρα*, not *μία ἡμέρα*. And Matt. xxviii. 1, it dawned or drew near *εἰς τὴν μίαν* to *the one*, not to *some one day* indefinitely, but to *that certain day* which was known by the name of

[1] Luke xxiii. 56. [2] Matt. xxviii. 1.

μία σαββάτων, and so here [Acts xx. 7] ἐν τῇ μία *in the one*, etc. . . . But since you are now content to allow, that by μία σαββάτων is *generally* meant the first day of the week, and in some places *certainly* so meant, and *may be* so meant in this place, and *probably is* so meant here (to which you may add, that it doth not appear *any where* to be otherwise meant, nor do you offer any reason or pretence of reason *why not* so meant here as it is every where else). I hope you will not be offended with me for calling it trifling to tell us again and again (and yet to insist upon it) that μία signifies *one*. If, in an argument at Westminster Hall, when it doth appear that such a thing was done *one hour* after twelve o'clock, you should still insist upon it that *six o'clock* is *one hour*, and that it is after *twelve*, and therefore this might be at *six o'clock* (or any other hour of the day) and would be thought *in earnest* when you so argue ; you would not be offended if the *Bar* or the *Bench* should take this to be *trifling*, and the best excuse that could be made for it would be, *surely he is not in earnest*."[1]

Again, from the manner in which the time of our Lord's second visit to his disciples is intimated in John xx. 26, "And after eight days, again his disciples were within, and Thomas with them. Then came Jesus, the doors being shut, and stood in the midst, and said, Peace be unto you," it is inferred that eight complete days must have intervened, and consequently that it did not take place on the day which is observed as the Christian Sabbath. In support of this view, it is attempted to explain away a peculiar phraseology common to the sacred writers, customary with other authors, as well as in the ordinary speech of various nations, and understood by all as exclusive, not inclusive, of parts of the first and last days in the series. Thus when it is said in Luke ii. 21, "And when eight days were accomplished for the circumcising of

[1] *Defense of the Christian Sabbath*, Part ii. pp. 34, 36. Dr. Wallis's *Defense* abounds in learning, ingenuity, and a vein of good-natured wit. In pleading that the word *Sabbath*, in Matt. xxiv. 20, and Acts xiii. 42, denotes the Christian Sabbath, he says, in reference to the latter text, "The Gentiles besought that these words might be preached to them the next Sabbath :" "'The next Sabbath' (τὸ μεταξὺ σάββατον) is the Sabbath between or the intermediate Sabbath. Now what can be that intermediate Sabbath (between *two next Sabbaths* of the Jews) on which they should preach to the Gentiles, in contradistinction to the Jews, but the Christian Sabbath on the first day of the week?" None of the commentators that we have consulted adopts this meaning but it appears to us to deserve more consideration than it has received.

the child, his name was called Jesus," the meaning is, not that the child was circumcised on the ninth day, but on the eighth, the day appointed in the law of Moses. It is repeatedly stated that Christ was to rise from the dead after the third day.[1] But Christ is expressly declared to have risen on the third day.[2] Jeroboam and Israel were desired by Rehoboam to come to him after three days.[3] Their coming on the third day (ver. 12), proved this to be the day intended. The Romans used the expression, "*post paucos dies*," after a few days, meaning a few days after. A third-day ague was, in Latin phrase, a *quartan*, one occurring every other day was a *tertian*. The French call a fortnight, *quinze jours*, and a week, *huit jours*, or eight days. And it is common with many amongst ourselves to say, "This day eight days," eight days, in fact, if they include the whole of the first and last day of the series, but only seven, "This day se'n-night," when they count from a certain hour of the first to the corresponding hour of the last.[4]

Dr. Paley and others adduce the following passages as evidence that 2500 years had passed away ere a Sabbatic appointment took place: "I caused them to go forth out of the land of Egypt, and brought them into the wilderness; and I gave them my statutes, and shewed them my judgments, which if a man do, he shall even live in them. Moreover, also, I gave them my Sabbaths, to be a sign between me and them, that they might know that I am the Lord that sanctify them."[5] "Thou camest down also upon mount Sinai, and spakest with them from heaven, and gavest them right judgments and true laws, good statutes and commandments: and madest known unto them thy holy Sabbath, and commandedst them precepts, statutes, and laws, by the hand of Moses thy servant."[6] To insist that such language establishes the origination of the Sabbath at the time to which it refers, requires us no less to believe, that all the other statutes mentioned in connexion with that institution were then also enacted. According to this doctrine, sacrifices, the Decalogue, and circumcision, must have then in the first instance been

[1] Matt. xxvii. 63; Mark viii. 31.
[2] Luke xxvii. 7; 1 Cor. xv. 4.
[3] 2 Chron. x. 5.
[4] *Compare* Esther iv. 16; v. 1.
[5] Ezek. xx. 10, 12.
[6] Neh. ix. 13, 14.

appointed. But sacrifices had been offered as early as the days of Abel; the ten commandments had been in force from the creation, for there are traces of them all in the Book of Genesis: "For until the law sin was in the world, but sin is not imputed when there is no law;" and circumcision had been instituted four hundred years before. How strikingly, as to this last-mentioned ordinance, does the rule of induction expose the fallacy of Dr. Paley's argument! Circumcision, like the Sabbath, is mentioned as given at the commencement of the Levitical dispensation: "Moses *gave* unto you circumcision; not because it is of Moses, but of the fathers."[1] No less decisive is another example. While it is said, "Thou madest known unto them thy holy Sabbath," it is in other parts of Scripture declared, "He showeth his word unto Jacob, his statutes and his judgments unto Israel." But Abraham knew the word, statutes, and judgments of God, though not so fully, yet as substantially as his descendants, else it could not have been said of him: "I know him, that he will command his children and his household after him, and they shall keep the way of the Lord, to do justice and judgment; that the Lord may bring upon Abraham that which he hath spoken of him."[2] The explanation of "the giving of Sabbaths," "the making known of God's holy Sabbath," "the giving of right judgments and true laws, good statutes and commandments," "the showing of his word, his statutes and his judgments" to Israel, as compared with earlier gifts and commandments to mankind, is, that laws and institutions previously appointed and known were at Sinai, with superadded ceremonies and political statutes, formally promulgated, committed to writing, and organized into a regular system. This was a great boon, indeed, but it no more disproves the antecedent institution of the Sabbath than it does that of circumcision, or of the existing laws requiring honour to parents, and respect for property and human life. Still less do the words, "I gave them my Sabbaths to be a sign between me and them," convey the idea of an entirely new gift. This is manifest from Deut. vi. 4-9, where it is said, "Hear, O Israel; The Lord our God is one Lord: and thou shalt love the Lord thy God with all thine heart, and with

[1] John vii. 22. [2] Gen xviii. 19.

all thy soul, and with all thy might. And these words, which I command thee this day, shall be in thine heart; and thou shalt teach them diligently unto thy children—and thou shalt bind them for *a sign* upon thine hand, and they shall be as frontlets between thine eyes. And thou shalt write them upon the posts of thy house, and on thy gates." The law, which was a sign to Israel, was to "go forth out of Zion," and did go forth. And so the Sabbath, notwithstanding any local or temporary purpose served by it, might be destined to be, as it has in reality become, a law and blessing to mankind.

Some of these remarks serve to introduce another mistaken view of the laws of Moses. The writers in question confound things that differ, blending together the moral, ceremonial, and civil laws of the Jews. Dr. Paley, for the purpose, we presume, of showing that the Sabbath must have taken its rise in the wilderness, and in connexion with the Jewish economy, adduces some adjuncts of the institution as it existed under that economy. He mentions, in the first place, the strict cessation from work, enjoined by the law of the Jewish Sabbath upon Jews and all residing within the limits of the State, the permission of such cessation to their slaves and their cattle, and the punishment of the violation of this rest with death.[1] Now, here, that able writer conceives of the Fourth Commandment, and of certain judicial regulations, peculiar to that people and time, as if they were the same thing. But the penalty of death, forming a part of the political law, which assigned the same punishment to idolatry and disobedience to parents, is not specified in the Fourth Commandment. The political law, except in so far as it expressed the eternal principles of morality, was the law of a nation only in which the Church and State were one, and is not therefore generally applicable to any other nation. It might be as justly affirmed that duty to parents was a peculiarity of Judaism, beginning and ending with it, as that the observance of the Sabbath was such a peculiarity, since the one as well as the other was, by the law of Moses, required on pain of death.[2] As Dr. Paley does not cite instances from Scripture of strictness in the injunction of rest, but only facts in the conduct of the Jews, we will not go with him into this

[1] Exodus xxxi. 15.

[2] Deut. xxi. 18, 21.

subject, observing only that what the Fourth Commandment required in this matter must not be identified with anything really burdensome, or with oppressive ceremonies added by the Jews, since the institution which it regulated was to be called "a delight, the holy of the Lord, and honourable."[1]

"Besides which," says Dr. Paley, "the seventh day was to be solemnized by double sacrifices."[2] These sacrifices, however, as compared with those offered in some other festivals, were not burdensome. Whether the former were required before the time of Moses we are not informed. In the temple-worship described by Ezekiel, and not without good reason supposed emblematically to portray the state of things in the Christian Church, the sacrifices of the Sabbath were to be still more numerous.[3] The double sacrifices under the law make nothing against the early origin and permanent obligation of a day of sacred rest. They were shadows of good things to come, to pass away when the substance was realized, but as types have their corresponding realities, so these sacrifices and those described by Ezekiel appear to have prefigured not only the sacred services of the future Christian Sabbath, but the multiplication on that day of religious observances which their own simplicity, the spirituality of the worshippers, and a larger supply of Divine influence, would render a yoke that should be easy and a burden that should be light.

The "holy convocations"[4] which Dr. Paley further adduces as a characteristic of the Mosaical Sabbath, although in the case of the Jews connected with ritual observances that were more frequent and organized than in the times of the patriarchs, and belong not to Christianity, have always been practised from the period when men began to call on the name of the Lord down to our own day. The same law which gave authority to the Patriarchal and Jewish convocations requires "the assembling of ourselves together" for the simpler services of the Christian worship.

The distinction, however, between the various laws of Moses, although lost sight of in some cases, as we have seen, is at other times recognised by Dr. Paley, who does not hesitate to rank the Jewish Sabbath among merely ritual appointments. "The dis-

[1] Isa. lviii. 13.
[2] Num. xxviii. 9, 10.
[3] Ezek. xxvi. 4.
[4] Lev. xxiii. 3.

tinction of the Sabbath," he observes, "is, in its nature, as much a positive ceremonial institution, as that of many other seasons which were appointed by the Levitical law to be kept holy, and to be observed by a strict rest; as the first and seventh days of unleavened bread; the feast of Pentecost; the feast of Tabernacles: and in Exodus xxiii. the Sabbath and these are recited together."[1] One important difference between the Sabbath and the other institutions here compared, however, is that none of the latter has a place in the Decalogue. Dr. Paley sees something in the recital of the twenty-third chapter of Exodus, but nothing in the recital of the twentieth chapter. He himself overturns his only proof of the preceding statement by afterwards producing cases in which "ceremonial and political duties, confessedly of partial obligation, are enumerated along with others which are natural and universal," "the distinction between positive and natural duties, like other distinctions of modern ethics, being unknown to the simplicity of ancient language."[2] We object not to his taking one or other of the grounds that the juxtaposition of subjects is or is not an evidence of their character, but it is too much to urge that the Sabbath is a positive duty because classed with ceremonies, and not a moral duty because included in an enumeration of matters belonging to morals. There are undoubtedly instances in which the two classes of subjects are intermingled, but not when laws are formally enacted or proclaimed, and when accuracy, order, and the interest and intelligent obedience of those to be ruled by them, require that they should be placed in their respective categories. And our minds must be peculiarly constructed or biassed, if, considering the Decalogue as consisting of laws not only of universal concern, but carefully detached from political and ceremonial statutes, and alone announced in circumstances of special solemnity and grandeur, we can discern no difference in character between a precept prohibiting idolatry or murder, and one forbidding to touch a dead body, or to plough with an ox and an ass together.

The other reasons assigned by the same writer for regarding the Sabbath "as part of the peculiar law of the Jewish policy," if more consistent, are not much more weighty, than the one now

[1] Paley's *Works*, vol. iv. p. 296. [2] *Ibid.* pp. 297, 298.

examined. He says, "If the command by which the Sabbath was instituted be binding upon Christians, it must be binding as to the day, the duties, and the penalty ; in none of which it is received." He might have as well said, The command of worship given to the Jews, if binding on us, must bind us to go to Jerusalem at certain times for that purpose, to practise circumcision, and to observe the passover with all the other sacrifices. He might have said, The command of reverence in worship, if applying to us, must require us to put off our shoes, and to direct our eyes to a holy place, made with hands. He might have said, If the law which obliged the Jews to abstain from idolatry and to honour their parents be obligatory upon us, it must be so in both cases on pain of death. Again, he alleges, the observance of the Sabbath was not one of the articles enjoined by the apostles in Acts xv. upon them "which from among the Gentiles were turned unto God." The enumeration referred to in this passage makes nothing against the institution, as it is not complete in respect of either ritual or moral duties, and is utterly irrelevant to the writer's purpose. But it is relevant to the purpose of proving the opposite of what it is adduced to establish. The decision of the Synod of Jerusalem was, that the Gentile believers were to abstain from certain things which were offensive to their Jewish brethren. And as nothing would have been more offensive to those Christians who had formerly been Jews than the neglect of a day of rest on the part of the converts from among the heathen, the absence of any injunction to keep such a day indicates that no offence existed on that score. Finally, it is affirmed that "St. Paul evidently appears to have considered the Sabbath as part of the Jewish ritual, and not obligatory upon Christians as such : 'Let no man judge you in meat, or in drink, or in respect of a holy day, or of the new moon, or of the Sabbath-days, which are a shadow of things to come ; but the body is of Christ.'"[1] These words have been already noticed. Let us add a very few remarks. The passage goes to protect Christians against attempts to impose upon them the Jewish *ceremonies* of distinctions of meat, and the distinctions of such days as holy days, new moons, and Sabbath-days. But the Fourth Commandment was not ceremonial. There was no

[1] Col. ii. 16, 17.

ceremony in a season of rest and devotion on a seventh day more than in the diligent labour of the other six. If the Apostle vindicated their right to keep no day holy, he also vindicated their right to occupy no day in a secular calling. If they were left free to have every man his own day of worship, they were left free also to disregard the anciently appointed season of industry. That some professing Christians had taken up these loose notions appears from the reproof which the same Apostle addresses in another epistle to the disorderly persons who made every day a day of rest. How obvious that by the Sabbath days the Apostle cannot mean a day of holy rest absolutely viewed, but the days fixed of old among the Jews, including the particular day of the ancient Sabbath, which as being all typical had been fulfilled in Christ, and any imposition of which now involved a rejection of Him! It was with the former weekly resting-day as with circumcision, there was to be a bearing with Jewish prejudice; but as the attempt to compel Gentiles to be circumcised was condemned by the Apostle as an infringement of their rights, and as even involving a renunciation of Christianity, so for the Jews to judge Gentile converts in regard to meats and days was also an infraction of their liberty, and an act of constructive treason against Christ as their risen Saviour, and the author of a finished redemption. This was more than the law of Moses itself had required, as Gentiles might be proselytes without being bound to the ceremonies of that law.

It thus appears that various theories and arguments militating against our doctrine are incapable of standing before the application of the just and Divine rule which requires us to "compare spiritual things with spiritual." To give one more example, how completely does a writer, acting on this rule, overthrow the tenet of an every-day Sabbath in two sentences! "Some indeed here argue: it [the New Dispensation] is more spiritual, because we consider every day a Sabbath; we are every day to live to the glory of God. But was not this the duty of the people of God in former times as well as now, and this did not prevent a seventh part of their time being immediately consecrated to the Divine service."[1]

Fourth Rule.—It must be remembered that the mind and will

[1] Innes's *Christ. Sab.* p. 62.

of God are made known to us in various modes. It would be a serious mistake in any reader of the Bible to conceive that the Divine Being must be limited to an express declaration for every truth that He propounds, and to an express command for every duty that He enjoins—that He cannot convey his thoughts in the different forms of explicit affirmation, figurative language, examples, or statements from which conclusions are to be drawn—and that He may not utter to a few individuals matters of universal concern, as well as, for the benefit of a small circle, frame laws of general and abiding importance—that He may not, for example, announce to Adam a catholic Sabbath, or to the small nation of the Jews an everlasting gospel and a world-embracing Decalogue. This would be to deny to the Supreme a right which we ourselves frequently exercise; this would be to refuse to the All-wise and the All-kind, the ability or the disposition to communicate with us after the manner of men—a mode of communication which in condescension and mercy to the creatures of the dust He has ever employed. If we will not follow this obvious rule for coming to the knowledge of the truth and our duty, we must walk on in darkness.

This rule is transgressed by an opinion which has led to much error on our subject, and which is itself demonstratively erroneous. The opinion is, that, because there is no formal command in the narrative of Genesis ii. 1-3 for the observance of the seventh day, or in the New Testament for the observance of the first day of the week, we have no proof that either a primitive Sabbath or the Lord's day has, or ever had, the force of a law. The error takes its rise in a preconceived notion of what is necessary as evidence on this subject. When we look into the sacred volume, we find that the Divine will may be made known by actions or by statements, from which we have to infer our duty or privilege, as well as in a directly preceptive or declaratory form. If express statute were in every case required to constitute obligation, then no law of marriage was enacted in Paradise, because the Creator merely performed an action and pronounced a benediction; no real, because only an inferential, prohibition of murder was uttered in the words, "Whoso sheddeth man's blood, by man shall his blood be shed;" and in the promise, "They shall not teach every man his neighbour, and every man his brother, saying, Know the Lord," there is no actual, because no explicit, injunction to every Christian to impart religious instruction to others so long as all know not the Lord from the least to the greatest. On the same principle, there never existed even a Jewish Sabbath, for both in the wilderness of Sin and at Sinai the commands respecting a day of rest refer to a previous gift and law, of which, however, we have no record except in the narrative of Genesis. The principle, therefore, must be false. It is false, for from the case of the law of marriage, which our Lord declares was from the beginning, and from the other cases named, we learn that actions and statements, without the formality of a precept, have been employed to express "the will of God concerning us." It is false, for nothing is more certain than the existence of a Jewish Sabbath, promulgated in the Decalogue, not, however, as a new, but as an old institution, founded on the work and rest of the first week of time. "If they hear not Moses and the prophets, neither will they be persuaded though one rose from the dead."

Let us present another instance of the violation of a divinely given law of Scripture interpretation. It has been held to be a just objection to the general and permanent character of legislation, that it has been connected with local and temporary circumstances. This is an unfounded objection, and calls in question a rule according to which the infinite Intelligence has seen it meet to act in divulging saving truth and human obligations. It has been the Divine method to make known matters of universal concern in connexion with particular places and occurrences, and to present them, not in cold abstractions, but as naturally springing up amidst the business and occasions of human life. Thus the appointment of deacons grew out of the circumstances of the Apostles and the increasing accessions to the Church. The Lord's Supper was instituted by Christ in the presence only of his disciples, and a renewed revelation of its divine authority arose from the abuses which certain individuals had introduced, and was given only to one church. A great part, indeed, of the instruction which we find in Scripture respecting the everlasting and catholic truth as it is in Jesus, was addressed to churches and individuals of the first age of Christianity. It was the same in times still more remote. The very earliest notice of a Saviour was not directly addressed to the world, which it was intended to encourage and bless, but to the great enemy of the Saviour and of man. And other animating promises, which have cheered the people of God in all subsequent time, were made to individuals. From the remarks now made we should be led to expect, and prepared to account for, the embedding as it were of laws, susceptible of the most extensive and enduring application, in a phraseology and in allusions of a local and temporary character. And yet the actual specialties in the Decalogue are so few and so clearly consonant to the universality of its import and bearings, as to show how careful the Lawgiver was to render it inexcusable for any one to reject its right and claim to be the law of the world. There is the preface, "I am the Lord thy God, that brought thee out of the land of Egypt and out of the house of bondage." Strictly speaking, the preface or preamble does not enter into the law. In the present case, it is the Gospel rather than a part of the Law. How obvious the principle implied, which is, that the mercy of the Lawgiver, especially as exhibited in the work of Redemption, is the mighty inducement to do His will; for when we consider the faithful among Israel as constituting with Christians one Church, "the seed of Abraham," and "heirs according to the promise," and that the redemption from Egypt was a type of the great redemption, as well as a step to its accomplishment, it does not require what is called an "accommodation" to apply this preface far beyond the typical deliverance, and to regard it as pointing to the infinitely more influential motives to obedience that are supplied by a spiritual and everlasting salvation. There is also this promise to filial obedience, "That thy days may be long upon the land which the Lord thy God giveth thee." The apostle Paul does not hesitate to apply the fifth commandment, and its promise too, to the children of Christian parents, "Children, obey your parents in the Lord: for this is right. Honour thy father and mother, which is the first commandment with promise, that it may be well with thee, and thou mayest live long on the earth." And, once more, the second commandment has annexed to it a threatening and a promise, which may be conceived by some to be applicable only to the Jews: "Visiting the iniquity of the fathers upon the children unto the third and fourth generation of them that hate me; and showing mercy unto thousands of them that love me and keep my commandments." But both the curse and the blessing were attached to the law of God long before it was given at Sinai, and have extended far beyond the boundaries of Judea, as well as endured long after the Mosaic economy had ceased. Was there anything Judaical in the blessing pronounced upon Shem and Japheth, or in the curse uttered against Ham? Did not both the curse and the blessing begin to take effect before the time of Moses? Have they not continued to operate in all nations? And are not their effects perceptible in the circumstances of the descendants of Noah even at this hour?

Fifth Rule.—There are matters, external to the Word of God, which serve to illustrate its import, as well as to establish particular meanings, and which cannot be innocently, or without injury, overlooked. The understanding of Scripture, as of other writings, is aided by our "intermeddling with all wisdom." It is the glory, indeed, of that Book that a person devoid of erudition may learn there all that he needs to know for his salvation, duty, and eternal happiness. But such a person, though uninitiated in the learning of the schools, has access to valuable means of illuminating to him the page of Revelation—means, in the events of Providence, in the knowledge of himself, in the experience of the truth, in the observed conduct of others, and in his own obedience to the Divine law—all of which pour a flood of illustration on the meaning, and of evidence on the authority, of the Sacred Volume. The more generally intelligent the reader is, however, the more is he prepared to profit by its study. "Ye shall know them by their fruits." "The secret of the Lord is with them that fear Him." "If any man will do the will of God, he shall know of the doctrine, whether it be of God." "Wisdom and knowledge shall be the stability of thy times."

The testimony of the Fathers to the meaning of the expressions, "the first day of the week," and "the Lord's day" (see pp. 368-370), the "fruits" of the weekly holiday considered as a Divinely-appointed day of entire rest and worship for all ages (pp. 173-266), and the history of septenary observances in Pagan and Christian countries (pp. 359-455), satisfy the conditions of this rule to the effect of showing that the above-defined institution has the appointment and sanction of Revelation. As to all other doctrines and practices in the matter, we ask, Where is the external evidence by which they are proved to be authorized in the Word of God—evidence in the events of Providence, in the experience of good, and the consciences of bad men, in the superior virtue and happiness of individuals and families, in the purity, progress, and active benevolence of churches, in the peace, enterprise, and prosperity of nations? The only answer that is or can be returned, is that of Echo shouting, Where?

Sixth Rule.—This is contained in the words: "The light of the body is the eye: therefore when thine eye is single, thy whole body also is full of light; but when thine eye is evil, thy body also is full of darkness. Take heed, therefore, that the light which is in thee be not darkness."[1]

Seventh Rule.—If we would study the sacred volume to any right and good purpose, we must continually apply for help to its Author, who, as is in a limited sense true of human authors, must be best acquainted with His own work. Without His direct teaching neither its truths nor its laws can be understood and estimated. This is owing not to any imperfection in the Record, for "the law of the Lord is perfect," but to the blinding prejudices and passions of the human mind. It is only as we are purged from this influence by the Holy Spirit, that we shall clearly see the light, and truly receive the testimony, of Heaven. The best of all means for understanding the Word of God in regard to the Sabbath, as to all other matters, is thus described: "Trust in the Lord with all thine heart; and lean not unto thine own understanding. In all thy ways acknowledge him, and he shall direct thy paths." "Open thou mine eyes, that I may behold wondrous things out of thy law." "If any of you lack wisdom, let him ask of God, that giveth to all men liberally, and upbraideth not; and it shall be given him. But let him ask in faith, nothing wavering. For he that wavereth is like a wave of the sea, driven with the wind and tossed. For let not that man think that he shall receive any thing of the Lord."

Let it not be said, The world is without the means of know-

[1] Luke xi. 34, 35.

ing that this or that person is favoured with "the single eye" or with the spirit of dependence upon "the Father of lights," in the study of Scripture, and, therefore, Rules 6 and 7 can afford no help in deciding between contending opinions in this controversy. Not only, however, are these rules necessary to the discovery of the truth, and thus to the practical and experimental settlement of the dispute, on the part of each individual, but they are also relevant and important as means of enabling us to adjudicate on conflicting opinions even in open court. Honest and earnest inquirers "cannot be hid." There are churches and communities in which the love of truth and the spirit of devotion have manifestly prevailed. And as the Divine promises to men of such a character cannot fail, the irresistible conclusion is that in these societies right views of the Sabbath have been on the whole attained, and attained in proportion to the simplicity of the aim and the measure of the piety. To identify these successful inquirers, we should have only to repeat the names, already given in this volume, of those classes of men, at home and abroad, who are most signalized at once by the sacred observance of the weekly rest, by their reverence and love for the other institutions and laws of Jesus Christ, and by their zeal in extending them over the earth.

CHAPTER VII.

THEORIES TRIED BY DIVINE PREDICTIONS.

The Pentateuch is by far the oldest historical record. There we find it stated that the seventh day of time was blessed and sanctified by the Creator of the heavens and the earth. Various references in the history of the Patriarchs, and many vestiges of the institution among heathen nations, admit of but one explanation, which is, that it had been continued from the beginning of time. When the children of Israel came out of Egypt, their lawgiver and leader referred to the day of rest as an appointment with which they were acquainted. The Saviour declared without challenge, that Moses was read in the synagogue every Sabbath-day. We have also the testimony of Josephus and Philo to the existence of the institution during the Jewish ecomony. In the writings of Isaiah, besides promises to those who should observe the Sabbath, of an everlasting name, and of a place in the house of prayer for all people, which plainly point to the times of Christianity, we have this prediction and pledge: "For as the new heavens, and the new earth, which I will make, shall remain before me, saith the Lord, so shall your seed and your name remain. And it shall come to pass, that from one new moon to another, and from one Sabbath to another, shall all flesh come to worship before me, saith the Lord."[1] And to mention only one other intimation regarding the perpetuity of the Sabbath, the Founder of Christianity said, eighteen hundred years ago, concerning the law, of which the Sabbath was a part, "Till heaven and earth pass, one jot or one tittle shall in no wise pass from the law, till all be fulfilled."[2] These words have been verified down to this day. We can trace the never-failing observance of the Sabbath for eighteen centuries prior to

[1] Isa. lxvi. 22, 23.
[2] Matt. v. 18.

the present time. Thus far, then, the language of Christ and of Isaiah has held true. The ordinance, indeed, has not been universal, and only by some maintained in its purity, but its preservation and true observance among any and so many in all ages, establish the truth of the foregoing promises respecting it, and thus its own Divine authority. Nor are the instances in which the Sabbath is abolished or lost unavailing as evidence on its behalf. They are adducible to establish its Divine authority, as they are the fulfilment of another class of predictions—those, we mean, which have foretold its withdrawal as the result of its abuse. But the fulfilment of prophecy does more than prove the truth of the Divine Word as respects the promised continuance of the institution. It enables us to decide between contending theories relative to other aspects of the subject, and it is to this point that we are now to call the attention of our readers.

First of all, the accomplishment of prophecy settles the questions that have been raised respecting the proportion of time and the particular day of the Christian Sabbath. The words lately quoted from the prophecies of Isaiah stand connected with his glowing descriptions of the sufferings of Christ, and the glory that should follow, both in His own exaltation and in His benignant reign over the earth. Of the happy times of the new heavens and the new earth, or the Christian dispensation, when the Gentiles should be brought for an offering unto the Lord out of all nations, it is declared, "And it shall come to pass, that from one Sabbath to another, shall all flesh come to worship before me, saith the Lord."[1] Then, again, when the prophet Ezekiel had his vision of the Temple—a vision, which, as we have already shown, applying neither to the Jewish dispensation, nor *literally* to the Christian, must be considered as a *figurative* representation of the latter; he was inspired to utter these words: "And it shall be, that upon *the eighth* day, and *so forward*, the priests shall make your burnt-offerings upon the altar, and your peace-offerings; and I will accept you, saith the Lord God."[2] Here we have a day, a weekly day, and the eighth day, not the eighth day of a week of eight days, but the eighth day in reference to the ancient, then common, and still prevalent week, the day after its

[1] Isa. lxvi. 23. [2] Ezek. xliii. 27.

seventh day; in other words, the first day of the week. Two facts are unquestionable: *first*, that the seventh day of the Jews has never been the generally recognised day of rest and worship among Christians; and, *second*, that the first day of the week, frequently by the Fathers called the eighth day, has ever been the Christian Sabbath. The theories, therefore, which propound respectively an "every-day Sabbath," a "no-day Sabbath," "the seventh-day Sabbath," "a half-day, or a two-or-three-hours' Sabbath each week," do not agree with the predictions to which we have referred, and are on this, as they are on other grounds, excluded from the right to compete for the honour of being Divine institutions.

Further, Prophecy defines the engagements of its promised weekly holy day. That holy day is not merely named a Sabbath, a rest; but has concomitants of duty which are incompatible alike with idleness and with secular pursuits. It was to be a day of worship. They "shall come and worship before me;" "I will make them joyful in my house of prayer;" "It shall come to pass in the last days, that the mountain of the Lord's house shall be established in the top of the mountains, and shall be exalted above the hills; and all nations shall flow unto it. And many people shall go and say, Come ye, and let us go up to the mountain of the Lord, to the house of the God of Jacob; and he will *teach us of his* ways, and we will walk in his paths: for out of Zion shall go forth the law, and the word of the Lord from Jerusalem."[1] Here, again, the every-day Sabbath is shown to be contrary to Scripture prediction, as it is to Scripture rule. A Sabbath of worldly pleasure and amusement has no place assigned to it under Christianity. A Sabbath devoted in whole or in part to the study of science and art is not provided for. Christians were to be made joyful, but it was to be in the house of prayer, and were not to do their own pleasure on God's holy day. They were to be occupied in studying nobler and more important things than science or art. Popery has fulfilled the Sabbatic predictions of Scripture in some respects, but not in the amount of time, not in intelligent devotion, not in religious instruction. The Scripture is fulfilled by those only who devote the weekly holy day, with

[1] Isa. ii. 2, 3.

the exception of so much time as is due to the objects of necessity and mercy, entirely to rest and religion.

Prophecy, which indicates the means, indicates also the manner of worship in Christian times. A blessing is pronounced on the man who should not only keep the Sabbath from polluting it, "but keep his hand from doing any evil."[1] In the same chapter, promises of better blessings and higher honours than those of this world are made to those who should keep God's Sabbaths, and choose the things that please Him, among which things are "loving-kindness, judgment and righteousness in the earth:" for "in these things," He declares, "I delight;" and to "the sons of the stranger," the Gentiles, "that join themselves to the Lord, to serve him, and to love the name of the Lord, to be his servants, every one that keepeth the Sabbath from polluting it, and taketh hold of my covenant," it is pledged that they should be made joyful, and be accepted in their worship, by Jehovah. In another chapter (lviii.) we are informed that the observance of the Sabbath was to consist not only in turning away the foot from the Sabbath, from doing one's pleasure on God's holy day, but in calling the Sabbath a delight, the holy of the Lord, honourable. The doctrines of an "every-day Sabbath," of "the Sabbath as an ecclesiastical or political arrangement," or of the Sabbath as a day that may be given partly to pleasure or business, and partly to religion, are utterly irreconcilable with the standard of excellence thus presented. It is only the doctrine of a solemn and yet benignant statute, of a careful, conscientious, and yet cheerful, affectionate Sabbatism, that, according to the words of Scripture, fulfils the claims of the institution. It is the Puritan's and Covenanter's holy day, not the Continental holiday, that copies the Divine model, and it is just in proportion as this is done, that the man is happy.

Pledges of happiness, prosperity, and honour, are given to the individual who thus hallows the day of rest. "Blessed is the man that keepeth the Sabbath from polluting it." "Every one" that did so was to be "made joyful." "A place and a name" "better than of sons and daughters," "an everlasting name," were to be given to all such persons. He that delighted in the

[1] Isa. lvi. 2.

Sabbath, and honoured God, not doing his own ways, or finding his own pleasure, or speaking his own words, was to delight himself in the Lord. And we have found, accordingly, when pointing out "the advantages" of the institution, that it brings good in every form to the individual who duly observes it, good to his body and mind, to his moral and religious character, to his circumstances and name. The experience of the conscientious observers of the Lord's day, attests the faithfulness of Him who promises thus to reward his servants. Those certainly who have made frequent use of an instrument are competent to speak of its worth, and if, besides being men of known veracity, their evidence of its efficiency is such as every one may see in their case and try in his own, their testimony must be unexceptionable. Few have been more qualified by both character and profession to pronounce a correct judgment respecting the value of the Sabbath than the distinguished Sir Matthew Hale, whose views, besides, were the result of careful attention to the subject, and confirmed by the experience of a long life. "I have," are his words, "by long and sound experience found, that the due observance of this day, and of the duties of it, have been of singular comfort and advantage to me; and I doubt not but it will prove so to you. God Almighty is the Lord of our time, and lends it to us; and as it is but just that we should consecrate this part of that time to him, so I have found, by a strict and diligent observation, that a due observation of this day hath ever had joined to it a blessing upon the rest of my time, and the week that hath been so begun, hath been blessed and prosperous to me; and on the other side, when I have been negligent of the duties of this day, the rest of the week hath been unsuccessful and unhappy to my own secular employments; so that I could easily make an estimate of my successes in my own secular employments the week following, by the manner of my passing of this day: and this I do not write lightly or inconsiderately, but upon a long and sound observation and experience."[1] Similar was the experience of a lawyer of great talents, who on his death-bed said to his friend, "Charge every young lawyer not to do anything in the business of his profession on the Sabbath. It will injure him, and lessen the pro-

[1] *Contemplations* (Lond. 1676), pp. 480, 481.

spect of his success. I have tried it. I do not know how it is, but there is something about it very striking. My Sabbath efforts have always failed."[1] We find the same experience, in the medical profession, expressed by Dr. Farre, Mr. Hey, and, as has been said, by one of its brightest ornaments, Boerhaave. Persons invested with the sacred office have felt in the same way. "I never find it well," was the remark of Dr. Doddridge, "on common days, when it is not so on the Lord's."[2] To the like conclusion, "that there was a special blessing vouchsafed to the keeping of that day devoted to spiritual purposes," was Mr. Wilberforce led in his different field of labour;[3] and he relates that he remained at home one Sabbath to write a letter to the Emperor Alexander on the abolition of the slave-trade, conceiving it to be his duty, and even supplicating the Divine blessing on the act, "yet it did not answer," he observes; "my mind felt a weight on it, a constraint which impeded the free and unfettered movements of the imagination or intellect; and I am sure that this last week I might have saved for that work four times as much time as I assigned to it on Sunday."[4] The instances in which mercantile men, sailors, tradesmen, and mechanics, have been sensible of a connexion between their use of the day of rest, and their success in their several undertakings, are too numerous for detail. We select one. The learned and enterprising Captain Scoresby, in an account of one of his whaling expeditions, makes the following remarks: "It is worthy of observation, that in no instance, when on fishing stations, was our refraining from the ordinary duties of our profession on the Sunday ever supposed eventually to have been a loss to us, for we in general found, that if others who were less regardful, or had not the same view of the obligatory nature of the command respecting the Sabbath-day, succeeded in their endeavours to promote the success of the voyage, we seldom failed to procure a decided advantage in the succeeding week. Independently, indeed, of the Divine blessing on honouring the Sabbath-day, I found that the restraint put upon the natural inclination of the men for pursuing the fishery at all opportunities, acted with some advantage, by proving an extraor-

[1] *Permanent Sabbath Documents*, No. 4, p. 51.
[2] *Memoirs* by Orton, 2d ed. p. 236, n.
[3] *Life*, vol. ii. p. 292.
[4] *Life*, vol. iv. p. 179.

dinary stimulus to their exertions when they were next sent out after whales. Were it not out of place here, I could relate several instances, in which, after refraining to fish upon the Sabbath, while others were thus successfully employed, our subsequent labours succeeded under circumstances so striking, that there was not, I believe, a man in the ship who did not consider it the effect of the Divine blessing."[1]

In the same ancient document, in which a blessing is pronounced on the individual observer of the sacred day, are benefits assured to the Sabbath-keeping community. Such a community was to ride on the high places of the earth.[2] And it has been shown that the tendency and actual results of national respect for the weekly day of rest and devotion have been most beneficial to all the interests of society. Britain and America, the countries in which that day is most sacredly regarded, do indeed verify the language of the prophet, and realize the promised pre-eminence among the nations. Let the confession of M. de Montalembert, already cited,[3] bear a just testimony to the truth of prophecy respecting the Sabbath, and thereby to the Divine original of the appointment. Let the following words of other foreigners confirm his judgment, and conduct us to the conclusion which so many facts in the preceding pages conspire to establish. "Impartial men," says one, "are convinced that the political education by which the lower classes of the English nation surpass other nations—that the extraordinary wealth of England, and its supreme maritime power—are clear proofs of the blessing of God bestowed upon this nation for its distinguished Sabbath observance. Those who behold the enormous commerce of England, in the harbours, the railways, the manufactories, etc., cannot see without astonishment the quiet of the Sabbath-day."[4] Another says: "Amongst the French whom the Great Exhibition has brought to London, there are some who are usefully impressed with the quiet and order which reign on the Sunday in the capital of Great Britain. I know a Roman Catholic politician, formerly Minister under Louis Philippe, who has been singularly struck by this.

[1] *Journal of a Voyage to the Northern Whale Fishery* (Edin. 1823), 382, 383, and note.
[2] Isa. lviii. 13, 14. See also Jer. xvii. 24, 25. [3] Page 250.
[4] *Religious Condition of Christendom*, p. 469.

He said, a few days ago, to one of my acquaintance, who repeated it to me, that if it were possible to lead the French to pass their Sunday like the English, much would be gained for the repose of the mind, which would act as a moral preservative upon the soul." The writer states that, in addressing from twelve to fifteen hundred persons at the Oratoire in Paris, on the 29th of June 1851, he remarked as follows: "It is but three weeks ago that he who now addresses you was on the other side of the Channel, in the capital of Great Britain. He saw there a wonder greater than that of the immense and magnificent Crystal Palace, which encloses, as it were, the epitome and compendium of all the industrial treasures of the known world; he saw a free, a peaceful, a happy people, moving forward, without hindrance, and without revolution, in the path of progressive improvement, loving their laws, loving their Government, respecting authority, rich, prosperous in all their concerns. Would you know why, my brethren? It is especially, and above all, because they are a people who know and invoke, at least among the majority of their members, the God that I preach to you; it is because public worship is there offered in His temples; it is because the day which is consecrated to Him is religiously observed; it is because His Word is read, and prayer is offered in the family; it is because that people are convinced that Jehovah reigns, and that there is no happiness for a nation, as there is none for a family or for an individual, but in the love of His Word and obedience to His commandments. 'Happy is the nation,' says the prophet, 'whose God is the Lord.'"[1]

The universal prevalence of a day of rest and worship is foreshown in the sacred oracles. There are declarations which suppose that some time everywhere is to be religiously occupied: "All the ends of the world shall remember, and turn unto the Lord: and all the kindreds of the nations shall worship before thee. For the kingdom is the Lord's; and he is the governor among the nations."[2] "From the rising of the sun, even unto the going down of the same, my name shall be great among the Gentiles; and in every place incense shall be offered unto my name, and a pure offering: for my name shall be great among the heathen,

[1] *Religious Condition of Christendom*, pp. 305, 306. [2] Ps. xxii 27, 28.

saith the Lord of hosts."[1] But not only is there to be universal worship, but a seventh proportion of time, and a particular day, are to the same extent to be consecrated to sacred purposes. In confirmation of our statement, we again quote these words: "From one Sabbath to another shall all flesh come and worship before me, saith the Lord."[2] "It shall be, that upon the eighth day,"—the first day of the week,—"and so forward, the priests shall make your burnt-offerings upon the altar, and your peace-offerings; and I will accept you, saith the Lord God."[3] Although these predictions are not yet fulfilled, they have not failed, as the time for their accomplishment, fixed and declared in the same record, is still future. The conversion of the Jews, and the removal of a professedly Christian but corrupt system, must take place, it is intimated, before the true religion can be universal. As so great an enterprise as the regeneration of the world requires much time, we might presume that there would be evidence of its gradual progress. What, then, is the religion that has for the longest period maintained its ground, and at the same time, by present appearances, promises to take possession of the earth? Only the religion which fully recognises the perpetual and the sacred weekly rest. Paganism, with its unenlightening, uncheering, bloody rites, whether annual, monthly, or even weekly, everywhere yields to Christianity and civilisation. Mohammedanism, with its inefficient Friday, is on the wane. Popery has been a long-continued proof of the ignorance, immorality, and pauperism, which holy-days, with superstition and without the gospel, inflict on society; and totters to its fall. Socinianism, depending on the merely human both for its heartless Christianity and its cold Sabbath, shows itself unable to extend or even to maintain itself. The Friends, who are not all Gurneys or Clarksons as to the Sabbath, date their denominational existence so late as from about the middle of the seventeenth century, and by 1852 numbered in Great Britain and Ireland only from 18,000 to 20,000. The seventh-day Sabbatists have ever been a small body. The every-day Sabbatists have hitherto been not only few, but far between. And the friends of a merely ecclesiastical or political holy day have never done much to bless the world, and, happily, not much more to extend their

[1] Mal. i. 11 [2] Isa. lxvi. 23. [3] Ezek. xliii. 27.

faith. There is but one class of religionists who make steady progress, and these are Christians who believe in a Divine, permanent, holy Sabbath. These have their missions, their converts, their sacredly observed Lord's day in every part of the world,—tokens that they are fulfilling the ancient oracles of a blessed and extended Sabbatism, and that men of like views who shall come after them are destined to realize the completed purpose and boon.

Thus the terms of prophecy respecting the Sabbath of Christianity have been fulfilled only by the theory which recognises the first day of the week as consecrated by Divine authority to sacred rest and service. While other theories, when tried by this test, are found wanting, that which has been generally received and practised by Christians proves itself to be of God, and destined to continue to the end of time, as well as to be universal in the earth.

THE CLAIMS OF THE SABBATH PRACTICALLY ENFORCED.

DESECRATION OF THE SABBATH—ITS NATURE.

It has been indiscriminately and confidently affirmed that the Jews were required to keep the Sabbath with a strictness which is not demanded of Christians. It is true that the institution as belonging to the Mosaic economy involved more physical labour than is now necessary, and that its judicial penalty imparted to it a severity which is not congenial to the free spirit of Christianity. But with the exception of such circumstances—which belonged to a temporary economy, to the accidents not the substance of the Sabbatic law—we are under that law as much as the Jews were. It has not modified to Christians the other precepts of the Decalogue that they too have been detached from the Levitical ceremonies and the political law of Judaism. No one will affirm that a Christian is not to be as strictly obedient to parents, or as rigidly truthful and honest in his dealings, as was the Jew. The prohibition to the latter of going out of his place on the seventh day, refers to the unnecessary work of gathering manna, on that day. The law forbidding the kindling of a fire on the Sabbath must, from its connexion with the account of the rearing of the tabernacle, and from our Lord's exposition of the Fourth Commandment, in which he vindicates the performance of works of necessity and mercy on the day of rest, be understood of such an action as had respect to secular work, or as was not indispensable. The Jews, no doubt, made the law of the Sabbath rigorous by their additions to its requirements, but we are to take our views of

Sabbatical duties from the Bible, and not from the opinions or practices of its corrupters. The privileges of Christians are greater than those of the ancients; but as it would be no privilege to be less truthful and honest than they were required to be, so it would be no blessing, whether for body or soul, to have the day of sacred rest abridged. The addition which Christianity makes to our privileges is designed and fitted to raise us to closer conformity to the demands of the law. It is never the exactness of compliance with the letter of any law that the Scriptures condemn, but attention to the mere letter—the form without the power of godliness.

Having set forth so fully the duties of the Sabbath, it is not necessary that we should enlarge on those omissions and acts by which the institution is profaned. We will do little more than name them as they are admirably presented in the *Westminster Shorter Catechism.* The Sabbath is profaned by *the omission of its duties.* If the house of God be forsaken, if the preaching of the Gospel, the public celebration of Divine praise, and the offering of prayer, collecting for the poor, observing the Lord's Supper, and the cultivation of domestic and personal piety be neglected, not only are these ordinances and claims of our religion set at nought, but the day of the Lord is not devoted to some of its most sacred and important objects. The day is profaned by *idleness.* To take advantage of its leisure for doing nothing, is to pervert the day of Him who rose early on the first day of the week, and, both before and after his resurrection, redeemed in holy and beneficent works the season sacred to the immediate service of God. The Lord's day is profaned by *the careless performance of its duties.* All these should be performed with the vigour and ardour which love and delight inspire, and not in the spirit and manner thus described: "Behold, what a weariness is it!"[1] "When will the new moon be gone, that we may sell corn? and the Sabbath, that we may set forth wheat?"[2] The Lord's day is profaned by *the doing on it of anything which is in itself sinful.* Whatever the sin—intemperance or theft, for example—it is made double by being perpetrated on that day. "Moreover, this they have done unto me; they have defiled my sanctuary in the same

[1] Mal. i. 12, *et seq.* [2] Amos viii. 4, 5

day, and have profaned my Sabbaths. For when they had slain their children to their idols, then they came the same day into my sanctuary to profane it; and, lo, thus have they done in the midst of mine house."[1] The Lord's day is profaned by *unnecessary thoughts about secular matters.* The people of Israel are blamed because their hearts on the Sabbath and in the sanctuary went after their covetousness. We are not to find our own pleasure on that day; these things "choke the word," interfere with every spiritual exercise and enjoyment, and are offensive to Him who demands our whole attention and interest on His own day. And he who has faith in God will comply with His requirement, casting all his care upon Him, and seeking his happiness in the things that are above. The Lord's day is profaned by *unnecessary words about the world.* "Not speaking thine own words." This "honours the Lord."[2] And the Lord's day is profaned by *unnecessary secular work.* Not doing our own ways on that day honours Jehovah.[3]

SABBATH DESECRATION AT HOME.

It is the confession of foreigners, as we have before noticed, that in no country, except it may be America in some places, is the Lord's day so well observed as in our own. But to compare the state of Sabbath observance with that of other lands, and not with the standard of piety and morals in the Scriptures, and to rest satisfied with our condition, would not be wise. While others, judging of us by themselves, bestow commendation, we, estimating ourselves by "the law and the testimony," shall see so much in our own conduct to condemn as ought to fill us with shame on account of our transgressions of the Divine law. And as this volume is especially intended for the good of our own countrymen, it is proper to be more particular in the scrutiny of our errors than we should deem necessary in searching into those of our neighbours.

The Lord's day is extensively desecrated in this country by secular labour. We should be very inconsiderate or ungrateful if we did not cordially acknowledge the manifold advantages enjoyed by

[1] Ezek. xxiii. 38, 39. [2] Isa. lviii. 13. [3] *Ibid.*

us under the British Government, and the benefit which it has done to the Sabbath cause by its resistance of attempts to assimilate its character to that of the Continent. But one of the expressions of right feeling towards our rulers is to show them wherein they err. And it is under the influence of this feeling, we trust, that we must condemn any measure of theirs by which the law of a higher power is transgressed. We will advert to two forms in which they are accessory to the infraction of the Divine law by patronizing secular labour on the holy Sabbath.

One is in the department of Police. The Metropolitan and City Police Force form a large body, who, although appointed to be guardians of property and of the public peace, in general "live almost without regard to religion or thought of another world, few if any of them enjoying at any time an uninterrupted Sabbath." Measures were adopted some years ago for securing the presence at Divine service, upon the Lord's day, of those of them who were not on duty, but no means of this nature will avail so long as the number of men is so inadequate to the amount of the duty to be done. It is certainly most unjust to these servants of the public, and most impolitic, as all wrong must be, to commit to them an amount of service which precludes a due attention on their part to their moral and religious interests.

The other form in which the Divine law is set aside by the law of man in this land is in the business which is authorized to be done on the Sabbath in the department of the Post-Office, involving thousands of persons in multifarious labours connected with the running of mails, and the sorting, despatching, and delivery of letters, not to mention a far greater number who by these means are induced to occupy themselves in the reading and writing of letters, and the reading of newspapers on the Lord's day. To this may be added the labour which the system produces as acted on in the Colonies.

It is truly gratifying to reflect that there is a considerable, we trust a growing number of our nobility and gentry, who esteem it their highest honour to obey the laws of the Most High, but with too many the Lord's day is the selected time for travelling or for entertainments, and forms no exception to the parade with which they appear in the scenes of public resort. For their convenience and pleasure the labours of thousands, whom the preceding week has sufficiently employed and exhausted, must be drawn upon, to the abridgement of liberty and life, and to the ruin of the soul.

Medical men, it is admitted, are occasionally under the necessity of practising their art on this day. But how many calls are made, prescriptions written, and surgical operations performed, which might have been arranged to occur on another day! Some of our best-employed and ablest practitioners have guided their affairs with such discretion and diligence as to admit of their regular attendance in the house of prayer. It is sad that persons who so well know the need which the physical system has of a periodical rest should act in opposition to their knowledge, and in violation of their own rules; and that, familiar with disease and death, they should lose the best season for pondering their own coming change, and teach others to go and do likewise.

There are many of the legal profession to whom the Sabbath brings no rest. Forgetful of the law of God, their care is to study the rules of human jurisprudence, and the laws of the land. When they ought to be making ready for the last assize, and securing the inheritance that fadeth not away, they are too often engaged in preparing to plead before an earthly tribunal, or in examining the titles to property that must soon pass from the possessors into other hands. Important transactions in themselves, but wofully mistimed! "I do not think," said a Scottish lawyer, when examined by a Committee of the House of Commons, "that in Edinburgh there are any who transact as much business on Sunday as on other days; but there are many, I believe, who do carry on business, more or less, upon that day. I know at the same time that there is a proportion who decline business on that day."[1]

Even the ministers of religion themselves may not be found blameless in this matter. It is possible that as the physicians of the body avail themselves of their professional liberty to labour unnecessarily on the day of rest, so the physicians of the soul may take improper advantage of the maxim, that "on the Sabbath-days the priests in the temple profane the Sabbath, and are blameless."[2] Is there no unnecessary travelling to fulfil sacred appoint-

[1] *Report on the Sabbath for* 1832, p. 201.

[2] Matt xii. 5.

ments? Are there no studies, which, though their subjects are theological, are as really secular labours as the studies of law or science? And have there not been Protestant as well as Roman Catholic clergymen, who, when they have dropped their canonicals, have shouldered their fowling-pieces or other implements of to-morrow's sport?

Judging from the biographies and writings of men of science and literature, it appears that not a few of them make little distinction between God's time and their own.

How much prostitution of sacred time is involved in the labours of the newspaper press may be in some degree estimated if we bear in mind the fact, that there is a circulation of eighteen millions of newspapers which leads in one way or another to the desecration of the Lord's day.[1]

The most numerous class of persons, however, who are chargeable with doing habitual dishonour to the Sabbath are those who are engaged in trade of various kinds on the day, and those who spend it in idleness, recreation, and pleasure. Referring to Baylee and other writers for the statistics on these points, we can only add a few words to show the extent of Sabbath desecration in this country. As the results of an exact calculation made in some of the largest towns in England, it is found that in place of five-eighths of the population repairing regularly to places of worship, as would be the proportion so employed were religion in a healthy condition, the case is nearly the reverse. Out of a population, for example, of 30,000, the number absent for good reasons would be 11,000, and the number in attendance ought to be 19,000; but only 10,000 are found in the house of God, while 20,000 live in the constant neglect of this part of their duty. In London, the proportion of absentees is not so great, but the absolute number may be reckoned at the enormous amount of 650,000. In Edinburgh, according to a late City Mission Report, there are localities where two-thirds of the people live in the neglect of Divine ordinances, and others where the proportion is still greater, the number altogether of those who are living in this manner being 60,000. In the smaller towns, and in rural districts, the people have not in such numbers cast off the fear of God. According to

[1] Baylee's *Statistics*, p. 8.

the census of 1851, 5,288,294 are absent every Sunday from the house of God.

This fearful extent of ungodliness is chargeable in different measures on all classes of the community. Much of it belongs to persons of rank, to professional men, to merchants, clerks, and others. But a very large proportion of the evil attaches to the labouring population. In the Report for 1849 of the London City Mission, we are informed that "the neglect of public worship among the working classes of the metropolis, and especially the men, is almost universal." Similar and equally recent is the testimony of the Directors of the Edinburgh City Mission, where they say, "What strikes one most is the breaking off of the working classes from the public ordinances of Divine worship, their disregard and even hostility to Christian ministers." It is stated of a working man in England that he had made a point of learning how his shop-mates spent the Sabbath, and that he had found that an awfully irreligious feeling had taken possession of the minds of a great majority of them, not one in ten, and sometimes not one in twenty attending a place of worship, and the majority looking down upon the churches and chapels as built not for them, but for the masters and middle classes who get their living by oppressing the poor workmen. This is the alleged reason of one class. But there are many who will tell you that they cannot go to church and also cook their dinner. Yet there are many, too, in the situation of the dying boatman, who, when his master endeavoured to give him religious instruction and consolation, observed, "You forced me to break one of God's commands, and when I broke one, I thought there was little use in trying to keep the others."[1] "In the least unfavourable aspect," says Mr. Mann in his remarks prefixed to his Report on the Census of 1851, "and assuming that the 5,288,294 absent every Sunday are not always the same individuals, it must be apparent that a sadly formidable portion of the English people are habitual neglecters of the public ordinances of religion. Nor is it difficult to indicate to what class of the community this portion in the main belongs. The middle classes have augmented rather than diminished that devotional sentiment and strictness of

[1] Baylee's *Statistics and Facts*, p. 65.

attention to religious services by which, for several centuries, they have so eminently been distinguished. With the upper classes, too, the subject of religion has obtained of late a marked degree of notice ; and a regular church attendance is now ranked amongst the recognised proprieties of life. But while the labouring myriads of our country have been multiplying with our multiplied material prosperity, it cannot, it is feared, be stated that a corresponding increase has occurred in the attendance of this class in our religious edifices. More especially in cities and large towns it is observable how absolutely insignificant a portion of the congregations is composed of artisans. This [secularism] is the creed which probably with most exactness indicates the faith which virtually, though not professedly, is entertained by the masses of our working population. They are *unconscious secularists*, engrossed by the demands, the trials, or the pleasures of the passing hour, and ignorant or careless of a future."

SABBATH DESECRATION ABROAD.

Although our proper subject is the manner in which the Christian Sabbath is treated, it may not be altogether out of place simply to glance for a moment at the kind of Sabbatism which obtains among two classes who recognise in part only the Divine revelation.

Among the Jews there is a variety of practice in regard to the observance of their Sabbath. Messrs. M'Cheyne and Bonar state that when they visited Altona, which contained 2600 Jews, they found many of their shops were opened though it was their Sabbath.[1] They also mention the following fact : Mr. Moritz, before his conversion from Judaism, was on a visit to London, and on inquiring of a Jewess, in whose house he lodged, why there was such quietness in the streets on a Lord's day, was answered, " The people of England are a God-fearing people, and if we had kept our Sabbath as they keep theirs, Messiah would have come long ago."[2] And yet it is affirmed that there are Jews in foreign lands who are more strict than their English brethren ; some going to the extreme of observing the day with

[1] *Narrative of a Mission to the Jews*, p. 518. [2] *Ibid.* p. 512.

uncommanded rigour, and regarding even the extinguishing of a fire as a violation of the Sabbath.[1]

The Mohammedans have also their weekly Sabbath. In Constantinople, we are told, it is a day of universal sport and diversion.

"Friday," says a traveller, "is the Sabbath of the Mohammedans, as that was the day on which Adam, they say, was made, and the day on which the resurrection will take place. Christians are prohibited from attending their mosques during public worship, and females, without being expressly forbidden, are ordered to pray at home on the Sabbath, which it is alleged they never do."[2]

Turning to those who profess themselves Christians, we advert, first of all, to the Greek and other Eastern Churches. How the Sabbath is spent by the members of the Greek Church may be learned from the following statements of Bremner: "In Russia it is impossible to escape being struck with the way in which the Sabbath is kept. People are everywhere busy at work in the fields, and the market-places, in all the provincial towns, are crowded with peasants selling potatoes, mushrooms, apples, turnips, cucumbers, etc., just as on the ordinary week-days. In short, Sunday seems to be the great fair-day in most parts of Russia."[3] Among the Nestorians there are various festivals in which, as on the Sabbath-day, they do not labour; but, as one of them said, "the Sabbath-day we reckon far, far above the others." In the Armenian churches "there are at least fourteen great feast-days in the course of the year in which all ordinary labour is suspended, and the day is more strictly observed than the Sabbath."[4]

The disregard of the true law of the Lord's day is proverbially prevalent in all Roman Catholic countries. The notorious practice of the body of Romanists in every region of the earth where they are to be found is to limit the sacred duties of the day to the time of mass. The remaining hours are devoted to secular business or to pleasure. The desecration is various in circumstances

[1] *The Jew*, pp. 40, 41. [2] Anderson's *Visit to Eastern Lands*, p. 26.
[3] *Excursions in Russia*, vol. ii. p. 291.
[4] Coleman's *Antiquities of the Christian Church* (Lond.), p. 205.

and measure, but what we have stated is the usual character of a Popish Sabbath. It is unnecessary, therefore, to fill our pages with illustrative cases. A few may suffice. In Madeira, when the priest's voice is silenced, and the candles are extinguished, the Sabbath is over. Multitudes parade the street with guitar and song, and the evening gathers in its votaries of gaming, and dancing, and folly. It is otherwise with the holiday, on which no work must be done, and the churches are full. Thus there is idleness where God has commanded toil, and profaneness where He has commanded rest.[1] To the French Canadian people, the Sabbath, at least after those hours which the Church of Rome claims for her service, is a day of sport and pleasure ; and with the dance, the chase, or at the tavern, do they often cheat away its sacred hours. Nor is the conduct of the priest less suicidal, for at the whist-table, or in equally unsuitable occupations, this "blind leader of the blind" not unfrequently gives to his people the example of trampling on the Lord's day.[2] Among the 575,000 Roman Catholics in Lower Canada there is no holy Sabbath, and the afternoon of the day, both by priests and people, is made a season of recreation and pleasure. And the Sabbath with them is not considered half as sacred as their set holidays. The afternoon of the day is a peculiar time for trading and trafficking in horses and cattle.[3]

We have in another place cited the account of the Sabbath in Spain given by Mr. Meyrick, who states that to the poor man in that country it brings no rest, all in-door trades being carried on, and that to the rich it is a day of pleasure, of bull-fights and theatrical amusements. The author of *Souvenirs of a Summer in Germany* says of a Sunday which she spent in Brussels : "All the shops are open, stalls in the streets, etc., and the every-day business of life no way interrupted. While we were at breakfast, Guillaume came in to say, that if Monsieur wished to have his coat repaired, the *ouvrier* was outside and would have it done in an hour ; and he seemed quite disappointed at not being allowed to take it. Shortly after, tickets were sent

[1] State of Religion in Madeira, *Christian Herald* for 1843, p. 251.
[2] *Record of French Canadian Society.*
[3] Rev. Joel Fisk, *Christian Treasury* (1851), 189.

in for the theatre that night, with the compliments of the British Minister."

The writer has spent Sabbaths in several continental towns, and must say that nowhere did he witness so utter a prostitution of the sacred day as in Paris, where the morning was signalized by the sale and reading of newspapers, the day by busy merchandise and labour, and the evening by crowded cafés and brilliantly lighted places of amusement. A correspondent writes in the *Record* newspaper in 1841 : "In Paris, tailors, shoemakers, and all who supply articles of dress and ornament, are fully occupied on Sunday morning. Many of the working classes work on Sabbath, and rest during the week. This is the case, too, with those employed about theatres, shows, etc. The great majority of the French abstain on Sunday, as on every other day, from any religious act ; and the few who differ are content to go and hear a mass. They do this on the way to the country, or at some village where they go for sport. They praise a man by saying he is a horse, and works on feast-days and Sunday." In the best description which we have seen of a Paris Sabbath, but which is too long for transcription here, it is mentioned that that day in the capital, and almost universally in French territory, the shops are open ; the *restaurants* and coffee-houses are more than usually splendid ; the theatres more numerously and eagerly frequented than on other days ; that all the artisans work on Sunday and rest on Monday; that marriages invariably take place amongst the lower and the middle classes on the Saturday, because they have Sunday before them for rest or amusement ; that balls are similarly given on Saturday, because after a night of dissipation they have Sunday for rest ; that, in short, Sunday is the chosen day for military reviews, the inauguration of public buildings and public festivals ; the day for excursions, balls, promenades, concerts, and festivities of all sorts."[1]

Let us now see how it is with the day of rest in foreign Protestant countries. The following account of a Sabbath in Berlin is too applicable to other parts of Protestant Germany : "The

[1] *Religious Condition of Christendom*, pp. 303-305. "Ce bienfait est méconnu en France —comme il ne l'a éte nulle parte et jamais."—Montalembert, *De l'Observ. des Dimanches*, etc. p. 7.

Sabbath desecration of Berlin is most lamentable. It is not like the gay pleasure-days of Paris, nor like the day of show and parade in London, but it is like a common business day. Most of the shops are open and busily frequented, and most of the people wear their week-day clothes. In the evening, it was saddening to see the large theatres open and lighted up. Guilty city! Paris sins in comparative ignorance, but Berlin sins against the light of a faithfully preached gospel, and the testimony of many holy believers."[1] "For aught I know," says Mr. Plitt, "there is not one town in all Germany where the theatres are closed on the Sabbath."[2]

Mr. Rae Wilson, in his *Travels in Norway, Sweden*, etc., says, "No regard is paid in these countries after church to the Divine command, 'Thou shalt keep the Sabbath holy,' for the afternoon is spent by all classes in singing, dancing, visiting the theatre, and other kinds of merriment. This appeared to me highly indecorous, considering that the Norwegians and Swedes profess the Protestant faith, and cannot be said to labour under the darkness of the Romish Church" (p. 125). Sabbath observance would appear, indeed, to be of a lower tone in all the Lutheran communities than in those of the Reformed Church. Mr. Laing, in his *Travels in Norway*, says, "It is a peculiarity in all Lutheran churches which strikes the traveller, especially from Scotland, that the evening of Sunday is not passed as with us, in quiet and stillness at least, if not in devotional exercises. He must be a very superficial observer, however, who ascribes this to a want of religious feeling. It arises from the peculiar, and in the Free Lutheran Church universally received interpretation of the scriptural words, that 'the evening and the morning made the first day.' The evening of Saturday and the morning of Sunday, make the seventh day or Sabbath, according to the Lutheran Church. This interpretation is so fully established and interwoven with their thinking and acting, that entertainments, dances, card-parties, and all public amusements take place regularly on Sunday evenings" (p. 190). Mr. Laing adds that "a Lutheran minister gives a party on Sunday evening at his house at which you find music, dancing,

[1] *Narrative of a Mission to the Jews*, p. 507.

[2] *Religious Condition of Christendom*, p. 479.

and cards," and "would think it superstiticus to object to it." But do the Lutherans shorten their own days as they do the Lord's day? If not, the apology of the charitable traveller will not avail them. The state of the Sabbath in America is much what it is in the mother country. And yet, we were not prepared for a late statement in one of the Boston papers, to the effect that a musical society in that city were giving public concerts on the Sabbath evenings.[1]

CAUSES OF SABBATH DESECRATION.

The human mind is naturally unwilling to stoop to authority, even when that authority may be interposed in favour of a work not repulsive to it. Many dislike to be told to do what they are inclined to, and will on this very account do the opposite. But to be required to do what is contrary to our inclinations is doubly offensive, and to have to continue in such a course exasperates the feelings beyond all endurance. There is nothing in any Divine requirement that is not holy, just, and good—that is not in itself reasonable, beneficial, and pleasant. In the heart of man, however, there is that which converts all into gloom, oppression, injustice and misery. "The carnal mind is enmity against God; for it is not subject to the law of God, neither indeed can be." Now, because the Sabbath requires total abstinence from thought and occupation relative to the things of the world, which are supremely loved, and the concentration of the spirit on all that is spiritual, and thoroughly hated, the whole opposition of the person to the Divine law is stirred against the all-comprehending statute, "Remember the Sabbath-day to keep it holy." The result is either such a constrained observance of it as excites the feeling, Behold what a weariness is it!—When will the Sabbath be gone? or a bold renunciation of the yoke, and a joining with others in the unholy confederacy of plotting against the day itself, "Let us break their bands asunder, and cast away their cords from us."

This is the secret source of bitterness against one of the wisest and most benign of institutions; the principle which gives potency

[1] *Montreal Witness*, March 11, 1855.

to all influences of an external nature, and to all arguments against the consecration of an entire day to the service of Him who is regarded as an enemy. But for this state of mind, how would it be possible for any rational being to resist the evidence for the Sabbath, presented in its own apparent wisdom, simplicity and beauty, in the plain statements of Revelation, and in the actual results of its observance in the formation of a personal excellence in thousands such as is produced by no other means, and in a social dignity, purity, and happiness by which Sabbath-observing communities are so distinguished above all others? Let us learn, however, from this cause of opposition to the Lord's day, that our chief endeavour must be to encounter it by the only means capable of fully meeting and dislodging it, and of securing both a genuine and abiding respect for the Divine Commandment, that Word of the Lord which transforms the dispositions of the heart, that armoury of spiritual weapons which are mighty through God for pulling down strongholds.

It would be well if the opponents of the Sabbath were to consider the imposition which they practise upon themselves in giving heed to the calumnies listened to, or invented by them against the friends of the institution as persons of narrow, bigoted notions, and in mistaking their own prejudices and prepossessions for argument and truth. It would be well for them to ponder their proceedings, the more that able men may advance much that is ingenious and plausible in support of a bad cause, and that such ability may serve only to place a man more hopelessly beyond the reach of that truth which is obvious to simpler and more unsophisticated minds. Let them consider, too, that many have thought like them respecting the Sabbath, but have lived to lament their opinions, or have died retracting them. No inconsistency in professed Christians, none of the subsidiary agencies or neglects now to be mentioned as contributing to their state of mind, will free them from responsibility. Their own dislike to the Sabbath is at the foundation of all their views and feelings on the subject, and that dislike is voluntary, uncoerced, and criminal.

We fear that much of the prevailing desecration of the Sabbath is owing to the apathy and evil example of its professed friends.

We have no sympathy with those who take advantage of the errors of individuals to condemn and expose classes of men. But we trust that we commit no such fault, when, recollecting the power of the sacred office for evil or for good, we affirm that some of those holding that office have done much to promote the desecration of the Lord's day; that others have done too little to arrest the evil; and that many, than whom none will be readier to acknowledge the fact than themselves, have not done what they could to vindicate the claims and to diffuse the spirit of the day of rest. Truth requires us to say that the desecration of the Sabbath in Roman Catholic countries is attributable in a great measure to the priesthood, who having so much control over their people, withhold from them the Word of God, and both by precept and example teach them that they sufficiently fulfil the demands of the Sabbath law by attending once on the service of the mass, while, instead of appealing to the legal tribunals when the evil becomes too much even for them, they could by moral means have secured at least an external decency of character on the Lord's day. But there are Protestant clergymen who are even worse than they, inasmuch as they offend amidst the clearer light and better profession of the Reformation. When such men are found significantly pointing their flocks to the discarded festivals of Rome as worthy of their admiration; when they are seen performing the most sacred offices of religion with manifest indifference or with pompous display; when they are not careful to declare all the counsel of God, the grace of the gospel as well as the claims of the law; when they prophesy smooth things, and when they are chargeable with immoralities, worldly conformity, or profaneness, what is to be expected but that there shall be, like priest, like people? The misconduct of the clergy had no small influence upon the celebrated Earl of Rochester, as he himself confessed, to make him an atheist. The increase of Sabbath desecration in Germany had its origin in times when infidelity was spread by the universities amongst the clergy, and by the clergy amongst the people.

But the members of churches have their influence and responsibilities. Those who profess to be Protestants, hold it as a part of their creed that they have a right to bring the sentiments and practice of their spiritual guides "to the law and to the testimony." They are ready enough to exercise this right in matters of worldly concern, and it will not avail them to allege, in reference to moral and religious things, that they followed the example of their pastors. Many of these pastors, besides, have taught and done what was right, and their people are found failing to profit by their instructions, and to walk in their steps. We are entitled, therefore, to separate the members of churches from their ministers, and to view them as a distinct and independent source of influence in regard to the observance of the Sabbath. Every professed Christian who is careless in this respect contributes to the discouragement of faithful ministers, to the impairing of the power of Christianity, and to the corruption of society in a degree which is incalculable. Let us refer to one principal mode in which the improper conduct of such persons operates. We refer to the want of parental care and example. While many, like Abraham, command their children and households after them to do what is right, there are others who resemble Eli, of whom it is said that when his sons made themselves vile he restrained them not. "You attribute," said the chairman of the Sabbath committee of the House of Commons, when examining Mr. H. F. Isaac, a Jew, "the observance of the Sabbath on the part of the Jew, to the force of early religious education?" "I am satisfied it is so," was the reply. We may conceive a variety of ways in which heads of families professing religion, do what tends to defeat as to them its great end. One is frequently called from home, and his house on the Lord's day is exposed to intrusion from the worldly men with whom he is connected in business. The result is, that a numerous family grow up practical pagans. Another leaves his family very much to themselves; and while some are constrained by early affliction to direct their attention to matters of chief moment, others become the disgrace of his name. A third is so much occupied with attending religious meetings, and with the theory of religion, that his children are in a great measure neglected, and what they learn is a sort of form of godliness, so that none of them gives decided indications of Christian character. A fourth is so stern and harsh in his discipline respecting Sabbath-keeping and other duties, that the effect of freedom from parental control is the bounding to a worse extreme. But cases accumulate to the view beyond the possibility of being recorded in our allowed space, and impress us with the conviction that parents have much to answer for in reference to prevailing Sabbath desecration. A London City Missionary says, "I have never discovered a single case of juvenile delinquency where the child had been the subject from infancy of the double teaching by precept and example in the ways of Christ, at the hands of parents, both of whom were evidently truly converted to God. I do not strain the promise so far as to believe such is *never* the case; I simply state the result of systematic inquiry and studies of human nature, pursued most extensively for years, at no small pains."[1]

There are other forms, however, in which the injurious influence of professed friends of the Sabbath is exerted. The conversation which takes place when persons are congregated about the house of God, or when they meet with their friends, goes to produce the impression that they recognise no difference of day, so far as that is concerned. There are those who take liberties with the Sabbath by visits to their acquaintance, under the delusive persuasion that they still maintain the sanctity of the day by attending church at the stated time of service. There are others who indulge themselves on that day with walking or in feasting. To these we must add a class who subject many to unnecessary labour by employing vehicles in going to church. We cannot conceive a better use of such conveniences than conveying the infirm and the sickly to the house of God, when this is so done as to interfere with no servant's religious rights and benefit on the Sabbath. But this condition is often violated. It should seem that "it is a common thing for persons to ride on Sundays to their places of worship,"[2] and that some go considerable distances for this object.[3] That this is not necessary, appears from the different conduct of "the religious persons of Islington, who are proverbial for not riding in omnibuses on Sundays."[4]

A large proportion of Sabbath profanation is chargeable to the account of the higher and wealthier classes of society. Many of

[1] Notes, etc., by R. W. Vanderkiste, p. 250.
[2] Baylee's *Statistics*, p. 79.
[3] Baylee's *Statistics*, p. 79.
[4] *Ibid.* p. 80.

these classes corrupt others by their example. The disposition to throw off the restraints of religion is ready to avail itself of some apology or encouragement. And nothing is more likely to furnish it than the conduct of our superiors in station. A writer on Sabbath desecration in Germany says, "Persons of high rank gave a very bad example, and the people followed it willingly. The officers of the government were seen very seldom at public worship. During the morning you found them generally in their offices, in the afternoon on some pleasure party, and in the evening at the theatre."[1] In the evidence on the Sabbath given before a committee of the House of Commons in 1832, the influence of the example of the upper classes in inducing their inferiors to mis-spend the Lord's day is amply attested. "The opportunity of knowing, through the public press and other sources, how the higher classes of society generally, but more particularly in the metropolis, are employed on the Lord's day, has a powerful influence on the minds of the lower classes, as a temptation or encouragement in their habits of Sabbath profanation."[2] "When you have endeavoured to enforce the duty of observing the Sabbath upon the lower classes, do they frequently allege the example of those in a higher sphere of life in justification of their own neglect, and violation of that day?' "Continually; and, in more than one instance, the meeting of Cabinet ministers on that day."[3] "I have met with instances where the lower classes have said, 'The greater ones do it'—buying fish on Sunday—'and why should we not do it?'"[4]

Then how many unnecessary works and pleasures of the great and rich make it in some sort imperative on tradesmen and others to encroach on sacred time. The journeys undertaken that might have been arranged for another day, the entertainments that might be postponed, the luxury of a particular dress, or article of food, or newspaper, these things, so utterly contemptible, involve many human beings in Sabbath labour, to the loss of the weekly rest required by their physical powers, and of the means of spiritual good indispensable to their higher being and interests.

[1] *Religious Condition of Christendom* (1852), p. 466.
[2] Report, Evidence of Mr. D. Rowland, p. 94.
[3] Evidence of Rev. J. W. Cunningham, Harrow, p. 177.
[4] Evidence, p. 101.

What is the penalty of the gratification of such desires to their victims, but slavery, sin against their great Master, shortened life here, and the forfeiture of the better life hereafter? "Masters and men are wholly employed during the day, and more so on the Sunday, because many noblemen and gentlemen who are members of Parliament, have more company on Saturday and Sunday, these being the only leisure their parliamentary duties afford them, consequently there is more done on these days than on others."[1] "Amongst the nobility and gentry there is most business done on Saturday and Sunday."[2] "From the nature of your business, do you see any means of diminishing your occupation, as long as the upper classes continue to give dinners on that day [Sunday]?" "I do not see that there is." . . . "Then, speaking as a conscientious man, it would be agreeable to you if the upper classes of society did fix on other days rather than Sunday for their great dinners?" "I should most decidedly say so, as far as regards myself individually, and the comfort and happiness of my servants; for I consider it to be a duty that I owe them to relieve them as much as possible from their duties on Sunday; whether they employ it in religious subjects, or in any other manner, it gives them the opportunity, if they think proper, to improve it; and if they do not, it still affords them the same advantages which most other people enjoy, that is, a day of repose after a week of hard work."[3]

To masters and employers of workmen another large share of Sabbath desecration must be ascribed. While many tradesmen, forty-nine out of fifty in London, desire to be relieved from Sunday trading, there are many others who are influenced by the cupidity and speculation so prevalent in our time voluntarily to bind fetters on working men in place of the holy and merciful restraints of the Sabbath law. Let us hear the following statements on this latter point: "Does the journeyman get additional wages for working on Sunday?" "None at all." "Then it is only the desire of gain on the part of the master that induces them to go

[1] Report, Evidence of Mr. J. B., Fishmonger, p. 96.
[2] Report, Evidence of W. D., Fishmonger, p. 104.
[3] Report, Evidence of Mr. J. Chaplain, proprietor of Clarendon Hotel, Bond Street, pp. 127-8.

on?" "That circumstance is the whole of it."[1] "Is there a general desire on the part of the tradesmen in Richmond to see the Sunday better observed than it is at present?" "I think there is with one part, but the other part are more anxious to get money."[2]

In defence of this reckless spirit, which, for the sake of money, disregards the law of God and the rights of man, it is pleaded that it is impossible to avoid it, and that in the general race and rush they must do like others if they would not be distanced in the course, or run over in the crowd. But what is in opposition to those Divine statutes which forbid and condemn the too eager pursuit of gain, the hastening to be rich, and the "adding of house to house, and laying field to field, till there be no place, that they may be placed alone in the earth," admits of no apology. The spirit is not only ungodly, but selfish and unfeeling as regards the interests of those whom it employs to be the instruments of its gratification, turning them into beasts of burden or mere machines, and caring not, if they serve such a turn, what becomes of their mental improvement, their souls, their everlasting interests. Mammon is indeed a cruel God, who has no regard for the flesh and blood, the noble faculties and feelings, the precious souls which his votaries sacrifice in his honour. Many examples there are to be found indeed in the commercial world of men who really feel for their workmen, and provide for them the means of promoting their health, comfort, and instruction. There are our Buxtons and other kindred spirits. Where, however, human beings are persuaded that the great object of life is to be rich, how can we suppose that they will allow their dependants time and opportunity for that mental and moral culture, of the value of which to themselves, and especially to working men, they have no just conception?

There is one way in which employers promote the desecration of the Sabbath that has not even the plea of the smallest contribution to their advantage or pleasure. We refer to the payment of their men at a time that exposes the latter to various temptations and injuries, and in some cases necessitates the infraction of the Divine law. There have been instances in which

[1] Report, Evidence of Mr. J. C., Jr., Baker, Richmond, p. 189. [2] *Ibid*, p. 190.

wages were actually paid on the Lord's day. It is not long since this was done in some parts of England, cases few, we trust, and now discontinued. It was proved in the evidence from which we have been quoting, that masters, by not paying their men till Saturday night, obliged them to make Sunday marketings, which occasioned crowds on Sabbath, subjected the workman to increased expense, and made him abstain from going to church ; and that there was no necessity for Sunday marketing.[1]

There are influences from without which do much to lower the general tone of religion and morals, and to foster Sabbath desecration. One kind of influence affects chiefly the upper and middle ranks of the community, that originating in their intercourse with foreigners. It is not to be supposed that the visits of our countrymen to the Continent, so multiplied of late by the facilities of communication, can have been without considerable injury to our national customs and manners. Familiarity with a secular Sabbath tends to abate a sense of the evil. A partial attendance in the house of God, and occasional absences, cease to be considered as anything wrong. And the frivolity and demoralizing amusements of other lands fascinate the mind and corrupt the heart.

Another species of influence has had its sphere of action among the remaining class of society. The immigration of so many natives of the sister island has been felt in an immense addition to the poor-rates, in defeating attempts to repress crime and disease, and in bringing down our comparatively instructed and moral population to their own level, and in some cases below it, as the impetus in consequence of the greater height fallen from must be greater. All this must be unfavourable to a regard for sacred institutions. But as the persons imported bring with them a religion which recognises only a fraction of a Sabbath, their practices on that day come to be regarded with decreasing aversion and fear, and in course of time to be imitated.

The defective, erroneous, and worthless opinions propagated through the press form the only other cause of the evil in question which we have to name. Among these opinions are deficient and incorrect views with regard to the institution itself We pre-

[1] Report, Evidence, pp. 29, 30.

sent a specimen or two. The first concerns the Continent. "You know," observes the Rev. T. Plitt of Bonn, "that an opinion prevails in our country that there is no real connexion between the Christian Sunday and the command of God, 'Remember the Sabbath-day to keep it holy;' but that the Sunday celebration is a human institution which must be left to Christian liberty, because it is good, and because it is enjoined by the Church. This view, in different gradations, you find too general in Germany; and I am quite convinced you agree with me in believing that a truly Christian Sabbath observance is only possible if we hold that the law given to Adam, and repeated on Mount Sinai, 'Remember the Sabbath-day to keep it holy,' has an eternal obligation."[1] We give another specimen, one relating to our own country: "The thought of writing at all was suggested to me by a few words only, which I heard interchanged in the street of a country town, but which were sufficient to convince me that Dr. Whately's pamphlet, *Thoughts on the Sabbath*, was doing extreme mischief; and that through it an opinion was gaining ground that the Episcopacy of our Church was opposed to the principle of keeping holy the Sabbath-day. Under such circumstances, I was induced to write these pages, to vindicate the Divine institution of the Christian Sabbath."[2] We find in the pamphlet itself, on which Mr. Barter animadverts, evidence that its views are not fitted to produce the most elevated morality. In an address to the inhabitants of Dublin and its vicinity, the Archbishop says, "If, for instance, after devoutly attending Divine worship with your family, you just turn into a shop to buy some trifling article, you indeed may not feel that you are doing anything that interferes with your own devout observance of the day; but you should remember that the expectation of some such chance-customers may induce the tradesman to remain all day in his shop, occupied in his ordinary worldly affairs, and deprived of his best, and perhaps only opportunity, of attending to the concerns of his soul."[3] From a sentence in the *Thoughts on the Sabbath*, to which the Address is appended, we learn the following fact relative to persons known to the writer as entertaining his opinions on the ques-

[1] *Religious Condition of Christendom*, pp. 479, 480.
[2] Barter's Answer to Whately, p. 35. [3] Pp. 43, 44.

tion: "I have formerly hinted my suspicions, in an essay already before the public [*On the Love of Truth*], that some persons who do not really believe the Mosaic law relative to the Sabbath to be binding on Christians, yet think it right to encourage or tacitly connive at that belief from views of expediency, for fear of unsettling the minds of the common people. Indeed, I know, as a fact, respecting several persons, what is probably the case with many others, that they fully coincide with my views on the present question, though they judge it not advisable, at present at least, to come forward and avow their opinion."[1]

The influence of the unguarded expressions of Luther and others on the subject before us was very extensively, and has been also permanently, injurious to the interests of religion and morality. We have only to look to the Protestant countries of the Continent for the proof. "Their view about the Sabbath of the Fourth Commandment as a Jewish ordinance," observes Fairbairn, "told most unfavourably upon the interests of religion on the Continent. There can be little doubt that this was the evil root from which chiefly sprung so soon afterwards such a mass of Sabbath desecration, and which has rendered it so difficult ever since to restore the day of God to its proper place in the feelings and observances of the people. . . . The evil, once begun, proceeded rapidly from bad to worse, till it scarcely left in many places so much as the form of religion. No doubt many other causes were at work in bringing about so disastrous a result, but much was certainly owing to the error under consideration. And it reads a solemn and impressive warning to both ministers and people, not only to resist to the utmost all encroachments upon the sanctity of the Lord's day, but also to beware of weakening any of the foundations on which the obligation to keep that day is made to rest; and here, as well as in other things, to seek, with Leighton, that they 'may be saved from the errors of wise men, yea, and of good men.'"[2]

There is another class of opinions which, without referring to our institution at all, operate against it, by fostering the supposition that religion is not the principal concern of man. The mere absence of religion from a publication which is constantly

[1] *Thoughts on the Sabbath*, p. 1. [2] *Typology*, vol. ii. pp. 475, 476

read, and the treatment of every topic as if there were nothing of importance beyond the present scene, have a most secularizing effect on the public mind. Robert Hall informs us that the evil effect of a perusal of Miss Edgeworth's writings, which are marked by "a universal and studied omission of religion," was experienced by him for weeks.[1] We have been informed by a working man that he was obliged from the same cause to discontinue the reading of a popular miscellany which prides itself on its harmlessness and moral purity. If works of this cast tend to make their readers mere "men of the world who have their portion in this life," such a publication as *Punch* would deprive them of any little dignity which the other writers had left to their time-bounded existence. Even where there may be nothing profane or licentious in the literature of the day, its entirely worldly or frivolous character imparts its own impress to the mind of the reader.

And how much more prejudicial the influence of those numberless works which more avowedly or covertly seek to sap the foundations of all religion and morals! Of this class of publications it was stated, in 1847, that there was an annual issue of not less than 28,000,000. This would give an average weekly number of above 500,000, and supposing five readers to each, there must have been in that year upwards of two and a half millions of people under the perpetual operation of the fatal leaven. Let us conclude this part of our subject with the impressive words of Dr. Warren: "I can most conscientiously express my belief, that for a long time no periodical of note has been established in this country which has not disclosed the desire of its conductors to fit it for the purpose of innocent recreation and information to readers of both sexes, and of all ages and classes. It is a fact, however, stated with concern and reluctance, that there is a poisonous growth of libertine literature—if the last word be not indeed libelled by such a use of it—designed for the lowest classes of society; supplied, moreover, to an extent scarcely equal to the demand for it, and which exists to an extent unfortunately little suspected. I know not how this dreadful evil is to be encountered, except by affording every possible encouragement, from every quarter, to the dissemination, in

[1] *Life*, p. 174.

the cheapest practicable form, of wholesome and engaging literature. If poison be cheap, let its antidote be cheaper."[1]

REMEDIES FOR SABBATH DESECRATION.

We have nothing new to propose on this part of our subject. We are firmly convinced that the grand panacea for the ills of the world has been long ago discovered and prescribed, and that what is wanting is only its more general and earnest application. Besides this chief remedy, there are others important in their place, but even on these little room has been left for originality. As truth, however, needs to be often presented, we offer no apology for the following suggestions.

The preaching of the Word by the appointed servants of Christ is perhaps next to prayer the most important remedy for a desecrated Sabbath. This was the great instrument by which Christianity was established in the world. It was the chief means of the Reformation. It has done more than any other human agency for the conversion of the heathen in our own time. It is the glory of our land. It would enlighten and bless all nations were it wielded as extensively as there are human beings. It would still more elevate Christian countries were it more fully and earnestly employed. And we have only to examine the doctrines and spirit of the apostle Paul to know what the true and effectual preaching of the gospel is. His great subject was a crucified Saviour, and he preached well and successfully because he believed, felt, prayed. Let a philosopher who knew human nature well, and had observed much, be heard on the kind of preaching that does good. His remark has been quoted already, but deserves repetition. "Those," he says, "who preach faith, or in other words a pure mind, have always produced more popular virtue than those who preached good works, or the mere regulation of outward acts." It is not difficult to trace the connexion between right preaching and a sanctified Sabbath. Let a man hear and believe the Word of God, and he immediately feels the value and obligation of the Lord's day, as of every Christian ordinance. If a person live under a faithful ministry he learns more and more of the value and obliga-

[1] *Intellectual and Moral Development of the Present Age.* By Samuel Warren, etc. p. 7

tion of that institution. To what mainly does Great Britain owe a Sabbath to such an extent honoured by her people, and blessing them in return with temporal and spiritual good, but to the teachings of an evangelical ministry? Let it be the endeavour of all who wish well to their country to have such an instrumentality extended to every part of the land. It is a melancholy fact, as we have already seen, that there are multitudes who will not attend on Divine ordinances in the usual places of worship. In these circumstances let us remember the wise words of Dr. Chalmers, "The gospel is a message, not a thing for which the people will come to them, but a thing with which they must go to the people."

Another mode of diffusing sacred knowledge, and an important pioneer and auxiliary to the other, is realized in the labours of missionaries. And they would, we conceive, still more efficiently promote their object by being trained and sent forth as foreign agents are. It is delightful to think of what has been accomplished by those excellent men who are employed in the London City Mission, in inducing Sabbath observance and its associated practices. In the Reports of the Society it is mentioned that in the course of one year they prevailed on 1914 adults regularly to attend public worship; and, in the progress of another, persuaded 2736 to follow their example. They have, in thousands of instances, influenced persons to give up their secular work, and families to keep their shops shut on the Lord's day. These are only specimens of results of the same nature which annually attend their exertions. And yet a much larger field might be occupied if there were only more abundant pecuniary means. Is it not painful in the extreme to reflect that multitudes, by trampling on the laws of God in our large cities, are continually provoking His displeasure, spreading moral and physical disease, burdening society, and destroying themselves, when there are so many able to provide the means of healing, in the fountain, these waters of bitterness?

The less official style of personal appeal and remonstrance by individuals of any class of society is an important aid in the promotion of this cause. Many instances of the efficacy of this means might be adduced. We cite the following. The late excellent Bishop Porteus, when so infirm as to require to be carried, waited on the Prince of Wales at Carlton House, and by his faithful representations procured the alteration, to another day of the week, of a meeting which was held by the Prince and some military friends regularly on the Sabbath. It is recorded of the Rev. Henry Venn, the author of the *Complete Duty of Man*, that by employing persons to attempt, through persuasion, the repression of the open violation of the Sabbath, he accomplished a great reformation in Huddersfield.[1] Even by children and servants may the Sabbath-breaker be reclaimed. We have read of the former addressing salutary and successful instruction and reproof to their seniors of that character. And the following is an instance of the wise and faithful rebuke of a servant who, in influencing the object of it to amend his ways, has been through him a blessing to many. It is mentioned in the *Life* of Fletcher of Madeley, that, when a young man about twenty-three, and employed one Sabbath in writing some music, a servant coming into his room looked at him with serious concern, and said, " Sir, I am sorry to see you so employed on the Lord's day." At first his pride and resentment were moved at being reproved by a servant; but on reflection he felt that the reproof was just, immediately put away his music, and from that time became a strict observer of the Lord's day.[2]

The press is confessedly an organ of great power in the cause of either truth or error, and one therefore of which the friends of religion and of the Sabbath ought largely to avail themselves. And certainly as its earliest was, so its principal application ought to be, in the multiplication and circulation of the most powerful of all writings, the sacred Scriptures. Human writings are imperfect. There is none of them in which there is not some defect or mistake. Enemies fasten on these things. But if fault be found with Scripture, it is without cause. "We question if any person of any class or school ever read the Scriptures regularly and thoroughly without being or becoming not only religious but sensible and consistent."[3] It was the reading of a Bible which originated the Reformation. And in our own days its truths

[1] *Life*, pp. 50, 51. [2] *Life*, 18mo, p. 23.
[3] Editorial Article in the *Times*, August 20, 1847.

have diffused knowledge, piety, happiness, and civilisation among men of every character, colour, and clime. Wherever they have penetrated, human beings have reverently acknowledged the claims of their Creator on their spirits and bodies, their substance and time. The truth as it is in Jesus is able to overthrow all error and evil, and to transform the character of mankind into the likeness of the Divine nature. It has a commission from its Author to accomplish this revolution over the whole world, and the commission is accompanied with His promise of entire success. What, then, is required to its further victories over sin in every form, is to present to the minds of men the Word of the Lord, with entire confidence in its mightiness through God to the pulling down of strongholds. And that it is still "quick and powerful" let the following facts show:—"Dr. Carey mentions that two of the most active and useful native preachers, and several other brethren, had been the fruits of a New Testament left at a shop, and states also that early in 1813 some Brahmins and persons of caste, not many miles from Serampore, obtained the knowledge of the truth, and met for Christian worship on the Lord's day before they had any intercourse with the missionaries, simply by reading the Scriptures. These were baptized, and reported that hundreds of their neighbours were convinced of the truth of the Christian religion, and were kept back from professing it only by the fear of losing caste, and its consequences." Mr. Dudley, in his *Analysis of the System of the Bible Society*, remarks, that "a greater regard for the Sabbath and more general and regular attendance on Divine worship was another and early result of the Society's labours, and an evidence that they were not in vain."[1]

But the circulation of the Scriptures does not supersede the employment of other publications for advancing the cause of truth and righteousness, provided they are agreeable to that supreme standard, and provided especially they set forth and enforce its doctrines and laws. Every department of knowledge and every form of publication may be rendered tributary to the designs of Revelation, and to the confirmation and defence of its great discoveries and lessons. The Reformation was eminently

[1] Pp. 94 95.

forwarded by the writings of Luther. What a blessing to the world have been the works of Baxter, Owen, Bunyan, Hervey, Leighton, and Chalmers! How potent an instrumentality in our own day has been the publication of tracts! Nor must the leading truths of Christianity, prominent though the exhibition of them ought to be made, be the exclusive subjects of such works. It may be necessary to single out such a topic as that of the Sabbath for frequent admonition or occasionally for full illustration. The lucubrations of Heylyn rendered imperative the elaborate treatises of Owen and Baxter. The speculations of Paley and Whately have demanded the strictures of Dwight, Holden, and Wardlaw. Prevalent error in opinion, and sin in practice, have called forth the various essays by ministers and working men with which the name of Henderson stands so honourably associated. And have these labours been in vain? It is stated that the works of Greenham and Twisse contributed greatly to promote the observance of the Sabbath in their times. The treatises, on the institution, of the seventeenth century, constitute to this day an armoury of weapons to defeat the continually reappearing, though frequently demolished, arguments of its enemies. How much in recent times have the works of Horsley, Edwards, and many others, corroborated the influence of the pulpit, and reassured the courage of the members of their respective communions, and of the friends of the Sabbath generally, as well as rolled back the tide of error and evil! And most encouraging, too, has been the success of smaller works. The movement in Germany, afterwards to be mentioned, was essentially aided by the issuing of addresses, in thousands of copies, on Sabbath celebration, and by the circulation of the *Pearl of Days*, and other prize essays. The sowing broadcast of many treatises and tracts over England and Scotland, within these few years, has resulted in a rich harvest. But perhaps the most effective use of the press has been made by the Sabbath Union of America, which, with the energy characteristic of the nation, has not only sent forth its secretary over the whole country to promote the observance of the Sabbath, by addressing meetings, and by interviews with influential individuals, but scattered in great profusion its Reports and Permanent Documents, in which the whole question is dealt with scripturally, and brought home by striking facts to men's business and bosoms.

One of the most important agencies for promoting reverence for the Sabbath and religion in general, and thus for advancing all the great interests of society, is lodged in the hands of parents. To them it belongs to train up the young in their earliest and most susceptible days, by instruction, example, and government, in the knowledge and practice of all excellence. And not the least effectual of the means which they ought to employ is the exercise of the authority with which they have been intrusted by the Supreme Ruler. The language of God to Abraham is their warrant for making use of this power: "I know him, that he will command his children and his household after him, and they shall keep the way of the Lord, to do justice and judgment; that the Lord may bring upon Abraham that which he hath spoken of him."[1] Their duty is taught them by a case, than which nothing in conduct and results can be conceived more unlike the procedure of the father of the faithful, and its consequences—the case of Eli, who when his sons made themselves vile restrained them not. Parental neglect is one of the chief occasions of the ignorance, immorality, and irreligion of a country. And we may add that there is nothing in which parents are so apt to fail, as in the exercise of their authority over their offspring. Although all other means were employed, if they are on the one hand too indulgent, or on the other too severe, what would avail those means? The young will too frequently in such a case despise the inconsistent teaching and example, or be driven from a path which they are not allowed in their homes to find a way of pleasantness and a path of peace. Equally necessary is the practice of two injunctions if a population is to be trained to fear God and keep His commandments: "Correct thy son, and he shall give thee rest; yea, he shall give delight unto thy soul."[2] "Ye fathers, provoke not your children to wrath; but bring them up in the nurture and admonition of the Lord."[3]

The example of consistent character and deportment is a means of good which all Christians may employ, and which every one is capable of appreciating as well as most prepared to feel and respect. The law of Christ applies to this, as to all other departments of

[1] Gen. xviii. 19. [2] Prov. xxix. 17. [3] Eph. vi. 4.

duty: "Let your light so shine before men, that they also may see your good works, and glorify your Father which is in heaven." The exemplary conduct of the humblest person has the most powerful influence over a family, and over all who have occasion to observe it. But the power of such example is the greater that the individual occupies a high standing in the church or in society—such, for instance, as the cases of a Sir M. Hale, a Howard, a Wilberforce, and a R. Hall, all of whom were distinguished by their sacred regard to the Lord's day. No apparent improvement may in some instances be the result in those who witness the example, but benefit is frequently the obvious, and still more frequently the actual effect. No good action is lost. It is ever beneficial to him who performs it. It is approved by the Judge of all. When seen, it is a witness for Him. And the influence of the character and the deeds of the good operates in ways and to an extent, which, whether known or not to them, are incalculable in their beneficent amount. Such men are the light of the world, the salt of the earth.

Of many instances in which persons under the authority of others have been ready to sacrifice their means of support for the sake of a good conscience, we particularize that of an overseer in a factory at Manchester, related by the Bishop of Chester at a public meeting. Being told by one of the proprietors on a Saturday that his attendance would be necessary next day, when certain repairs in the machinery were to be made, he replied that he regretted much to disobey his employer, but he could not attend at work on the Sunday. "Then," said the proprietor, "you will come on that day, or you will not come again at all." In the course of the Monday following, his employer sent for him, and asked why it was that he had not returned: the man said that after what had been told him on the Saturday, he did not consider himself at liberty to return. "Oh!" said his employer, "perhaps I was a little hasty in what I said: attend in your place as usual." See the value of a man of principle! It was felt by one who perhaps disregarded the religious feeling on which the principle was founded, but who still set a just value on the individual who conscientiously adhered to it.[1] Instances of many others in various situations in

[1] *Missionary Register for* 1836, p. 313.

life, who have acted with equal firmness in similar circumstances, must be known to our readers. The person who so acts performs a valuable service to the cause of the Sabbath. Let others, putting their trust in the Lord of the institution, the Proprietor of the earth and its fulness, go and do likewise.

Ellis, in his *Polynesian Researches*, states that the example of the missionaries in Tahiti led to the strict and general observance of the Lord's day by the nation at large, and that the prevailing attention to the public worship of God, and the exemplary Christian deportment of many of the people, have proved not only delightful, but beneficial to their visitors; there being probably many instances of good besides, which the revelations of the last day alone will disclose. It would be well that a similar example were set by the multitude of our countrymen who visit foreign lands for other purposes than those of missionary enterprise. How desirable that they should bear with them the thought, "Thou God seest me," and that, constrained by His love, they should spend His day according to the commandment, and as every Christian delights to do. The following cases might supply a directory and stimulus: "This day, being Sunday," writes a Christian traveller, "was devoted to repose. The want of religious ordinances is the greatest of all privations. May I henceforth duly estimate the privileges of my native land."[1] "We remained all day (Sunday) in Wady Sŭdr. We had determined before setting off from Cairo, always to rest on the Christian Sabbath, if possible; and during all our journeys in the Holy Land, we were never compelled to break over this rule but once. Strange as it may at first seem, these Sabbaths in the desert had a peculiar charm, and left upon the mind an impression which never can be forgotten."[2]

Example may operate where its living form was not seen, and far beyond the sphere in which it shone. A medical gentleman acknowledged that it was his reading that Mr. Hey of Leeds rarely missed attending the morning and afternoon service of the church, which led him to arrange his time better, and follow the same plan. This occurred when he was a young man, and he never had altered the practice.[3] A correspondent of the *Record* news

[1] *Remains of the late A. L. Ross*, p. 379. [2] Robinson's *Palestine*, i. p. 94.
[3] W. Brown, Esq. late President of the Royal College of Surgeons

paper stated, some years ago, that the debate in the House of Commons on the Lord's-day Bill, and the serious manner in which it was conducted, had been noticed in more than one of the leading newspapers at Paris, and that one of them directs the particular attention of its readers to this part of the British character as worthy of imitation. "Thus," the writer justly remarks, "Sir Andrew Agnew and his associates in Parliament are in reality acting on all Europe, though apparently only on England and the sister kingdoms."

When a duty is performed in circumstances of strong temptation to an opposite course, the example has increased claims to our consideration and respect. It required no small measure of principle in Wilberforce, when, a Minister of State having called upon him on some public business on a Sunday, he at once excused himself, saying he would wait upon his Lordship at any hour he might fix the next day, but he was then going to church; this, too, after he had already attended the morning service.[1] Still stronger was the temptation of a command, addressed by a late King to an excellent person still living, to dine with his Majesty on a Sabbath-day, and the polite declining of the intended honour, received without offence, did credit to both the subject and his Prince.[2] But to act such a part towards one from whom something worse than displeasure may be apprehended, is to encounter a greater temptation still, and to evince a higher degree of courage. There were those who boldly refused to read the *Book of Sports* from their pulpits in the times of James I. and Charles I., though liable thereby to suspension. Dr. Twisse was one of these faithful men. He even warned his people against Sabbath profanation. It was to the credit of James that he gave secret orders not to molest the Doctor. When Charles renewed the edict, he preached and published on the subject, "which produced a powerful impression on the public mind in favour of the Sabbath."

There is a special obligation lying on persons of high standing in society to exemplify the principles of our holy religion, since the more elevated the station the more conspicuous and regarded is the individual. And it is a peculiar pleasure to refer to in-

1 Scott's *Discourse on Wilberforce*, p. 29.
2 *Life of Lady Colquhoun*, 156-159.

stances of the union of piety and rank in such men as were Lords Harrington, Dartmouth, Teignmouth, Gambier, and Earl Ducie. Nor is it impossible for those in the very highest grade of earthly distinction, amidst all the pleasures, temptations, and cares of a throne, to be patterns of Sabbath observance. It was a king who delighted to go with the multitude that kept holyday; who was glad when it was said, Let us go up to the house of the Lord; who would have preferred being a door-keeper in the house of his God, to dwelling in the tents of wickedness; and who esteemed a day in the courts of the Lord better than a thousand anywhere else. Kings and emperors have followed his example. King George III. evinced, in various ways, his veneration for the law of the Sabbath. "To every pious subject it must be a source of lively satisfaction to know that in the pavilion itself originated measures which have materially tended to promote the better observance of the Sabbath in Brighton. It is said that there were certain arrangements in the royal household which undesignedly entailed a large amount of Sunday labour; but when the facts were represented to Queen Adelaide, she immediately commanded that the orders in question should be given on Monday instead of Saturday as heretofore. And this act of Christian consideration has been extensively copied, to the great relief of many a laundress, who formerly could not remember the Sabbath day to keep it holy. In unison with this tribute to the Divine command, was the injunction of our present Queen, forbidding the exhibition, on the Lord's day, of the State apartments at Windsor Castle; an act which, along with Her Majesty's patronage of the Sabbath observance movement among the working classes, has given a much-loved sovereign an additional claim to the gratitude and attachment of a Christian people."[1]

"Except the Lord build the house, they labour in vain that build it: except the Lord keep the city, the watchman waketh but in vain." Whence but from Divine patronage has a day of sacred rest, so opposed to the avarice, love of pleasure, and irreligion of the world, which give birth to so many opinions and practices tending to obliterate its name from the calendar, maintained, notwithstanding, its ground, and been not only valued by

[1] *Life of Lady Colquhoun*, pp. 159, 160.

men of the world, but venerated, loved, and observed by Christians? And on what other power than that of its Author can we justly depend for the preservation and universal prevalence of the institution, when the human mind is naturally as much as ever liable to error, and prone to evil, in regard to this as well as all the doctrines and laws of a kingdom which is not of this world? All hearts and events are in the hands of the Almighty. His own institutions are under His special care, and He can easily secure for them favour and honour. To Him, therefore, ought we to come; in Him repose our confidence, for guidance, help, and success in every plan that we adopt, and in every exertion that we put forth on behalf of the day which He has consecrated for Himself, and blessed for man.

It promises well for our cause when the paramount importance of this remedy is practically recognised. In the Stuttgard Conference of 1850, at which about two thousand Christians of all the countries of Germany were assembled, an address was agreed to, in which, after various useful suggestions, it is stated, "But, above all, every one should pray often and ardently to the Lord our God, that the Sabbath celebration may be restored amongst his people, and that all Governments and Chambers of Deputies may understand how pernicious it is for the people if this duty is more and more disregarded, by the example of persons high in station, by working in the Government offices, by military reviews, by meetings of the public, and of societies, during the hours of Divine worship, by noisy or immoral public feasts, and by a lax legislature;" and at which, in addition, it was, on the motion of the Rev. S. C. Kapff, resolved "That the third Sabbath of every month should be a day for common prayer with all the evangelical Christians of Germany, especially on behalf of Home Missions and Sabbath observance." "We know," adds the relator, "that this resolution did not remain without consequences—that new prayer-meetings were established; and, we trust, if the number of Christians increase who pray for Sabbath celebration, that the Lord will also send us an abundant answer, in a better observance of His holy day."[1] That answer has been sent. For of the year 1855 we have to present the following gratifying statements:—

[1] *Religious Condition of Christendom*, pp. 471, 477, 478.

"In Prussia, Würtemberg, Baden, Sabbath observance has undoubtedly improved in the course of the last years. Not only stricter laws of former times have been enjoined, but what is of greater importance, public opinion, as also the manners and customs of the people, have been ameliorated." This was written in July of that year. The writer, referring again to the subject in the following month, observes, "Though much remains to be done for the better observance of the Sabbath in Germany, yet, as I remarked in my last letter, in many, if not in most, countries an improvement is going on."[1]

The same spirit has actuated Christians in this land, and has undoubtedly been the means of carrying our ark over many a raging billow, and deepened the interest of our people in its future safety. Members of Parliament, while pleading its cause with man, did not forget to present their suit at a higher tribunal. When the friends of the Sabbath were employing on its behalf the eloquence of the orator and the power of the press, they neglected not to unite their petitions at the throne of grace. In circumstances the most inauspicious to such a spirit has it been evoked and prevailed. We give an interesting example. For three years the men on the Mersey and Irwell had petitioned their employers to be emancipated from Sabbath slavery, and their petitions had no effect. At length some of them said, "We have tried men without effect; let us appeal to God." For six weeks before the next annual meeting of their masters, they humbly besought God to put it into their hearts to comply with their request; they did that which, whether it proceed from the cottage or the palace, from the prince or the peasant, is sure to produce a favourable result—they offered prayer in faith. The result was that, after some demur on the part of one or two individuals, the masters at length unanimously resolved to comply with their request. The sailing of thirty-nine boats on the canal was stopped on Sabbath.

These things are well. But it is not an outwardly-guarded and respected Sabbath, however important and desirable this is, that will satisfy the Divine claims or human necessities. The institution must be loved and venerated as the appointment of

[1] *News of the Churches*, vol. ii. pp. 186, 205

Heaven, and kept in the sanctuary of the heart. How can this be attained, however, without the saving knowledge and faith of the gospel, produced by the agency of the Spirit of God, or how can the bestowal of this agency be secured but by prayer? "Thus saith the Lord God, I will yet for this be inquired of by the house of Israel to do it for them." "Ye that make mention of the Lord, keep not silence, and give him no rest till he establish and make Jerusalem a praise in the earth." "Arise, O God, plead thine own cause, remember how the foolish man reproacheth thee daily."

PROGRESS AND PROSPECTS OF OUR CAUSE.

The friends of the Sabbath have, we trust, such a regard for truth, as to preserve them from consciously understating the amount of Sabbath profanation as it exists in this country or in foreign lands. Honesty is in this, as in everything else, the best policy, the policy in the present case being fully to set forth the evil, that every man who "desireth life, and loveth many days, that he may see good," and who would wish others to enjoy the same blessings, may be roused to efforts for its removal. For let it be true, that the words of Shakspere describe a case, not now of rare but of common occurrence on the Continent :—

> "Why such impress of shipwrights, whose sore task
> Does not divide the Sunday from the week?
> What might be toward, that this sweaty haste
> Doth make the night joint-labourer with the day?
> Who is 't that can inform me?"

and that the language of Wordsworth is not yet obsolete as a description of England,—

> "Where now the beauty of the Sabbath kept
> With conscientious reverence, as a day
> By the Almighty Lawgiver pronounced
> Holy and blest?"

—we have, nevertheless, the confidence, that great though the enormity is, there is in the truth and in prayer an adequate instrumentality for coping with it, and in the Divine agency and promises a perfect guarantee of victory. And we owe it as a tribute to the glory of the Author of the Sabbath, as well as an encouragement to those who are fighting its battles, to adduce some further illustrative instances of the success that has crowned the exertions of its friends, and that heralds its coming triumph.

A considerable volume might be filled with the facts which show how auspicious have been the attempts of missionaries to plant the institution among various classes of Pagans, notwithstanding the aversion to sacred exercises and restraints that must especially be felt by men previously accustomed to a wild freedom on all days, or to a galling bondage on six days of the week. Let a few of the many particulars that might be adduced suffice. When slavery was the law and practice in the West Indies, the Sabbath was the market-day, and the day selected for the punishment of the slaves. That was a noted time of immorality. Contrast with this the following :—"Among other pleasing features presented by this station," it was reported of Hampden, in Jamaica, "the progress of marriage among the negroes is not the least encouraging. The number of couples which have been married since its commencement amount to 511. A great improvement has taken place in regard to the observation of the Lord's day. Public worship is not only well attended, but the Sabbath is, in other respects, sanctified in a manner, which, considering the former habits of the negroes, is truly surprising. Prayer-meetings are established in every district of the congregation. Family-worship is observed in many of their dwellings, unity and brotherly love prevail, parents are more anxious for the instruction of their children, and more careful in watching over their morals. A Bible and Missionary Society has been formed in the congregation, which, in the first eleven months, raised £150 currency. Temperance societies have also been established, which number no fewer than 593 members. A session has been formed in the congregation, which takes the entire charge of the discipline of the church ; and though nearly all the elders are, or lately were, apprentices, they discharge the duties of their office with propriety, zeal, and prudence, firmness and fidelity. Mr. Blyth"—the Rev. George Blyth, the missionary at the station—"has also begun a system of family visitation similar to what prevails in many of the best regulated congregations in this country." "Altogether," Mr.

B. says, "this part of the island has assumed the aspect of a Christian country."[1] Of Lucea, another missionary station in Jamaica, the Rev. James Watson, the missionary, reported: "The improvement of the Black population is particularly remarkable. It is astonishing to see the change that has been wrought upon them in so short a space of time. In a merely civil point of view, it is exceedingly interesting. They seem much more cheerful, and much more attentive to matters of decency and propriety of conduct than formerly. Marriage is now rapidly advancing among them. Hundreds have left off their former mode of living, and have entered into this honourable relation within the last year. The Sabbath is almost universally observed as a day of rest by an entire cessation of everything in the shape of work."[2] As it is in Jamaica, so also in the South Sea Islands. Stewart, in his *Visit to the South Seas*, devotes a chapter (or letter) to a description of a Tahitian Sabbath in 1829, concluding with these words, "The whole external observance of the day by the natives, in a suspension of all ordinary occupations and amusements, was such as to be worth the imitation of older and more enlightened Christian nations" (p. 253). The well-known and excellent missionary, Mr. Pritchard, confirms this testimony: "On almost all the islands where the gospel has been introduced, and the people have made a profession of Christianity, a most diligent attention is paid to the public ordinances of religion. This is particularly the case in those stations which are not visited by foreign shipping. They very strictly observe the Sabbath. Their food for the Sabbath is cooked on the Saturday, consequently none are detained from a place of worship, to cook hot dinners on the Sabbath, as is so common in England even among professing Christians. They usually attend three services on the Sabbath. The first is a prayer-meeting held early in the morning. These meetings are generally well attended. It would be considered a great disgrace for a church member to absent himself from the prayer-meeting. All who profess to feel any concern about good things will be there. Most of the natives consider it as important to attend the prayer-meeting as the preaching of the gospel.

[1] Sketches by Dr. W. Brown, Secretary of the Scottish Missionary Society, in *Christian Teacher*, vol. i. p. 564.

[2] *Ibid.* p. 565.

It is exceedingly interesting at these meetings to hear how particularly and affectionately they pray for their missionaries, for the ministers of the gospel generally, and for the increase of vital religion in their own hearts, and especially for the best of blessings to rest upon their Christian friends in Britain, who have sent them the gospel. In the forenoon there is usually a very full attendance. Some of the chapels are so crowded that many persons have to sit outside. On these occasions most of them are neatly dressed. Many of them take paper and pencils, and write the particulars of the discourse. But few congregations in England surpass them, in serious attention and decent behaviour in the house of God. At the close of the afternoon service many of them frequently stop, to talk over what they have heard through the day, and to pray that the seed which has been sown may spring up and produce an abundant harvest. Besides attending schools daily, they have two religious services each week."[1] We find the same spirit among the converts of New Zealand: "It was customary with the missionaries on their first settling in New Zealand to erect a flag at their station on the Sabbath-day, and this was the sign for many distant tribes of natives to desist from work, or from war; indeed, they seem to have shown at a very early period of the mission a decided respect and honour for the Sabbath, which the missionaries told them was set apart by them in honour of the 'Atua nue,' the Great Jehovah."[2] Mr. Davis, a missionary, says, "Our chapel could not contain the whole of our congregation yesterday; so that we shall have to enlarge it as soon as possible. Ripi and his party continue to listen with attention, and are steady in their attendance on the means of grace. The manner in which the Lord's day is kept by this tribe would shame many country parishes in England, even where the gospel is faithfully preached. Their firewood is always prepared, and their potatoes scraped and got ready, on the Saturday afternoon, to be cooked on the Sunday; and this is no new thing, as they have proceeded in this way now for a long time."[3]

We must content ourselves with only a few more illustrations,

[1] Pritchard's *Missionary Reward*, pp. 78-80.
[2] *Missionary Guide-Book*, p. 279.
[3] Ramsden's *Missions*, p. 164.

derived chiefly from the lately published and very interesting volume, *Nineteen Years in Polynesia*, by the Rev. George Turner: "We had the pleasure of spending a Sabbath at Eromanga, and met with about a hundred and fifty of the people in their little chapel. All were quiet and orderly. It thrilled our inmost soul to hear them, as led by Mrs. Gordon, strike up the tune of 'New Lydia,' and also the translation and tune of 'There is a happy land.' Mr. Macfarlane and I addressed them through Mr. Gordon. They were startled and deeply interested, as I told them of former times, and to show them that we were different from other white men who had visited their shores" (pp. 487, 488). "We left Uea early on the morning bound for Guamha, Mr. Creagh's station, there to land Mr. Jones, and the supplies of Mr. Creagh, and his native teachers. We were close in by nine A.M., on Sabbath, when Mr. Jones, Mr. Turpie, the first officer, and I went on shore in the whale-boat. As we reached the beach, I had a vivid recollection of the naked savage crowd Mr. Murray and I saw there on my first visit fourteen years ago. *Then* some were painted from head to foot, and all were armed with clubs, spears, or tomahawks. Old Ieui gave the word of command, when an avenue was formed for us to walk up through the motley group, to his large round house, where we talked to them of Christ, and his peaceful kingdom, and entreated them to abandon heathenism and embrace the gospel. But how changed the scene now! As Mr. Jones, Mr. Turpie, and I walked up from the boat, all was quiet. It was the hour of Divine service, and the people were assembled in the chapel on the rising ground a little to the left. We walked up to the place, a stone building eighty feet by sixty, looked in at the door, and saw that it was filled with 900 attentive worshippers. Mr. Creagh was in the pulpit, and a black precentor stood leading the whole in one harmonious song of praise. I felt it quite overpowering, as we walked up the aisle, and took our places in the missionary's pew. Mr. Creagh preached, and as it was their day for administering the ordinance of the Lord's Supper, we had the further pleasure of uniting, at the close of the morning service, with the church of ninety-four members, in commemorating the death of Christ" (pp. 513, 514). "In summing up our progress in these islands just visited, where twenty years ago we had not a single missionary, or a single convert from heathenism, and at the very entrance to which John Williams then fell, we find that, out of a population, in the twelve islands which we now occupy, of about 65,500 souls, we have 19,743 who have renounced heathenism, and are professedly Christian. Of these there are 645 church members, and 689 who are candidates for admission to the church. And there are now labouring among them ten European missionaries, and 231 native teachers and assistants. Three printing-presses, also, are at work, especially devoted to the Papuan vernacular of the respective islands" (p. 533). To this summary of what has been done by missionaries in a single fraction of the field, let there be added a mere outline, sketched by us some years ago, of the achievements of such men within little more than half a century over the world, and we feel ourselves warranted, as we said then, to challenge any one to produce measures worthy for a moment to be placed in competition with Christian missions as the means of enlightening and civilizing human beings : Greenland and Labrador raised from their deep degradation—a hundred spots in the North and South Pacific, once the dark domains of ignorance, enlightened—the reproach of hopeless stupidity wiped away from the Hottentots, many of whom now equal Europeans in their skill as artisans—the elevation of New Zealanders, Negroes, and Bushmen, to the rank of intelligent beings—the education of between 300,000 and 400,000 young persons in heathen lands—the erection of numerous churches and school-houses—the reduction of many languages to writing—the preparation of millions of tracts and books—and the translation of the Scriptures into one hundred languages spoken by upwards of half the human family. In all these cases, the missionaries, after being themselves trained by the help of the Sabbath, introduced it into the scenes of their labours, where it has been as well observed by the converts as in any country, and where it has performed an indispensable and not the least important part in the happy transformation which the character and condition of many among the most uncivilized of our race have undergone.

We are aware of little that is pleasing to set over against the deeply shaded picture of a Popish Sabbath on the Continent which truth required us in some preceding pages to present. Allowance must be made, so far as the people are concerned, on the ground of the ignorance in which they are left by their spiritual guides, and the example which their leaders set before them. There have been exceptions, moreover, among the clergy—one, at least, appears, the already mentioned instance of the Archbishop of Paris, whose efforts, with those of M. de Montalembert, to secure a better-observed Sabbath in France, were deserving of no slight praise, notwithstanding that they have not been so successful as every friend of the institution would desire. A writer, in a work repeatedly drawn upon, observes, "It seemed to me that in Protestant countries public Sabbath desecration never proceeded to so great a length as in Catholic districts."[1] In his opinion, so far as our limited observation has gone, we are disposed to concur. We found Geneva, in 1851, not so bad in respect of Sabbath desecration as we have seen it described, or as Lucerne and Frankfort-on-the-Maine. The streets of the city of Calvin were tolerably quiet, as much so as in some of our English towns, though we have been informed that many of the inhabitants repair to the environs, and had the testimony of a rattling sound as we passed along that others retreated to the billiard room, for the purposes of amusement. In Basle and Amsterdam we saw in numerous strollers, and their levity, an evidence that there were many who had no reverence for the first day of the week; but the shops were not generally open or business carried on as in Lucerne. In 1861, we had an opportunity of contrasting Basle, which seemed improved since we had seen it ten years before, though we noticed some open shops, with Roman Catholic Mâcon in France, where, after mass was over, the population, with the exception of a few sober, devout Protestants, appeared to be "wholly given to idolatry"—the idolatry of spectacles, music, and wine. There are, moreover, such symptoms of conviction on the part of not a few of the inhabitants of Continental countries that religion is low, and so much anxiety for better things as themselves evince progress and improvement. Take Germany, where Protestantism is so encompassed by the contaminating influence of Popery; and it may be said that, while it had de-

[1] *Religious Condition of Christendom*, p. 466.

clined from the Sabbath-keeping of the Reformers, earlier and later, there have ever been "faithful Christians, who, in their small circles, observed the commandment—faithful working men who did no work on Sabbath-day, faithful merchants who sold nothing on Sabbath-day—that though the number of these faithful men was small, and though their voice expired in the vast desert, they ardently desired reformation—and that the object which they longed for is in our day beginning to be attained."[1] The events of 1848, and the circulation of the English Sabbath prize essays, gave a powerful impulse to the cause of the Sabbath in Germany. Conferences at Wittenberg and Stuttgard took up the question with great earnestness. Addresses to the German nation and Governments were published. The address to the people recommended the following things :—" *1st.* All should be prepared on Saturday, that it may not be necessary to do any labour in the household on Sunday. *2d.* Every one should dine very plainly on the Sabbath-day, that the servants may have time to attend the services of God, and also for rest. *3d.* Every one should be regularly present at public worship, and at domestic devotion. *4th.* All the labour done on week-days must be omitted; chiefly the payment of the labourers, the delivering of finished, or the bespeaking of new orders, and generally all business and trade. *5th.* Children and servants should be looked after most conscientiously in respect of their employment of the Sunday ; above all, that every one should pray often and ardently to the Lord our God, that the Sabbath celebration may be restored amongst His people." Petitions, moreover, were presented to the Prussian Government. The results were encouraging. The post-offices in Prussia were shut from 9 to 12 A.M., and from 1 to 5 P.M. The Government expressed its desire to stop the running of the railways, which was resisted by the mercantile boards. The Chamber of Deputies in Saxony, in consequence of the petition of a clergyman, resolved unanimously to recommend to the Government the strict enforcement of the law of 1811, with respect to the celebration of the Lord's day. Similar measures were adopted in the kingdom of Hanover, and in the Duchy of Brunswick. To all these efforts must be added the means employed with success by

[1] *Religious Condition of Christendom*, p. 467.

voluntary societies, and eminent individuals, to promote the great object. It is painful to have to say that the authorities of the Grand Duchy of Hesse were opposed to the movement, and that the only step towards reformation was a resolution, "that public dancing parties and music be closed on Saturday at midnight, and begin on Sunday only after the service." The only appearance in Germany in favour of the Sabbath by Roman Catholics is the following, which, however, was on this account the more honourable to the mover and to the Government. In the kingdom of Bavaria, the Roman bishop applied to the Government to protect Sabbath celebration, and the Government in consequence republished all the laws upon the subject, and distributed them to all the civic boards and parishes.[1]

It was mentioned at the meeting of the Evangelical Alliance in Paris, by M. Descombaz, in his report on the Sabbath, that the observance of the Lord's day was diminishing in Switzerland. We have reason to believe, however, that a beneficial change in this respect will come over that honoured land, and is already begun. There, indeed, we have had a Victor Mellet, who was one of the ablest and most ingenious pleaders for anti-Sabbatic opinions, and was the more dangerous an opponent of the commonly received views, that he seemed to have taken up the wrong side so conscientiously. But then, on the other hand, we have a Malan, who has appeared as an author on behalf of a sanctified Sabbath, the spirit of which and of heaven he has so much imbibed ; and a Merle D'Aubigné, who has more than once proclaimed his sympathy with our Sabbath and with our exertions on its behalf, as, for example, a few years ago in these words :—"In Geneva he had looked to this Sunday question as if England were his own country. He felt that it was very important, not only to England, but to the whole Continent. England was like a citadel—a strong tower ; and if that tower was broken down, what should be done ? How would the Church exist without the sanctification of the Lord's day ? He would say to England, Keep it holy, keep it holy."[2] We anticipate much good to Switzerland and the whole continent from the recent

[1] *Religious Condition of Christendom*, pp. 467, 473.
[2] Speech at a meeting in Liverpool.- *C. Times*, May 30, 1856

Conference of the Evangelical Alliance, at which the Sabbath was a subject of prominent notice. One result of that meeting was an agreement on the part of certain ministers of Geneva to preach a course of sermons early this year on the all-important theme. The volume containing the proceedings of the Conference will, without doubt, be largely circulated, and give an impulse to the cause. Indeed, the general meetings, and the ramifications of the Alliance, must have great influence in spreading Divine truth, not only on the Sabbath question, but on many subjects deeply affecting the interests of humanity.

In no part of the world, perhaps, has more been successfully attempted of late years for the reformation of Sabbatic abuses and for promoting the observance of the institution than in the United States. Through the efforts of the Secretary of the Sabbath Union and others nearly twenty years ago, an increased attention was awakened, and in many places a great change in sentiment and practice was effected with regard to this subject. We give a few sentences from the summary of the good accomplished, as contained in the first Annual Report of the Union: "The transportation of the mails on the Sabbath has, on numerous routes, been discontinued; and stage-coaches, steamboats, rail cars, and canal boats, have in many cases ceased to run on that day. Stockholders, directors, distinguished merchants, and civilians, have expressed the conviction that, should this be the case universally, it would greatly promote the welfare of all. The number of those who go or send to the post-office, who are disposed to labour, or engage in secular business, travelling, or amusement on the Sabbath, is diminishing, and the number is increasing of those who are disposed to attend the public worship of God. Sabbath-breaking is becoming more and more disreputable, and is viewed by increasing numbers as evidence of a low, reckless, and vicious mind. The conviction is extending that it is not only morally wrong, but unprofitable and dangerous. And should all the facts with regard to this subject be known and duly appreciated, that conviction, we believe, will become universal" (pp. 4, 5). It is to be regretted that this movement was interrupted, but it has not been without much advantage, and has been succeeded by another, which, though local, promises, through the energy of its chief promoter, the Rev. R. S. Cook, New York, to extend over and bless the whole continent of North America. We have referred, in our sketch of the Sabbath Literature of the United States, to "some important documents" issued by the Sabbath Committee of New York. From a "Circular Letter of the Committee to the Clergy," of date Nov. 20, 1861, printed in one of these documents, we give the following most gratifying *vidimus* of "the Sabbath reform" in that city: "It is not easy to exaggerate the deplorable and apparently hopeless condition of things here four years ago. The change already effected seems scarcely credible to ourselves. Then, Sunday laws were as obsolete and inoperative in New York as in Vienna: nobody attempted or expected their enforcement. Now, they are as efficiently executed as other statutes, with the cordial approval of our citizens generally. Then, hundreds of news-boys overran the city every Sabbath, disturbing the peace of the whole population; now, the nuisance is abated, and most of our streets are as quiet as those of a country village. Then, more than 5000 dramshops plied their deadly traffic openly, and without hindrance; now, their doors and shutters are generally closed, and if liquors are sold, it is by stealth, and at the hazard of instant arrest for the misdemeanour. Then, a score of theatres made Sunday their chief day of profit and pleasure, with no adequate law to restrain them; now, a stringent law is on our statute-book, its constitutionality affirmed, and its penalties inflicted, in spite of the most powerful combinations. Then, the arrests for Sunday crime exceeded the average by 25 per cent.; now, the week-day arrests are 50 per cent. more than on Sunday. Then, the secular press ignored the Sunday question as foreign to its objects; since and now, the entire press of the city, uninterested in Sunday issues—with, perhaps, a single exception—has been and is earnestly enlisted in support of this reform. Then, the entire German population was claimed to be wedded to Sunday pastimes and opposed to American Sabbath restraints; now, a large and influential body of Germans are avowedly friendly to the due observance of the Lord's day, and actively hostile to the demoralizing views and customs of the beer-garden classes. In a word, the more offensive forms of Sabbath desecration have been suppressed, in the face of the most virulent opposition of interested parties, by the co-operation of the orderly classes with the public authorities. And a permanent foundation has been laid for all needed future action—legislative, judicial, or executive—for the protection of our civil Sabbath."[1] In the document from which these words are taken, there are resolutions of more than 100 clergymen of New York (1858)—Minutes of the General Assemblies of the Presbyterian Church, O. S. and N. S. (May 1861)—Resolution of the General Synod of the Reformed Dutch Church (June 1861)—and resolutions of 2000 Germans in Cooper Institute—all expressive of the strongest attachment to the sacred day, and of determination to maintain and promote its observance.

It would be truly lamentable if Great Britain should, after all, put away from her that Sabbath which has been her bulwark, blessing, and honour—which foreigners have so greatly admired and coveted—and which she has done so much to revive in continental, as well as to plant in heathen nations. Some of her unworthy sons no doubt have a desire to witness this catastrophe, as incendiaries have a taste for the destruction of food, property, or life. Too many, besides, are by their neglect and violation of the institution inconsiderately working towards such a result. And opinions, which unsettle the foundations of a weekly holy day as they exist in primæval appointment, in the Decalogue, and in the words and example of Jesus Christ, have *a tendency* to the same fatal issue. It is true, that the Sabbath does not depend upon any particular country, and that the loss of it would only be our own ruin. But there is "hope in Israel concerning this thing." We are not without "tokens for good." Many of our working men have proved false to the trust, which their fathers, after nobly contending for the divinely given right, committed to their hands; but the recent prize essays, and the numerously subscribed petitions against threatened spoliations of the boon, have afforded gratifying evidence, that the profound regard for the Lord's day, which was derived from the religious instruction for so long a time the glory of this country, still largely distinguishes our peasantry and artisans.[2] Another cheering circumstance is the extent to

[1] Doc. No. xx., *The Sabbath and the Pulpit*, pp. 2, 3.

[2] There were presented during the Session of 1853, chiefly from working men, 764 petitions, with 165,757 signatures, against the opening of the Crystal Palace on the Lord's day: in favour of it, only 119 petitions, with 23,081 signatures.

which the middle classes are imbued with the spirit of the institution, evinced in their exertions on its behalf.[1] A third encouragement arises from certain services, as the Forbes Mackenzie Act, and the frequent negativing of proposals to open places of public amusement on the Lord's day, which have been rendered to our cause in Parliament.[2] Further, when some years ago the same newspaper recorded the coronation of the Emperor of Russia on the Sabbath-day, and informed us that the Emperor and Empress of the French were present on a Sunday at a bull-fight at Bayonne, remaining at it to the end, we had the pleasure of knowing that such things could not have been enacted in this land.[3] To these symptoms of good, we have to add the manifestations of a reviving religion, the strong desires for an extended and improved education (soon, we trust, to be fulfilled), so prevalent in our day, experiments showing that Sabbath labour, held for so long a time to be neces-

[1] For example: All the banking firms in London, with two exceptions, memorialized the Lords of the Treasury in 1838, against the opening on Sunday of the General Post-Office and branch offices in London, for the reception of letters, etc. Besides memorials from merchants, solicitors, and others to the same effect, the Common Council of London unanimously adopted a resolution in harmony with the memorials. In Glasgow forty-one of the fifty members of the Town-Council—the managers of nine of the eleven banks—twenty-two physicians and surgeons, including the most eminent—sixty-eight procurators, brokers, etc.,—and 382 merchants and manufacturers—Nos. 68 and 382 embracing "a very large section of the most affluent and influential portion of the community," declared, in a petition to Parliament against Sunday labour in the Post-Office, "that many of your petitioners are engaged in mercantile and professional pursuits, and are quite prepared to dispense with all postal communications on the Sabbath: and they are fully persuaded that the adoption of this course would be unattended with any serious commercial disadvantages, and, on the whole, greatly conducive to the interests of the entire community." We have already mentioned the petition of 641 medical men of London against the opening of the Crystal Palace—and add only one other fact out of many, which is, that the petitions against opening public exhibitions on the Lord's day, during the session of 1856, was 4996, with 629,178 signatures; in favour of the opening, 123 petitions, with 24,056 signatures.

[2] A Bill which was introduced into the House of Commons last session, and which passed a select committee, but at too late a period to become law, has been again introduced this Session, intituled "The Public Houses (Scotland) Amendment Acts Bill," and if passed into a law, will eminently serve the interests of the Sabbath, and of morality.

[3] On Saturday the Queen laid the foundation-stone of the mausoleum at Frogmore, in which are to be deposited the remains of her dearly-loved husband the Prince Consort, and ultimately her own. Her Majesty had wished that this mournful ceremony should take place upon the first anniversary of the death of her revered mother the Duchess of Kent, but, as that day was Sunday, the eve of the anniversary was selected.—*British Ensign*, March 19, 1862.

sary in certain callings, may be safely and even beneficially dispensed with[1]—and the continually increasing exertions of churches, and other societies for evangelizing the masses at home, and converting the heathen abroad.[2]

But our confidence as to the ultimate universality and triumph of the Sabbath is not reposed on men, however great or good. Nor does it rest on past success, or present promising appearances, however encouraging these may be. Hope has no sure ground of anchorage, in the changing, dying men, or in the shifting scenes, of this earth. It must "enter into that within the veil." The Word and Power of the invisible, the unchangeable, and eternal God of the Sabbath, are our all-sufficient security that the institution is to be universal in the world, and to endure for ever. "From one Sabbath to another shall all flesh come to worship before me, saith the Lord." "There remaineth"—even to all eternity—"a rest to the people of God." "God is not a man, that he should lie; neither the son of man, that he should repent: hath he said, and shall he not do it: or hath he spoken, and shall he not make it good?"

In bringing this extended discussion to a close, we wish briefly to urge upon our readers two considerations, which ought to dispose all to increased respect and gratitude for so benignant an institution as the Sabbath, and to lead those who have not already done so, earnestly to ponder its claims.

First, The present interests of all classes are deeply involved in their views of the Sabbatic institution. As to working men, it is eminently their charter—the security for their all—for their time, their health, their respectability, their defence against the exaction

[1] As in iron-works (pp. 210, 211)—in gas-works and cheese-making (Baylee's *Hist. of the Sab.* p. 274)—and in baking, as appear from trials made by master-bakers in Edinburgh (see report in the newspapers by the Secretary of the Sabbath Alliance, who has interested himself much in this matter).

[2] We give a second specimen of the results of such exertions in connexion with one benevolent institution—the London City Mission: "Communicants, 1535—Backsliders restored to church communion, 307—Families induced to commence family prayer, 681—Drunkards reclaimed, 1230—Unmarried couples induced to marry, 361—Fallen females rescued, 681—Shops closed on the Lord's day, 212—Children sent to schools, 10,158." Taken from Summary for 1860-61, circulated by Rev. F. Tyrell, one of the secretaries.

of undue toil, the improvement of their minds and morals, and, above all, their means of eternal salvation. Its importance is enhanced by the numerical greatness of their class, who form an immense majority, more than two-thirds of the population of the United Kingdom. According to their character and circumstances must their own millions comprise a vast amount of suffering or enjoyment, and it is impossible for them to be virtuous and comfortable, or the reverse, without affecting for good or evil the entire nation. The condition of the labouring portion of society has of late years largely and properly engaged the thoughts of statesmen and philanthropists. Among the elements of social good, and the remedies for prevalent evil, the value of a day of sacred rest has not been overlooked. Its friends have not neglected to remind their countrymen of its beneficial influence on the conduct and prosperity of those who honour its claims, and enjoy its privileges ; and of the injury that ever results from a compulsory deprivation, or a voluntary rejection of its advantages. The highest praise is due to those who have exerted themselves to diffuse information regarding the institution, with the view of securing its appreciation by the great body of the people themselves, and of imparting both the power and the inclination to apply it to its holy and benevolent ends. And there is good reason to believe that reverence for the Lord's day has thereby not only been increased, but extended to not a few who had declined from the piety of their fathers.

But the welfare and happiness of the remaining portion of the community are also deeply involved in the subject before us. Although less numerous, they are certainly in some respects the more influential members of society. The middle classes imitate their superiors in dress, manners, and conduct, and are in their turn followed by multitudes who have many opportunities of hearing their language, knowing their opinions, and observing their behaviour. Infidelity in France, prior to the first Revolution, began with the higher grades in the State ; and our country has been found to be licentious or moral as the Court and nobility have been profligate, or the reverse. It would not be easy to calculate the amount of moral injury inflicted on a rural district by a resident proprietor of profane and gambling propensities, or on the provincial town by its free-living men of wealth. How beneficial to the morals of a land if our merchants were Thorntons in their spirit; if our squires had the piety and philanthropy of a Wilberforce; if our noblemen were as devoted to the cause of benevolence as a Shaftesbury! It is a happy sign of the times that among all these ranks there are so many counterparts of such men. And it is our singular privilege to see the personal and relative virtues, as well as the proprieties of life, daily exemplified in the most elevated station by our Queen and her princely Consort.[1] Well were it for many if the maxim held good:—

> "Componitur orbis
> Regis ad exemplum; nec sic inflectere sensus
> Humanos edicta valeut, ut vita regentis."
>
> CLAUDIAN.

No classes are more concerned in the stability and observance of religious institutions than the middle and upper ranks of a nation. In all countries every man should have free scope for obtaining wealth by honest industry, and for reaching distinction by the force of intellect, and by the cultivation of moral excellence. It is in proportion as religion prevails in any land, that such facilities exist. And when riches and honours are gained, religion is the security for the conservation of all just possessions. The Sabbath is itself the means of upholding truth and piety, is a pillar of the throne, and a protection of property and honourable distinction against the tide of revolution. If the fear of God be rooted out, where is the guarantee that the king shall be honoured, the noble and the rich respected, or the laws obeyed? Indispensable to the children of toil, the Sabbath is scarcely less important to the other orders of a State. It concerns their safety amidst materials of combustion, which it would require only a little more infidelity and irreligion amongst themselves, and amongst their neighbours, to kindle into a conflagration de-

[1] Since these words were first printed, death has been commissioned to bereave our Queen of her beloved husband, and the nation of one of its chief ornaments and benefactors; but that Prince Albert contributed by his position and virtues to "our singular privilege," is a fact which remains unchanged in itself, and is too important and interesting to be cancelled or altered in one of its humblest memorials.

structive of all the securities for station and property that are maintained, under Providence, by a well-observed Sabbath.

But, *Second*, the subject concerns still higher and more enduring interests. In the world that is unseen and eternal there are only two conditions of human beings, as the results, thus foretold, of the Grand Assize: "These shall go away into everlasting punishment, but the righteous into life eternal." With these destinies of men the Sabbath has momentous connexions. It is one of the laws of God, for the transgression of which men deserve the former lot, and by perfect obedience to which Jesus delivered his followers from the wrath to come: "The wages of sin is death, but the gift of God is eternal life through Jesus Christ our Lord," "in whom we have redemption through his blood, the forgiveness of sins, according to the riches of his grace." The Sabbath is one of those laws of God, the affectionate keeping of which is necessary to prove our saving relation to Christ, and our title to heaven: "Blessed are they that do his commandments, that they may have right to the tree of life, and may enter in through the gates into the city." "Not every one that saith unto me, Lord, Lord, shall enter into the kingdom of heaven; but he that doeth the will of my Father which is in heaven." When some of the Pharisees said, "This man is not of God, because he keepeth not the Sabbath-day,"[1] they were right in so far as the principle was concerned, but utterly wrong in its application. Of those who by "scorn of God's commands" show that they are unblessed with spiritual life, Cowper has terribly but truly said—

"That want uncured till man resigns his breath,
Speaks him a criminal assured of everlasting death.
Sad period to a pleasant course! Yet so will God repay
Sabbaths profaned without remorse, and mercy cast away."[2]

On the other hand, how happy the condition of the man who, under "the conviction that he stood almost on the verge of eternity, and that the days could not be many before the secret and awful things of futurity should be unveiled to him," invoked the spirit of God to enable him to cherish, with other habits, that of "dedicating the Sabbath to its proper duties—not wasting its precious

[1] John ix. 16. [2] *Poems*—Nichol's edit. vol. ii. p. 124.

hours, not worshipping God with a wandering and unsteady mind, not stealing its moments for secular purposes," and that, of "calling himself to account for the use of his money, of his time, of his powers."[1] The Sabbath, moreover, is a law the love of which, besides attesting the title to heavenly glory and blessedness, proves that a character congenial to the employments, society, and joys of the world above has begun to be formed, or rather is far advanced—the character equally as the title being among those "gifts and callings of God which are without repentance." The person who has pleasure in a weekly day of holy rest and service will not feel himself out of his element when he sits down with Abraham, Isaac, and Jacob in the kingdom of God. But how could he who dislikes the Sabbath, spend eternity in beholding, loving, and lauding the Creator and Redeemer of men? "For what fellowship hath righteousness with unrighteousness? What communion hath light with darkness? And what concord hath Christ with Belial? or what part hath he that believeth with an infidel?" The Sabbath, in short, has been given as a necessary means of directing us "in the way of life which is above to the wise, that he may depart from hell beneath."[2] It brings leisure to immortal beings, too engrossed with the perishing objects of the earth, to attend to the claims of the soul and of the future. It gives us a periodical pause in the race of life that we may "wear off by meditation the worldly soil contracted during the week."[3] It is "the combs, and hive, and home of rest." It is heaven let down from week to week, that we may dwell in its light, breathe its air, and learn its music. And only as we redeem the precious fleeting season are we becoming qualified

"to rest eternally
With him that is the God of Sabbath hight."

But if we would intelligently and sincerely join the poet in his following fervent aspiration,—

"O that great Sabbath! God grant me that Sabbath's sight,—

and if we would "rest eternally" in the favour, in the perfections, in the service, and holy happiness of God, a change in our re-

[1] *Memoirs of Sir T. F. Buxton*, 5th edit., pp. 306, 307.
[2] Prov. xv. 24.
[3] Dr. Johnson.

lation and feelings to Him must be effected. And it must be effected in the present state. It cannot take place in a future world, for in that world there is an impassable gulph between the two classes of men, and, while "the holy" remain holy, "the filthy" must be "filthy still." Nor would it be reasonable to indulge the hope that it will be realized in the article, or immediate prospect, of death. The thief on the cross obtained mercy as he was about to die. But how foolish to regulate our procedure by the only authenticated case of so late a repentance,—the one exception; and to forget the all but universal rule! Because one man has thrown himself over a precipice, and been mercifully preserved, would it be wise in us to try the same experiment? While every period, then, even of this life, is not favourable for beginning the preparation for heaven, it is only in this life that it can be commenced. The Scriptures represent this world as the only training-place for eternity. It is the lower form in the school of knowledge, where the rudiments of celestial wisdom must be learned. There is no provision in a future state for instructing tyros. There is beyond death "no more sacrifice for sins," and no gospel to be "the power of God unto salvation." Let us, therefore, now hear, that our souls may live, the joyful sound as it comes from the lips of the Divine and compassionate Saviour: "Come unto me, all ye that labour and are heavy laden, and I will give you rest. Take my yoke upon you, and learn of me; for I am meek and lowly in heart: and ye shall find rest unto your souls. For my yoke is easy, and my burden is light."

GENERAL INDEX.

C

H

M

N

INDEX OF TEXTS.

www.ingramcontent.com/pod-product-compliance
Lightning Source LLC
LaVergne TN
LVHW021056110826
845150LV00001B/85

* 9 7 8 1 4 2 5 5 6 7 0 2 6 *